WORLD HISTORY

WITH STUDENT ACTIVITIES

Third Edition

Greenville, South Carolina

WORLD HISTORY
Third Edition

David A. Fisher, EdD

Contributing Authors
Carl Abrams, PhD
Lynn Garland
Nathan Lentfer
Dennis Peterson
Bryan Smith, PhD

Editor
Manda Kalagayan

Bible Integration
Margaret E. Calhoun
John C. MacInnis
Bryan Smith, PhD

Cover Designer
John Bjerk

Designer
Dan Van Leeuwen

Composition
Monotype
Katie Cooper
Peggy Hargis
Maribeth Hayes
Carol Jenkins

Page Layout
Megan Eshleman
Anne Nolan
David Siglin

Design Contributor
Christy Bruckner
John Cunningham
Aaron Dickey
Elly Kalagayan

Project Manager
Elena Emelyanova

Photo Acquisition
Brenda Hansen
Joyce Landis
Susan Perry
Sarah Strawhorn

Illustration
Megan Eshleman
Caroline George
Preston Gravely, Jr.
Jim Hargis
David Joyal
Anne Nolan
Kathy Pflug
Lynda Slattery
Mark Tucker
Dan Van Leeuwen

Consultant
Frank Eberhardt

Photograph credits are listed on pages 349–51.

Produced in cooperation with the Bob Jones University Departments of History and Social Studies of the College of Arts and Science, the School of Education, and Bob Jones Academy.

Greenville, South Carolina 29614

Printed in the United States of America

ISBN 978-1-59166-432-1

15 14 13 12 11 10 9 8 7 6 5 4 3 2 1

CONGRATULATIONS

Your search for the very best educational materials available has been completely successful! You have a textbook that is the culmination of decades of research, experience, prayer, and creative energy.

THE FACTS

Nothing overlooked. Revised and updated. Facts are used as a springboard to stimulate thoughtful questions and guide students to broader applications.

THE FOUNDATION

Nothing to conflict with Truth and everything to support it. Truth is the pathway as well as the destination.

THE FUN

Nothing boring about this textbook! Student (and teacher) might even forget it's a textbook! Brimming with interesting extras and sparkling with color!

BJU PRESS

1.800.845.5731 www.bjupress.com

GIVE EAR,

O my people, to my law:
incline your ears to the words of my mouth.
I will open my mouth in a parable:
I will utter dark sayings of old:
Which we have heard and known,
and our fathers have told us.
We will not hide them from their children,
SHEWING TO THE GENERATION TO COME
the PRAISES of the Lord,
and his STRENGTH,
and his WONDERFUL WORKS that he hath done.

For he established a testimony in Jacob,
and appointed a law in Israel,
which he commanded our fathers,
that they should make them known to their children:
THAT THE GENERATION TO COME MIGHT KNOW THEM,
even the children which should be born;
who should arise and declare them to their children:
THAT THEY MIGHT SET THEIR HOPE IN GOD,
AND NOT FORGET THE WORKS OF GOD,
BUT KEEP HIS COMMANDMENTS.

—PSALM 78:1-7

CONTENTS

BOOK A

UNIT I: THE ANCIENT WORLD

UNIT II: THE EASTERN WORLD

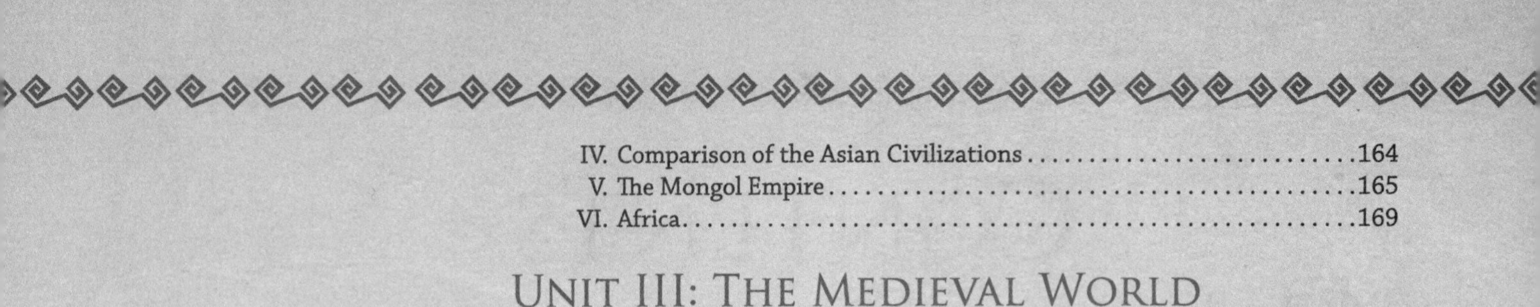

Unit III: The Medieval World

Unit IV: The Awakening World

Student Activities

Book B

Unit V: The Enlightened World

Unit VI: The European World

Unit VII: The Modern World

FEATURES OF THE BOOK

At the beginning of each chapter, an interesting **quotation** highlights the theme of that chapter.

The **chapter outline** lists the major topics that will be covered.

Major feature boxes highlight an aspect of history in the chapter and provide more information about it.

7

"The unknown lands"

THE CIVILIZATIONS OF ASIA AND AFRICA

I. India
A. Early Civilization
B. Key Features of Indian Society
C. Religion and the Indian Way of Life
D. Lack of Political Unity

II. China
A. The Land
B. Societal Features
C. Chinese Thought and Life
D. Dynastic History of China
E. Chinese Culture and the Western World

III. Japan

A section of the Great Wall of China snakes across the Chinese landscape.

The Roman Army

In his conquest of the ancient world, Alexander the Great relied upon the Greek military formation called the "phalanx." This formation packed hundreds of men into a tight wedge with their long spears facing forward. The phalanx was very powerful and almost impossible to defeat on level ground. But it had one weakness that made it almost useless to the Romans: it could not maneuver. It could march forward or backward, but because the men and spears were tightly intertwined, it could not turn easily. Because Rome's enemies used a number of different fighting tactics, Rome needed a formation which could adapt to many different situations. Thus Rome invented the "legion." Each legion (about five thousand men) was divided into several groups. Up front was a line of "skirmishers," carrying short spears. Next came two lines of soldiers, marching in groups called "centuries." Each century, which was headed by a "centurion," stood in a checkerboard formation with the other centuries. These soldiers carried heavier spears. Behind all these soldiers came a line of men carrying heavy thrusting spears with which they could mow down the enemy. As the front lines tired, they could retreat through the gaps in the checkerboard formation and rest behind the last line. There were two advantages to this formation. First, it was much more maneuverable than the phalanx, so it could adjust more easily to variations in the land and the enemy's formations. Second, the men could move in and out more easily, fight more freely, and get rest if they needed it.

that served for financial gain rather than for a patriotic cause. Their devotion to the commander of the army was greater than their devotion to Rome. This shift in loyalty would later be the undoing of Rome as generals used their armies to further their own interests rather than those of the people and the state.

In 88 BC war broke out in Asia Minor. The Senate appointed **Sulla** (138–78 BC), a general who was sympathetic to the senatorial side, to command the Roman army in the east. The Tribal Assembly, however, rejected the Senate's choice and appointed Marius instead. The years that followed saw much bloodshed as the tension between the Tribal Assembly and the Senate, fueled by the rivalry between Marius and Sulla, developed into civil war. In the end Sulla emerged victorious.

Sulla had himself declared dictator. He then set about reorganizing the Roman government. He hoped to restore stability and order by reviving the power and prestige of the Senate. The influence of the Tribal Assembly and the tribunes was now all but gone. With the power of the Senate firmly established, Sulla resigned as dictator. The Senate, however, was unable to maintain control of the government.

The Second Civil War

The first civil war ended with the Senate triumphant over the Tribal Assembly. Yet it was obvious that a powerful man at the head of the army could control the state. Ambitious men sought to gain that control. The people, weary

The Roman Republic • 91

Fascinating **photos and illustrations** add life to the people and places being studied.

Terms in bold type draw attention to important facts, ideas, or definitions.

Byzantine Empire at Its Height (6th Century)

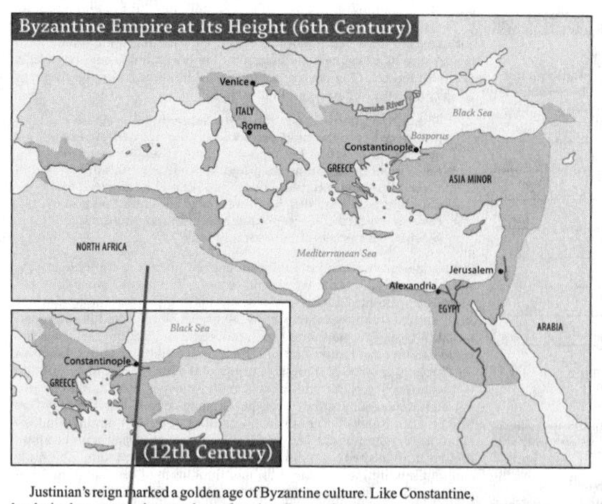

Justinian's reign marked a golden age of Byzantine culture. Like Constantine, he desired to restore the grandeur of ancient Rome. Sparing no expense, he initiated an extensive building program to construct churches, public buildings, aqueducts, and roads both in the capital city and throughout the empire. He also patronized Byzantine art. From this period comes the finest example of Byzantine architecture, the Church of **Hagia Sophia** (HAH-juh so-FEE-uh), meaning "Holy Wisdom."

Even so, Justinian left his successors with an empire beset by many problems. In his attempts to reclaim the West, he had neglected the defense of the empire's eastern and northern borders. Likewise, his costly military campaigns, coupled with his massive building program, left the empire financially drained. Thus it may be said that Justinian took the Byzantine Empire to the height of glory but left it at the brink of ruin.

An Excerpt from the Justinian Code

The imperial majesty should be not only made glorious by arms, but also strengthened by laws, that, alike in time of peace and in time of war, the state may be well governed, and that the emperor may not only be victorious in the field of battle, but also may by every legal means repel the iniquities of men who abuse the laws, and may at once religiously uphold justice and triumph over his conquered enemies.

Eastern and Western Churches Separate

When Constantine founded "New Rome," he established not only a new political capital but also a new religious center. He desired Constantinople to be a Christian city, a "new Jerusalem." Under his influence, Christianity became the favored religion of the Roman Empire. It was quite natural for "Constantine City" to rise to a place of honor in the structure of the organized church; it became one of the five patriarchal cities, second only to Rome in prestige. The bishop of Rome (later to become the pope) became the most important religious leader in the West; the patriarch of Constantinople held that position in the East.

The Byzantine a

Margin text boxes offer intriguing bits of extra information.

Section quizzes help the student remember what he has learned so far.

Section Quiz

1. ______________
2. ______________
3. ______________
4. ______________
5. ______________

1. What did the Romans call the Mediterranean Sea?
2. In what year was the city of Rome founded?
3. According to legend, what two brothers founded Rome?
4. What were the two main social classes of ancient Rome?
5. What became the symbol of the king's authority in early Roman society?

Blanks in the margin allow space to answer questions and include personal thoughts.

II. The Early Roman Republic

Establishment

About a century after the founding of Rome, the Etruscans crossed the Tiber River from the north and conquered the Latin villages. During the period of Etruscan rule, Rome grew from a weak league of villages to become the leading Latin city. As the influence of Rome increased, so did the hatred of the Roman nobility for the Etruscan monarch. In **509 BC** they overthrew the king. In the place of the monarchy, they established a new form of government called a **republic**. Under the Roman Republic the administration of government was divided among three governing branches: the consuls, the Senate, and the assemblies.

Two elected **consuls** (government officials) replaced the king and held the imperium. They supervised the everyday affairs of government, commanded the Roman army, and served as the supreme judges of the land. Power was equally divided between each consul; one could not act without the consent

Flow of Political Power in the Early Roman Republic

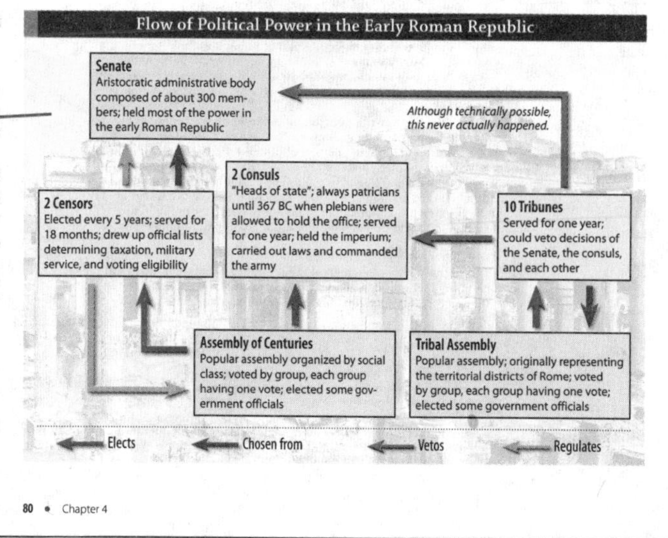

80 • Chapter 4

Diagrams and maps help with visualizing geography, numbers, and comparisons.

"This Moment in History" boxes provide a deeper look at a person, event, or concept mentioned in the text.

THIS MOMENT IN HISTORY:

Charlemagne

How did Charlemagne's interest in education impact his generation and future generations?

Perhaps it was under Alcuin's influence that Charlemagne developed his deep concern for a better-educated clergy. He encouraged the church to establish schools to upgrade the literacy of the priests and monks. In a letter to church leaders, Charlemagne set forth what has been called the charter of education for the Middle Ages. In it, he said:

> Whence it happened that we began to fear lest perchance, as the skill in writing was less, so also the wisdom for understanding the Holy Scriptures might be much less than it rightly ought to be. And we all know well that, although errors of speech are dangerous, far more dangerous are errors of the understanding. Therefore, we exhort you not only not to neglect the study of letters but also with most humble mind, pleasing to God, to study earnestly in order that you may be able more easily and more correctly to penetrate the mysteries of the divine Scriptures.[3]

Charlemagne's educational reforms renewed interest in the Bible and the works of classical writers. For several centuries in western Europe there had been little interest in learning; few people could read or write. During that time many ancient manuscripts were lost or damaged; others were full of copyists' mistakes. One of the most important contributions of Charlemagne's reign was the rediscovery and preservation of these ancient works. In addition, God used the Carolingian scholars to preserve copies of the Bible.

Monasteries were the primary centers for studying, copying, and preserving ancient manuscripts; they were the "printing houses" and libraries of the Middle Ages. Monks undertook the painstaking process of making handwritten copies of earlier works. During this period, they developed a new and beautiful style of handwriting known as the **Carolingian minuscule**. This clean and simple writing style became the model for much of our "lowercase" writing today. Many manuscripts were illuminated with colorful illustrations.

"Through Eyes of Faith" boxes view important issues from a Christian perspective.

THROUGH EYES OF FAITH:

The Value of Education

Some Christians are suspicious of higher education. What do Charlemagne's educational reforms suggest about how a Christian should view all levels of education?

Disintegration of Charlemagne's Empire

Although the effects of this renewed interest in learning lasted for centuries, Charlemagne's impressive empire deteriorated rapidly. Within a century after his death, the empire had collapsed, torn by civil war and pillaged by invaders.

Problems from Within

When Charlemagne died in 814, his empire passed to his only surviving son, Louis the Pious. During Louis's reign, a bitter rivalry broke out among his sons over which portion of the empire each would inherit. Even before Louis's death this rivalry led to civil war. The Bible tells us, "A brother offended is harder to be won than a strong city: and their contentions are like the bars of a castle" (Prov. 18:19).

After years of fighting, the brothers met at the city of Verdun to settle their differences. In the **Treaty of Verdun (843)**, they agreed to split the empire into three separate kingdoms: **Charles the Bald** received West Frankland; **Louis the German**, East Frankland; and the eldest brother, **Lothair**, retained the title of emperor and ruled the land between his brother's kingdoms. (See the map on p. 191.) Notice how closely the modern states of France, Germany, and Italy correspond to these divisions.

When Lothair died, Charles and Louis wasted little time in seizing portions of his kingdom. (Part of this territory is still know today as Lorraine, "Lothair's kingdom.") Political fragmentation characterized the last days of the empire as the Carolingian rulers persisted in their family strife. In addition, the successors to Charlemagne's grandsons were weak and incompetent rulers, as is demonstrated by the disrespectful surnames they were given; Louis the

praise. Zoroaster taught that good and evil are two opposing forces; the world was their battleground. Every man takes part in this struggle, Zoroaster taught, for he serves either the forces of good or the forces of evil. Like so many of the world's false religions, Zoroastrianism held that at the end of life one would be assured of eternal happiness if his good works outweighed his evil.

The Persian Empire continued some two hundred years after the death of Cyrus. Under **Darius the Great**, the empire reached its height, expanding all the way to Greece, where the Persian expansion was halted. Although the Greeks stopped the Persian advance, the Persians continued to rule the ancient world until a new world conqueror, Alexander the Great, created an even greater empire toward the close of the fourth century BC.

Section Quiz

1. What city became the capital of the Assyrian Empire?
2. What prophet was sent by God to Nineveh to preach repentance?
3. What term describes the scattering of the Jewish people by Nebuchadnezzar?
4. What Hebrew captive foretold the fall of Babylon?
5. What Persian king created the largest empire known to his day and earned the title "the Great"?
6. What was the religion of ancient Persia? What was the name of its sacred writings?

1. ________
2. ________
3. ________
4. ________
5. ________
6. ________

A Glance Behind

The civilizations discussed in this chapter may be viewed almost like the rings that radiate out from a pebble dropped in a pool of water. In this case, the spot where the pebble dropped would be Sumer, site of one of the earliest recorded ancient civilizations. Sumer, in turn, was swallowed by the Akkadian Empire. Successive empires swelled larger and larger, while smaller civilizations, such as the Israelites, existed on their borders or flourished during the lulls in empire building.

In Daniel 2 we read of a vision sent by God to King Nebuchadnezzar, the Chaldean king. In it a huge statue is described as having a head of gold, chest of silver, legs of iron, and feet and toes of an iron/clay mixture. God provided an interpretation of this dream to Daniel, who relayed it to the king. King Nebuchadnezzar was pleased to hear that he was the head of gold, but no doubt troubled to hear that his golden reign would end and that his empire would be eventually replaced. In 539 BC it was replaced by the Persian Empire—further testament to the sureness of God's word and unchanging plan for history.

The Persian Empire, the chest and arms of silver, encompassed the territory held by nearly every other civilization discussed in this chapter. Yet Persia was destined to fall as well, and it did in 331 BC. It fell to the Greeks, the subject of the next chapter, through the conquests of Alexander the Great—the waist of bronze.

and a Glimpse Ahead

"A Glance Behind and a Glimpse Ahead" summarizes the completed chapter and gives a sneak preview of the next one.

Notes

1. Samuel N. Kramer, *History Begins at Sumer* (Garden City, N.Y.: Anchor Books, 1959), pp. 8–9.
2. James B. Pritchard, ed., *Ancient Near Eastern Texts Relating to the Old Testament* (Princeton: Princeton Univ. Press, 1969), pp. 164–77.
3. W. J. Martin, trans., "The Law Code of Hammurabi," in *Documents from Old Testament Times*, ed. D. Winton Thomas (Edinburgh: Thomas Nelson and Sons, 1958); reprint ed. (New York: Harper and Row, 1961), pp. 29–35 passim.
4. Pritchard, p. 93.
5. Herodotus, *The History of Herodotus* (trans. George Rawlinson), p. 98.

52 • Chapter 2

Chapter Review

Can You Define?

polytheism
cuneiform
ziggurats
empire
astronomy
astrology
pharaoh
hieroglyphics
theocracy
monotheism
Babylonian Captivity
Diaspora
satrapies

Can You Identify?

Sargon I
Hammurabi
Epic of Gilgamesh
Menes
Khufu (Cheops)
Hatshepsut
Thutmose III
Amenhotep II
Rameses II
Baal
Abraham
Abrahamic Covenant
Jacob (Israel)
Joseph
Judah
Moses
Joshua
David
Solomon
586 BC
722 BC
Sargon II
Sennacherib
Nebuchadnezzar
Belshazzar
Cyrus
Croesus
Zoroaster
Avesta
Darius the Great

Can you Locate?

Mesopotamia
Tigris River
Euphrates River
Persian Gulf
Sumer
Akkad
Ur
Babylon
Egypt
Nile River
Memphis
Giza
Thebes
Asia Minor
Tyre
Damascus
Sinai Peninsula
Jerusalem
Samaria
Fertile Crescent
Nineveh

How Much Do You Remember?

1. List the three major rivers in this chapter and identify the civilizations which began along their banks.
2. List at least one way in which each of the following civilizations played a role in the history of Israel: Sumerians, Egyptians, Hittites, Phoenicians, Assyrians, Chaldeans, and Persians.
3. Make a list including each person listed in the "Can You Identify?" section. Beside each name, identify the civilization to which that person belonged.

What Do You Think?

1. What can be learned about the land of Egypt from the prophecy of its destruction in Isaiah 19:1–10?
2. From Ezekiel 27, list at least five items included in the trade of the Phoenicians.
3. Arriving at the correct date for an event in ancient history is a difficult task. How did the Hebrews calculate dates? See Isaiah 6:1; 7:1; Ezra 1:1–2; and 1 Kings 6:1.
4. From Genesis 50:2–3 and 50:26 we find that some of the Hebrews followed one of the Egyptian customs. Which one was it?
5. Outline the civilizations and kings mentioned in the book of Daniel. From the following references, can you name the kings Daniel served? (Dan. 1:1, 5:1–2, 31; 10:1)

The **Chapter Review** asks students about terms, people, places, and concepts to help them prepare for the test.

Name __________

WORLD HISTORY 2 ACTIVITY 1

Questions and Timeline

Identify the person, civilization, place, event, and/or date for each of the following questions. Identify in parentheses the civilization each person represents. Then record the appropriate information on the timeline on the next page.

Section I:

1. United the land of Mesopotamia and is remembered for his code of laws (year reign began) __________
2. Established the first known empire (year reign began) __________

Section II:

3. Age when Egypt became a great world power (year age began) __________
4. Age in Egypt when Khufu built the great pyramid at Giza (year age began) __________
5. Age when Egyptian pharaohs directed their attention to projects that would benefit the country as a whole (year age began) __________

Section III:

6. The Israelites led out of Egypt by Moses __________
7. Jews carried into Babylon __________
8. Began to settle Asia Minor with their army commanders as kings (year began) __________
9. Came from Ur and began Israel's history (birth year) __________
10. King whose army destroyed Jerusalem and carried the Jews into exile for seventy years (year reign began) __________
11. Israel's southern kingdom capital that the Chaldeans destroyed __________

Section IV:

12. Led the Assyrian army to destroy Samaria and took captive the ten northern Hebrew tribes (year destroyed) __________
13. Used by God to free His people from their captivity in Babylon __________
14. City destroyed by the Chaldeans and the Medes __________
15. Was killed by the Medes and Persians after using the golden vessels from God's temple in Jerusalem __________

Activity pages reinforce and enrich chapter content using a wide variety of exercises.

HOW TO USE THIS BOOK

Units and Chapters

World History is divided into seven units. The main theme of each unit is presented in a brief summary and timeline and illustrated by a two-page color picture. Each unit in turn contains from two to six chapters. These begin with a brief introduction and an outline of the period to be studied. The chapters are divided into main sections and subsections. For instance, one of the main sections in Chapter 2 is Mesopotamia. The first subsection under this is Sumerian Civilization. Often subsections are further divided to help you quickly identify the major topics of discussion.

Section Quizzes

At the end of each major section of a chapter is a section quiz. These are primarily recall questions designed to test your understanding of the material you have just read. Space is provided in the text to answer the quiz questions. There are normally three to four section quizzes in each chapter.

Chapter Reviews

Each chapter ends with a review section. These sections should help you study the chapter. The Chapter Review is divided into three parts: terms, recall questions, and thought questions.

1. Key terms are listed in the order in which they appear in the text. They are grouped under three headings: Can You Define?, Can You Identify?, and Can You Locate? You should be able to define the words in the first list, identify the terms or dates in the second list (answering the questions Who? Why? Where? When? How?), and locate on a map and state the importance of the places in the third list. All terms found in Can You Define? and Can You Identify? are in boldface type in the text.

2. The purpose of the questions from How Much Do You Remember? is to help you recall what you have read in the chapter. Try to answer these questions without looking back into the chapter. This will help you to determine what you know and what parts of the chapter you need to review.

3. The questions under What Do You Think? require you to formulate your own opinions. Be sure that these opinions are based on facts and are not just ideas that you think up. Some questions ask you to examine what the Bible has to say on a particular subject. Remember that it is important for a Christian to always use the Bible as his guide when formulating ethical and moral standards.

Illustrations, Charts, Timelines, and Maps

Each illustration and chart in the book has been included to aid you in your understanding of world history. Take time to look at these and read the captions associated with them. The timelines will help you place events in a broader historical context. The maps will help you visualize the size and location of various countries or the region in which a particular people live.

Highlights

Each chapter has a number of interesting articles contained in feature boxes. These will not only help to broaden your knowledge of history, but many will also make your reading of *World History* more exciting. If you are curious, for instance, about how we got our calendar, who wrote "Joy to The World," or how during World War II the United States knew ahead of time that the Japanese were going to attack Midway, you will be able to read all about it in these boxes. Two other features are Through Eyes of Faith and This Moment in History. Through Eyes of Faith helps you develop a Christian perspective on various events of history (such as "The Conversion of Constantine"). This Moment in History highlights a major person or event in the time period discussed (such as the *Pax Romana*) and asks questions about that moment.

Activity Pages

In the back of this book activity pages are included. These pages will be assigned by your teacher when appropriate. They are perforated for ease of use.

Dates

In your reading of this *World History* textbook you will encounter many dates. We do not intend for you to memorize all these. The dates are provided so that you will be able to fit people and events into a time frame. In addition, there are some facts you need to know about dates.

1. *How to use BC and AD*
   Today it is customary to label events that happened before the birth of Christ BC (meaning "before Christ") and events that happened after His birth AD ("Anno Domini"; Latin, meaning "in the year of our Lord"). BC is written after every date before the birth of Christ. We do not write AD next to a date, however, unless it might be confused with a BC date. Therefore, when you see a date in the book without BC after it or AD before it, you may assume it is AD. When AD is used, it is proper to write it before the date (e.g., AD 70). Some contemporary writers use "Before the Common Era" (BCE) and "Common Era" (CE) for their dating schemes to stand for BC and AD, respectively.

2. *How to count in BC*
   The dates of events before the birth of Christ are much like the countdown of a rocket launch (10, 9, 8, . . . 3, 2, 1). Ancient civilizations, of course, did not count backwards like this. But because of the historical significance of the birth of Christ, we today date ancient events from the number of years they occurred before His birth.

3. *How to recognize an approximate date*
   Because of incomplete historical records, it is sometimes impossible to establish an exact date for a historical event. When this is the case, we express an approximate date by placing the abbreviated form of *circa* (Latin for "around") before the date (e.g., ca. 1446).

4. *How to understand dates printed after a person's name*
   The date in parentheses after a person's name usually indicate his lifespan. Dates for monarchs or popes, however, are the dates they held office. If a question mark appears after a date, it means we are uncertain about the time of a person's birth or death, for example, John Wycliffe (1320?–1384).

5. *How to determine in what century an event took place*
   The first century includes the years 1 to 100; the second, 101 to 200; the third, 201 to 300; and so on. The twenty-first century will therefore be from 2001 to 2100. The same procedure is used for establishing centuries BC. Can you determine the centuries for the following dates? 586 BC, ca. 1446, 1900.

Pronunciation Guide

Vowels

symbol	example	symbol	example
a	cat = KAT	aw	all = AWL
a-e	cape = KAPE	o	potion = PO shun
ay	paint = PAYNT	oa	don't = DOANT
e	jet = JET	o-e	groan = GRONE
eh	spend = SPEHND	oh	own = OHN
ee	fiend = FEEND	u	some = SUM
i	swim = SWIM	uh	abet = uh BET
ih	pity = PIH tee	oo	crew = CROO
eye	icy = EYE see	*oo*	push = P*OO*SH
i-e	might = MITE	ou	loud = LOUD
ah	cot = KAHT	oy	toil = TOYL
ar	car = KAR		

Consonants

symbol	example	symbol	example
k	cat = KAT	th	thin = THIN
g	get = GET	*th*	then = *TH*EN
j	gentle = JEN tul	zh	fusion = FYOO zhun

The pronunciation key used in this text is designed to give the reader a self-evident, acceptable pronunciation for a word as he reads it from the page. For more nearly accurate pronunciations, the reader should consult a good dictionary.

Stress: Syllables with primary stress appear in LARGE CAPITAL letters. Syllables with secondary stress and one-syllable words appear in SMALL CAPITAL letters. Unstressed syllables appear in lowercase letters. Where two or more words appear together, hyphens separate the syllables within each word. For example, the pronunciation of Omar Khayyam appears as (OH-mar kie-YAHM).

THE ANCIENT WORLD

I

Every story has a beginning, and a well-crafted story progresses toward a climax. Indeed, a talented writer will carefully build up to his climax, arranging the details of the plot so that the climax will have the greatest possible effect on the reader. Ancient history, the subject of this first unit, builds toward such a climax. In steady succession, empires rise and fall, each new empire appearing even greater and more extensive than the last. Finally, with the Roman Empire, ancient history reached its climax—but not with the empire itself. The Roman Empire provided the setting for the turning point of history, the death and Resurrection of Jesus Christ: "But when the fullness of the time was come, God sent forth his Son, made of a woman, made under the law, to redeem them that were under the law, that we might receive the adoption of sons" (Gal. 4:4–5).

2700–2200 Old Kingdom

2166 Abraham Born

2100–1640 Middle Kingdom

1570–1075 New Kingdom

1446 Hebrew Exodus from Egypt

753 Rome Founded

700–500 Greek City-States

586 Hebrew Captivity in Babylon Begins

539 Cyrus the Great Frees Hebrews

2700 BC | 2212 BC | 1723 BC | 1235 BC | 746 BC

480 Battle of Salamis Bay

460–429 Periclean Age

431–404 Peloponnesian War

264–146 Punic Wars

31 BC–AD 180 *Pax Romana*

31 BC–AD 476 Roman Empire

4 BC Birth of Jesus Christ

AD 30 Crucifixion of Jesus Christ

70 Romans Destroy Jerusalem

306 Constantine Becomes Emperor

476 Fall of Rome

500 BC

243 BC

AD 14

AD 272

AD 529

336 Alexander the Great Becomes King of Macedonia

44 Julius Caesar Assassinated

31 BC Battle of Actium

54 Nero Becomes Emperor

313 Edict of Milan

325 Council of Nicaea

1

"In the beginning God created the heaven and the earth."

FOUNDATIONS OF WORLD HISTORY

A building cannot be stronger than its foundation. This statement is certainly true in architecture, and it is also true in the study of history. Every telling of history—whether by a grandfather at a fireside or by a college professor in front of a classroom—is based on a number of "foundation stones." This chapter will talk about the foundational concepts that form the basis for this study of world history. These concepts fall into two categories. First, there are *philosophical foundations*, concepts that help us understand why we study history in the first place and how we should pursue that study. Second, there are *historical foundations*, the world's earliest events. These events are foundational because they form the bedrock on which all the rest of world history is built.

Just as a building rests on foundation stones, so also the teaching of history must rest on certain foundational concepts.

I. The Study of World History

The Value of Studying History

Our word *history* comes from a Greek word (*historia*) meaning "inquiry." History is the inquiry into what has happened in the past and why it has happened. Through the centuries the study of history has been praised by many influential people. Consider the following quotations.

"There is much profit in a knowledge of the past. Every kind of experience is there for all to see. Historical documents contain examples for our instruction: models for a person or a nation to imitate and shameful things for all to avoid."
Livy
Roman historian, 59 BC–AD 17

"History is a witness of the times, the light of truth, the life of memory, the teacher of life, the messenger of antiquity."
Cicero
Roman statesman and orator, 106–43 BC

"Observing the working of God through history ministers to the readers thereof wholesome admonitions for life: with experience and wisdom both to know God in His works, and to work the thing that is godly: especially to seek unto the Son of God for their salvation, and in His faith only to find that they seek for, and in no other means."
John Foxe
English historian and scholar, 1516–87

"The present is the past rolled up for action, and the past is the present unrolled for understanding."
Will Durant
American historian, 1885–1981

Many students, however, cannot bring themselves to agree that studying history is profitable. To them, the seemingly endless lists of names, wars, and dates found in any history textbook are hopelessly boring and irrelevant. "Who cares about what happened a thousand years ago? We don't live in the past; we live in the present. And education should prepare us for the future." If you are a student who doubts the value of studying history, the following paragraphs are especially for you.

History Prepares Us for the Future

Being concerned about the future is a virtue. But a careful examination of the past is one of the best preparations for living successfully in the future. Many people (and some of them are historians) claim that history cannot prepare us for the future. They say that since all humans are individuals, and since each human civilization is unique, it is not possible to use history to prepare for the future. The past is simply too different from the future for that to be possible.

The Christian, however, knows better. Although he acknowledges that each human is in many ways unique, he also knows that all humans are related. We all have come from Adam, and we all are beings made in God's image who have also fallen into sin. Most basically, therefore, we all tend to love and hate the same things, and we tend to behave in similar ways. Consequently, the Christian has good reason to expect that human choices will fall into patterns. Those who understand history can benefit from observing those patterns and may then use those observations to help them make good choices in the future. As Solomon said long ago, "The thing that hath been, it is that which shall be; and that which is done is that which shall be done: and there is no new thing under the sun" (Eccles. 1:9). Those who desire to be wise will prepare for "that which shall be done" by studying "that which is done."

History Gives Us Cultural Identity

But the study of history not only prepares us for the future, it also helps us understand who we are. A person's memory of his past is his identity. Probably most of us have read books or watched films that feature a central character suffering from amnesia. At some point in the story—usually early in the plot—the main character exclaims in anguish, "I don't know who I am!" Such conflicts make for enjoyable reading, but none of us would want to trade places with that character.

Memory of one's personal history is essential to knowing one's identity. Similarly, if we are to know who we are as a civilization, we must know our history. Through studying our cultural past, we come to learn what forces have made us who we are, and thus we learn what about us is truly valuable, what is only of marginal value, and what is vice or corruption. If we neglect our history, collective amnesia will set in. We will forget who we are and what we should want to become. The struggles of the past will be forgotten, and that which is truly valuable may be mistaken for vice, while vice may become mistaken for virtue.

At this point you may be asking, "But why must we study the history of the whole world? Could we not maintain our cultural identity by studying only the particular culture we live in?" Fundamentally, we are not Americans, Canadians, or Chinese. We are *humans*—children of Adam, creatures of God. We therefore are interested in all civilizations, for all civilizations are part of our own. As the apostle Paul told the Athenians, God "hath made of one blood all nations of men for to dwell on all the face of the earth, and hath determined the times before appointed, and the bounds of their habitation" (Acts 17:26).

If we truly desire to know what it means to be human, we must be willing to study not just the history of our own nation, but also of all nations. Their history is our history.

History Declares God's Glory

The Christian's best reason for valuing history is that history declares the glory of God. He is the ultimate historian. The Bible—the infallible book that He has given to teach us about Himself—makes extensive use of history. Nearly sixty percent of the Bible is concerned with recording history, and all of Scripture fits into a historical framework. The epistles, the Psalms, and all the other portions take place against the historical backdrop provided by the books of history.

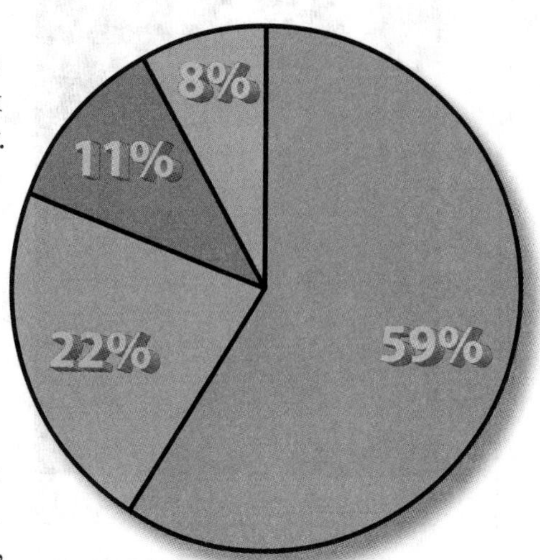

Historical Narrative: 59%
(Genesis–Esther and Matthew–Acts)
Prophecy: 22%
(Isaiah–Malachi and Revelation)
Poetry: 11%
(Job–Song of Solomon)
Epistles: 8%
(Romans–Jude)

God is a God who acts in history, and those who wish to know Him must know history. Scripture itself makes this point repeatedly by frequently commanding the people of God to *remember*. In explaining the importance of the Ten Commandments, God told the Israelites, "Remember that thou wast a servant in the land of Egypt, and that the Lord thy God brought thee out thence through a mighty hand and by a stretched out arm" (Deut. 5:15). When God was preparing them to enter the land of Canaan, He commanded them, "Thou shalt remember all the way which the Lord thy God led thee these forty years in the wilderness, to humble thee, and to prove thee" (Deut. 8:2). And centuries later, in one of the grandest statements of God's supremacy over the nations and their false deities, the Lord commends the right kind of historical awareness: "Remember the former things of old: for I am God, and there is none else; I am God, and there is none like me, declaring the end from the beginning, and from ancient times the things that are not yet done, saying, My counsel shall stand, and I will do all my pleasure" (Isa. 46:9–10).

These passages apply in our day as well. God is no less involved in His world today. He remains on His throne, and He will never cease to be what He has been throughout human history: "the blessed and only Potentate, the King of kings, and Lord of lords" (1 Tim. 6:15). Those who love God love His works, and since His works are displayed in history, those who love God have good reason to love history as well. The study of history is not just for the history buffs. It is for all who believe that the whole world is God's cathedral of praise and who also are constantly looking for new and fresh ways to "praise him for his mighty acts" (Ps. 150:2).

The Historian and His Task

History is of great value, especially for the Christian, but how do historians produce the books we use to learn about the history of our race? Historians act much like detectives. They search for clues that they hope will unlock the secrets of the past. These clues, or resources, provide the raw material of historical study. By collecting, analyzing, and interpreting this material, the historian can produce an account of the past that others may use.

The Historian's Resources

The resources that historians use are of two basic kinds. First, historians examine **primary sources**. These sources are records produced during the time period being studied, and they are often produced by the people involved in the events being studied. Second, historians study **secondary sources**. These are records that explain or interpret primary sources. Obviously, historians prefer to base their work on primary sources, though for some periods they are not able to do so. Primary sources may be derived from three basic historical resources: artifacts, tradition, and written records.

Johann Sebastian Bach (1685–1750)

Primary Sources	Secondary Sources
Manuscripts of Bach's choral pieces	Article analyzing the music of Bach
Emancipation Proclamation	Biography of Abraham Lincoln
Poems by American Puritans	Book about the Puritans
Memoirs of Napoleon	Essay on military tactics

Artifacts

The historian studies **artifacts** to learn about the background and culture of a people. Artifacts are objects made by man. They may be small relics, towering monuments, or priceless works of art. Most artifacts are simple, everyday items. Pottery, tools, weapons, furniture, clothing, coins, and jewelry unearthed by archaeologists (people who search for and study the artifacts of the past) give us valuable information about everyday life in past centuries.

The historian also derives information from architecture. He considers, for example, the pyramids in Egypt, the Acropolis in Athens, the Colosseum in Rome, the Great Wall in China, the Mayan temples in Central America, the soaring cathedrals in Europe, the Taj Mahal in India, or the towering skyscrapers of New York City. These impressive structures reflect the creative skill that God has given to men as well as the character of the people who built them.

As a historical artifact, these Mayan pyramids contain important clues for understanding the culture that produced them.

Even works of art aid the historian in understanding the past. Statues, drawings, paintings, and tapestries—"pictures of the past"—depict the customs, beliefs, hobbies, fashions, and way of life of past generations.

Tradition

Think of your own family's history. You may be able to trace your heritage back many generations. How did you learn about your family's past? Most likely this information was passed down by parents or grandparents who talked of the "good old days." Such oral communication was the earliest method of transmitting historical information. It is called **tradition**, which is simply the handing down of information by word of mouth from generation to generation. Over the centuries tradition has taken many forms. Legends, ballads, folk songs, and tales are but a few of these forms. But tradition is more than the reciting of songs and stories about the past. It includes the imparting of religious beliefs, family heritage, and social customs.

Written Records

Because word-of-mouth information can easily be forgotten or distorted, men have written down their accounts of the past to preserve a more accurate record for future generations. These **written records** are abundant and diverse. They include private letters, inventory lists, inscriptions, diaries, and journals. Historians also use information preserved in family and church records, in lists of kings and dynasties, and in political and legal documents. They gain insight into the thoughts, attitudes, and feelings of past generations by examining their works of literature. They also make use of historical works—detailed accounts of people, places, and events written during the period being investigated. They are also valuable tools in understanding the past.

Of the three kinds of primary sources, written records are by far the most important to the historian. Artifacts usually give only a sketchy testimony to the past and can be interpreted in very different ways. Tradition tends to offer detailed accounts, but since these accounts are subject to the embellishing of hundreds (sometimes thousands) of retellings, the testimony they yield is often not reliable. However, written records produced by those who lived during the period give a clearer testimony than artifacts, and since they do not have to be retold generation after generation, they are far more reliable than tradition. The great importance of written records is demonstrated by the fact that most historians consider it impossible to write a reliable history of a period unless written records are available.

A portion of Thucydides' History of the Peloponnesian War

The Historian's Use of His Resources

Producing a historical account, however, involves more than just collecting primary and secondary sources. The historian must also make proper use of what he has amassed. He does this, first of all, by **evaluation of historical sources**. He examines a given record for its internal consistency and believability. Then he compares that record to others like it, examining their points of agreement and disagreement. Having exposed the strengths and weaknesses of what is available to him, the historian is ready for the next step—**historical synthesis**. In this step he gathers the useful information he has found in his investigations and weaves that information together into a narrative of the past. The narrative he produces constitutes the vast majority of his history. But the historian's task is not yet complete. He must also engage in **historical interpretation**. He needs to interpret the events he records by integrating into that account what he believes is the meaning and significance of these events. He must not simply state what happened, but he must also explain why it happened and how the event remains significant for humans today. Once the historian has completed the steps of evaluation, synthesis,

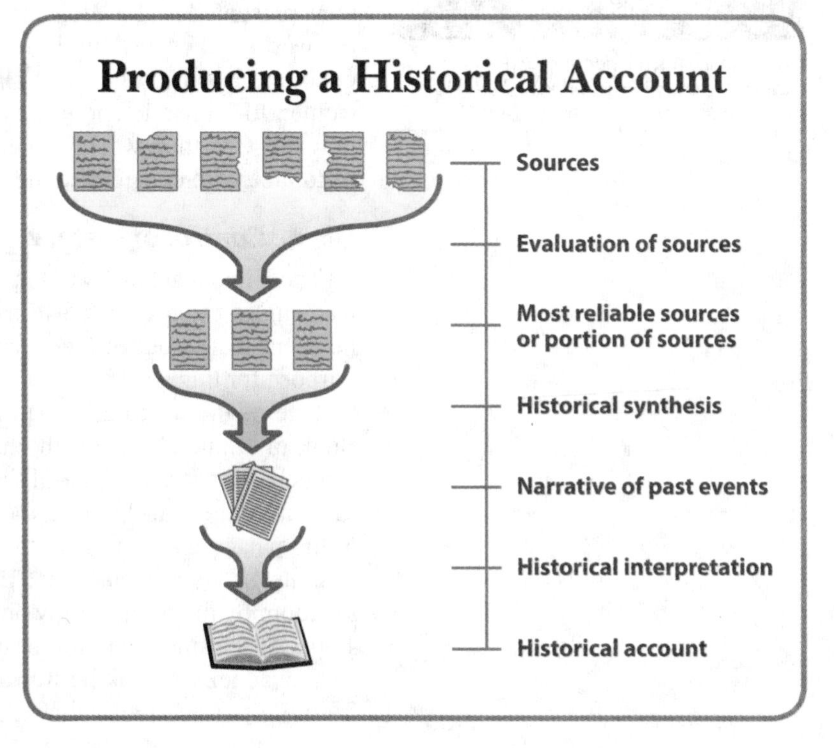

and interpretation, his work is ready to be studied, critiqued, and perhaps received by those who desire to know more about the subject of his work.

The Historian and His Philosophy

In working through the previously mentioned steps, the historian realizes right away that he is limited. He cannot know everything about the past. Furthermore, he cannot (and should not) record every bit of knowledge that is available about a given subject. He must select the events and facts that he will record. After selecting his information, he must then decide which areas will receive more emphasis. Some facts and events require several pages of description, while others need only a paragraph. Decisions about selection and emphasis are driven by a historian's philosophy of life—how he answers life's most important questions. Where did the universe come from? Why is it here? Where is this world headed? These are questions that humans can answer only by faith. A historian's faith—whether the faith of a Hindu, Muslim, atheist, or Christian—will profoundly shape his telling of history.

Studying History with a Christian Worldview

It is the conviction of the authors of this textbook that God has written a completely accurate and ultimately useful history. His history is contained in the Bible, in the sixty-six books of the Old and New Testaments. The Bible is the Christian's historical anchor. It records thousands of events that the Christian knows did indeed happen. Though the majority of the events studied in any world history textbook concern events that happened after the Bible was written, the Bible's record of these early periods is still very significant. That record concerns the most important events in the history of this world. By knowing about them, we know a great deal about all other events.

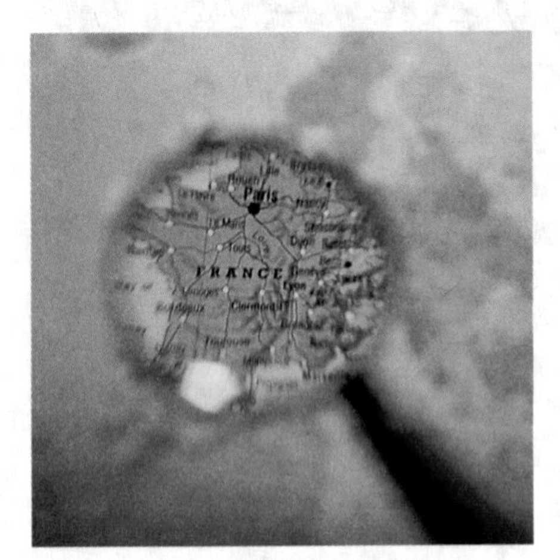

Biblical teaching functions as a lens that enables the Christian historian to study history as it was meant to be studied.

In addition to recording without error many important events, the Bible also presents us with a way of understanding and studying history. It does not give us a pattern to follow exactly. The biblical books are inspired, and ours are not. But the Bible does give us a **worldview**, a perspective from which we may examine and interpret the universe and everything in it. The **Christian worldview** presented in the Bible is composed of three central truths: (1) God made the world and everything in it; (2) this world has fallen into a sad and broken condition because of human sin; and (3) God is working to redeem men and women to Himself. The paragraphs that follow are our attempt to show you how this Christian worldview shapes our telling of history and how it enables us to face with confidence the limits of historical research.

Divine Control of History

The Bible teaches that God has planned all of human history. This biblical teaching is often referred to as the doctrine of **divine providence**. There is no event that is out of God's control or that does not help to accomplish His purpose for this world.

One of the best demonstrations of this truth in Scripture is found in the Book of Daniel. The fourth chapter records how the God of Israel humbled Nebuchadnezzar, the ruler of the Neo-Babylonian Empire and the most powerful man in the world during the sixth century BC. One day as he was walking in his palace and admiring the splendor of his kingdom, he arrogantly said to himself, "Is not this great Babylon, that I have built for the house of the kingdom by the might of my power, and for the honour of my majesty?" (Dan. 4:30). At that moment God struck his mind with a strange malady that made Nebuchadnezzar think he was a wild animal. His servants had to remove him from the palace, and Nebuchadnezzar lived outside, eating grass like a cow

Nebuchadnezzar's Babylon was the glory of the ancient world.

for seven years. After seven years God mercifully healed his mind. And it is instructive what Nebuchadnezzar concluded when he was able to think and reason clearly. He said of the God of the Bible, "He doeth according to his will in the army of heaven, and among the inhabitants of the earth: and none can stay his hand, or say unto him, What doest thou?" (v. 35). All who are able to think and reason clearly about history are led to the same conclusion. The Christian God is the One Who "worketh all things after the counsel of his own will" (Eph. 1:11).

The reality of divine providence affects our study of history in two important ways. First, it reminds us that we should be historical optimists. As we learn about the problems of the past (and there are more than anyone can count), we will be tempted to become very pessimistic about human history. But the fact that God is in control teaches us that we have no good reason to despair about the condition or direction of our world. The doctrine of divine providence does not deny that the world is evil; it does, however, deny that the world is out of control.

Second, divine providence encourages us to develop the habit of studying history with God's will in mind. The Christian should regularly ask himself, "What was God doing in this part of history?" Certainly there are some limitations that we face in seeking to answer this question. The first limitation concerns our lack of knowledge of the past. There is much about the past we do not know that may play a significant role in understanding how God has been at work. A second limitation concerns our own fallenness. We are all sinners, and therefore what we do know about the past we tend to interpret in selfish ways. A final limitation concerns our ignorance of God's will. We cannot know what God is doing in the earth unless He reveals it to us. That revelation is contained in the Bible. But connecting what the Bible says about God's working in the earth with the written records of the past is often difficult. Because of these limitations, we should be careful to answer the question concerning God's providence tentatively, viewing our answers as suggestions for understanding the past. However, though they are suggestions, these answers are not insignificant. They do help us grow in our understanding of the past, and they also help us show God our love and devotion even in history class. Such answers are our sacrifices of praise that we offer to God to show Him that we agree with the humbled Nebuchadnezzar: "Now I Nebuchadnezzar praise and extol and honour the King of heaven, all whose works are truth, and his ways judgment: and those that walk in pride he is able to abase" (Dan. 4:37). The recurring section of questions titled "Through Eyes of Faith" serves, in part, as our attempt to help you think about history with divine providence in mind.

Divine Providence and the Life of Joseph

God's humbling of Nebuchadnezzar (Dan. 4) teaches us that God controls the history of nations. God's working in the life of Joseph (Gen. 37-50) teaches that He controls the personal history of every individual.

Even at the age of seventeen, Joseph was a godly man. But his godliness did not protect him from humiliation and suffering. His brothers hated him because their father, Jacob, showed him preferential treatment. When the opportunity arose, the brothers sold him to be a slave in Egypt, and then they told Jacob that a wild animal had killed him. Joseph remained true to God in Egypt, but because he refused to be immoral while a slave, he was put in prison.

Jehovah, however, never abandoned Joseph. God enabled him to successfully interpret dreams while in prison, and when Pharaoh himself had a disturbing dream, Joseph was brought in to interpret. Joseph correctly perceived that the dream was referring to a coming worldwide famine. Pharaoh then appointed him to serve directly beneath him as the governor of all Egypt and to be in charge of preparing for the famine.

When the famine came, Joseph's brothers traveled to Egypt to buy grain. They did not recognize Joseph, but he immediately recognized them. Joseph used this advantage to test them. When he perceived that they had changed, he revealed himself to them and promised that he would take care of them through the famine. The brothers, however, could not believe that Joseph would forgive them. In that moment Joseph revealed how a firm belief in divine providence enables a person to overcome bitterness and to love the unlovely: "Now therefore be not grieved, nor angry with yourselves, that ye sold me hither: for God did send me before you to preserve life. . . . So now it was not you that sent me hither, but God" (Gen. 45:5, 8).

God is in control of all that happens. Even when wicked people harm those who love God, God is at work causing their wrong choices to accomplish His will. Part of being a Christian historian is learning to see how God takes the evil that people do and turns it into good (cf. Gen. 50:20). This perspective, however, applies not just when studying history. If we are abused for doing right, we, like Joseph, must resist bitterness and be willing to see how God may be using our own pain and suffering for good. That is part of being a Christian.

Jacob Mourning over Joseph's Coat, *Giovanni Francesco Barbieri, called Il Guercino, Bolognese, 1591–1666*
From the Bob Jones University Collection

Man's Fall into Sin

We cannot understand history unless we understand what the Christian worldview teaches regarding the source of the world's problems. Ultimately, it is not scarcity, disease, social inequality, or poor education that is to blame for pain in the world. The problem lies within each one of us. Our world is a troubled place because of our fall into sin. Because our first parents disobeyed and were cursed, all of us are depraved. **Human depravity** is a term that is used to describe the results of the Fall. It does not mean that all humans are as bad as they can possibly be. It means that every aspect of every human's being (body, mind, will, and emotions) has been stained by the Fall. Because we are all depraved, the story of our race is a story filled with wickedness and woe.

An understanding of human depravity will prevent the Christian from having an overly optimistic view about past generations. He will resist the temptation to accept an unrealistic picture of the past. At the same time, Christian students of history should take care that the truth of human depravity does not cause them to be overly negative about the future. While it is true that modern-day society is very degenerate, the Christian should not assume that this condition must continue forever. The God Who brought Nineveh to repentance, Who saved millions of souls in the Roman world during the first few centuries of the church, and Who has regularly revived His people ever since, is the same God Who hears our prayers now. No individual or society is too wicked for God's strong arm to save.

Redemption in Christ as the Goal of History

We have already mentioned that God is in control of history. We have even suggested that Christians should study history attempting to discern what God has been doing in the past. We cannot, of course, discern God's working unless we know the final goal that He is guiding this world toward. We cannot suggest *what* God may have done in the past unless we first know *why* He has chosen to be in control in the first place. Repeatedly, Scripture teaches that God is in control of history to redeem this world to Himself through the work of His Son. Or to state it more fully, God has planned all that happens in order to establish Christ's kingdom on earth so that through that kingdom He may declare His own glory (Rom. 11:36; 1 Cor. 15:28; Eph. 1:10; Rev. 11:15). The goal of human history is redemption in Christ.

God's redemptive love in Christ stands at the center of human history. The rise and fall of nations take on their proper significance only as they are related to what God is doing in the earth by His Son and through His people. History is about God seeking and saving His lost world. In His plan He has included many sorrows and disappointments. But viewed from the perspective of the end of all things, His plan is marvelously glorious. At the center of this plan are His Son and the people that His Son has purchased from sin. The Christian

Where Is This World Headed?

To express despair over the wickedness of our society, we often ask, "Where is this world headed?" Christians, however, should not despair. The world is wicked, but we know that it is still God's world and that in His plan it has a glorious future. Isaac Watts, commonly called the Father of English Hymnody, eloquently reminds the believer in "Jesus Shall Reign" that this world is headed for redemption because of the coming kingdom of Jesus Christ. This hymn is based on Psalm 72.

Jesus shall reign where'er the sun
Doth his successive journeys run;
His kingdom spread from shore to shore,
Till moons shall wax and wane no more.

People and realms of every tongue
Dwell on His love with sweetest song;
And infant voices shall proclaim
Their early blessings on His name.

Where He displays His healing power,
Death and the curse are known no more;
In Him the tribes of Adam boast
More blessings than their father lost.

Isaac Watts (1674–1748) by unknown artist
© National Portrait Gallery, London

1. ______________________________

____

____

____

2. ______________________________

____

____

____

____

3. ______________________________

____

____

____

____

4. ______________________________

____

____

5. ______________________________

____

____

6. ______________________________

____

____

7. ______________________________

____

____

____

8. ______________________________

____

____

____

____

worldview does not tell us what will happen in the next few years, but it does reveal that Christians are on the winning side of the conflicts of world history and that whatever does happen in the next few years will somehow contribute to Christ's ultimate triumph.

A Concluding Word About Studying History

As we think about our Christian worldview and how it affects our investigation of the past, we conclude that **history** is the study of the record of the past acts of God and man on earth from its creation to the present, based on the best surviving evidence. Our primary purpose for presenting to you a Christian view of history is not to enable you to do well on standardized tests or to make you appear educated before unbelievers (though we believe that if this book is used properly both will result). Our primary goal is to accomplish what the biblical historians sought to accomplish. When the psalmist Asaph introduced his survey of Israelite history, he told his readers, "I will utter dark sayings of old: which we have heard and known, and our fathers have told us. We will not hide them from their children, shewing to the generation to come the praises of the Lord . . . that they might set their hope in God, and not forget the works of God, but keep his commandments" (Ps. 78:2–4, 7).

If you are trusting in Christ for salvation from sin, then you are part of the next generation of the people of God. We sincerely hope that this year of studying world history will motivate you to set your hope in God. He has never failed His people, and He will not begin to do so in your generation. May the chapters that follow give you hundreds of reasons to live in obedience to His commands, and may they open your eyes to the ways in which God may use you to extend the kingdom of His Son. Some of you may exercise great influence on the future course of history. Many of you will have a small sphere of influence. But all of you will have influence, and that influence will have meaning and will be significant. May the history books of the next century be filled with hope because you used your influence for the glory of God.

Section Quiz

1. What is the Christian's best reason for studying history?
2. How do primary and secondary sources differ?
3. What are the three steps a historian must go through in order to produce a historical account?
4. What drives a historian's decisions about selection and emphasis?
5. In what ways does the Bible function as the Christian's historical anchor?
6. What question should the Christian regularly ask himself as he studies various periods in history?
7. What is the goal of human history?
8. Define *history*.

II. The Beginnings of World History

The first pages in most world history textbooks are some of the most difficult to get through. They deal with events in the very-distant past for which historians have only sketchy records. Paragraph after paragraph presents impersonal accounts of human-like groups struggling to move their race toward civilization.

The Bible's opening chapters present a very different account of long ago. Genesis 1–11 is anything but impersonal. It tells the story of individuals known to us by name: Adam, Eve, Cain, Abel, and Noah, to name a few. More impor-

A fish much like this longnose hawkfish is just one of the billions of creatures that came into being when God simply said, "Let the waters bring forth."

tantly, however, these chapters introduce us to history's most important Person. This Person too we know by name—**Jehovah**, the only true God. And unlike the cautious presentation of most history books, the Bible's record is bold, going far beyond the shadowy past to a time when there were no cities, no farms, no humans, and no earth.

Creation

The Bible begins where it must: "In the beginning God—." Before the universe was born, there was God and God alone. No other truths in Scripture have further-reaching ramifications than the two simple truths that God existed when nothing else did and that all that has come into being was made by Him. If the universe came about by chance—as many have claimed—its inhabitants are not responsible to a higher power. But if the world has been made by an almighty God—as the Bible claims—then this Supreme Being holds the title deeds to every galaxy, every planet, and every human. All are responsible to honor and obey the One Who has graciously chosen to let them exist.

God completed His world simply by speaking. In six days the earth went from a dark, watery sphere to a beautiful, inhabited world that God Himself could describe as "very good" (Gen. 1:31). And God accomplished all this work with only a series of commands—

"Let there be light" (v. 3)
"Let there be a firmament" (v. 6)
"Let the dry land appear" (v. 9)
"Let there be lights in the firmament" (v. 14)
"Let the waters bring forth abundantly" (v. 20)
"Let the earth bring forth the living creature after his kind" (v. 24)

Jehovah's voice of command is more than law. It determines what is and what will be. The events of this world's first week emphatically teach **divine sovereignty**—a phrase referring to God's complete and permanent authority over this world. Whatever opposition He has faced in history, He has chosen to face it so that He may use it for His own purposes. Although rebels within His creation may seem to triumph, He will in His own time prove to all that

He alone is victorious, "for he spake, and it was done; he commanded, and it stood fast" (Ps. 33:9).

The Climax of Creation—The Human Race

The climax of God's creative work came after He made the land animals on the sixth day. To that point, all that God had made came into existence with some form of the impersonal command "Let there be." Just before His final creation, however, God expressed special interest in what He was about to do: "Let us make man" (Gen. 1:26).

Mankind's Distinction

The reason for this special interest was that man was to be God's great masterpiece. Unlike the mammoth whales of the ocean, the majestic peaks of the mountains, and the brilliant stars scattered throughout the huge expanse of space, man would be made in God's own image: "So God created man in his own image, in the image of God created he him; male and female created he them" (Gen. 1:27). The **image of God** in man is a complex of qualities possessed by all humans that reflects part of God's own personality. Like God, humans would possess the characteristics of reason, moral consciousness, spiritual desire, sociability, and emotion. By mirroring part of His own being in man's, God set in this creature's soul both the desire and the ability to know Him intimately. The other creatures praise God for being the mighty Creator. Man, however, is privileged to praise Him for being both Creator and Friend.

Mankind's Purpose

The image of God in man also equipped the human race to fulfill its calling on earth. God did not make humans simply with the ability to fellowship with Him; He also made them with a job to do. After making the first man and woman, God told them, "Be fruitful, and multiply, and replenish the earth, and subdue it: and have dominion over the fish of the sea, and over the fowl of the air, and over every living thing that moveth upon the earth" (Gen. 1:28). This first command from God, often called the **Creation Mandate**, reveals mankind's reason for being.

The Meaning of the Creation Mandate—The central command of Genesis 1:28 is the command to "subdue" the earth by exercising "dominion" over it. Perhaps the best definition of this dominion is the work of maximizing the usefulness of the earth and all of its parts. Whether the part in question is a tomato or Niagara Falls, humans are called by God to imagine and implement prudent ways to tame the earth and make it useful.

To exercise good and wise dominion requires all sorts of knowledge and skill—knowledge of science, math, technology, language, and history, to name a few. These areas of human endeavor are not found explicitly in Genesis 1–2, but they are implied in the Creation Mandate. Properly understood, the Creation Mandate is not a command about fish and birds only. It is a command about pursuing the advancement of **culture**—the physical and mental environment developed through human thought and labor.

Historians who reject the Bible's history usually assert that humans had to evolve over thousands of years before they were capable of changing their environment. The Bible, however, teaches that human management of the environment—one of the leading themes of world history—goes back to our race's first day. At that time God placed in man's heart the desire and the ability to pursue every aspect of culture. This pursuit was never meant to serve man's selfishness or pride. It was to be God's way of declaring His glory through us. All of creation exists to declare God's glory (Rom. 11:36). But humans

Prehistoric Peoples?

Most world history textbooks offer an evolutionary account of the beginnings of our race. These accounts are called "**prehistory**" because they concern events that took place before humans developed writing. For these periods there are only artifacts: tools, clothing, weapons, and skeletons. These scant pieces of evidence are supposed to tell a story millions of years in length.

According to this view of the past, hominids (early humanlike creatures) first lived in East Africa as far back as three to four million years ago. The period from this time to about 10,000 BC is called the Early Stone Age (or the Paleolithic Age) because humans during this period used very simple stone tools. From the early hominids evolved the species *Homo erectus* ("upright human"). These hominids had more advanced tools than their predecessors, and they were the first to leave Africa for Asia and Europe. About 250,000 years ago, another human species arose, *Homo sapiens* ("wise human"). All humans today are members of this species.

Toward the end of the Old Stone Age, two kinds of *Homo sapiens* are said to have become prominent. In the caves of Europe and Southwest Asia, Neanderthals lived from about 130,000 to 35,000 years ago. Their significant contribution to human history was the great care that they took in burying their dead. Anthropologists believe that this practice is the first indication of belief in life after death—and thus some take it as the first evidence of religion in human history. About 35,000 years ago, the Cro-Magnons arose in Europe. These humans made advancements in tools and weapons. But perhaps their most interesting advancements were in art. Paintings by Cro-Magnons have been found in the caves of Spain and southern France.

The period from 10,000 BC to about 4000 BC is called the New Stone Age (or the Neolithic Age). The most significant development during this period was the agricultural revolution. Prior to this time, humans had been hunter-gatherers. They wandered from place to place hunting animals for food. But somehow, during the New Stone Age, humans learned that if certain seeds were planted, they could grow into edible plants. As agriculture and the domestication of animals developed, humans began settling down in permanent communities. These communities became the forerunners of the cities of antiquity. With the founding of the first cities between 4000 and 3000 BC, human civilization began.

It is difficult to imagine an account more at odds with biblical history. The Bible presents the human race as intelligent and able to engage in agricultural pursuits from its earliest times. Art and religion did not take millennia to develop. Toward the end of our race's first day, the first man spontaneously authored a poem (Gen. 2:23), and both man and woman spoke daily with God while in the Garden of Eden (Gen. 3:8). But the greatest problem with such accounts is that they attempt to show how humans came into being apart from any reference to God. In so doing, they remove from the history of our race the Person Who gives our race meaning and significance. God has made us in His image; therefore, we have dignity; and therefore, we can know peace and happiness only as we serve and love Him. Without Him we are nothing, and without Him in our history, our history has no meaning.

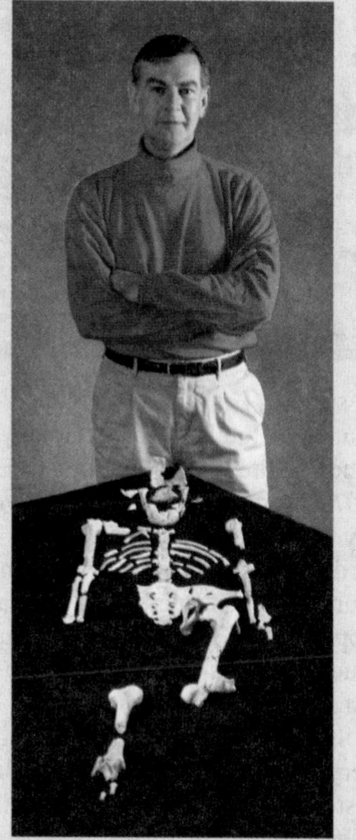

Top: *Mary Leakey, one of the most influential paleontologists of the twentieth century, convinced the scientific community that hominids first appeared in Africa rather than Asia.*

Middle: *Don Johanson, while excavating in Ethiopia in 1974, discovered what is considered an early hominid skeleton. He named it "Lucy" after a famous Beatles song. The skeleton (considered two or three million years old) is one of the most complete ever found.*

Bottom: *Though primitive to the untrained eye, the cave paintings attributed to Cro-Magnons show remarkable artistic sensitivity and skill.*

Ultimately, even the skyline of Singapore is not of human origin. The specialization and organization that make a city a city have their roots in the Creation Mandate of Genesis 1:28.

are special. The stars glorify God by declaring the greatness of His power and creativity. Humans glorify God by being like Him and imitating His deeds. He is the infinite Lord of the universe; we are the finite lords of His earth.

The Creation Mandate and Civilization—Central to the study of world history is the study of civilization. The word **civilization** comes from a Latin word (*civitas*) meaning "city," and it refers to human culture lived in cities or under their influence. Historically, a **city** is more than a place where many people live. It is a complex cultural institution in which humans share core values and a desire to improve the quality of their existence through specialization and organization.

Specialization refers to the division of labor that is part of the culture of every city. Individuals can specialize in a given endeavor necessary for human existence. The benefit of specialization is that individuals no longer need to do everything for themselves. Some specialize in food production, some in education, some in housing, some in the making of tools, and so forth; and each one benefits from the achievements of the others. To keep the network of specialization from unraveling, organization is necessary. This **organization** refers to a system of rules, regulations, and accountability that governs all who take part in the functions of the city. The results of specialization and organization are great advancements in science, technology, government, language, art, philosophy, and the accumulation of wealth.

It is important for Christians to realize that the city is ultimately not a human invention. Civilization—the object of study in this course—has its roots in the Creation Mandate. The specialization and organization that make a city a city are suggested in the opening commands of Genesis 1:28: "Be fruitful, and multiply, and replenish the earth, and subdue it." God recognized that the earth was a huge, complex place. If humans were to exercise the kind of dominion that would glorify Him, there would need to be a network of humans working together to maximize the usefulness of God's world. While it is true that the first city was still many years away (the first mention of a city is in Genesis 4:17), God intended from the beginning that civilization—and the enrichment that it brings—be part of human experience.

When God called the Israelites out of bondage in Egypt, He called them to live in a land filled with cities. He later chose a city, Jerusalem, to be the place where He was to be worshiped by His people. And in the age to come, the cultural center of the earth will be a city, the new Jerusalem (Rev. 21:1–3). God's heart is in the city, and as a Christian studies the history of civilization, he must remember that it is possible for a city to glorify God—indeed, that is His plan.

Mankind's Initial Work of Dominion

Genesis 1:1–2:3 records in general terms what God did on each day of the world's first week. Genesis 2:4–25 returns to the sixth day to record details not included in Genesis 1. These details focus on how mankind began the work of dominion.

Immediately after bringing **Adam**, the first man, to life, Jehovah began showing him how he was to exercise dominion over the earth. Just as God demonstrated His authority over the world by naming certain parts of it (cf. Gen. 1:5, 8, 10), so Adam was to begin to establish his dominion over the earth by giving names to the creatures God brought to him. To complete this task successfully would require much wisdom and creativity. Scripture indicates that God was not disappointed in Adam's performance: "Whatsoever Adam called every living creature, that was the name thereof" (Gen. 2:19).

Although the sixth day was drawing toward its close, God's creative work was not yet complete. He had made man to have dominion, but at this point Adam still lacked something essential to fulfill his calling. Adam had no human companion. Exercising successful dominion over the earth depended to a great degree on producing human offspring. Without another human as his sexual partner, Adam could not "replenish the earth, and subdue it" (Gen. 1:28).

God caused Adam to fall into a deep sleep. While he slept, God took one of his ribs and made a woman from it. Adam greeted this new creature by naming her. But recognizing that she was far more beautiful and glorious than anything he had yet named, he did not simply name her. He named her with a poem (Gen. 2:23):

> This is now bone of my bones,
> And flesh of my flesh:
> She shall be called Woman,
> Because she was taken out of Man.

The Fall

Adam and his wife, whom he later named **Eve** (Gen. 3:20), were part of a wonderful paradise. Best of all for Adam and Eve was not the beauty of the garden or the pleasures of a perfect marriage. Their greatest joy must have come from the relationship they had with their Creator. Genesis 3:8 indicates that Jehovah came regularly to visit with Adam and Eve, perhaps much like a parent spending time with a child. There was no fear and no danger. God and His highest creation enjoyed an unbroken, holy communion.

Like this plum, the fruit of the tree of the knowledge of good and evil looked both beautiful and delicious.

The First Sin

This ideal situation changed in a moment. When God called the human race to govern the earth, He called it to govern itself also. God had prohibited Adam and Eve from eating from the tree of the knowledge of good and evil (Gen. 2:16–17). This divine demand for self-control was taken by Satan as an opportunity to tempt the first woman to sin.

After listening to Satan's lies, Eve found herself doubting the only Person Who is completely trustworthy and trusting the person who can never be trusted. She was then ready to commit the act that would change the world: "She took of the fruit thereof, and did eat, and gave also unto her husband with her; and he did eat" (Gen. 3:6).

The Consequences of Sin

Immediately after eating the fruit, Adam and Eve became painfully aware that they had made the wrong decision. The consequences of their sinful choice affected both their inner being and their physical existence. As the apostle Paul explained centuries later, the consequences of that choice have been passed on to all humans: "Wherefore, as by one man sin entered into the world, and death by sin; and so death passed upon all men, for that all have sinned" (Rom. 5:12).

Twisted Affections

Since God had made the man and the woman good, they originally obeyed God's most basic moral command naturally. They naturally loved God with their entire being and loved each other as much as themselves (cf. Mark 12:30–31). But when they chose to disobey, these affections became twisted. Instead of enjoying God's presence in the garden, Adam and Eve were afraid of God and attempted to hide from Him. And when God confronted Adam about his sin, he gave a truly tragic answer: "The woman whom thou gavest to be with me, she gave me of the tree, and I did eat" (Gen. 3:12). Adam blamed his fellow human for a deed he was equally responsible for, and he blamed her in such a way that he implied God was partly at fault. With this one sentence Adam demonstrated the chief inward effect of the Fall. Humans love themselves supremely, and they cannot bring themselves to love God or their fellow humans as they should. This central moral defect has characterized all of human culture ever since. The history of science, technology, art, politics, religion, and philosophy all bear the tragic marks of mankind's inability to love as he was meant to love.

Thwarted Dominion

God had made Adam and Eve to have dominion over the earth. Just as they had rebelled against God, so God made the earth rebel against them: "Cursed is the ground for thy sake; . . . thorns also and thistles shall it bring forth to thee" (Gen. 3:17–18). In this struggle Adam—along with all his offspring—was destined for defeat. Though called to subdue the earth, he would in the end be subdued by it: "In the sweat of thy face shalt thou eat bread, till thou return unto the ground; for out of it wast thou taken: for dust thou art, and unto dust shalt thou return" (v. 19).

The couple's most tragic punishment came last. Because they were now sinners, Adam and Eve were no longer fit to enjoy the bliss of the garden and the unhindered fellowship with God that it provided. Jehovah expelled them from paradise and stationed angels with flaming swords at its entrance. To gain the knowledge of good and evil, our first parents chose to disobey God. They got what they wanted; they lost what they had.

The Hope of Salvation

In the middle of this devastating tragedy, God gave our race a glimmer of hope. While pronouncing His curse on Satan and the serpent he used, God offered a glimpse of the gracious salvation He had planned for mankind: "I will put enmity between thee [Satan] and the woman, and between thy seed and her seed; it shall bruise thy head, and thou shalt bruise his heel" (Gen. 3:15). Had it not been for this verse, there would have been no need of another. The human race had chosen its own destruction by sinning. But God revealed only moments after confronting this sin that those made in His image would have the hope of future triumph.

The Two "Seeds"

God promised both the serpent and the woman a "seed," or a group of descendants. Most likely, the **seed of the serpent** is a phrase referring to humans yet to be born who would prove to have the same deceptive, God-defying nature that Satan evidenced that day in the garden. The **seed of the woman**, on the other hand, most likely refers to future humans who would prove to be loyal to their Creator. Of course, the most important member of the seed of the woman would be God's own Son, who would enter the human race to lead His people to victory over sin, Satan, and death.

The Central Conflict of History

Genesis 3:15 is the Bible's thesis statement for human history. Man had been called to exercise dominion over God's creation. But because of sin there would now be two dominions: the seed of the woman and the seed of the serpent. God predicted that these two seeds were destined for conflict ("enmity"). Through the long centuries ahead, Satan's offspring would wound the followers of Jehovah many times. Often Satan's bruising of God's people would seem more like fatal blows to the head than injuries to the foot. And at such times

Because of the many Christians who died for their faith in that place, Rome's Colosseum has become a symbol of the struggle of belief against unbelief seen throughout history.

Satan and his followers would seem to go on with no injuries at all. During these periods—and they would prove to be many—the seed of the woman would be able to discern God's working in the world only through eyes of faith. Jehovah had promised victory for His followers, but that victory would be many, many battles away.

Moral Decay and Judgment

Adam and Eve believed God's promise of a conquering seed. Eve demonstrated this faith at the birth of her first son. She named him **Cain** (meaning "acquired") and explained, "I have gotten a man from the Lord" (Gen. 4:1). Perhaps this was her way of saying that she had mothered the seed of the woman destined to crush the serpent's head. If so, her faith was commendable, but she had tragically underestimated the magnitude of the struggle that lay ahead for the human race. Eve had in fact brought into the world the first of the serpent's seed, as she was about to learn.

Cain and His Seed

Cain grew to be a religious man. He demonstrated outward devotion to his Creator by offering to Him a portion of the crops he harvested. However, for a reason not stated in Genesis, Jehovah rejected these offerings. Instead, He took delight in the offerings of Cain's younger brother, Abel. This rejection made Cain very jealous and angry.

The First Murder

Cain would not heed God's correction. His self-centeredness fed his frustrated pride until he lashed out in anger. He could not hurt God, but he could—as Satan did in the garden—harm a person that God delighted in. One day, while Cain and Abel were working together in the field, Cain killed his brother. In one generation mankind had gone from eating forbidden fruit to murder.

As He had done with Adam in the garden, God confronted Cain with a question: "Where is Abel thy brother?" (Gen. 4:9). Adam had responded to a similar question with fear; Cain responded to this question with brash disrespect:

The Dead Abel, *Peter Paul Rubens*
From the Bob Jones University Collection

"I know not: Am I my brother's keeper?" The judgment God chose for Cain was an intensification of the curse given in the garden: "When thou tillest the ground, it shall not henceforth yield unto thee her strength" (v. 12).

Though built long after the time of Cain (after the Flood), the city of Jericho is considered to be the oldest city that has been excavated. This part of the city is thought to be its most ancient section.

The Growth of Godlessness

Cain went on to father a line of descendants whose activities are in many ways typical of human history. The Cainites, it seems, were the first to live in civilization. The first city mentioned in Scripture was built by Cain. The specialization that is always part of city life was carried on by Cain's descendants. Jabal worked in agriculture as a herdsman. Jubal labored in the arts, making musical instruments. And Tubal-cain worked in industry, producing all sorts of objects made of brass and iron. Whether they realized it or not, they were living out the implications of the Creation Mandate. They had been fruitful and therefore had multiplied over the face of the earth. Through specialization and organization, they had raised up the earliest human civilization.

Nevertheless, their civilization was not pleasing to God. Their sin was not building and maintaining a city. Their sin was attempting to live out the Creation Mandate independent of God. Perhaps the best summary statement in Genesis for the problem with Cainite culture is the verse that introduces us to that culture: "And Cain went out from the presence of the Lord, and dwelt in the land of Nod" (Gen. 4:16). Living apart from the will and love of Jehovah was one of the core values that held Cainite civilization together.

The best personal example of this culture is given in what the Bible records about **Lamech**, the great-great-great-grandson of Cain. He violated God's created order for marriage. As the first known polygamist (a man with more than one wife), Lamech fulfilled Jehovah's sad prediction that men would "rule over" women (cf. Gen. 3:16). He also demonstrated that Cain's descendants were more corrupt morally than Cain himself. Cain had murdered his brother, tried to cover it up, and later begged God for mercy (Gen. 4:13–14). Lamech, however, murdered a man and then bragged about it to his wives (vv. 23–24).

Seth and His Seed

The story of Cain and his descendants is only part of the history of mankind after the Fall. God gave Adam and Eve another son. Eve named him **Seth** ("appointed"). She explained, "God . . . hath appointed me another seed instead of Abel" (Gen. 4:25). Seth proved to be a spiritual as well as a physical replacement for Abel. Just as Abel worshiped God in an acceptable manner, so Seth fathered a line of people who were known to "call upon the name of the Lord" (v. 26). Through Seth, the seed of the woman increased and prospered.

The Growth of Godliness

Seth's seed was the opposite of Cain's. Just as the Bible singles out Lamech as typical of the Cainites' sinfulness, so also Enoch, Seth's great-great-grandson, is held up as an example of this line's godliness. While Lamech was living away from the presence of God, Enoch "walked with God" (Gen. 5:22). But Enoch was not the only descendant of Seth. Genesis 5 records a

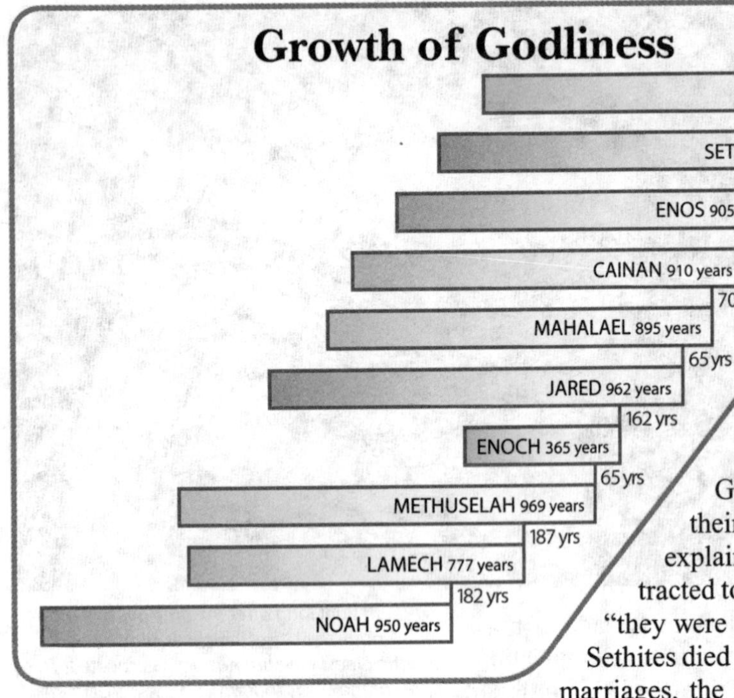

Because each person lived a very long time, the population growth among the Sethites must have been remarkable—that is, if the birthrate was similar to the modern birthrate. These long lives would also have made possible a great cultural continuity. Noah could have learned about God and history from his father, who could have learned from Adam himself.

long genealogy of Sethites, each of whom lived an amazingly long life. If calling on the name of Jehovah was typical of each of these men's life and influence, the seed of the woman must have eventually rivaled the numbers of the Cainites, the seed of the serpent.

Compromise and Tragic Loss

The Sethites, however, did not remain true to their God. Because of the reality of death, a godly people cannot remain godly unless it passes on to each new generation its love and devotion to God. At some point in their history, the Sethites allowed their children to intermarry with the Cainites. The Bible explains that Seth's descendants ("the sons of God") were attracted to the Cainite women ("the daughters of men") because "they were fair" (Gen. 6:2). As the previous generations of godly Sethites died and were replaced by the children of religiously mixed marriages, the line of Seth was transformed. Soon the behavior of Seth's descendants was no different from that of Cain's people. The entire race became morally corrupt. Eventually, as the Bible declares, "every imagination of the thoughts of [man's] heart was only evil continually" (Gen. 6:5).

The Great Flood

Since the earth was no longer serving its purpose, God determined to remake His world. God was now preparing to cover the whole earth with a great flood. One member of the Sethite line remained a committed worshiper of his Creator. **Noah** rejected the corrupting influences of the world and, like Enoch, "walked with God" (Gen. 6:9). To Noah God revealed His plan for the survival of the human race. He instructed Noah to build a massive ark (literally a "box" or a "chest"). God told Noah that when he completed this project, he was to take his family and representatives of the animal kingdom into the ark, where they would be safe. Noah and his family obeyed. God held back His judgment for 120 years (Gen. 6:3). The human race had more than a century to repent and accept the promise of life offered through the ark. But in the end only Noah, his wife, his three sons, and their wives entered the ark. At the predetermined moment, the "fountains of the great deep" were broken up, and torrents of rain fell. It rained for forty days, and by the time it stopped, the entire earth was covered in water. The almighty Creator had caused the earth to return to its original state. Once again it was "without form and void" (Gen. 1:2).

The Hebrew word translated "ark" means "box." This indicates that—contrary to many artists' renderings—the ark was probably not a large boat. It was designed to be a floating box.

A Second Beginning

As the flood waters receded, the ark came to rest on the Ararat mountain range. As Noah left the ark, he entered a world newly reborn. The contaminating vestiges of the old world had been purged away. The earth was now populated only by members of the divinely promised seed of the woman—or so it seemed at first.

A Glimpse at the Future

One of Noah's earliest actions after the Flood was less than noble. He became intoxicated from the fruit of his own vineyard and fell asleep naked in his tent. This failure became the backdrop for one of history's most important moments. Noah's son **Ham** saw his father in his shameful stupor and talked about him to his brothers, **Shem** and **Japheth**. Having proper respect and love for their father, these two sons entered Noah's tent with their backs turned and covered him with a garment.

Noah's Prophecy

When Noah realized what had happened, he punished Ham by placing a curse on **Canaan**, one of Ham's sons: "Cursed be Canaan; a servant of servants shall he be unto his brethren" (Gen. 9:25). But recognizing the noble deed of the other two sons, Noah blessed Shem and Japheth. He spoke of Shem's future first: "Blessed be the Lord God of Shem; and Canaan shall be his servant" (v. 26). Thus Noah indicated that Shem's future blessing would consist in his descendants' special relationship to Jehovah and that God would use the curse on Canaan to benefit Shem. Concerning Japheth, Noah prophesied, "God shall enlarge Japheth, and he shall dwell in the tents of Shem" (v. 27). Japheth would be blessed with wealth and power, and he would find additional blessing in sharing in Shem's blessing.

Mount Ararat is located in modern-day Turkey, near its eastern border.
Photo from the book Noah's Ark Uncovered, *Scandinavia 2005*

The Serpent's Seed Continues

This incident demonstrated that though all the Cainites had perished in God's judgment, the seed of the serpent had survived. To accomplish his ends, Satan is not limited to using only those who openly oppose Jehovah's working. Ham was the son of the godliest man on earth and had served Jehovah for decades building the ark. But in the end we learn that Ham's heart was corrupt and that many of his descendants would not enjoy the blessings that God had planned for the other sons of Noah.

Triumph Through Shem

This incident also shows that Jehovah remained the master of history. Though opposed by the serpent, He continued to be in control and still had a plan for His ultimate triumph. New aspects of that plan were revealed in Noah's prophecy. Here God suggested that Shem would somehow play a special role in the triumph of the seed of the woman. This triumph is foreshadowed in the curse on Canaan. The Canaanites, who eventually settled in a land they named for their ancestor, would end up serving the descendents of Shem. It should not surprise us, therefore, to find that much of biblical history traces God's working among the Hebrews, descendants of Shem, in a land that God took from the Canaanites.

Babel and Its Consequences

As years passed into decades, mankind once again multiplied and began to fill the earth. Civilization reemerged as city-building began again. But mankind did not want to establish many different civilizations. The race desired to live together and form a single, unified society.

The Sin of Babel

At this time all of mankind spoke the same language. It was not difficult, therefore, for them to organize themselves. They gathered in the land of Shinar (probably located in southeastern Mesopotamia) and began to build the city that would later be called **Babel**. Central to this city was to be a magnificent tower, which would serve as this civilization's religious center. The reasons

The Tower of Babel,
Pieter Bruegel the Elder, 1563
From the Kunsthistorisches Museum, Vienna

Many have imagined that the Tower of Babel was a very tall, cylinder-like structure. It may, however, have been more like the ziggurats built some time later by the Sumerians.

they gave for this undertaking were revealing: "Go to, let us build us a city and a tower, whose top may reach unto heaven; and let us make us a name, lest we be scattered abroad upon the face of the whole earth" (Gen. 11:4).

Eve brought immeasurable woe on the human race when she tried to fulfill God-given desires by disobeying God-given commands (Gen. 2:16–17; 3:6). Now these descendants of Noah were seeking to enjoy the blessings of the Creation Mandate while refusing to obey the command to fill the earth (cf. Gen. 1:28; 9:1; 11:4). They were also seeking fulfillment and fame by trying to enter heaven,

God restrained mankind's sinfulness at Babel because He had promised never again to destroy the world with a flood (Gen. 9:15–16). The symbol of this promise is the rainbow.

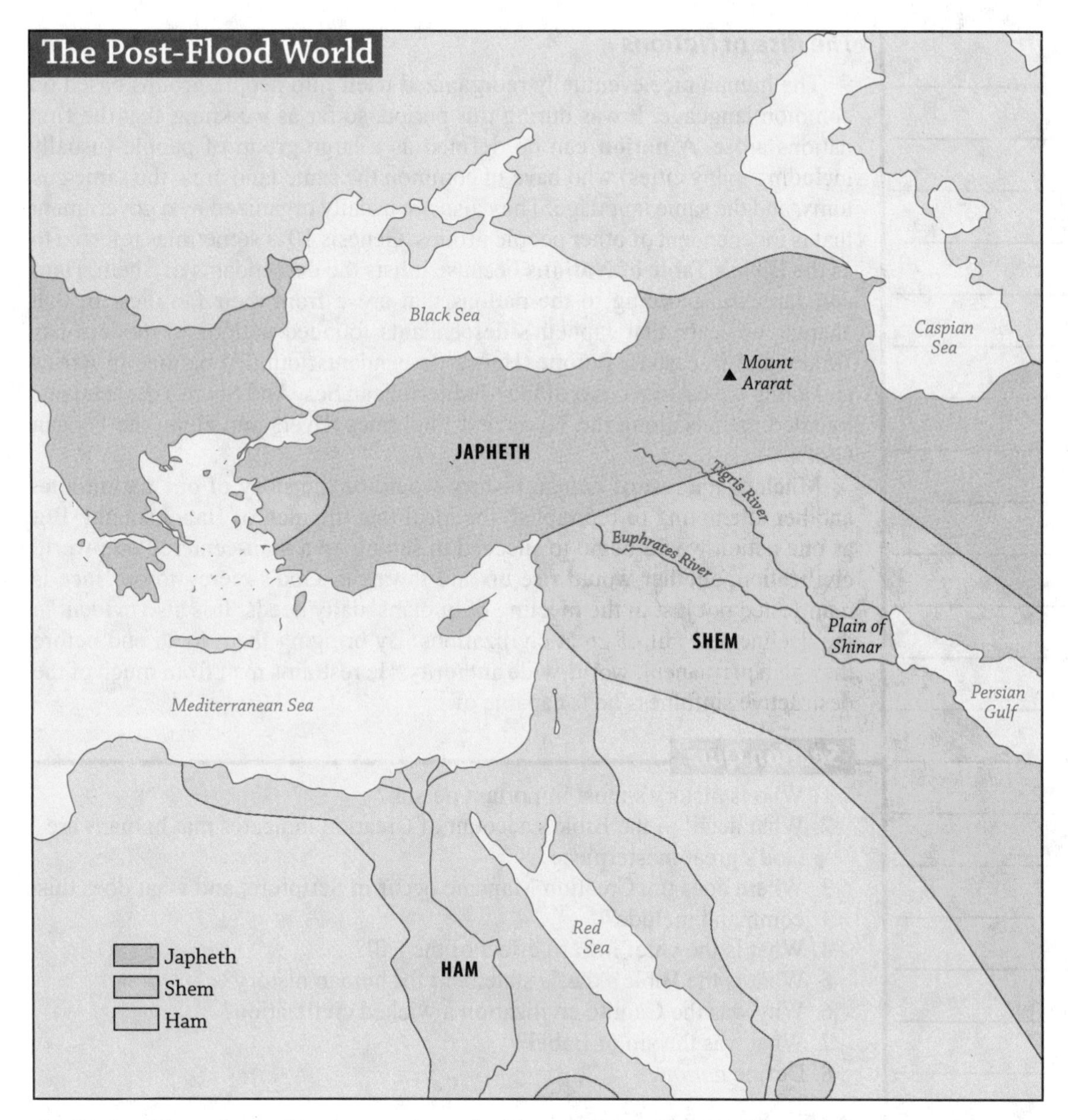

God's dwelling place. The core values that bound this civilization together were the desires to disobey the Creation Mandate and to challenge the distinction between God and man. Jehovah was, of course, aware of what they were doing. He found their endeavors to be disturbing: "Behold, the people is one, and they have all one language; and this they begin to do: and now nothing will be restrained from them, which they have imagined to do" (v. 6).

God's Response to Babel

God did not feel threatened by what was happening at Babel. Through the Flood, He had proved His ability to rule rebellious humans effectively. His concern was for mankind. The race was once again on the verge of destruction. They were pushing the earth toward the same cataclysm of divine wrath that had snuffed out nearly all life on earth.

Jehovah, however, had promised that He would never again destroy the world with a flood (Gen. 9:15–16). Rather than unleashing His righteous anger, He chose to restrain our race's ability to do evil. He confused the minds of those at Babel so that they could no longer communicate with one another. In that hour, long ago, the complex and confusing differences among human languages were born.

1.
2.
3.
4.
5.
6.
7.
8.

The Rise of Nations

The human race eventually reorganized itself into people groups based on common language. It was during this period, so far as we know, that the first nations arose. A **nation** can be defined as a large group of people (usually including many cities) who have in common the same land area, the same customs, and the same language. They also are usually organized by a government that is independent of other people groups. Genesis 10 is sometimes referred to as the Bible's **Table of Nations** because it lists the descendants of Shem, Ham, and Japheth according to the nations that arose from their families. In that chapter we learn that Japheth's descendants founded nations in modern-day Turkey and in eastern Europe. Ham's descendants founded nations in Africa and along the eastern coast of the Mediterranean Sea. And Shem's descendants founded nations along the Tigris and Euphrates Rivers and along the Persian Gulf.

Much of the rest of human history would be the story of one nation after another attempting to reestablish the ideal that the men of Babel sought. But as one nation would begin to succeed in setting up a man-centered one-world civilization, another would rise up and thwart it. God's mercy to our race is manifested not just in the meeting of humans' daily needs. It is also evident in the decline and fall of great civilizations. By bringing them to an end before they gain permanent, world-wide authority, He restrains man from much of the destructive sinfulness he is capable of.

Section Quiz

1. Who is history's most important person?
2. What detail in the Bible's account of Creation indicates that humans are God's great masterpiece?
3. Where does the Creation Mandate occur in Scripture, and what does this command include?
4. What is the chief inward effect of the Fall?
5. What is the Bible's thesis statement for human history?
6. Why was the Cainite civilization a wicked civilization?
7. What was the sin of Babel?
8. Define *nation*.

A Glance Behind

God made man in His image so that He could declare His glory through man's work of dominion. This high calling was the basis for the rise of human civilization. Man, however, chose to disobey God. Because of his rebellion, paradise was ruined, and the course of civilization was cursed by death and man's inability to love as he was meant to. But in the midst of this curse, God promised to restore mankind to his original stature and calling. Through the seed of the woman, God would defeat the serpent and his seed.

As the centuries passed, the disturbing strength of the serpent's seed became evident. Jehovah's plan, however, could not be frustrated. Though often outnumbered and seemingly defeated, the seed of the woman continued to enjoy God's blessing and protection. And though the external delights of Eden would remain lost until God's final triumph, the inner blessings of walking with God were restored to these worshipers of Jehovah. These inward blessings would be necessary to sustain them as they looked forward to the next stage in the fulfillment of God's promise of a conquering seed—the call of Abraham.

and a Glimpse Ahead

Chapter Review

Can You Define?

primary sources
secondary sources
worldview
divine providence
human depravity
history
divine sovereignty
image of God
culture
prehistory
civilization
city
specialization
organization
nation

Can You Identify?

artifacts
tradition
written records
evaluation of historical sources
historical synthesis
historical interpretation
Christian worldview
Jehovah
Creation Mandate
Adam
Eve
seed of the serpent
seed of the woman
Cain
Lamech
Seth
Noah
Ham
Shem
Japheth
Canaan
Babel
Table of Nations

Can You Locate?

Ararat
Shinar
Region of the Hamites
Region of the Japhethites
Region of the Shemites

How Much Do You Remember?

1. How does the study of history protect us from collective amnesia?
2. Of the three kinds of primary sources discussed in this chapter, which one is most important to historians? Why?
3. Name three limitations that Christians face as they attempt to study history with divine providence in mind. Why is studying history in this way still important?
4. Why has God planned all that happens in history?
5. Historically, what is a *city,* and how is the Creation Mandate related to this historical concept?
6. Through what task did Adam begin to establish his dominion over the earth?
7. What was the most tragic punishment that God placed on Adam and Eve?
8. What practice, committed by the Sethites, caused the entire human race to become morally corrupt?
9. What was the content of Noah's prophecy concerning his sons? How is this prophecy significant for human history?

What Do You Think?

1. Respond to the following statement: "It is not possible to use the study of history to prepare for the future. Every civilization is unique. The legitimate parallels between our lives and the lives of previous generations are too few and far between."
2. For a city to form, those who will populate the city must have in common a number of core values. Name some core values that have throughout history bound civilizations together.
3. How have the twisted affections resulting from the Fall affected the development of human civilizations?
4. What may the Christian learn from the compromise and tragic loss of the Sethites?
5. Was the confusion of languages at Babel a divine judgment or a divine mercy? Defend your answer.

2

"In thy seed shall all the nations of the earth be blessed."

EARLY CIVILIZATIONS

The Plain of Genneseret below the Arbel Cliffs

Blessed is the man that walketh not in the counsel of the ungodly, nor standeth in the way of sinners, nor sitteth in the seat of the scornful. But his delight is in the law of the Lord; and in his law doth he meditate day and night. And he shall be like a tree planted by the rivers of water, that bringeth forth his fruit in his season; his leaf also shall not wither; and whatsoever he doeth shall prosper.

Psalm 1:1–3

It is no coincidence that the psalmist compares the life of a godly man to a tree planted on a riverbank. To the people of the ancient world, rivers were the source of life. It was along riverbanks that civilization began anew after the Flood. This chapter highlights development of the early Middle Eastern and Egyptian civilizations and God's work in their midst.

Karnak temple ruins

I. Mesopotamia

After God scattered the nations at the Tower of Babel, many of the descendants of Ham and Shem remained and settled in the fertile region of the Tigris and Euphrates rivers (Gen. 10: 6–32). Later the Greeks described this region with the word *Mesopotamia* (MES uh puh TAY mee uh), meaning the "land between the rivers." By about 3000 BC the people in the southern part of this area had established the Sumerian civilization.

Sumerian Civilization

Sumer consisted of about a dozen independent city-states that had no political unity but possessed a similar culture. The cities fought constantly among themselves, each trying to gain dominance over the others. The Sumerians believed that their cities belonged to the gods. For this reason the temple was not only a place of worship but also the center of education, government, and trade. Each city had its own ruler, usually a priest, who acted as the representative of the gods.

The Sumerians' religion was a clear rejection of the one true God. They, along with almost all other civilizations until the coming of Christ, were committed to **polytheism** (belief in many gods). The fact that they were polytheistic, though historically near to the Flood and the witness of Noah, testifies to the truth of Romans 1:20–21: "The invisible things of [God] from the creation of the world are clearly seen, being understood by the things that are made . . . so that they are without excuse; because that, when they knew God, they glorified him not as God, neither were thankful; but became vain in their imaginations." False religion is not motivated by a desire to find and know the true God. It is an attempt to hide from the testimony to this God, found everywhere in this world.

Cuneiform

Much of what we know about Sumer has come from the discovery of thousands of clay tablets bearing **cuneiform** (KYOO nee uh FORM), the earliest known form of writing. Using a wedge-shaped stylus (a split reed), the Sumerians made impressions on tablets of wet clay, which they later baked until hard. They could express ideas by the manner in which they arranged these wedge-shaped impressions. Young men learned this complex writing in a formal educational system. Professors were called "school-fathers," and the students were called "school-sons." Sumerian boys also studied the Sumerian numerical system—a system based not upon ten like ours today, but on the number sixty.

An Account of a Sumerian Schoolboy

I recited my tablet, ate my lunch, prepared my (new) tablet, wrote it, finished it. . . . When school was dismissed, I went home, entered the house, and found my father sitting there. I told my father of my written work, then recited my tablet to him, and my father was delighted. . . . When I awoke early in the morning, I faced my mother and said to her: "Give me my lunch, I want to go to school." My mother gave me two "rolls" and I set out. . . . In school the monitor in charge said to me, "Why are you late?" Afraid and with pounding heart, I entered before my teacher and made a respectful curtsy.[1]

A reconstructed ziggurat at Ur

Farming and Architecture

The major occupation of the Sumerians was farming. They built an elaborate network of canals and dikes to provide irrigation for their crops. Although agriculture was the basis of their economy, the people lived in fortified cities. They built their homes and public buildings with baked clay bricks. The most outstanding examples of Sumerian architecture are the temple towers called **ziggurats** (ZIG uh RATS). These impressive pyramidlike structures had terraces at different levels along their exterior. The bricks used in these buildings were often glazed in different colors.

Sargon

During the period of Sumerian dominance, a new people migrated into the northern Sumerian cities. They adopted much of the Sumerian culture. At the same time, they began to assert their own influence upon the cities in which they settled. Around 2350 BC the ruler **Sargon I** came to power in the city-state of Kish. Sargon conquered other city-states and established the first known **empire**—the rule of one people over another. Making the city of Akkad his capital, he created a united kingdom—the Akkadian (uh KAY dee un) Empire—which stretched from the Persian Gulf to northern Mesopotamia. Under Sargon, the king's authority surpassed that of the priests. Many people began viewing the kings as gods.

About a century after Sargon's death, the city of Ur rose to prominence. This powerful city-state may have been the same Ur that is mentioned in Genesis 11:31 as the birthplace of Abraham, the father of the Hebrew people. But whether "Ur of the Chaldees" (as the Bible calls it) was the well-known city of southern Mesopotamia is ultimately of little importance. What is important to know and remember is that the world into which Abraham was born was a world dominated by polytheism and idolatry. God revealed Himself to Abraham around 2100 BC. And when He called him to move out of Ur, He was not simply telling him to leave his home. He was also telling him to leave his way of life—probably the only way of life he had known.

Sumerian Contributions

By 2000 BC the Sumerian civilization had died out. However, aspects of its culture continued in later civilizations. The Amorites, Hittites, Assyrians,

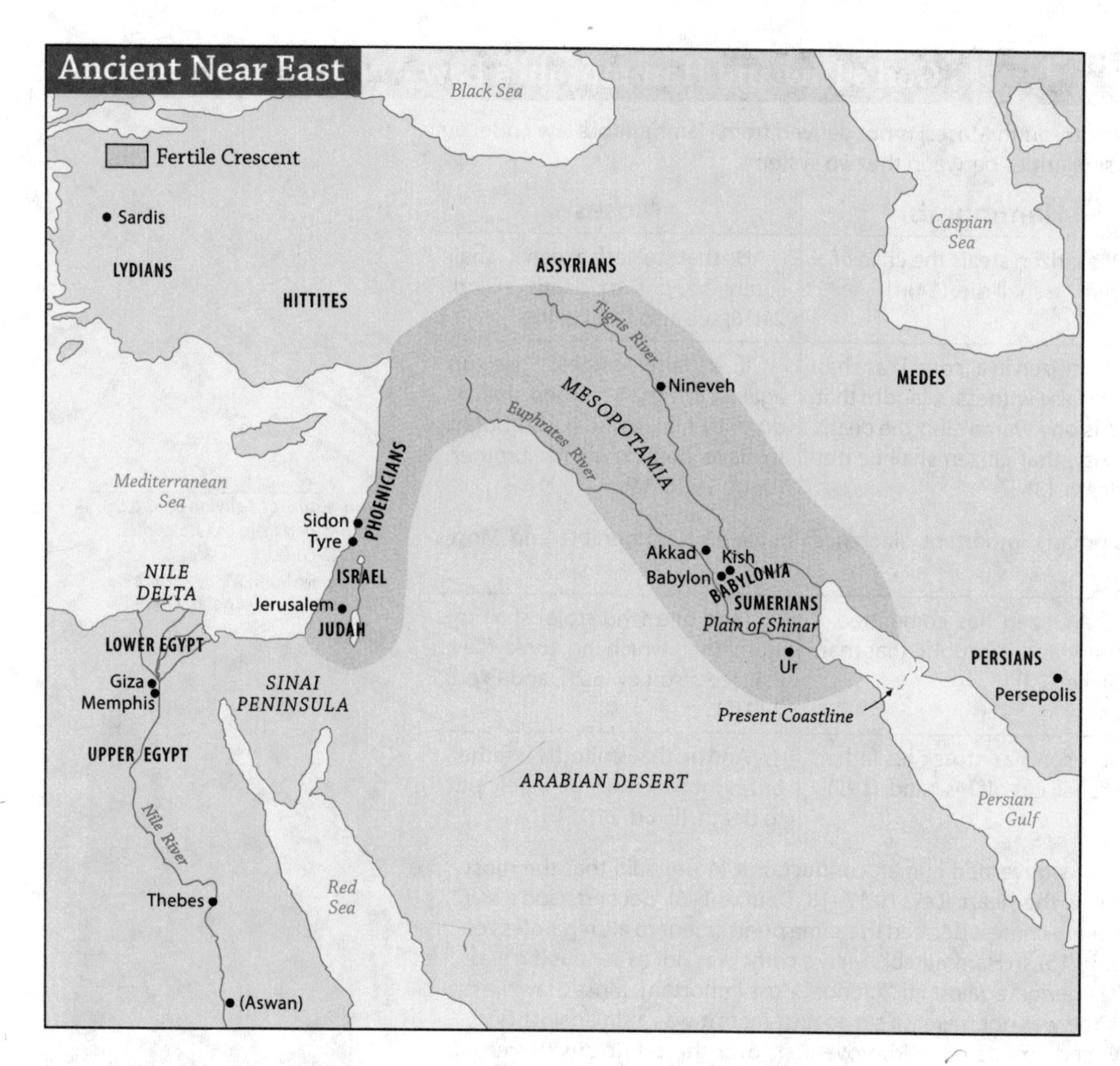

and Persians used cuneiform. Roman architects adopted Sumerian building techniques, such as the arch. Even today we use Sumerian inventions: the wheel, the division of a circle into 360 degrees, and the division of hours and minutes into sixty units. These influences testify of Sumerian knowledge and technological skill.

Amorite Civilization

Weakened by a series of wars with its neighbors, the Sumerian civilization, centered at Ur, fell to Amorite invaders. The Amorites established the "Old Babylonian" Empire. Its capital was the city of Babylon (BAB uh lun), one of the greatest cities of the ancient world. The history of this city began shortly after the Flood, when Nimrod established a kingdom that included Babylon (Gen. 10:10). It was in or near this city that the Tower of Babel was built.

Hammurabi (1795?–1750 BC)

The sixth king of the Amorites, **Hammurabi** (HAH moo RAH bee), united the land of Mesopotamia under his rule. He was a successful military leader and an able administrator. His large staff assisted in the building and maintenance of the canals for irrigation, in the collection of taxes, and in the regulation of the administrative and business matters of the kingdom.

Hammurabi is best remembered for his code of laws. He did not write these laws but compiled, organized, and simplified existing laws. Hammurabi's code

God's Law and Hammurabi's Law

God's law, given through Moses, is not derived from Hammurabi's law code, but there are several similarities between the two systems.

	Hammurabi	Moses
Kidnapping	If a citizen steals the child of a citizen, he shall die. (14)	He that stealeth a man . . . shall surely be put to death. (Exod. 21:16; see also Deut. 24:7)
Lying	If a citizen in a [court] case has borne false witness . . . [and] if that case is one warranting the death penalty, that citizen shall be put to death. (3)	If a false witness rise up against any man . . . then shall ye do unto him, as he had thought to have done unto his brother. (Deut. 19:16, 19)

There are also many important differences between Hammurabi's and Moses' (God's) law codes.

	Hammurabi	Moses
Theft	If a citizen has committed a robbery and is caught, that man shall die. (22)	[The one who stole] shall restore that which he took. (Lev. 6:4; see also Lev. 6:2ff. and Exod. 22:1ff.)
Disrespect	If a son has struck his father, they shall cut off his hand. (195)[3]	And he that smiteth his father, or his mother, shall be surely put to death. (Exod. 21:15)

Hammurabi's laws governed human conduct, but Moses said that the most important thing was the heart (Lev. 19:17–18; Deut. 6:1–6). Second, God's law was truly fair; for every crime it decreed the same punishment to all, regardless of social status (Lev. 19:15). In Hammurabi's view a crime was not as serious if it was committed by a "superior" against an "inferior." Most important, Moses' law was God-centered. Crime was not merely a sin against man; it was a sin against God. Hammurabi's law code was a great improvement over the capricious decrees of other ancient kings, but the law of Moses, because it was given by God, is far superior to any law code of man.

Hammurabi of Babylon before the sun-god from the stele with the law-code.

THIS MOMENT IN HISTORY

Hammurabi

How did Hammurabi influence Mesopotamian society through his laws? How did he justify the need for the laws?

____

____

____

____

____

____

became the standard of judgment in moral, social, domestic, and commercial matters throughout the empire.

"To cause justice to prevail in the land, to destroy the wicked and the evil, that the strong might not oppress the weak"[2]—this inscription introduced the 282 laws set forth in this code. Hammurabi's law was one of retaliation—"an eye for an eye and a tooth for a tooth." The penalty for a particular offense varied with the social class of the offender. For example, if a man of the wealthy class broke a bone of a member of his own social class, his own bone was to be broken. If, however, such a man broke the bone of a commoner, he had only to pay a fine. Hammurabi had the code engraved in stone pillars and placed throughout the kingdom so that everyone would know the law.

The Epic of Gilgamesh and the Universal Flood

A noted example of Babylonian literature is the ***Epic of Gilgamesh.*** This epic poem (a long narrative poem dealing with the deeds of a heroic figure) describes the adventures of the legendary hero Gilgamesh (GIL guh MESH) and his search for eternal life. In his travels Gilgamesh meets Utnapishtim (OOT nah PEESH teem), the only man to have attained immortality.

One of the most interesting sections of the poem is Utnapishtim's account of how Ea, one of the gods, delivered him from a universal flood. Ea warned him that Enlil, one of the other gods, was angry and was planning to cover the earth with water. He gave Utnapishtim the following instructions:

> *Tear down (this) house, build a ship!*
> *Give up possessions, seek thou life.*
> *Despise property and keep the soul alive!*
> *Aboard the ship take thou the seed of all living things.*[4]

Having built a ship, Utnapishtim gathers aboard his family, the craftsmen who helped him, and the animals of the field. The rains and flood rage for six days and nights and subside on the seventh.

Most ancient civilizations had similar legends. In all of these stories a great flood destroys the human race except for a Noah-like figure through whom the human race is preserved. For the Christian, these similarities simply confirm the truth of the biblical account of Noah and the universal Flood (Gen. 6–8). The differences between these legends and the biblical record should be viewed as the result of mankind's tendency to mix truth with error. It is instructive to note that one of the most obvious differences between these ancient flood legends and Scripture is who is at fault for the deluge. While Genesis states clearly that man and his wickedness are to blame, the ancient legends tend to blame the caprice and selfishness of the gods. As the apostle Paul stated centuries later, when unbelieving human culture is confronted with the truth about itself, it tends to "hold [suppress] the truth in unrighteousness" (Rom. 1:18).

Amorite Accomplishments

The Amorites are also noted for their trade in gold, silver, tin, and textiles. They worked with algebra and geometry and made important contributions to the field of **astronomy** (the study of celestial bodies). However, they refused to acknowledge that "the heavens declare the glory of God" (Ps. 19:1). Instead the Amorites tried to interpret human events and destiny by the position of the planets and stars—a practice that is called **astrology**.

Lacking able leadership after the death of Hammurabi, the Amorite civilization declined in both power and influence. Invaders came into the land and occupied the territory of this once powerful kingdom. As with Sumer, this civilization remained alienated from God and therefore was not permitted to continue.

How the Mesopotamians and Egyptians Measured a Year

In Genesis 1:14 we read that God set the sun, moon, and stars in the heavens so that man could measure years. Most of the civilizations of the ancient world did not measure their years by the solar calendar as we do today. It was too difficult for them to judge the different positions of the sun. Instead they observed the phases of the moon to determine a year. They divided each year into twelve lunar months of 29 ½ days each. Their months did not actually have half days but alternated between 29 and 30 days. Thus their years consisted of 354 days. One can see that after a few years they were markedly out of step with the solar year of 365 ¼ days. The Babylonians noticed this and sought to correct it by adding an extra month every few years. In a letter written by Hammurabi, one reads that he gave instructions to add an extra month whenever it was noticed that the year was "deficient."

The Egyptians were the first people known to have a solar calendar. Egyptian astronomers noticed that a certain star, Sirius, appeared on the horizon just before sunrise at the time of the annual flooding of the Nile. Counting the days between two such sightings, they arrived at 365 days. Their calendar consisted of twelve months of 30 days each plus 5 extra days called "days of the year." These days were used for feasting and religious festivals.

By the time of the famous astronomer Ptolemy in the second century AD, even the Egyptian calendar was inaccurate. They failed to realize that they needed to add an extra day every four years. The Egyptians refused to allow Ptolemy to correct it for them—to do so would interfere with the ancient traditions of the gods.

The Nile River

Section Quiz

1. ______________________
2. ______________________
3. ______________________
____
4. ______________________
5. ______________________
____
____
____
____
____

1. What did the Greeks call the fertile region between the Tigris and Euphrates rivers?
2. What is the name of the Sumerian wedge-shaped form of writing?
3. Who established the first known empire? What became his capital city?
4. The Amorite civilization was centered in what capital city?
5. What is the difference between astronomy and astrology.

II. Egypt

Egypt is a desert land. Had it not been for the dry climate, the remains of Egypt—the monuments, the documents, and even the bodies of her rulers—would have crumbled or decayed long ago. Because so much has been preserved from this ancient civilization, we can learn a great deal about its fascinating history and culture.

The land of Egypt has served as another type of "preserver." God used Egypt as a special place of preservation for His people. The descendants of Abraham journeyed to Egypt to escape a severe famine in their land. They went with God's promise: "Fear not to go down into Egypt; for I will there make of thee a great nation" (Gen. 46:3). Centuries later Mary and Joseph with the Christ child likewise found safety in Egypt as they fled from the threats of King Herod (Matt. 2:13–21).

The Land of Egypt

Ancient Egypt was not the square-shaped territory that we call Egypt today. It was the narrow strip of land along the banks of the Nile River. It was about seven hundred fifty miles long but in many places less than twelve miles wide. Because the Nile flows northward from the southern plateau, the southern region is called "Upper Egypt" and the northern region "Lower Egypt." These were really two entirely different lands. Upper Egypt lay close against the Nile, completely cut off from the outside world by desert to the east and west and by rapids (called "cataracts") to the south. Lower Egypt, on the other hand, spread out across the Nile Delta in easy contact with other nations by way of the Mediterranean Sea and the Sinai Peninsula.

One Greek historian called Egypt the "gift of the river." He was exactly right. If there had been no Nile, there would have been no Egypt. Because there was almost no rain there, only the Nile held back the menacing desert wasteland. The river rose and fell every year. As the snow at the river's source in the mountains melted every spring, the river flooded its banks from June through August. This flooding deposited tons of rich silt on Egypt, annually providing fertile soil for the crops.

The Nile River was vital to the existence of the ancient Egyptian Civilization. This Egyptian papyrus portrays noblemen hunting and fishing on the river.

The Nile was also important as a highway. Boats at the northern end of the river (called the "delta" after the triangular Greek letter delta, Δ) could hoist sails and let the winds from the north push them upriver. To return they needed simply to drop their sails and let the current carry them back. Since nearly all ancient Egyptians lived on the banks of the river, it was easy for those living at one end of the kingdom to communicate with those at the other end. Thus the Nile greatly contributed to a unified Egypt.

The History of Egypt

The people of Egypt were descendants of Mizraim, the son of Noah's son Ham. In fact, the Hebrews called Egypt "Mizraim" (Gen. 50:11). Shortly before 3000 BC a man named **Menes** (MEE neez) united the two lands of Upper and Lower Egypt, ruling them from a capital which he called "White Walls" (later named Memphis).

Old Kingdom

Historians divide ancient Egyptian history into three major phases: the Old, Middle, and New Kingdoms. Each is separated from the others by a time of unrest called an Intermediate Period. The Old Kingdom (ca. 2700–2200 BC) had been called "The Age of the Pharaohs." There were **pharaohs** throughout all of ancient Egyptian history, of course, but in the Old Kingdom these rulers were especially powerful. The people considered them to be gods in human form. As "gods" they owned all of Egypt and used it for their own purposes. It was during this time that the great pyramids were built, huge tombs attesting to the splendor and might of the pharaohs. The most famous pharaoh of this age was **Khufu** (KOO foo), or Cheops, who built the Great Pyramid at Giza. Its construction required thousands of men working for twenty years.

The Great Pyramid

The Great Pyramid of Khufu (or Cheops) at Giza is a marvelous example of Egyptian architectural skill. It sits virtually astride the 30th parallel, or almost exactly one-third of the way from the equator to the North Pole. All four sides of the pyramid face the points of the compass (north, south, east, and west). It rises to a height of 481 feet, and at its base, each side spans a length of nearly two and one-half football fields. It covers approximately thirteen acres, and amazingly, its foundation is almost perfectly flat from side to side; its level varies less than an inch from one corner to another over 1,069 feet away. In its construction the Egyptians used over two million stone blocks, the average weight of each being two and one-half tons. These mammoth blocks were so well placed that between some of them it is impossible to insert the blade of a knife. While the white limestone that graced its exterior has long since been stripped away (to be used in other building projects), the Great Pyramid remains a monument to the genius of the ancient Egyptians.

THROUGH EYES OF FAITH

Hyksos

Why might the conquest of Egypt by the Hyksos have been important for God's working in the human race at that time?

___

___

___

___

___

___

Middle Kingdom

After a time of rebellion called "The First Intermediate Period," the Middle Kingdom, "The Age of the People," began (ca. 2100–1640 BC). Aware of the social unrest that preceded them, the Egyptian pharaohs directed their attention to projects that would benefit the country as a whole. The pharaohs did not have a great concern for the people under their rule; they simply desired a peaceful reign. On the whole, the Middle Kingdom was an age of peace and construction. The Egyptians built irrigation canals and systems of ponds to store the Nile's waters for use in the dry season.

It was during this time of peace that the Israelites moved to Egypt (Gen. 46–50). God used the influence of Joseph (Abraham's great-grandson) to save the Egyptians from starvation and to provide a haven for the children of Israel during a time of famine (Gen. 47:1–6). The Israelites stayed in the land of Egypt for four hundred thirty years from 1876 to 1446 BC (Exod. 12:40–41). During that time their numbers grew from a handful to well over a million.

After the Middle Kingdom (in what we call "The Second Intermediate Period"), an Asian people, the Hyksos (HIK sose), came into the land and eventually became its rulers. It is not known exactly who they were or how they became so powerful. From the Hyksos the Egyptians learned the art of war. The Hyksos brought with them horses, chariots, and bronze weapons. It seems that the Hyksos were responsible for beginning the enslavement of the Hebrews. This would explain how a pharaoh could come to power who "knew not Joseph" (Exod. 1:8).

Stela of Senu. *Egyptian. XVIII Dynasty, from Tuneh, c. 1400 BC, limestone.*

The Metropolitan Museum of Art, Rogers Fund, 1912 (12.182.39) Photograph ©1982 The Metropolitan Museum of Art

Senu was a high priest during the time of Hatshepsut.

New Kingdom

Egypt eventually expelled these foreign rulers and restored an Egyptian to the throne. This New Kingdom (ca. 1570–1075 BC) is also called "The Age of the Empire" because it was in this age that Egypt became a great world power. The pharaohs became "warrior-kings." They extended their control to Palestine, Syria, and the lands of the Nile (that is, to the south). In this age Upper Egypt became more important; the Egyptian capital was moved to Thebes in the south.

There are several pharaohs in this age which are of particular interest. One of the early rulers of the New Kingdom was **Hatshepsut** (hat SHEP SOOT), the first great woman ruler of Egypt. She may have been the "daughter of Pharaoh" who discovered the baby Moses in the bulrushes and raised him as her own son (Exod. 2:5–10). Her rule was a peaceful one, and during her reign Egypt carried on extensive trade with nearby nations.

Hatshepsut's reign was followed by that of **Thutmose III** (thoot MO suh), the greatest Egyptian warrior-king. Under Thutmose, the Egyptian armies conquered Palestine and Syria, extending Egyptian rule all the way to the Euphrates River. One modern historian called Thutmose the "Napoleon of Egypt." Moses, another great leader, lived at this time. But Moses, by faith, "refused to be called the son of Pharaoh's daughter; choosing rather to suffer affliction with the people of God, than to enjoy the pleasures of sin for a season" (Heb. 11:24–25). Thutmose III was probably the pharaoh from whom Moses fled after he killed the Egyptian. Following Thutmose's death Moses returned to Egypt, commissioned by God to lead the Hebrew people out of their bondage. The new pharaoh, probably **Amenhotep II** (AH men HO tep), refused to allow the children of Israel to go. He finally yielded after God sent ten plagues upon the land of Egypt (Exod. 7:8–11:10, 12:29–36). However, Amenhotep changed his mind and pursued the Hebrew people. God overwhelmed the pharaoh's chariots and horsemen by returning the waters of the Red Sea on them (Exod. 14). About a century and a half after the Hebrews left Egypt, **Rameses II** came to power. During his long reign, Egyptians once again embarked on building mammoth temples and monuments. Egypt gradually declined from her rank as a Near Eastern power after his death.

The Culture of Egypt

The social structure of ancient Egypt was shaped like a pyramid: at the top was the pharaoh, supremely powerful; below him were the priests and nobles; then came the merchants, the common people, and the foreign slaves, in that order.

Most Egyptians were poor, but anyone from a lower class—even a foreign slave—could rise to a higher class if he gained the pharaoh's favor. This fact is illustrated by Joseph, a Hebrew slave who became the second most powerful man in Egypt.

"King Tut"

About the middle of the fourteenth century BC, a nine-year-old boy named Tutankhamen became the pharaoh of Egypt. After a reign of ten years, he died and was buried in the Valley of the Kings at Thebes. The Egyptians stored great treasures in his tomb, as they did for every pharaoh. They did their best to conceal the burial sites of their pharaohs, but sooner or later most of them were plundered. Shortly after Tutankhamen's death, grave robbers broke into his tomb and stole many of the smaller precious objects that had been placed there. Even so, Tutankhamen's tomb remained nearly intact. Rock chips from another building project nearby soon covered his tomb; it remained forgotten until the twentieth century.

Golden burial mask of Tutankhamen

In 1922 British archaeologists Howard Carter and the earl of Carnarvon found the tomb after many years of digging in the valley. Many experts consider this the greatest archaeological discovery of all time: no Egyptian tomb had ever been found in such a marvelous state of preservation. Over a period of eight years, Carter and his assistants removed, catalogued, and restored several thousand objects found in the tomb. (Carnarvon had died in 1923.) Carter and other archaeologists were amazed at the great wealth that they found—especially because Tutankhamen was a relatively unimportant pharaoh. They could only imagine what might have been buried in the tombs of Egypt's great pharaohs.

Unlike women in other ancient cultures, Egyptian women were especially favored in their society. As we have seen, one woman even became a great pharaoh.

The legacy left by the Egyptian civilization is truly great. The Egyptians made important advances in the field of medicine; they increased the knowledge of anatomy and prescribed drugs as remedies for diseases. They also developed a solar calendar, dividing the year into 365 days. They used a form of picture writing called **hieroglyphics** (HY er uh GLIF iks) and developed a type of paper made from reeds of the papyrus plant. (It is from the word *papyrus* that we get our word *paper*.) They drew upon their understanding of geometry and astronomy to build the pyramids, some of the most amazing architectural achievements of the ancient world.

The Egyptian religion was polytheistic. The people considered the pharaohs to be gods, but there were many other gods as well: animals, natural forces, and especially the Nile itself. The most important gods were Amen and

The Rosetta Stone and the Unlocking of Hieroglyphics

For centuries men sought to decipher the meaning of the hieroglyphic writing of ancient Egypt. It was not until 1799 that the first glimmer of light was cast on this mystery. In that year a group of French soldiers digging in the sand near the Egyptian village of Rosetta discovered a large black stone containing a proclamation inscribed in three scripts: Greek, demotic (common Egyptian), and hieroglyphic. The Greek text, which was readily understood, revealed that the same decree was set forth in all three scripts. By comparing the hieroglyphic text to the Greek text, scholars hoped to finally unlock the secrets of the hieroglyphics. Their task was not easy. They could not tell if the hieroglyphic characters were symbols for entire words or were symbols of an alphabet. Furthermore, the words from the two texts did not match up word for word.

The breakthrough came when one translator began looking for the proper names within the texts. He discovered that the hieroglyphics for a proper name were contained in a symbol called a cartouche.

The first name he was able to identify was that of Ptolemy (Ptolemaios in the Greek).

This enabled him to determine the next cartouche as Berenice, Ptolemy's wife.

The Rosetta Stone – From Fort St Julien, el-Rashid (Rosetta), Egypt Ptolemaic Period, 196 BC.

The most famous scholar to study the Rosetta Stone was the French translator Jean Champollion. From his examination of the stone and the cartouches from other Egyptian sources, he devised a preliminary hieroglyphic alphabet that enabled scholars to read other Egyptian inscriptions and documents. With this accomplishment, archaeologists gained a wealth of information about Egyptian history, politics, social customs, and religion.

Ra (who later became one god, Amen-Ra, the sun-god), and Osiris and Isis, the husband and wife who ruled the underworld.

The Egyptians believed that after death they would be judged according to their works. If their works were good enough, they would spend their afterlife in a place of peace—fishing, hunting, and relaxing. The pharaohs' tombs and those of other important men were filled with objects for them to enjoy in the next world. However, the Egyptians believed that these pleasures could not be enjoyed unless the body were preserved. Thus they developed the practice of embalming, or preserving dead bodies. Today mummies of the Egyptians lie in museums, preserved by the embalmer's skill and centuries of desert dryness.

The greatness of ancient Egypt is no more. After the New Kingdom, Egypt fell successively to the Assyrians, the Persians, the Greeks, and the Romans.

Tomb of Rameses VI in the Valley of the Kings

God's reasons for judging the Egyptians are stated in many different places in the Old Testament. In addition to their worship of false gods, the Egyptians were condemned for their pride, a vice that has often kept people and nations from repenting and trusting the true God: "Thus saith the Lord GOD; Behold I am against thee, Pharaoh king of Egypt . . . which hath said, My river is my own, and I have made it for myself" (Ezek. 29:3). Such arrogance always leads to divine humiliation: "[Egypt] shall be the basest of the kingdoms; neither shall it exalt itself any more above the nations" (v. 15). But in God's judgment He does not forget His mercy. The Bible also speaks of a coming day of blessing for Egypt: "And the Lord shall smite Egypt: he shall smite and heal it: and they shall return even to the Lord, and he shall be intreated of them, and shall heal them" (Isa. 19:22).

Section Quiz

1. To what river was a Greek historian referring when he called Egypt the "gift of the river"?
2. List the three major periods of ancient Egyptian history.
3. Who is called the "Napoleon of Egypt"?
4. Who was atop the social structure of ancient Egypt?
5. What important discovery enabled Jean Champollion to read Egyptian hieroglyphics?

1. ____________________
2. ____________________
____
____
3. ____________________
4. ____________________
5. ____________________

III. Land of Canaan

The land of Canaan was named for Canaan, one of Ham's sons. Most of the inhabitants of this land were descendants of this son of Ham. This land is very important to the story of God's working in our race and was the land of promise for God's chosen people, the Israelites. "Every place that the sole of your foot shall thread upon, that have I given unto you. . . . From the wilderness and this Lebanon even unto the great river, the river Euphrates, all the land of the Hittites, and unto the great sea [Mediterranean] toward the going down of the sun, shall be your coast" (Josh. 1:3–4). After leaving Egypt, the children of Israel wandered in the wilderness for forty years before they reached

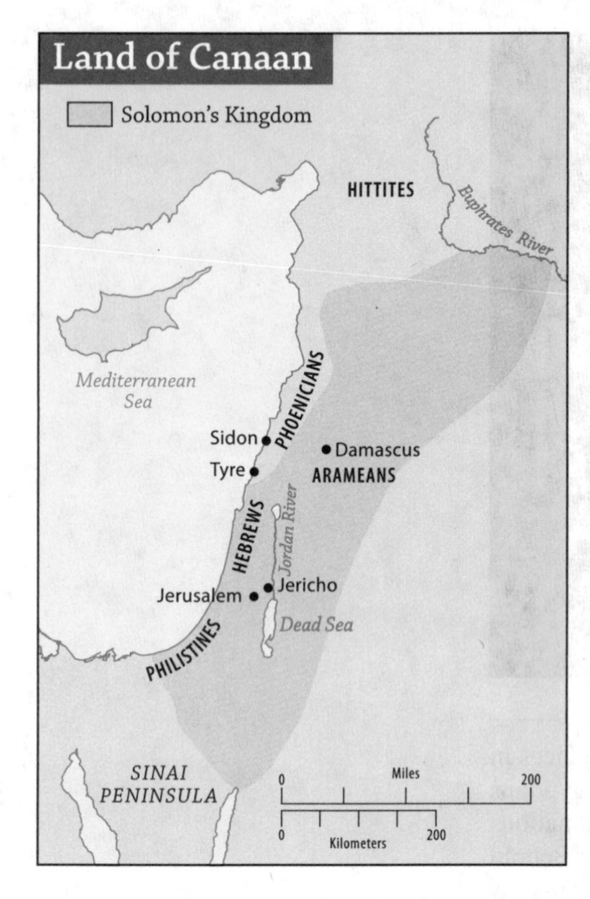

the Promised Land. As the Hebrew people entered the land, they encountered numerous peoples. Three of them—the Hittites, the Phoenicians (fih NISH unz), and the Arameans (AIR uh MEE unz) (or Syrians)—interacted with the Hebrew people and made notable contributions to the culture of the ancient world.

The Hittites

Before the twentieth century little was known about the Hittites. Many people did not even believe that they had ever existed. The Old Testament was the only source of information concerning this people. The Hittites were the descendants of Heth, the son of Canaan and the grandson of Ham (Gen. 10:15). Biblical references to the Hittites include Abraham's purchase of a burial site from Ephron the Hittite (Gen. 23:1–20; 25:7–10) and King David's murder of Uriah the Hittite to cover up his sin with Bathsheba (2 Sam. 11:3–27).

Archaeological discoveries around the turn of the twentieth century confirmed the existence of the Hittite empire. The Hittites began to settle in Asia Minor about 2000 BC. They were not ruled by priests or gods like the Sumerians and Egyptians. The Hittite king was the commander of the army. His power depended on the support of the chief warriors. Controlling rich supplies of iron ore, the Hittites excelled in the production of iron. With their military skill and their work in iron, they became feared by other peoples.

Using iron weapons and horse-drawn chariots, the Hittites extended their empire throughout Asia Minor and into the Fertile Crescent (which takes its name from the crescent-shaped fertile region encompassing Mesopotamia and the land of Canaan). They raided the Amorite capital of Babylon and later took control of Syria. This expansion brought them into conflict with the Egyptian Empire, which was also expanding into that area. Constant fighting between the Hittites and the Egyptians weakened them both and led to their mutual decline. This event gave the Phoenicians, the Arameans, and the Hebrews an opportunity to establish independent kingdoms. Once a major power in Asia Minor and the northern Fertile Crescent, the Hittites were absorbed by more advanced cultures and gradually passed into obscurity.

Alaja Huyuk Hittite temple carving of a two-headed eagle in Turkey

The Phoenicians

> *O thou that art situate at the entry of the sea, which art a merchant of the people for many isles, . . . thy borders are in the midst of the seas, thy builders have perfected thy beauty. . . . When thy wares went forth out of the seas, thou filledst many people; thou didst enrich the kings of the earth with the multitude of thy riches and of thy merchandise.*
>
> *Ezekiel 27:3–4, 33*

This is the prophet Ezekiel's description of the city of Tyre. For more than a thousand years, Tyre was the leading city-state of

Phoenicia. Comprising many independent city-states, Phoenicia was located along the eastern coast of the Mediterranean Sea (where Lebanon is today). The Phoenicians were a Canaanite people. The earliest Phoenician city was probably Sidon, founded by Canaan's firstborn son, Sidon (Gen. 10:15).

Merchants of the Mediterranean

The Phoenicians became the greatest merchants of their day. With their large merchant fleet, they traded with areas all over the Mediterranean Sea—Egypt, Greece, Sicily, Spain, and North Africa. Spices, fine linen, wheat, cattle, horses, ivory, gold, precious stones, and tin (used to harden copper) were just some of the items handled by these traders.

Cedar in Lebanon

The Phoenicians also gained great wealth through two valuable natural resources. The first was a type of mollusk (a sea animal similar to a snail) found off the Phoenician coast. The Phoenicians obtained a purple dye from this sea animal. Purple-dyed cloth became one of their chief exports. (The word *Phoenicia* comes from the Greeks, who called these people the "purple people" or the "traders of purple.") The second natural resource was the cedar and fir trees found in the Lebanon mountains. Phoenicia supplied the cedars that King Solomon used to build the temple in Jerusalem. In fact, Solomon used many precious materials from the commercial city of Tyre in building the temple (1 Kings 5).

In their travels Phoenician merchants sailed to the farthest reaches of the Mediterranean Sea and to Britain; some historians believe they sailed around Africa and also might have traveled west to the North American continent. The Phoenicians planted colonies all along the Mediterranean coastline. Colonies such as Carthage would later reach greater heights than the Phoenician cities in Palestine.

The Phoenician Alphabet

The Phoenicians are believed to be the originators of the alphabet. By this time the cuneiform writing of the Sumerians and the hieroglyphics of the Egyptians had been in use for centuries. The Phoenicians developed uniform symbols to stand for distinct sounds. By arranging letters representing sounds, they could form an almost infinite number of words. Writing then became simple enough for most people to understand. The Greeks and the Romans later adapted this alphabet for their own use and passed it on to us.

The City of Tyre

Phoenician independence was lost during the ninth and eighth centuries BC as the Assyrians invaded the territory along the coast and exacted tribute from the wealthy city-states. However, Tyre, the leading Phoenician city-state, continued to thrive, her trade unhampered by the Assyrians. Long before the Assyrian invasion, Tyre had expanded her city to an island about a half mile off the coast. From her island fortress she was safe from land attack. Massive walls around the island city and her strong navy protected her from sea attack as well.

The wealth and prosperity of Tyre was short-lived. The people of Tyre and the other Phoenician cities rejected the knowledge of the true God by worshiping **Baal**, the word the Hebrews used to refer to any of the Canaanites' gods. The Phoenicians were also largely responsible for the growth of paganism in Israel. It was Jezebel, the daughter of the king of Sidon, who married King

Ruins of Tyre: "And I will make thee like the top of a rock; thou shalt be a place to spread nets upon, thou shalt be built no more: for I the Lord have spoken it" (Ezek. 26:14).

Ahab and introduced Baal-worship in Israel. Because of their great commerce, pride entered their hearts. The prophet Ezekiel addressed them: "Thine heart is lifted up because of thy riches" (Ezek. 28:5). Tyre laughed at the calamity of the people of God when Nebuchadnezzar destroyed Jerusalem. For these reasons the prophet Ezekiel declared:

> *Therefore thus saith the Lord God; Behold, I am against thee, O [Tyre], and will cause many nations to come up against thee, as the sea causeth his waves to come up. And they shall destroy the walls of [Tyre], and break down her towers: I will also scrape her dust from her, and make her like the top of a rock. It shall be a place for the spreading of nets in the midst of the sea: for I have spoken it, saith the Lord God: and it shall become a spoil to the nations.*
>
> *Ezekiel 26:3–5*

In addition, Ezekiel foretold that Nebuchadnezzar, king of Babylon, would come and besiege the city (Ezek. 26:7–11). Nebuchadnezzar did come, and he besieged Tyre for thirteen years. He destroyed the mainland portion of the city but failed to destroy the island portion. Alexander the Great, more than two hundred years later, fulfilled the rest of this prophecy. By pushing the ruins of mainland Tyre into the sea (leaving it like bare rock), Alexander's men built a causeway out to the island city. His forces conquered the city, killing thousands and taking many thousands captive. The plunder of Tyre continued in the centuries to follow.

The Arameans

Syria (or Aram) is often called the "crossroads of civilizations." Through the centuries this land has been the link between Asia and Africa, the "melting pot" of the Middle Eastern cultures, and the passageway of the conquering armies. The Arameans, called Syrians in the King James Version, were descendants of Aram the son of Shem (Gen. 10:22). They settled throughout

Syria and northern Mesopotamia. Around 1000 BC the Arameans established a number of small independent states. Although of little political importance, this people had a profound effect upon the ancient world in other ways.

As the Phoenicians created a commercial empire by sea, the Arameans established one by land. Damascus, one of the oldest continuously inhabited cities in the world, became a capital of international trade. It was centrally located among the land routes of the Near East. Aramean camel caravans transported goods throughout the ancient world.

To facilitate trade, the language of the Arameans, called Aramaic, was used as a "go-between" language among the nations of the Fertile Crescent. Later Aramaic became the common spoken language of the entire region. This is probably the language which Jesus and His disciples spoke.

The Israelites were the neighbors of the Arameans. David and Solomon conquered many of the Aramean cities, but with the division of the Hebrew nation after Solomon, constant fighting took place between the Syrians and the Hebrews. God used the Arameans to punish His people (2 Kings 13:3). Later, because of the wickedness of the people of Damascus, God pronounced the destruction of the Aramean civilization (Amos 1:3–5). In 732 BC the Assyrians crushed Damascus and took her people away as captives.

The Hebrews

The Call of Abraham

> *Get thee out of thy country, and from thy kindred, and from thy father's house, unto a land that I will shew thee: and I will make of thee a great nation, and I will bless thee, and make thy name great; and thou shalt be a blessing: and I will bless them that bless thee, and curse him that curseth thee: and in thee shall all families of the earth be blessed.*
>
> *Genesis 12:1–3*

With these words God called **Abraham** out of Mesopotamian paganism and set in motion a series of events that will one day culminate in the second coming of His Son to earth in triumph, glory, and peace. In this call God made a covenant with Abraham (called the **Abrahamic Covenant**) that expresses very briefly God's plan for redeeming His fallen world to Himself. The covenant is composed of three basic promises. First, God promised Abraham a great seed, or group of descendants. This seed would grow to become a mighty nation from which God would raise up the Messiah (Hebrew for "the anointed one"). The Messiah would bless God's people by saving them from their sins and ruling over them in goodness and justice. Second, God promised to give Abraham's seed a land to live in, the land of Canaan. Third, God promised that, through this seed and through this land, He would bless all the peoples of the earth. This final promise is, for the Christian, the summary statement for human history. It is a summary statement that finds its earliest expression in God's promise to the serpent in Eden: "I will put enmity between thee and the woman, and between thy seed and her seed; it shall bruise thy head, and thou shalt bruise his heel" (Gen. 3:15). And it finds its consummation in history's greatest "hallelujah": "The kingdoms of this world are become the kingdoms of our Lord, and of his Christ; and he shall reign for ever and ever" (Rev. 11:15). The story of our race is the story of how God is working to make the disobedient kingdoms of this world the kingdom of His Messiah, His own Son.

Abraham was born around 2166 BC. When God called him (ca. 2091 BC), Abraham was himself an idolater (cf. Josh. 24:2). God chose Abraham not because he was a better person than the other inhabitants of Ur but because He is a gracious God. He told Abraham that he would be the father of a great nation, even though at that time his wife could not have children and the land God brought him to was occupied by other people groups. Despite these obstacles, Abraham believed God and obeyed. In time God fulfilled His promise by providing the aged Abraham with a son, Isaac, through whom the chosen line was to come. This line of blessing continued through Isaac's son, **Jacob**. The descendants of these patriarchs are called the children of Israel, taking their name from Jacob, whose name God changed to Israel.

Bondage in Egypt

Jacob and his family went down into Egypt to escape a famine in Canaan. God had already provided for His people in Egypt by giving **Joseph** (one of Jacob's sons) a place of leadership. It was here in Egypt that God revealed through Jacob that the future nation of Israel would be composed of twelve tribes, descendants of Jacob's twelve sons (Gen. 49). The most important of these tribes, Jacob revealed, would prove to be **Judah**. From this patriarch Israel's kings would come, the greatest of these kings being the Messiah Himself (v. 10). In Egypt, Jacob's descendants became a numerous people—the Israelites. Once a place of refuge and prosperity for the Israelites, Egypt became a place of hardship. A pharaoh who did not remember what Joseph had done for Egypt inflicted heavy burdens upon the Hebrew people. God remembered His people, however, and raised up **Moses** to lead them from the land of bondage to the Promised Land. The children of Israel, in about 1446 BC, left Egypt and crossed the Red Sea bound for the land of Canaan.

The Covenant at Sinai

One of the most important events in Hebrew history occurred in the wilderness at Mount Sinai (Exod. 19–20). There God established Israel as a **theocracy**—a people governed directly by God. God established His covenant with the children of Israel, promising to be ever present with them. God governed His people by communicating His will through leaders He ordained, such as Moses and Joshua. The centerpiece of the covenant at Sinai was the law of God. God's law gave them instruction, guidelines, and judgments in moral, civil, and ceremonial matters. God's law provides for all time a perfect moral standard by which men can distinguish right from wrong.

Moses erected the brazen serpent to halt a plague of the fiery serpents in the wilderness (Num. 21).

The Brazen Serpent, *Benjamin West, P.R.A. American, active in England 1738–1820*

From the Bob Jones University Collection

The Conquest of Canaan

Though blessed with the very presence of God, the children of Israel fell into sin. Moses sent twelve spies into the land of Canaan to search out the land (Num. 13:1–16). As the reports came back that the land was filled with giants and walled cities, the people forgot God's promises and rebelled against the Lord out of fear. Because of this rebellion, the children of Israel had to wander in the wilderness before entering the Promised Land (Num. 14:20–35). After forty years the children of Israel finally crossed over the Jordan River into the land "flowing with milk and honey." Under their new leader, **Joshua**, they began their conquest of the land of Canaan. They destroyed Jericho and Ai and defeated the many different peoples of the land. They divided the land among the twelve tribes of Israel (Josh. 14–22).

The Judges

After the death of Joshua "every man did that which was right in his own eyes" (Judges 17:6; 21:25). God had intended that the

Hebrew people demonstrate to the ancient world that there is but one living God. In an age dominated by polytheism, He wanted them to be sincerely committed to **monotheism** (belief in only one God). But the children of Israel turned from God to worship the false gods of the Canaanites. Because of their disobedience, God raised up enemies to oppress Israel. This oppression caused the children of Israel to turn back to God and cry out for mercy. God heard their cries and raised up leaders, called judges, through whom He ruled His people and delivered them from their oppressors (Judg. 2:16–18).

During the judgeship of Samuel, the Israelites again rejected God's rule, desiring a human king to rule over them instead (1 Sam. 8:4–8). Saul became the first king of Israel. He united all the tribes of Israel under his leadership and led Israel in victories over the Philistines and the Amalekites. Nevertheless, he failed to obey the commands of God, and God rejected him as king (1 Sam. 15).

Divisions of Hebrew History	
I. Patriarchal	2166–1876 BC
II. Egyptian	1876–1446 BC
III. Wilderness	1446–1406 BC
IV. Conquest	1406–1389 BC
V. Judges	1389–1050 BC
VI. United Kingdom	1050–930 BC
VII. Divided Kingdom	930–586 BC
VIII. Exile	586–538 BC
IX. Persian	538–332 BC
X. Hellenistic	332–168 BC
XI. Maccabean	168–63 BC
XII. Roman	63 BC–AD 70

David and Solomon

God chose **David**, a man "after God's own heart," as the next king. From his family the promised Messiah would come. King David firmly established the Hebrew kingdom. He conquered Israel's enemies, enlarged Israel's borders, and established peace throughout the land. Jerusalem, the "city of David," became the center of worship and government for the Hebrew kingdom (2 Sam. 5:6–10).

The kingdom of Israel reached its peak during the reign of David's son **Solomon**. Visiting dignitaries, such as the Queen of Sheba, marveled at the wealth and wisdom of this Hebrew king (1 Kings 10:1–13). Supplied with materials from Phoenicia, Solomon built the magnificent temple of God that his father David had planned. Before the end of Solomon's reign, however, he began to permit the worship of false gods in Israel. God, therefore, revealed to Solomon that He would judge his people by dividing the nation in two.

Division and Judgment

God used Solomon's oppressive taxation policy to bring this division about. Following the death of Solomon, the Hebrew people came to Rehoboam, the new king, and begged him to lower their taxes. Rehoboam decided to increase the taxes instead (1 Kings 12:1–15). Outraged at this decision, the ten northern tribes of Israel rebelled and made Jeroboam their king. The southern tribes of Benjamin and Judah became the kingdom of Judah, remaining loyal to Rehoboam and the house of David (1 Kings 12:19–24).

The Hebrew nation, now divided, lost the greatness and peace achieved under the reigns of David and Solomon. Wickedness increased among both the people of Israel and the people of Judah. Peace was replaced by strife and constant warfare. Isaiah and Jeremiah, as well as other prophets, warned God's people of coming judgment, but their warnings went unheeded.

Judgment came upon the disobedient people of God. In 722 BC the Assyrians destroyed Samaria (the capital of the northern kingdom of Israel) and carried her people away captive. The Chaldeans (kal DEE unz) under Nebuchadnezzar destroyed Jerusalem in **586 BC** and carried many of the Jews back to Babylon. This period of exile, known as the **Babylonian Captivity**, lasted seventy years.

Nevertheless, God did not forsake His people, and He did not forget the Abrahamic Covenant. God raised up the Persians to free His people and restore them once again to their land. By renewing His promise of a seed for Abraham and of a land for that seed, God was keeping alive His promise to bless all the nations of the earth through the coming of the Messiah.

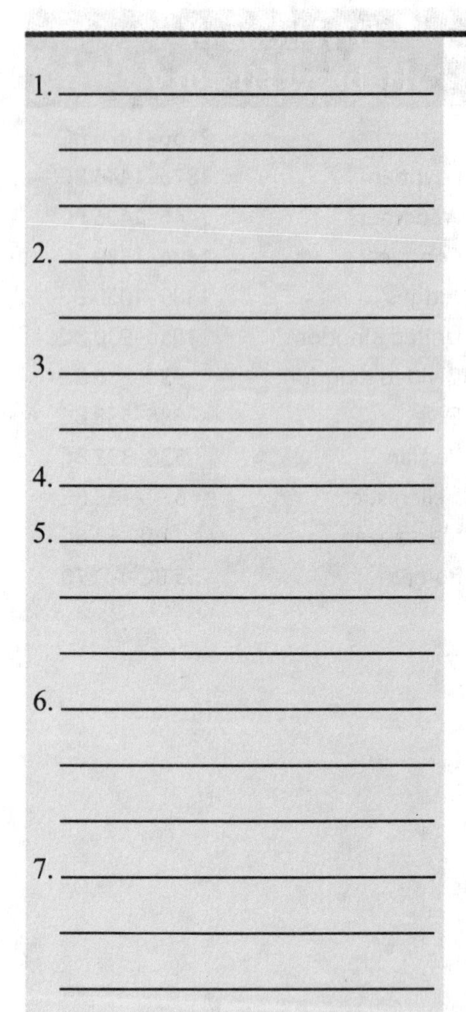

Section Quiz

1. List three civilizations that the Hebrew people encountered as they entered the Promised Land.
2. What two major weapons did the Hittites use as they expanded their empire into Asia Minor?
3. What were the two valuable natural resources that brought wealth to the Phoenicians?
4. What language served as a "go-between," or international language, among the people of the Fertile Crescent?
5. Define theocracy.
6. Name the three promises that make up the Abrahamic Covenant.
7. How is the third promise different from the first and second?

IV. Near Eastern Empires

The most High ruleth in the kingdom of men, and giveth it to whomsoever he will, and setteth up over it the basest of men.
Daniel 4:17

God uses nations to accomplish His purpose in history. We can see in the ancient world how God used the Assyrians and the Chaldeans as His instruments of judgment upon the Hebrews. In a similar manner God used the Persians as His instrument for preserving the Jews. Even so, these kingdoms were not excused from the consequences of their own wickedness. God's judgment eventually fell on them too.

The Assyrian Empire

The Assyrians created the largest empire the world had seen up to that point. For centuries they lived in northern Mesopotamia along the Tigris River, but by the eighth century BC they had built a vast empire that encompassed the Fertile Crescent, Egypt, and part of Asia Minor. Nineveh, the city built by Nimrod shortly after the Flood (Gen. 10:11), became the capital city of the empire.

The Assyrians were indebted to the previous Mesopotamian cultures; their gods, language, art, architecture, science, and literature were in large part adapted from the Sumerian and Amorite cultures. The Assyrians preserved many contributions of the earlier civilizations and spread these accomplishments throughout the ancient world by their military conquests.

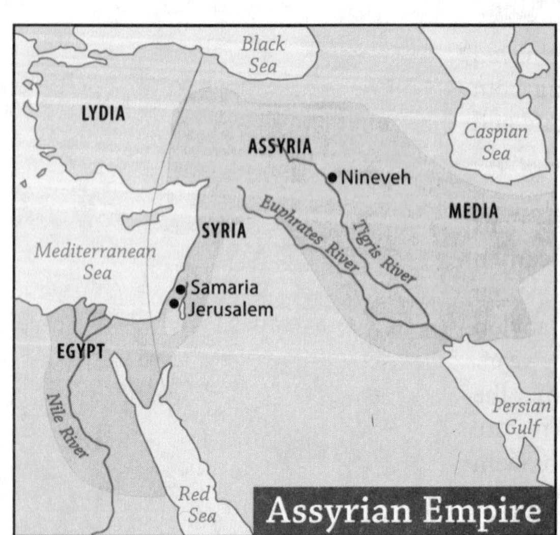

Assyrian Empire

Assyrian military might was unmatched by any other civilization of the day. The Assyrian army was equipped with iron weapons, siege towers, battering rams, and war chariots. This army of well-trained foot soldiers, spearmen, archers, and cavalry wreaked havoc on the people of the Near East. They terrorized nations with threats of destruction hoping to gain their submission without the use of force. They earned a reputation for fierceness and cruelty; it was not uncommon for them to butcher, mutilate, burn at the stake, or skin alive their defeated foes. They also practiced mass deportation—removing conquered people from their own land and settling them in a foreign country.

God's Judgment

God used this ungodly, war-loving people as His instrument for venting His wrath against sinful nations and for punishing His own disobedient people.

> *O Assyrian, the rod of mine anger, and the staff in their hand is mine indignation. I will send him against an hypocritical nation, and against the people of my wrath will I give him a charge, to take the spoil, and to take the prey, and to tread them down like the mire of the streets.*
>
> *Isaiah 10:5–6*

Under Tiglathpileser (TIG lath puh LEE zer), the Assyrians captured the Aramean capital of Damascus. Ten years later, in **722 BC**, the Assyrian army led by **Sargon II** destroyed Samaria and took captive the ten northern tribes of Israel (2 Kings 17). Later, Assyrian armies invaded Egypt and subdued much of her territory.

Mercy and Judgment

The Assyrians did not acknowledge God and were not aware of His workings. They became arrogant because of their conquests. Under **Sennacherib** (sih NAK er IB) they tried to take Jerusalem from Hezekiah, king of Judah. As the Assyrians prepared to take the city, the agents of Sennacherib, standing outside the walls of Jerusalem, boasted of the conquests and might of the Assyrian army (2 Kings 18:13–35). But God through His prophet Isaiah pronounced: "I will punish the fruit of the stout heart of the king of Assyria, and the glory of his high looks. For he saith, By the strength of my hand I have done it, and by my wisdom; for I am prudent" (Isa. 10:12–13). God sent an angel who killed 185,000 men of Sennacherib's army. Sennacherib went home in defeat and was later murdered by his own sons.

Although Assyrians were among the most ruthless people of the ancient world, God showed mercy to them. God sent Jonah to Nineveh to preach repentance: "Arise, go to Nineveh, that great city, and cry against it; for their wickedness is come up before me" (Jon. 1:2). As this heathen city "turned from their evil way" (Jon. 3:10), God turned away His wrath. What a great example of God's mercy, which can save even the vilest of sinners.

The people of Nineveh, however, eventually returned to their wicked ways, and God's mercy turned to wrath (Nah. 1–3). In 612 BC Chaldean and Median armies completely destroyed Nineveh, bringing the Assyrian Empire to an end.

The Chaldean Empire

Nebuchadnezzar of Babylon

Babylon was one of the oldest and grandest of all the cities of the ancient world. Empires had come and gone, but Babylon had remained. Babylon had been the capital of previous civilizations, but it was not until the sixth century BC that it reached the height of its glory.

Shortly before 1000 BC a group of Semitic people, the Chaldeans, began to settle around Babylon. Disunited, they were constantly subdued by Assyrian kings. Later, however, in 612 BC the Chaldeans allied themselves with the Medes and helped destroy Nineveh. During the reign of **Nebuchadnezzar** (NEB uh kud NEZ er; 605–562 BC), the "New Babylonian" Empire reached its height.

The ancient world was amazed at the sudden rise to power of the Chaldeans. Jeremiah, the prophet of the Lord, explained Nebuchadnezzar's success:

> *I [the Lord God] have made the earth, the man and the beast that are upon the ground, by my great power and by my outstretched arm, and have given it unto whom it seemed meet unto me. And now have I given all these lands into the hand of Nebuchadnezzar the king of Babylon, my servant. . . . And all nations shall serve him.*
>
> *Jeremiah 27:5–7*

Reconstruction of the Ishtar Gate of Babylon

THROUGH EYES OF FAITH

God's Work

Many people believe that in ancient times God was working only in Israel. Although God was revealing Himself primarily to the Israelites, He was still concerned with the other nations as well. At several points this chapter has quoted Old Testament passages that record God calling non-Israelites to repent of their pride, cruelty, and immorality and to worship Him alone. What does this fact suggest about the nations of the world today?

____

____

____

____

____

____

____

____

____

God used Nebuchadnezzar, whom He called His "servant," to punish other nations for their disobedience to Him. For example, in 605 BC Nebuchadnezzar defeated the Egyptian armies under Pharaoh Necho, who tried to conquer Syria and Palestine. Likewise God allowed Nebuchadnezzar to destroy Jerusalem in 586 BC and carry the Jews away captive (2 Kings 25:8–21). This dispersion of the Jewish people is known as the **Diaspora**, or "scattering." Under Nebuchadnezzar, the Chaldeans became the masters of the Fertile Crescent.

Nebuchadnezzar is remembered not only for his military accomplishments but also for building up Babylon as "the glory of kingdoms, the beauty of the Chaldees' excellency" (Isa. 13:19). The ancient Greek historian Herodotus said of Babylon, "In magnificence there is no other city that approaches it." Inner and outer walls, some of which towered over three hundred feet, surrounded the city. The walls were so thick that chariots, two abreast, could ride on top of them. The city was further protected by a moat surrounding the outside walls.

The Babylonian "hanging gardens" were one of the wonders of the ancient world. The gardens were probably built by Nebuchadnezzar for his Median wife, who missed the trees and flowers of her homeland. Supported by brick arches, these terraced gardens containing tropical plants and trees were the pride of ancient Babylon. The river Euphrates, which ran under the wall and through the midst of the city, watered the gardens and provided a water supply for the city.

Astronomy

The Chaldeans continued the interest in astronomy that had been popular during the Amorite civilization and made further contributions to the field. They charted the positions of planets and stars, named constellations, and predicted eclipses. As did others that preceded and followed them, they accepted the belief that the position of the sun in relationship to the stars and planets influenced human destiny.

From the book of Daniel, we learn that the "wise men"—astrologers, magicians, and sorcerers—had an important place in Chaldean society. They were often called upon to advise the king. Although they claimed the power to interpret dreams and tell the future, these so-called wise men were false prophets. Time and again they proved themselves unable to interpret the king's dreams (Dan. 2:10–11; 4:7). On one occasion Daniel came before King Nebuchadnezzar and said, "The secret which the king hath demanded cannot the wise men, the astrologers, the magicians, the soothsayers, shew unto the king; but there is a God in heaven that revealeth secrets, and maketh known . . . what shall be in the latter days" (Dan. 2:27–28).

God's Wrath

The glories of the Chaldean Empire did not last even a century. Nebuchadnezzar had learned of God's power from the Hebrew captive Daniel. But he viewed his accomplishments with a heart of pride. He said, "Is not this great Babylon, that I have built for the house of the kingdom by the might of my power, and for the honour of my majesty?" (Dan. 4:30) God's judgment fell upon Nebuchadnezzar. He temporarily lost his throne and became like a beast of the field until he recognized the folly of his pride and acknowledged the greatness of God (Dan. 4:31–37).

Under Nebuchadnezzar's successors, Babylon—which had been a "golden cup in the Lord's hand" (Jer. 51:7)—became an object of God's wrath. This mighty empire with its seemingly invincible capital fell in one night. The coruler of the empire, **Belshazzar**, had made a great feast. He used the golden vessels taken from the temple of God in Jerusalem to drink wine and toast the pagan gods of the Chaldeans. Amidst the drunken revelry, fingers appeared and wrote on the palace wall an inscription with the following interpretation:

> *God hath numbered thy kingdom and finished it. . . . Thou art weighed in the balances, and art found wanting. . . . Thy kingdom is divided, and given to the Medes and Persians.*
>
> *Daniel 5:26–28*

On that same night, in 539 BC, Belshazzar was killed by the conquering Medes and Persians. The Chaldean Empire was no more.

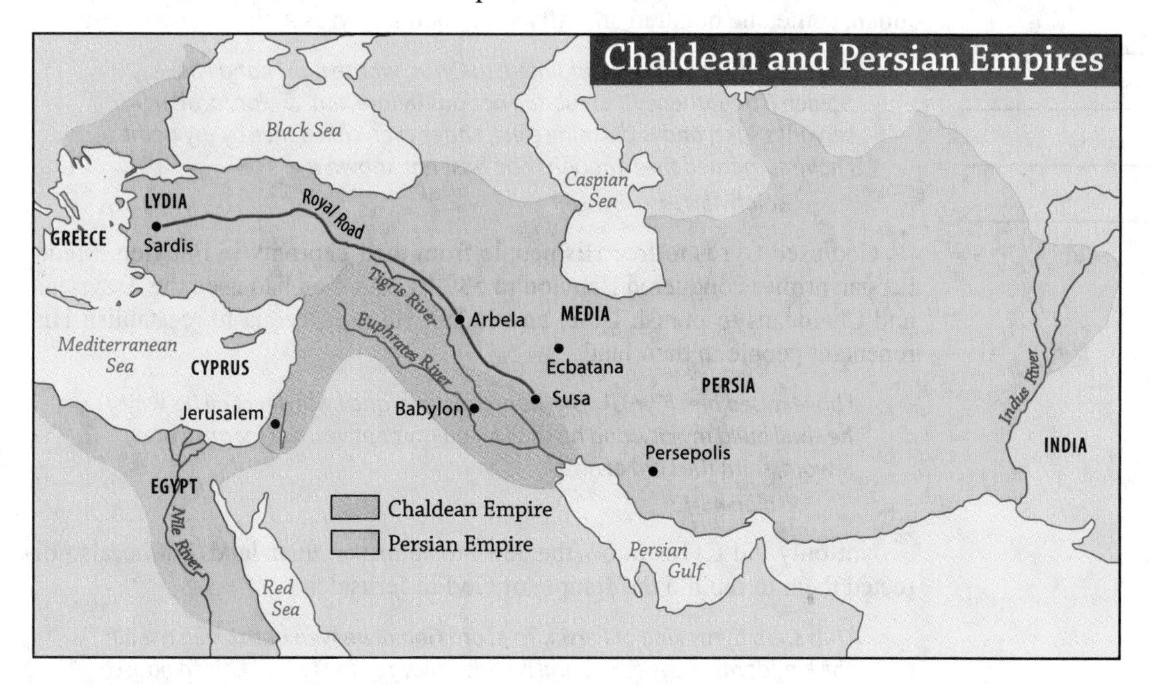

The Persian Empire

Out of the land of what is today Iran came an empire which spread across the entire Near Eastern world. At its height the Persian Empire stretched from the coastline of Greece to the Indus River Valley in India and from Egypt to Mesopotamia. The rise of this great empire was hastened in the mid-sixth century BC by the Persian defeat of the Medes, Lydians, and Chaldeans.

Cyrus the Great

The Persian king **Cyrus** was one of the greatest conquerors who ever lived. Cyrus rose to power among the Persian tribes in the southern region of the Median Empire (see map). After the Assyrian Empire fell in 612 BC, the Medes had control of the land north and east of Mesopotamia. Cyrus took advantage of a rebellion in the Median army and conquered the Median capital of Ecbatana in 549 BC. As he extended his conquests into Asia Minor, he came into contact with the Lydians.

The western region of Asia Minor bordering the Aegean Sea was the homeland of the Lydians. Here rich mineral resources, especially gold, were found in abundance. This land was the supposed home of King Midas, who had the legendary touch of gold. The most important contribution made by the Lydians to the ancient world was the use of coinage as an international medium of exchange. Prior to this time, the barter system (the exchange of one commodity for another) was used. The Persians, Greeks, and Romans later adopted coinage.

The Lydian king **Croesus** (KREE sus) confronted Cyrus and the advancing Persian army. Cyrus defeated the Lydian army in 546 BC. Unlike the Assyrians,

THIS MOMENT IN HISTORY

Cyrus the Great

How did Cyrus's methods of ruling conquered peoples distinguish him from other conquerors?

____

____

____

____

____

____

who had difficulties ruling their vast empire because of their harsh treatment of conquered peoples, Cyrus was a wise and merciful conqueror. He allowed his defeated enemies some measure of self-rule, tolerated their religious beliefs, and restored captive peoples to their homeland. Instead of killing Croesus, Cyrus took him as a prisoner and allowed him to enjoy the life of the Persian royal court.

Cyrus and the Nation of Israel

The Bible refers to Cyrus as the "Lord's anointed." Isaiah, a prophet from Judah, some one hundred and fifty years before Cyrus's birth, prophesied:

> *Thus saith the Lord to his anointed, to Cyrus, whose right hand I have holden [strengthened], to subdue nations before him. . . . For Jacob my servant's sake, and Israel mine elect, I have even called thee by thy name: I have surnamed thee, though thou hast not known me.*
>
> *Isaiah 45:1, 4*

God used Cyrus to free His people from their captivity in Babylon. Medo-Persian armies conquered Babylon in 539 BC. As God had used the Assyrians and Chaldeans to punish Israel and Judah, He used Persia to reestablish His repentant people in their land.

> *I have raised him [Cyrus] up in righteousness, and I will direct all his ways: he shall build my city, and he shall let go my captives, not for price nor reward, saith the Lord of hosts.*
>
> *Isaiah 45:13*

Not only did Cyrus allow the Jews to return to their land, but he also directed them to rebuild the Temple of God in Jerusalem.

> *Thus saith Cyrus king of Persia, The Lord God of heaven hath given me all the kingdoms of the earth; and he hath charged me to build him a house at Jerusalem, which is in Judah. Who is there among you of all his people? his God be with him, and let him go up to Jerusalem, which is in Judah, and build the house of the Lord God of Israel, (he is the God,) which is in Jerusalem.*
>
> *Ezra 1:2–3*

Through the Persians, God protected and provided for His chosen people. It was through Esther and the Persian King Xerxes (ZURK seez), called Ahasuerus (uh HAZ yoo EE rus) in the Bible, that God delivered the Jews from the wicked plot of Haman. Later Artaxerxes I (AR tuh ZURK seez) allowed Nehemiah to return to Jerusalem to help rebuild the walls (Neh. 2:1–8).

Persian Government

The Persians developed an effective organization to rule the vast territories they had conquered. The empire was divided into provinces called **satrapies**.

Description of the Persian Postal System

Nothing mortal travels so fast as these Persian messengers. The entire plan is a Persian invention; and this is the method of it. Along the whole line of road there are men (they say) stationed with horses, in number equal to the number of days which the journey takes, allowing a man and horse to each day; and these men will not be hindered from accomplishing at their best speed the distance which they have to go, either by snow, or rain, or heat, or by the darkness of night.[5]

The ruins of the ancient city of Persepolis. It was the residence of the Persian kings from Darius I (521–486 BC) until its destruction by the armies of Alexander the Great in 330 BC.

Each province was overseen by a satrap, or governor, who was appointed by the Persian king. It seems that "Darius the Mede," an important character in Daniel 5 and 6, was one of these satraps whom Cyrus had appointed to rule for him in the city of Babylon. The king had secret police, known as the "king's eyes," that kept the king informed of matters that took place in each province.

An excellent network of roads facilitated trade and travel throughout the empire. The primary road of the empire—the Royal Road—ran for 1,677 miles from Susa (one of the Persian capitals) to Sardis near the Aegean Sea. These roads aided the Persian mail service, which was similar to the American pony express. In fact, the account of the Persian mail system given by the ancient historian Herodotus has been used to describe the United States Postal Service: "Neither snow nor rain nor heat nor gloom of night stays these couriers from the swift completion of their appointed round." The book of Esther gives us an example of this mail system in action. When Xerxes made the decree to protect the Jews from Haman's evil decree, he sent letters throughout the provinces telling of his decision (Esther 8:3–10).

Persian Culture

Much of Persian culture was adopted from previous civilizations. The Persians borrowed the idea of coinage and gold currency from the Lydians. Their early writing system was the Sumerian cuneiform. Phoenicians and Greeks supplied the Persians with her navy. The Persians also popularized the Egyptian calendar.

The religion of ancient Persia was founded by and took its name from the religious leader **Zoroaster** (ZOR oh AS ter), who lived during the sixth century BC. Zoroaster rejected the polytheism prevalent in much of the ancient world and instituted the worship of one god, Ahura Mazda. The sacred writings of Zoroastrianism, called the ***Avesta***, consist of myths, regulations, and hymns of praise. Zoroaster taught that good and evil are two opposing forces; the world was their battleground. Every man takes part in this struggle, Zoroaster taught, for he serves either the forces of good or the forces of evil. Like so many of the world's false religions, Zoroastrianism held that at the end of life one would be assured of eternal happiness if his good works outweighed his evil.

The Persian Empire continued some two hundred years after the death of Cyrus. Under **Darius the Great**, the empire reached its height, expanding all the way to Greece, where the Persian expansion was halted. Although the Greeks stopped the Persian advance, the Persians continued to rule the ancient world until a new world conqueror, Alexander the Great, created an even greater empire toward the close of the fourth century BC.

Section Quiz

1. What city became the capital of the Assyrian Empire?
2. What prophet was sent by God to Nineveh to preach repentance?
3. What term describes the scattering of the Jewish people by Nebuchadnezzar?
4. What Hebrew captive foretold the fall of Babylon?
5. What Persian king created the largest empire known to his day and earned the title "the Great"?
6. What was the religion of ancient Persia? What was the name of its sacred writings?

1. ______________
2. ______________
3. ______________
____
____
4. ______________
5. ______________
6. ______________
____

A Glance Behind

The civilizations discussed in this chapter may be viewed almost like the rings that radiate out from a pebble dropped in a pool of water. In this case, the spot where the pebble dropped would be Sumer, site of one of the earliest recorded ancient civilizations. Sumer, in turn, was swallowed by the Akkadian Empire. Successive empires swelled larger and larger, while smaller civilizations, such as the Israelites, existed on their borders or flourished during the lulls in empire building.

In Daniel 2 we read of a vision sent by God to King Nebuchadnezzar, the Chaldean king. In it a huge statue is described as having a head of gold, chest of silver, legs of iron, and feet and toes of an iron/clay mixture. God provided an interpretation of this dream to Daniel, who relayed it to the king. King Nebuchadnezzar was pleased to hear that he was the head of gold, but no doubt troubled to hear that his golden reign would end and that his empire would be eventually replaced. In 539 BC it was replaced by the Persian Empire—further testament to the sureness of God's word and unchanging plan for history.

The Persian Empire, the chest and arms of silver, encompassed the territory held by nearly every other civilization discussed in this chapter. Yet Persia was destined to fall as well, and it did in 331 BC. It fell to the Greeks, the subject of the next chapter, through the conquests of Alexander the Great—the waist of bronze.

and a Glimpse Ahead

Notes

1. Samuel N. Kramer, *History Begins at Sumer* (Garden City, N.Y.: Anchor Books, 1959), pp. 8–9.
2. James B. Pritchard, ed., *Ancient Near Eastern Texts Relating to the Old Testament* (Princeton: Princeton Univ. Press, 1969), pp. 164–77.
3. W. J. Martin, trans., "The Law Code of Hammurabi," in *Documents from Old Testament Times*, ed. D. Winton Thomas (Edinburgh: Thomas Nelson and Sons, 1958); reprint ed. (New York: Harper and Row, 1961), pp. 29–35 passim.
4. Pritchard, p. 93.
5. Herodotus, *The History of Herodotus* (trans. George Rawlinson), p. 98.

Chapter Review

Can You Define?

polytheism
cuneiform
ziggurats
empire
astronomy
astrology
pharaoh
hieroglyphics
theocracy
monotheism
Babylonian Captivity
Diaspora
satrapies

Can You Identify?

Sargon I
Hammurabi
Epic of Gilgamesh
Menes
Khufu (Cheops)
Hatshepsut
Thutmose III
Amenhotep II
Rameses II
Baal
Abraham
Abrahamic Covenant
Jacob (Israel)
Joseph
Judah
Moses
Joshua
David
Solomon
586 BC
722 BC
Sargon II
Sennacherib
Nebuchadnezzar
Belshazzar
Cyrus
Croesus
Zoroaster
Avesta
Darius the Great

Can you Locate?

Mesopotamia
Tigris River
Euphrates River
Persian Gulf
Sumer
Akkad
Ur
Babylon
Egypt
Nile River
Memphis
Giza
Thebes
Asia Minor
Tyre
Damascus
Sinai Peninsula
Jerusalem
Samaria
Fertile Crescent
Nineveh

How Much Do You Remember?

1. List the three major rivers in this chapter and identify the civilizations which began along their banks.
2. List at least one way in which each of the following civilizations played a role in the history of Israel: Sumerians, Egyptians, Hittites, Phoenicians, Assyrians, Chaldeans, and Persians.
3. Make a list including each person listed in the "Can You Identify?" section. Beside each name, identify the civilization to which that person belonged.

What Do You Think?

1. What can be learned about the land of Egypt from the prophecy of its destruction in Isaiah 19:1–10?
2. From Ezekiel 27, list at least five items included in the trade of the Phoenicians.
3. Arriving at the correct date for an event in ancient history is a difficult task. How did the Hebrews calculate dates? See Isaiah 6:1; 7:1; Ezra 1:1–2; and 1 Kings 6:1.
4. From Genesis 50:2–3 and 50:26 we find that some of the Hebrews followed one of the Egyptian customs. Which one was it?
5. Outline the civilizations and kings mentioned in the book of Daniel. From the following references, can you name the kings Daniel served? (Dan. 1:1, 5:1–2, 31; 10:1)

3

"All men are Greeks."

The Greek Civilization

The Acropolis in Athens

The Bible states that after the Flood the descendants of Javan (one of Japheth's sons) journeyed westward from Mesopotamia and settled in the "isles of the Gentiles" (Gen. 10:4–5). This phrase may refer to the land we now call Greece. This land is a mountainous peninsula in the eastern Mediterranean. Between it and Asia Minor lies the island-dotted Aegean Sea. Here was the cradle of Greek civilization. Geography influenced Greek history from its very beginning. Mountains made farming difficult, but abundant natural harbors encouraged the Greeks to become seafarers. Furthermore, the rugged terrain hindered communication among the Greek cities, causing them to remain isolated. As a result, the Greeks developed a spirit of independence and local patriotism and became known for their love of individualism and self-sufficiency.

An island in the Sea of Crete

I. The Early Greek World

Aegean Civilizations

Archaeologists have found remains of two remarkable civilizations, the Minoan and Mycenaean, which preceded the Greek civilization in the Aegean region. Although these civilizations did not last long, they left a permanent stamp upon later Greek culture.

Crete

The earliest center of civilization in the Aegean region was located on the island of Crete. By 2000 BC the **Minoan civilization** (named after the legendary King Minos) flourished on the island. Through their trade and colonization, the Minoans came into contact with the people of the Fertile Crescent. The Minoans established trade routes with the Egyptians, who desired Cretan olive oil and fine pottery. Many scholars believe that the Philistines, who troubled the Hebrew people in Palestine, were colonists from this Cretan civilization.

The grand palace at Knossos, the capital city, gives us an indication of the wealth and achievement of the Minoans. The palace had hundreds of rooms and covered several acres. Flush toilets, bathtubs, and piped water were some of the "modern" conveniences found there. The beautiful carvings, pottery, and frescoes (painting done on wet plaster walls) found among the ruins of the palace reflect the Minoan love for beauty.

The Lion Gate, entrance into the fortified citadel of Mycenae

Mycenae

At Mycenae (my SEE nee) on the mainland of Greece, another center of Aegean culture emerged. The Mycenaean civilization was established by invaders from the north. Much of the Mycenaean's knowledge of art, building, and commerce came from the Minoan culture. When Knossos was destroyed around the year 1400 BC (possibly by the Mycenaeans), Mycenae became the leading commercial center of the Aegean region.

While the Minoan culture displayed a love for beauty, the Mycenaean culture reflected the military fervor of her people. Her palaces were built on high hills and fortified with massive walls. Rival kings fought constantly. The Mycenaeans expanded their trade through sea raids, piracy, and colonization.

A major commercial rival of Mycenae was the city of Troy. Located on the western coast of Asia Minor, Troy sat on a hill overlooking the Hellespont (HEL us PAHNT), the strait that separates Asia Minor from Europe. (See the map on p. 55.) This strategic site linked the land trade of the Fertile Crescent with the sea trade of the Aegean world.

According to Greek legend the Mycenaeans went to war against the city of Troy. After ten years of bitter struggle, Troy finally fell to the Mycenaeans. They had gained entrance to the city by use of the fabled Trojan horse. The glory of Mycenae was short-lived, however. Around 1200 BC, invaders called the **Dorians** came down from the north and conquered the main Mycenaean fortresses. The Dorian invasion marked the decline of the Mycenaean civilization and ushered in a new period of Greek history.

The Trojan War

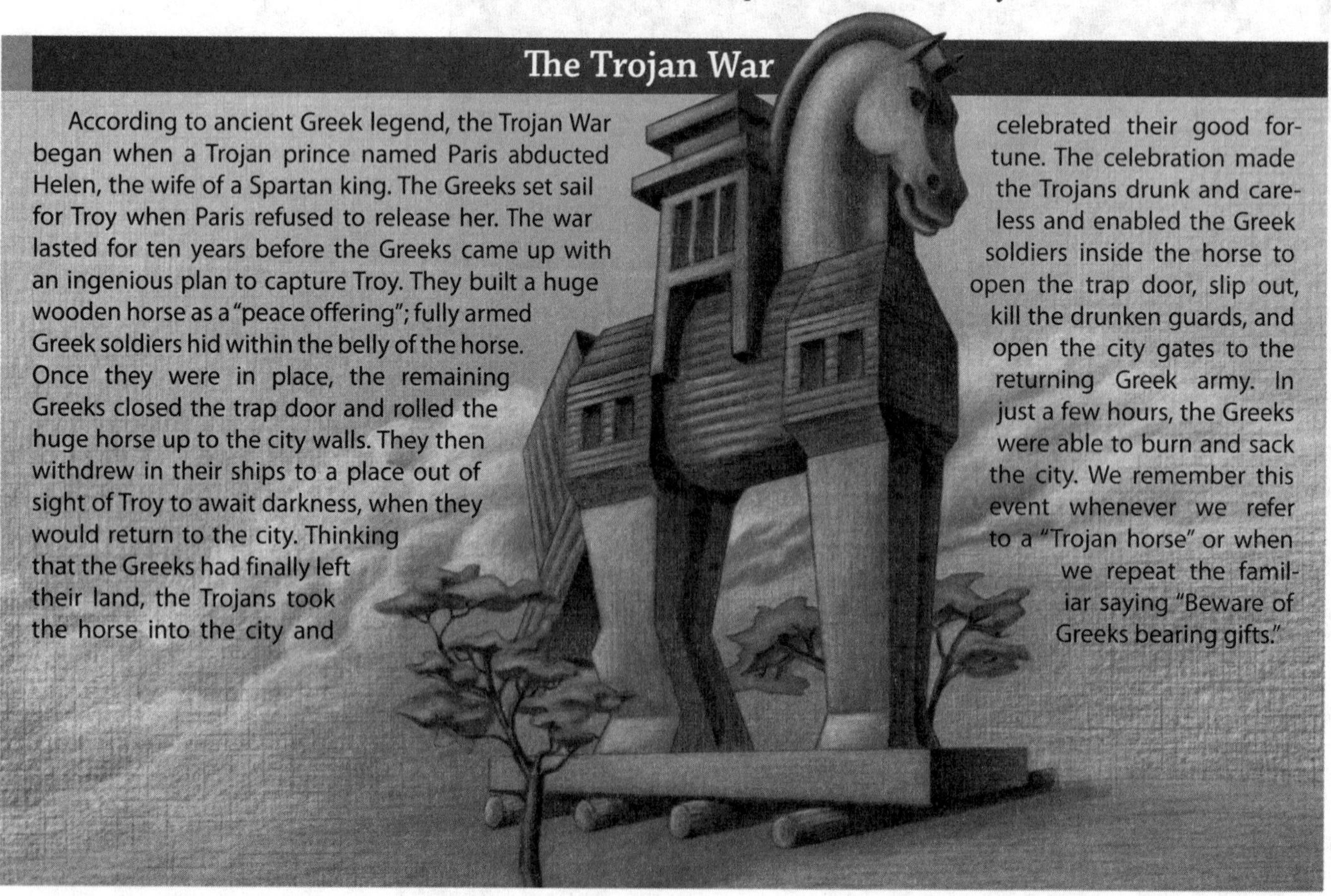

According to ancient Greek legend, the Trojan War began when a Trojan prince named Paris abducted Helen, the wife of a Spartan king. The Greeks set sail for Troy when Paris refused to release her. The war lasted for ten years before the Greeks came up with an ingenious plan to capture Troy. They built a huge wooden horse as a "peace offering"; fully armed Greek soldiers hid within the belly of the horse. Once they were in place, the remaining Greeks closed the trap door and rolled the huge horse up to the city walls. They then withdrew in their ships to a place out of sight of Troy to await darkness, when they would return to the city. Thinking that the Greeks had finally left their land, the Trojans took the horse into the city and celebrated their good fortune. The celebration made the Trojans drunk and careless and enabled the Greek soldiers inside the horse to open the trap door, slip out, kill the drunken guards, and open the city gates to the returning Greek army. In just a few hours, the Greeks were able to burn and sack the city. We remember this event whenever we refer to a "Trojan horse" or when we repeat the familiar saying "Beware of Greeks bearing gifts."

Schliemann and Troy

Heinrich Schliemann (SHLEE mahn) (1822–1890), the son of a Protestant clergyman, developed a love for the stories of ancient heroes. As a boy, Schliemann had been thrilled as his father told him in a simple and dramatic way about the Trojan War. The stories so fascinated him that Schliemann talked about them regularly. Many of the children his age laughed at him, but young Heinrich determined that one day he would find Troy.

After his commercial ventures had made him a millionaire, Schliemann retired from business and devoted himself to his lifelong ambition—finding Troy. Few scholars in the nineteenth century believed that Troy or even Homer ever existed. Schliemann, however, did not listen to their opinions. He received permission from the Turkish government to carry out excavations.

He first went to the place where Troy was believed by some to be located. Upon reaching the spot, Schliemann was troubled; the landscape was different from that described by Homer. Using the topographical information found in the *Iliad* as a guide, Schliemann found a site about three miles from the sea coast which seemed to harmonize with Homer's description. He hired workmen, and the digging began. After three years' work, Schliemann found not just one city of Troy but nine cities, each built upon the ruins of the previous city. His childhood dream had at last come true.

THIS MOMENT IN HISTORY

Homer

Why are Homer's writings so valuable?

______

______

______

______

______

______

The Greek Dark Ages

The period from 1150 to 750 BC is known as the "Dark Ages" of Greek history. During this period there were new intruders in the land. They neglected the great palace fortresses, once the centers of culture in the Aegean world. Instead they adopted a simpler life in local villages and encouraged little contact with areas outside the Aegean region. Despite the decline of the Minoan and Mycenaean civilizations, this period did witness the blending of the distinctive elements in the Aegean world into a common Greek culture.

Our knowledge of the Greek Dark Ages rests largely upon the epic poems the ***Iliad*** and the ***Odyssey***, attributed to the Greek poet **Homer**. Because Homer's poems provide nearly the only glimpse of the early Greek way of life, historians have also called this period the "Homeric Age." With stories of heroic figures, brutal warfare, and adventurous exploits, Homer describes the shaping of Greek culture. Values such as dignity, strength, valor, bravery, generosity, and wisdom as expressed in the lives of Homer's characters are the qualities the Greeks honored most.

> Tell me, O Muse, of that ingenious hero [Odysseus] who traveled far and wide after he had sacked the famous town of Troy. Many cities did he visit, and many were the nations with whose manners and customs he was acquainted; moreover, he suffered much by sea while trying to save his own life and bring his men safely home.[1]

THROUGH EYES OF FAITH

Greek Morality

In some ways the morality of the Greeks is impressive. They admired many of the same values Christians have always held dear. Was the ancient Greek civilization, therefore, a civilization that pleased God? Why or why not?

______

______

______

______

______

______

______

Greek Mythology

Greek mythology played a dominant role in shaping Greek culture during the Homeric Age. The Greeks devised stories (myths) to explain their beliefs about life, the world, and God. According to Greek mythology the twelve chief gods and goddesses dwelt on Mount Olympus, the heaven of the gods. **Zeus**, the "king of gods and man," was the ruler of Mount Olympus. His son, Apollo, was the god of the sun, music, and medicine. **Athena**, patron of the city of Athens, was the goddess of wisdom. Ruling over the sea and earthquakes was the god Poseidon, Zeus's brother. The Greeks believed in many gods, all of whom

were endowed with certain human characteristics (**anthropomorphic**, "having human form or attributes"); yet these gods also possessed extraordinary powers and immortality. The gods had power to both help and harm man. Zeus, for example, often expressed his anger with men by sending lightning bolts to earth. Because these gods were the invention of sinful men, it is not surprising that they exhibited human sins: they were immoral, impatient, whimsical, unjust, and deceitful. The apostle Paul probably had Greek polytheism especially in mind when he said that the Gentiles were guilty before God because they had "changed the glory of the uncorruptible God into an image made like to corruptible man" (Rom. 1:23). Even so, the Greeks sought the favor of these gods through prayers and sacrifices. How different was the Greek religion from that of the Hebrew people, who worshiped the one true God.

Top: *Poseidon or Zeus from Cape Artemission: detail of head*
National Archaeological Museum, Athens, Greece
Bottom: *Temple of Poseidon located at Cape Sounion, Athens, Greece*

In honor of Zeus, the Greeks held national religious festivals every four years at Olympia, the site of a temple of Zeus. Physical contests, thought to please the gods, became the chief feature of these festivals. The Olympic Games, as they became known, attracted competitors from all over the Aegean world. Each participant represented his home city. The intense competition indicated the high regard the Greeks had for physical prowess. To attain physical perfection was the ultimate goal of every athlete. The games became so popular that the **Olympiad**, the four-year interval between the games, became a Greek means of dating historical events. The Olympic Games were a rare example of cooperation between the Greek city-states.

1. ______________________
2. ______________________
3. ______________________
4. ______________________
____
____
5. ______________________

Section Quiz

1. Where was the earliest center of civilization located in the Aegean region?
2. What Aegean culture displayed a love for military pursuits?
3. What ancient city did Heinrich Schliemann discover?
4. From what two epic poems do we get a glimpse of Greek life during the period from 1150 to 750 BC? To whom are these poems attributed?
5. What athletic contests began as an attempt to please the Greek gods through physical prowess?

II. Greek City-States

Role

Though they shared the same language, customs, and religious beliefs, the Greeks lacked political unity. The Nile River in Egypt had brought the Egyptian people together and had encouraged their political unification. In sharp contrast, the mountains of Greece tended to isolate the Greek city-states, thus hindering national unity.

The Greeks usually built their cities at the foot of a hill. For protection, they would construct a fortress at the top of the hill, to which they could flee when under attack. They called their city a "polis," and the fortified hill, an "acropolis" (from *acro*, meaning "high").

The **polis**, or "city-state," was the basic political unit of Greece. Although relatively small, Greek city-states exercised powers usually associated with national states. The ultimate source of authority, protection, and livelihood for an individual Greek was his city.

The Greek Word *Polis*

The Greek word *polis* had many interesting meanings. It referred not only to a city with its buildings but also to the people and their government. Today we use this Greek word in much the same way.

Greek usage	Our usage
"City government"	We talk about *politics*.
"City governor"	We talk about a *politician*.
"A citizens' assembly"	We call it the *polity* or *body politic*.
"City"	Some of our cities have the word *polis* at the end of their names. For example: • Indianapolis—"city of Indiana" • Minneapolis—"city of water" • Annapolis—"city of Anne" (named for Queen Anne of England, 1702–1714)

Government

The Greek city-states experienced four basic forms of government. The earliest form was a **monarchy**, "rule (*archy*) by one (*mono*)," which was prominent during the Homeric Age. The king received advice from a council of nobles and a popular assembly. Gradually the council of nobles assumed the king's powers and ruled as the privileged class. This "rule of a few," called an **oligarchy** (AHL ih GAR kee), produced great tension between the wealthy noble class and the lower classes.

The dissatisfaction and unrest of the lower classes often led to **tyranny**. At the head of this government was a tyrant who gained complete control of the government—usually by force. A tyrant was not necessarily a corrupt ruler, as our modern conception of that word implies. He often championed the cause of the common people and brought about reform that allowed more people to participate in government.

A unique political contribution of the Greeks was the development of **democracy**, rule by the people. Here was a government in which each adult male citizen could share in the responsibility of ruling his city.

The Athenian Pledge

I will not dishonor my sacred weapons, nor will I abandon the one standing beside me where I am positioned in battle. . . . I will not pass on my fatherland inferior, but greater and better. . . . If anyone tries to do away with its laws, I will not allow it, whether I stand by myself or with everyone else.

Development

The period from 750 to 500 BC in Greek history saw the development of the Greek city-states. Important in later Greek history, the city-states of Sparta and Athens represented two opposing political systems and ways of life. Other Greek city-states were to follow the example and leadership of either Sparta or Athens.

Sparta

Sparta was located in the southern part of Greece on the peninsula called the Peloponnesus (PEL uh puh NEE sus). Conquered by the Dorians, her inhabitants were made slaves, or **Helots** (HEL uts). The new rulers of Sparta

Greek Colonization

Greek settlement was not restricted to the land we call Greece. From about 750 to 550 BC, Greeks established colonies throughout the Mediterranean world. The most important Greek colony in the western Mediterranean was the city of Syracuse on the island of Sicily. In fact, the Greeks established so many colonies on Sicily and in southern Italy that the area became known as Magna Graecia (Great Greece). Some colonies were founded to alleviate overcrowding, some were founded as trading posts, and some were founded as places to send the undesirable members of society.

Sicily

The colonization procedure was as follows: A mother city—called a metropolis—would choose a leader (often a noble) to direct the expedition. After listening to the reports of merchants, the leader then chose a site for the colony. When final preparations had been made, the colonists, taking with them a small amount of soil as well as fire from the altars of the mother city, boarded the ships and set sail.

Once the colonists arrived at their destination, the leader assigned land and established various laws and religious rites. (Sometimes the people even worshiped their leader after his death in honor of his services to the colony.) Finally, when the colonists were securely settled, they broke their ties with the metropolis. The new city-state was on its own.

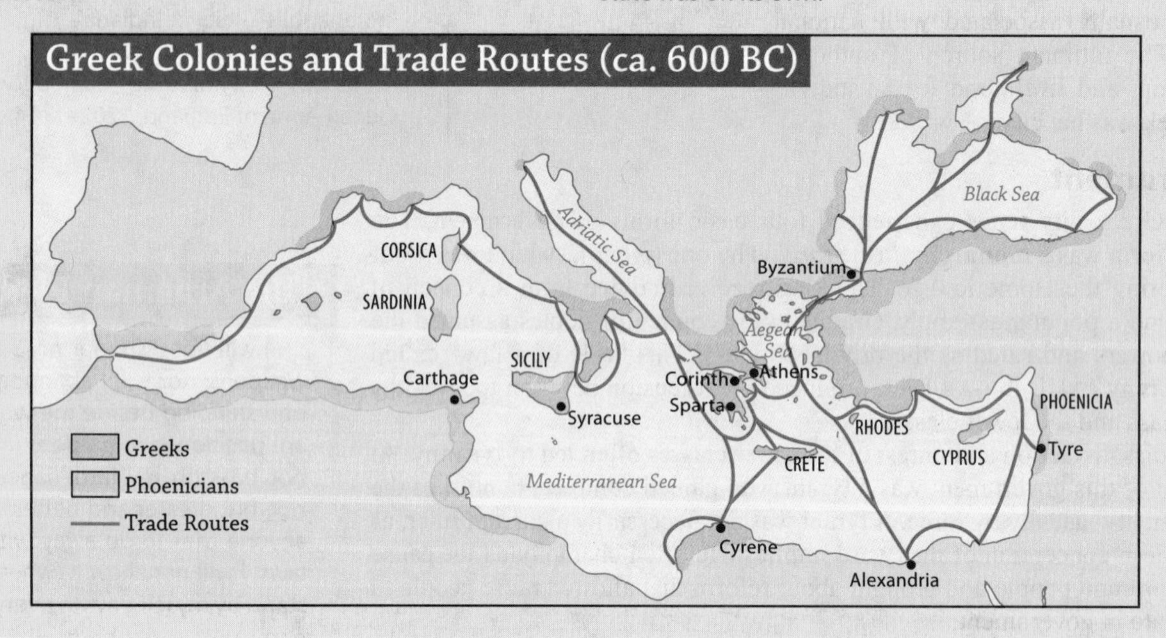

conquered surrounding areas, reducing many of the inhabitants to slave status. Soon the Helots outnumbered the Spartans. In constant fear of an uprising, the Spartans created a thoroughly militaristic state.

The way of life at Sparta centered on the training of warriors. The highest goal of any Spartan was to be the best warrior for the Spartan state. Sparta controlled all aspects of her citizens' lives in order to maintain an army ready for battle. Spartan elders determined whether babies were healthy enough to be reared. An unhealthy baby would be left on a hillside to die. When boys reached the age of seven, the state took them from their homes and placed them in army barracks. Here they underwent rigorous physical training to make them into fit warriors. They were beaten so that they would learn to endure pain. They were encouraged to steal in order to prove their resourcefulness. At the age of twenty, they became a part of the Spartan army but were not full citizens of the Spartan state until they reached the age of thirty. Even then they had to eat and sleep in the army camp instead of at home; they had to be prepared to fight at all times.

Spartan girls went through similar training so that they might learn the same Spartan spirit. Their discipline included running, jumping, and boxing. Their chief goal was to become strong mothers, rearing warriors for the state. Spartan women reportedly sent their sons and husbands off to battle with the words "Return with your shields or on them."

Sparta became the champion of the oligarchical form of government. A board of five Spartan nobles guarded against changes in the Spartan society and any harmful outside influences that would disrupt the *status quo* (existing state of affairs). To ensure the continuing success of her military state, the Spartans often used force or intimidation to help establish oligarchies in neighboring city-states. These city-states organized the **Peloponnesian League**, with Sparta at its head. Its purpose was to thwart the advance of the democratic principles fostered by the Athenians.

Greek countryside and harbor; the mountainous terrain of Greece contributed to the political fragmentation of Greek civilization.

Athens

Life in Athens contrasted sharply with the rigid, disciplined life of Sparta. Sparta became associated with militarism, isolation, oligarchy, and glorification of the state. Athens, however, nurtured creativity, commercial endeavors, democracy, and individualism. The Athenians maintained the creative and intellectual heritage of the Minoan and Mycenaean civilizations.

Like other Greek city-states, Athens was ruled by a king during the Homeric Age. Later the noble class rose in power and established an oligarchy. Power was vested in a council of nobles, with the chief magistrate, or **archon**, being elected from the nobility. As the nobles gained more and more power, hostility arose between them and the common people.

Under the leadership of the statesman **Solon**, Athens took a step toward democracy. Solon assumed the office of archon around 594 BC. Charting a moderate course in Athenian affairs, he provided economic and political stability during a time of tension and hostility. Although Solon was of the noble class, he instituted reforms that helped the common man. For example, he forbade the practice of making debtors into slaves. He also created the Council of Four Hundred, which gave representation to all sections of Athens. He later wrote of his years in government:

> On the one hand I gave the common people such privilege as is sufficient, neither detracting from nor adding to their honor. On the other hand I declared that those having power and being admired for their riches should also have nothing shameful done to them. I stood casting a strong shield back and forth between both sides, and I would not allow either an unjust victory.

The moderate policies that Solon instituted satisfied neither political side. After Solon's death tension mounted again between the nobles and the common people. Tyrants supporting the cause of the lower classes arose and seized control of the government. They initiated reforms and reorganized the government to allow greater citizen participation. It was not until the fifth century BC under the leadership of Pericles (PARE ih KLEEZ) that Athens established a "rule of the people."

Section Quiz

1. ______________________________
2. ______________________________
____
____
____
____
____
____
____
3. ______________________________
____
4. ______________________________

1. What was the basic political unit of Greece?
2. List and define the four basic forms of government found in the Greek city-states.
3. What two Greek city-states represented two opposing ways of life within Greek society?
4. What Greek city-state was characterized by creativity, commercial endeavors, democracy, and individualism?

III. The Fateful Century

The Persian Wars

At the outset of the fifth century BC, the westward advance of the Persian Empire threatened Greek independence and isolation. The Persians, expanding into Asia Minor, conquered the Lydians as well as the Greek colonies located along the coast bordering the Aegean Sea. The Greek colonies were well treated by the Persians, but the Greeks, who valued independence and self-sufficiency, could not tolerate Persian authority. With the support of Athens, the Greek colonies rebelled and overthrew Persian rule.

Under King **Darius I** the Persians not only crushed the revolt but also sought to punish Athens for her part in the rebellion. (This is the same Darius that is mentioned in Ezra 6:1, 6–12. God used his government to aid immensely in the reconstruction of the temple of God at Jerusalem.) In **490 BC** a Persian force landed at the Bay of Marathon, about twenty-five miles north of Athens. Though outnumbered and seemingly doomed for destruction, the Athenian army marched out to meet the mighty Persian army. The Greek histo-

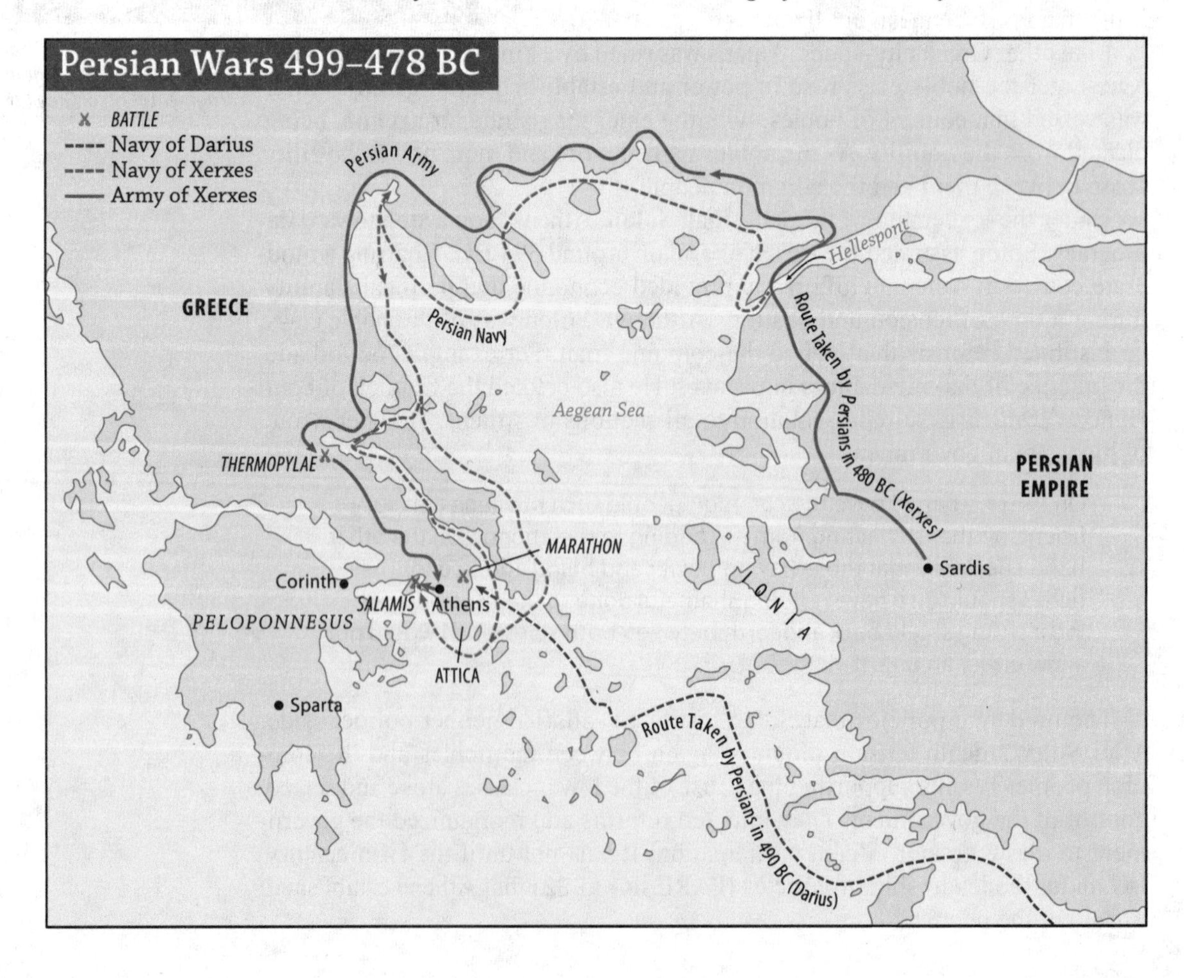

rian Herodotus (hih RAHD uh tus) wrote about the Persian Wars and gave this description of the battle:

> So when the battle was set in array . . . instantly the Athenians . . . charged the barbarians [Persians] at a run. Now the distance between the two armies was little short of [one mile]. The Persians, therefore, when they saw the Greeks coming on at speed, made ready to receive them, although it seemed to them the Athenians were bereft of their senses, and bent upon their own destruction; for they saw a mere handful of men coming on at a run without either horsemen or archers. Such was the opinion of the barbarians; but the Athenians in close array fell upon them, and fought in a manner worthy of being recorded.[2]

Surprised by the Greek charge, the Persians were unable to fully use their cavalry, upon which they heavily relied. Instead, they found themselves engaged in hand-to-hand combat; they were no match for the physical strength and battle skill of the Greek soldiers. The Greeks won a decisive victory.

Battle of Thermopylae

Furious over this setback, Darius, according to legend, appointed a slave to sit at his feet and say to him each day, "Master, remember the Athenians!" Darius organized a full-scale invasion of Greece but died before this could be carried out. **Xerxes**, his son, renewed the struggle. He amassed a great invasion force of men, ships, and supplies. Crossing the Hellespont upon a bridge made of boats, the Persian army marched toward Greece.

In **480 BC** the Persians, accompanied by their large fleet of ships, made their way down the Greek coast. The Greeks differed on how best to defend their cities. The Spartans suggested that the Greeks mass their forces across the Corinthian isthmus and defend the Peloponnesus. The Athenians objected to this plan because it would leave Athens exposed to the Persian army. The Greeks finally decided to take their stand at the mountain pass of Thermopylae (thur MOP uh lee), north of most of the city-states.

At Thermopylae a force of about seven thousand Greeks confronted the advancing Persian army. According to Herodotus, who could never resist improving a story, the Persians numbered about three million. It was more likely that they numbered about two hundred thousand. The Greeks had a good position, however, since only a small number of the Persian army could advance through the narrow pass at one time. The Persians attacked three times but could not take the pass. Then a Greek traitor showed the Persians another way through the mountains. When the Greeks realized that they were almost surrounded, they retreated, but three hundred Spartans remained to hold the pass. These Spartans fought to the death. According to Herodotus "they defended themselves to the last, such as still had swords using them, and the others resisting with their hands and teeth."[3] A monument at

The Hellespont Bridge

To move his army across the Hellespont from Asia Minor to Greece, Xerxes attempted a seemingly impossible feat: to build two bridges over which his army and its supplies could pass. Under the direction of Phoenician and Egyptian engineers, his men anchored a total of 674 ships in two lines across the mile-wide waterway. After tying the ships together with ropes, they laid down a plank roadway across their decks. On the planks they laid brush, which they covered with dirt, pressed down to make a solid surface. The process was nearly completed when a storm destroyed both bridges. The furious Xerxes had the chief engineers beheaded and then had the Hellespont beaten with 300 lashes! Then, under the direction of a Greek engineer, the Persians built two new bridges in the same way. In late May 480 BC, Xerxes dedicated the bridges by throwing a golden cup, a golden bowl, and a war sword into the water. Then, taking several days, the army marched across one bridge, while the supply wagons used the other. Xerxes, viewing his troops from a nearby mountain, began to cry. When a friend asked him why, he said, "There came upon me a sudden pity, when I thought of the shortness of man's life, and considered that of all this host, so numerous as it is, not one will be alive when a hundred years are gone by." Xerxes and the Persian army were now on the European continent, a step closer to their confrontation with the Greeks.

the spot bore these words: "Tell them in Sparta, passerby, that here, obedient to their orders, we lie."

Battle of Salamis Bay

Once past the Spartan barrier, the Persians swept on to Athens. Xerxes burned it to the ground. The Athenians had left the city, realizing that they would not be able to defend it. They withdrew to an island called Salamis, just off the coast.

Hoping to exploit Xerxes' desire for a quick victory, Themistocles (thuh MIS tuh KLEEZ), the leader of Athens, devised a trap. In September 480 BC, he sent a trusted slave to Xerxes with the story that the Greeks were frightened and were planning to escape in the morning by sailing northward. The slave also suggested that if Xerxes were to send his ships into the strait between the mainland and Salamis, he would be able to block their escape. The next morning Xerxes ordered his fleet, with many of his soldiers on board, to attack the Greeks. The Persians entered the strait just as Themistocles had hoped. But the rising morning tide made their large ships hard to maneuver. As the Persian sailors struggled to steer their crafts, the Greeks launched their ships from the beaches of Salamis. The small, easily maneuvered Greek crafts created great confusion as they rammed and sank a great many Persian vessels. From a high vantage point overlooking the bay, Xerxes watched as the Greeks carried the day.

The following year the Greeks, led by Sparta, defeated a sizable Persian army, which had remained in northern Greece. Although they had stopped the Persian invasion force, they did little to weaken the vast Persian Empire. The Persians continued to interfere in Greek affairs for two hundred years following the war. Yet the Greeks maintained their hard-fought independence. Freedom bolstered the Greek spirit, furthered the growth of democracy, and encouraged Greek creativity. The way was prepared for the "Golden Age" of Greece—a period of great cultural achievement.

The Periclean Age

Nowhere in Greece following the Persian Wars was the spirit of patriotism and self-confidence stronger than in Athens. She became the leading city-state of all Greece; because of her heroic efforts against the Persians, other city-states looked to her for protection. The Athenians encouraged the formation of a defensive alliance among the Greek city-states to protect themselves against any further Persian attacks. This alliance became known as the **Delian League**, and Athens became its leader.

This period of Greek history (460–429 BC) is often called "The Age of **Pericles**." For over thirty years Pericles was the influential leader of Athens. He called Athens the "school of Greece." During his lifetime Athens attained cultural heights unparalleled in the ancient world. Her permissive climate encouraged advances in thought, art, science, literature, drama, and architecture. So numerous and notable were the Greek accomplishments during this period that special attention will be devoted to them later in this chapter.

Under Pericles' leadership every adult male citizen of Athens gained the privilege and responsibility of sharing in the Athenian government by being able to vote and hold office. No longer was the government controlled only by those of wealth or of noble birth. Now all adult male citizens could participate in government on an equal basis. The majority of Athenians, however—women, slaves, and foreigners—were still excluded from this privilege.

Pericles on the Athenian Democracy

Our form of government does not enter into rivalry with the institutions of others. We do not copy our neighbors, but are an example to them. It is true that we are called a democracy, for the administration is in the hands of the many and not of the few. But while the law secures equal justice to all alike in their private disputes, the claim of excellence is also recognized; and when a citizen is in any way distinguished, he is preferred to the public service, not as a matter of privilege, but as the reward of merit. Neither is poverty a bar, but a man may benefit his country whatever be the obscurity of his condition.[4]

The Peloponnesian War

The Periclean Age came between two violent upheavals in the fifth century BC. The first was the Persian Wars, which temporarily united the Greek city-states in a common defense of their liberty. Following the Golden Age came the **Peloponnesian War** (431–404 BC), a devastating civil war pitting Greek against Greek. As Athens had grown in influence and wealth, she had transformed the Delian League into an Athenian empire. Sparta became alarmed over the commercial and political power Athens had acquired. The tension between these two rivals and their allies finally flamed into war.

The war has been likened to a struggle between an elephant and a whale. Sparta's strength rested in her land army whereas Athens reigned supreme on the sea with her large fleet. Early in the war a devastating plague wiped out a large portion of the population of Athens, including her leading citizen, Pericles. Though weakened by these losses, Athens continued to fight. Through intermittent fighting, Sparta eventually gained the upper hand by forming an alliance with the Persians. Sparta was finally able to bring Athens to her knees by destroying the Athenian fleet.

Although Sparta emerged victorious, she had nothing but problems after the war. City-states that had looked to Sparta for deliverance from Athenian domination now found themselves under a greater oppressor. Democratic governments were replaced with oligarchies. The Greeks who had experienced freedom found it difficult to submit to Spartan oligarchical rule. Constant uprisings reduced Sparta's control over the Greek city-states, leaving them disunited once again.

Section Quiz

1. What eastern civilization threatened the Greeks at the outset of the fifth century?
2. At what battle did an unorthodox charge by the Greeks help them to win a decisive victory?
3. Across what body of water did Xerxes make a bridge of boats to move his army?
4. Who was the influential leader of Athens during her so-called Golden Age?
5. What type of war was the Peloponnesian War?

1. ____________________
2. ____________________
3. ____________________
4. ____________________
5. ____________________

IV. Alexander's Empire

Rise of Macedonia

North of Greece was Macedonia, inhabited by a people related to the Greeks. King **Philip II** united Macedonia under his rule and extended his kingdom into Greece. Many Greek city-states supported Philip, hoping that he would bring unity to their land. Some resisted him, fearing that their freedom would be lost under Macedonian rule. The weakened and divided Greek city-states were no match for the well-organized army of Philip.

Philip's appreciation for Greek culture led him to treat his many subjects with great tolerance. He hoped to gain Greek support for an invasion of the Persian Empire, the Greeks' constant enemy. But in 336 BC, before he could fulfill his plans, Philip was assassinated. His son **Alexander** assumed the throne at the age of twenty. As a boy, Alexander had been taught by one of the greatest Greek philosophers, Aristotle, who had instilled in him a love for Greek culture. With his conquering armies he carried this culture to the far reaches of the Near Eastern world.

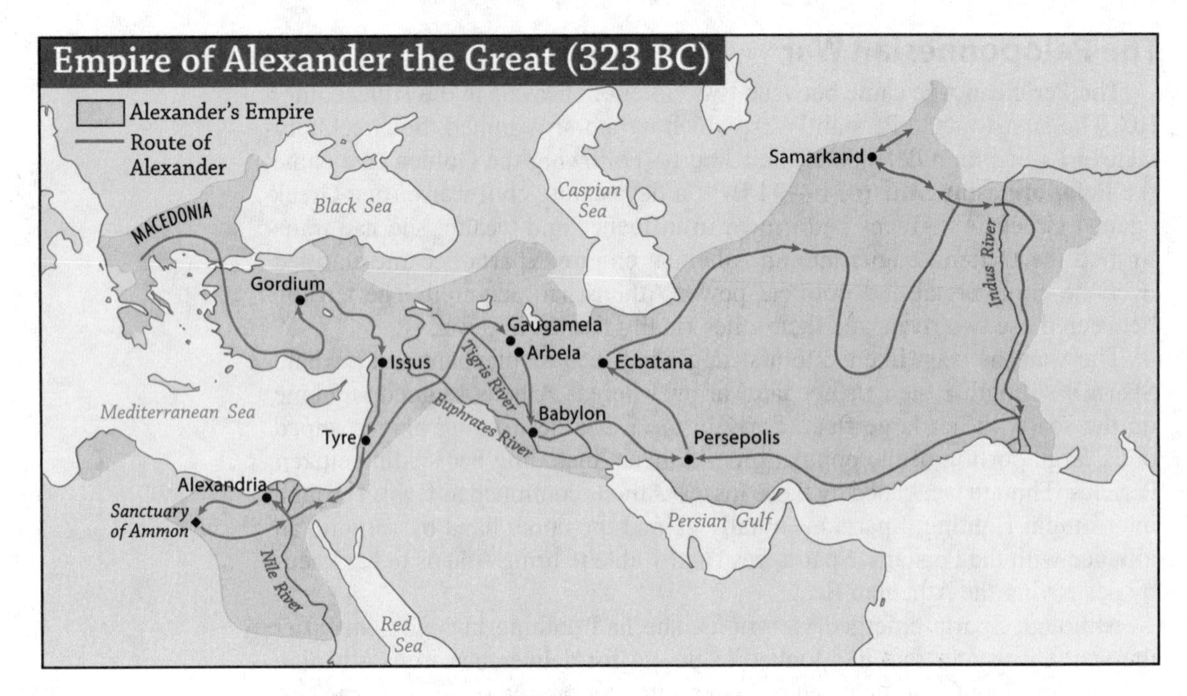

Alexander's Conquests

With amazing speed Alexander led his army across Asia Minor and confronted the Persian army, led by King **Darius III**. In the heat of one battle, Darius fled, leaving behind his wife, mother, and children to be taken captive by Alexander. Alexander took Syria, destroyed the city of Tyre (see p. 42), and marched unopposed into Egypt. The final blow to the Persian Empire came as Alexander, near the Tigris River, defeated the larger army of Darius. Alexander had accomplished what he had set out to do—avenge the Persian invasion of Greece and become the king of Asia.

But his thirst for conquest was not yet satisfied. He marched all the way to India and would have gone beyond, but his weary army refused to go farther. They had been gone eight years and had marched over eleven thousand miles. Alexander sulked for several days over the unwillingness of his army to continue. Although he had conquered almost all the known world of his day, his achievements had not brought any lasting satisfaction to his heart. How often men have tried to satisfy their soul's desires by seeking the fleeting pleasures of this world. Alexander probably would not have been satisfied even if he had conquered the whole world. God's Word says, "For what is a man profited, if he shall gain the whole world, and lose his own soul? or what shall a man give in exchange for his soul?" (Matt. 16:26).

Empire Divisions

In 323 BC, at the height of his power, Alexander died of a fever; he had not yet reached his thirty-third birthday. Over two hundred years before Alexander's death, God's prophet Daniel had foretold that Alexander's empire would be divided into four kingdoms (Dan. 8:21–22; 11:4). Because Alexander left no plans for a successor to his empire, his chief generals fought among themselves to determine who would rule. Four generals emerged victorious and declared themselves kings over portions of the empire; thus Daniel's prophetic vision was fulfilled.

These greedy new kings fought one another as each tried to restore the whole empire under his own rule. From the families of Alexander's generals came dynasties that ruled portions of the former empire until the time of the Roman conquests: the Ptolemies (TOL uh meez) in Egypt, the Seleucids (sih LOO sidz) in Syria and Persia, and the Antigonids (an TIG uh nidz) in Macedonia and Greece.

Section Quiz

1. Over what kingdom did Philip II rule?
2. Who was the teacher of Alexander the Great who instilled in his young pupil a love for Greek culture?
3. List the three ruling families that ruled portions of Alexander's empire after his death. Identify the region over which each family ruled.

1. ______________________
2. ______________________
3. ______________________

V. Greek Culture

The Essence

The culture of a civilization is a reflection of the values and character of her people. The Greeks cultivated an appreciation for beauty, freedom, justice, truth, and knowledge. They exalted the man who had a creative spirit, versatile talents, a thirst for knowledge, physical ability, and a zest for life. The Greek respect for such qualities as self-control, restraint, balance, and moderation is evident in the Greek motto: "Nothing in excess, and everything in proportion." These were the qualities that characterized Hellenic culture.

The term **Hellenic** is used to describe Greek culture. The Greeks called themselves Hellenes and their land Hellas. The height of Hellenic culture occurred during the Golden Age of Athens. The spirit of independence and self sufficiency, bolstered by the defeat of the Persians, produced the flowering of Hellenic culture in Athens. Most of the Greek men whose achievements history remembers lived in this vibrant city.

Ancient Greece has been called the cradle of Western culture. Greek culture left a lasting imprint on the Western world. The Greeks set forth many of the basic concepts of science, mathematics, and philosophy. Greek literature, architecture, and sculpture became models that later civilizations have tried to imitate.

Although the Greek army never conquered the world, Greek culture did. Alexander's conquests spread the Greek language and way of life throughout the ancient world. As a result, Hellenic culture mixed with the cultures of the East. A new culture emerged; it was no longer just Hellenic, meaning "Greek," but **Hellenistic**, "like the Greek."

Hellenistic culture permeated the Near East from the time of Alexander until the coming of the Romans in the first century BC. Its influence was so great that this period is known as the Hellenistic Age. This culture united the peoples of the Near East by blending their arts, religions, philosophies, and customs. The Hellenistic Age brought the East and West together in learning, in government, and in trade.

Grecian urn

The Expression

Focus on Man

"Wonders are many of earth, and the greatest of these is man." To the Greeks the ability to think and reason made man unique. His "humanity" was thus worthy of special study. The Greeks were among the first to begin the formal study of human thought and culture called the **humanities**. Philosophers and scientists praised the human mind and its reasoning powers. Greek literature dealt with how man lives and acts. The goal of physical activity was to develop the human body toward physical perfection. Greek art focused upon the human form.

The Greeks stressed the dignity and uniqueness of man. They assumed a great truth: man is the highest of created beings. However, they looked upon man's uniqueness apart from God, glorifying the "creature more than the Creator" (Rom. 1:25). As a result they perverted this noble truth into a form of humanism. They did not accept the fact that God created man in His own image; therefore, they praised man for his ability, rather than praising God, Who gave man that ability. Similarly, they did not acknowledge their responsibility to their Creator. Instead they believed that "man is the measure [judge] of all things."

Interest in Philosophy

Throughout history men have sought answers to the basic questions of life: (1) Where did I come from? (2) Why am I here? (3) Where am I going? and (4) What is the highest good in life? Early in their history the Greeks developed many myths to help them answer these questions. Following the sixth century BC, however, many lost confidence in these myths. Men called **philosophers**, "lovers of wisdom," tried to find the answers to these questions through man's reasoning ability. They believed that the highest good was to seek truth and attain knowledge. This, they hoped, would enable men to live properly.

The Greeks believed in the basic goodness of man. They trusted in man's wisdom as a guide for their behavior and as a means for finding happiness. They did not understand that "the wisdom of this world is foolishness with God.... The Lord knoweth the thoughts of the wise, that they are vain. Therefore let no man glory in men" (1 Cor. 3:19–21). The Greeks relied on man's reasoning ability in their search for wisdom. However, God's Word says that "the fear of the Lord is the beginning of wisdom: and the knowledge of the holy is understanding" (Prov. 9:10).

***Thales of Miletus (640?–546 BC)*—Thales** (THAY leez) is often called the Father of Philosophy. Among the Greeks, Thales was one of the first who sought to explain the origin of the universe in natural terms. He concluded that water was the original substance of all things. He and other early philosophers did not deal with the questions of ethics—what is right and wrong. This was left to later philosophers, the most famous of whom are Socrates, Plato, and Aristotle.

***Socrates (470?–399 BC)*—Socrates** (SAHK ruh TEEZ), a contemporary of Pericles, lived in Athens during her Golden Age. This snub-nosed man with bulging eyes devoted his life to seeking truth and teaching men how to conduct their lives. He took as his motto "Know thyself." According to Socrates, "The unexamined life is not worth living."

Socrates was not a writer but a teacher. We know what he taught by what his students wrote about him. His method of teaching involved the asking of leading questions followed by the analyzing of the students' answers. Socrates believed that truth (absolutes) could be attained through human reason. To Socrates virtue was knowledge, and ignorance produced evil. Thus reason was the best guide to good behavior.

Many in Athens objected to Socrates questioning of some of the fundamental institutions of the city. They accused him of corrupting the youth and rejecting the gods of Athens. He was tried and condemned to death. Refusing to flee, Socrates calmly drank the cup of hemlock (poison) by which the sentence of death was to be carried out. He died at the age of seventy in the midst of his followers.

Jacques-Louis David (French, 1748–1825), The Death of Socrates, *1787.*

The Metropolitan Museum of Art, Catharine Lorillard Wolfe Collection, Wolfe Fund, 1931 (31.45) Photograph ©1995 The Metropolitan Museum of Art

Plato (427?–347 BC)—The most famous pupil of Socrates was **Plato** (PLAY toh). He established a school of philosophy and science called the Academy in Athens. In the *Republic*, he devised one of the first plans for an ideal society and government. Although Plato lived in democratic Athens, he realized that too much liberty and freedom without restraint often leads to **anarchy** (the breakdown of government and order). He stated that the "excess of liberty, whether in states or individuals, seems only to pass into excess of slavery."

In his works Plato discussed what he considered the nature of true reality. He determined that something would have to be permanent (eternal) if it were to be truly real. Since nothing in this world is permanent, Plato concluded that true reality lies outside the physical world. The things on earth are mere shadows, or imperfect reflections, of their eternal counterparts, or "forms," in the unseen realm of eternity. Through this reasoning process Plato came close to the biblical truth expressed by the apostle Paul in 2 Corinthians 4:18—"For the things which are seen are temporal; but the things which are not seen are eternal."

Was Plato a Christian?

Plato's philosophy is in some ways similar to Christianity's emphasis on the importance of faith in the unseen. The apostle Paul did say in 2 Corinthians 4:18, "For the things which are seen are temporal; but the things which are not seen are eternal." But Plato's point was that the unseen world is the real world and the seen world is only a representation. The Bible, however, presents the world of human experience as real—temporal, yes, but not unreal. Plato also had a very un-Christian view of the unseen world. He had no conception of a personal God Who loves mankind and is working to redeem the human race from its sinfulness. Some historians claim that the New Testament reflects the philosophy of Plato. But such claims are based on superficial similarities.

Aristotle (384–322 BC)—The last of the three famous Greek philosophers was **Aristotle** (EHR uh STOT ul). Aristotle was not an Athenian like the other two but came to Athens from northern Greece. At the age of eighteen, he began

Logic

We remember many things about Aristotle. One of his best-known contributions is the syllogism (a way of reasoning). A syllogism consists of three parts: (1) a major premise (statement); (2) a minor premise; and (3) a conclusion. Here is an example of a syllogism:

$a \longrightarrow b$

Major Premise: All spiders have eight legs.

$c \longrightarrow a$

Minor Premise: A tarantula is a spider.

$c \longrightarrow b$

Conclusion: Therefore, a tarantula has eight legs.

From this simple example we are able to devise a formula for logical reasoning: ($a \longrightarrow b, c \longrightarrow a, \therefore c \longrightarrow b$). If we do not follow this formula, we could come up with reasoning like this:

$a \longrightarrow b$

Major Premise: All cows have four legs.

$c \longrightarrow b$

Minor Premise: My cat has four legs.

$c \longrightarrow a$

Conclusion: Therefore, my cat is a cow!

Only if the major premise is reversible (true whether you read it forward or backward) can we reason the way we did in the second example. The following is an example of this type of premise: All right angles have ninety degrees; all ninety-degree angles are right angles.

his study at Plato's Academy. Plato called his most famous student "the mind of the school." Like Plato, Aristotle has had a continuing impact on Western thought through his writings. Aristotle, as we learned earlier, was also the tutor of Alexander the Great and instilled in the young prince an appreciation for Greek culture.

Unlike Plato, Aristotle believed that reality was in the physical world. Therefore, he developed wide interests in many fields. He wrote treatises on politics, biology, physics, art, drama, mathematics, and ethics. He is best remembered for his works on logic, which are collectively called the *Organon* ("Instrument"). To aid man's reasoning ability, Aristotle developed the **syllogism**, a three-step logical process of thinking. The following is a good example: (1) All Greeks are human; (2) Aristotle is a Greek; (3) Therefore, Aristotle is human.

Epicureans and Stoics—The Epicurean (EP ih k*yoo* REE un) and Stoic philosophies emerged shortly after the death of Alexander the Great. **Epicurus** believed that great happiness and pleasure could be achieved through the avoidance of pain and fear. **Zeno**, the founder of Stoicism, taught that the affairs of men and the universe were ordered by fixed laws. Man must accept his fate and live a life of duty and self-control. These philosophies had greater impact upon the Roman world than on the Hellenistic world. (See p. 108.) When the apostle Paul visited Athens in the first century AD, certain Epicurean and Stoic philosophers mocked him because his preaching concerning the resurrection (Acts 17:18, 32) contradicted their teaching.

THIS MOMENT IN HISTORY

Aristotle

How did Aristotle influence Alexander's empire?

____

____

____

____

____

____

____

____

Contributions to Science, Medicine, and Mathematics

The questions raised by the Greek philosophers concerning man and his world encouraged others to seek natural or logical explanations through observation. Even before the Golden Age, **Pythagoras** (pih THAG er us), a philosopher and mathematician of the sixth century BC, had concluded that the universe could be explained in mathematical terms. His geometric theorem, the Pythagorean Theorem, is still studied by students taking geometry.

Hippocrates (460?–377? BC), the famed physician of the Golden Age, is known as the Father of Medicine. After studying in Athens, Hippocrates be-

The Hippocratic Oath

I swear . . . to fulfill, according to my power and judgment, this oath and this written contract. . . . I will use diets for the help of the sick according to my power and judgment, not for injury or to do an unjust thing. I will not ever give a deadly drug to anyone, even if asked, nor will I lead the way in such counsel; and likewise I will not give a woman a device to cause an abortion. I will keep my life and my art purely and piously. . . . If I fulfill this oath and do not break it, may it be mine to enjoy the fruit of both my life and my art, being honored among all men for all time; but if I transgress and break it, may the opposite of these things come to pass.

came a wandering physician who traveled throughout Greece and Macedonia. Contrary to common Greek myths which held that disease was the punishment of the gods, Hippocrates (hih PAHK ruh TEEZ) taught that every illness has a natural cause. He rejected magic and superstition and instead recommended rest and proper diet as the proper treatments. He wrote manuals that preserved his findings for other physicians. On the walls of many doctors' offices today hangs a copy of Hippocrates' oath, which governed his practice of medicine.

Euclid (YOO klid) has often been called the Father of Geometry. He founded a school of mathematics in Alexandria, Egypt. His textbook *Elements* has been the basis for geometry textbooks up through the twenty-first century. The Greek inventor and mathematician Archimedes (AR kuh MEE deez), born in the Greek colony of Syracuse, was known throughout the Hellenistic world for his many discoveries. One of his discoveries was the principle of the lever, the practical value of which is illustrated today by the raising of a car with a jack. Proud of his discovery of the laws of levers, he once boasted, "Give me a spot to stand on and a lever long enough, and I will move the earth." The Greek astronomer and geographer **Eratosthenes** (ehr uh TAHS thuh NEEZ) determined the circumference of the globe with amazing accuracy by using the geometry that Euclid popularized. He also formulated the lines of longitude and latitude that are still used today on maps. The belief that the earth is round was established by the Greeks some seventeen centuries before Columbus.

Achievement in Literature

History—We get our word *history* from the Greek word meaning "inquiry." The Greeks believed that men could learn lessons from the past to help them live in the present. **Herodotus**, the Father of History, wrote his history of the Persian Wars in the hope of "preserving from decay the remembrance of what men have done, and of preventing the great and wonderful actions of the Greeks and the Barbarians from losing their due need of glory, and withal to put on record what were their grounds of feud."[5] Although Herodotus tried to present an accurate historical account, his work contains many myths and exaggerations and an obvious bias toward the Greeks.

Thucydides (thoo SID ih DEEZ), a contemporary of Herodotus, wrote the *History of the Peloponnesian War*, a more accurate and objective record than Herodotus's work. Although Thucydides was an Athenian and fought briefly for Athens during the war with Sparta, he did not let his personal affections influence his account of the war.

Drama—The Greek achievement in literature was unsurpassed in the ancient world. Homer's epic poems are the monuments of early Greek literature. Later the Greeks excelled in poetic drama. An outgrowth of religious festivals, drama became an important part of Greek life. In Athens, for example, several days were set aside each year for the drama festivals. Shops were closed and schools had a holiday as the entire population of the city attended the outdoor performances. The Greeks held contests to determine the best plays and actors.

Greek drama provided more than just entertainment. The plays educated the Greek people in religious beliefs, moral behavior, and civic pride. Both tragedy and comedy were popular forms of Greek drama. **Sophocles** (SAHF uh KLEEZ), a writer of tragedy, and **Aristophanes** (EHR ih STAHF uh neez),

Thucydides on the Writing of History

Of the events of the war I have not ventured to speak from any chance information, nor according to any notion of my own; I have described nothing but what I either saw myself, or learned from others of whom I made the most careful and particular inquiry. The task was a laborious one, because eyewitnesses of the same occurrences gave different accounts of them, as they remembered or were interested in the actions of one side or the other. And very likely the strictly historical character of my narrative may be disappointing to the ear. But if he who desires to have before his eyes a true picture of the events which have happened, and of the like events which may be expected to happen hereafter in the order of human things, shall pronounce what I have written to be useful, then I shall be satisfied. My history is an everlasting possession, not a prize composition which is heard and forgotten.[6]

Ancient Greek theater in Athens

A Selection from a Comedy of Aristophanes

They're always abusing the women, / As a terrible plague to men:
They say we're the root of all evil, / And repeat it again and again;
Of war, and quarrels, and bloodshed, / All mischief, be what it may:
And pray, then, why do you marry us, / If we're all the plagues you say?
And why do you take care of us, / And keep us so safe at home,
And are never easy a moment, / If ever we chance to roam?
When you ought to be thanking heaven / That your Plague is out of the way—
You all keep fussing and fretting— / "Where is my Plague to-day?"
If a Plague peeps out of the window, / Up go the eyes of the men;
If she hides, then they all keep staring / Until she looks out again.

a writer of comedy, were among the most famous of the Greek dramatists. Many of the Greek dramas are still enjoyed today; their analysis of human behavior is just as penetrating today as it was in ancient Greece.

Excellence in Art

The Greeks excelled in many forms of art; the most highly prized are their urns, sculpture, and temples. Grecian urns are among the most beautiful ever fashioned. On the exteriors of these graceful forms, the Greeks painted scenes of everyday life, battles, athletic competitions, and activities of their gods.

Greek sculpture falls into three main periods: archaic, classical, and Hellenistic. In the archaic period, Greek sculpture shows a strong Egyptian influence. Figures stand stiff and expressionless, their fists clenched by their sides. From these somewhat crude forms Greek sculpture gradually became more realistic. This change came about during the classical period, a period when Greek sculpture reached its highest achievement. Through their sculpture the Greeks sought to represent the ideal man. In the Hellenistic period Greek sculpture lost its simple beauty. Its calm self-confidence was replaced by a frenzied emotional tone.

The "Golden Age" of Greek culture (see p. 64) was also the "golden" or "classical" age of Greek architecture. The Greek building style became a standard of excellence that later generations copied. Nothing better reflects the beauty of Greek architecture than the buildings of the Athenian Acropolis. During the Persian Wars, Xerxes had destroyed Athens, but under Pericles new and more beautiful buildings were erected. Formerly a fortress for refuge, the

Athenian Acropolis became the site of temples to the Greek gods. The most spectacular of these temples is the **Parthenon**. We can get a glimpse of its former beauty and grandeur today, even in its ruined state.

The Athenians dedicated the building to the city's patron goddess, Athena. During the days of Pericles, a forty-foot-high gold and ivory statue of Athena stood inside the temple. The building itself is rectangular in shape and is supported by towering columns in beautiful symmetry. The Greeks gave it the

The Winged Victory of Samothrace (sculpted ca. 190 BC) illustrates the sense of movement and emotion that distinguishes Hellenistic Greek art from the calm of classical Greek art.

Top: *The Parthenon in Athens, temple dedicated to the Greek goddess Athena*
Bottom: *The Porch of Maidens, one of the fine examples of Greek statuary found on the Acropolis of Athens*

Greek Architectural Orders

From the columns and capitals (the head or top of a column) of Greek buildings, we can distinguish three styles or orders of architecture: (1) the Doric style with solid, strong masculine-looking feature; (2) the Ionic style with its splendor and graceful elements and its scroll-shaped capital; and (3) the Corinthian style, whose capitals were richly carved and ornately designed.

Doric (left), Ionic (below), and Corinthian (right)

appearance of solidity and symmetry through the subtle use of optical illusions. The steps leading to the entrance are slightly curved up at the center; this feature gives the eye the illusion of their being flat. (If they were truly flat, they would appear to dip.) The columns are placed closer together at the sides of the building than at the middle. This spacing gives the appearance of regularity. Likewise the floor rises gently at the center, giving the whole the appearance of a swelling, living edifice.

The Parthenon is a symbol of the cultural achievement of the Greek civilization. It is also a symbol of the spiritual blindness of the Greek people. The apostle Paul visited Athens some five hundred years after her "Golden Age." He preached against the idolatrous practices that the Parthenon and the statue of Athena represented.

> *God that made the world and all things therein . . . dwelleth not in temples made with hands; . . . we ought not to think that the Godhead is like unto gold, or silver, or stone, graven by art and man's device.*
>
> *Acts 17:24, 29*

Section Quiz

1. What was the name given to the new culture that emerged in the Near East that mixed Greek culture with the cultures of the East?
2. What philosopher developed the three-step logical process of thinking called a syllogism?
3. Who is known as the Father of Medicine?
4. Who was the more objective historian: Herodotus or Thucydides?
5. Identify the three styles of Greek architecture.

1. ______________________
2. ______________________
3. ______________________
4. ______________________
5. ______________________

____

____

A Glance Behind

The story of the Greeks is exciting, and their cultural achievements are remarkable. Greek culture has profoundly influenced Western society. We cannot study art, literature, philosophy, or government without encountering Greek ideas. Nevertheless, through their idolatry and immorality they perpetuated the rebellion against God that began in the Garden of Eden. But God was not indifferent to their rebellion. He sent wars, plagues, and various other hardships to remind them of their sinfulness.

In referring back to the vision found in Daniel 2, we will remember that the huge statue had his arms and chest of silver (Persia) below which was a waist of bronze (the Greeks). Even Greek power was overshadowed by the Romans—the legs of iron.

In the next two chapters we will see how the Romans adopted much of Greek culture into their own society. It is this Graeco-Roman culture that formed the foundation of the modern Western world and provided the historical setting for the promised Messiah, Who would come to earth to redeem for Himself a people "out of every kindred, and tongue, and people, and nation."

and a Glimpse Ahead

Notes

1. Homer, *Odyssey* (trans. Samuel Butler), 1. intro.
2. Herodotus, *The History of Herodotus* (trans. George Rawlinson), 6. 112.
3. Herodotus, 7. 225.
4. Thucydides (trans. Benjamin Jowett), 2. 37.
5. Herodotus, 1. intro.
6. Thucydides, 1.22.t

Chapter Review

Can You Define?

anthropomorphic
Olympiad
polis
monarchy
oligarchy
tyranny
democracy
Helots
archon
Hellenic
Hellenistic
humanities
philosophers
anarchy
syllogism

Can You Identify?

Minoan civilization
Mycenaean civilization
Dorians
Iliad
Odyssey
Homer
Zeus
Athena
Peloponnesian League
Solon
Darius I
490 BC
Xerxes
480 BC
Delian League
Pericles
Peloponnesian War
Philip II
Alexander the Great
Darius III
Thales
Socrates
Plato
Aristotle
Epicurus
Zeno
Pythagoras
Hippocrates
Euclid
Eratosthenes
Herodotus
Thucydides
Sophocles
Aristophanes
Parthenon

Can you Locate?

Aegean Sea
Crete
Knossos
Mycenae
Troy
Hellespont
Mount Olympus
Olympia
Sparta
Peloponnesus
Athens
Marathon
Thermopylae
Salamis
Macedonia

How Much Do You Remember?

1. Draw two columns and list at least three contrasting characteristics of the Spartan and Athenian societies.
2. How did the Persian and Peloponnesian Wars affect the unity of the Greeks?
3. How did Hellenic culture differ from Hellenistic culture?

What Do You Think?

1. What are the strengths and weaknesses of monarchy, oligarchy, and democracy?
2. Why was Athens and not Sparta the cultural center during the Golden Age?
3. Read 1 Corinthians 1:22–31. How does this passage apply to a Christian's study of Greek philosophy?

"All roads lead to Rome."

The Roman Republic

I. Beginning of Roman Civilization
   A. Geographic Features
   B. Early Inhabitants
   C. Founding of Rome
   D. Early Society and Government

II. The Early Roman Republic
   A. Establishment
   B. Struggle

III. The Mediterranean—A Roman Sea
   A. Rome—Master of Italy
   B. Rome—Master of the Western Mediterranean Sea
   C. Rome—Master of the Eastern Mediterranean Sea

IV. Decline into a Dictatorship
   A. Problems
   B. Failure of Reform
   C. Civil War

Roman aqueduct at Caesarea

Today if you were to travel in Spain, France, Britain, Italy, Greece, Asia Minor, Palestine, Egypt, or North Africa, you could find roads built almost two thousand years ago by the Romans. In fact, some of the modern roads in these lands are built on top of the firm and deep base of the old Roman roads. The Romans constructed a network of roads that connected the far corners of their vast empire with their capital city. It could literally be said of the ancient world that "all roads lead to Rome."

In a figurative sense the road of ancient history also leads us to Rome. Rome was the culmination of ancient civilization. Despite all her power and influence, Rome was deeply bound in spiritual darkness. She readily embraced the pagan gods and false teaching of her many conquered peoples.

The road of God's plan for the ages leads us to Rome as well. God chose to send His Son, Jesus Christ, into the world when the Roman civilization was at its height. God had been at work in history preparing the world for the coming of the Savior. It could be said that the Roman world was the cradle of Christianity. From the Roman province of Judea, the truth of the gospel spread to every part of the empire—on Roman roads.

Before we go any further, consider again Daniel's vision in Daniel 2. Most biblical scholars accept the statue's legs of iron to be a picture of Rome and her influence. Like no other previous world power, Rome broke and crushed all in her path to dominance. With ruthless efficiency, Rome conquered all world powers that preceded it.

I. Beginning of Roman Civilization

Geographic Features

The land of Italy, centrally located in the Mediterranean world, was the heart of the Roman Empire. Shaped like a boot, the Italian Peninsula extends into the Mediterranean Sea between the lands of Greece and Spain. At the southern tip of Italy is the island of Sicily, which nearly joins Italy with North Africa.

Geographic obstacles did not hamper the Romans as they did the Greeks. Because of the lack of good soil, the Greeks looked to the sea for their livelihood. However, the soil and climate of Italy were more suitable for farming. The mountains in Greece divided the Greek people and hindered their political unity. The Apennine (AP uh NINE) Mountains, which run down the middle of the Italian Peninsula, are less rugged than the mountains of Greece and did not hamper the growth of trade and travel among the people of Italy. From the Italian Peninsula, the Romans expanded their territory to include all the land surrounding the Mediterranean Sea. It is little wonder that the Romans would later call the Mediterranean ***Mare Nostrum***, which means "our sea."

Early Inhabitants

The earliest inhabitants of the Italian Peninsula had come from across the Alps and had settled in northern Italy. Many of these early settlers—called Latins—moved south and settled in Latium, a plain lying south of the Tiber River near the western coast of Italy. From this region arose a civilization that would one day rule the entire Mediterranean world.

Portions of Italy were also inhabited by the Phoenicians, Greeks, and Etruscans. Both the Phoenicians and the Greeks were known in the ancient world for their sea trade and colonization. Phoenicia established colonies on Sicily and along the coast of North Africa. (The Phoenician colony of Carthage in North Africa later rivaled Rome for mastery of the western Mediterranean world.) The Greeks established independent colonies on the island of Sicily also, as well as along the coast of southern Italy.

Most people have never heard of the **Etruscans**. They came to Italy between 900 and 800 BC and established one of Italy's earliest civilizations. Little is known of their origin, although many historians believe they came from the East, possibly from Asia Minor. The Etruscans settled along Italy's western coast, just north of the Tiber River. They soon became trade competitors with the Greeks living in Italy. The Etruscans learned much about Greek myths, architecture, sculpture, and language. In fact, it was probably the Etruscans who first introduced Greek culture to the Romans. Much of later Roman culture would reflect Greek tradition and customs.

The Founding of Rome

The city of Rome began on the banks of the Tiber River, about fifteen miles from the seacoast. Here trade routes that ran along the western coast of Italy crossed the river. At this point the river was easy to ford. People from Latium began to settle on the hills that overlooked this spot. A colony of Latin people established a village on the Palatine Hill near the Tiber. Soon other Latin villages were founded on the surrounding hills. Sometime during the eighth century BC, seven of these villages formed a league—the **"League of the Seven Hills."** This was the beginning of the city of Rome.

Like the Greeks, the Romans developed legends to explain their early history. According to Roman tradition, Rome was founded in 753 BC by the twin brothers **Romulus** and **Remus**. The legend tells how a relative of Romulus

Roman Roads

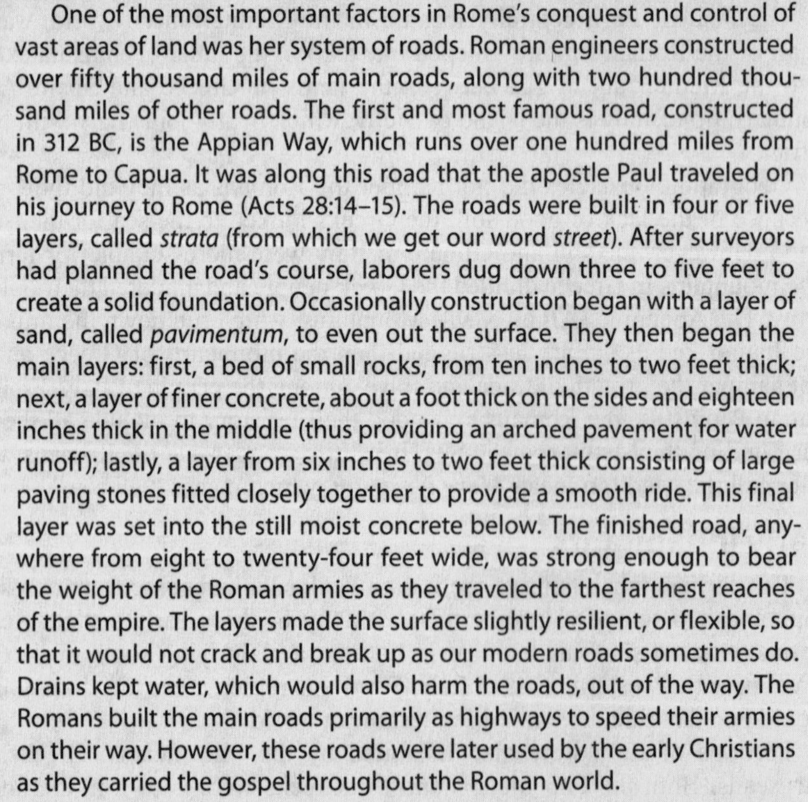

One of the most important factors in Rome's conquest and control of vast areas of land was her system of roads. Roman engineers constructed over fifty thousand miles of main roads, along with two hundred thousand miles of other roads. The first and most famous road, constructed in 312 BC, is the Appian Way, which runs over one hundred miles from Rome to Capua. It was along this road that the apostle Paul traveled on his journey to Rome (Acts 28:14–15). The roads were built in four or five layers, called *strata* (from which we get our word *street*). After surveyors had planned the road's course, laborers dug down three to five feet to create a solid foundation. Occasionally construction began with a layer of sand, called *pavimentum*, to even out the surface. They then began the main layers: first, a bed of small rocks, from ten inches to two feet thick; next, a layer of finer concrete, about a foot thick on the sides and eighteen inches thick in the middle (thus providing an arched pavement for water runoff); lastly, a layer from six inches to two feet thick consisting of large paving stones fitted closely together to provide a smooth ride. This final layer was set into the still moist concrete below. The finished road, anywhere from eight to twenty-four feet wide, was strong enough to bear the weight of the Roman armies as they traveled to the farthest reaches of the empire. The layers made the surface slightly resilient, or flexible, so that it would not crack and break up as our modern roads sometimes do. Drains kept water, which would also harm the roads, out of the way. The Romans built the main roads primarily as highways to speed their armies on their way. However, these roads were later used by the early Christians as they carried the gospel throughout the Roman world.

Via Appia Antica; a section of the Appian Way near Rome

and Remus usurped the throne and ordered the two babes, who were of royal descent, to be drowned. The infants were placed in a basket and thrown into the Tiber River to die. But a wolf saved the boys and cared for them until a shepherd found them and took them in. As young men Romulus and Remus allegedly returned to found a city near the place where the wolf had discovered them. While marking out the boundaries for the city, Romulus, in a burst of jealous anger, killed Remus. Romulus founded the city of Rome, named it after himself, and became its first king. Few of the legends concerning the founding of Rome, however, are historically reliable.

Ancient Roman home at Pompeii

Early Society and Government

The basic unit of early Roman society was the family. The family was a small community—self-sufficient and self-ruled. It included not only the father, wife, and children, but also all the people who lived in the household, such as slaves. (Even property was considered to be part of the family.) The father (***pater*** in Latin) was the sole authority over the family, and his control extended to every aspect of family life. He ruled his family without interference from the state. He was in charge of the family's worship and dispensed discipline and law, holding even the power of life and death over members of his household.

Every Roman took great pride in his family heritage. Parents instilled into their children the values of loyalty, submission to authority, self-control, and duty. Rome's strong families coupled with the patriotism and hardworking spirit of her people provided the foundation for her greatness.

The family also provided the basis for larger social groups. A number of families from a common ancestor are called a **clan**. Likewise, a number of clans united by common beliefs and living in a particular region are called a **tribe**.

Within the Roman society there were two social classes. They differed greatly from each other in the social and political privileges of their members. The wealthy landholders and noble families made up the aristocratic class (a privileged class) called the **patricians**. They held the highest positions in the early Roman society. The majority of the people, however, belonged to a supposedly inferior class called the **plebeians** (plee BEE unz). These were the "common people"—the farmers, traders, and craftsmen.

The early government of Rome was a monarchy. The king served as the chief priest, the commander of the army, and the administrator of justice. The king's authority was called the imperium. A small bundle of rods which enclosed an axe, called the **fasces**, symbolized his power. As far as we know, the kings were elected by the people. The kings could gain advice on official matters from a council of clan leaders known as the Senate. A popular assembly that represented the people at large also existed. It elected the kings and bestowed the imperium on them.

Fasces

THROUGH EYES OF FAITH:

Family

How does the Roman view of a family compare and contrast with the biblical view?

Section Quiz

1. ______________________
2. ______________________
3. ______________________
4. ______________________
5. ______________________

1. What did the Romans call the Mediterranean Sea?
2. In what year was the city of Rome founded?
3. According to legend, what two brothers founded Rome?
4. What were the two main social classes of ancient Rome?
5. What became the symbol of the king's authority in early Roman society?

II. The Early Roman Republic

Establishment

About a century after the founding of Rome, the Etruscans crossed the Tiber River from the north and conquered the Latin villages. During the period of Etruscan rule, Rome grew from a weak league of villages to become the leading Latin city. As the influence of Rome increased, so did the hatred of the Roman nobility for the Etruscan monarch. In **509 BC** they overthrew the king. In the place of the monarchy, they established a new form of government called a **republic**. Under the Roman Republic the administration of government was divided among three governing branches: the consuls, the Senate, and the assemblies.

Two elected **consuls** (government officials) replaced the king and held the imperium. They supervised the everyday affairs of government, commanded the Roman army, and served as the supreme judges of the land. Power was equally divided between each consul; one could not act without the consent

Flow of Political Power in the Early Roman Republic

Senate
Aristocratic administrative body composed of about 300 members; held most of the power in the early Roman Republic

Although technically possible, this never actually happened.

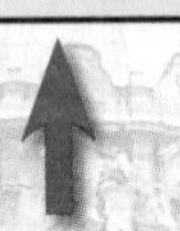

2 Censors
Elected every 5 years; served for 18 months; drew up official lists determining taxation, military service, and voting eligibility

2 Consuls
"Heads of state"; always patricians until 367 BC when plebians were allowed to hold the office; served for one year; held the imperium; carried out laws and commanded the army

10 Tribunes
Served for one year; could veto decisions of the Senate, the consuls, and each other

Assembly of Centuries
Popular assembly organized by social class; voted by group, each group having one vote; elected some government officials

Tribal Assembly
Popular assembly; originally representing the territorial districts of Rome; voted by group, each group having one vote; elected some government officials

 Elects
Chosen from
 Vetos
Regulates

What Is a Republic?

A republic is a form of government in which voting citizens control the power of government through elected officials under law. The word comes from the Latin *res publica*, which literally means "a public thing." The Romans believed that while kings often advanced themselves and their families, a republic would best protect the interests of the people. There have been many different forms of republics in history. In some only a small portion of the people have held full citizenship and have thus been able to vote. In others the vast majority of the people have had this privilege. You are probably most familiar with the word *republic* in connection with the government of the United States. The framers of the American Constitution feared government by monarchy or oligarchy, for rulers under these types of governments often abused their powers and oppressed the people. Likewise, these men feared pure democracy because it might lead to "mob rule." They studied the Roman Republic and saw the wisdom of a government which blended the elements of monarchy, oligarchy, and democracy into one government under written law. The framers of the Constitution recognized the biblical truth that men are evil by nature and therefore cannot be trusted. For this reason they valued a limited government that would keep any one man or group of men from obtaining absolute power. Many of the principles of government found in the American Constitution came from the model of the Roman Republic.

of the other. Each consul served only a one-year term at a time. The shortness of the term prevented a consul from becoming too powerful. During the early years of the republic, members of the patrician class held the office of consul almost exclusively.

The **Senate** became the most important and most powerful body of the republic. Though the Senate served the interest of all the people of Rome, it was in particular an aristocratic body that safeguarded the powers of the patrician class. The Senate was composed of three hundred members who were appointed for life by the consuls. The permanency of the Senate served to increase its powers beyond its early advisory role. It controlled the government's finances, passed laws, and supervised the foreign affairs of the republic.

The republic also had assemblies through which the people could express their views. Wealth, birth, and the place of one's residence determined the membership and voting procedures of these various assemblies. The chief assembly of the early republic was the Assembly of Centuries. This assembly voted on legislation submitted by the consuls, made declarations of war, and elected high-ranking government officials. However, the Senate had veto power over the acts passed by this assembly.

Struggle Within the Republic

The patrician nobles who expelled the Etruscan king took firm control of the government. Patricians held the consulships, dominated the Senate and assemblies, made most of the laws, and controlled the courts. In contrast, the plebeians had few social privileges and virtually no voice in government. They were excluded from holding public office, and marriage between plebeians and patricians was forbidden. For failing to repay loans, plebeians could lose their property and even be sold into slavery.

For two centuries following the founding of the republic, the plebeians struggled to gain political and social equality. During these two centuries Rome was constantly waging war against her neighbors in Italy. Because the patricians could not handle the burden of war alone, they had to rely more and more on the common people to help in fighting these wars. As the plebeians shared in the dangers of fighting, they wanted to share in the privilege of being represented in the government. By threatening to desert the army, the plebeians gradually gained concessions from the patricians.

One of the first concessions gained by the plebeians was the right to have their own assembly and elected officials. They met as the Council of Plebeians and passed resolutions called **plebiscites**. These were binding only on the plebeians, however, and not on the patrician class. The Council of Plebeians elected ten men to the office of **tribune**. The tribunes protected the rights and interests of the common people. By crying out **"Veto!"** ("I forbid!"), the tribunes could stop unjust acts of patrician officials.

In the past, patrician judges had taken advantage of the plebeians, who were not familiar with the traditions that made up Rome's unwritten laws. However, continued pressure from the plebeians finally forced the patricians to put the Roman laws into writing. Around 450 BC these laws were written down on twelve tablets and hung in the **Roman Forum**, the section of the city that was the center of government. Now all could know the law. Likewise the law was to be applied equally to all. Young boys in the republic memorized the whole code as part of their school work. These tablets of law, called the **Law of Twelve Tables,** became the foundation of Roman civil law.

Gradually the plebeians improved their political and social standing in the republic. They gained the right to hold public offices which had previously been held only by the patricians. A few plebeians even became senators. Debtor slavery was abolished, and the law against intermarriage between plebeians and patricians was repealed. In **287 BC** the plebeian assembly, now called the **Tribal Assembly**, gained the power to pass laws binding upon all the people of Rome—patricians as well as plebeians.

As the result of these two centuries of struggle, the plebeians officially gained social and political equality with the patricians. The peaceful changes seemed to make the republic more representative of the people. But as the distinctions between patricians and plebeians began to disappear, a new class

The Roman Forum

distinction began to develop—the rich versus the poor. Wealthy plebeians and patricians formed a new alliance that maintained control of the Senate and held the reins of power in the republic.

Section Quiz

1. In what year was the Roman Republic founded?
2. What was the most powerful body within the governmental structure of the republic?
3. What power did tribunes get to exercise over unjust acts of patrician officials?
4. What was the name of the Roman law that was written down and placed in the Roman Forum?
5. What was the name of the plebeian assembly that gained the power to pass laws binding on all the people of Rome, regardless of their social class?

1. ____________________
2. ____________________
3. ____________________
____
4. ____________________
____
5. ____________________

III. The Mediterranean—A Roman Sea

The Romans had not originally set out to conquer the world. But through constant warfare from 509 to 133 BC, Rome grew from a small city along the Tiber River into the largest empire of the ancient world. How did this expansion take place?

Rome—The Master of Italy

During the years of internal struggles between the patricians and the plebeians, Rome was also involved in external struggles with her neighbors in Italy. Under Etruscan rule Rome became the leading Latin city. With the expulsion of the Etruscan king in 509 BC, other Latin cities joined with Rome in a defensive alliance for protection against the Etruscans. Just as the members of the Delian League had revolted against the growing power of Athens, so the Latin cities, fearful of the growing power of Rome, revolted. Rome defeated the Latin cities and secured a strong position in central Italy. She later acquired the land to her north by defeating the Etruscans.

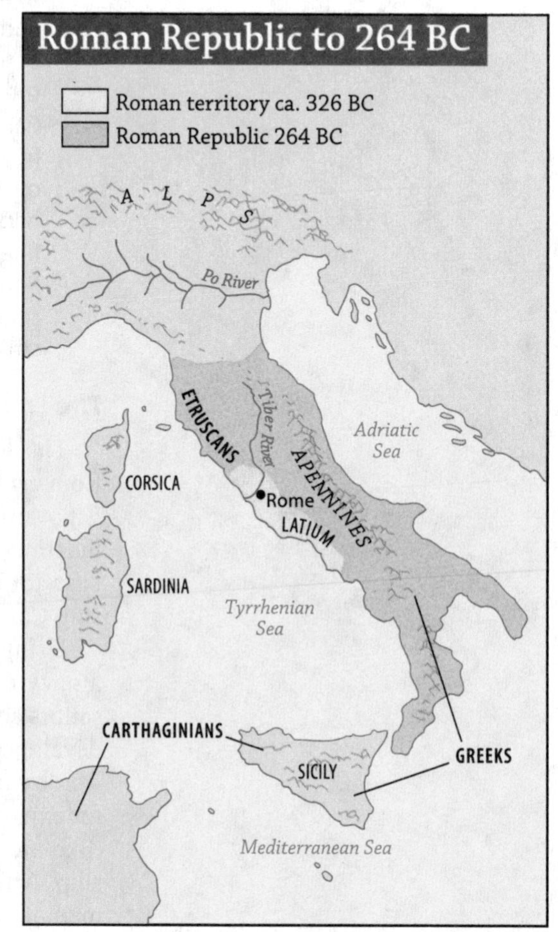

Rome soon began expanding into southern Italy, threatening the Greek colonies located there. The Greek colonies feared Roman conquest and appealed to **Pyrrhus**, a distant relative of Alexander the Great, for help. With the aid of war elephants (the "tanks" of ancient warfare), Pyrrhus defeated the Romans twice. In gaining the second victory, however, Pyrrhus's army suffered such great losses that he reportedly exclaimed, "Another such victory and I shall be ruined." Since that time, the term "Pyrrhic victory" has referred to a victory whose costs outweigh any advantage that may have been gained. Pyrrhus returned to Greece when Rome, joined by another Greek rival, further weakened his force. With Pyrrhus back in Greece, Rome was able to conquer all of the southern Italy.

By 265 BC Rome controlled all of the Italian Peninsula. Her task now was to rule effectively a land which included Latins, Etruscans, and Greeks. Unlike most conquering people, Rome treated her conquered subjects with mercy and fairness instead of force and oppression. As long as they did not rebel against Roman authority, her subjects lived in relative peace. To many of her conquered subjects in Italy, Rome granted citizenship—the right to vote and hold office. To others Rome allowed a great degree of local independence.

Although Rome did not demand tribute (payment of money or grain showing submission) from the conquered states within Italy, she did require them to furnish troops to help her fight her wars. The protection of Roman law and the stability and prosperity that Rome brought to the Italian Peninsula secured the loyalty of her subjects and allies.

Rome—The Master of the Western Mediterranean

Rome's conquest of the Italian Peninsula brought her into conflict with Carthage, another power in the Western world. This rival of Rome, located in North Africa, possessed good harbors, rich mining resources, and the best navy in the western Mediterranean. While Phoenicia, her mother country, grew weak as a result of Assyrian and Chaldean conquests, Carthage built her own empire in the West. Her empire included the North African coast, southern Spain, the islands of Sardinia and Corsica, and part of the island of Sicily.

Between 264 and 146 BC, Rome and Carthage fought each other in three wars. Both cities controlled much territory in the western Mediterranean. Both were expanding rapidly. In addition, Rome and Carthage were competing commercially for control of trade in the Mediterranean. This rivalry, which was built upon both jealousy and fear, led to a series of wars known as the **Punic Wars**. (*Punici* was the Roman word for Phoenicians.) The Greek historian Polybius, sympathetic to the Roman Republic, gave this description of the differences between Carthage and Rome.

> The Carthaginians naturally are superior at sea both in efficiency and equipment, because seamanship has long been their national craft, . . . but as regards military service on land the Romans are much more efficient. . . . The troops [the Carthaginians] employ are foreign and mercenary [hired for pay], whereas those of the Romans are native of the soil and citizens. So that in this respect also we must pronounce the political system of Rome to be superior to that of Carthage, the Carthaginians continuing to depend for the maintenance of their freedom on the courage of mercenary force but the Romans on their own valour and on the aid of their allies. Consequently even if they happen to be worsted at the outset, the Romans redeem defeat by final success, while it is the contrary with the Carthaginians. For the Romans, fighting as they are for their country and their children, never can abate their fury but continue to throw their whole hearts into the struggle until they get the better of their enemies.[1]

The First Punic War (264–241 BC)

The First Punic War was fought over control of the island of Sicily. The Romans feared that the Carthaginians would become too strong on the island. A powerful rival force could control the waters between Sicily and Italy and thus hinder Roman trade in the Mediterranean. Sicily could also become a base for a Carthaginian attack on southern Italy. The only way Rome could stop Carthage was to break her naval supremacy.

Using the design of a captured Carthaginian warship, Rome began to build a navy of her own. Although Rome soon possessed the same ships, Roman sailors could not match the experience and skill of the Carthaginians. So Rome developed new tactics for fighting at sea. Up to that time, naval battles were won by ramming and sinking the enemy's vessels. Rome substituted soldiers for experienced sailors. When an enemy ship came near, a plank was dropped (like a drawbridge) so that its spiked tip fastened to the deck of the enemy's ship. Armed Roman soldiers then crossed over and captured the ship. By this method Rome crippled the navy of Carthage.

Despite many setbacks, Rome finally defeated Carthage. Although much of the Roman fleet had been destroyed by fierce storms and though military and diplomatic blunders had prolonged the war, Rome was able to break the spirit of the Carthaginians by overcoming Carthage's naval supremacy. Growing weary from the long war, Carthage sued for peace in 241 BC. From the peace settlement, Rome gained control of Sicily, and Carthage was forced to pay for Roman losses.

Italian coastline along the Mediterranean Sea; a strong navy was vital for Rome's defense of its coasts and trade routes.

The Second Punic War (218–201 BC)

Carthage recovered from her defeat in the First Punic War and extended her control over much of Spain. In 219 BC Carthage attacked a Roman ally, a Spanish town on the Mediterranean coast. The city fell after an eight-month siege, and a second war broke out between Carthage and Rome. Rome, who now had the superior navy, planned to isolate Carthage's forces in Spain. By sending one army to Spain and another to Carthage, Rome hoped for a quick end to the war against the divided Carthaginian forces. This strategy might have worked had it not been for a young Carthaginian commander named **Hannibal**.

Historians have likened Hannibal to Alexander the Great. His strong character and leadership won the devotion of his soldiers. This military genius devised tactics that are still being studied by army experts today. (Some of his tactics were used in tank battles during World War II.) Hannibal realized that his only hope of success was to invade Italy and capture Rome. By invading Italy, he planned to present himself as liberator of Rome's conquered allies and give them an opportunity to break with Rome and gain their freedom. Without the soldiers and resources supplied by her allies, Rome could be conquered—so Hannibal thought.

With cavalry, elephants, and some forty thousand men, Hannibal set out from Spain. He marched his army over the rugged, snow-covered Alps and into northern Italy. The dangerous mountain passes, wintry weather, and attacks from mountain tribes combined to cut his army by about half and left him with only a few supplies and elephants. Nevertheless, he surprised the Romans. They had believed it impossible for any army to cross the Alps—especially during the winter. For the next fifteen years, Hannibal brilliantly led his outnumbered army to many victories in Italy.

Battle of Cannae—In the spring of 216 BC, the Romans suffered one of the worst defeats in their long history. At Cannae (KAN ee), a small town southeast of Rome, the Roman legions confronted Hannibal's army. Because the Romans outnumbered his army almost two to one, Hannibal had to rely on superior battle tactics. He arranged his forces in the same fashion as the Roman troops—cavalry units on the flanks and infantry at the center. But unlike the Roman line, Hannibal's line bulged forward at the center, inviting the Romans to attack there. The Roman infantry charged the center of Hannibal's line, hoping to break it and divide the Carthaginian forces. While the outside of Hannibal's line held its ground, the center (according to plan) retreated, drawing the advancing Romans into a U-shaped pocket. The Romans soon found

The Siege of Syracuse

When Rome attacked Syracuse during the Second Punic War, the Roman commander Marcellus expected to capture the city with only a five-day siege. However, the Romans found their land-and-sea attack repulsed by a variety of unusual war machines. The land forces were met by stones and other missiles hurled from great distances. The naval attack faced catapults hurling five-hundred-pound stones. Syracuse also used cranes, some of which dropped huge stones on the ships, while others with chains and iron claws picked ships up, spun them around, and smashed them upon the rocks along the shore. Legend tells us that the city's defenders also used large mirrors that focused the sun's rays upon Rome's ships and caused them to catch fire. The inventor and director of all this somewhat strange war machinery was Syracuse's most famous mathematician, Archimedes. So effective was his defense that the Romans never tried another assault upon the city. In 212 BC Rome finally captured Syracuse, but with a blockade and trickery rather than a direct attack. Part of the reason for the Syracusans' defeat was the fact that they so trusted in their machines that they were unprepared in the final hours to use their more conventional weapons.

themselves hemmed in by the enemy on three sides. Meanwhile, Hannibal's cavalry, which had routed Rome's cavalry, circled around and attacked the rear of the Roman infantry. The surrounded Roman army was almost completely wiped out. It has been estimated that Hannibal lost six thousand men, while the Romans lost nearly sixty thousand. A generation passed before Rome recovered from this terrible defeat.

Following the Battle of Cannae, the situation looked very grim for the Romans, who had suffered numerous defeats at the hands of Hannibal. To make matters worse, Rome had to contend with a new Carthaginian ally, Macedonia, and to suppress Syracuse, a powerful Greek city on Sicily that revolted against Rome. Despite these advantages, Hannibal was unable to conquer the city of Rome. He lacked the heavy siege equipment needed to break down her walls. Furthermore, he gained few recruits from the people he freed from Roman rule. Rome's fair and generous treatment of her subjects encouraged them to remain loyal to Rome.

Scipio—The turning point in the war came through the daring strategy of a young Roman commander named Scipio (SIP ee OH). A member of a powerful family, he became the most famous Roman of his time. After defeating the Carthaginian forces in Spain, he could have moved his army into Italy to take on Hannibal. But instead he crossed over to North Africa and prepared to attack Carthage. Hannibal, who had not lost a battle in Italy, was ordered back home to defend Carthage. By the time he arrived, the Romans had already gained the advantage. Not even the leadership of Hannibal could stop Scipio

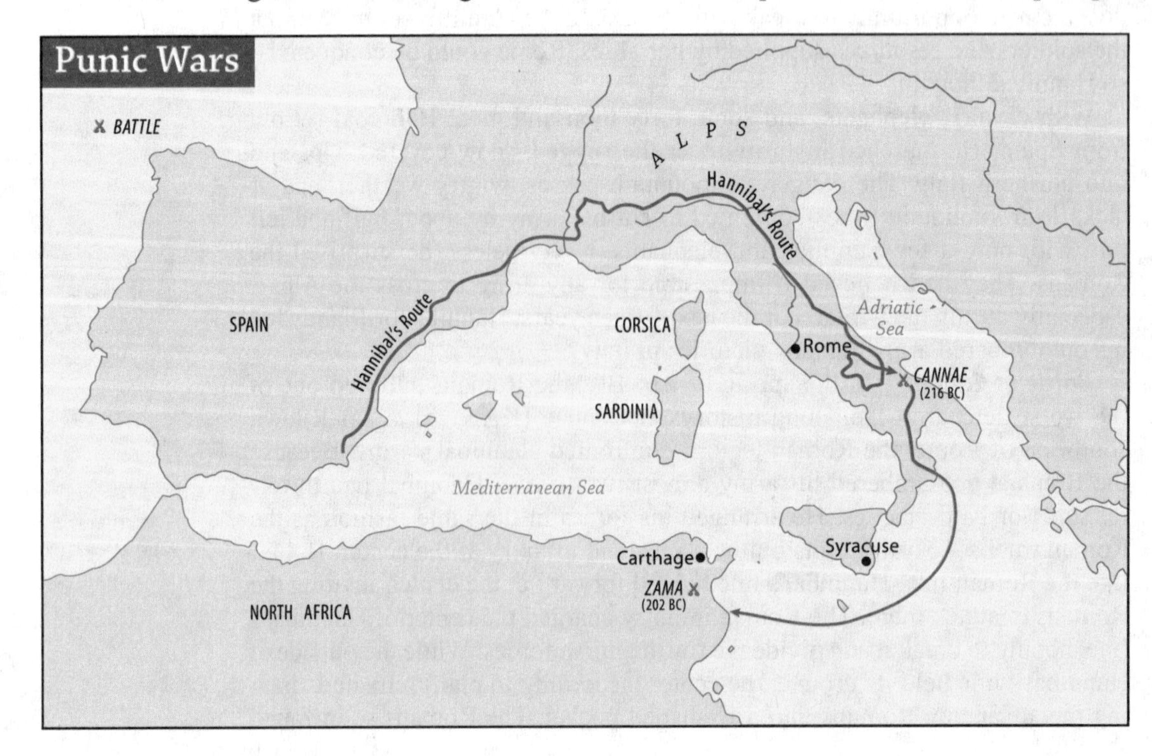

and the Roman legions. At the Battle of Zama (202 BC), the Romans defeated the Carthaginian army. Carthage surrendered and was forced to give up all her territory outside of North Africa, reduce her fleet to only ten vessels, and pay a great sum to Rome for war damages. Rome was now the master of the western Mediterranean world.

The Third Punic War (149–146 BC)

Fifty years after the Second Punic War, many Romans became fearful and jealous of the recovering prosperity of Carthage. One man especially, the Roman senator Cato, sought to arouse the Roman people to take action against Rome's old rival. No matter what the topic of debate was in the Senate, Cato ended all his speeches with the statement, "but I declare that Carthage must be destroyed." When the city broke one of the provisions of her treaty with Rome, Rome harshly demanded that the Carthaginians move their city ten miles inland. Since such a move would mean the death of this commercial center, the citizens decided to fight instead. But the Carthaginians were no match for the Romans. After a three-year siege, the Romans captured the city and utterly destroyed it. They plowed up the land and sold the surviving inhabitants into slavery. The land around Carthage became a new Roman province called Africa.

Ruins at Carthage

Rome—The Master of the Eastern Mediterranean

After the Second Punic War, Rome turned her attention to the eastern portion of the Mediterranean. Here the kingdoms carved out of Alexander the Great's empire—Macedonia, Syria, and Egypt—were engaged in a power struggle of their own. Because Macedonia had joined Carthage against Rome during the Second Punic War, Rome sent her legions to deal with Macedonia after Carthage had been defeated. With Macedonia weakened by her wars with Rome, the king of Syria marched into Asia Minor, crossed the Hellespont, and invaded the kingdom of Macedonia. Rome met this challenge by soundly defeating the Syrian armies. Egypt, the weakest of the three, thought it best to make an alliance with Rome. With this completed, Rome became the master of the entire Mediterranean world.

At first, Rome allowed her eastern conquests a certain amount of self-government. But because of constant uprisings and petty rivalries, Rome reorganized her holdings throughout the Mediterranean region into provinces. Governors appointed by the Roman Senate administered these provinces and served as the chief military and civil rulers for each province. The provinces retained local freedom as long as they did not rebel against Roman authority. The main obligation of the provinces was to pay tribute—money or grain—to Rome. In return Rome provided order and protection.

Hair Styles in Ancient Rome

The early Romans were down-to-earth and practical people. Their fashions—especially their hair styles—confirmed this fact. During the republic women wore their hair pulled back in a bun; young girls sometimes wore ringlets. It is interesting to note, though, the degradation. By the time of Octavian, there was a noticeable change. Aristocratic women, aided by special slaves, curled (with curling irons) and oiled their hair and then piled it in elaborate fashions on top of their heads. Dark-haired Latin ladies often dyed their hair blonde or red or wore wigs fashioned from the hair of their slave girls. Hair styles changed so often that one Roman poet complained, "I cannot keep track of fashion. Everyday, so it seems, brings a different style!" Some sculptors, when carving a statue of a lady, made the head with a detachable scalp; by carving different hair pieces, he could keep the statue in the height of style.

Lest you think it was only the ladies who suffered from vanity, it must be pointed out that men were equally vain. During the republic most men were clean-shaven and wore their hair cropped close. Later when men began to let their hair grow, they too used curling irons to fashion their hair and beards. Like many of their modern counterparts, men who were losing their hair went to great lengths to conceal their baldness. Some grew their hair long on the sides and combed it over the bald spot; others wore wigs. Some even painted the likeness of hair on their heads! It is interesting to note that daily vain concerns are not a new thing for a degrading society.

Section Quiz

1. ____________________
2. ____________________
   ____
   ____
   ____
   ____
   ____
   ____
3. ____________________
4. ____________________
5. ____________________

1. What man led the defense of Greek colonies against Roman expansion in southern Italy?
2. From the description of the Greek historian Polybius (p. 84), list the differences between Carthage and Rome at the outset of the Punic Wars.
3. Over what island was the First Punic War fought?
4. What famed Carthaginian leader invaded Rome by an unexpected march over the Alps into northern Italy?
5. At what battle during the Second Punic War did the Roman general Scipio decisively defeat the Carthaginians, making Rome the master of the western Mediterranean world?

IV. Decline into a Dictatorship

By the first century BC, Rome was the greatest power in the Mediterranean world. Nevertheless, during the last two centuries before Christ, the very foundation of the republic was shaken—not by any foreign enemy but by problems that arose within the republic as a result of Roman expansion.

Problems

The economic and military backbone of the early republic was the hard-working citizen-farmer. During the period of Roman expansion, the greatest military burden as well as economic hardships fell upon the small farmers. Many of them lost their land. When these citizen-farmers returned from fighting Rome's wars, they faced numerous obstacles. Some of them lacked the money needed to get their land back in shape; others were unable to pay their back taxes and thus lost their farms to the government. Those who were able to grow crops were unable to compete with the large farms of the wealthy aristocrats or with the cheap grain imported from the new Roman territories. In poverty and in debt, small farmers sold their land (usually for a cheap price) and sought jobs in the cities or as tenant farmers. But jobs were hard to find because of the increased number of slaves that were brought into Italy following Rome's conquests. Landless and unemployed, the citizen-farmers became dissatisfied and restless. Their self-reliant spirit broke down, and they turned to the government for help.

Frescoes adorned the walls of many Roman houses.

Cubiculum (bedroom) from the Villa of P. Fannius Synistor, *Roman, ca. 40–30 B.C., fresco.*

The Metropolitan Museum of Art, Rogers Fund, 1903 (03.14.13a-g) Photograph ©1986 The Metropolitan Museum of Art

But they received no help from the government. Since its early years, the republic had undergone many changes in order to provide equal rights and privileges for all Roman citizens. The Tribal Assembly, which represented the common people, had greatly increased in power. But no sooner had these gains been achieved than the Punic Wars broke out. The common people failed to assume the responsibilities they had struggled so long to gain. They relied instead on the more experienced and stronger leadership of the Senate to see them through times of crisis. Thus, during the period of the Roman conquests, the Senate was able to increase its power and again dominate the republic.

The conditions that devastated the poor provided opportunities for increased prosperity for the already wealthy landholders, whose interests the Senate represented. These wealthy landowners expanded their own estates by buying out the small farmers. They also controlled large tracts of land in the new Roman provinces. Aristocratic senators, once concerned for the best interests of the republic, became greedy and pleasure-loving. The pleas for reform from the masses of unemployed and landless went unheeded by the Senate, whose self-centered interests opposed any change. The Senate was unwilling to address the social and economic problems at home.

The corruption in the government at Rome spread to the Roman provinces. Many of the provincial governors appointed by the Senate used their powers for their own selfish gains. One of the greatest abuses was in the collection of taxes that each province paid to Rome. Roman officials often made agreements with men called **publicans** to collect taxes in a given province. The publicans would agree to pay a fixed amount to Rome. Whatever they collected above this fixed sum they could keep for themselves. In return for a percentage of the extra money received, some senators and governors made deals to see that certain men were appointed publicans. Soon the publicans were the most despised people in the Roman territories; they had become rich, but at the expense of the people. These abuses were still part of Roman society during the time of Jesus Christ in the first century AD.

Publicans

The reader of Scripture is no doubt aware of the term *publican*. These tax collectors found it easy to make themselves unpopular. That is why it is interesting that the New Testament Scripture should be favorable to them overall. First we read of the conversion of Matthew, also called Levi. Jesus chose him to be one of His special twelve (Matthew 9, Mark 2, and Luke 5). We read that it was publicans who came to hear Jesus preach (Luke 15:1)—that He even ate with them (Mark 2:16, Luke 5:30). It was publicans who were baptized (Luke 3:12). In fact, Jesus makes a remarkable statement in Matthew 21:32. He tells the Pharisees (the hypocritical religious leaders of the day) that it is tax collectors and sinners who are entering the Kingdom of Heaven and not them! We read again of Jesus loving these hated people in Luke 19. He calls out to a publican tucked away in a sycamore tree, watching Him pass by. This tax collector received Him with joy and was never the same again.

Even these most hated people, these deceitful and lying tax collectors, received His love like anyone else.

Failure of Reform

The poor found champions for their cause in the brothers **Tiberius** and **Gaius Gracchus** (GRAHK us). The Gracchi (plural form of *Gracchus*) were from one

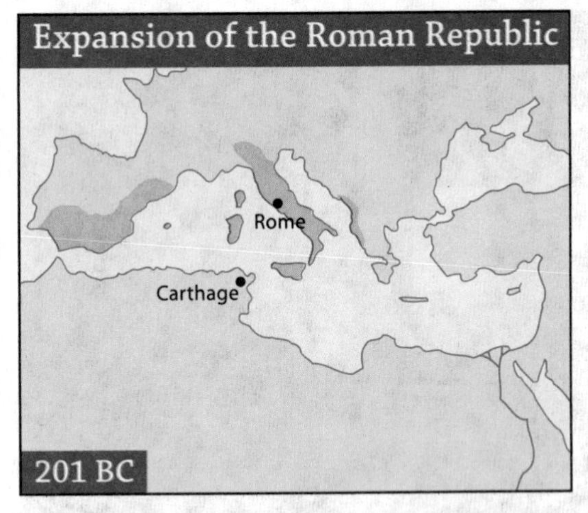

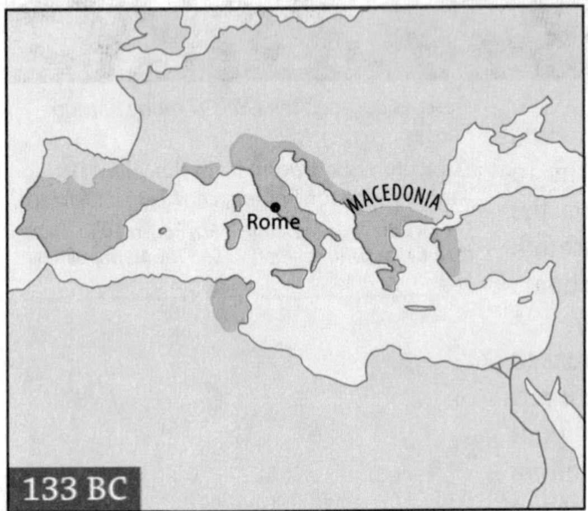

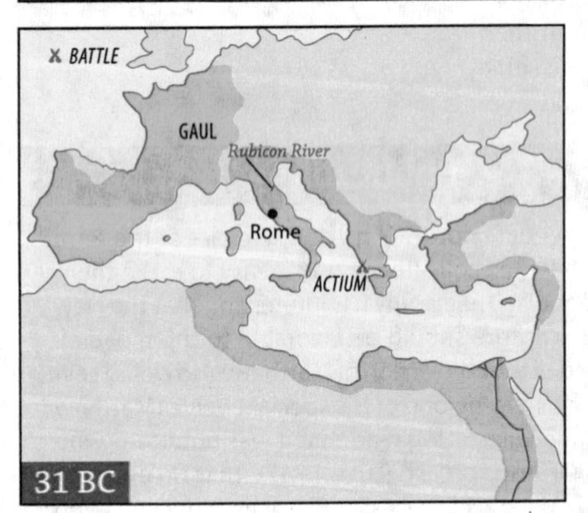

of the noble families of Rome. Their father had been a consul, and their grandfather was Scipio, who had led Rome to victory in the Second Punic War. Elected as a tribune in 133 BC, Tiberius strove for reforms in the republic and became the spokesman for the common man. In one of his speeches he said,

> The wild beasts that roam over Italy . . . have every one of them a cave or lair to lurk in; but the men who fight and die for Italy enjoy the common air and light, indeed, but nothing else; houseless and homeless they wander about with their wives and children. . . . They fight and die to support others in wealth and luxury, and though they are styled masters of the world, they have not a single clod of earth that is their own.[2]

Tiberius proposed changes in Rome's land policy. For years wealthy aristocrats had monopolized the lands gained through Rome's conquests. Tiberius wanted these "public lands" to be divided among the poor. He also sought to limit the amount of public land controlled by any one person. Although the Tribal Assembly adopted his reforms, his proposals gained him powerful enemies. Wealthy landholders foresaw their own financial ruin, and senators disliked his reviving the powers of the Tribal Assembly. When Tiberius tried to be reelected as a tribune—an act contrary to Roman tradition at that time—angry senators killed him along with three hundred of his followers and threw their bodies into the Tiber River.

When Gaius became tribune in 123 BC, he sought to carry on his brother's land reform measures. He also proposed that the government sell grain at low prices to the poor. But the Senate undermined the popular support of Gaius by offering its own programs. (The Senate, however, had no intention of carrying through with these reforms.) During a riot carefully planned by his enemies, Gaius lost his life. Some accounts say he committed suicide to keep from falling into the hands of the senatorial forces. Once again the Senate had prevailed.

Civil War

In the early years of the republic, the Senate, in order to preserve the stability of the government, met the challenges of the plebeians by granting concessions. In response to the new challenge of the Gracchi brothers, the Senate abandoned peaceful measures and resorted to violence to preserve the power and wealth of the aristocrats. The failure of the Senate to deal with reform for the poor further weakened the republic. The disorder of the Roman state finally led to civil war.

The First Civil War

In the first century BC, three civil wars shook the very foundations of Rome, exposing the corruption in Roman society. The rivalry between the Tribal Assembly and the Senate gave occasion for the outbreak of the first civil war.

Following the deaths of the Gracchi brothers, the common people found a new champion for their cause in **Marius** (155?–86 BC). Marius was a well-known military hero who had gained fame for victories in North Africa and Europe. He reorganized the dwindling Roman army, allowing the poor and landless to enlist for long terms of service. He promised them a share in the spoils of war—land and money. Up to this time citizens served in the army out of loyalty for their country. Now Marius created a "professional" army, one

The Roman Army

In his conquest of the ancient world, Alexander the Great relied upon the Greek military formation called the "phalanx." This formation packed hundreds of men into a tight wedge with their long spears facing forward. The phalanx was very powerful and almost impossible to defeat on level ground. But it had one weakness that made it almost useless to the Romans: it could not maneuver. It could march forward or backward, but because the men and spears were tightly intertwined, it could not turn easily. Because Rome's enemies used a number of different fighting tactics, Rome needed a formation which could adapt to many different situations. Thus Rome invented the "legion." Each legion (about five thousand men) was divided into several groups. Up front was a line of "skirmishers," carrying short spears. Next came two lines of soldiers, marching in groups called "centuries." Each century, which was headed by a "centurion," stood in a checkerboard formation with the other centuries. These soldiers carried heavier spears. Behind all these soldiers came a line of men carrying heavy thrusting spears with which they could mow down the enemy. As the front lines tired, they could retreat through the gaps in the checkerboard formation and rest behind the last line. There were two advantages to this formation. First, it was much more maneuverable than the phalanx, so it could adjust more easily to variations in the land and the enemy's formations. Second, the men could move in and out more easily, fight more freely, and get rest if they needed it.

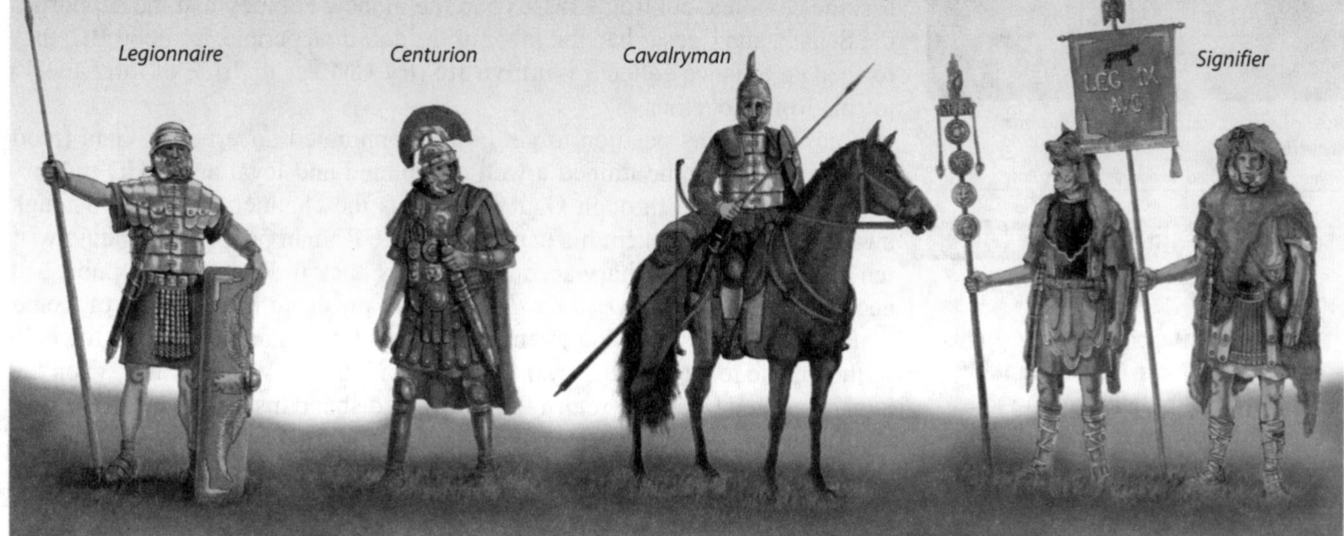

that served for financial gain rather than for a patriotic cause. Their devotion to the commander of the army was greater than their devotion to Rome. This shift in loyalty would later be the undoing of Rome as generals used their armies to further their own interests rather than those of the people and the state.

In 88 BC war broke out in Asia Minor. The Senate appointed **Sulla** (138–78 BC), a general who was sympathetic to the senatorial side, to command the Roman army in the east. The Tribal Assembly, however, rejected the Senate's choice and appointed Marius instead. The years that followed saw much bloodshed as the tension between the Tribal Assembly and the Senate, fueled by the rivalry between Marius and Sulla, developed into civil war. In the end Sulla emerged victorious.

Sulla had himself declared dictator. He then set about reorganizing the Roman government. He hoped to restore stability and order by reviving the power and prestige of the Senate. The influence of the Tribal Assembly and the tribunes was now all but gone. With the power of the Senate firmly established, Sulla resigned as dictator. The Senate, however, was unable to maintain control of the government.

The Second Civil War

The first civil war ended with the Senate triumphant over the Tribal Assembly. Yet it was obvious that a powerful man at the head of the army could control the state. Ambitious men sought to gain that control. The people, weary

Bust of Julius Caesar (100-4 BC), Roman statesman
Mueso Archeologico Nazionale, Naples, Italy

of economic and political crises, were willing to exchange their freedom for temporary relief.

Crassus and **Pompey**, two commanders who served in Sulla's army, competed with one another for fame and power after Sulla's death. Crassus was one of the richest men of Rome. He added military glory to his riches by raising an army and defeating a slave revolt that had threatened the Italian Peninsula. But his military glory was surpassed by Pompey, who had many conquests in the east. He had turned Asia Minor, Syria, and Palestine into Roman provinces. He also rid the Mediterranean Sea of pirates.

The wide accomplishments of both Crassus and Pompey, however, failed to win them the popular support that **Julius Caesar** received. This young leader, nephew of the popular Marius, undertook ambitious projects to win the public favor. Caesar (100–44 BC) was a wise politician who knew how to sway the common people in order to accomplish his aims. Crassus, Pompey, and Caesar each wanted to be sole ruler of Rome. None, though, had sufficient power to assume complete control: Crassus had the money, Pompey had the support of the Senate, and Caesar had the favor of the common people. So in 60 BC, they formed an alliance called a **triumvirate** (try UM ver it; "rule of three men") to rule Rome together.

Caesar used his position to get himself appointed governor of Gaul (modern France). There he trained a well-disciplined and loyal army. His military campaigns led him through Gaul and across the channel to Britain. Though away from Rome, he kept his name before the Roman people by sending written accounts of his military accomplishments back to Rome. These published accounts, his *Commentaries on the Gallic Wars,* made him the talk of Rome. Jealous of Caesar's growing strength and popularity, Pompey sought the help of the Senate to weaken his rival. (Crassus had died in war in Asia.) When the Senate ordered Caesar to return to Rome and disband his army, Caesar crossed the Rubicon (a river in northern Italy) and marched his army toward Rome. By this act Caesar declared war on Pompey and the Senate. Since that day "crossing the Rubicon" means making a fateful decision from which there is no turning back.

Pompey and members of the Senate fled to Greece to give themselves time to raise an army to battle Caesar. When the two armies finally met, Pompey's forces were no match for Caesar's seasoned veterans. Pompey fled to Egypt, where he was later killed. With power firmly in his hands, Caesar had himself proclaimed dictator for life.

Caesar accomplished many reforms during his short rule. He curbed the corruption of the provincial governments, established colonies for the landless army veterans, granted citizenship to many non-Italians living in Rome's new colonies, and initiated many public works programs. He also established the calendar that is the basis for our 365¼ days calendar year.

Although popular with the people, Caesar had enemies among the nobles and senators. Some were former followers of Pompey; others feared that Caesar was going to make himself king and do away with the republic. Since the time of the Etruscans, the Romans had regarded kings as evil. Although they permitted a temporary dictatorship, the Romans would not accept a king. On the Ides (fifteenth) of **March** in **44 BC**, a group of conspirators assassinated the dictator in the Senate chamber.

THIS MOMENT IN HISTORY

Julius Caesar

Describe the changes that Julius Caesar brought to Rome's Republic. Explain his popularity among the common people.

____

____

____

____

____

____

____

Plutarch's Account of Caesar's Death

Those who had prepared themselves for the murder bared each of them his dagger, and Caesar, hemmed in on all sides, whichever way he turned confront[ed] blows of weapons.... When he saw that Brutus had drawn his dagger, he pulled his toga down over his head and sank, either by chance or because pushed there by his murderers, against the pedestal on which the statue of Pompey stood. And the pedestal was drenched with his blood, so that one might have thought that Pompey himself was presiding over this vengence upon his enemy, who now lay prostrate at his feet, quivering from a multitude of wounds.[3]

The Third Civil War

After Caesar's death a third civil war broke out to determine the next ruler. Caesar's friend and right-hand man, Mark Antony, teamed with Octavian (Caesar's nephew and only male relative) to capture and punish Caesar's murderers. Octavian and Antony then divided the Roman territory in half—Octavian ruling in the west and Antony (who had fallen under the charm of Cleopatra, the queen of Egypt) ruling in the east. Each man, however, was too ambitious to share power with the other. Again civil war was to settle the question of who was to be sole ruler of Rome. In **31 BC**, off the coast of Greece, Octavian's navy won a decisive victory over Antony and Cleopatra at the Battle of Actium. Antony and Cleopatra fled the battle, realizing their cause was lost. They both later committed suicide. Octavian, only thirty-one years of age, then ruled the entire Roman world.

With Octavian, one era of Roman history ended and a new one began. Historians have called the period from the Battle of Actium (31 BC) to the Fall

How the Romans Measured Time

The Romans had two different ways of measuring time. First, they divided the daylight hours into twelve equal parts. (This meant that the "hours" were longer in the summer than in the winter.) Second, the Romans invented a water clock, which kept time in much the same manner as our modern clocks. However, these water clocks were so inaccurate that the Roman philosopher Seneca once observed that it was easier to find two philosophers who agreed than it was to find two water clocks that agreed. It is interesting to note that our use of a.m. (*ante meridiem*) and p.m. (*post meridiem*) comes from the Roman system of counting hours from the middle of the day.

In numbering their years, the Romans started counting from the founding of Rome. After the year number, they wrote A.U.C. (*ad urbe condita*), which means "from the foundation of the city." Their years had 355 days, and even though the calendar was periodically corrected, it was still out of step with the sun. So when Julius Caesar ruled Rome, he asked astronomers to help him set the calendar straight. Upon their recommendations, he decreed that the year 707 A.U.C. (46 BC) would have 445 days. This was done so that the Roman year would once again match the solar year. In Roman history that year was known as the "Year of Confusion."

Thus began the Julian calendar, which remained in use for the next sixteen hundred years. Instead of ten months, each year then had twelve months that alternated between thirty and thirty-one days. Even today we still use the same names for the months that the Romans did. The only difference is that the Romans began their year with March and ended with February.

Perhaps you have always wondered why February has only twenty-eight days when the rest of the months have thirty or thirty-one. According to tradition, Julius Caesar named the month of July after himself; because he did not want his month to have fewer days than any other, he took a day from February and added it to July, making a total of thirty-one days. Later, when Octavian named the month of August after himself, he also took a day from February so that his month would be just as long as Julius's.

January—Named after Janus, the Roman god of gates and doors.

February—From the Latin word that means "to purify." February was originally the last month of the year. It was during this month that the Romans purified themselves in preparation for the festivals that marked the beginning of the new year.

March—Named after Mars, the Roman god of war.

April—From the Latin word that means "to open." April was originally the second month of the year.

May—Two possible sources of the name: (1) Named after Maia, the Roman goddess of spring, or (2) from the Latin word that referred to older men (*majores*); the month of May was sacred to these older men.

June—Two possible sources of the name: (1) named after Juno, the Roman goddess of marriage, or (2) from the Latin word that referred to young men (*juniores*); the month of June was sacred to these young men.

July—Named by Julius Caesar after himself. (It was his birth month.)

August—Named by Caesar Augustus (Octavian) after himself.

September—Means "the seventh month."

October—Means "the eighth month."

November—Means "the ninth month."

December—Means "the tenth month."

of Rome (AD 476) the Roman Empire. Rome did not become an empire during these years, for she had already built a vast empire under the republic. But beginning with Octavian (some say with Julius Caesar), Rome was no longer a republic—a "public matter"—but was transformed into a government ruled by an **imperator** (an ancient title given to the commander of a victorious army). During this period, which lasted nearly five hundred years, imperators (from which we get our words *empire* and *emperor*) ruled with supreme power. This will be the period of history on which we will focus in the next chapter.

Section Quiz

1. What responsibility did the publicans have in Roman society?
2. What were the names of the two brothers who became spokesmen for reform in the later days of the republic?
3. Who were the two generals who fought in the First Civil War? Identify which one had the backing of the Senate and which one the backing of the Tribal Assembly.
4. Who were the three rulers of the triumvirate?
5. At what place and in what year did Octavian defeat Antony in the Third Civil War?

1. ______________________

____

2. ______________________

____

3. ______________________

____

4. ______________________

____

____

5. ______________________

A Glance Behind

During these years of the republic, Rome grew from a small city along the Tiber to become the master of the Mediterranean world. New prosperity and power resulted from Rome's conquests. But with her rise to prominence, Rome was faced with new challenges. The Roman historian Livy described their predicament: "For true it is that the less men's wealth was, the less was their greed. Of late, riches have brought in avarice, and excessive pleasures the longing to carry wantonness and license to the point of ruin for oneself and of universal destruction."[4]

The foundations of the republic began to crumble. Traditional values, such as discipline, personal morality, and respect for authority, diminished. Citizens who once served their country with a sense of patriotic duty and responsibility now sought their own selfish interests. Corruption in government abounded. The breakdown of the moral fiber of the republic encouraged the use of force to settle Rome's problems.

In the midst of economic and political disorder, the Romans allowed the powers of the state to increase. They surrendered many of their rights and freedoms to obtain political and economic stability. The republic that offered so much liberty and rule by the people was replaced by tremendous government control and rule by emperors.

Every person and every society is responsible to believe in God correctly and to live accordingly. They are not always able—but this does not diminish their responsibility before God. Human depravity is not restrained by anything but God's working in human lives. To base a society on anything other than faith in God and obedience to His Word, no matter how wise concerning human nature the planners may be, is to doom that society to eventual destruction.

and a Glimpse Ahead

Notes

1. Polybius (trans. W. R. Patton), 6.52.
2. Plutarch, *The Parallel Lives* (trans. Bernadotte Perrin), "Tiberius Gracchus," 9
3. Plutarch, "Caesar," 66.
4. Livy (trans. B. O. Foster), 1. pref.

Chapter Review

Can You Define?

Mare Nostrum
pater
clan
tribe
patrician
plebeian
imperium
fasces
republic
consul
plebiscite
tribune
veto
publican
triumvirate
imperator

Can You Identify?

Etruscans
Romulus
Remus
League of Seven Hills
509 BC
Senate
Roman Forum
Law of Twelve Tables
287 BC
Tribal Assembly
Pyrrhus
Punic Wars
Hannibal
Scipio
Cato
Tiberius Gracchus
Gaius Gracchus
Marius
Sulla
Crassus
Pompey
Julius Caesar
March 15, 44 BC
Mark Antony
Octavian
31 BC
Cleopatra

Can You Locate?

Italian Peninsula
Mediterranean Sea
Apennines
Latium
Tiber River
Rome
North Africa
Carthage
Spain
Sicily
Sardinia
Corsica
Alps
Battle of Cannae
Syracuse
Battle of Zama
Macedonia
Gaul
Rubicon River
Battle of Actium

How Much Do You Remember?

1. In what ways is it true to say that "all roads lead to Rome"?
2. Outline the steps by which the plebeians gained a voice in the Roman government.
3. Make an outline of the three Punic Wars. Include dates, causes, major events/ battles, and results.
4. For each of the three civil wars that occurred during the first century BC of the republic, list the opposing army generals and underline the winner.

What Do You Think?

1. In what way does Daniel 7:7 describe Rome?
2. What do you think were the strengths and weakness of the Roman Republic?
3. After reading the conclusion to the chapter, what parallels do you see between the conditions contributing to the fall of the Roman Republic and the present conditions in the American Republic?

"The fullness of time"

THE ROMAN EMPIRE

Detail of **Christ Leaving the Praetorium,** *Gustave Dorè, French 1832-1883, From the Bob Jones University Collection*

JESUS OF NAZARETH KING OF THE JEWS—By the command of Pontius Pilate, this inscription was placed upon the cross on which Jesus died. Under this sign the long-awaited Messiah—the son of Abraham, Judah, and David—suffered for the sins of His people. But who were His people? The words of this sign would seem to indicate that they were Jews only. But the fact that these words were written not just in Hebrew but also in Greek and Latin would seem to suggest something else—something that is taught everywhere in Scripture. When God called Abraham, He promised that all nations would be blessed in him (Gen. 12:3). When Isaiah prophesied the coming of God's Servant, he foresaw One Who would "bring forth judgment for the Gentiles" and Who would serve as "a light of the Gentiles" (Isa. 42:1, 6). And when Jesus revealed Himself to the Jews, John the Baptist proclaimed, "Behold, the Lamb of God, which taketh away the sin of the world" (John 1:29). In this chapter we will see the beginnings of the fulfillment of God's promise to bless all nations through His Son. We will also see how God used the culture of the Jews, Greeks, and Romans to prepare the human race to face the turning point of history—the life, death, and Resurrection of Jesus Christ. This divine preparation culminated with the Roman Empire. This was the time when the world was made ready (Mark 1:15), when the "fulness of the time was come" (Gal. 4:4).

I. Pax Romana

Octavian's rule brought a period of peace to the Mediterranean world that lasted from 31 BC to AD 180. During these two centuries the Roman Empire reached its height; its boundaries encircled the Mediterranean Sea and included parts of the old Persian Empire in the east as well as most of western Europe and Britain. In contrast to the period of civil wars that preceded Octavian's reign, the first two centuries of the empire were marked for the most part by internal harmony and unity. Trade prospered, travel and communications improved, and cultural activities flourished. The ancient world experienced a period of peace and prosperity known as the ***Pax Romana*** ("Roman Peace"). Nevertheless, this was in a sense an artificial peace. Won by war and maintained by force, it did not long endure. But during the *Pax Romana*, the Author of Peace—Jesus Christ—was born. By His death on the cross, He secured for mankind a true and lasting peace. He said, "Peace I leave with you, my peace I give unto you: not as the world giveth, give I unto you. Let not your heart be troubled, neither let it be afraid" (John 14:27). Of Him the prophet Isaiah foretold, "For unto us a child is born, unto us a son is given: and the government shall be upon his shoulder: and his name shall be called Wonderful, Counsellor, The mighty God, The everlasting Father, The Prince of Peace. Of the increase of his government and peace there shall be no end, upon the throne of David, and upon his kingdom, to order it, and to establish it with judgment and with justice from henceforth even for ever" (Isa. 9:6–7).

Augustus: The "First Citizen" of Rome

With his defeat of Antony and Cleopatra at the Battle of Actium, Octavian brought an end to a century of civil war. He returned to Rome as the triumphant ruler of the Roman world, much as Julius Caesar had two decades earlier. But unlike Julius Caesar, who had made himself dictator for life, Octavian announced in 27 BC his desire to restore the republic. He voluntarily chose to share his powers with the Senate. This division of power had existed during the republic. He took the title princeps (PRIN keps), or "first citizen." This title was popular among the common people, for it conveyed the idea that he was one of them and not a noble. But in fact, the Roman government was a monarchy disguised as a republic. In his position as the head of the army, Octavian maintained firm control of the government. He was the first Roman ruler to be called an emperor—a title also given to his many successors. We find in the New Testament (Luke 2:1) two other titles or names of Octavian: "Caesar" and "Augustus." Caesar was Octavian's family name—he was the great-nephew and adopted son of Julius Caesar. (The term *caesar* later became a political title used by many Roman emperors.) He is best remembered by the name **Augustus**. The Senate conferred this title on him when he restored the republic. It was a title of divinity, expressing honor and majesty usually associated only with the Roman gods.

Augustus (Gaius Julius Caesar Octavianus) (63 BC-14 AD). Roman Emperor. Marble bust.
Photo: Alfredo Dagli Orti. Musei Capitolini, Rome, Italy

Augustus and the *Pax Romana*

During Augustus's reign (31 BC–AD 14), the entire Mediterranean world enjoyed economic prosperity. Agriculture remained the livelihood of most of the people. But the unity and stability maintained during the *Pax Romana* also encouraged the growth of trade. Rome established a stable currency of gold and silver coins, which traders could use as a medium of exchange almost anywhere in the empire. Rome freed the Mediterranean Sea of piracy and provided for safe travel in Roman territory. Ease of communication also aided trade. Greek and later Latin became almost universal languages. Not only did trade flourish within the empire, but trade also extended to the world outside the empire. The Romans imported such luxury items as silks, spices, and jewels from India and China; they brought in gold and ivory from Africa. During the *Pax Romana* the material wealth of Rome reached its peak.

In addition to prosperity and peace, Augustus's reign brought stability and order to Roman government and society. Attempting to restore honesty and efficiency in government, he placed ability above social class when selecting government officials. Augustus removed unqualified, self-seeking men from office and replaced them with well-qualified officials paid by the state. He created a police and fire service for the city of Rome. In addition, he established a postal service and undertook major building programs.

Augustus also sought to abolish corruption in the provincial governments. He reorganized the provinces of the empire, placing some under the supervision of the Senate and others under his own supervision. To provide fairer methods of taxing the provinces, Augustus ordered a census-taking throughout the empire every fourteen years. From the Scriptures we know that Augustus ordered such a census around the time of the birth of Jesus Christ: "And it came to pass in those days, that there went out a decree from Caesar Augustus, that all the world should be taxed [registered]" (Luke 2:1).

Augustus correctly realized that a civilization is only as strong as the moral character of her people. Therefore, he sought social reforms to revive the traditional Roman virtues of duty, discipline, and hard work. He encouraged the passage of laws that promoted family life and rewarded those families that had many children. Other laws punished immorality and placed limits on extrava-

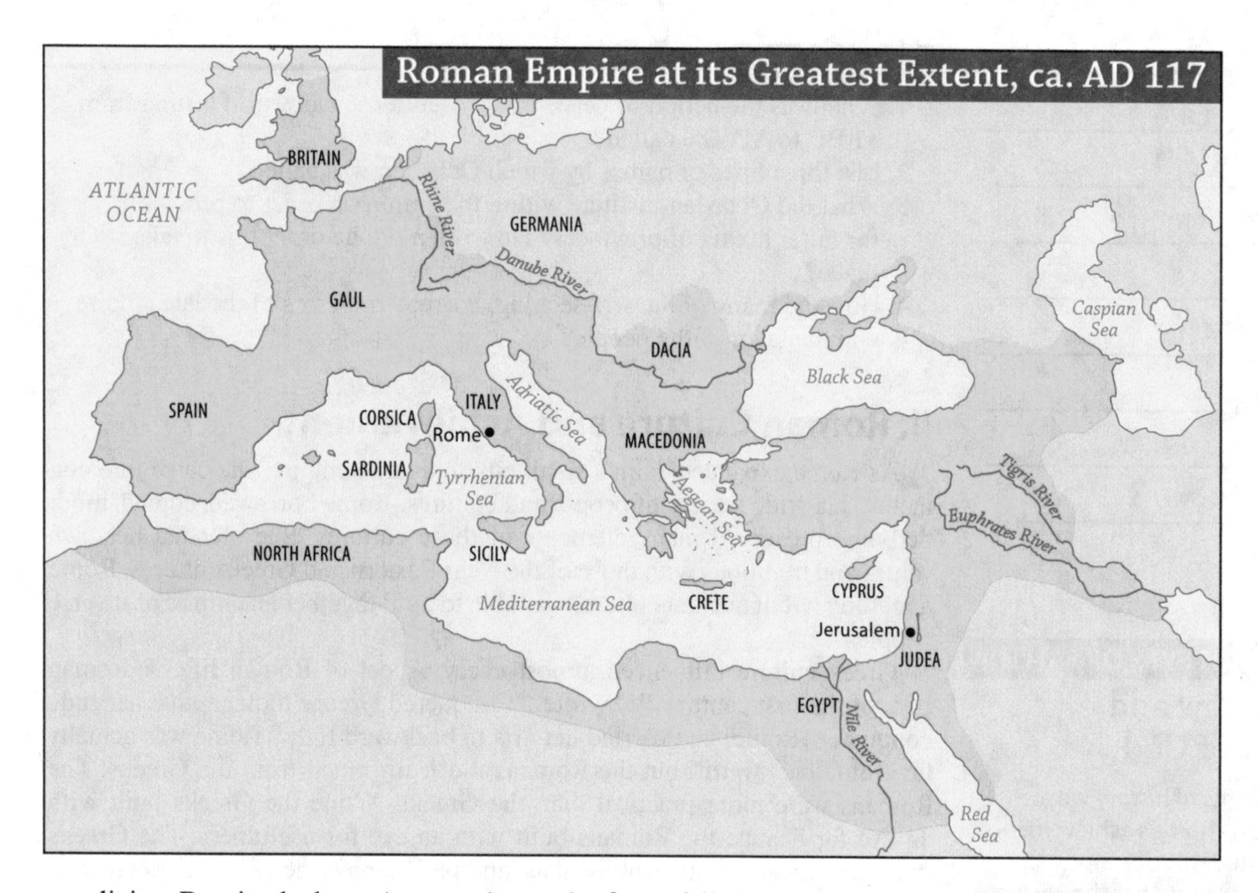

gant living. Despite the laws, Augustus's moral reforms failed. Moral behavior without love for God is not true morality. God's most basic moral command is that humans love Him with their entire being (Mark 12:30–31). If a culture—or an individual—refuses to love the God who made the world and preserves it every day, its attempts at morality will never rise above hypocrisy and selfishness. In time such a culture will fall into a low moral condition that will shock and offend the very people responsible for the moral decline. It is instructive to note that the Bible's most extensive description of the moral deterioration of Gentile culture is found in a letter written to Christians living in Rome (Rom. 1:18–32).

Successors of Augustus

Though Augustus established an effective and well-organized government, he left no plan for choosing a successor. For nearly a half century after his death, men who were in some way related to Julius Caesar occupied the imperial office. Most of these men led wicked lives and squandered the wealth of Rome on their own selfish pleasures. In spite of incompetent leadership, the "Roman peace" continued—it was held intact by the might of the Roman army. Toward the end of the first century, the Roman army began to elevate its favorite generals to the office of emperor. These emperors were men of proven ability. During most of the second century, they provided strong leadership for Rome.

Nevertheless, too much power placed in the hands of ambitious and self-seeking men often leads to corruption. The emperors won popular favor by providing "free" grain and amusements for the people of Rome. The Romans failed to realize however, that these things were not really free. (The necessary funds came out of the public treasury.) Civil war often erupted as rival generals fought to gain the emperor's crown. For example, from AD 235 to 285 Rome had twenty-six different emperors. Of these, twenty-five died a violent death.

THIS MOMENT IN HISTORY

Pax Romana

Describe the impact of the *Pax Romana* on the Roman Empire and other areas in the world.

____

____

____

____

____

____

____

____

____

____

____

1. ____________________

2. ____________________

____

____

3. ____________________

____

4. ____________________

____

Section Quiz

1. What was the period of peace in the Mediterranean world lasting from 31 BC to AD 180 called?
2. List three titles or names by which Octavian was called.
3. What did Octavian institute within the empire in order to provide for fairer taxing of provinces? How often did he order this to take place?
4. How did many of the self-seeking, corrupt emperors of the late empire win the favor of the people?

THROUGH EYES OF FAITH

Roman Law and the Law of God

As students of history we are impressed by Rome's achievements in law. As students of Scripture, however, we know that the ancient polytheistic civilizations were "vain in their imaginations, and their foolish heart was darkened" (Rom. 1:21). We also know that such civilizations were under God's judgment: "God gave them over to a reprobate mind" (v. 28).

How did Rome, polytheistic and ultimately reprobate, produce such a valuable and enduring system of justice? Consider Romans 2:14–15.

____

____

____

____

____

____

____

____

____

____

II. Roman Culture and Achievement

As Rome expanded from a small city to a large empire, she came into contact with a wide variety of people and cultures. Rome borrowed, copied, modified, and preserved many elements of these cultures. She blended her own values and traditions with those of the Near Eastern and Greek cultures. Rome, a melting pot of ancient culture, was able to hold together an empire of diverse peoples.

Greek culture influenced almost every aspect of Roman life. A Roman poet of the first century BC wrote, "Conquered Greece took captive her rude conqueror [Rome] and carried her arts to backward Italy." Rome was actually far from "backward," but the Romans did learn much from the Greeks. The Romans were more practical than the Greeks. While the Greeks built with an eye for beauty, the Romans built with an eye for usefulness. The Greeks made significant contributions in art and philosophy; the Romans, in law and politics.

Contribution to Law

One of the most valuable and enduring of Rome's achievements was her system of justice. Rome protected the individual rights and property of her citizens. The New Testament writer Luke points out that it was "not the manner of the Romans to deliver any man to die, before that he which is accused have the accusers face to face, and have license [opportunity] to answer for himself concerning the crime laid against him" (Acts 25:16). The Romans believed that all citizens should have equal rights before the law. Cicero, the famous orator of the republic, wrote: "The legal rights at least of those who are citizens of the same commonwealth ought to be equal. For what is the State except an association or partnership in justice?"

The legal codes of many modern European countries include many principles based on Roman law. Even the American system of justice has benefited from Rome's example. Here are some Roman legal principles. Do you notice any similarity between these and America's laws? Which legal principles can be defended biblically—which ones cannot?

- Justice is a constant, unfailing disposition to give everyone his legal due.
- Liberty is a possession on which no evaluation can be placed.
- Freedom is beloved above all things.
- The burden of proof is upon the party affirming, not on the party denying.
- In inflicting penalties, the age and inexperience of the guilty party must be taken into account.

- No one [is] to be convicted on suspicion alone . . . [for it is] better for the crime of a guilty person to be left unpunished than for an innocent person to be condemned.
- The credibility of witnesses should be carefully weighed.
- In case of equal [conflicting] claims, the party in possession ought to be considered in the stronger position.
- Every individual is subjected to treatment in accordance with his own action, and no one is made the inheritor of the guilt of another.[1]

Latin Literature and Language

The Romans modeled their literature after Greek examples. As they studied in Greece or under Greek tutors, many Romans fell under the influence of Greek literature and literary style. They added their own literary ideas and spirit to what they borrowed from the Greeks and thereby created a distinct literature of their own.

Latin literature expresses the life and history of the Roman people. Although Latin literature lacks the originality of Greek literature, the Romans produced some literary masterpieces that are still studied and appreciated today.

The greatest Latin literature was produced during the lifetimes of two of Rome's most famous citizens—Cicero and Augustus. **Cicero** (106–43 BC) dominated the first half of this literary age. He was not only one of the leading political figures of the late republic but was also an outstanding scholar, author, lawyer, and statesman. An eloquent and effective speaker, he also won acclaim as the greatest orator of his day. A master of Latin prose, he influenced later Roman writers and students of Latin literature.

The peaceful, stable conditions established during Augustus's reign (27 BC–AD 14) fostered another outpouring of literary activity. Optimism, patriotism, and appreciation for traditional Roman values dominated Latin literature. Roman writers of the Augustan Age best expressed these feelings through poetry.

Poetry of the Augustan Age

Virgil—Often called the "Homer of Rome," **Virgil** (70–19 BC) is considered the greatest Roman poet. He glorified Rome in his epic poem the *Aeneid* (uh NEE id), one of the most widely read Latin literary works. Virgil modeled

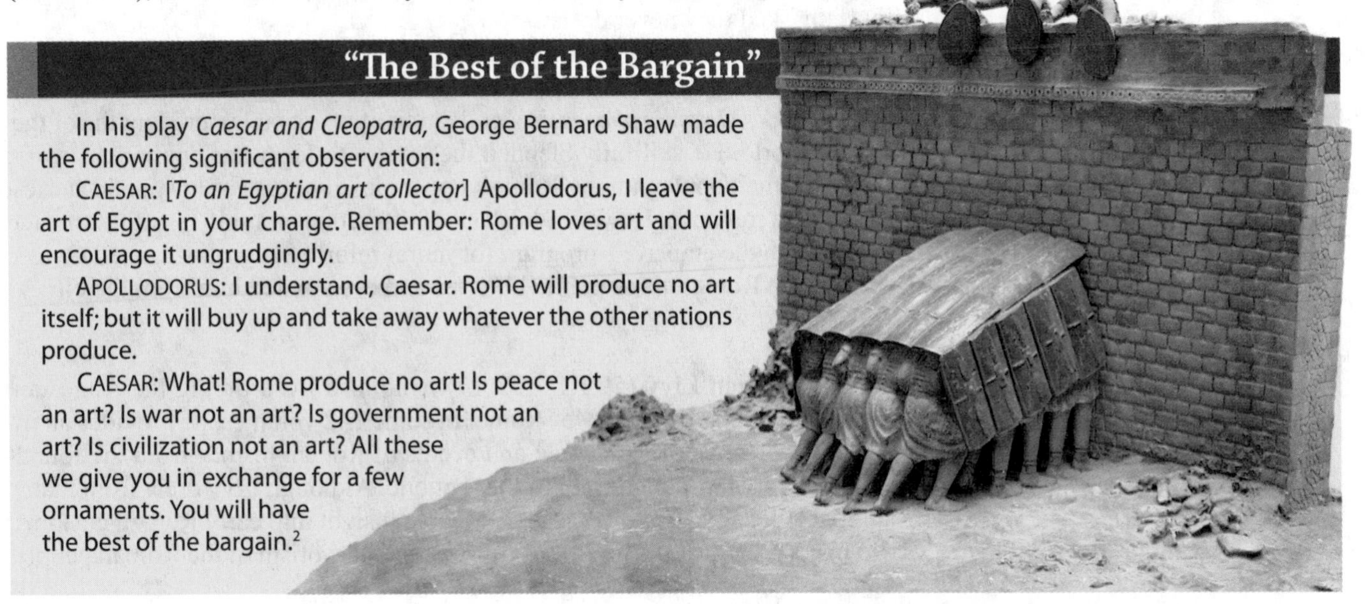

The Romans were renowned for their military innovations, such as this Roman infantry tactic for attacking a walled city more safely.

"The Best of the Bargain"

In his play *Caesar and Cleopatra,* George Bernard Shaw made the following significant observation:

CAESAR: [*To an Egyptian art collector*] Apollodorus, I leave the art of Egypt in your charge. Remember: Rome loves art and will encourage it ungrudgingly.

APOLLODORUS: I understand, Caesar. Rome will produce no art itself; but it will buy up and take away whatever the other nations produce.

CAESAR: What! Rome produce no art! Is peace not an art? Is war not an art? Is government not an art? Is civilization not an art? All these we give you in exchange for a few ornaments. You will have the best of the bargain.[2]

the *Aeneid* after Homer's great epic poems the *Iliad* and the *Odyssey*. But while Homer's works stressed the virtues of the Greek ideal man, Virgil's work exalted Rome as the ideal state. The *Aeneid* reflects the common belief of the Augustan Age that Rome was destined to rule the world:

> Others, I doubt not, shall beat out the breathing bronze with softer lines; shall from marble draw forth the features of life; shall plead their causes better; with the rod shall trace the paths of heaven and tell the rising of the stars: remember thou, O Roman, to rule the nations with thy sway—these shall be thine arts—to crown Peace with Law, to spare the humbled, and to tame in war the proud.
>
> *Aeneid 6. 847–853*

Horace—After the death of Virgil, his close friend **Horace** (65–8 BC) became the "Poet of the Augustan Age." In a poem written in praise of Augustus, he (like Virgil before him) spoke of the triumph of Rome.

> For earth at peace, hath closed Rome's Janus-gate;—
> Curbed license which past ordered limit strays;
> Uprooted vice, and Rome's old ways
> Recalled to guide the state;
> The ways whereby Rome's name and fame increased,
> And her great empire's majesty grew strong,
> Stretching from sunset's couch along
> Right to the rising East.

Yet Horace did not overlook the seeds of decay in Roman society.

> What benefit are empty walls
> If crime we prune not with a knife severe?
> Where life is tainted, what avails
> Law without morals?

Horace warned of the danger of luxury and ease: "As riches grow, care follows, and a thirst for more and more." He praised the simple virtues of morality, justice, courage, and moderation. In his satires (works using ridicule or wit to correct or expose human folly or vice), he described the many follies of contemporary Roman society. For example—"This is a fault common to all singers, that among their friends they are never inclined to sing when asked, [but] unasked they never desist."

Ovid—The poetry of **Ovid** (43 BC–AD 17) is quite different from the poetry of Virgil and Horace. Ovid wrote about mythology and love. His best-known work, *Metamorphoses*, is a collection of over two hundred myths of the ancient world. He skillfully blended these tales to form one continuous story. Ovid became popular among Rome's upper class because of his poetic stories of love and romance. However, his lack of discretion and self-restraint was out of step with the emperor's program for moral reform. Augustus banned Ovid's works from Rome's three public libraries and even exiled him from the city.

History

The historian **Livy** (59 BC–AD 17), who also lived during the Augustan Age, wrote a lengthy history of Rome. In some 142 volumes, he provides an interesting narrative of the people and events of Roman history from the founding of the city through the end of the republic. Although Livy drew from many unreliable legends, his work offers valuable insight into early Roman customs and history. He saw the traditional virtues and patriotism of the Roman people as the foundation of Rome's greatness.

Livy on the Value of History

What chiefly makes the study of history wholesome and profitable is this, that you behold the lessons of every kind of experience set forth as on a conspicuous monument; from these you may choose for yourself and for your own state what to imitate, from these mark for avoidance what is shameful in the conception and shameful in the result.[3]

Pompeii

On the afternoon of August 24, AD 79, Mount Vesuvius (a volcano about 125 miles south of Rome) violently erupted. Having no advance warning, few of the residents of the nearby city of Pompeii had time to flee. Many died from breathing poisonous gases and fumes. Others were trapped in their houses by the deadly shower of hot cinders and ashes. In three days the entire city was completely buried. This thick layer of volcanic ash hardened, and the city of Pompeii passed from memory.

The site of the city was rediscovered in 1748. Archaeological excavations since that time have uncovered much of Pompeii. The city has been so well preserved that we can almost "relive" that fateful day over nineteen hundred years ago. Through their excavations, archaeologists have gained many insights into everyday life in Pompeii. They have uncovered many houses, complete with what were once beautiful gardens, furniture, utensils, colorful wall paintings, and even "beware-of-the-dog" signs and doghouses. In the city squares are walls covered with political posters and advertisements. City streets are lined with shops of all kinds—cloth dyers, cobblers, tanners, potters, surgeons, metal smiths, and many others. There is even a bakery with loaves of bread still in the oven.

In the process of their excavations, the archaeologists also found mysterious air pockets inside the hardened ash. Curious, they filled the air pockets with plaster of Paris. After the plaster dried and the surrounding ash could be removed, the archaeologists realized that the air pockets were forms of the men and women who had been buried by ash during the eruption. When the bodies later decomposed, only air pockets remained in the ash. The plaster casts are graphic portrayal of the final agonies of the citizens of Pompeii.

The sudden destruction of Pompeii stands as a sobering reminder to all students of history. Human life is fragile and fleeting. As James said long ago, "Ye know not what shall be on the morrow. For what is your life? It is even a vapour, that appeareth for a little time, and then vanisheth away" (James 4:14). We should attempt to live each day aware of our mortality, remembering that at any moment we may leave this life and be ushered into the presence of God.

Later Roman Writers

The mood of Roman writers changed after the death of Augustus. Latin writers of the first century AD were more critical and pessimistic than their predecessors. The poet **Juvenal** (60?–140?) wrote bitter satires on the loose morals and social problems of the empire.

> And when could you find more vices abounding?
> When did the gullet of greed open wider?
> When did the dice draw more to the tables?
> They don't bring their wallets along,
> They bring a whole safety deposit box.[4]

Juvenal longed for a return to the days of the republic. He was not alone. The famed historian **Tacitus** (55?–120?) favored the old republic over life under the self-centered emperors. His work *Annals* is a valuable but pessimistic history of Rome from the death of Augustus to the reign of Nero. In *Germania*, Tacitus gives us a rare glimpse of the lifestyle of the Germanic peoples, who later conquered the Western Roman Empire. He contrasts the simple virtues and customs of these "barbarians" with the corrupt morals of Rome's upper class.

The importance of Latin did not diminish after the collapse of the Roman Empire. Latin continued as the dominant language of medieval Europe—in learning, government, and religion. From Latin many of the native (or common) languages of Europe arose. Latin was the "parent" of the Romance languages—Italian, French, Spanish, Portuguese, and Romanian. Although English is not a Romance language, thousands of English words are of Latin origin.

The dome of the Pantheon in Rome, rebuilt by the Emperor Hadrian ca. 125 AD.

Greek Contributions

During the *Pax Romana*, centers of Greek learning, such as Alexandria, Egypt, flourished. **Plutarch** (45–125) was probably the most famous Greek writer in the Roman Empire. He wrote biographies that compared the lives of important Greek and Roman men. His *Parallel Lives of Illustrious Greeks and Romans* is not only an excellent literary work but also the source of valuable historical information. Advances in medicine continued under the work of the Greek physician **Galen**. Experimenting with animals, Galen studied the lungs, heart, arteries, and blood. His encyclopedia, a collection of the medical ideas of the ancient world, became the accepted medical authority of the Middle Ages. The Alexandrian astronomer and mathematician **Ptolemy** (85?–165?) promoted the theory that the earth was the center of the universe. He taught that the sun, moon, and planets revolve around the earth. Though based on false assumptions, his **geocentric** (earth-centered) **theory** of the universe went unchallenged for almost fourteen centuries.

Art and Architecture

As Roman generals returned from their conquests, they brought captured art and artists back to Rome. Greek art became so popular among the Romans that they commissioned artists to make copies of Greek statues. But not all Roman art was imitative. The Romans excelled in portrait busts (head-and-shoulder statues). These popular

statues portrayed Roman heroes, honored statesmen, and valiant soldiers. Unlike Greek sculpture, most Roman statues are realistic. Some even show warts, scars, and wrinkles. The Romans also excelled in relief sculpture (sculpture in which figures project out from a flat background). Realistic reliefs adorned gigantic monuments—triumphal arches and columns—which the Roman emperors built to commemorate their conquests. The reliefs on these monuments gave a visual story of Rome's military exploits.

Even in ruins, these monuments attest to Roman engineering skill. The Romans used new building techniques as well as techniques borrowed from other cultures. Arches and vaults strengthened with concrete enabled Roman engineers to create large indoor spaces enclosed by massive domes. The Romans built **aqueducts** to supply water to many of their cities. Some aqueducts carried over fifty million gallons daily. They also built bridges and an extensive network of roads. Public baths and large amphitheaters provided relaxation and entertainment for many Romans throughout the empire. Unlike Greek buildings, which are known for their simple beauty, Roman buildings are distinguished by their large size, durability, and practicality.

Top: *Aqueduct.* **Bottom:** *Relief from the Arch of Titus in Rome showing the looting of the Temple in Jerusalem.*

The Colosseum

The Roman Colosseum is probably the most famous example of Rome's architectural genius. Shaped much like a football stadium, this mammoth structure originally towered over 160 feet high and covered six acres of land. In many ways the Colosseum was like a modern stadium; however, unlike that of most modern stadiums, admission to the Colosseum was free.

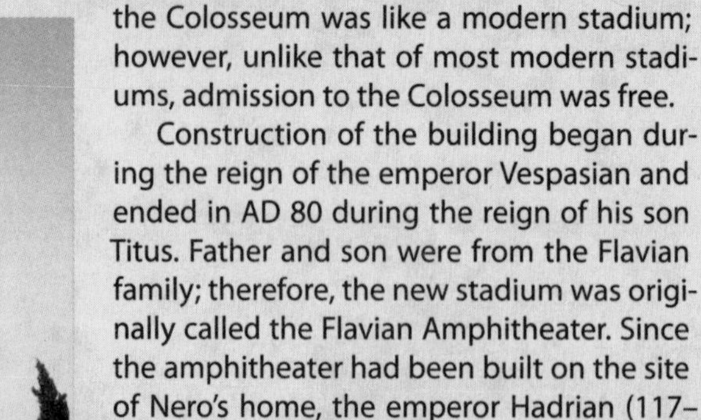

Construction of the building began during the reign of the emperor Vespasian and ended in AD 80 during the reign of his son Titus. Father and son were from the Flavian family; therefore, the new stadium was originally called the Flavian Amphitheater. Since the amphitheater had been built on the site of Nero's home, the emperor Hadrian (117–138) erected a large statue (colossus) of Nero outside the building. It is for this reason that the Flavian Amphitheater soon came to be called the Colosseum.

When filled to capacity, the Colosseum could hold nearly fifty thousand people. Spectators poured in through the many numbered gates and took their places in the stadium based upon their social class. In order to increase spectator comfort, workers positioned awnings on top of the stadium wall to give relief from the hot sun. During lunch breaks (these spectacles often lasted all day) the people could buy food and drink at the stadium.

All the activity took place on the large oval floor of the Colosseum. This floor was made of wood and covered with sand. In fact, our word *arena* is the Latin word for sand. Parts of the floor could be quickly raised and lowered to bring up wild animals from their cages below. In addition, the whole arena could be flooded in order to reenact famous naval battles. The "actors" in all these bloody spectacles were usually criminals or war captives. However, professional gladiators also fought in the arena. Here Christians were martyred for Christ.

The Roman Games

In arenas throughout the empire, the Romans flocked to see their favorite events—chariot races, gladiator contests, and wild beast fights. At the Circus Maximus in Rome, over a quarter of a million people gathered regularly to watch the chariot races. At the Roman Colosseum they delighted in the brutal struggles of the **gladiators** and wild beasts. The victors in these life-and-death contests became instant public heroes. In many of these arenas Christians died for their faith as they were slain by the gladiator's sword, thrown to the wild beasts, or burned at the stake. These bloody "amusements" were staged by the Roman emperors to win the public favor and keep the unemployed masses of Rome out of mischief.

Seneca's Account of the Roman Games

I chanced to stop in a midday show [of gladiators], expecting fun, wit, and some relaxation, when men's eyes take respite from the slaughter of their fellow men. It was just the reverse. The preceding combats were merciful by comparison; now all the trifling is put aside and it is pure murder. . . . In the morning men are thrown to the lions and the bears, at noon they are thrown to their spectators. "Kill him! Lash him! Burn him! Why does he meet the sword so timidly? Why doesn't he kill boldly? Why doesn't he die game? Whip him to meet his wounds!" And when the show stops for intermission, "Let's have men killed meanwhile! Let's not have nothing going on!"[5]

THIS MOMENT IN HISTORY

Rome's Bloody Amusements

What would have been some good and appropriate ways for the emperors to deal with unemployment and win the favor of their subjects? Do modern societies have amusements similar to the Roman games? If so, what are they and how are they similar?

____

____

____

____

____

____

Religious Beliefs

Roman religious beliefs gradually changed during her history. In the early days of the republic, the Romans had worshiped gods of nature. Many of the planets in our solar system bear the names of these gods: Mercury, Venus, Mars, Jupiter, Saturn, Neptune, and Pluto. As the Romans came into contact with the Greeks, they associated their gods with the mythical gods of Mount Olympus. But like the Greeks, many Romans grew dissatisfied with the old gods and turned instead to philosophy to find happiness and meaning in life. The Romans were not very interested in the abstract ideas of Greek philosophy, but in two Greek philosophies—Epicureanism and Stoicism—they discovered practical guidelines for living.

The Maison Carrée, a beautiful Roman temple at Nîmes, France, was built in honor of the grandsons of Caesar Augustus.

Minerva

Greek and Roman Deities

Greek Deity	Function	Roman Deity
Zeus	King of the gods	Jupiter
Hera	Queen of the gods, wife of Zeus (Jupiter)	Juno
Ares	God of war	Mars
Apollo	God of the sun, the arts, and medicine	Apollo
Aphrodite	Goddess of love and beauty	Venus
Athena	Goddess of wisdom	Minerva
Hermes	Messenger of the gods, god of commerce and travel	Mercury
Poseidon	God of the sea	Neptune
Kronos	God of agriculture	Saturn
Artemis	Goddess of the moon	Diana
Eros	God of love	Cupid

Epicureanism

The **Epicurean** philosophy may be summed up by the following:

> There is nothing to fear in God,
> There is nothing to be alarmed at in death;
> Good is easily obtained,
> Evil is easily endured.[6]

The founder of this philosophy, Epicurus, taught that true happiness comes only as man frees his mind from fear and his body from pain. Epicurus believed happiness rested in the virtues of simple pleasure and peace of mind. He rejected the ideas of an afterlife and divine judgment. For him, happiness was to be found only in this life.

The poet **Lucretius** (99–55 BC) was probably the greatest exponent of Epicureanism in the Roman world. In his philosophical poem *On the Nature of Things*, Lucretius preserved the teachings of Epicurus. He hoped to reform the declining moral standards of the republic. However, many Romans interpreted the Epicurean teaching "seek happiness as the only good" as meaning they could do *anything* that would bring them pleasure. What was intended to restore Rome's traditional values became an excuse for the worst excesses of behavior.

Stoicism

The Stoic philosophy had a stronger and more lasting impact on Roman society than Epicureanism. One of the leading Stoics of the Roman Empire was **Seneca** (3 BC–65 AD), the tutor of the emperor Nero and an outstanding writer and thinker. Seneca saw Stoicism as the solution to Rome's moral decline. He wrote:

> A brave man fears nothing more than the weakness of being affected with popular glory. His eyes are not dazzled either with gold or steel; he tramples upon all the terror and glories of Fortune; he looks upon himself as a citizen and soldier of the world; and in despite of all accidents and oppositions, he maintains his station. He does not only suffer, but court, the most perilous occasions of virtue, and those adventures which are most terrible to others: for he values himself upon experiment, and is more ambitious of being reputed good than happy.

Stoicism teaches that the highest good is the pursuit of the virtues of courage, dignity, duty, simplicity of life, and service to fellow men. Stoics believed in the brotherhood of man and the moral responsibility of each individual to his society. By proper living, man could bring himself into harmony with the divine law that governs the universe and directs his fate. The Stoics were sincere in their efforts, but they were sincerely mistaken; good behavior does not make a person good in the sight of God. It does not change the fact that he is a sinner.

Another eminent Roman devoted to Stoicism was the emperor **Marcus Aurelius**—scholar, philosopher, administrator, and last of the so-called Good Emperors of Rome. (His death in AD 180 marks the end of the *Pax Romana*.) Known as the "philosopher-king," Marcus Aurelius expressed the Stoic ideals in his book *Meditations*, a collection of personal reflections.

Eastern Influence

With the large number of peoples and lands embraced by the Roman Empire came a great variety of religious beliefs and ideas. From the East came the "mystery religions" that won popular acceptance among the Romans. These religions, based upon polytheism and mythology, promised immortality to those who performed secret and mysterious ceremonies. Rome tolerated these foreign religious beliefs as long as the people acknowledged that the Roman emperor was a god too.

Also from the East came the practice of emperor-worship. The Roman emperors held the title ***pontifex maximus*** ("greatest priest"). In this office, they interpreted the will of the gods in the affairs of state. People expressed their loyalty and patriotism to the state by worshiping the emperors. (Beginning in the Middle Ages, Roman Catholic popes also claimed this title for themselves.) Although Christians were loyal to the state, the government persecuted them because they did not worship the emperors—their first loyalty was to God, for He alone is worthy of worship.

Section Quiz

1. What culture greatly influenced Roman culture?
2. Who was called the "Homer of Rome"?
3. What city was covered by the volcanic ash of Mount Vesuvius and not rediscovered until the eighteenth century?
4. What was the name of the theory that stated that the earth was the center of the universe? Who developed this theory?
5. Who was a leading Stoic philosopher of the Roman Empire and also served as tutor to an emperor? Who was his famous pupil?

1. ____________________
2. ____________________
3. ____________________
4. ____________________
   ____
5. ____________________
   ____

III. The Introduction of Christianity

The World Made Ready

God directed the affairs of men and civilizations in ancient times to make the world ready for the coming of His Son and the spread of the gospel. Roman society at the time of Christ was characterized by safe travel and social and political stability. The widely known Greek language made possible the easy exchange of ideas. While these factors would aid the spread of Christianity, other factors would encourage the popular acceptance of Christianity. The moral decay throughout the empire demonstrated the inability of human religions and philosophies to satisfy the longings of man's soul and to provide a worthy standard of moral behavior. Into this climate of despair, God sent His Son, who alone could satisfy that hunger and teach men how to live.

Bethlehem, the birthplace of Christ.
Published by permission, Historic Views Of The Holy Land: The 1960s: Photographs of Charles Lee Feinberg, *www.bibleplaces.com, 2004.*

God used the Greeks and the Romans, but the Jews were His special tool. Though often disobedient and rebellious against God, they preserved the knowledge and worship of the one true God in the midst of a heathen world. They offered the hope of the coming Messiah and through their sacrifices testified to the sinfulness of man and his need of reconciliation to God.

The Babylonians destroyed Jerusalem in 586 BC and exiled thousands of Jews from their homeland. Separated from the temple in Jerusalem, these "scattered" Jews built new centers of worship called **synagogues**. (Christians later used these synagogues for the preaching of the gospel message.) Like many other peoples, the Jews came under the influence of Hellenistic culture. Many Jews embraced the Greek culture and language. A group of men translated the Hebrew Old Testament into Greek because many Jews could no longer understand Hebrew. This translation is called the **Septuagint** (SEP too uh JINT). Through this translation, both Hellenistic Jews and Gentiles were made aware of the hope of the coming Messiah and the moral standard of God's law.

The Turning Point of History

At the completion of His work of preparation, God sent **Jesus Christ** as a sacrifice to redeem fallen man from his sinful condition and to provide eternal life to those who trust in Him. The Bible states that "when the fulness of the time was come, God sent forth his Son, made of a woman, made under the law, to redeem them that were under the law, that we might receive the adoption of sons" (Gal. 4:4–5).

Jesus was born in the small Roman province of Judea during the reign of the emperor Caesar Augustus. The events of His earthly life and ministry are recorded in the four Gospels (Matthew, Mark, Luke, and John). At the age of thirty, Jesus began His public ministry—preaching, teaching, and working miracles—demonstrating to all by word and deed that He was the promised Messiah, the Son of God.

However, most Jews rejected Jesus as their Messiah. The apostle John tells us, "He came unto his own, and his own received him not" (John 1:11). The Jews looked for a messiah who would free them from Roman oppression and restore in their midst the glorious kingdom of Solomon. They failed, however, to realize that the Messiah's first concern would be to release His people from inward oppression—their sinfulness. Unless the problem of sin is dealt with, no human can be part of the Messiah's kingdom. Jesus Himself said, "Except a man be born again, he cannot see the kingdom of God" (John 3:3). To make this new birth possible, the Messiah had to die a bloody and humiliating death. The Old Testament prophet Isaiah foretold this aspect of the Messiah's coming:

> *He is despised and rejected of men; a man of sorrows, and acquainted with grief. . . . We did esteem him stricken, smitten of God, and afflicted. But he was wounded for our transgressions, he was bruised for our iniquities: the chastisement of our peace was upon him; and with his stripes we are healed.*
>
> *Isaiah 53:3–6*

Since Jesus came to save people from sin, His preaching was filled with calls for men and women everywhere to admit their sinfulness and follow Him. The thesis of much of His preaching was the bold statement, "The kingdom of God is at hand: repent ye, and believe the gospel" (Mark 1:15). Jesus did not exempt the Jewish religious leaders from His preaching: "Woe unto you, scribes and Pharisees, hypocrites! for ye are like unto whited sepulchres, which indeed appear beautiful outward, but are within full of dead men's bones" (Matt. 23:27).

These religious leaders were offended by such preaching, and they plotted to have Jesus killed. They paid Judas Iscariot, one of Jesus' disciples, to betray Him. They then brought Him before the Roman governor **Pontius Pilate**, charging that He was working to overthrow Roman rule. They said that since He claimed to be the Messiah, the King of the Jews, He was setting Himself up in opposition to the Roman emperor **Tiberius** (14–37). Although Pilate found no fault in Jesus, he desired to maintain the peace. Giving in to the Jewish demands, he sentenced Jesus to death by **crucifixion**.

Christ before Pilate, *Constantijn Daniel van Renesse (attr. to).*
From the Bob Jones University Collection

But three days later, Jesus' tomb was empty. Some claimed that His followers had stolen the body. His followers themselves, however, gave a very different explanation. They said that when they came to the tomb on the third day (not to steal the body but to anoint it with perfume), they found that Jesus was already gone. An angel confronted them with good news: "Fear not ye: for I know that ye seek Jesus, which was crucified. He is not here: for he is risen, as he said" (Matt. 28:5–6).

The significance of this event cannot be overstated. When God raised Jesus from the dead, He proved that the life and death of this Man from Nazareth do indeed constitute the turning point of history. Up to that point, the nations of the earth were spiraling downward into depravity and destruction. But now there was hope. God had sent His Son to be born of a virgin (Matt. 1:23), to live a sinless life (1 Pet. 2:22), and to die in the place of sinful humans so that they might be forgiven of their sins and be able to claim as their own the righteousness of Jesus Christ (1 Pet. 2:24). This is the **gospel**. As the apostle Paul stated later in one of his epistles, "I declare unto you the gospel . . . how that Christ died for our sins according to the scriptures; and that he was buried, and that he rose again the third day according to the scriptures" (1 Cor. 15:1, 3–4). What Jesus did during His Crucifixion changes forever the lives of all humans who will believe He died for them. Since the day that the angel first proclaimed, "He is risen," many have believed—more than any historian could number. By changing lives, Jesus has changed history.

The Spread of the Gospel

"All power is given unto me in heaven and in earth. Go ye therefore, and teach all nations, baptizing them in the name of the Father, and of the Son, and of the Holy Ghost" (Matt. 28:18–19). With these words, Jesus Christ charged His disciples to teach all the nations (not just the Jewish nation) how to be forgiven of sin and how to live in obedience to their Maker. This is a command for Christian disciples of every age. During the first three hundred years of the Christian era, the followers of Christ carried the gospel to many parts of the world. Conditions were favorable for the rapid expansion of the Christian faith. It was not until the nineteenth century that the missionary outreach of Christianity again experienced such favorable conditions.

Jerusalem was the center of the early church. Christ told His disciples, "Ye shall be witnesses unto me both in Jerusalem, and in all Judaea, and in Samaria, and unto the uttermost part of the earth" (Acts 1:8). Through the disciples' preaching, thousands of Jews at Jerusalem turned from their unbelief and trusted in Jesus Christ as their Savior. But as the number of believers grew, so did the opposition of Jewish religious leaders. They began to persecute the Christians, imprisoning many of the disciples and stoning **Stephen**—the first Christian martyr. But the persecution at Jerusalem served only to spread the Christian faith, scattering Christians and their gospel message throughout Judea and Samaria. The spread of Christianity beyond its Jewish cradle was greatly aided by two events: the conversion of Paul and the Roman destruction of Jerusalem.

THROUGH EYES OF FAITH

How the Gospel Spread

The two primary means that God used to spread the gospel were two events that must have challenged the faith of many Christians. First, He saved Saul of Tarsus—a man who had persecuted and murdered many early Christians—and made him an apostle. Second, He allowed the Romans to destroy Jerusalem. What do these two events indicate about God's working in the world and in our lives?

___

___

___

___

___

___

___

___

___

The Apostle Paul (AD 5?–67?)

Paul, originally named Saul, was born into a Jewish home of Tarsus (in present-day Turkey), inherited Roman citizenship, received one of the best educations a Jew could obtain, and became a Pharisee (a member of the strictest of the Jewish religious sects). His religious zeal made him a persecutor of the Christian church. But one day on his way to Damascus, Saul, the zealous persecutor, became a zealous Christian (Acts 9:1–6).

Perhaps no person has exceeded Paul in the impact of his work for Christ. The Holy Spirit inspired him, as He also inspired certain other men of his day (such as Peter, Luke, John, and others) to write part of the New Testament Scriptures. Paul wrote a greater number of books than any other biblical writer; most of the New Testament epistles (letters) were written by him. Through his missionary endeavors, Paul introduced the gospel to a large portion of the Roman world. He traveled thousands of miles on Roman roads preaching the gospel and establishing churches in Asia Minor, Macedonia, Greece, and Rome. The success of Paul's labors among the Gentiles demonstrated that the gospel was for all people and not just for the Jews. It was not until the Jewish uprising in AD 66–70, however, that the Roman world outside the Judean province was able to distinguish clearly the Christian faith from Judaism.

Remnant of a Roman road near Tarsus.

The Destruction of Jerusalem (AD 70)

Since the destruction of Jerusalem by Nebuchadnezzar in 586 BC, Judea had been under the rule of foreign powers—first the Chaldeans, then the Persians, Alexander the Great, the Ptolemies, the Seleucids, and finally the Romans. The Jews tolerated foreign rule as long as they could maintain their religious freedom and administer their own local affairs. But the Jews grew dissatisfied with Roman rule as the Roman governors of Judea gradually became more oppressive and insensitive to the strong religious beliefs of the Jews.

In AD 66 Jewish discontent flared into open rebellion. The Jewish historian **Josephus**, who later recorded the conflict between the Jews and the Romans, warned the Jews of the folly of armed resistance against the mighty Romans. But the Jews failed to heed his advice. Roman legions were quickly dispatched to suppress the Jewish insurrection. In **AD 70** the war came to a climax as the Roman legions under their commander **Titus** breached the walls of Jerusalem, looted the temple, and completely destroyed the city. God had judged the Jews for their rejection of Jesus Christ and their persecution of the early church. The Jews lost their homeland and became wanderers among the nations of the earth—objects of ridicule and persecution. Nevertheless, they retained their distinctiveness as a people. God used the destruction of Jerusalem to separate the early church from its Jewish environment and to scatter Christians throughout the Roman Empire.

The Arch of Titus in Rome, constructed soon after his death, commemorated his capture of Jerusalem. One of the reliefs depicts the spoils of the temple being carried away *(see p. 105).*

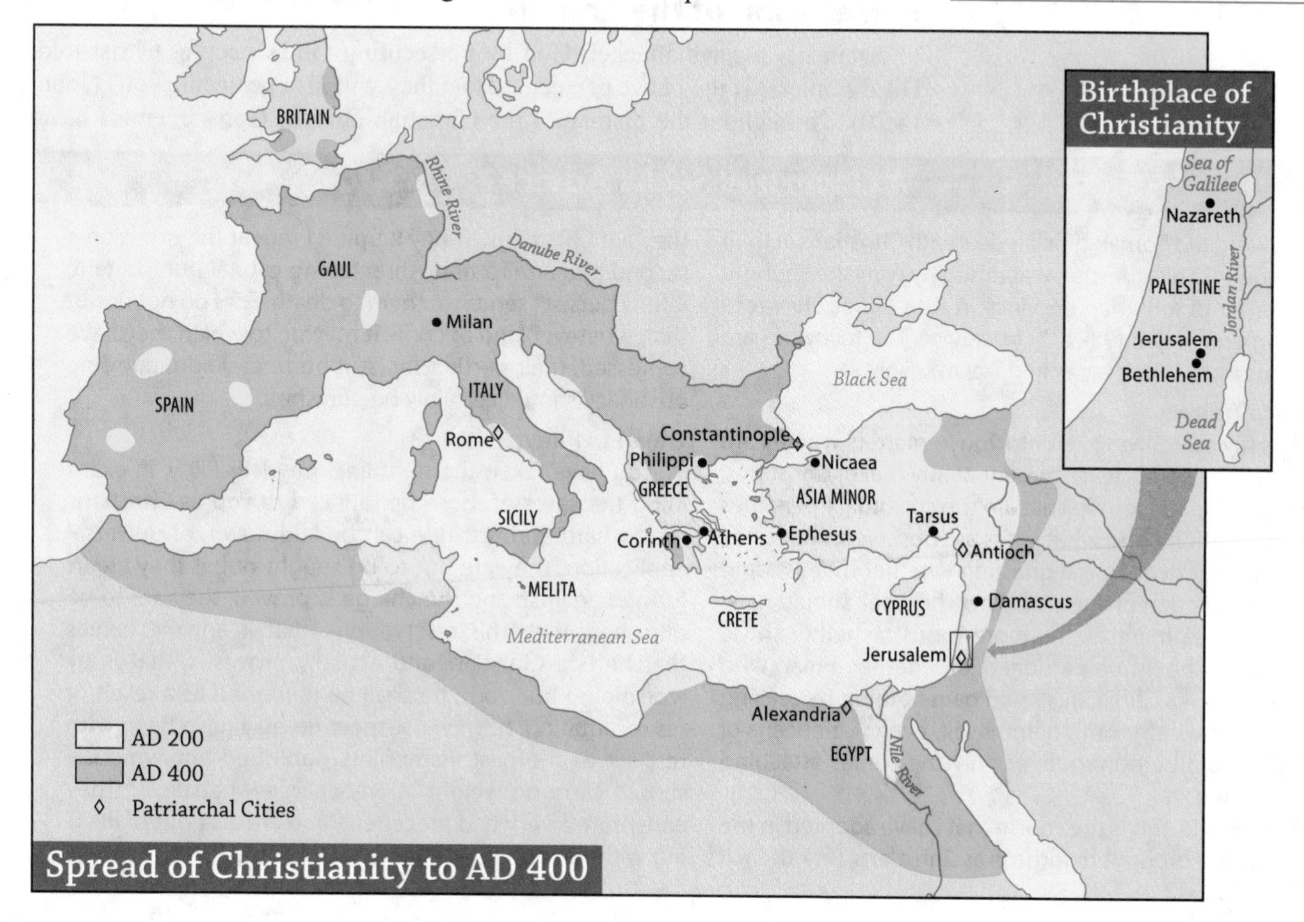

Church Organizational Development

The organization of the early church was very simple. Christians met in private homes or in the Jewish synagogues for fellowship and worship. They gathered to read portions of God's Word, pray, sing songs of praise, and partake of the Lord's Supper. As the number of believers multiplied, the apostles recognized that they could not minister to all the physical and spiritual needs in the church. Therefore, they appointed "seven men of honest report, full of the Holy Ghost and wisdom" to take care of the daily business of the church. This delegation of responsibility allowed the apostles to devote more time and effort to praying and the preaching of the Word (Acts 6:1–7).

The earliest leaders of the church were the apostles, who were chosen directly by Christ. As the church spread and the apostles died, men of faith and experience were chosen to administer the affairs of the local assemblies. The pastor was just one of a number of elders (or presbyters) chosen to direct the worship, discipline, and business matters of the local assembly. At first all the elders were of the same rank but gradually the pastor, or bishop ("overseer") as he was called, rose to a greater position of authority. When difficult times arose, local assemblies looked to their pastor-bishops to protect them from doctrinal error and to provide stable leadership in the midst of persecution. As the number of churches grew, the influence and prestige of the pastor-bishops grew as well. Those men who pastored large and important churches—those founded by one of the apostles, those located in cities of political or economic importance, or those which had started many daughter churches—had special places of prominence. These church officers attempted to meet the needs of local assemblies as they faced the challenges of a rapidly increasing membership, intense persecution, and heretical attacks upon Christian doctrine.

Persecution of the Church

Satan has always attacked God by persecuting God's people. Christ told His disciples, "If they have persecuted me, they will also persecute you" (John 15:20). Throughout the history of the Christian church, God's enemies have

A Governor Seeks Advice

How should Roman officials deal with Christians in their community? This question was raised by Pliny the Younger, a governor of a Roman province in Asia Minor. He wrote the emperor Trajan (98–117) for advice. The following are excerpts from Pliny's letter and Trajan's reply.

Pliny to Trajan:

It is my rule, Sire, to refer to you in matters where I am uncertain. . . . I was never present at any trial of Christians; therefore I do not know what are the customary penalties or investigations, and what limits are observed. I have hesitated a great deal on the question whether there should be any distinction of ages; whether the weak should have the same treatment as the more robust; whether those who recant should be pardoned, or whether a man who has ever been a Christian should gain nothing by ceasing to be such; whether the name itself, even if innocent of crime, should be punished, or only the crimes attaching to that name.

Meanwhile, this is the course that I have adopted in the case of those brought before me as Christians. I ask them if they are Christians. If they admit it I repeat the question a second and a third time, threatening capital punishment; if they persist I sentence them to death. For I do not doubt that, whatever kind of crime it may be to which they have confessed, their pertinacity [stubbornness] and inflexible obstinacy should certainly be punished.

Trajan to Pliny:

You have taken the right line, my dear Pliny, in examining the cases of those denounced to you as Christians, for no hard and fast rule can be laid down, of universal application. They are not to be sought out; if they are informed against, and the charge is proved, they are to be punished, with this reservation—that if anyone denies that he is a Christian, and actually proves it, that is by worshiping our gods, he shall be pardoned as a result of his recantation, however suspect he may have been with respect to the past. Pamphlets published anonymously should carry no weight in any charge whatsoever. They constitute a very bad precedent, and are also out of keeping with this age.[7]

Polycarp: "Faithful unto Death"

In his message to the church at Smyrna in Asia Minor, Jesus said, "Behold, the devil shall cast some of you into prison, that ye may be tried; and ye shall have tribulation ten days: be thou faithful unto death, and I will give thee a crown of life" (Rev. 2:10). A little more than fifty years later, Christians at Smyrna experienced that tribulation in bloody persecution. Among those "faithful unto death" was the leader of the church at Smyrna, Polycarp.

Polycarp had received many spiritual blessings in his life. As a young man, he had actually heard the apostle John speak. When he was about forty, Polycarp had received a visit from Ignatius, bishop of Antioch, who was on his way to Rome under arrest, where he died for his faith. After the visit, Ignatius wrote a letter, thanking Polycarp for his hospitality and urging, "Stand thou firm, as an anvil when it is smitten. It is the part of a great athlete to receive blows and be victorious. But especially must we for God's sake endure all things." Around AD 160 a wave of persecution swept over the Christians in Smyrna. City authorities seized Polycarp, bishop of the church, and brought him before a howling crowd gathered at the stadium. The Roman official governing Smyrna tried to get Polycarp to publicly disavow his faith. "Swear the oath [to the emperor]," he said, "and I will release thee; revile the Christ." Polycarp looked at the official and replied, "Fourscore and six years have I been His servant, and He hath done me no wrong. How then can I blaspheme my King who saved me?" When further argument proved fruitless, the official turned Polycarp over to the fury of the crowd. They seized the aged bishop, bound him to a stake, and burned him to death in the middle of the stadium. A faithful witness to his Lord, Polycarp proved worthy of "a crown of life."

demonstrated their hatred for God by persecuting Christian people. "All that will live godly in Christ Jesus shall suffer persecution" (2 Tim. 3:12).

One of the most severe periods of persecution of the church occurred during the time of the Roman Empire. The Romans believed that the claims of Christ upon His followers set Christians at odds with the Roman state and society. They charged that Christians were disloyal citizens because they refused to burn incense on the altars of the emperors, acknowledging "Caesar as Lord." The Romans, who worshiped many different gods, opposed the exclusive claims of Christians: "Neither is there salvation in any other: for there is none other name under heaven given among men, whereby we must be saved" (Acts 4:12).

The Romans considered Christians "social misfits" and Christianity a threat to their way of life. Christians did not attend the "amusements" of the arenas, celebrate the pagan festivals, or indulge in the many other vices of the day. Because Christians separated themselves from these public activities, the Romans branded them "haters of humanity." They resented the Christians' fervent desire to tell others about Christ and became alarmed over the rapid growth of the Christian church. Christians became the scapegoats for many of the evils that plagued the empire, from fires to earthquakes.

The first official Roman persecution of Christianity began under the emperor **Nero** (54–68). He accused the Christians of setting fire to Rome, although he himself may have been responsible. What followed was a hideous display of cruelty and death. The Roman historian Tacitus records that Christians were "torn by dogs, or were nailed to crosses, or were doomed to the flames and burnt, to serve as nightly illumination, when daylight had expired."

From the time of Nero until AD 250, the persecution of Christians was sporadic and confined to small areas. However, beginning in 250, persecution became empire-wide. Thousands of Christians—both the young and the old—met death by sword, crucifixion, wild beasts, fire, and burning oil. But they had the steadfast confidence that it is better to "fear him which is able to destroy both soul and body in hell" than to fear "them which kill the body, but are not able to kill the soul" (Matt. 10:28).

The last and perhaps the most widespread Roman persecution occurred during the reign of the emperor **Diocletian** (284–305). In successive waves of edicts, Diocletian dismissed Christian soldiers from the army and ordered

The Catacombs

The early Christians buried their dead rather than cremating them as the pagans did. Because they believed in the resurrection of the body, Christians thought it was wrong to destroy the body deliberately by burning it. They established their own burial grounds, which they called *koimeteria*—a Greek term meaning, "place of rest," or "sleeping place." From this word we get our modern English word *cemetery*. We call the cemeteries that these early Christians established catacombs. (The word *catacomb* derives from the Greek *kata kumbos*, meaning "near the low place." The Italians first used this Greek phrase in reference to a Christian cemetery located near a low place outside the city of Rome.)

The catacombs are underground passageways about a yard wide and six to eight feet tall. In the walls of these passageways the Christians carved openings in which they placed the bodies of their friends and relatives. As more burial space was needed, more of these corridors were dug. Eventually there were many miles of walking space underground. Between the years 150 and 400, over half a million Christians were buried in the catacombs.

As the Roman Empire collapsed and barbarians swept into the Italian Peninsula, the catacombs were abandoned. The church removed some of the remains to safer places, while grave robbers and vandals destroyed the rest. By the year 900 all the tombs were empty.

Today the catacombs are tourist attractions. They contain some of the earliest examples of Christian art. More importantly, the catacombs illustrate the faith of the early Christians. One symbol often found painted or carved on the walls of the catacombs is the fish. The early Christians used the Greek word for fish *(ichthus)* as a confession of their faith in Jesus Christ.

Iesous **Ch**ristos, **Th**eou **U**ios, **S**oter
Jesus Christ, God's Son, Savior

the destruction of Christian churches and the burning of the Scriptures. Later a co-emperor ordered all Christians to sacrifice to the pagan gods under pain of torture and death.

Of course, the Romans hoped that persecution would cause Christians to renounce their faith and deter others from converting to Christianity. Yet even as Romans persecuted the Christians, the Christian church grew both numerically and in spiritual purity. More than a hundred years before the final persecution a Christian writer had declared, "The blood of the martyrs is the seed of the Church."

From Imperial Persecution to Acceptance

In **313** one of the most significant events in the history of the Christian church occurred. In the **Edict of Milan**, the Roman emperor **Constantine** (306–337) made Christianity legal, ending almost three hundred years of Roman persecution of Christians. Just a year earlier, before a crucial battle with a rival for the emperor's throne, Constantine said he saw in the sky a vision of a shining cross that bore the inscription "By this sign, conquer!" Upon defeating his foe, Constantine publicly embraced Christianity, attributing his military success to the Christian God. We do not know what Constantine's true motives were for adopting the Christian faith nor whether he truly became a Christian. But we do know that his outward acceptance of Christianity dramatically changed the history of the church. Rome, previously a persecutor of the church, became the protector and patron of the church. Constantine restored church property that had been confiscated under the Diocletian persecution, made Sunday a legal holiday, contributed funds for new church buildings, and encouraged others to embrace Christianity.

Once threatened by persecution, Christians now found themselves protected by Roman law, favored by the Roman emperor, and granted privileges by the Roman state. The emperor even helped the church sort through a major doctrinal difficulty. When a heretic by the name of **Arius** disrupted the unity of the church by challenging the deity of Christ, Constantine intervened and called for a general council of church leaders to settle this doctrinal controversy. In 325, the **Council of Nicaea**, presided over by Constantine, affirmed Christ's deity and the doctrine of the Trinity; it also branded Arianism a heresy. As the emperors became more involved in church matters, the church gained more favor and power in the Roman world. At the end of the fourth century, Christianity became the official and exclusive religion of the Roman state by edict of the emperor **Theodosius I** (379–395).

Portrait Head of Emperor Constantine I, *Roman, ca. 324–337, Constantinian, late Antique period, marble.*

The Metropolitan Museum of Art, Bequest of Mary Clark Thompson, 1923 (26.229) Photograph by Schecter Lee. Photograph © 1986 The Metropolitan Museum of Art

As a result of the freedom and privileges granted by the Roman government, the church grew rapidly in membership and material prosperity. This position of favor set the stage for a decline in the purity of the church's membership, practices, and organization. Great numbers of people joined the church—some because they embraced the truth, others because it was the popular thing to do. Although Christianity triumphed over the pagan religions of Rome, some pagan ideas and practices crept into the church. One such practice was **monasticism**, which exercised a strong influence on the church from the fourth century to the end of the Middle Ages. Monasticism is not of Christian origin nor biblically based but came from Eastern pagan religions. Because of the moral and economic decay of the Roman Empire and the growing worldliness of the church, many sought escape from the turmoil and evil of the world by living apart from society in monasteries. Many men and women sincerely believed that the greatest form of piety and the best means to gain victory over the flesh was to withdraw from all worldly cares and possessions and practice strict discipline and religious exercises.

The organization of the church became more complex as the church grew numerically. By the fourth century, the church had a definite **hierarchical** (HY er AR kih kul) structure—levels of authority among the pastor-bishops and churches in the empire. The organization of the church followed the pattern of the political and geographic divisions of the Roman Empire rather than being based on the teachings of the apostles preserved in the New Testament. The smallest division was the parish, served by a pastor. Next was the diocese (DY uh sis) or district, a territorial division supervised by a bishop and comprising a number of parishes within and around a city. An archbishop administered a number of dioceses called a province. The largest administrative districts of the church were the patriarchates. The **patriarchs** were the bishops of the most important cities of the empire—Jerusalem, Alexandria, Rome, Antioch, and Constantinople (the new capital founded by Constantine). These positions had

THROUGH EYES OF FAITH

The Conversion of Constantine

Do you think the conversion of Emperor Constantine was a divine blessing on the Christian church or a satanic ploy to spoil God's people with favor from the ungodly?

1.

2.

3.

4.

5.

6.

7.

the most prestige and authority within the church. At first the patriarchs were all of equal rank, but over a period of time the patriarch of Rome came to be regarded as the "first among equals."

Because of the worldliness of many Christians, the adoption of pagan ideas, and religious hierarchy, the church gradually departed from the truth of the Christian faith. The seeds of error that took root during the fourth and fifth centuries blossomed during the Middle Ages into the Roman Catholic Church. (In Chapter 8 we will examine the rise and growth of this church and its leader, the pope.)

Section Quiz

1. What were the centers of worship called for the Jews who were scattered abroad?
2. Why did the Jewish religious leaders reject Jesus as their Messiah?
3. According to the apostle Paul, what is the gospel?
4. What two events greatly aided the spread of Christianity beyond its Jewish cradle?
5. What emperor made Christianity a legal religion in the empire? What emperor made Christianity the official religion of the empire?
6. What heresy challenged the deity of Christ? At what council in 325 was the truth of Christ's deity affirmed?
7. What were the pastor/bishops of the most important cities called? List these five cities.

IV. Collapse of the Roman Empire

Reasons for Decline

In the third century a series of political, economic, and social crises shook the foundations of the empire. Signs of internal weakness and decay were already present within the empire. In the fourth and fifth centuries, barbarian invaders entered Roman territory, and Rome was too weak to expel them. What were the reasons for this decline and the eventual collapse of Roman Empire?

One important reason was Rome's political disorder. By the third century, Rome could no longer boast of a strong and stable government. Inefficiency and waste had accompanied the sharp rise in the size of the government. Rome also suffered from unstable leadership, for the Romans had never adopted a definite plan for choosing a successor to the emperor. Hence, ambitious generals plotted and struggled to gain control of the government. As the army became increasingly involved in political affairs, greedy soldiers were quick to elevate a military leader to emperor in return for rewards. If the army became dissatisfied with an emperor, they could remove him from power and put someone else in his place. In many cases war broke out between different legions as each tried to secure the emperor's throne for its own commander. Political turmoil, assassination, and civil war became commonplace. The army, once the protector of the Roman state, controlled the state in order to satisfy its own greed.

Closely associated with Rome's political problems were her economic troubles. The cost of maintaining an increasingly large army to defend her extensive borders, as well as the expenses of a huge government bureaucracy, drained the Roman treasury. To solve the economic crisis, the government attempted to raise revenue by increasing the tax burden of the people. In addition, emperors reduced the silver content in the Roman coins, adding cheaper

Ancient Roman coins

metals instead. As the value of coinage declined, prices rose. This inflation was aggravated by Rome's one-sided trade with India and China, which depleted the empire's gold and silver supplies. Because Roman money became almost worthless, the barter system replaced the use of money. Trade slackened, shops closed, and poverty increased. Confidence in the economic future of Rome all but collapsed.

Moral decay was another factor in the decline of Rome. As we saw in the last chapter, Rome's strength during her early history was due in large part to the virtues of her citizens—their discipline, patriotism, self-denial, hard work, and respect for authority. However, the moral decay that began during the days of the republic continued during the *Pax Romana*. Contentment was replaced by greed. People looked to the government to supply free grain and public amusements. (This also contributed to the large economic burden of the empire.) Family life disintegrated, divorce and immorality abounded, and superstition increased. Once the backbone of Rome, a hard-working patriotic citizen was now hard to find.

THIS MOMENT IN HISTORY

Decline in the Roman Empire

Do you think that some of the reasons for Rome's decline can be found in our culture as well? What are they? How should we deal with them?

Reform and Reorganization Attempts

By the end of the third century the Roman Empire was at the point of collapse. But two powerful emperors—Diocletian and Constantine—introduced strong reforms that delayed the fall of the empire for almost two centuries. While earlier emperors tried to work within the framework of the old institutions of the republic, Diocletian and Constantine wielded supreme authority over the state in their attempts to restore order and stability to the empire.

In 284 the Roman army proclaimed Diocletian emperor of Rome. Diocletian, an able administrator and organizer, reshaped the political structure of the empire. He realized that the empire was too large for one man to rule effectively. He therefore chose a co-emperor, known as an **augustus**, to rule the western half of the empire while he ruled in the east. Diocletian's plan called for each co-emperor to appoint an assistant, called a **caesar**, to help the augustus and to become his successor. Diocletian divided the empire into four large administrative divisions, called prefectures, which were to be ruled by the two co-emperors, and the two caesars. Through these measures, Diocletian brought temporary stability to the government.

Diocletian also introduced strong measures to combat Rome's economic problems. To curb inflation, he set maximum prices on goods and services. Anyone selling an item above the price limit could be put to death. He tried to revive confidence in Rome's monetary system by introducing new gold and silver coins. He also reformed the tax system, although the people still suffered under an excessive tax burden. In each instance, Diocletian's measures to solve Rome's economic worries involved greater government control and regulation. In the long run, his measures only added to the problems they were intended to solve.

When Diocletian retired from office in 305, his system of joint rule fell apart. Civil war broke out among the co-emperors and caesars. After years of struggle, Constantine emerged victorious and became the sole ruler of the empire. Through his political and economic reforms, Constantine continued in the same direction as Diocletian. One of the most significant actions taken by Constantine was the moving of the capital of the empire to the east. He selected the site of the ancient city of Byzantium (bih ZAN shee um) to build his "New Rome," which

THROUGH EYES OF FAITH

Rome and the Visigoths

By the time of the Battle of Adrianople (378), many of Rome's most powerful people were at least nominal Christians. What would have been a truly Christian way to treat the Visigoths? How could this treatment have changed the course of Roman history?

became known as Constantinople. But this removal of the imperial throne to the east weakened the already struggling western half of the empire.

Diocletian and Constantine prepared the way for the division of the Roman Empire into two separate empires. The empire did not become permanently divided until **395** when the emperor Theodosius I divided it between his two sons. After this division, the Western Roman Empire soon fell. The Eastern Roman Empire—later called the Byzantine Empire—was to endure for another thousand years, as we shall see in Chapter 6.

Barbarian Invasions

During the latter years of the Roman Republic growing numbers of Germanic peoples had moved down from northern Europe and settled along Rome's borders. These people were divided into independent tribes such as the Angles, Saxons, Franks, Vandals, and Goths. Roman historians described the Germanic tribes as courageous but restless, given to much drinking and gambling, yet possessing many simple virtues. The Romans called these people "barbarians"—a term they used to describe all those outside the empire who did not share in the Greek or Roman cultures.

Rome greatly increased the size of her army in an effort to maintain the security of her borders from barbarian intruders. At first Rome had a hard time finding recruits for this frontier army. To solve the problem, some emperors allowed the most "Romanized" of the Germanic tribes to settle within Roman territory to serve as a buffer between Rome and other barbarian tribes. Other emperors allowed barbarians to enlist in the army. Gradually, this foreign element in Rome's army became Rome's primary means of protecting the empire against the more restless tribes outside her borders.

Out of the Far East in the late fourth century came a new threat to Rome's security—the **Huns**. This fierce nomadic tribe, which had menaced the Chinese empire for centuries, now moved across Asia into Europe, bringing terror and destruction upon all who were in its path. The advance of the dreaded Huns prompted many Germanic tribes to seek refuge in Roman territory.

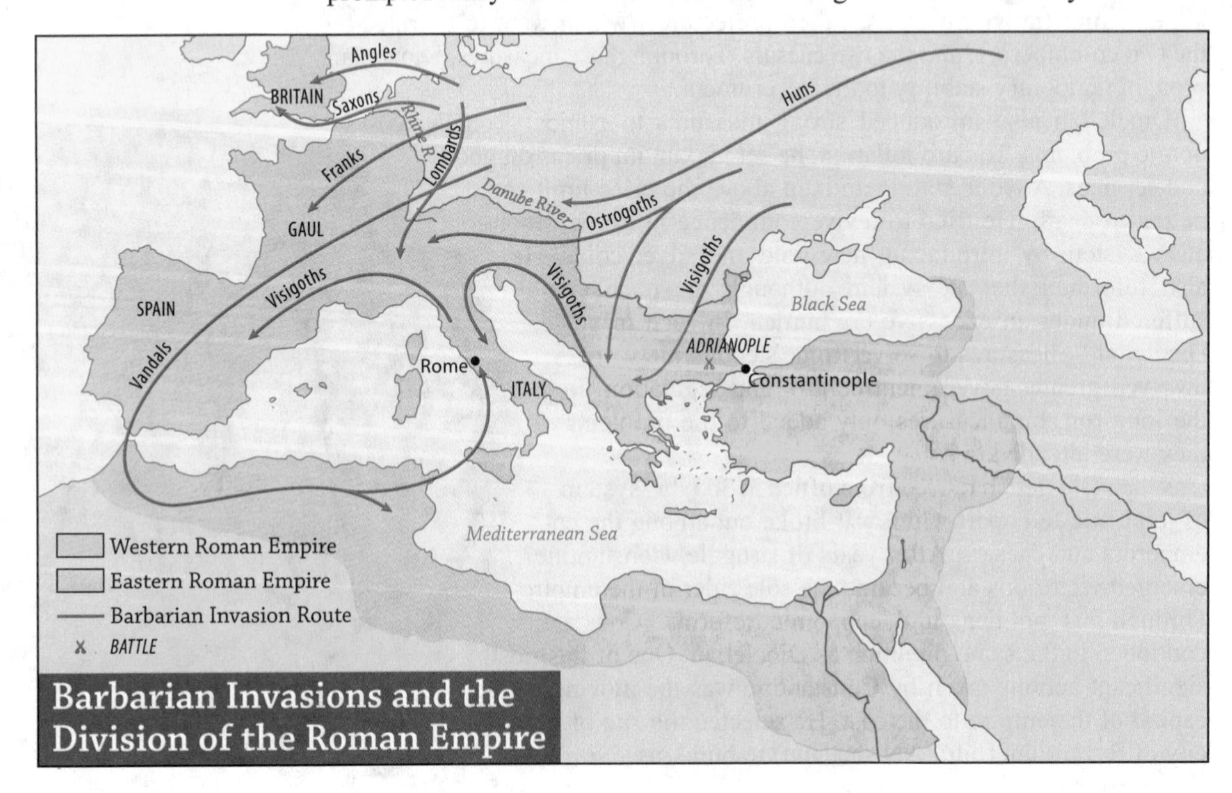

Barbarian Invasions and the Division of the Roman Empire

Augustine of Hippo

Augustine of Hippo (354–430) was one of the outstanding figures of the early Christian church. As a bishop, writer, and preacher, he earnestly defended the Christian faith against its many enemies.

Augustine was born at Tagaste in North Africa. His father was a pagan, but his mother was a Christian. Despite his mother's influence, Augustine led a sinful life until his conversion in the year 386. He underwent an intense spiritual struggle. He wanted peace in his soul but loathed giving up his sin. At one point he actually prayed, "Grant me chastity and continence—but not yet." While sitting in a friend's garden, Augustine was in despair over his sin. He prayed, "But Thou, O Lord, how long? . . . How long, how long? Tomorrow, and tomorrow? Why not now? Why is there not this hour an end to my uncleanness?" Then he heard a child nearby chanting in play, "Take up and read. Take up and read." Taking this as a sign from God, Augustine picked up a copy of the Scriptures. His eye fell on Romans 13:13–14—"Not in rioting and drunkenness, not in chambering and wantonness, not in strife and envying. But put ye on the Lord Jesus Christ, and make not provision for the flesh to fulfil the lusts thereof." In the Lord Jesus Christ, Augustine placed his faith and found salvation.

St. Augustine, *Gaspar de Crayer, Flemish, 1584–1669,* From the Bob Jones University Collection

After his conversion, Augustine became a priest and eventually bishop of Hippo in North Africa. Augustine opposed the religious falsehoods of his day through both his preaching and his writing. For example, about this time a British monk named Pelagius began teaching that man was not born sinful and therefore could be pleasing to God through his own efforts. Augustine condemned this idea and affirmed the biblical position that man can be saved only by God's mercy and grace.

In 410 barbarian invaders attacked the city of Rome. Pagan Romans blamed this disaster on the Christians. They said that the gods were punishing Rome for abandoning the old ways of worship. Augustine answered this charge in his greatest work, *The City of God*. He said that all human history is the story of two cities representing opposing ways of life. One is the city of earth, the home of sinful, unsaved men. The other is the city of God, namely His church. God's purpose in history is to build His city by saving men from sin. These two cities exist side by side in this life but will be separated by God at the final judgment. The earthly city and its citizens will go to the destruction reserved for sinners. Citizens of the heavenly city will go to eternal glory and bliss with God. With this in mind, Augustine says that we should not look at individual historical events as demonstrating the favor or disfavor of some god. Instead we should see in every event the hand of the true God directing the course of history for His purpose and glory.

One such tribe was the **Visigoths**, who crossed the Danube River and settled in the eastern part of the Roman Empire. Because of mistreatment by Roman officials, the Visigoths rebelled. In order to put down the revolt, the emperor led the Roman army against the Visigoths. At the Battle of Adrianople in **378**, the Visigoths soundly defeated the Roman army and killed the emperor. This was obviously a disaster for Rome: her legions, thought to be invincible, had fallen in defeat before a barbarian people.

THIS MOMENT IN HISTORY

Attila

Of the many barbarian groups invading the Roman Empire, explain why Attila of the Huns was given historical significance.

____

____

____

____

____

The Fall of Rome

In 410, under the leadership of **Alaric**, the Visigoths moved southwestward into the Italian peninsula and plundered the city of Rome. They eventually settled in what is now Spain. Meanwhile, the Franks moved into northern Gaul, and the Angles and Saxons crossed over into Britain. The Huns, led by their fierce leader **Attila** (433–453; called the "scourge of God," for he was considered to be the instrument of God's wrath upon a sinful people), also invaded Roman territory. However, the Romans with the help of the Germanic peoples were able to stop the advance of the Huns. Just a few years later, the **Vandals**—a Germanic tribe that established a kingdom in North Africa—raided and pillaged Rome again. To later generations, their name came to mean "a destroyer of property."

With the onslaught of the barbarian invasions, the Western Roman Empire collapsed. Many historians give the date **476** for the fall of Rome. In that year, the army ended the long period of Roman rule by placing a non-Roman upon the emperor's throne in the west.

Section Quiz

1. List three economic problems troubling Rome in the late days of the empire.
2. What emperor sought to solve the political problems of the empire by dividing the empire into four administrative divisions called prefectures?
3. What emperor divided the empire between his two sons, leading to the division of the Roman Empire into two separate empires?
4. What did the Romans call the Germanic peoples who began to settle along the borders of the empire and threatened the security of the empire?
5. In what year did the western Roman Empire collapse, when a non-Roman was placed on the imperial throne?

1. ______________________

____

____

2. ______________________

3. ______________________

4. ______________________

5. ______________________

A Glance Behind

It must be remembered that the foundation of Rome had eroded internally before collapsing under the pressure of external invasion. The English historian Edward Gibbon, who wrote the monumental *Decline and Fall of the Roman Empire*, stated, "The story of its ruin is simple and obvious; and instead of inquiring *why* the Roman Empire was destroyed, we should rather be surprised that it had subsisted so long." Nevertheless, when Rome fell, many Christians were distraught. When the civilization that had at first opposed Christianity and then nurtured it unraveled, it seemed that Christianity itself was doomed. But just as the destruction of Jerusalem was used by God to advance the kingdom of His Son, so also the fall of Rome was part of God's plan to bless all nations through the seed of Abraham. Rome had come to an end, but the work of the triumphant Christ was just beginning.

and a Glimpse Ahead

Notes

1. Naphtali Lewis and Meyer Reinhold, eds., *Roman Civilization*, vol. 2 (New York: Columbia Univ. Press, 1955), pp. 535–50 *passim*.
2. George Bernard Shaw, *Seven Plays with Prefaces and Notes* (New York: Dodd, Mead, and Co. 1951), p. 466.
3. Livy, *History of Rome*, trans. B. O. Foster, I. pref.
4. Juvenal, *Satires*. trans. L. R. Lind, I. 93–96.
5. Seneca, *Moral Epistles*, trans. Chester G. Starr, 7.
6. F. F. Bruce, *New Testament History* (Garden City, N. Y.: Doubleday, 1961), p. 42.
7. Pliny, *Letters*, trans. William Melmouth.

Chapter Review

Can You Define?

princeps	*pontifex maximus*	hierarchical
geocentric theory	synagogues	patriarchs
aqueducts	Septuagint	augustus
gladiators	crucifixion	caesar
Epicureanism	gospel	barbarians
Stoicism	monasticism	

Can You Identify?

Pax Romana	Seneca	Edict of Milan
Augustus	Marcus Aurelius	Constantine
Cicero	Jesus Christ	Arius
Virgil	Pontius Pilate	Council of Nicaea
Horace	Tiberius	Theodosius I
Ovid	Stephen	395
Livy	Paul	Huns
Juvenal	Josephus	Visigoths
Tacitus	AD 70	378
Plutarch	Titus	Alaric
Galen	Nero	Attila
Ptolemy	Diocletian	Vandals
Lucretius	313	476

Can You Locate?

Rome	Tarsus	Alexandria
Roman Empire	Damascus	Constantinople
Judea	Asia Minor	Danube River
Jerusalem	Milan	Adrianople

How Much Do You Remember?

1. List four ways Octavian sought to improve Roman government and society.
2. For each of the following names, list the person's occupation and a brief statement of his achievement: Cicero, Virgil, Livy, Plutarch, Galen. (Include any titles of important works they wrote.)
3. List two reasons why the Romans persecuted Christians.
4. List three reasons for Rome's decline.

What Do You Think?

1. Read the following passages from the book of Acts, and tell what you learn about the rights of a Roman citizen: Acts 16:37–38; 19:38–41; 22:25–29; 23:27–29; 25:7–12, 16.
2. How did the Roman games compare to the Greek games?
3. How did God use the Jews, Greeks, and Romans respectively to prepare the world for the coming of His Son?
4. Read Micah 5:2 and Luke 2:1–7. How did God use Caesar Augustus to fulfill Micah's prophecy about the birth of Messiah?
5. Arius taught that Christ did not always exist but that He was created by God the Father. How does John 1:1–4 show this teaching to be false?

THE EASTERN WORLD

II

Medieval Europeans thought of Asia as a mysterious place. This unit progresses eastward from Rome into the mysterious, alluring Orient as well as southward to the continent of Africa. Beginning with the Byzantine Empire (a blending of Eastern and Western culture), we will move to the Middle East (the realm of Islam), to the faraway lands of India and China, and finally to an examination of early African civilizations. What seemed strange and incomprehensible to the medieval Europeans will become familiar to us.

2300–1500 Early Indus River Civilization

1500 Aryan Civilization Begins (to 500 BC)

1000–250 Chou Dynasty

483 Siddhartha Gautama (Buddha) Dies

221–206 Ch'in Dynasty

202 BC–AD 220 Han Dynasty

622 Hegira
960–1279 Sung Dynasty
661–750 Umayyad
Caliphate
618–907 T'ang Dynasty
1192 Shogunate
Begins (to 1868)
700 Ghana Empire
Begins (to 1200)
1368–1644 Ming
Dynasty
732 Battle of Tours
1453 Fall of
Constantinople
862 Rurik Takes Novgorod

"Orthodox and infidel"

THE BYZANTINE AND ISLAMIC EMPIRES

The Ortaköy mosque in Istanbul, Turkey, was built in 1853. Behind it is the Bosporus Bridge connecting Asia Minor and Europe.

In 476 the Roman Empire collapsed in the West. It endured in the East, however, for another thousand years. This Eastern Roman Empire became known as the **Byzantine** (BIZ un TEEN) **Empire**. The Byzantine civilization was a blending of the cultural heritage of ancient Greece and the cultures of the Near East. Byzantine culture strongly influenced the people of Russia and southeastern Europe.

The growth of Christ's kingdom continued here in the East as it did in the West. And the spiritual contamination that was common in the West was common in the East. Christ had promised that His kingdom would grow in this manner. He taught His disciples that the kingdom of heaven would be like a mustard seed once it is planted. It would start out very small but would experience amazing growth (Matt. 13:31–32). Christ also revealed that this kingdom would be like a field of wheat into which an enemy plants many weeds (Matt. 13:24–30). Much of the story of our race from the Resurrection of Christ to the present is the working out of these two truths. God is at work in the earth growing the kingdom of His Son, and this kingdom is constantly being corrupted by people whose faith in Christ is insincere.

But God allows more than just insincerity to challenge Christ's kingdom. He also raises up rival civilizations. During the seventh century the Islamic religion arose in the desert land of Arabia. Its zealous followers, the Muslims, spread their faith through military conquest; they built an empire that stretched from Spain to India. At the same time, they forged a remarkable civilization by combining their own customs and traditions with the arts and learning of the people they conquered. This chapter will trace the beginnings, growth, and interaction of these two civilizations.

The Byzantine Hagia Sophia (top, 532–37) and the Islamic Blue Mosque (1609–16) face each other in Constantinople, present-day Istanbul.

I. The Byzantine Civilization

The Rise of "New Rome"

In 330 the emperor Constantine formally dedicated a new capital for the Roman Empire. He called the city **New Rome**, but it became more widely known as Constantinople, "Constantine's City." This second Rome was ideally located on a peninsula that juts out into the waters of the Bosporus, a narrow strait that separates southeastern Europe from Asia Minor. Constantinople was the meeting place of East and West, the vital link in both land and sea trade routes. Wealth from all over the world passed through her port.

In addition to being a flourishing commercial center, Constantinople also became an important political and religious center. After the days of Constantine, Roman emperors continued to live there. When the emperor Theodosius formally divided the empire into two parts (see p. 120), the city became the permanent capital of the Eastern Roman Empire. It was also recognized as one of the five major patriarchates of the Christian church.

While the Eastern Roman Empire continued to prosper, conditions in the western empire steadily declined. During the fourth and fifth centuries barbarian tribes threatened Rome's borders. The weak western empire crumbled under the onslaught, but the richer and stronger eastern empire was able to withstand the attacks. Constantinople, the "queen of the Mediterranean," became the foremost city of the empire.

The Byzantine Empire took its name from the ancient Greek city Byzantium, on which Constantinople was built. The inhabitants of this empire still considered themselves Romans, for in many respects their civilization was a continuation of the Roman Empire. In addition to having many of the same customs and traditions, the eastern empire retained the political and legal structures of

The name of Constantinople, ancient capital of the Byzantine Empire, was changed to Istanbul by the Turkish government in 1930.

ancient Rome. But Byzantine culture was influenced even more by the Hellenistic culture that still permeated the region; it was more Greek than Roman, more Asiatic than European. While a more civilized way of life declined in the West, it endured and flourished in the East under the Byzantine Empire.

The Reign of Justinian

The first great period of Byzantine history and culture came during the reign of the emperor **Justinian** (juh STIN ee un; 527–65). He rose from humble origins to become one of the most famous Byzantine emperors. However, he owed much of his success to the timely counsel and strong character of his wife **Theodora**. In 532 a riot broke out in Constantinople, threatening to topple Justinian from power. This riot flamed into a popular uprising, named the **Nika Revolt** after the people's battle cry: "Nika!" ("Conquer!"). Justinian was about to flee the capital and admit defeat when Theodora's bold advice encouraged him to stay:

> My opinion then is that the present time, above all others, is inopportune for flight, even though it bring safety. . . . For one who has been an emperor it is unendurable to be a fugitive. May I never be separated from this purple [sign of royalty]. . . . If, now, it is your wish to save yourself, O Emperor, there is no difficulty. For we have much money, and there is the sea, here the boats. However consider whether it will not come about after you have been saved that you would gladly exchange that safety for death. For as for myself, I approve a certain ancient saying that royalty is a good burial-shroud.[1]

This was the turning point in Justinian's reign; he remained and crushed the revolt, firmly establishing himself as emperor.

Justinian then turned his attention to his chief objective: restoring the greatness of the Roman Empire. To accomplish this goal, he sought to recover the Roman territory in the West that had fallen into the hands of barbarian tribes. For over two decades his generals led military campaigns throughout the Mediterranean world. His forces defeated the Vandals in North Africa, captured Italy from the Ostrogoths, and penetrated the southern portion of the Visigoth kingdom in Spain. Justinian's conquests extended the boundaries of the Byzantine Empire to their greatest extent; nevertheless, he was unable to recover all the land once held by Rome.

One of the most enduring achievements of the Byzantine Empire was the preservation of Roman law. By the sixth century, the reliable Roman legal system had become a complex and disorganized mass of legal opinions. Its many laws were often confusing and contradictory. Like the New Testament Pharisees, the Romans had created so many regulations that they almost forgot the foundational concepts of truth and justice. For this reason Justinian appointed a commission of ten scholars to compile, reorganize, and condense the vast body of law that had accumulated from the days of ancient Rome. Their work resulted in the **Justinian Code**, a systematic arrangement of laws that clarified Roman legal principles. This code preserved the heritage of the Roman legal system, which was to provide a foundation on which most modern European nations would build their political and legal systems.

THROUGH EYES OF FAITH

Theodora's Advice

What do you think of Theodora's advice to Justinian? Evaluate the advice from a biblical perspective.

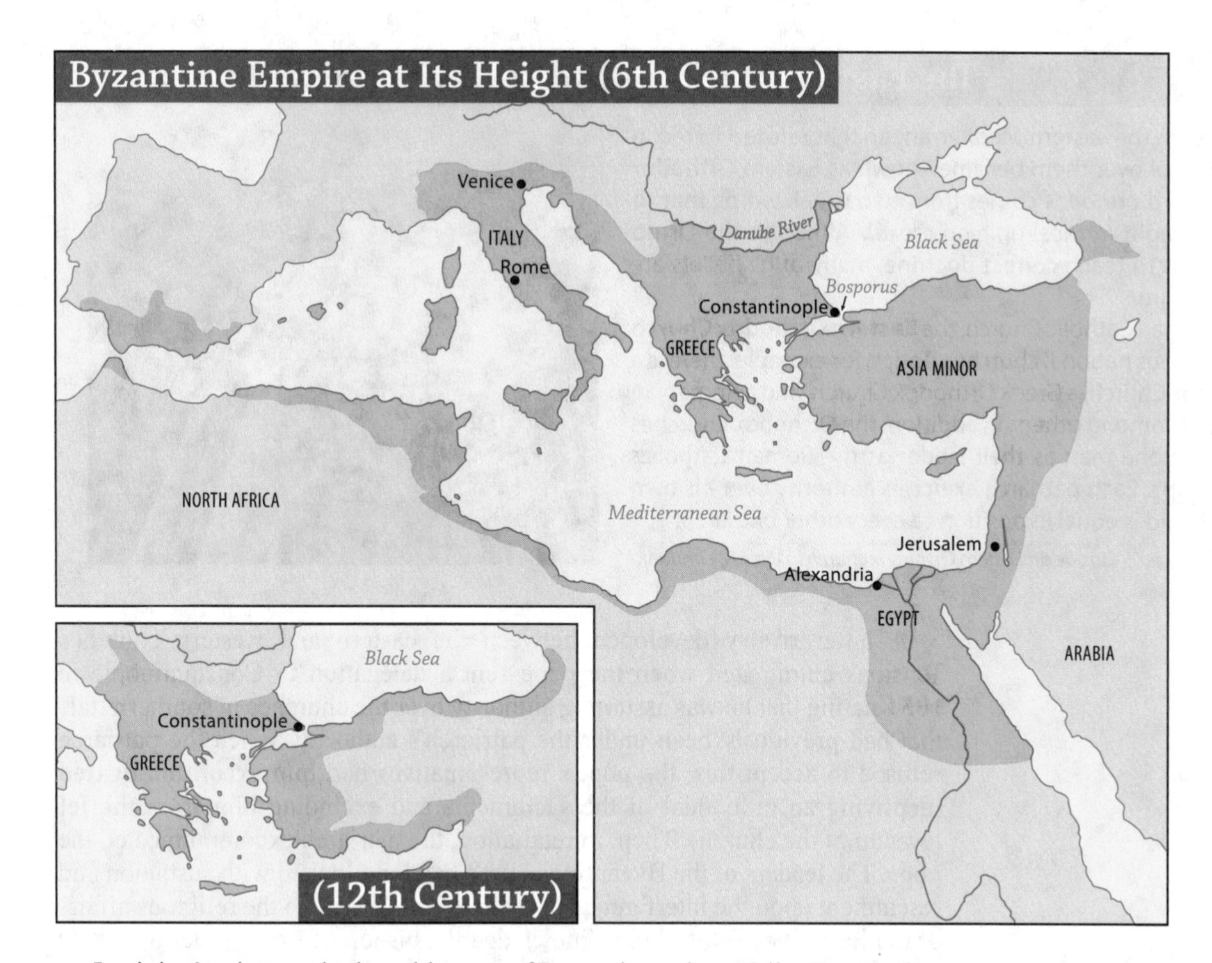

Justinian's reign marked a golden age of Byzantine culture. Like Constantine, he desired to restore the grandeur of ancient Rome. Sparing no expense, he initiated an extensive building program to construct churches, public buildings, aqueducts, and roads both in the capital city and throughout the empire. He also patronized Byzantine art. From this period comes the finest example of Byzantine architecture, the Church of **Hagia Sophia** (HAH-juh so-FEE-uh), meaning "Holy Wisdom."

Even so, Justinian left his successors with an empire beset by many problems. In his attempts to reclaim the West, he had neglected the defense of the empire's eastern and northern borders. Likewise, his costly military campaigns, coupled with his massive building program, left the empire financially drained. Thus it may be said that Justinian took the Byzantine Empire to the height of glory but left it at the brink of ruin.

An Excerpt from the Justinian Code

The imperial majesty should be not only made glorious by arms, but also strengthened by laws, that, alike in time of peace and in time of war, the state may be well governed, and that the emperor may not only be victorious in the field of battle, but also may by every legal means repel the iniquities of men who abuse the laws, and may at once religiously uphold justice and triumph over his conquered enemies.

Eastern and Western Churches Separate

When Constantine founded "New Rome," he established not only a new political capital but also a new religious center. He desired Constantinople to be a Christian city, a "new Jerusalem." Under his influence, Christianity became the favored religion of the Roman Empire. It was quite natural for "Constantine City" to rise to a place of honor in the structure of the organized church; it became one of the five patriarchal cities, second only to Rome in prestige. The bishop of Rome (later to become the pope) became the most important religious leader in the West; the patriarch of Constantinople held that position in the East.

The Eastern Orthodox Church

The churches in the eastern Mediterranean that refused to recognize Rome's control over them became known as Eastern Orthodox churches. The word *orthodox* comes from two Greek words that together mean "straight *(orthos)* opinion *(doxa)*." Although the Orthodox church claims to teach correct doctrine, many of its beliefs are contrary to Scripture.

Unlike the Roman Catholic Church, the **Eastern Orthodox Church** is made up of various national churches. Today, for example, there is a Russian Orthodox Church, a Greek Orthodox Church, and a Romanian Orthodox Church, among others. In addition, the Orthodox churches do not recognize one man as their leader as the Roman Catholics recognize the pope. Each patriarch exercises authority over his own national church and is equal in position to every other patriarch.

Inside an Eastern Orthodox church in Vilnius, Lithuania

A bitter rivalry developed between the eastern and western churches. Tensions culminated when the pope sent a delegation to Constantinople in **1054** stating that he was assuming authority over the churches in southern Italy that had previously been under the patriarch's authority. When the patriarch refused to accept this, the pope's representatives had him **excommunicated** (depriving an individual of the sacraments and excluding him from the fellowship of the church). Then, in retaliation, the patriarch excommunicated the pope. The leaders of the Byzantine church had long looked with suspicion and resentment upon the interference of the bishop of Rome in the religious affairs of the East. They refused to acknowledge the bishop of Rome's claim that his authority was supreme over all churches (see p. 180). East and West differed over such things as when to celebrate Easter, whether parish priests should marry, and whether the church should use **icons** (EYE kahnz)—painted images of Christ and the saints, which some thought to be idolatrous.

Each church developed a distinctive character. In the West the organized church incorporated into the Christian faith some of the pagan practices of ancient Rome and the Germanic tribes. Greek and Oriental ideas strongly influenced the eastern church. This adoption of nonbiblical elements helped to create the Roman Catholic Church in the West and the Byzantine or Eastern Orthodox Church in the East.

The church in the East became one of the most powerful institutions in the Byzantine Empire. Closely linked to the political framework of the empire, it gradually emerged as the state church. The Byzantine emperor was at the same time the head of the state and the protector of the church and its teachings. This relationship was not found in the West after the fall of Rome. People in the West looked primarily to the bishop of Rome, instead of a king or emperor, for leadership.

The Empire Under Siege

The Byzantine Empire experienced both success and failure during the period from the sixth to the fifteenth centuries. She enlarged her empire repeatedly, only to see the gains erased by outside forces. During the fourth and fifth centuries she endured strong barbarian attacks. After Justinian's reign in the sixth century, the empire was besieged on almost every side for several hundred years. From the West came the Lombards, a Germanic tribe that conquered most of Italy. From the North came the Slavs and the Bulgars, who settled in the Balkan Peninsula. Out of the East came the Persians, who sought to restore the glory of the Persian Empire. Although often weak and on the brink of collapse, the Byzantine Empire managed to stave off all these invaders.

In the seventh century the Byzantine Empire had to reckon with a new and energetic force—the Arab Muslims. The Muslims, advancing from the Arabian Peninsula, smashed the Byzantine defenses both on land and at sea. Soon they threatened Constantinople itself. But the "city protected by God" (as it was called) withstood the Arab attacks.

Constantinople was aided by its defensible location, its strong fortifications, and a new secret weapon called "Greek fire." Though the Byzantines stopped the Muslim expansion into southeastern Europe, they lost Syria, Palestine, Egypt, and North Africa. The Byzantine Empire at one time encompassed the Mediterranean Sea; by the eighth century its territory had been greatly reduced.

Between 850 and 1050 the Byzantine Empire gradually recovered her former strength and prosperity. No longer did she remain on the defensive; she pushed back the Muslims and reasserted herself as the dominant power in the Mediterranean. This period of military success reached its height under **Basil II** (976–1025). Known as the "Bulgar Slayer," Basil crushed the Bulgars in the Balkan region and added their kingdoms to the empire. The Byzantines not only reclaimed some of the territory they held during Justinian's day but also revived their commercial and cultural interests. Constantinople abounded with the riches of trade, art, and architecture. Merchants and missionaries carried these achievements to other lands; many of these lands still bear the marks of Byzantine culture.

After two centuries of expansion, new obstacles confronted the empire. The growth of commercial rivals—especially the city of Venice, in Italy—challenged Byzantine trade supremacy in the eastern Mediterranean. Competition from Venetian merchants cost the empire sorely needed resources and markets. At the same time, the **Seljuk Turks** emerged as a powerful force in the East. These Turks, originally nomadic tribes from central Asia, had adopted Arab culture and the Islamic religion. The important Byzantine territory of Asia Minor fell to these fierce warriors in 1071, when they annihilated the Byzantine army at the **Battle of Manzikert** (MAN zih kurt). (Since that day, Asia Minor has remained under the control of the Turks.) Fearful that Constantinople would fall, the desperate Byzantine emperor appealed to the Christians in the West for aid. The West responded by sending several military expeditions, known as the **Crusades**, to free the East—especially the Holy Land—from these Muslim invaders.

In 1204 an invading army breached the defenses of Constantinople. The invaders captured and looted the city, slaughtering both young and old. They reveled in drunken orgies before the altars of the Hagia Sophia. Surprisingly, these soldiers were not the infidel Muslims, but supposed Christian warriors from the West on a "holy" Crusade. Venetian merchants had enlisted the aid of these greedy Crusaders and had transported them to Constantinople so that they might destroy Venice's commercial rival. Neither their cause nor their conduct was holy.

Although Byzantine forces later recaptured Constantinople, the Byzantine Empire never fully recovered from the destruction it had suffered.

For two centuries the empire continued to exist, but in a state of steady decline. The empire finally came to an end in **1453**, when a new wave of Muslim invaders, the **Ottoman Turks**, sacked Constantinople and killed the last Byzantine emperor.

Greek Fire

One reason Constantinople was able to withstand enemy sieges was her secret weapon known as "**Greek fire**." This weapon, which the Byzantines acquired in the seventh century, was an explosive mixture of naphtha oil, sulfur, and saltpeter. Soldiers squirted it from tubes or threw clay pots containing this flammable liquid at the enemy. Greek fire ignited spontaneously and burned even on water. In fact, it could not even be extinguished with water. This weapon proved to be particularly effective against wooden ships and enabled the Byzantines to control the Mediterranean Sea for many centuries.

THROUGH EYES OF FAITH

The Fall of Constantinople

If Constantinople was a Christian city, why did God let it fall to the Muslims?

____

____

____

____

____

____

____

____

____

The Fall of Constantinople, May 30, 1453

The Hagia Sophia was crowded. Every able-bodied person was in attendance—even the emperor Constantine XI. The light from many candles illuminated the mosaics of Justinian and his empress. This was a somber occasion. Weary from months of fighting the Ottoman Turks, the people of Constantinople gathered for the last time in their great church and asked God for help on the morrow. When the service was over, every man hurried back to his position on the wall.

At dawn the Turkish bombardment began again. Since April 12, the Turks had been using catapults to hurl rocks weighing up to twelve hundred pounds at the walls of the city. At one particular place they had succeeded in breaching the wall. However, they were unable to enter Constantinople because of the wide moat surrounding the city. As they built bridges over the moat and brought up siege towers to scale the walls, the Byzantines burned them with Greek fire. The Turks also tried tunneling under the walls, but the Byzantines dug tunnels to meet them and again used Greek fire and poison gas on those underground.

However, the Byzantines knew that the city's downfall was inevitable. The Turks had been able to fill in the moat at the place where the city wall had been broken down. At dawn on May 30, 1453, waves of Turkish soldiers charged the gap in the wall, but the Byzantines repulsed them several times. Sometime during the fighting, Constantine XI joined his soldiers; his presence, however, did not influence the outcome of the battle. The greater number of Turks finally overpowered the city's defenders. By nightfall Constantine XI was dead, and Constantinople was in the hand of the Turks

Byzantine Civilization Contributions

When the Turks brought an end to the Byzantine Empire, they destroyed the protective barrier that for hundreds of years had shielded the West against the spread of Islam. This protection had given the West time to recover from the long period of chaos that followed the collapse of Rome. In addition, the Byzantine civilization was important in its own right. It was the means by which the classical heritage of Greece and Rome was preserved and transmitted to the West.

While the size of the Byzantine Empire had gradually diminished from its peak under Justinian, the influence of the Byzantine civilization had expanded. The many achievements of the Byzantine society had attracted the less civilized peoples who came into contact with the empire. They marveled at the material wealth that abounded at Constantinople and tried to copy the effective governmental system that the Byzantines had adapted from ancient Rome.

Mosaic of Christ from the Hagia Sophia

Furthermore, many of the pagan peoples of eastern Europe had embraced Orthodox Christianity along with Byzantine culture. Two Byzantine missionaries, the brothers **Cyril** and **Methodius** (muh THO dee us), had gone to the Slavic peoples of Russia and southeastern Europe. The Slavic tribes did not have a written language, so Cyril and Methodius developed one for them. Their system, a modification of the Greek alphabet, became the foundation of the Slavic written language.

Byzantine art and architecture demonstrate the wealth and splendor of this once-mighty empire. Byzantine art was primarily intended to glorify God; it adorned the interiors of churches. Craftsmen excelled in wall paintings, carved ivory, illuminated manuscripts (manuscripts decorated with ornate letters or designs in bright colors or precious metals), and marble and metal work. A favorite decorative art—the **mosaic**—graced the walls and ceilings of Byzantine churches. By inlaying tiny pieces of glass or stone in wet cement or plaster, artists could form beautiful patterns and pictures.

The churches housed some of the best examples of Byzantine art, and they were themselves the best examples of Byzantine architecture. Byzantine architects demonstrated a mastery of design and engineering skill. They especially excelled in domed structures. The most famous of Byzantine structures is the beautiful Hagia Sophia, sometimes

The Meaning of Icons

A characteristic feature of Eastern Orthodoxy is its use of icons. They occupy prominent places in churches and homes and are held in great reverence by the Orthodox faithful. Religious art in itself is not wrong, but many of the Orthodox seem to have turned their icons into objects of worship by kissing them and burning incense before them.

Although we frequently speak about looking at a painting, the Orthodox believe that one should not look at icons. Instead, the viewer should direct his mind beyond the icon to the heavenly reality it represents. For example, one viewing a picture of the apostle Peter should not see a painted figure but should see in his mind's eye the real Peter in heaven. The icon is seen as a means of achieving a spiritual connection with the person depicted and the heavenly realm.

Left: *Mary, Tikhvinskaya Theotokos (Bogoroditsa), Novgorod School, Mid 16th century,*
Right: *Mary, Iverskaya Theotokos (Bogoroditsa), Russian, 20th Century,*
Both: *From the Bob Jones University Collection*

In an effort to make the painted figures appear otherworldly, the artists developed several techniques that remained unchanged for many centuries. For example, there are no shadows in icons because the shadows imply something material and earthly. Second, historical scenes that occurred inside a building are often shown outside with the building in the background. In this way, the painters hoped to elevate the event beyond its historical context and give it universal meaning. Third, the figures in icons are portrayed unrealistically with very thin noses, small mouths, and large eyes. This illustrates the fact that the figures supposedly conquered their five senses (their earthly selves) and lived in holiness according to their spiritual nature.

Even the colors used by the icon painters had special meaning. For example, the monks usually portrayed Christ wearing garments of red, blue, and gold. The red symbolized love, and the blue and gold represented truth and heaven. In pictures of the transfiguration, Christ is usually shown wearing white—a symbol of light and holiness.

Notice the icons pictured here. The one on the left is from the sixteenth century, and the one on the right is from the twentieth century. Notice that in spite of some obvious differences, both portray the Madonna and child in a similar fashion. (The one on the right has a decorative cover.) Unlike Western art with its changing styles, icon painting has for centuries remained basically unchanged.

called the Santa Sophia. In size and rich adornment, no other church in the empire could equal it. It became a model of architectural design that was copied in other cities and lands. Still standing today, its great dome reaches a height of 180 feet and has a diameter of 108 feet. Procopius, a sixth-century historian, describes the splendor of the Hagia Sophia as "a spectacle of marvellous beauty, overwhelming to those who see it, . . . for it soars to a height to match the sky, and as if surging up amongst the other buildings it stands on high and looks down upon the remainder of the city, adorning it. . . . It exults in an indescribable beauty."

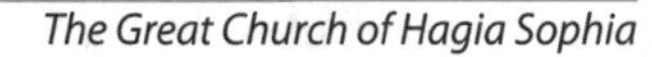

The Great Church of Hagia Sophia

Section Quiz

1. List four titles which were given to the city of Constantinople.
2. What Byzantine emperor sought to restore the greatness of the Roman Empire by extending the boundaries of the Byzantine Empire to their greatest extent?
3. What is the name of the organized church that developed within the Byzantine Empire?
4. What decorative art did Byzantine artists create by using tiny pieces of glass or stone in wet cement or plaster?
5. What is the name of the most famous of the Byzantine architectural structures?

II. Early Russia

Beginnings

Looking at a map of the modern world, one cannot help noticing the enormous size of the land of Russia. Covering about one-sixth of the globe, it is the world's largest country. Russia occupies a large portion of two continents—Europe and Asia. Within her borders is a population composed of people of many different racial and linguistic backgrounds. The largest group is the **Slavs**, whose ancestors played a major role in establishing the early Russian state.

No one knows for sure where the Slavs first lived. They moved into eastern Europe as the Germanic tribes there migrated farther westward. Eventually three groups emerged: the West Slavs—the Poles and Czechs—settled in the Danube region; the Yugo-Slavs, or "South Slavs," moved down into the Balkan area; and the East Slavs, the ancestors of the Russians, occupied the territory between the Baltic and Black seas. Running through the land of the East Slavs is a network of rivers along which they built their village communities. The Slavs participated in the prosperous trade that flourished along these river highways.

Russia About 1000

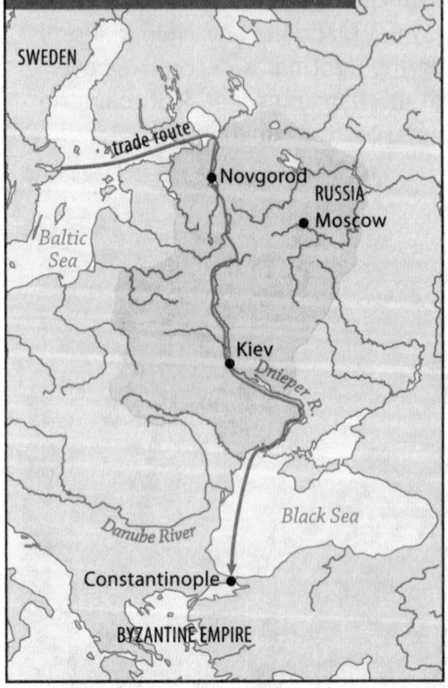

During the eighth and ninth centuries, bands of Swedish Norsemen, known to the Slavs and Byzantines as **Varangians** (vuh RAN jee UNZ), sailed south from the Baltic Sea using the waterways. Like the Vikings who terrorized western Europe (see p. 191), the Varangians plundered Slavic villages along the rivers. Attracted by the possibilities of opening trade routes with the Byzantine and Muslim civilizations, many Varangian warriors settled along the inland waterways. Slavic settlements often hired Varangian warriors to protect their villages from other raiding tribesmen.

In the city of Novgorod (NAWV guh RAWT), according to the one traditional account, the Slavs invited Varangian rule: "Our whole land is great and rich, but there is not order in it. Come to rule and reign over us." Whether by invitation or by force, the Varangian warrior **Rurik** gained control of Novgorod about 862. That year is the traditional date for the beginning of Russian history. Rurik established the first ruling dynasty of Russia. His successors captured and ruled other cities in the region, the most important of these being Kiev (KEE ef). Yet despite their military superiority, the Varangians were greatly outnumbered by the Slavs and were soon absorbed by the populace.

Shortly after Rurik's death, Kiev became the center of the early Russian state. This city was located on the shores of the Dnieper (NEE pur) River, the major route for trade with the Byzantine Empire. For three centuries Kiev held the prominent position in a loose confederation of city-states. Established by Varangian princes, this confederation sought to further the region's common commercial interests and protect important trade routes. The area under Kievan influence became known as Russia, perhaps deriving its name from the Slavic designation of the Norsemen, ***Rus***, meaning, "rowers" or "seafarers."

Russian Orthodox church with a dome shaped like an onion

Byzantine Cultural Influences

Russian culture bears a strong Byzantine imprint. Because of early commercial contacts, Kiev and Constantinople developed close cultural ties. A significant event in Russian history was the adoption of Byzantine Christianity by the Kievan ruler **Vladimir I** in 988. He ordered the destruction of pagan idols and temples and established Orthodox Christianity as the official state religion. By adopting Orthodox Christianity rather than Roman Christianity, Russia was virtually cut off from the mainstream of Western thought. She came under the influences of the Eastern church and Byzantine culture.

The influence of the Orthodox church upon Russia was great. The Russian language profited from the Slavic alphabet, which the Byzantine missionaries Cyril and Methodius had adapted from the Greek alphabet. This alphabet enabled the Russians to translate Greek works into their Slavic language. It also prompted the growth of native Russian literature. Russian artists made beautiful icons like those adorning Byzantine churches. The Russians even patterned their cathedrals after Byzantine models. One feature of their cathedrals, however, is uniquely Russian—the onion-shaped dome.

For All the Wrong Reasons

According to legend, the Russian ruler Vladimir decided that he would establish a monotheistic religion among his people to replace their polytheistic, pagan beliefs. Before he decided what that new religion would be, he investigated what the world had to offer. He summoned representatives of Islam, Judaism, Roman Catholicism, and Eastern Orthodoxy and had each of them explain why his religion was best. After listening to the claims of each, Vladimir sent out envoys to observe these religions on a firsthand basis. When they returned, he made his decision.

First of all, Vladimir rejected Islam because the Koran forbade the drinking of alcoholic beverages. Second, he rejected Judaism because the Jewish people had been defeated and scattered across the world. Since their God did not seem strong enough to protect them, He could not be counted on to protect the Russian people, thought Vladimir. Third, the king rejected Roman Catholicism because the Catholic churches were dark and damp and the services were dull. Vladimir chose Eastern Orthodoxy.

The reason for his choice was simple. When his envoys returned from Constantinople, they enthusiastically described a service they had attended at the Hagia Sophia. They told him how the whole church seemed to shine as the mosaics reflected the light of the burning candles. They told him of the beautiful music, the clouds of incense, and the gorgeous robes of the patriarch who led the service. Impressed by what he heard, Vladimir adopted Eastern Orthodoxy. The Russian Orthodox Church was established, and Vladimir was "converted" to Christianity.

Today many people are just like Vladimir. They choose religion that makes them comfortable or that appeals to their intellect. However, Christ told His disciples. "If any man will come after me, let him deny himself, and take up his cross daily, and follow me" (Luke 9:23). Christ does not promise His followers a life of ease and pleasure. But those who know Christ as Savior would not exchange the riches of their faith for all the manmade religions the world has to offer.

Height of Kievan Russia

Kiev reached the zenith of its power and prestige during the reign of **Yaroslav** (yuh ruh SLAHV) "the Wise" (1036–54). Yaroslav greatly strengthened the city's position of leadership; Kiev became known as the "Mother of Russian Cities." His reign saw the greatest territorial expansion of the early Russian state. He gained international recognition by negotiating marriage alliances between his princely house and the royal families of France, Sweden, Norway, Poland, Hungary, and the Byzantine Empire. He also sponsored the earliest Russian code of laws, which combined Slavic tribal law and Byzantine law.

Yaroslav desired to make Kiev a rival of Constantinople. In size, wealth, and culture, Kiev became one of the leading cities of its day. It was a prosperous center of commerce—a meeting place of the world's merchants. Yaroslav's patronage of art, education, and the church attracted Byzantine painters, architects, teachers, and priests. With the aid of Byzantines, the Russians constructed their own cathedral of Hagia Sophia. Kiev also boasted schools, libraries, monasteries, cathedrals, and fortifications that Yaroslav built.

After the death of Yaroslav, Kiev lost its prominence among the Russian cities. Civil war broke out among Yaroslav's heirs over succession to the throne. Cities that had formerly looked to the Kievan rulers as the Grand Princes of Russia began to assert their independence. New trade routes and commercial centers drew away much of Kiev's wealth and population. The death blow to the early Russian state came in the thirteenth century, when the **Tartars**—fierce Mongolian warriors from central Asia—swept into Russia (see p. 168). They destroyed Kiev in 1240 and ruled Russia for more than two centuries, up to the late 1400s. After the decline of Mongol power, a new center of Russian society arose in the north—Moscow.

Section Quiz

1. What ethnic group played a major role in establishing the early Russian state?
2. What city became the center of the early Russian state?
3. What Russian ruler adopted the Eastern Orthodox Church as the official religion of the Russian state?
4. What two Byzantine missionaries developed a written language for the Slavic people of Russia?
5. Under whose leadership did the city of Kiev reach the height of its power and prestige?

1. ______________________
2. ______________________
3. ______________________
4. ______________________
   ____
5. ______________________

III. The Islamic Civilization

The Land of Arabia

The cradle of Islam was Arabia, a large peninsula that extends south of the Fertile Crescent in the Middle East. This peninsula lies between Asia and Africa, bounded by the Persian Gulf in the east and the Red Sea in the west. In land area, it is about one-third the size of the United States. Much of the land is a barren wilderness of deserts and stony plains. Vegetation is sparse and agriculture is limited because of the extreme heat and lack of adequate rainfall. This uninviting environment kept Arabia in relative isolation until the birth of the Islamic religion in the seventh century.

The land of Arabia is adjacent to the Bible lands. As do the Hebrews, many Arabs trace their beginnings back to Abraham: the Hebrews, through his son Isaac; the Arabs, through his son **Ishmael**. Although he was not the child of God's special promise as was Isaac (Gal. 4:22–23), God blessed Ishmael: "I have blessed him, and will make him fruitful, . . . and I will make him a great nation" (Gen. 17:20). Ishmael's descendants lived in the Arabian Peninsula and became a numerous people, just as God had foretold.

Because they had no organized government, there was little unity among Arabs before the advent of Islam. Each Arab's loyalty was to his tribe, and warfare among tribes was frequent. These tribes did not have a common religion. In addition, there were two distinct lifestyles among the people of Arabia. Many of the Arabs traveled through the harsh desert wilderness in independent bands. These nomads, called **Bedouins** (BED oo inz), roamed the desert in search of pastureland and water for their herds of goats, sheep, and camels. Over the centuries the Bedouin way of life has remained relatively unchanged; today they can be seen traveling from oasis to oasis across the desert.

Not all Arabs were desert nomads, however; some lived a more settled life along the outer rim of the peninsula. They established cities along important trade routes or along the coast, where rainfall was more abundant and the land was more fertile. A few of these cities became important trade centers for camel caravans, which carried goods across the desert to and from other lands. Out of one of these cities arose an Arab religious leader whose teaching united the people of Arabia.

The Founding of Islam

Muhammad

Shortly after the Byzantine emperor Justinian died in 565, **Muhammad** (m*oo* HAM id) was born in Arabia. Muhammad (570–632) claimed to be the last and greatest of the prophets of the god **Allah** (AH luh). His teaching became the basis for a new religion known as **Islam** (is LAHM), meaning "submission" (that is, to the will of Allah). His followers are known as **Muslims** ("submitters to Allah").

Muhammad, whose name means "highly praised," was born to a poor family in the city of Mecca in western Arabia. Little is known of his early life except that he became an orphan at the age of six and was reared by his grandfather and uncle. As a young man he entered the employment of a wealthy merchant widow. At the age of twenty-five, he married his employer (fifteen years his senior). For the first time in his life he had financial security. He spent much of his leisure time meditating on religion. The Jewish and Christian influences that he encountered while traveling with caravans impressed him deeply. The Judeo-Christian belief in one God (monotheism) was quite different from the polytheism so prevalent in Arabia.

The Messenger of Allah

In his fortieth year, Muhammad claimed that he had received a vision in which the angel Gabriel gave him a divine revelation to "Recite!"

> Recite thou, in the name of thy Lord who created;—
> Created man from Clots of Blood:—
> Recite thou! For thy Lord is the most Beneficent,
> Who hath taught the use of the pen,—
> Hath taught Man that which he knoweth not.

This incident was the beginning of a series of visions and revelations that allegedly continued throughout his lifetime. Muhammad became convinced that he was the "messenger of God" entrusted with a new revelation for man. He began preaching that there was only one god, Allah, and that he, Muhammad, was Allah's prophet.

On a pilgrimage, modern Muslims visit the Kaaba, located in the courtyard of the great mosque in Mecca.

Muhammad had little success in gaining converts at first. His early followers were family members and close friends. For the most part, the people of Mecca ridiculed him, viewing his teaching as a threat to the city's commercial interests. Mecca was a leading trade center, situated at the crossroads of trade routes in western Arabia. It was also a center of religious worship. At Mecca was located the **Kaaba**, a sacred shrine that housed hundreds of pagan idols. People from all over Arabia made pilgrimages to this shrine. Meccan merchants promoted pagan worship in order to reap financial gain. Large crowds in Mecca meant money in their coffers. The principal attraction was the famous Black Stone, a meteorite built into the wall of the Kaaba. According to later Muslim tradition, the angel Gabriel sent the stone to Abraham, who, along with his son Ishmael, built the shrine. Fearing that Muhammad's teaching about one god would stop the profitable business surrounding the shrine, the leaders of Mecca persecuted Muhammad and his followers.

The Flight to Medina

In **622** Muhammad made a fateful decision. He and his followers decided to flee Mecca and move to Medina (mih DEE nuh), a city several hundred miles to the north. This move is known as the **Hegira** (hih JIE ruh), or "Flight." (It is celebrated as year 1 in the Muslim calendar.) At Medina, Muhammad's following grew rapidly. The citizens of Medina not only accepted Muhammad as their spiritual leader but made him their political and military leader as well. Once in power, Muhammad the persecuted became Muhammad the persecutor. He had previously presented his cause peaceably through preaching, but now he advanced it by military conquest. With an army of militant Muslim followers, he crushed all opposition. A bitter struggle with the rival city of Mecca ended in 630. Muhammad reentered the city of his birth in triumph. He destroyed the idols of the Kaaba and turned it into the center of Islamic worship. Mecca became the holy city of this new religion.

The Teachings of Islam

The Koran

The heart of Islam is the **Koran**, the sacred book of the Muslims. Muslims believe that the archangel Gabriel revealed the words of Allah to Muhammad through many dreams and visions. These revelations formed the basis of his teaching. Many of his followers memorized his teaching; others wrote it down. After Muhammad's death, they compiled his teaching into a book, the Koran, meaning "recitation." Composed of 114 chapters, or *suras*, the Koran is the primary authority on Muslim belief and practice. Dedicated Muslims memorize the entire Koran, which is about the length of the New Testament.

The central doctrine taught by the Koran is the belief in one god, Allah (*al*, "the"; *Ilah*, "god"). According to the Koran,

> *[Allah] is God beside whom there is no god. He knoweth things visible and invisible: He is the Compassionate, the Merciful. He is God beside whom there is no god: He is the King, the Holy, the Peaceful, the Faithful, the Guardian, the Mighty, the Strong, the Most High! Far be the Glory of God from that which they unite with Him!*
>
> *Sura 59:22–23*

Muslims believe that Allah sent more than one hundred thousand prophets to reveal his will to man. But Islam reveres Muhammad as the last and greatest of Allah's prophets and the Koran as Allah's final revelation, superseding all others.

The moral teaching of the Koran serves as a guide for the conduct of its believers. It encourages Muslims to cultivate humility, duty, kindness, and benevolence. It condemns idolatry, murder, gambling, drinking of wine, and adultery. Muslims are taught to fear Allah, because he will reward good and punish evil in the life to come. The Koran describes this "day of judgment":

> *As for him who shall come before his Lord laden with crime—for him verily is Hell: he shall not die in it and he shall not live. But he who shall come before him, a believer, with righteous works,—these! the loftiest grades await them: Gardens of Eden, beneath whose trees the river flow: therein shall they abide for ever. This, the reward of him who hath been pure.*
>
> *Sura 20:76–78*

The Koran reflects many ideas that Muhammad drew from Jewish and Christian sources. It frequently mentions stories and characters of the Old and New Testaments. The Koran honors Noah, Abraham, David, and even Jesus as prophets of Allah. (Muhammad considered Jesus no different from the prophets.) Likewise, the Koran echoes many truths found in the Bible. It emphasizes prayer, moral conduct, a coming day of resurrection and judgment, and the existence of heaven and hell. Islam also stresses the worship of one god and regards the Bible as a holy book.

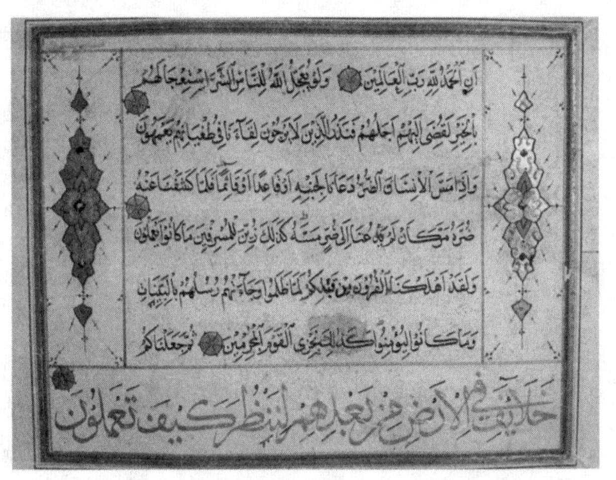
Part of a page from a copy of the Koran

But while Muhammad used many biblical terms in his teaching, he distorted biblical truth. Satan often uses this tactic to deceive people—he dresses error in the clothes of truth. Muhammad claimed to worship the same God as the Christians. But the god of the Koran is not the God of the Bible, for Muhammad rejected the doctrine of the Trinity and denied that Christ is the Son of God (see 1 John 4:2–3). In reference to Christians, the Koran says:

> *O ye people of the book! overstep not bounds in your religion. . . . The Messiah, Jesus, son of Mary, is only an apostle of God. . . . Believe therefore in God and his apostles, and say not, "Three": [there is a Trinity]—forbear—it will be better for you. God is only one God! Far be it from His glory that He should have a son!*
>
> *Sura 4:169*

The Five Pillars

The Koran teaches that heaven is a paradise in which the faithful will enjoy gardens of delight, rivers of wine, and the company of beautiful women. Islam requires every Muslim to perform certain religious duties in order to reach heaven. These are called the **Five Pillars of Islam**:

1. *Shahadah*: The shahadah is the thesis of Islam and must be sincerely believed and recited regularly: "There is no God but Allah, and Muhammad is his prophet."
2. *Salat*: This word means "prayers." Every Muslim must pray five times a day while facing Mecca.
3. *Zakat*: This word means "purification," and it refers to alms (money) that the devout are to give to the poor.
4. *Sawm*: The sawm is a required fast that all Muslims are to observe from sunrise to sunset during the sacred month of Ramadan (RAM uh DAHN).
5. *Hajj*: The hajj is the pilgrimage to Mecca. Every able Muslim is commanded to make at least one hajj in his lifetime.

The Koran teaches Muslims to fear Allah's punishment if these religious practices are not observed.

The shahadah expresses Islam's fundamental error. Muslims believe that the ultimate spokesman for divine truth is Muhammad. The message given to him, preserved in the Koran, is the final word from heaven. The Bible, however, reserves this high calling for Jesus Christ. He is the Word of God, the ultimate revealer of the Father (John 1:1–3, 18; Heb. 1:1–5). Islam does honor Jesus as a good man and an important prophet, but it refuses to give Him the full honor He demands.

This refusal has led Islam to two critical contradictions. First, Islam praises Jesus as a prophet of God and accepts the writings of His apostles, but it rejects Jesus's most important claims. Many Muslims seeks to resolve this conflict by asserting that modern versions of the New Testament are quite different from the New Testament available in Muhammad's time. However, there exist today many copies of the New Testament books that were available in Muhammad's day. All of them teach the doctrines that Muslims deny; chiefly, that Jesus is the Son of God and that He died to pay for the sins of His people.

A second contradiction concerns the death of Jesus and its implications. Islam denies that Jesus came to save people from sin. In fact, it denies even that He died on the cross. Nevertheless, the Koran regularly speaks of Allah as a God of justice who is at the same time a God of mercy and forgiveness. But Allah cannot be just *and* forgiving if Jesus never died to pay the penalty for sin. Without the death of Jesus, Allah could be just *or* forgiving. He could not, however, be both.

Sunni or Shiite Islam

The basic difference between Sunni and Shiite Islam is based on beliefs concerning Muhammad's successor.

The Sunnis believe that Muhammad did not appoint a successor and one should be appointed by the Muslims themselves. Therefore, the caliphate was established. The *caliph* was a temporal leader who fulfilled the role of judge, administrator, and general but was neither the community's spiritual leader nor a prophet like Muhammad.

Shiite Islam believes that Muhammad intended Ali, his son-in-law, to be his successor with worldly power and his spiritual heir. The Shiite leader was called *imam* rather than *caliph*.

Today, in Sunni Islam the imam is the leader of worship in a mosque. In Shiite Islam there is an unbroken succession of imams after Ali, and certain imams are thought to be hidden by Allah for protection.

The Spread of Islam

By the time of his death in 632, Muhammad had united much of Arabia under Islam. But he died without having appointed a successor. This presented a serious problem for Islam and the Arab people. Who should succeed Muhammad as the rightful leader of new religion and the emerging Arab state? The closest friends of Muhammad chose his first four successors from among themselves. These men, who were called **caliphs** (KAY lifs; "successors"), directed the affairs of Islam, exercising spiritual, political, and military authority. The first caliph was **Abu Bakr** (AH-boo BAH-kur) 632–34, father of one of Muhammad's wives and early convert of Muhammad. He and the three caliphs (Umar 634–44, Uthman 644–56, and Ali 656–61) who followed him initiated a policy of military conquest that led to the creation of a vast Arab empire founded upon the Islamic religion.

With amazing speed, Arab warriors burst forth from the desert homeland, conquering Palestine, Syria, Egypt, Iraq, and Persia. Many factors contributed to this rapid expansion:

1. A desire for fertile, productive land. Since their land was barren and unable to support a growing population, the Arabs sought an escape from the poverty of the drought-stricken Arabian peninsula through conquest.
2. The weakness of the Byzantine and Persian empires in the seventh century. Years of constant warfare had left those two rivals exhausted and their territories vulnerable to attack.
3. Islam, which united the Arab people around a common cause. The Arabs viewed each conquest as a ***jihad*** (jih HAHD; "holy war"). With their swords they defended the honor of Islam. Their religious fervor prduced a fierce fighting spirit—a fanatical zeal intensified by the promise that a Muslim's death in battle assured him of entrance into paradise.

THIS MOMENT IN HISTORY

Abu Bakr

Explain Abu Bakr's importance in the spread of Islam and the founding of the Islamic Empire.

____

____

____

____

____

____

____

____

Umayyad Caliphate (661–750)

In 661 a Muslim general seized the office of caliph (the caliphate). He moved the political capital of the empire from Medina to Damascus and established the rule of the **Umayyads** (oo MY yadz). The Umayyads created a

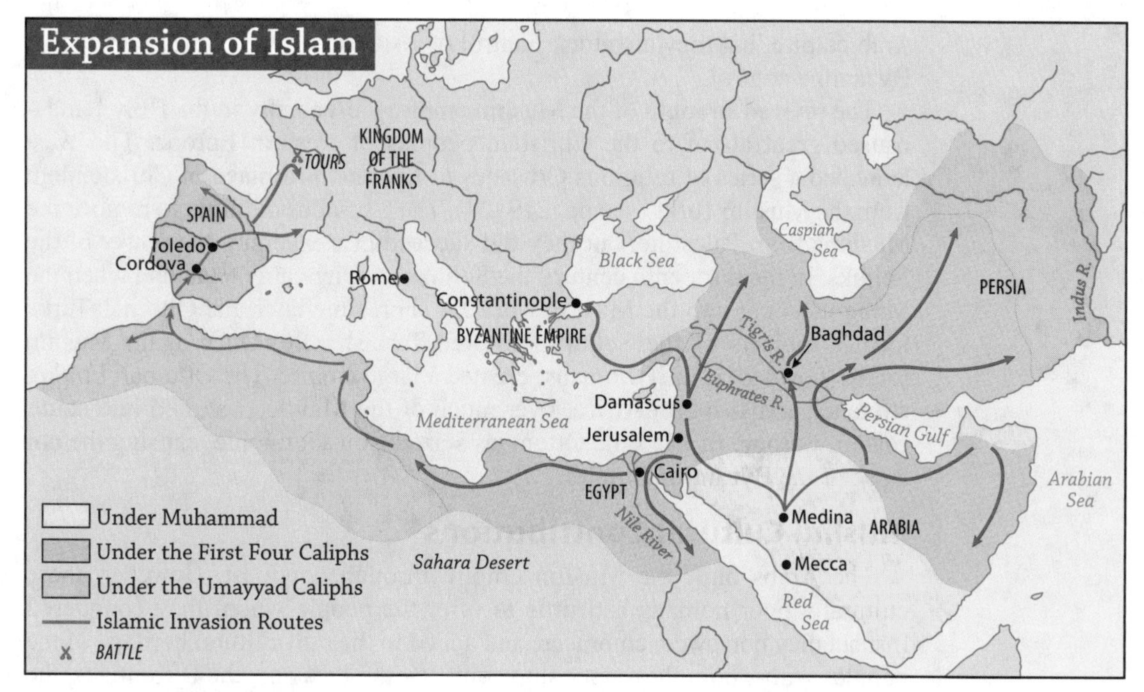

hereditary dynasty, ending the practice of selecting the caliph from among the close friends and relatives of Muhammad.

The Umayyads continued Arab expansion. Muslim forces pushed eastward into India, laid siege to Constantinople, and advanced across North Africa. In 711 they crossed the Mediterranean and invaded Spain. They pressed on into southern France until they were stopped by the Franks at the **Battle of Tours** (see p. 186). The year of this battle was 732, exactly one hundred years after the death of Muhammad. Although the Muslim advance into Europe was stopped, the Arabs could boast of an empire that stretched from Spain to India.

Abbasid Caliphate (750–ca. 1000)

Discontent over Umayyad rule soon mounted: a growing number of non-Arab Muslims were dissatisfied with being treated as second-class citizens by Arab rulers. In addition, many Arab Muslims did not consider the Umayyads the rightful successors of Muhammad. In 750 Abbas, a descendant of Muhammad's uncle, overthrew the Umayyad caliph and founded the **Abbasid** (AB uh sid) caliphate. Under the Abbasids, Arab supremacy within the Muslim empire gradually declined. The Abbasids appointed many non-Arabs to high government positions. Also, non-Arabs became increasingly influential in Islamic society.

The Abbasid caliphate marks the peak of the Muslim empire. The Muslims controlled more territory than the ancient Romans did. Its new capital, Baghdad, became one of the world's leading commercial centers, rivaling Constantinople. Likewise, during the Abbasid rule, Islamic culture flourished.

The Turks and the Crusades

The Arabs had been the primary agents in the early spread of Islam. Their military conquests had created the expansive Muslim empire. But during the Abbasid dynasty, the political unity of the Muslim world began to crumble. Disputes over the succession to the caliphate broke out among rival Muslim factions. Soon independent dynasties appeared, each proclaiming its own caliph. Meanwhile the Seljuk Turks entered the territory of the weakened Abbasids. These fierce and energetic warriors accepted Islam and began a new wave of Islamic expansion. The Seljuks not only reunited much of the former

THROUGH EYES OF FAITH

The Spread of Islam

How did the spread of Islam differ from the spread of Christianity? What does this difference suggest about the origins of these religions?

Arab empire, but they also took control of Asia Minor, which had been under Byzantine control.

The revived strength of the Muslim empire—especially in the Holy Land—caused great alarm to the Christian peoples of western Europe. The West launched a series of religious Crusades to free the birthplace of Christendom from the Muslim Turks (see pp. 219–24). The Crusades did little to remove the Muslims from Palestine, but they did succeed in weakening the power of the Seljuks. In the thirteenth century the Seljuks' empire came to an end when the Mongols swept into the Muslim world. A short time later, the Ottoman Turks, former subjects of the Seljuks, restored Turkish rule. Once again Muslim forces (now led by the Ottomans) created a large empire. The Ottoman Empire stretched across North Africa, over much of the Middle East, and into southeastern Europe. In 1453 the Ottomans seized Constantinople, causing the collapse of the Byzantine Empire.

Muslim Cultural Contributions

The Arabs built the Muslim empire through conquest. However, these culturally poor nomads had little to offer the people whom they conquered. Instead they borrowed, embraced, and added to the rich cultural heritage of the peoples with whom they came into contact—the Persians, the Byzantines, the Egyptians, and the Syrians. By blending the many cultural influences within the empire with the Islamic religion, the Arabs were able to create a unified civilization.

By the middle of the eighth century, the Muslim empire was no longer predominantly Arab. Its capital was moved from Damascus to Baghdad, and it assumed a more Persian aspect. As the empire continued to expand, so did its trade routes. Now Muslim merchants traveled to China, India, and East Africa, bringing back new products and ideas (such as paper from China and mathematics from India). These products and ideas, as well as the achievements of Muslim culture, later found their way to the West as European merchants opened up trade routes to the Middle East.

As Western travelers came to Muslim lands, they were astounded to find silk, muslin (fine cotton), linen, and damask (cloth woven with silver and gold thread). They admired magnificently woven carpets ("Persian" or "Oriental" rugs), finely tooled leather, delicate filigree jewelry (ornamental work done with fine wire), engraved silver and gold, and exquisite knives and swords. Travelers also discovered dates, oranges, lemons, apricots, peaches, and melons, all of which were unknown in the West at that time.

One of the chief ways the Muslims gained knowledge was to translate manuscripts from other lands into Arabic. They translated the writings of Aristotle, Plato, Galen, Hippocrates, Archimedes, Euclid, Ptolemy, and others. They also translated important works from Persia and India. Many of these manuscripts might have been lost had they not been preserved by the Muslims. They built great libraries to house these manuscripts and their Arabic translations.

Medicine

In the field of medicine, the Muslims profited from the Greek writings of Galen and Hippocrates. Muslim doctors put into practical use what they learned from the classics and developed new medical procedures. Two of the most famous Muslim physicians were **al-Rāzi** (AL RAY-zee) and **ibn Sina** (IB-un SEE-nuh; also known as Avicenna). Both men wrote many medical books in which they recorded their practical experience in identifying and treating various diseases. Al-Rāzi is best remembered for his work with smallpox, and ibn Sina for his work with tuberculosis.

Muslim doctors developed amazing surgical skills. They performed such delicate operations as removing cancer from the body and cataracts from the eye. The Muslims also built hospitals throughout the empire. Although they did not know about germs, they suspected that dirt led to disease. Therefore, they tried to keep their patients and hospitals as clean as possible. Furthermore, Muslims had drugstores that filled prescriptions. Government inspectors supervised these druggists to ensure the purity of the drugs.

Literature

In addition to their religious, scientific, and medical writings, the Muslims produced rich and colorful imagery in both their poetry and their prose. Perhaps the most renowned Muslim poet (also a famed mathematician) was **Omar Khayyam** (OH-mar kie-YAHM). His *Rubaiyat* (roo by YAHT; a poem with verses of four lines) remains quite popular in the West. Like most Muslim poetry it is very picturesque.

> The Moving Finger writes; and, having writ,
> Moves on: nor all your Piety nor Wit
> Shall lure it back to cancel half a Line.
> Nor all your Tears wash out a Word of it.
>
> And that inverted Bowl they call the Sky,
> Whereunder crawling coop'd we live and die,
> Lift not your hands to It for help—for It
> As impotently moves as you or I.

Better known to both young and old is *The Thousand and One Nights* (popularly known as *The Arabian Nights*). Among these fanciful tales gathered from all over the Muslim world are the stories of "Aladdin and His Wonderful Lamp" and "Ali Baba and the Forty Thieves."

Tales of Arabia

The Thousand and One Nights is about a sultan named Shahriyar who each day weds a new bride and then executes her the next morning. One day he marries Scheherazade, a beautiful and intelligent young maiden. That night for Shahriyar's entertainment, she tells him a story but stops at the climax. Eager to hear the conclusion, the sultan decides to wait another day and then execute her. The next night Scheherazade finishes her story but then begins another, stopping again at an exciting part. Shahriyar once more decides to wait so that he can hear the conclusion. This goes on for a thousand and one consecutive nights. At the end of that time, the sultan is so much in love with Scheherazade that he abandons all thought of executing her, and they live happily ever after.

Mathematics

The Muslims borrowed much of their basic mathematical knowledge from India. The so-called Arabic numerals are of Hindu origin. So are the decimal system and the concept of zero, which the Muslims popularized. The Muslims studied and improved algebra, which came from India, as well as the geometry and trigonometry of the Greeks.

Art and Architecture

Religion plays an important part in Muslim art. Muhammad is said to have forbidden the representation of humans and animals in art. He feared that the people might worship the statues or painting of living things. Therefore, Muslim artists developed decorative designs that are more abstract than representational. The most common patterns found in Muslim art are abstract designs of stems and leaves and geometric figures. Muslim artists also excelled in **calligraphy**, the art of beautiful writing. They adorned the walls of buildings with verses from the Koran written in beautiful Arabic script. One of the most honored forms of Islamic art was manuscript illumination; Muslim artists used miniature paintings and decorative colors and ornamentation to illustrate or "illuminate" their books—especially the Koran.

The Dome of the Rock in Jerusalem makes that city important to Muslims.

In architecture, however, Muslim art reached its highest achievement. The Muslims drew from the architectural styles of Persia and Byzantium but gradually produced their own unique style. The best examples of Muslim architecture are the **mosques** (MAHSKS; places of Muslim worship). Muhammad did not believe Muslims should build elaborate mosques, since these buildings were only places of prayer. He said on one occasion, as recorded by ibn Sa'd, "The most unprofitable thing that eateth up the wealth of the believer is building."[3] Nevertheless, his followers spent fortunes on their houses of worship.

The typical features of a mosque are its courtyard, minaret, and dome. In the courtyard is a pool for ceremonial washing before prayer. Either as part of the mosque or adjacent to it is a tall **minaret** (tower). From this tower the **muezzin** (myoo EZ in; "crier") calls the faithful to prayer five times a day. One of the characteristic features of Muslim architecture is the dome. It usually covers the main portion of the mosque. Inside, the walls are white and inscribed with quotations from the Koran. Some, however, are highly decorated with tile and mosaic designs. In one wall of each mosque is a niche that indicates the direction of Mecca, toward which a Muslim prays.

Section Quiz

1. What name is given to the Arab nomads who roam the desert in search of pastureland and water?
2. Who claimed to be the last and greatest of the prophets of Allah?
3. What became the "holy" city of the Islamic faith? What is the most sacred shrine in that city?
4. What is the name of the holy book of Islam?
5. What is the shahadah? What two critical contradictions does it lead to in Islam?
6. List the two caliphates that ruled the Islamic empire from the seventh to the eleventh centuries. Beside each caliphate, write the name of the capital city of its empire.
7. What is the name for Muslim places of worship, which are the best examples of Muslim architecture?

1. ______________________
2. ______________________
3. ______________________
____
4. ______________________
5. ______________________
____
____
____
6. ______________________
____
7. ______________________
____

A Glance Behind

This chapter has focused on two remarkable yet opposing civilizations. The first—the Byzantine—preserved Roman culture and learning after the Western Roman Empire collapsed. The second—Islam—also preserved much from the classical world. Although the Byzantine Empire gradually declined in size and political influence, her culture spread northward, particularly into Russia. On the other hand, as the Muslims expanded politically, they spread their culture from Spain to India.

As western Europe slowly recovered from the chaos brought about by the barbarian invasions of the fifth century, she renewed her contacts with the East. These ties stimulated the intellectual rebirth called the Renaissance and the spiritual revival known as the Reformation. Before we turn our attention back to western Europe, however, we will take a brief look at ancient civilizations in the Far East and Africa—civilizations that derived very little from the cultures of the Mediterranean world.

and a Glimpse Ahead

Notes

1. Procopius, *History of the Wars*, trans. H. B. Dewing, 1.24.
2. Ibid., 1.1.
3. K.A.C. Creswell, *A Short Account of Muslim Architecture* (Beirut, Librairie du Liban, 1958), p. 4.

Chapter Review

Can You Define?

excommunicate
icon
Greek fire
Crusades
mosaic
Rus
Bedouin
Allah
Islam
Muslim
Hegira
caliphs
jihad
calligraphy
mosque
minaret
muezzin

Can You Identify?

Byzantine Empire
New Rome
Justinian
Theodora
Nika Revolt
Justinian Code
Hagia Sophia
Eastern Orthodox Church
1054
Basil II
Seljuk Turks
Battle of Manzikert
1453
Ottoman Turks
Cyril
Methodius
Slavs
Varangians
Rurik
Vladimir I
Yaroslav
Tartars
Ishmael
Muhammad
Kaaba
622
Koran
Five Pillars of Islam
Abu Bakr
Umayyad
Battle of Tours
Abbasid
al-Rāzi
ibn Sina
Omar Khayyam

Can You Locate?

Byzantium
Constantinople
Bosporus
Balkans
Venice
Russia
Novgorod
Dnieper River
Kiev
Arabia
Mecca
Medina
Damascus
Baghdad

How Much Do You Remember?

1. List three achievements of Justinian's reign as Byzantine emperor.
2. The Byzantine Empire was constantly besieged during its history. List six groups of foreign invaders that threatened its borders.
3. List the contributions to Russian history of each of the following: Rurik, Vladimir I, and Yaroslav.
4. List the Five Pillars of Islam.
5. Identify the occupation and contribution to Muslim culture of each of the following men: al Rāzi, ibn Sina, and Omar Khayyam.

What Do You Think?

1. Of what significance is Genesis 16:10–12 to the Arab people?
2. Many in the Orthodox church have held great reverence for icons, often to the point of worship. Is this in keeping with the teaching of the Bible? Explain your answer. (See Exod. 20:3.)
3. Because Muhammad drew many of his ideas from the Bible, esteemed Christ as a prophet, and regarded the Bible as a holy book, is Islam a Christian religion? Explain your answer.

7

"The unknown lands"

THE CIVILIZATIONS OF ASIA AND AFRICA

A section of the Great Wall of China snakes across the Chinese landscape.

The "unknown lands" of Asia and Africa have fascinated Westerners for centuries. The Orient, with her silks and spices and her unique cultures, has attracted travelers since early days. Africa's rich natural resources have long spawned a profitable trade with that continent. Despite these few contacts, Africa remained mostly untouched until after the Middle Ages, and most of Asia remained virtually unaffected by Western influences until the twentieth century. In recent times, concern for the millions lost in the darkness of Asian and African religions has prompted Western missionaries to carry the gospel to those lands. In this chapter we first will examine the early histories of the three major Asian civilizations: India, China, and Japan. We will also consider the Mongols, a warring people who built an empire that stretched from the Pacific Ocean westward to eastern Europe. Finally, we will study the culture and heritage of the enormous continent of Africa.

Sunrise in Africa

I. India

India is a land of great diversity. In its **topography** (the physical features of a land), climate, and population, it is a study in contrasts. This triangular subcontinent extends from southern Asia into the Indian Ocean, forming a giant peninsula. Its terrain varies from subtropical rain forest to barren deserts, from low coastal plains to the highest mountain range in the world, the Himalayas. Between the rugged mountain regions in the north and the coastal plains and tropical plateaus of the south lie fertile valleys watered by two great river systems, the Indus and the Ganges. Like the Mesopotamian and Egyptian cultures, the earliest Indian civilization began along riverbanks. The first inhabitants of India settled in river valleys along the Indus and Ganges rivers.

These people must have felt secure from invaders and foreign influences. They were protected by tall mountain ranges in the north and by seas on the east and west. But despite these natural barriers, India did not remain an isolated land. Throughout her history, merchants, foreign invaders, and wandering tribes crossed the mountains along India's northwestern border (through such mountain passes as the Khyber) and settled in the fertile river valleys. As a result, India became a land of many peoples, customs, and languages. From the diverse elements within Indian society, a unique culture developed.

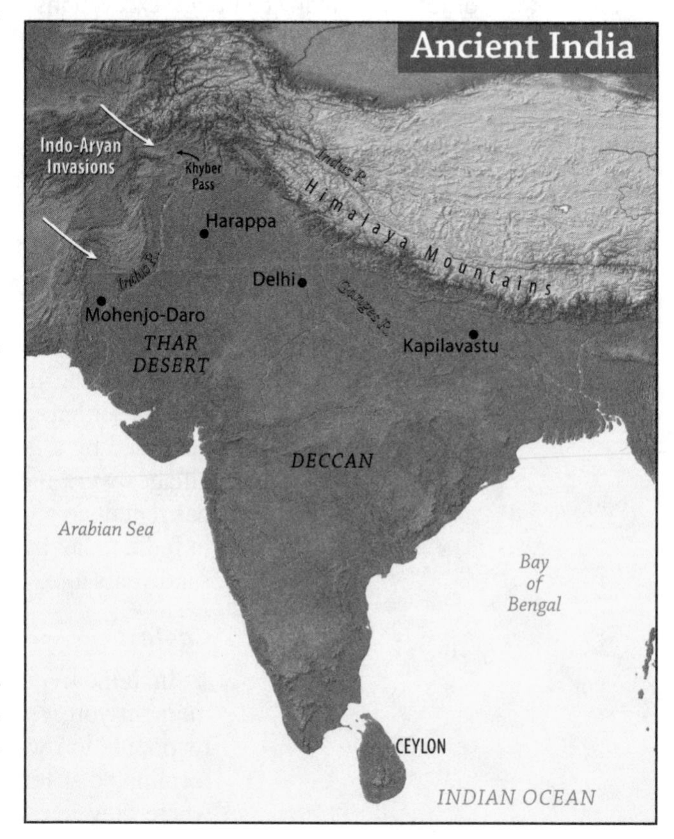

Early Civilization

India derives its name from the Indus River, along whose fertile banks the earliest Indian civilization flourished (ca. 2300 BC). Much of our limited knowledge of this civilization has come from excavations of two of its leading cities: Mohenjo-Daro (moh HEN joh DAH roh) and Harappa (huh RAP uh). These were carefully planned cities with wide, straight streets lined with brick houses. Evidence indicates that these cities had elaborate drainage and sewer systems, which were more advanced than those in most modern Indian villages. Although a great distance separates India and the Near East, the early inhabitants of India carried on trade with Egypt and Mesopotamia. We know from archaeological evidence that the Indus civilization ended suddenly—perhaps by flood or by enemy invasion. It was at this time that a warlike people called the **Aryans** migrated into the Indus Valley.

Mohenjo-Daro

When the city of Mohenjo-Daro in the Indus Valley was first built (ca. 2300 BC), the founders had carefully planned everything. Wide main streets ran from north to south, and small lanes ran east and west. Houses were built with thick, solid walls to keep the dwellings cool during the long, hot summers. The thick walls also made it possible for buildings to have several stories. The builders used kiln-baked bricks, which were of a higher quality than those dried in the sun. Each house was equipped with a well, and drains took dirty water down the streets and out of the city. In the center of the city were huge public baths, which the men used in religious ceremonies. Also in the center of the town was a huge granary.

All this was suddenly and violently destroyed, possibly by Aryan invaders. From unearthed skeletal remains, archaeologists have learned of the swiftness of Mohenjo-Daro's destruction. The remains of two men who were evidently attempting to hide in a well have been found. A group of people, slowed by a small child, died in the streets. Archaeologists have found the skeletons of another group, who thought they could find safety by crouching down behind a wall. One family grabbed all their possessions and tried to escape, but they were caught and brutally murdered. A young couple tried to hide themselves and their child in a corner of the darkest room in the house, but they too did not escape death. The city's destruction was complete. Never rebuilt, it lay forgotten for many centuries; excavations of the site in recent times have revealed the grim ending of Mohenjo-Daro.

The Aryans were a fair-skinned people who came from central Asia sometime after 1500 BC and subdued the non-Aryan people of northwest India. Many historians believe that the Aryans were related to tribes that were invading the Near East, Greece, and Rome about the same time. The Aryans were herdsmen; they kept large numbers of cows and horses. Although they left behind no cities as the Indus civilization did, they did establish a new language in India—**Sanskrit**.

Our knowledge of the Aryans and their influence on Indian society comes not from archaeology, but from a collection of religious literature known as the ***Vedas*** (VAY dus), meaning "knowledge." Preserved in the *Vedas* are early traditions and religious beliefs of the Indians, which were orally passed down from one generation to the next. From Sanskrit literature, we gain insights into the Aryan way of life, which became the basis of Indian culture and tradition. This formative period of Indian history lasted from 1500 to 500 BC.

Key Features of Indian Society

India has one of the oldest cultures in the modern world. The basic characteristics of Indian society, described in the *Vedas*, have changed little from ancient to modern days.

Joint Family

The family has always been one of the most important social units in India. The extended or **joint family** included the children, grandchildren, wives, and close blood relatives of a common ancestor. The oldest male of the group was the dominant authority over the family. When married, sons did not establish their own homes; instead they remained in their father's or grandfather's household. Each family member had his own duties and obligations. The interests of the family came before those of the individual family members. Parents chose the husbands or wives for their children in order to maintain the family's position and honor in society.

Village Life

Unlike the inhabitants of the Indus civilization, who dwelt in cities, the Aryans settled in small rural villages. Family groups living in a village were governed by a headman or a council of village elders. For the most part, the villages were independent and self-governing. Over the centuries village life has remained a vital part of Indian society. It is said that eight out of ten people in India today live in small villages, much as their ancestors did over two thousand years ago.

Caste

Imagine living in a country in which your status in life was determined the moment you were born. India was, and in many ways still is, such a country. Its population was divided into rigid social groups called **castes**. The Indians formulated strict rules governing the life of the members of each caste group: where they lived, what they did (profession), what they wore, what and with whom they could eat, as well as whom they could marry. (Marriage was forbidden outside one's own caste.)

There were between two and three thousand different castes and subcastes in India. Each one fell into one of four broad "class" groups. The most important group was the priests, called the *Brahmans*. Next in rank were the rulers and warriors, followed by the merchants and traders. The lowest class group was the *Sudras* (SOO dras)—composed of servants and serfs. Outside the caste system and at the bottom of the Indian social ladder were the outcastes, or "untouchables." They performed the most menial tasks in society. Members of the caste structure avoided the "untouchables," for mere contact with them was thought to bring defilement. While anyone could improve his status within his caste, no one could change castes. Thus with the caste system there was little change in the village and family life of India. This fact explains in part why Indian society remained nearly the same for thousands of years.

Religion and the Indian Way of Life

Religion has played a dominant role in shaping Indian culture. From India came two religions that have had a major impact on Asian culture: Hinduism and Buddhism.

Hinduism

Hinduism is ingrained in the Indian way of life. It developed from the early culture and traditions of India: her social structure, literature, arts, and customs. It has not only preserved the traditional elements of India's past but also served as a unifying influence in India's diverse society. Because Hinduism has no formal statement of doctrine, it was able to absorb into its system of belief a wide variety of gods and religious concepts found among the many peoples of India. (Hindus believe all religions to be equally true and equally false.) To this day, the vast majority of the people of India are Hindus.

The basic tenets of Hinduism are found in the religious literature of ancient India, namely the *Vedas* and the ***Upanishads*** (oo PAN uh SHADZ; philosophical essays elaborating on the teaching of the *Vedas*). Hindus believe that a great god called **Brahman** permeates everything in the universe. The Hindus acknowledge many gods; all deities, however, are considered only manifestations of the eternal, unchanging Brahman. Since Brahman is not a personal

THROUGH EYES OF FAITH

The Outcastes

Certain aspects of India's caste system remain to this day. Although estimates vary, there may be over 160 million outcastes living in India today. Many of these people have adopted the label "Dalit"—a Hindi word meaning "oppressed." Though it is technically illegal, mistreatment of Dalits occurs routinely in India. Most are denied proper health-care and education. Any Dalit who attempts to rise above his status (perhaps by purchasing property) is likely to be persecuted. What does the Bible say about this issue?

____

____

____

____

____

____

____

____

Hindu temple of Khajuraho

being, he is often referred to as the great soul or **world soul**. The ultimate purpose and goal of man, according to the *Vedas*, is to reunite his soul with the world soul. This is done through the process of reincarnation, in which a man's soul passes through many states (or rebirths) before it escapes the physical world and unites with Brahman. This cycle of rebirths is called the **wheel of life**.

The Hindu believes that a person's deeds in this life determine his status in the next. If he has lived a good life (that is, his good works outweigh his bad), then he will move to a higher caste in the next life. The soul of an evil person may be reborn into a lower caste or even into some form of animal life. By observing the religious rituals and ceremonies prescribed by the Hindu priests and by fulfilling the duties and obligations of his caste, a Hindu believes that he (through repeated rebirths) can ultimately gain release from the "wheel of life" and attain union with the world soul.

Buddha statue

Buddhism

India was also the birthplace of **Buddhism**. The founder of this religion was **Siddhartha Gautama** (sid-DAR-tuh GOU-tuh-muh) (563?–483 BC), later known as Buddha, the "Enlightened One." At the age of twenty-nine, Gautama became troubled over the misery, poverty, and death that he saw in the world. He became convinced that he should devote all his efforts to find the way of deliverance from suffering. Therefore, he renounced his life of luxury, gave up his princely heritage, left his wife and child, and set out to find peace and true happiness. After six frustrating years living as a hermit in self-sacrifice and meditation, Gautama was at the point of despair. Sitting down under a tree, he vowed that he would not move until the truth came to him. According to Gautama, he was pondering the questions of life when he realized the truth and attained enlightenment (ca. 528 BC).

Central to Buddha's teaching are his **Four Noble Truths**: (1) Suffering is part of all existence. (2) Suffering has a cause—selfish desires. As long as man has a craving for pleasure, possessions, and power, he will have sorrow and misery. (3) Suffering can be overcome by destroying selfish desires. (4) If man follows the Eightfold Path, he will destroy selfish desires and end all suffering. This pattern for living includes correct beliefs, intentions, speech, conduct, livelihood, effort, thoughts, and meditations.

Buddhism is a religion built on works and moral behavior. Buddhists believe that man does not need the help of the gods or membership in a higher caste in order to obtain freedom from suffering. Once a man has absolutely freed himself from his selfish cravings, he will no longer be reborn but will enter into *Nirvana* (neer VAH nuh), the state of absolute peace and happiness where one loses himself into nothingness.

Both Hindus and Buddhists believe that man can eventually achieve eternal peace (whether in union with the "world soul" or by freeing himself into nonbeing) by living a good life. The Bible clearly teaches that the final state of all people is either in eternal union or eternal separation from God; and the only way to have union with God is through Jesus Christ, not by living a good life (1 John 5:11–12).

Lack of Political Unity

While many aspects of Indian society have remained the same for centuries, the political history of India has been one of constant change. Through much of her history India has been little more than a patchwork of small rival kingdoms. Successive waves of foreign invaders streamed into the Indian subcontinent. The powerful empires established by these invaders provided brief periods of unity and stability for the Indian peoples.

Mauryan Empire

In 326 BC Alexander the Great threatened India. His armies crossed the Indus River and conquered many small kingdoms in India's northwestern region. Alexander intended to advance farther into India, but when his army refused to continue, he had to turn back. According to traditional accounts, he met a young man named **Chandragupta Maurya** (CHUN-druh-GOOP-tuh MAH-oor-yuh) while in India. As Alexander's empire began to disintegrate after his death, Chandragupta conquered the disorganized and weak kingdoms in the north and created the first strong empire of India—the Mauryan Empire.

The most famous of the Mauryan rulers was Chandragupta's grandson **Asoka**. He extended the Mauryan Empire to include all but the southern tip of India. Sickened by the results of his own bloody conquests, Asoka renounced war and became a convert to Buddhism. He spent much of his reign promoting the Buddhist religion. Asoka is credited with building thousands of Buddhist shrines called stupas (STOO puz). He also had Buddhist teachings inscribed on stone pillars throughout the empire. Many of these stone pillars still stand, providing valuable information concerning Asoka's reign. One of his most far-reaching acts was the sending of Buddhist missionaries abroad. Buddhism soon spread across much of Southeast Asia, where it became a powerful force in other Asian cultures. It did not gain a wide following in India, however. Hindu priests viewed Buddhist teaching as dangerous to the caste system. Fearing that they might lose their prestige and rank in society, they worked against the acceptance of Buddhist beliefs.

Gupta Empire

The first great period of Indian unity was short-lived. Not long after Asoka's death (232 BC), the Mauryan Empire collapsed. The years between the second century BC and the third century AD witnessed new invasions and the rise of small competing kingdoms. However, during this time of turmoil, India did enjoy a profitable trade with Rome and China. Even so, it was not until the fourth century AD, with the rise of the **Gupta** (GOOP tuh) **Empire**, that India entered a new, and perhaps her greatest, era of prosperity and achievement.

One historian has stated that "at the time India was perhaps the happiest and most civilized region of the world." The rulers of the Gupta dynasty reunited northern India under a strong and effective government. Trade flourished and the people prospered materially. India's culture spread throughout Southeast Asia. Her universities attracted students from all over the continent, and she made great strides in the fields of textiles and ironwork. The Gupta Age was also one of the finest periods of Indian art, architecture, literature, and science.

Gupta literature became renowned for its adventurous and imaginative fables and fairy tales. The foremost Indian poet and dramatist of this period was **Kalidasa** (KAH lih DAH suh), whose plays have earned him the title "the

The Buddhist monastic caves at Ajanta, which contain some of India's greatest paintings, were discovered by British tiger hunters in 1819.

Indian Shakespeare." The popularity of various Indian stories soon spread outside India, where many of them found their way into the literature of other lands. (Western authors such as the brothers Grimm and Rudyard Kipling drew upon Indian stories for ideas for their writing.)

This was also an age of advance in mathematics, science, and medicine. Our so-called Arabic numerals originally came from India. Indian mathematicians were among the first to use negative numbers, the decimal, and the zero. Centuries before Isaac Newton, Indian scientists developed their own theories of gravity. Indian astronomers knew that the earth was round and that it rotated on its axis. If in need of medical attention, the people of the Gupta Empire could go to free hospitals where Indian physicians were able to perform many surgical procedures.

During the sixth century the Gupta Empire collapsed under the repeated attacks of the White Huns (perhaps related to the Huns who plagued the Roman Empire during the fifth century). India again entered a period of political disorder; the country became divided into small warring kingdoms. Waves of foreign invaders again entered the land; but as in the past, Hinduism absorbed these foreign elements into Indian society. However, the history of India took a dramatic turn when northern India fell under the domination of Muslims, who brought with them a religion and culture as strong as Hinduism.

After years of constant raids, Muslim warriors conquered much of northern India, where they established a Muslim kingdom in 1206 near the city of Delhi. Almost immediately a conflict arose between the Muslim and Hindu elements within Indian society. This was a struggle not only between two religions, but between two distinct ways of life. The Hindus believed in many gods, but the Muslims acknowledged only one. The Hindus followed the rigid caste system, while the Muslims believed in the equality of all men before their god, Allah. Although Muslim control of northern India ended at the close of the fourteenth century, the hostilities between Hindus and Muslims in Indian society have continued to the present.

Section Quiz

1. Along the banks of what river did the earliest Indian civilization begin?
2. List the four broad class groups under the Indian caste system.
3. What is the cycle of rebirths (the process of reincarnation) called?
4. Identify the two empires which temporarily brought national unity to India.
5. What famous Indian poet earned the title of "the Indian Shakespeare"?

II. China

The Land

At the heart of eastern Asia is the land of China. In ancient days the Chinese named their land the **Middle Kingdom** because they believed China to be the center of the earth. Today more people live in China than in any other country in the world—close to one-fifth of the world's population. In land size, modern China is about the same size as the United States; but China's population is four times greater.

China is one of the world's oldest civilizations. The earliest Chinese lived in the fertile valleys of China's two major river systems: the Huang He (or Yellow) and the Yangtze (YANG see). In this respect, ancient China was similar to other early river-valley civilizations—Mesopotamia, Egypt, and India. But while all these were conquered by hostile armies, China during her early history remained relatively free from outside influences.

China was isolated from other centers of civilization until modern times. The vast Pacific Ocean, the tall Himalaya Mountains, and the huge Gobi Desert hemmed in China on all sides. These geographic barriers gave her security from foreign invasion and influences. She did, however, carry on trade with many countries. Because of the relatively small foreign influence upon Chinese society, the Chinese developed and maintained a unique and stable culture that has remained virtually unchanged from ancient to modern times.

Yangtze River in China

Societal Features

Strong Family Ties

The family was and still is the center of life in Chinese society. Chinese families were large, embracing many generations: parents and their children, grandparents and grandchildren, aunts and uncles, nephews and nieces, cousins and in-laws. Ancestors were also included in the Chinese concept of the family. Many Chinese could trace their family history back hundreds of years.

A major responsibility of every Chinese was to bring honor to his family. One of the worst offenses that a person could commit was to dishonor his ancestors by bringing reproach on the family name. The cult of **ancestor worship** became the leading religion in China. Every Chinese house contained an ancestral altar before which the Chinese burned incense to the spirits of their dead. By caring for their family graves and worshiping before these altars, the Chinese hoped to receive blessings and guidance from their ancestral spirits.

An American historian gives this description of the traditional Chinese family:

> The family had functions which in the modern West are commonly assumed by the state. It educated its youth, cared for its unemployed, disciplined its erring members, and supported its aged. In turn, the state held the family accountable for the misdeeds of its members. . . . The individual was of far less importance than the family. The individual member was to make his earnings available to his less fortunate relatives. . . . Marriage was primarily not for the happiness of those who entered into that relationship, but for the purpose of continuing the family line. No sin was greater than that of dying without leaving male issue to revere the memory of one's ancestors.[1]

Language and Learning

The most noticeable feature of Chinese spoken language is its tonal quality. By varying the tone of voice on a particular syllable, the Chinese can convey more than one meaning. For example, *ma* may mean "mother," "hemp" (an Asiatic plant), "horse," or "to scold," depending upon the pitch of the voice. Communication in China is made difficult by variations in the spoken languages from one region to another. It is often impossible for one Chinese to understand what another is saying.

Although the spoken language varies greatly, China does possess a common written language. Traditional Chinese writing is not based on a simple alphabet as our English system is; the Chinese writing consists of some sixty-five thousand **characters** that represent complete ideas, objects, and sounds. For instance, the word for "good" is a combination of the characters for "girl" and "boy." One has to memorize each character in order to be able to read—a fact that makes reading and writing extremely difficult. Over the centuries the vast majority of the Chinese people have been illiterate. Even the most literate Chinese know only about four thousand characters. It is little wonder that those who master the written language have always been given a place of distinction in Chinese society.

China has been called a "scholar's world." In most other civilizations soldiers, priests, or merchants held prominent positions in society. Through much of Chinese history, however, no social group exceeded the influence of scholars. For the would-be scholar, education (consisting mainly of memorizing classical Chinese literature) began at an early age and demanded total dedication of time and energy. The goal of the learned man was a career in government service. Scholarship was the determining factor in obtaining a position,

Chinese Characters

我們既因信稱義、就藉着我們的主耶穌基督、得與上帝相和。

Romans 5:1

When God scattered Noah's descendants throughout the world (Gen. 11:1–9), they carried with them a knowledge of man's earliest history. They knew of Creation, the Fall, and the Flood. Those who migrated to China seem to have preserved some of these truths in their writing system. Since most Chinese characters tell a story, we can break down the more complex characters into simpler ones and discover the meaning of each part.

to forbid

林

wood or tree

God

For example, the Chinese character meaning "to forbid" tells the story of God's command to Adam in Genesis 2:16–17. God planted two special trees in the Garden of Eden: the tree of life and the tree of the knowledge of good and evil. God commanded Adam not to eat of the tree of the knowledge of good and evil but gave him permission to eat fruit from any other tree in the garden. It is interesting to note, therefore, that the character "to forbid" is made up of "wood" or "tree" (notice that two are indicated) and one of the basic Chinese symbols for God. (This character for God also had the idea of "to command" or "to express").

The scriptural idea of sacrifice (the killing of a spotless animal) is also found in Chinese writing. The verb "to sacrifice" is made up of four major parts: "ox" or "cattle," "sheep," "beautiful" or "unblemished," and "spear" (the weapon by which the animal was killed).

sacrifice ox or cattle sheep beautiful spear

Closely associated with the idea of sacrifice is the concept of righteousness. The character meaning "righteous" or "righteousness" is made up of "lamb" and "me." Notice that when the two characters are combined to create the word *righteous(ness)*, the lamb is placed over the person. In the same manner, Christ, Who is the perfect Lamb of God, covers our sins with His blood.

righteous lamb me

Another interesting study is the character for a boat or ship. It is made up of "small vessel," the number eight, and "person," "population," or "mouth." The largest boat built in antiquity (as far as we know) was the ark. It saved Noah and his family—a total of eight persons.

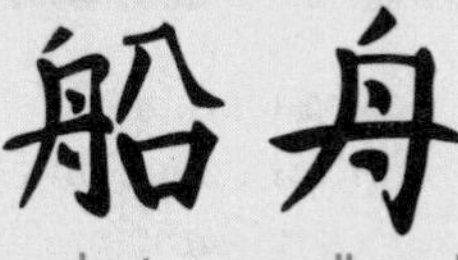

boat small vessel

eight person

The written Chinese language indicates that at some time in the past the Chinese knew God's truth. Although most Chinese people today do not have access to the Scriptures, the written language preserves not only the truth of man's sin but also the wonderful fact of God's saving grace.

whether it be that of a local magistrate or a high government official. Because there were more scholars than government positions, the Chinese developed civil service examinations to choose the best qualified. Those obtaining the highest test scores received these positions.

Chinese Thought and Life

Two native philosophies greatly influenced Chinese life: **Confucianism** (kun FYOO shun iz um) and **Taoism** (TOU iz um). These systems of thought became the heart of China's religious beliefs and practices.

Confucianism

K'ung Fu-tzu (KOONG FOO DZUH) (551?–479 BC) is the most honored teacher in Chinese history. The Chinese call him "the Master"; we know him as **Confucius**. Confucius grew up in poverty during a time of social and political unrest in China. Unable to obtain a political office, he devoted his life to teaching. He believed that through proper conduct man could solve the problems of society and live in complete happiness. His disciples recorded and

The Sayings of Confucius

The philosophy of Confucius is contained in a collection of his sayings and activities called the *Analects*. Some of what Confucius said is remarkably sound advice. This demonstrates how the image of God in man, although fallen, still allows him to discern a certain amount of wisdom in how to live.

• When you have erred, be not afraid to correct yourself.

• It does not greatly concern me . . . that men do not know me; my great concern is my not knowing them.

• To go beyond is as wrong as to fall short.

• It is moral cowardice to leave undone what one perceives to be right to do.

• Where there is habitual going after gain, there is much ill-will.

• Learn, as if never overtaking your object, and yet as if apprehensive of losing it.

• The nobler-minded man . . . will be agreeable even when he disagrees; the small-minded man will agree and be disagreeable.

• Impatience over little things introduces confusion into great schemes.

• The cautious seldom err.

• Faults in a superior man are like eclipses of the sun and moon: when he is guilty of a trespass, men all see it; and when he is himself again, all look up to him.

• When you meet with men of worth, think how you may attain to their level; when you see others of an opposite character, look within and examine yourself.

• They who care not for the morrow will the sooner have their sorrows.

• Learning without thought is a snare; thought without learning is a danger.

• With a meal of coarse rice. . . and water to drink, and my bent arm for a pillow—even thus I find happiness. Riches and honors without righteousness are to me as fleeting clouds.

expanded upon his teaching, developing a system of ethics that became a major influence on Chinese culture.

Fundamental to Confucius's teaching was his belief in five basic human relationships: father and son, elder and younger brothers, husband and wife, friend and friend, and ruler and subjects. Confucius believed that maintaining proper relationships in these five areas would bring harmony and order to society. In addition, he placed great confidence in China's past, trusting it as the basis and guide for human behavior. From the ancients he derived the fundamental principle for all human relationships: "What you do not want done to yourself, do not do to others."

The major defect in Confucius's teaching was his neglect of the most important relationship of all—man and God. Only as we fulfill our duties and responsibilities to God are we able to properly relate to our fellow men. God's Word teaches,

> *Thou shalt love the Lord thy God with all thy heart, and with all thy soul, and with all thy mind. This is the first and great commandment. And the second is like unto it, Thou shalt love thy neighbour as thyself.*
>
> *Matthew 22:37–39*

Only by drawing nigh to God is man able to fulfill God's teaching found in Luke 6:31: "As ye would that men should do to you, do ye also to them likewise."

Taoism

Second in importance to the teaching of Confucius was that of **Lao-tzu** (LOU DZUH) (604?–531 BC), the legendary founder of **Taoism**. Lao-tzu taught that tao (meaning "the way") was the pervading force in nature. He encouraged men to find peace and happiness by living in harmony with nature. According to Taoist teaching, men can achieve this harmony by ceasing to strive after power, wealth, and learning; instead they should adopt a simple, inactive lifestyle. By being passive and submissive, men can accomplish great things. Taoists illustrated this teaching with the example of water: "There is nothing in the world more soft and weak than water, yet for attacking things that are hard and strong there is nothing that surpasses it. . . . The soft overcomes the hard; the weak overcomes the strong."

Confucianism became the guiding philosophy of China's educational, social, and political systems; Taoism became the basis of mystical, magical, and superstitious elements in Chinese society. In many ways, these two philosophies are opposed. Confucianism promotes living an active life and fulfilling one's social obligations. Taoism favors a more passive lifestyle and attempts to free man from the busyness of responsibility. Confucianists strive for improved government, laws, and education, while Taoists minimize external authority and involvement in society.

Dynastic History of China

The Chinese have a passion for history. Their interest in antiquity sparked a great tradition of historical writing, much of which traces the history of China's ruling dynasties (or families). From the periods of **dynastic rule**, historians have established the major divisions of Chinese history.

The Chinese were able to maintain a strong sense of national unity; however, they did experience numerous periods of political upheaval and disorder. Each dynasty went through the same cycle: it began, matured, prospered, and then declined. The unrest that brought an end to one dynasty prepared the way for the founding of a new one. Although each dynasty had its own special qualities and left its mark on Chinese culture, the fundamental character of Chinese society remained essentially the same throughout the country's long history.

Shang Dynasty

The Shang dynasty, one of the earliest known Chinese dynasties, was established along the Yellow River (called Huang He in Chinese) around 1500 BC. The rulers of this dynasty united much of northern China. Archaeologists have unearthed fine examples of Shang bronze work and marble carvings. Much of our knowledge of Shang culture comes from early Chinese writing found inscribed on pieces of animal bones and tortoise shells. To obtain answers about the future from their ancestors, the Chinese wrote questions on bones or shells; then they touched them with a hot metal rod, causing them to crack. By "interpreting" the pattern of the cracks, the Chinese believed they could determine the will of their ancestors.

Chou Dynasty

Shortly before 1000 BC, the people who lived along the Shang's western border overthrew the Shang rulers. The Chou dynasty that they established lasted over eight hundred years—longer than any other dynasty in Chinese history. This period is often called the "classical" or "formative" age of Chinese history. Much of China's culture, such as family life, ancestor worship, the writing system, and Confucian and Taoist thought, became firmly established during this time.

The Chou government was decentralized. While the Chou rulers retained the ultimate authority, they allowed powerful nobles great freedom in ruling local territories. However, the Chou rulers were unable to control the nobles, and fighting broke out among rival states.

Ch'in Dynasty

Order was restored by **Shih Huang Ti** (247–210 BC), the founder of the short-lived but memorable Ch'in dynasty—the dynasty that gives China its name. Shih Huang Ti (SHEE HWAHNG TEE), which means "First Emperor," was the first to unite China proper under one strong centralized government.

The Tomb and Terra-Cotta Army of Shih Huang Ti

Shih Huang Ti, the first emperor of China, died in 210 BC. His body was entombed in an elaborate mausoleum that had taken workers his entire reign to construct. (Thirty-six years before his death he had drafted nearly a million Chinese laborers for the project.) According to contemporary Chinese historians, it contained a model of his palaces and various government buildings. It also housed a replica of his empire complete with rivers and seas of mercury, which actually flowed by mechanical means.

To protect his grave, the Chinese installed crossbows which would release automatically if an intruder entered the tomb. According to the custom of the day, Shih's son ordered his father's concubines who had not borne him sons to be buried with the emperor. He also ordered that those who had worked on the safety devices in the tomb to be buried too. Once the emperor was interred, the Chinese covered the mausoleum with earth and planted trees over it to give the appearance of a hill. Today it is called Mount Li. It stands fifteen stories high in the midst of a plain.

In 1974 a group of Chinese farmers, while digging a well in the Mount Li area, unearthed a subterranean passageway. Inside were huge terra-cotta statues (made of hard, waterproof ceramic clay) of ancient Chinese soldiers. In the years since the discovery, Chinese archaeologists have uncovered about six thousand soldiers—life-size replicas of the men in Shih Huang Ti's army. No two statues are alike. Some are old with wrinkles, and others are young and fair. Some are smiling, and some are serious. In addition to the soldiers, archaeologists have found clay horses and chariots. Because the ceiling of the tomb collapsed and crushed many of the terra-cotta statues, the task of excavating is a difficult one. The Chinese built a museum on the excavation site, and it has become one of the most visited tourist stops in China.

He standardized the Chinese weight, measurement, and coinage systems and brought uniformity to China's writing system. Perhaps the most remarkable achievement of the Ch'in dynasty was the construction of the Great Wall. The wall was was twenty-five to thirty feet high and fifteen feet wide. A road ran along its top, providing for rapid movement of troops and swift communication. A consolidation of existing structures, the Great Wall covered over 1,400 miles of often rugged terrain. It was erected as a defensive barrier against the invasions of the barbaric Huns (whose descendants later invaded the Roman Empire). Although Shih Huang Ti brought order and protection to China, he did so through harsh and ruthless measures. Just a few years after his death, the people revolted, bringing an end to the Ch'in dynasty.

THIS MOMENT IN HISTORY

Shih Huang Ti

Give Shih Huang Ti's achievements while ruler of China. What was positive and what was negative about his rule?

____

____

____

____

____

____

____

____

____

____

____

Han Dynasty

The next dynasty to rule China was the Han dynasty, established in 202 BC. This dynasty was so popular that to this day some Chinese call themselves the "sons of Han." The most famous Han ruler was **Wu Ti** (140–87 BC). He drove back the Huns and extended China's territory. To meet the growing need for well-trained government officials, the Han rulers introduced a civil service system in which competitive public examinations determined appointments to government posts. The Han established the ***Pax Sinica*** ("Chinese Peace") throughout China and much of central Asia. During this period trade routes were opened with the West. Over the "Silk Road"—named for China's chief export—traders brought China into direct contact with the Greek and Roman civilizations. The Han period also marked the entrance of Buddhism into China. It soon became one of China's leading religions.

Description of a Chinese Civil Service Examination

The candidates had to get up in the middle of the night and come to the palace at dawn, bringing their cold meals with them, for they would not be able to leave until the examinations were over. During the examinations they were shut up in cubicles under the supervision of palace guards. There was a rigorous system to prevent bribery or favoritism. . . . While the candidates were let out after the examinations, the judges themselves were shut up within the palace, usually from late January [until] early March, until the papers were properly graded and submitted to the emperor. The candidates were examined first on questions of history or principles of government. There was a second examination on the classics, and finally, after the successful ones had been graded, there was one—under the direct supervision of the emperor—on lyrics, descriptive poetry, and again essays on politics.[2]

T'ang Dynasty

In 220, revolts overthrew the last of the Han rulers. For nearly four hundred years China suffered from internal wars and barbarian invasions. Attempts to establish a lasting central government were unsuccessful. At the beginning of the seventh century, however, the T'ang rulers came to power and restored unity and prosperity once again to China. The T'ang dynasty (618–907) was a golden age that produced a stable government, an expanding empire, increased trade, contact with other civilizations, advances in learning, and magnificent works of arts and literature. The T'ang was one of the finest periods of Chinese poetry. The most popular and prolific poet was **Li Po**, who wrote thousands of poems expressing emotional and sentimental themes.

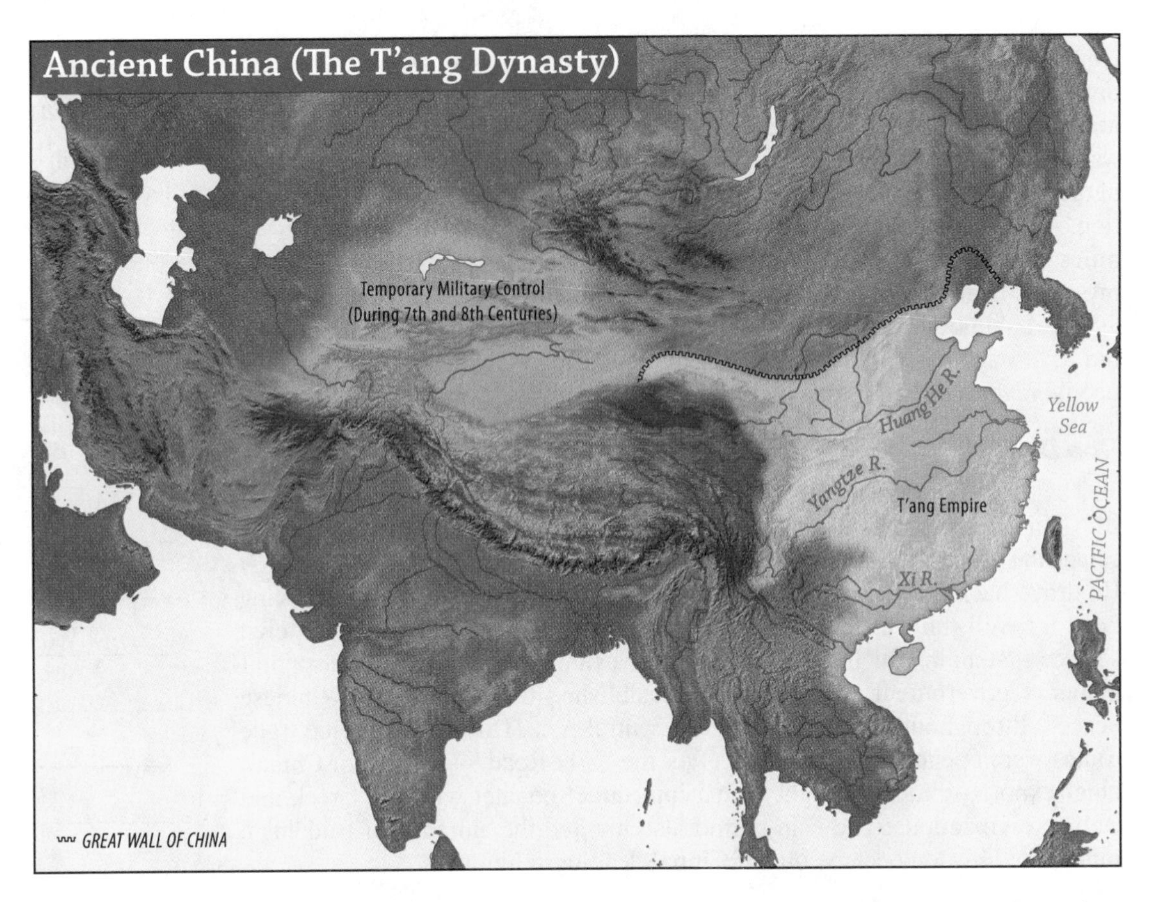

The glory of the T'ang lasted about three centuries. As self-seeking rulers began squandering much of the country's wealth, the T'ang dynasty lost both prosperity and power. The weakened dynasty collapsed in 907.

Sung Dynasty

About fifty years later, in 960, a new dynasty—the Sung—restored order. Compared to the other dynasties of China's past, however, the Sung dynasty was politically weak. The Sung rulers were unable to prevent the northern portions of China from falling under barbarian control. Despite these problems, the Sung dynasty carried on active trade, and the Chinese culture flourished. During this period the Chinese excelled in painting, printing, and porcelain.

Chinese Culture and the Western World

Only in recent years has the Western world significantly influenced Chinese society. Over the centuries China had resisted the introduction of foreign elements. This distrust of outsiders is the reason the traditional Chinese way of life remained virtually unaffected by the Western ideas and influences for centuries. The contrast between Eastern and Western cultures caused many westerners to view China as a land of mystical enchantment.

> Many of [China's] traditional customs are the opposite of those of the Occident [the West] and, accordingly, seem bizarre. In the old China the men wore skirts and long gowns, the women baggy trousers. At banquets what we think of as a dessert came first and rice concluded the meal. Men in greeting one another shook their own hands, not the hands of the other (a much more sanitary proceeding than that of the West, be it said). The place of honor was on the left, not on the right. In meeting on the streets gentlemen removed their spectacles and not their hats. White, not black, was the color of mourning.[3]

Unlike the Chinese, who generally looked with suspicion on Western ways and ideas, Westerners eagerly profited from their contacts with the Chinese. Europe became an open market for many Chinese goods; silk and porcelain were among the most popular. As far as we know, the Chinese were the first to produce silk. They carefully guarded the secret of the silkworm, whose cocoon provided the silk thread needed to make this beautiful fabric. The Chinese also developed the process for making porcelain: a white, translucent form of pottery which is still known as "china." In Europe, Chinese silk became fashionable, and china was one of the most valued possessions.

The West also learned of printing from the Chinese. The Chinese developed a method called block printing in which they carved raised characters on a block of wood. By inking the block and pressing it on paper, the Chinese were able to print multiple copies. However, the printing of new pages involved the slow process of carving another block of wood. To speed up this process, the Chinese invented **movable type**—that is, they carved smaller separate blocks for each Chinese character. The blocks could then be rearranged and reused. However, because there were thousands of characters, movable type was not widely used, nor was it practical.

Like printing, many other products associated with the Western world originated in China. Can you imagine a school classroom without paper or an ink pen? The Chinese were the first to develop paper (as we know it) and one of the first peoples to use ink. Think what navigation would be like without the Chinese invention of the magnetic compass. Another important Chinese discovery was gunpowder; this substance was first used in the manufacturing of fireworks. The Chinese were remarkably ahead of the West with regard to many discoveries and inventions. While it is true that the West made more productive (and sometimes destructive) use of these inventions, we should remember that they were originally Chinese contributions.

Section Quiz

1. What did the ancient Chinese call their land? Why?
2. What social group held the most esteemed position in Chinese society?
3. What is perhaps the most remarkable building achievement that occurred under the Ch'in dynasty?
4. List seven specific contributions that China made to the Western world.

1. ______________________

____

____

2. ______________________

3. ______________________

4. ______________________

____

____

____

____

____

____

III. Japan

Over one hundred miles off the coast of Asia—opposite China, Korea, and Siberia (Russia)—is the island nation of Japan. Japan consists of four main islands and hundreds of lesser ones. If placed alongside the Atlantic coast of the United States, Japan would stretch from Maine to Florida. In land area Japan is about the size of the state of California. Most of this land, however, is mountainous; less than 20 percent of it is suitable for farming. Through much of her history, Japan was more geographically remote than China; for centuries she remained isolated from the mainstream of the world's civilizations. It was not until the late nineteenth century that Japan made her presence felt in the arena of world affairs.

Early History

Although Japan is younger than most Asian civilizations, little is known about its early history. Instead of keeping historical records as the Chinese did, the early Japanese passed down myths and legends, many of which played an influential role in shaping the country's culture. According to Japanese

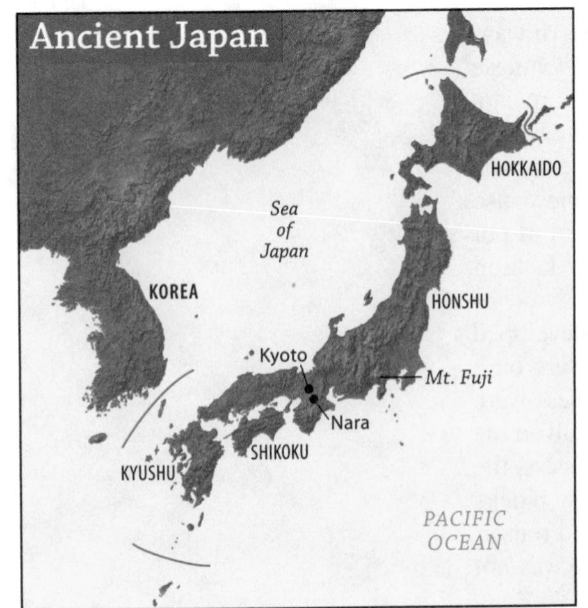

mythology, the god Izanagi and goddess Izanami, while standing on the rainbow bridge of heaven, dipped a jeweled spear into the ocean. Drops falling from the tip of the spear formed the islands of Japan. The god and goddess descended to live on the islands. Their offspring were the Japanese people.

Our first historical glimpse of ancient Japan finds the land divided by a number of warring clans. In early Japanese society, the **clan**—a group of families claiming descent from a common ancestor—was the basic unit of social, religious, and political organization. Each clan had its own land, its own god, and its own chieftain. The chieftain served as both political and religious leader. By the fifth century AD, one clan had risen in power and prestige over rival clans. Centered on the island of Honshu (the main Japanese island), the **Yamato clan** extended its authority and forged a unified Japanese state.

The leaders of the Yamato clan used Japanese mythology to secure the loyalty of other clan chieftains. According to legend the first emperor of Japan, **Jimmu Tenno** (*tenno*, "heavenly prince"), was a direct descendant of the sun goddess. The Yamato clan claimed that its rulers were descendants of Jimmu Tenno; they were, therefore, believed to be divine. From this clan arose the imperial family of Japan. Subsequent Japanese emperors all claimed Jimmu Tenno as their divine ancestor. Unlike China, which has had many ruling families or dynasties, Japan has had but one imperial family in its entire history. For this reason, the imperial family has served as a symbol of unity and continuity in Japanese society.

Supporting the belief in the divine origin of the emperor was Japan's native religion, **Shintoism** (meaning "the way of the gods"). Shintoism was originally a form of nature worship that attributed deity to anything in nature that

Shinto shrine

was awe-inspiring or extraordinary, such as fire, a waterfall, or a high mountain. However, Shintoism also stressed the supremacy of the sun goddess and the divine descent of the emperor. In many respects it became a religion of feeling, inspiring love for one's homeland, loyalty to one's clan, and reverence for one's emperor. It is little wonder that in modern times the Japanese government made Shintoism the national religion, which requires belief in the ancient myths, encourages patriotism, and maintains the prestige of the emperor.

Influence of China

Japan remained in relative isolation during her early history. In the fifth to the eighth centuries, however, the Chinese invaded the Japanese islands. This was not a military invasion by soldiers but a cultural invasion of ideas, learning, and art. China was experiencing the golden age of the T'ang dynasty, and the Japanese welcomed the influx of the "superior" Chinese culture.

There were two important vehicles that transmitted Chinese culture to Japan. The first was the Chinese writing system, which the Japanese adopted to complement their spoken language. For the first time, the Japanese were able to keep written records and produce their own literature. From an understanding of Chinese characters, they were also able to read and study Chinese literature and learn of the life and thought of the Chinese people.

Buddhist temple in Japan

Secondly, Chinese culture flowed into Japan through Buddhism. The Japanese learned much about the Chinese way of life from Buddhist monks who came over from China. For example, the Japanese learned to appreciate Chinese art and architecture from the numerous Buddhist temples built in Japan. Buddhism became firmly established in Japan during the seventh century when a member of the imperial family, **Prince Shotoku**, made Buddhism the favored national religion. He had many Buddhist temples, hospitals, and schools constructed. He also sent many young men to China to study Chinese ways: agriculture, science, architecture, law, government, philosophy, and religion. Japan borrowed not only Chinese writing, literature, and religion, but also China's system of weights and measurements, medical practices, calendar, styles of furniture and dress, and methods of building roads and bridges.

In the mid-seventh century, the leaders of Japan sought to weaken the influence of the local clan chieftains and extend the power of the emperor to all of Japan. They modeled their government after the strong centralized bureaucracy of the T'ang dynasty. This turnabout in the Japanese political and economic structure became known as the "Great Change" or **Taika** (tie EE kuh) **Reform**. Like the Chinese, the Japanese established civil service examinations, granting government posts to men of ability. A new judicial code and tax system came into existence, and at Nara the Japanese established their first permanent capital, which was copied after the main city of China. (Later the capital was moved to Kyoto, where the Japanese emperors maintained their court until 1868.)

The Taika reforms changed the nature of Japan's political structure from semi-independent clans to a centralized government headed by the emperor. Or so it was in theory. In actual practice, government authority came to rest in the hands of powerful families who controlled the key posts of government. One such family, the **Fujiwara**, had married their daughters to the sons of the imperial family. When a male child was born, they forced the ruling emperor to abdicate. The Fujiwara elders then ruled Japan as regents of the infant emperor.

A samurai

Rise of the Samurai

The Fujiwaras enjoyed the wealth and extravagance of the imperial city. However, the luxurious life of the royal court brought corruption and bankruptcy to the government. Disorder followed as the central government was no longer able to provide protection for outlying provinces. Many provincial governors began to rely on strong military clans for protection. Soon power struggles broke out among rival military families. In the twelfth century **Yoritomo**, the leader of the Minamoto clan, became the supreme military leader of Japan when he defeated the only remaining powerful clan. The powerless emperor granted Yoritomo the title of **shogun** ("great general"). Yoritomo created a warrior state, ruled by military rather than civilian officials. Although the line of the imperial family continued, powerful shoguns held the real power over the Japanese government from 1192 to 1868.

With the rise of the office of shogun, the warrior class became the leading class in Japanese society. The Japanese warrior was called **samurai** or *bushi*. Besides mastering the military skills of horsemanship, fencing, archery, and jujitsu (a form of martial arts), the samurai studied history, literature, and the art of writing. He used these skills in providing protection for his master and lord. An unwritten military code known as the **Bushido** (BOOSH ih DOH; "the way of the warrior") governed the conduct of the samurai. It demanded that he live by loyalty, honor, duty, justice, courage, sincerity, and politeness. To avoid the disgrace of capture, atone for deeds of misconduct, or prove questioned loyalty to his master, a warrior could end his life with honor by committing suicide according to the ceremonial practice of *hara-kiri*.

The Way of the Warrior

A Japanese warrior learned *Bushido* almost from birth. One authority on *Bushido* describes the early training this way: "Does a little [baby] cry for any ache? The mother scolds him in this fashion: 'What will you do when your arm is cut off in battle? What [will you do] when you are called upon to commit *hara-kiri*?' "

Section Quiz

1. What was the basic social, religious, and political unit in early Japanese society?
2. According to legend, who was the first Japanese emperor? What do the Japanese believe about his ancestry?
3. The culture of what foreign civilization had a profound effect on Japan's early history?
4. What was the name of the reform movement that sought to weaken the influence of local clan leaders while strengthening the authority of the emperor and the central government?
5. What were Japanese warriors called? What was the unwritten military code that governed their conduct?

1. ______________________
2. ______________________
____
____
3. ______________________
4. ______________________
5. ______________________
____

IV. Comparison of the Asian Civilizations

As we have seen in this chapter, each of the major Asian civilizations—India, China, and Japan—had a distinctive culture and history. Nevertheless, there are a few characteristics they share.

Traditionalism

These Eastern civilizations have often been referred to as the "changeless" lands. So deeply were their cultures rooted in the beliefs and customs passed down from generation to generation that there remained little room for new ideas and ways. Each possessed its own standard of traditional values—Hinduism and the caste system in India, Confucianism and historical literature in China, and Shintoism and mythology in Japan. Built on traditionalism, these civilizations frowned upon change; they were content to live in the past. The Asians relied on human tradition in determining what was true and good. Paul warns of this danger in Colossians 2:8, "Beware lest any man spoil you through philosophy and vain deceit, after the tradition of men, after the rudiments [principles] of the world, and not after Christ."

Stifling of Individuality

Within the Indian, Chinese, and Japanese societies, the group—not the individual—held the prominent place: the caste in India, the extended family in China, and the clan in Japan. The group was responsible for the welfare and actions of its members; likewise, each member became accountable as part of the group. Because these societies lacked personal initiative and responsibility they remained static. Although the Bible does teach us to "bear . . . one another's burdens," it also tells us how God desires each individual to be productive: "But let every man prove his own work, and then shall he have rejoicing in himself alone, and not in another. For every man shall bear his own burden" (Gal. 6:2, 4–5). Likewise, God will hold each individual accountable for his own actions: "So then every one of us shall give account of himself to God" (Rom. 14:12).

False Religion

The cultures of India, China, and Japan are among the oldest and most enduring in the world today. They are also among the most deceived by Satan. This is not to say they are nonreligious. Hinduism, Buddhism, Confucianism, Taoism, and Shintoism played an important role in shaping the lives of the people in the Orient. But in these lands the vast majority live apart from the knowledge of God and His truth. Instead of worshiping the true living God, they follow after polytheism, idols, superstition, vain philosophies, myths, and fables. Their man-centered religions offer no hope beyond this life. Only in Christ can man look to the future with confidence and expectation.

Section Quiz

1. List the standard of traditional values in India, China, and Japan.
2. Which group in the Indian, Chinese, and Japanese cultures held the prominent position?

1. ______________________________

____

____

____

____

____

2. ______________________________

____

____

V. The Mongol Empire

In this chapter and the preceding one, we have examined the major civilizations of Asia and eastern Europe to the thirteenth century. Despite being separated by great distances and diverse cultural backgrounds, the civilizations of India, China, Byzantium, Russia, and the Muslim empire shared something in common: each land was invaded by fierce warriors coming out of central Asia. Since ancient days, central Asia had been the homeland of many nomadic peoples. Vast grassy plains, known as the **steppes**, stretch from western China to eastern Europe. This pastureland was a highway along which roving tribes moved as they sought food for their flocks and herds.

One of these roving tribes was known as the Huns. They advanced into China and Europe while the Turks, also a nomadic people, moved into Byzantine and Islamic territories. By the thirteenth century another group, the Mongols, had united the peoples of central Asia. The Mongols spread across the Asian steppes, creating an empire that stretched from China across central Asia to Russia, southward into Byzantine and Muslim territories, and later into the land of India. In less than a century, the Mongols built the largest land empire in history.

Building the Mongol Empire

The Mongol people arose in the north of China, in the land known today as Mongolia. Their round felt tents dotted the eastern portion of the Asiatic grasslands. They raised sheep, goats, and horses. They had no government but were divided into small tribes. In approximately 1162, Temujin (TEM yoo jin) was born to the family of a tribal chief. Overcoming many hardships in his youth, Temujin succeeded his father as leader of his tribe at the age of thirteen. He gradually united all the Mongol tribes under his authority and established an empire in the steppes. He became "lord of all the people dwelling in felt tents." In 1206 the Mongols gave him the title "**Genghis Khan**" (JENG-gis KAHN), meaning "universal ruler."

Genghis Khan was one of the greatest conquerors in history. He believed that he had a divine commission to conquer the world. Having organized the Mongols into a well-disciplined fighting force, he conquered northern China. He then turned his army westward. The Mongols overran central Asia, advanced to the banks of the Indus River, pushed into Persia, and crossed into southern Russia. Returning from his western conquests, Genghis renewed his campaign against China. His death in 1227, however, prevented him from seeing the whole of China fall under Mongol control.

Mongol warrior

Much of Genghis's success lay in the organization and mobility of his army. He skillfully deployed his forces in battle. His army, which he divided into groups of tens, hundreds, and thousands, could strike with great speed. In addition, the Mongols were expert horsemen. Riding into battle on horseback, they had a distinct advantage over the armies of other civilizations. (The horse was the most prized Mongol possession.) Much like the ancient Assyrians, the Mongols gained a reputation for terrorizing the peoples they were about to conqueror. They often massacred the entire population of a city to teach others the futility of resistance. The Mongol conquests left fear, destruction, and death in their wake.

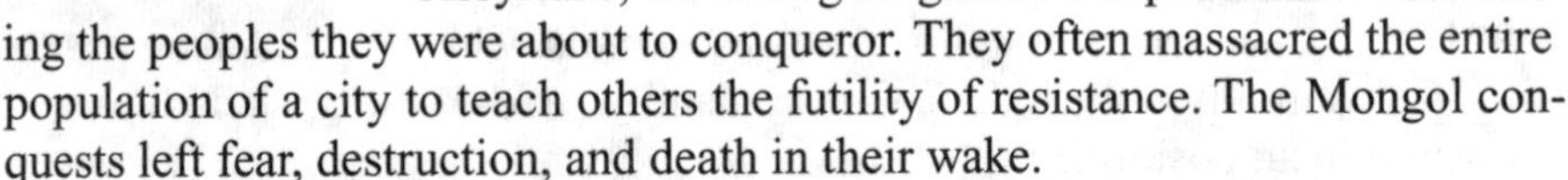

Mongol expansion did not cease with the death of Genghis. His sons and grandsons enlarged his empire. Their armies completed the conquest of China, swept farther into Russia, and overran the Muslim states in central and southwestern Asia. They sacked Baghdad, brought an end to the Abbasid dynasty, and broke the power of the Seljuk Turks.

The Mongols chose Genghis's son to succeed him as the Great Khan, the ruler of the entire Mongol Empire. But the empire eventually became too large for one man to rule effectively. By the time of the fifth ruler, the empire had already begun to fragment into many separate Mongol states, each ruled by a descendant of Genghis. In the following pages we will examine separately the Mongol states established in China, Russia, central Asia, and India.

The Yuan Dynasty in China (1279–1368)

The Mongol attack came as no surprise to the Chinese. For hundreds of years the Chinese had defended their borders against the attacks of central

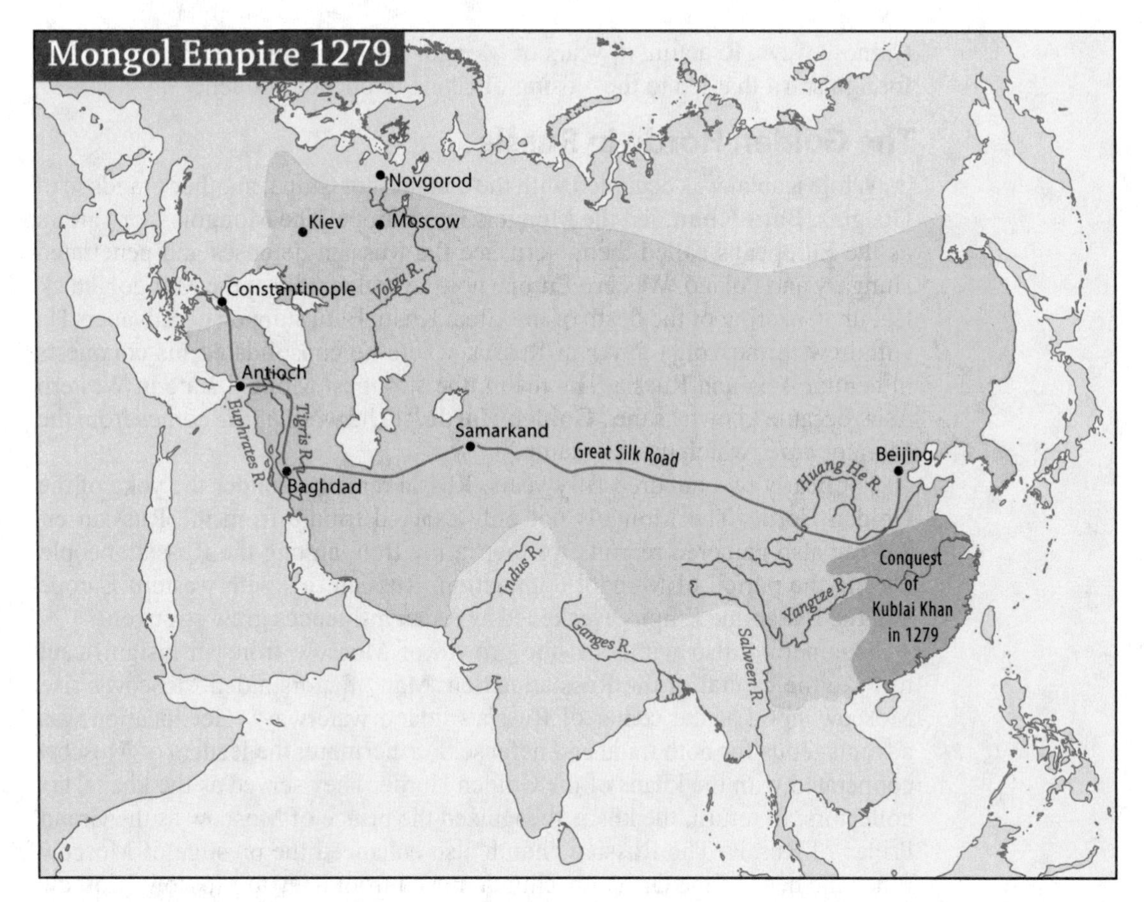

Asian nomads. But none of China's previous invaders had possessed the military strength of the Mongols. Not even the Great Wall could stop their advance. The conquest of China began by Genghis was completed by his grandson **Kublai Khan** (KOO-blie KAHN). Kublai was the last of the Great Khans, the heir to the entire Mongol world. After a long campaign, he succeeded in conquering southern China, the stronghold of the ruling Sung dynasty (see p. 160).

Kublai Khan established the Mongol (or Yuan) dynasty, the first foreign dynasty to rule all of China. He moved the capital to Cambaluc (modern-day Beijing), where he directed the affairs of the Mongol empire. His primary interest was China. He built highways to facilitate trade and communication between China and the rest of Asia. He invited missionaries, scholars, artists, merchants, and engineers from all over the world to his capital. Kublai employed many of these foreigners as government officials. The most famous European traveler to Mongol China was Marco Polo (see p. 303). Polo lived in China seventeen years. Many of those years he spent in the service of Kublai. He later wrote a glowing account of his travels and of the wonders of Kublai's court. His stories gave most Europeans their first glimpse of China.

With the death of Kublai, the world empire founded by Genghis Khan came to an end. The Mongols still ruled most of Asia, but no longer could they boast of a unified empire. The empire had broken into many independent Mongol kingdoms. The descendants of Kublai continued to rule in China. But despite the peace and prosperity that the Yuan dynasty brought to China, the Chinese resented the rule of foreigners. The Mongols had excluded the Chinese from holding government positions. Discontent mounted as Kublai's successors grew weaker and more decadent. Rebellion eventually broke out, and in 1368 the Chinese drove the Mongol rulers back into Mongolia. A new Chinese dynasty, the Ming ("brilliant") dynasty, restored Chinese rule and reestablished

Chinese ways. Reacting to years of Mongol rule, the Chinese adopted an antiforeign spirit that led to the closing of China to outside influences.

The Golden Horde in Russia

While Kublai was occupied with the conquest of China, another grandson of Genghis, **Batu Khan**, led the Mongols into Europe. The Mongols—or Tartars, as the Europeans called them—crushed the Russian defenses and penetrated Hungary and Poland. Western Europe now lay vulnerable to the Mongol attack. But upon hearing of the death of the Great Khan, Batu stopped his advance. He withdrew to the Volga River in Russia, where he consolidated his conquests in central Asia and Russia. His realm, the strongest Mongol state in Western Asia, became known as the "**Golden Horde**." (The word *horde* comes from the Mongol *ordu*, which means "camp.")

For nearly two hundred fifty years, Russia remained under the yoke of the Golden Horde. The Mongols not only exacted tribute from the Russian cities, but also gathered recruits for their army from among the Russian people. During the period of Mongol domination, Russian ties with western Europe and the Byzantine Empire weakened as Asian influences grew stronger.

This period also witnessed the growth of Moscow from an insignificant town to the capital of the Russian nation. Many factors aided Moscow's rise. Moscow stood at the center of Russia's inland waterways. Her location was advantageous for both trade and defense. Furthermore, the leaders of Moscow cooperated with the khans of the Golden Horde. They served as the khans' tax collectors. In return, the khans recognized the prince of Moscow as the Grand Prince of Russia. The Russian church also enhanced the prestige of Moscow. When the head of the Orthodox church moved from Kiev to Moscow, Moscow became the religious center of Russia.

While Moscow grew strong and prosperous, the Golden Horde weakened. By the late fourteenth century, the grand princes began to openly challenge their Mongol overlords. Under **Ivan III**, the Grand Prince from 1462 to 1505, Moscow refused to pay further tribute to the Mongols. By 1480 Moscow had thrown off the Mongol yoke and had become the political and religious capital of the new state. Ivan extended his control over much of northern Russia. He laid the foundation for an independent Russian state and emerged as its **autocratic** (ruling with unlimited authority) leader. After the collapse of Constantinople in 1453, many people considered Moscow the "Third Rome."

Later Mongol Empires

Tamerlane's Empire

In the late fourteenth century, there arose a central Asian conqueror who attempted to rebuild Genghis's empire. His name was Timur the Lame; he was known to the Europeans as **Tamerlane**. Tamerlane belonged to a Mongol-Turkish tribe and claimed to have descended from Genghis Khan.

Having established his power in central Asia, Tamerlane raised an army and began a new wave of Mongol invasions. His army swept over the Muslim lands in southwestern Asia, capturing Baghdad and Damascus and defeating the Ottoman Turks in Asia Minor. His march into southern Russia weakened the Golden Horde and indirectly aided the Russian princes in their struggle to gain freedom from Mongol control. Turning to the East, Tamerlane led his army into India, where in 1398 he reduced the city of Delhi to ruins and slaughtered an estimated one hundred thousand people. He died in 1405 while planning an invasion of China.

Tamerlane was an able, but cruel, conqueror. He left a trail of merciless plundering, destruction, and massacres. His conquests reached from India to Asia Minor. But the size of his empire was much smaller than the earlier Mongol Empire. It collapsed shortly after his death.

The Mughal Empire in India

India was a frequent target of Mongol attacks. From the time of Genghis Khan to Tamerlane, Mongol raiders had terrorized the people of northern India. But unlike most Asian lands, India had not fallen under Mongol rule; not until the sixteenth century did the Mongols gain control of India. **Babur**, "The Tiger," a descendant of the two greatest Asian conquerors, Genghis Khan and Tamerlane, became the leader of the Turkish-Mongol tribes in what today is Afghanistan. With an army of twelve thousand men, Babur crossed the mountain passes and invaded northern India. Having captured the capital city of Delhi, he established the **Mughal** dynasty in 1526. ("Mughal" is the name given to the Mongols in India.) Later Mughal rulers extended the empire over all but the southern tip of India.

Under the Mughals (who were Muslims), Indian civilization flourished. Unlike Tamerlane, who inflicted cruel destruction, the Mughal rulers established law and order, increased Indian unity, and fostered a period of rich achievement in art and architecture. The greatest Mughal ruler was Babur's grandson **Akbar** (1556–1605). Akbar expanded the empire to include all of northern and central India. Not only an excellent military general, Akbar was an able administrator who brought many reforms to the Indian government. He realized that force alone could not win the support of the Indian people. Through his policy of religious toleration, he won the support of the Hindu population.

Section Quiz

1. What name is given to the vast grassy plains that stretch from western China to eastern Europe?
2. Who united the Mongol tribes and established a Mongol empire in the steppes? What title was he given?
3. What Mongol ruler conquered China? What was the name of the Mongol dynasty in China?
4. What city rose to prominence during the period of Mongol domination over Russia?
5. What descendant of Genghis Khan and Tamerlane set up a Mongol dynasty in India? What was the name of this dynasty?

1. ______________________
2. ______________________
____
3. ______________________
____
4. ______________________
5. ______________________
____

VI. Africa

Although the Mongols spread over Asia and threatened Europe, they left untouched one great "unknown land"—Africa. The second largest continent, Africa covers over one-fifth of the earth's land surface. It is nearly four times the size of the continental United States. Although much of the continent is a large plateau, its mountains, deserts, grassy flatlands, and jungles give Africa a unique beauty.

We have studied some of Africa's history in earlier chapters. The Egyptians established on the banks of the Nile the earliest recorded civilization in Africa. Carthage built a thriving civilization in North Africa in the days of the Roman Republic, and the Romans later made the area part of their empire. After the collapse of Rome, Muslims swept across North Africa and brought the region under Islamic domination.

As important as these events are, they involve only a portion of that great continent. The history of the rest of Africa, known as **sub-Saharan Africa** (so named because it is south of the Sahara Desert), is not so well known but is nonetheless important.

Ancient African Civilization

Centuries before Europeans penetrated into sub-Saharan Africa, several African empires and kingdoms flourished. In ancient times, two important kingdoms arose in northeast Africa, south of the Egyptian civilization. The earliest was the kingdom of Kush, which centered in what is today northern Sudan. (Ruins of its capital, Meroë, still exist near the modern city of Khartoum.) Originally a province of the Egyptian Empire, Kush grew in power until by 700 BC it had not only overthrown Egyptian rule but also conquered all of Egypt and established its own dynasty of pharaohs. (The Tirhakah of Ethiopia mentioned in 2 Kings 19:9 is one such Kushite ruler, Taharqa.) The Assyrians drove the Kushites out of Egypt in the mid-600s BC, but the Kushite kingdom continued for nearly a thousand years longer.

Kush eventually fell to a kingdom to its east known as Aksum (or Axum). The ruler of Aksum recorded the shattering defeat he inflicted on the Kushites in AD 330:

> I made war on them. . . . They fled without making a stand, and I pursued them . . . killing some and capturing others. . . . I burnt their towns, both those built of bricks and those built of reeds, and my army carried off their food and copper and iron . . . and destroyed the statues in their temples, their granaries, and cotton trees and cast them into the [Nile].[4]

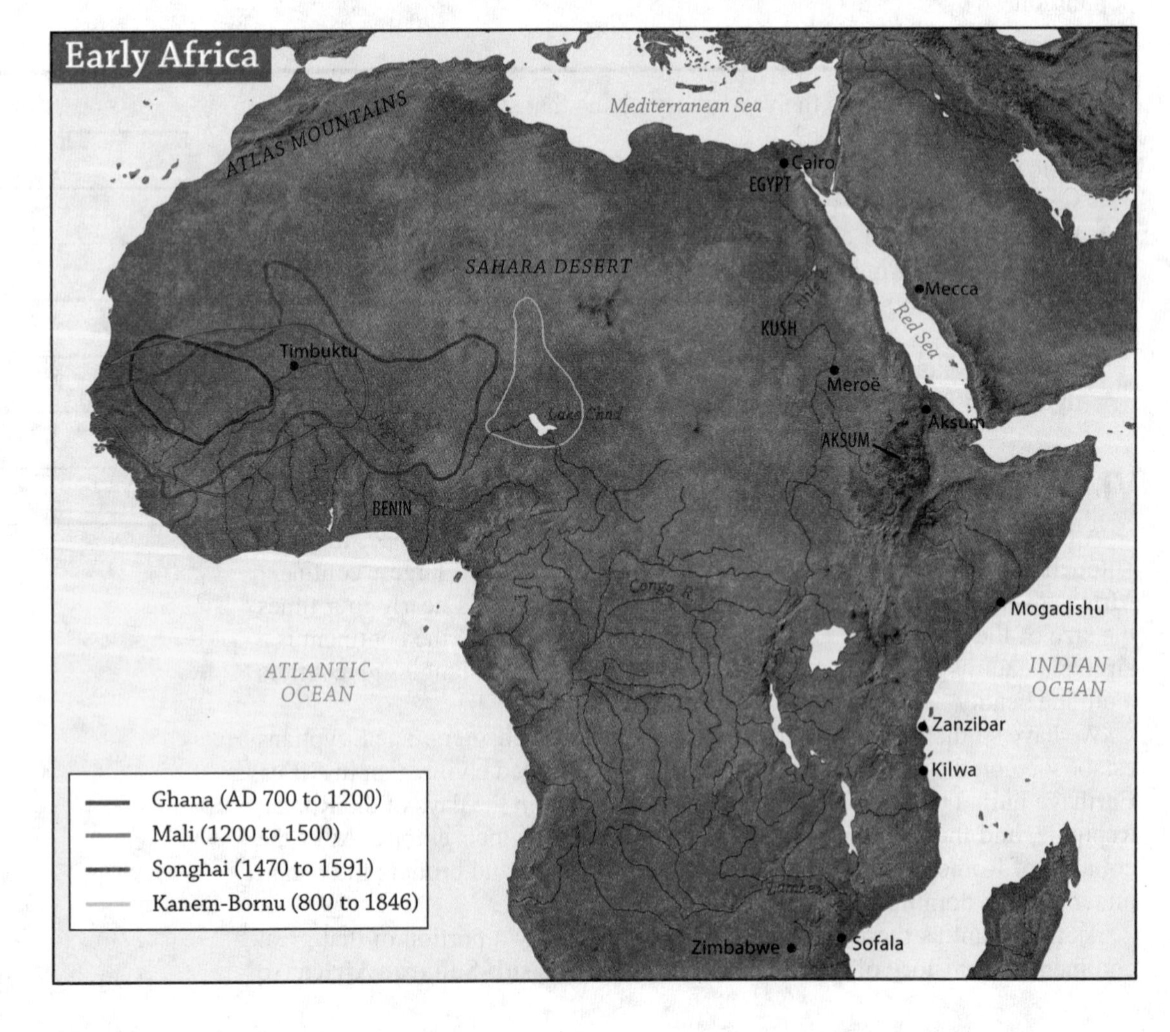

Aksum was unusual among the early African kingdoms in that it embraced Christianity. Later tradition claimed that the rulers of Aksum were descendants of King Solomon and the Queen of Sheba. Actually the kingdom's conversion to Christianity was the work of a Syrian Christian named **Frumentius**. Aksum's conversion intensified its already extensive trade with the Roman Empire. Later, however, the Muslim invasions in North Africa cut off Aksum from almost all European contact. The civilization nonetheless continued to exist and became the nucleus of the modern state of Ethiopia.

Central and Western Africa

During Europe's Middle Ages several important kingdoms arose in central and western Africa. Our knowledge of these civilizations is somewhat sketchy, because most of their histories were not written down but passed on orally. However, oral tradition, archaeology, and some accounts written by non-Africans provide us a general picture of these cultures. In central Africa, for example, the kingdom of Kanem-Bornu thrived on the shores of Lake Chad. Deriving its profit from the camel caravan trade and building a strong military force (including camel-mounted cavalry), this African kingdom lasted a thousand years, from ca. 800 to 1846.

Even more important were the three kingdoms of western Africa—Ghana, Mali, and Songhai, each progressively larger than the previous. All three built prosperous civilizations whose wealth derived from the gold mines within their empires and the camel caravan trade in gold, salt, and other precious items that crossed the Sahara Desert. The Niger (NIE jur) River in particular provided a base for these empires as its waters drew travelers crossing the arid Sahara.

Frumentius, "Apostle to the Abyssinians"

The conversion of Aksum (sometimes known as "Abyssinia") was the result of the ministry of an unlikely missionary named Frumentius. We have little information about his early years. We know that he was a professing Christian and Roman citizen, probably from Tyre, who was born around AD 300. While still a young man, he and his brother were traveling abroad with a relative. Pirates attacked their ship, massacring most of the crew and passengers. The pirates spared the brothers, however, and sold them into slavery in Aksum. Frumentius and his brother, like Joseph in Egypt, rose to high positions in government because of their abilities. As treasurer and secretary to the king of Aksum, Frumentius earned the trust of high officials in government. When the king died, the queen asked Frumentius to help administer the government until the young prince was old enough to rule himself.

While serving the kingdom, Frumentius also promoted his Christian faith. He encouraged Christian merchants from the Roman Empire to hold private services during their visits to Aksum. Under Frumentius's preaching and guidance, the citizens of Aksum also began to convert to Christianity. The young prince whom Frumentius served was probably Ezana, the king who won the great victory over Kush in 330. Ezana seems to have accepted Christianity later in life. Historians note that he did not credit his victory over Kush to pagan gods, as he had done with victories earlier in his reign, but "by the might of the Lord of Heaven Who in heaven and upon earth is mightier than everything which exists." He also praised the "Lord of Heaven, Who . . . to all eternity reigns the Perfect One." Ezana's conversion was perhaps the crowning work of Frumentius, a man since remembered as the "Apostle to the Abyssinians."

Camels were the perfect beasts of burden for the traders who brought precious cargo across the Sahara Desert.

THIS MOMENT IN HISTORY

Mansa Musa

How did Mansa Musa draw attention to his kingdom? Why did Timbuktu, Musa's capital, become Africa's most important center of trade?

The kingdom of Ghana rose to prominence first, enjoying its heyday from AD 700 to 1200. Fanatical Muslims from northern Africa attacked and fatally weakened Ghana in the eleventh century but proved unable to conquer the region. In its place rose the kingdom of Mali, dominating western Africa from 1200 to 1500. The most famous ruler of Mali was **Mansa Musa** (1312–37). Since the Mali rulers had converted to Islam, Mansa Musa made a pilgrimage to Mecca. So splendid was his traveling party that it caught the attention of the non-African world. Mansa Musa took with him sixty thousand men and over ten thousand pounds of gold, and he astonished the Egyptians with his wealth during a stay in Cairo. His capital, Timbuktu, became Africa's most important center of trade. Mansa Musa also encouraged learning in his realm, attracting so many scholars to Timbuktu that books began to rival gold as an item for trade.

If rulers such as Mansa Musa enjoyed an exalted status among their people, they also paid a price. A king was supposed to be superior to common men. He often spoke to his court hidden behind a curtain, and no one could watch him eat. Unfortunately, this emphasis on perfection meant that if the king fell seriously ill or became infirm with age, he was expected to commit suicide or be smothered to death.

In the fifteenth century, the Songhai Empire overthrew the Mali Empire. It extended farther than either Ghana or Mali, stretching to the Atlantic in the west and pressing Kanem-Bornu on Lake Chad in the east. Its wealth proved more attractive than its power proved fearsome, however. An invasion by greedy Moroccans in 1591 brought an end to Songhai, and with it, an end to the western African empires.

East African City-States

Along the eastern coast of Africa lay a series of important trading ports, each an independent city-state. These trading ports had existed as early as the days of the Roman Empire, and after the collapse of Rome, they continued to flourish as outlets for gold, iron, ivory, and animal skins to the Arabs and Persians. Prosperous city-states such as Kilwa (in what is today Tanzania) received goods from the tribes and kingdoms in the interior and sold them to Arab sea traders. As a result of this profitable trade, as well as a temperate climate, the seaside city-states grew wealthy and cultured. In the fourteenth century a Muslim visitor wrote, "Kilwa is one of the most beautiful and well-constructed towns in the world." A European visiting in 1500 wrote, "In this land there are rich merchants, and there is much gold and silver and amber and musk and pearls. Those of the land wear clothes of fine cotton and of silk and many fine things, and they are black men."

Arusha, Tanzania, Africa

Although they were independent of each other, the city-states shared a common culture, one that was a mixture of Arab, Persian, and African elements. The architecture, for example, was predominantly Arab. The language of the city-states, **Swahili**, was more dominantly native African but contained elements of Arabic, Persian, and Indian. The city-states enjoyed centuries of prosperity, but after 1500 they were crushed between the Europeans attacking the coasts to seize control of trade and the pressure of interior tribes pushing toward the coasts. The Swahili language has survived, however, and the term *Swahili* is used even today to describe the culture of some eastern Africans.

Forest Kingdoms

Providing the goods for the eastern city-states to sell were the "forest kingdoms" of the interior of Africa. Records of these kingdoms are even scarcer than of the central and western empires to the north. The best-known forest kingdoms are those with which Europeans came into contact right after the close of the Middle Ages. Perhaps the most important was the kingdom of Benin, in western Africa (today's southern Nigeria). It arose about 1300 and lasted until the nineteenth century. In addition to being a center for trade, Benin also produced fine statues and relief sculptures in bronze. The metalworking of Benin was in fact one of the highest artistic accomplishments of early African history.

African Culture

Daily life for most Africans centered less on kingdoms and empires than on smaller social organizations. Many Africans knew of little more than life as it existed in their villages. The family, of course, was most basic. Since **polygamy** (marrying more than one wife) was common, families were larger and more complex than in Europe at that time. Several families who could trace their descent back to a common ancestor formed a clan. A group of two clans or more, in turn, formed a tribe, or ethnic group. The tribe was perhaps the most important cultural organization. Many African kingdoms were dominated by one ethnic group.

Religious belief in Africa was diverse. Some regions, such as Aksum, embraced Christianity. Islam claimed a large number of converts, but Islamic visitors from the Middle East often complained that much African adherence to their religion was only superficial. Muslim patterns often influenced African kingdoms, however, in structuring their government, organizing their system of education, and establishing their currency.

The majority of the people in sub-Saharan Africa held to traditional tribal religions. In general, these traditional religions taught that there was a high god who created the universe and below him were a number of lesser gods and the spirits of dead ancestors. Prayers and sacrifices were offered to these gods to ward off illnesses and increase crop yields. In some cases, followers of traditional religions would even offer human sacrifices. During the collapse of the kingdom of Benin, for example, rulers ordered human sacrifices in attempts to appease the gods and stave off disaster.

Most Africans relied on farming or herding to sustain themselves and their families. Trade, however, was the mainstay of the African kingdoms. Gold, salt, ivory, and animal skins were perhaps the most valued products. Beginning late in the Middle Ages, African trade began to change. As Europeans began sailing to African ports, the camel caravan trade became less important. More significantly, a new trade opened with Arabs and later with Europeans—the slave trade. Although slavery had

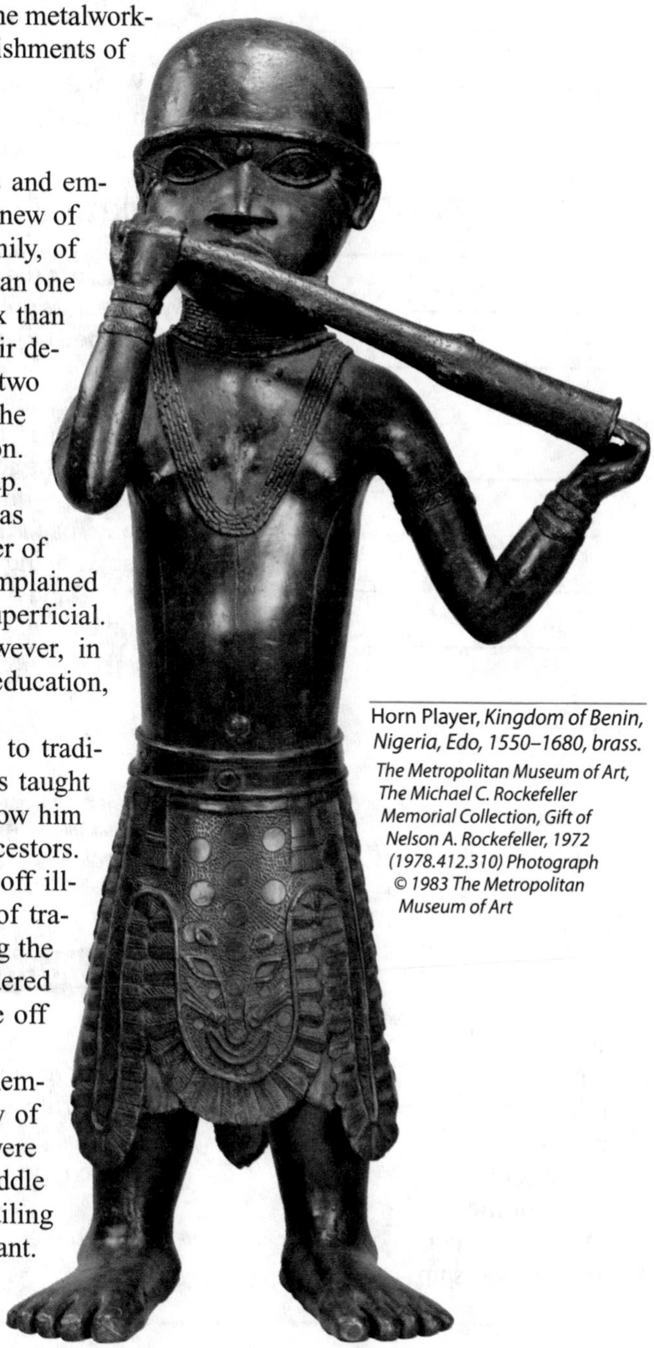

Horn Player, *Kingdom of Benin, Nigeria, Edo, 1550–1680, brass.*

The Metropolitan Museum of Art, The Michael C. Rockefeller Memorial Collection, Gift of Nelson A. Rockefeller, 1972 (1978.412.310) Photograph © 1983 The Metropolitan Museum of Art

existed in Africa for centuries, demand for slaves increased after the Middle Ages. This traffic in human lives tragically became the main point of contact for African-European relations after 1500. It led to suffering and exploitation of the African people.

As this survey of early African civilization demonstrates, portrayals of all of Africa as "primitive" are unfair. The African kingdoms displayed a level of complexity and organization that compare favorably with contemporary civilizations in Europe and Asia. Like the Asians, though, most Africans (with a few notable exceptions) remained in spiritual darkness, apart from the light of the saving truth of God's Word.

Section Quiz

1. What ancient African civilization conquered the Egyptians for a time? What ancient African civilization converted to Christianity?
2. Name the three western African kingdoms in chronological order. What were the two bases of their wealth?
3. What African kingdom was noteworthy for its fine metalworking in bronze?
4. Name at least three items that were important goods in African trade.

1. ______________________

____

2. ______________________

____

____

____

____

3. ______________________

4. ______________________

____

____

____

____

A Glance Behind

Not since the days of the *Pax Romana* had the contact between the East and West been as great as under the *Pax Mongolica* ("Mongol Peace"). The empire established by Genghis and his successors brought unity to Asia for a time. This made travel safer, improved communications, and encouraged trade. (In 1415, for example, one African kingdom was able to send a giraffe as a gift to the emperor of China. The emperor returned the favor by sending numerous gifts back to Africa in the company of a Chinese fleet.) Many historians believe that it was during this period that such Chinese inventions as gunpowder, the magnetic compass, papermaking, and movable-type printing came to the West. Renewed contact with the East prompted the West to search for new and better ways to reach the lands of silks and spices. Likewise, the Mongol policy of religious toleration encouraged missionaries to travel to the Far East.

and a Glimpse Ahead

Notes

1. Kenneth Scott Latourette, *A Short History of the Far East* (New York: Macmillan, 1957), p. 158.
2. Lin Yu-t'ang, *The Gay Genius* (New York: Day, 1947), p. 38.
3. Latourette, p. 181.
4. Robert W. July, *A History of the African People*, 2nd ed. (New York: Charles Scribner's Sons, 1974), p. 43.

Chapter Review

Can You Define?

topography
joint family
castes
world soul
wheel of life
Middle Kingdom
ancestor worship
Chinese characters
dynastic rule
Pax Sinica
movable type
clan
shogun
Bushido
steppes
autocratic
sub-Saharan Africa
Swahili
polygamy

Can You Identify?

Aryans
Sanskrit
Vedas
Hinduism
Upanishads
Brahman
Buddhism
Siddhartha Gautama
Four Noble Truths
Chandragupta Maurya
Asoka
Gupta Empire
Kalidasa
Confucianism
Taoism
K'ung Fu-tzu (Confucius)
Lao-tzu
Shih Huang Ti
Wu Ti
Li Po
Yamato clan
Jimmu Tenno
Shintoism
Prince Shotoku
Taika Reform
Fujiwara
Yoritomo
samurai
Genghis Khan
Kublai Khan
Batu Khan
Golden Horde
Ivan III
Tamerlane
Babur
Mughal
Akbar
Frumentius
Mansa Musa

Can You Locate?

India
Indian Ocean
Himalayas
Indus River
Ganges River
Khyber Pass
Mohenjo-Daro
Harappa
Delhi
China
Huang He
Yangtze River
Gobi Desert
Japan
Korea
Honshu Isand
Nara
Kyoto
Mongolia
Beijing
Volga River
Moscow
Kush
Aksum
Ghana
Mali
Songhai
Niger River
Timbuktu
Benin

How Much Can You Remember?

1. List three key features that characterized early Indian society.
2. Make a chart of the major Eastern religions (Hinduism, Buddhism, Confucianism, Taoism, and Shintoism). For each religion, list (if possible) its founder, its native territory, and its main teachings.
3. List the Chinese dynasties, and next to each write its main contribution(s).
4. Identify the most influential class of people in each of the following civilizations: India, China, and Japan.
5. Identify the key river systems of India and China.
6. List the Mongol rulers. Identify the territory ruled by each one.
7. List three characteristics shared by India, China, and Japan.
8. Why is our knowledge of much of African culture so sketchy? What are three available sources for studying African history?
9. Name the three major religions of Africa.

What Do You Think?

1. How does Hebrews 9:27 refute the Hindu teaching of reincarnation?
2. How does each of the Eastern religions mentioned in this chapter rely on human effort and works to find happiness in this life and the life to come?
3. The Chinese appointed scholars to government posts. What do you think should be the qualifications of your government officials?
4. What do you think is the most influential class of people in your society today? Explain your answer and relate how it demonstrates the values of your country.

THE MEDIEVAL WORLD

Writers give various titles to the era in Europe lasting from 500 to 1500. You are probably already familiar with names such as the "Dark Ages," the "Medieval Era," and of course the "Middle Ages." (The term *medieval* itself comes from Latin words meaning "middle age.") The "darkness" of the age lies more in our ignorance of the period than in its actual character. The era is, however, a "middle" age. The medieval world is the bridge between the ancient world of Greece and Rome and our modern world. Far from being an unhappy blot on the history of man, the Middle Ages are an important stage in the course of history.

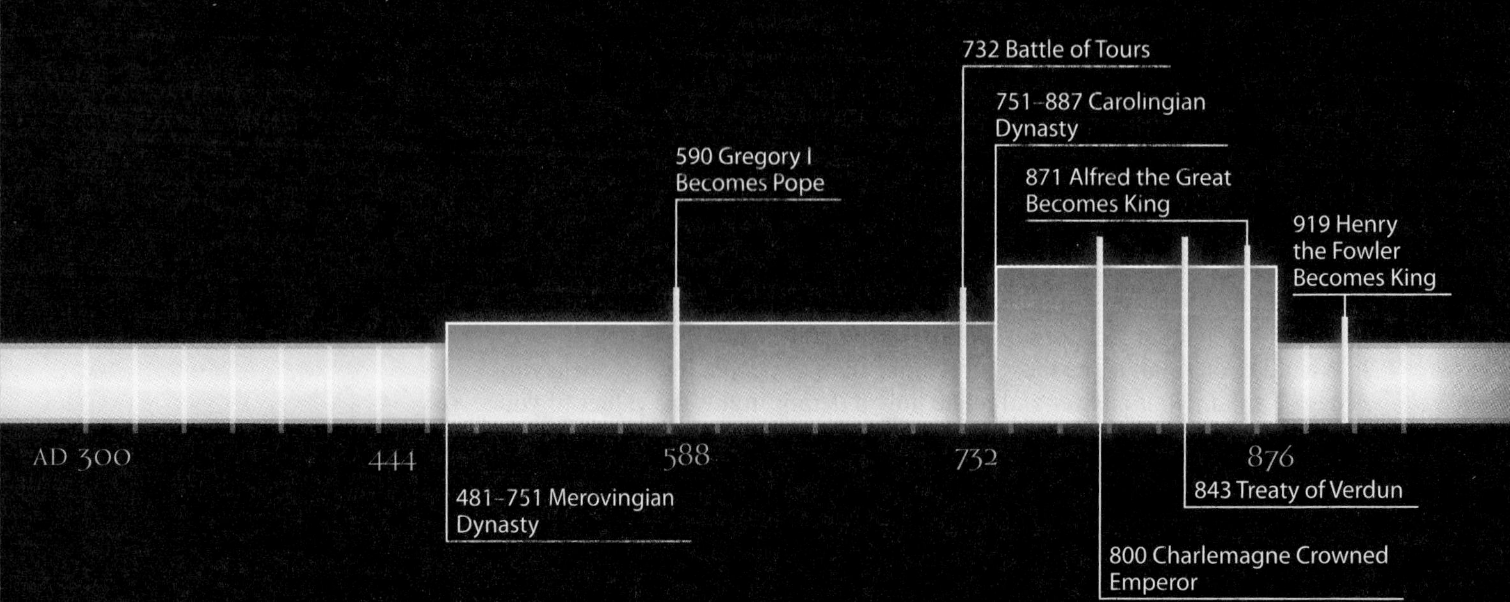

987 Hugh Capet Becomes King
1066 Battle of Hastings
1095–1291 The Crusades
1152 Frederick I Becomes King
1187 Saladin Recaptures Jerusalem
1215 Magna Carta
1302 *Unam Sanctam*
1309–77 Avignon Papacy
1414–18 Council of Constance
1453 Fall of Constantinople
1492 Ferdinand & Isabella Oust Moors
948
1092
1236
1380
1524
1122 Concordat of Worms
1377–1418 Great Schism
1077 Canossa
1226 Louis IX Becomes King
1337–1453 Hundred Years' War
1485 Henry VII Becomes King

8

"Some to pray, some to fight, some to work"

The Making of Medieval Europe

The joust was an important part of both medieval entertainment and the training of knights.

During the Middle Ages, Western society was composed primarily of three classes of people: the clergy, the nobility, and the peasants. Each played an important part in shaping European life and culture. Their roles in society have been described simply: the clergy were called to pray; the nobility, to fight; and the peasants, to work. Accordingly, each group represented an institution of medieval Europe—the church, the feudal system, or the manor.

Three classes of people shaped life in medieval Europe: the clergy, nobility, and peasantry.

I. Growth of the Medieval Church

Outwardly, things looked bleak for western Europe at the outset of the Middle Ages. Rome had fallen; the order and stability she had once provided were gone. Barbarian tribes began to carve out their own kingdoms from the territory once held by the caesars. Monuments of Rome's former grandeur—her aqueducts, amphitheaters, public baths, and roads—were in disrepair. Productivity and trade, as well as thought and learning, were on the decline. The lifestyle of the barbarians was gradually replacing Graeco-Roman culture.

Amidst the confusion and change there remained one stable institution. It represented order and authority and was a means of preserving many elements of classical culture. This institution was the Roman Catholic Church. It became the heart of medieval society, influencing almost every aspect of life. As the church grew in numbers and amassed great power, prestige, and wealth, it assumed leadership in political as well as religious matters. The Roman church cared for the poor, sick, and aged, and took the leading role in education. (There was little literacy and learning outside the church during the medieval period.)

To fully understand the Roman church, one must examine Christianity and its development in the days of the Roman Empire. At that time the word *church* had two different meanings. Specifically, it referred to a local assembly of believers. There were many such local churches scattered throughout the Roman world. The word also had a universal meaning, namely, the "body of Christ." In this sense, *church* referred to the spiritual body composed of all true believers everywhere who were united by faith in Christ. Scripture presents Jesus as "the head over all things to the church, which is his body, the fulness of him that filleth all in all" (Eph. 1:22–23). Recognizing the unity of their faith, the early Christians described this church as **catholic**, a word meaning simply "universal" or "encompassing all."

In the estimation of most people living in western Europe during the Middle Ages, there was but one church. Unlike the early Christians, Europeans conceived of the church solely as an outward, visible institution, which they called the Catholic church. They viewed the large number of local assemblies merely as part of one large ecclesiastical (religious) organization.

It is difficult to tell precisely when the "universal church" as perceived by Europeans took on the official title of the Roman Catholic Church. One thing is certain, however; the *true* universal church and the Roman Catholic Church are not synonymous. The former is a spiritual union of all true believers. The latter is an earthly organization; though it has included many believers through the centuries, it is nevertheless the mixed offspring of biblical truth and human error. Consequently, the Roman Catholic Church in its long history has given increasing importance to the traditions of man at the expense of God's truth. During the Middle Ages, the church became more interested in preserving outward unity among its members than in fostering the inner peace that comes by faith in Jesus Christ. Gradually people began to look to this institutional church for salvation, rather than to the Savior, Jesus Christ.

The Head of the Church

The church and bishop of the city of Rome played key roles in the development of the Roman church. As discussed earlier (see p. 117), the church had been organized according to the political and geographical divisions of the Roman Empire. The church of Rome administered one of the five patriarchates, the highest-ranking divisions within the church. (Jerusalem, Antioch, Alexandria, and Constantinople administered the other four.) At first the patriarchates were equal in rank and authority; however, the church of Rome gradually rose to a place of preeminence. Its bishop assumed sole authority over the church in the West.

There were many reasons for this rise in power and prestige. The bishop of Rome presided over the largest and wealthiest city in the empire. As the people of the Mediterranean world looked to Rome for political and economic leadership, it was quite natural for them to look to her for spiritual guidance as well. Furthermore, all the other patriarchal bishops were located in the East. With the collapse of the western empire in the fifth century, the Roman bishop became one of the few remaining sources of stability in the West. Under Bishop **Leo I** of Rome, the prestige of the office was further enhanced. In 452, when the barbarian Huns threatened the city of Rome, Leo persuaded their leader Attila to spare the city. Leo was hailed as *papa* or **pope** ("Father-Protector"). This title had been applied to other bishops in both the East and the West; by the sixth century, however, it referred almost exclusively to the bishop of Rome.

During the fifth and sixth centuries, the bishops of Rome desired to translate their prestige into authority over all churches. For the most part they were successful. By the end of the sixth century, the bishop of Rome was generally regarded as the pope, the head of the visible church in the West.

To support their claim of primacy ("first in rank"), the bishops of Rome advanced the **Petrine theory**. This theory holds that Christ made Peter the first pope and gave him supreme authority over the church on earth.

> *Thou art Peter, and upon this rock I will build my church; and the gates of hell shall not prevail against it. And I will give unto thee the keys of the kingdom of heaven: and whatsoever thou shalt bind on earth shall be bound in heaven: and whatsoever thou shalt loose on earth shall be loosed in heaven.*
>
> *Matthew 16:18–19*

Jerome and the Vulgate

Because most of the people in the Roman Empire spoke Latin, there was a great need for a Latin translation of the Bible. From the earliest days of the church, many people had attempted to meet that need. By the fourth century there had been so many mistakes in translating and copying the Scripture that many Latin manuscripts were no longer reliable. To correct the problem, the bishop of Rome asked a scholar named Jerome (340–420) to revise the Latin text. Jerome agreed to do so and worked for over twenty years, revising existing translations of portions of the Bible and making original translations of other portions. The result of his labor is a translation that came to be called the Latin Vulgate—a name which means "common" or "well-known." Although Jerome's work was also somewhat inaccurate, the Vulgate became the most widely used Bible of the Middle Ages. Later it became the official Bible of the Roman Catholic Church. Through Jerome's work medieval Europe was exposed to the Word of God.

St. Jerome, *Pietro Paolini, Luccan, 1603–1681, From the Bob Jones University Collection*

Saints

One of the greatest errors promoted by the Roman church during the Middle Ages was the veneration of "saints." The word *saint* means "set apart" or "holy." According to the New Testament, every Christian is a saint through the righteousness of Jesus Christ (e.g., see Rom. 1:7). However, after the time of the apostles, the Roman Catholic Church applied the term *saint* only to Bible characters or to noteworthy Christians (those who reportedly performed miracles or died a martyr's death).

To honor these people, the medieval church held special services and declared certain days to be sacred in their memory. Many of these days—such as St. Patrick's Day and St. Valentine's Day—are still celebrated today. The church taught that dead saints not only help people in time of trouble but also intercede on their behalf before the throne of God. Certain saints became known as "patron" saints because they supposedly interceded for a special group of people. People with specific needs could pray to St. Lucy if they had eye trouble, St. Martha if they needed help with cooking, or St. Valentine if they were in love. Likewise, each occupation had a patron saint; for example, St. Sebastian for athletes, St. Hubert for hunters, and St. Matthew for tax collectors. (The Roman Catholic Church continues to designate saints as patrons for modern times: for example, St. Michael is the patron saint of policemen, St. Joseph of Arimathea is the patron saint of funeral directors, and St. Clare—who died in 1253—is the patron saint of television.) Countries, too, had their own special saints: St. George of England, St. Patrick of Ireland, St. Denis of France, and St. Boniface of Germany.

The Roman church revered Mary above all other saints, as the inscription on this art from a Ukrainian church shows, calling her "Mother of God."

Honored above all saints was Mary, the mother of Christ. To medieval man Mary was the queen of heaven. Calling her the Mother of God, he prayed to her frequently. He believed that she never sinned and that she remained a virgin forever. In fact, Mary became more important in his everyday life than Christ Himself.

According to this theory, Peter became the vicar, or substitute, of Christ on earth. As the first bishop of Rome, he transferred his office with all its authority to those who succeeded him.

The Petrine theory rests upon a number of false assumptions. For instance, the Roman church misinterprets Scripture by asserting that in Matthew 16 Christ appointed Peter the first pope. Nowhere in Scripture does Peter ever claim to have such authority. In fact, it is Peter who in 1 Peter 5:2–3 exhorts God's servants to be of a humble spirit:

> Feed the flock of God which is among you, taking the oversight thereof, not by constraint, but willingly; not for filthy lucre, but of a ready mind; neither as being lords over God's heritage, but being [examples] to the flock.

Another false assumption is that Peter, as the first pope, passed down his authority to succeeding bishops of Rome. There is no historical evidence that Peter ever served as the bishop of the church at Rome.

The Church's Teaching

The Middle Ages is often called an "age of faith." Religion dominated society; nearly every aspect of a person's life was controlled by the Roman church. The power of the Roman bishops grew greater than that of monarchs. And the few bright spots of culture that existed at this time also were made possible by the church.

There was much church activity, but there was little true faith. The church had compromised with the world. Because few people other than the clergy

Little Horwood Church, Buckinghamshire, England

could read and examine the Bible for themselves, the majority of the people placed their trust in the visible church instead of in Christ; they looked to an institution for guidance instead of to the Word of God. Christians began to tolerate spiritual error; without the Bible, they knew no better. Gradually their faith became separated from the truth, and they believed in a distortion of biblical Christianity. This period is perhaps best characterized as an age of spiritual ignorance and darkness.

The papacy assumed the title *Vicarius Filii Dei*, a Latin title meaning "the one who takes the place of the Son of God." The Roman church believed in the inspiration and authority of the Bible as God's Word, but it contended that the traditions of the church had equal authority. As a result, the doctrine and practice of the Roman church was a dangerous mixture of truth and error.

Medieval Superstitions

Closely associated with the worship of Mary and the veneration of the saints was the importance that the church attached to relics. A relic is an object associated with a saint, such as a piece of clothing, or even a part of the saint himself, such as a bone or a lock of hair. During the Middle Ages many rulers as well as individual churches made great efforts to secure relics. The reason for such interest was twofold. First, the Roman church taught that mass could not be celebrated unless it were performed upon an altar stone that contained a relic of a saint. Second, the church taught that those who properly viewed and honored the relics would have time removed from the temporal punishment for sin in purgatory. This teaching helped to promote pilgrimages to shrines housing the relics of saints.

Most of the relics, however, were erroneous or falsified. Some churches claimed to have Noah's beard, a bit of manna, the bones of Balaam's donkey, and some feathers from the wings of the archangel Michael (to name only a few). In addition, various churches claimed to have relics related to the life of Christ: straw from the manger, some of the wine Jesus made at Cana, drops of sweat from Gethsemane, the crown of thorns, and some of Christ's blood. So many places claimed to have part of the true cross that one sixteenth-century churchman sarcastically remarked that if all the pieces were gathered together, there would be enough wood to build Noah's ark!

It was such superstition, believing that these relics acted as some sort of "good luck" charm, that blinded the people of the Middle Ages to the truth of God's Word.

An outgrowth of this mixture of human tradition and Bible doctrine is the **Roman sacramental system**. The Roman church defines a sacrament as a religious act that automatically grants grace (spiritual benefit) by its very performance. The church taught that the sacraments were necessary for salvation: they were thus made the core of worship and teaching in the Roman church. In addition, the church claimed the exclusive right to administer the sacraments and to do so only to those in fellowship with the visible church.

By the end of the twelfth century, the Roman church recognized **seven sacraments** and taught the following regarding them:

1. Baptism initiates one into the church by "washing away original sin."
2. Confirmation brings one into full fellowship with the church and confers upon him the Holy Spirit to strengthen his spiritual life.
3. Through penance a church member earns forgiveness for sin committed after baptism. Penance includes contrition (sorrow), confession (to a priest), satisfaction (actions done to make amends for sins), and absolution (forgiveness of the guilt of sins by a priest).
4. The Holy Eucharist (YOO kur ist), or Holy Communion, is both a sacrament and a sacrifice in which the priest sacrifices Christ anew. During this service, known as the **mass**, the priest claims to transform the bread and wine into the actual body and blood of Christ. This change is known as **transubstantiation**.
5. Matrimony unites a man and a woman as husband and wife.
6. Holy Orders sets an individual apart for the service of the church by ordaining him into the priesthood.
7. Extreme Unction, sometimes called the last rites, gives an anointing or blessing to a seriously ill or dying person. Its purpose is to grant absolution from any remaining sin and to offer spiritual comfort.

Through the sacraments, the Roman church wielded great power over the Western world, because no one could be saved without them, and they could be administered only by the church. Thus, it maintained that there was no salvation outside the one visible "catholic" church, and salvation became a product of works. The words of Jesus Christ show the error of this system:

> *In vain they do worship me, teaching for doctrines the commandments of men.*
>
> *Matthew 15:9*

Warriors of the Church

In many respects the Roman church was like an army—a religious army that spread across western Europe and held it captive for almost a thousand years. There arose a sharp distinction between the common church members and those who "enlisted" (through Holy Orders) in the special service of the church. The "enlisted" men were called the **clergy**; the "nonenlisted," the **laity**. The medieval world looked upon the clergy as the only servants of the church—its elite "warriors." However, this idea is contrary to God's Word; all Christians are to be active soldiers in the service of God. (See Eph. 6:10–18.)

In any volunteer army, men enlist for many different reasons. So it was in the Roman church. Some wore the uniform but were not in sympathy with the cause; they joined out of ambition, hoping to gain the wealth, luxury, and power that often accompanied prestigious church offices. Others enlisted to

THROUGH EYES OF FAITH:

Sola Scriptura

As the Middle Ages drew to a close, many Europeans began to realize that much of the church's teachings were based on tradition and not on Scripture. Not until the Protestant Reformation, when the cry of *Sola Scriptura!* (the Bible alone) began resounding, did people begin to realize the extent of the problem. This problem that developed in the Roman Catholic Church was natural. It has even happened repeatedly in the history of God's people; according to Matthew 15:9, it was common in Christ's day as well. Is valuing tradition over Scripture a problem in churches today? If yes, can you think of any examples of how that could be true?

____

____

____

____

____

____

____

____

____

____

Whitby Abbey was founded in the seventh century on cliffs by the sea in Northumbria.

find a haven from personal or family problems. Though many had poor motives, some men joined the ranks out of a sincere desire to serve God. Thus the medieval church had both good and bad warriors: the dedicated and the indifferent, the giving and the selfish, those who sought eternal rewards and those who desired material gain, those who furthered the cause of Christ and those who hindered it.

Much like the soldiers in an army, the clergy of the Roman church were organized into different branches of service. The clergy of one branch were called **secular** (from *seculum*, Latin for "world") **clergy**. These men conducted religious services, administered the sacraments to the laity, and supervised the business and property of the church. Too often, however, the secular clergy mixed the work of the church with worldly pleasure. The Bible admonishes: "No man that warreth entangleth himself with the affairs of this life; that he may please him who hath chosen him to be a soldier" (2 Tim. 2:4).

Another of the church's "fighting forces" was the **regular clergy**. This group of clergy renounced the things of this world. Some sacrificed their own personal ambitions in order to maintain an active mission of social service. Others retired to a life of solitude and study. They lived in monastic communities under strict regulations. (The word *regular* comes from the Latin *regula*, meaning "rule.") The most popular system of rules in medieval Europe came from Benedict of Nurisa (480?–543?), often called the "Father of Western Monasticism." Characterized by discipline and order, the **Benedictine Rule** strictly regulated the lives of monks. They engaged in such daily activities as manual labor, study, religious services, and prayer. Monks entering this order took vows of poverty, chastity (celibacy), and obedience to the abbot, the leader of the monastery.

The regular clergy, or monks, played an important role in the growth of the medieval church and in the progress of Western society. They were the missionaries of the medieval church. Two of the most renowned medieval missionaries were English monks: **Patrick** (389?–461?), who took the gospel to Ireland, and **Boniface** (680?–755), who was known as the "Apostle of the Germans." Monks also developed new farming techniques and contributed to the preservation of learning by collecting the writings of the ancient world for their libraries.

The "commander in chief" of the medieval "army" was the pope. Perhaps the best representative of the early medieval popes was **Gregory I** (590–604), called "the Great." As bishop of Rome, he greatly expanded the power and authority of his office. In fact, he is commonly recognized as the first true pope—a title which he, however, disclaimed. Unlike many of his successors, he was a man of deep devotion and fervent piety. Yet, like most of the age in which he lived, Gregory was blinded by superstition and ignorance. He promoted many unbiblical doctrines that the Roman church later officially embraced: the mass,

The Origin of Names

People have not always had first and last names as we do today. During Bible times, for example, most people had only one name. However, to avoid confusion with another person who had the same name, people often added a second name: for example, Simon the Canaanite (Matt. 10:4) and Alexander the coppersmith (2 Tim. 4:14). During the Middle Ages this practice of adopting a second name continued. Some names were descriptions of a person's appearance or character, such as "the Pious," "the Fat," or "the Red." (The modern English surnames, or last names, Reid, Reed, and Read mean "Red.") Some names, such as Cook, Miller, Tailor (Taylor), Carpenter, Smith (from blacksmith), or Clark (from clerk), described a person's occupation. Other names described the place near which a person lived: Stone, Hill, Wood, Ford. Finally, many people took the name of their father as their second name. For example, the son of John became Johnson; the son of Henry became O'Henry; the son of Greg became MacGregor. Later even this naming system became confusing. As a result it became customary for a son to keep his father's last name regardless of his own occupation or where he might live. While most modern surnames still have a particular meaning, for the most part they no longer bear any relationship to one's work, the first name of one's father, or one's place of residence.

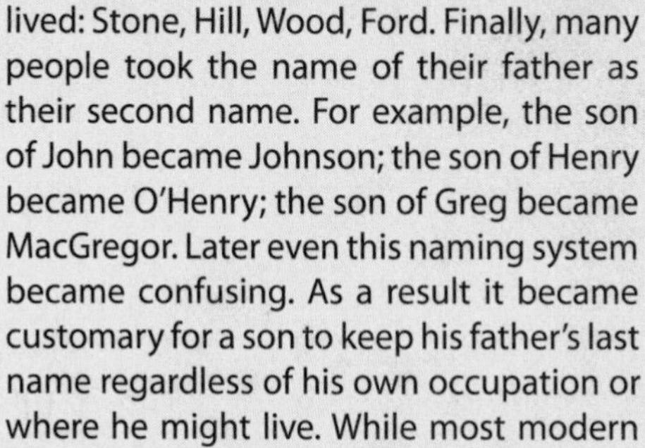

the equality of tradition and Scripture, the sacrament of penance, and **purgatory** (a place of temporary punishment where souls bound for heaven must go after death to atone for their "minor" unconfessed sins or for sins for which they have not done sufficient penance).

Section Quiz

1. List two reasons for the rise of the bishop of Rome to prominence over other bishops.
2. What term describes a religious act (necessary for salvation) that automatically grants spiritual benefit to the one who does it?
3. List the seven sacraments of the Roman church.
4. Into what two groups were the members of the Roman church divided?
5. Name the two English monks who were known for their missionary activity.

1. ______________________
2. ______________________
3. ______________________
4. ______________________
5. ______________________

II. A New Western Empire

As the Middle Ages began, western Europe faced widespread invasions, social unrest, and political disorder. The kingdoms established by leaders of Germanic tribes were generally small and lacked strong central governments. By far the most powerful of the Germanic peoples were the **Franks**. They established many independent kingdoms in Gaul (modern-day France). From these Frankish kingdoms arose a new empire that temporarily reunited much of western Europe.

Clovis and the Franks

In 481 **Clovis** became the head of a Frankish tribe in northern Gaul. Through treachery and exceptional military ability, he conquered other Frankish tribes, uniting them into one kingdom. He soon became known as "King of the Franks." Once Clovis pushed the Visigoths out of southern Gaul, his territory included most of the area of present-day France, which takes its name from the Franks.

Important to the history of both western Europe and the Frankish kingdom was Clovis's "conversion" to Christianity. Like the emperor Constantine, Clovis was in danger of being defeated in battle when he cried out to God for help. He vowed to believe in God and be baptized in His name if granted the victory. Emerging victorious in battle, Clovis remained true to his vow. He even required three thousand of his soldiers to be baptized into the Roman church. The "conversions" of Clovis and his men were typical of many medieval conversions made for convenience or by coercion. But Christ reminds us in Matthew 7:21–23 of the fate of people who make only outward conversions:

> Not every one that saith unto me, Lord, Lord, shall enter into the kingdom of heaven; but he that doeth the will of my Father which is in heaven. Many will say to me in that day, Lord, Lord, have we not prophesied in thy name? and in thy name have cast out devils? and in thy name done many wonderful works? And then will I profess unto them, I never knew you: depart from me, ye that work iniquity.

Clovis gained the support of the Roman church, which found him a powerful champion for its cause. Thus began an alliance between the Frankish rulers and the Roman church that lasted for centuries.

The Mayors of the Palace

Clovis died in 511, after having established a strong, unified kingdom. In accordance with Frankish custom, the kingdom was divided among his four sons. Their descendants continued to reign over the Franks well into the eighth century. This royal line of family was known as the **Merovingian House**, taking its name from an early ancestor of Clovis named Merovech. The Merovingian family was plagued by quarrels. The custom of granting a share of the kingdom to each of the king's sons caused brothers to become rivals. Each sought to gain the other's territory, using murder and treachery when necessary. Yet despite the domestic feuds and confusion under the Merovingian kings, Frankish rulers remained in power.

Even so, by the seventh century, they had lost much of their prestige and effectiveness through drunkenness, immoral living, and family strife. They became known as the **"do-nothing kings."** They reigned, but they did not rule. The real power behind the throne was assumed by the principal palace official, called the *major domo*, the **mayor of the palace**. Originally, the mayor of the palace supervised only the king's household, but he later extended his authority over the financial, military, and administrative functions of government.

Near the end of the seventh century, **Pepin II** became the mayor of one of the stronger Frankish states. He defeated all rival mayors and reunited almost all of the Frankish territories under one rule. The Merovingians still occupied the throne, but they were mere puppets of the mayors. Probably the best remembered of all the mayors of the palace is **Charles Martel**, son of Pepin II. In **732** Charles won his fame by stopping the advance of the Muslims into Europe. He defeated them at the Battle of Tours in western France. This feat earned him the title *Martel*, or "the Hammer."

Pepin the Short (751–68), like his father Charles Martel, served as mayor of the palace. He possessed all the powers of the king, but he wished to have the title as well. Pepin appealed to the pope, asking him to decide whether he, Pepin, or the "do-nothing" Merovingian king should be the rightful ruler of the Franks. The pope replied that the one who wielded the power should be king. Pepin therefore became king in 751. Three years later the pope traveled to France and sealed the change in ruling families by anointing Pepin "by the grace of God king of the Franks." The **Carolingian House**—named after its most illustrious member, Charlemagne—now officially ruled the Franks.

In return for his support, the pope asked Pepin to protect him against the **Lombards**. They were a Germanic people who through conquest had moved into northern Italy (a region still known today as Lombardy). In the first half of the eighth century, the Lombards had invaded central Italy and had threatened

THROUGH EYES OF FAITH:

Battle of Tours

What might Europe have been like had the Muslims won the Battle of Tours? Why do you think God allowed the Franks to defeat them? Can you think of other examples of God's providence evident in history?

the city of Rome. Coming to the pope's aid, Pepin defeated the Lombards and gave their lands to the pope. Known as the **Donation of Pepin,** these lands eventually became the Papal States. The pope, head of the Roman church, became a ruler involved in European politics. His successors continued to rule as kings over this region for the next one thousand years.

The Empire of Charlemagne

Charlemagne's Character

When Pepin died in 768, his sons Carloman and Charles succeeded him as corulers. After only a few years, Carloman died, and Charles became the sole ruler of the Frankish kingdom. Charles was not only the greatest Carolingian king but also one of the outstanding figures of the Middle Ages. His character and accomplishments won him the title **Charlemagne** (SHAR luh mane), or "Charles the Great."

According to Einhard, Charlemagne's close friend and biographer, "Charles was large and strong, and of lofty stature, though not disproportionately tall (his height is well known to have been seven time the length of his foot)." Undoubtedly his "lofty stature" did not come from his father, Pepin the Short, but from his mother, who was called *Berte au grand pied*, or "Big-Foot" Bertha. Einhard further described Charlemagne as

> stately and dignified, whether he was standing or sitting; although his neck was thick and somewhat short, and his belly rather prominent; but the symmetry of the rest of his body concealed these defects. His gait was firm, his whole carriage manly, and his voice clear, but not so strong as his size led one to expect. . . . He abominated drunkenness in anybody, much more in himself and those of his household.[1]

Equestrian statuette of Charlemagne

From the Treasury of Metz Cathedral. Carolingian, 9th AD. Bronze with traces of gold. ¾ view. H.: 23.5 cm. Inv.: OA 8260.

Charlemagne possessed many virtues, but he was not without his vices. On one occasion he is reported to have beheaded several thousand prisoners in cold blood. In addition, his personal life was marred by sin. He had little regard for the sanctity of marriage; he married, divorced, and remarried many times.

Charlemagne's Conquests

The Frankish kingdom reached its peak under Charlemagne's rule (768–814). As his father had done, Charlemagne rescued Rome, which had again been invaded by Lombards. He took for himself the title "King of the Lombards." With this foe subdued, he directed his military campaigns against the Saxons, a Germanic tribe in northern Europe. After thirty years of bitter struggle he conquered this people also. Near the Danube River in central Europe, he defeated the Avars, a nomadic people similar to the Huns. And in the south, he drove the Spanish Muslims back across the Pyrenees. By the time of his death, Charlemagne had created an empire that stretched over most of western Europe. He laid the foundation for the modern European nations of France, Germany, and Italy.

Charlemagne divided his empire into hundreds of administrative districts, or counties. He appointed counts to supervise each district. They administered justice, maintained the peace, and raised an army in times of war. To ensure the enforcement of his policies on the local level, Charlemagne created the office of ***missi dominici***, or the king's envoys (messengers). He sent pairs of these messengers into the districts to investigate local conditions and to hear

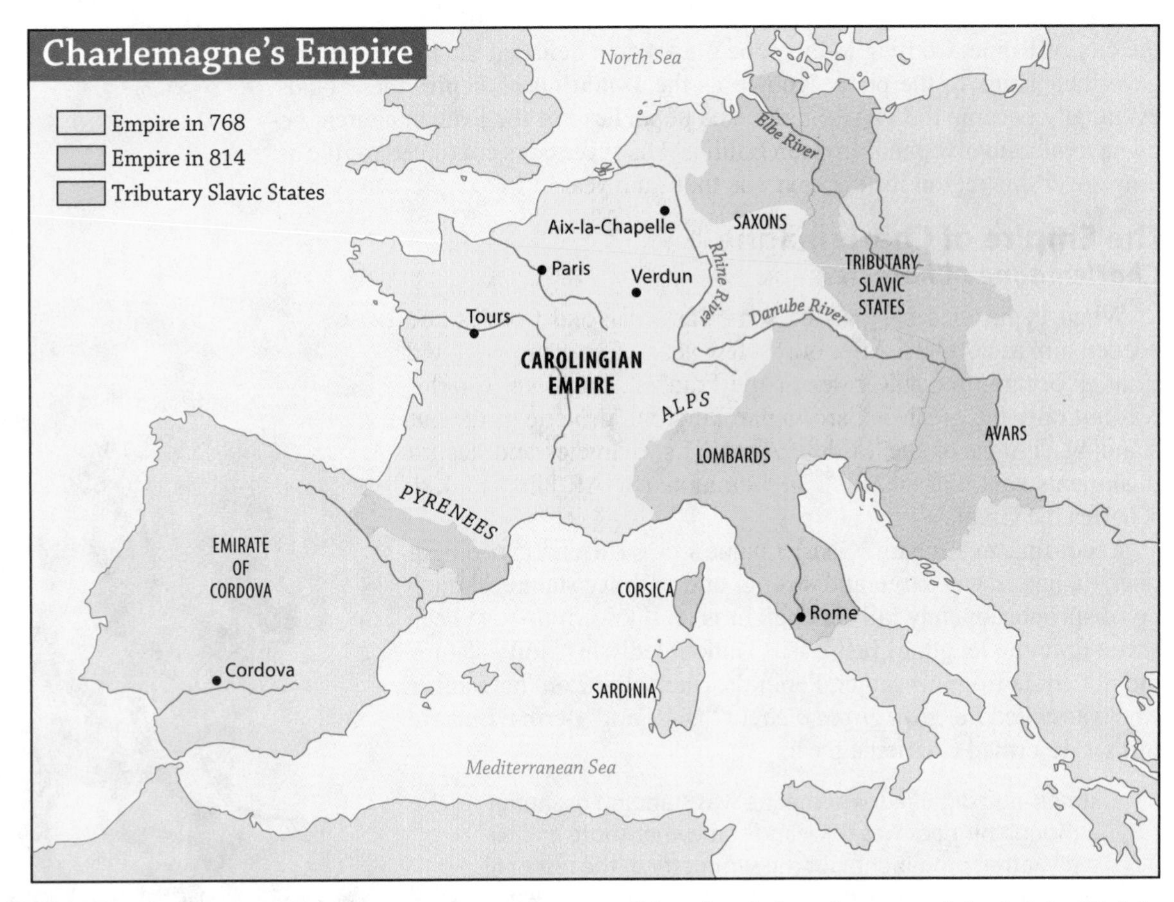

complaints leveled against any of the local officials. These *missi dominici* then sent back written reports to Charlemagne.

Because such officials were subject to bribery, Charlemagne chose only men of proven ability and character. Furthermore, he stated that no *missi dominici* could serve in any district in which he held property, nor could two serve together for more than one year.

Charlemagne's Crowning

Since the days of the Roman emperors, no one man in the West had ruled as much territory as Charlemagne. Western Europe looked upon him as another Constantine, ruling and protecting both church and state. While Charlemagne was attending a church service in Rome on Christmas Day, **800**, the pope placed a crown on his head and proclaimed him Roman emperor. The assembly present cried out: "To Charles Augustus, crowned by God, the great and pacific [peaceful] emperor of the Romans, life and victory."

Although the title "emperor" did little to increase the actual power of Charlemagne, it did have an important impact upon later medieval history. His empire fell apart after his death, but Charlemagne's

Throne of Charlemagne. Cathedral (Palatine Chapel), Aachen, Germany

Aachen Cathedral in Germany; the building was begun by Charlemagne and was the coronation church for thirty German kings.

crowning had revived the idea of a restored Roman Empire which would again unite the territories of western Europe. This crowning also raised a serious question: whose authority is supreme—the state's or the church's? Though Charlemagne's authority was unquestioned in his day, popes later insisted that their authority superseded that of the kings, pointing out that a pope had crowned Charlemagne. They claimed the power not only to confirm kings but also to depose them. This struggle for supremacy between the popes and the kings culminated during the late Middle Ages.

A Revival of Learning

Charlemagne's love of learning prompted him to promote education throughout his empire. His royal court at Aachen (Aix-la-Chapelle; AYKS lah shah PEL) became the leading center of learning in the realm. There he assembled the best scholars of western Europe. The most distinguished of these was **Alcuin** (AL kwin) from York, England. He took charge of the palace school and trained the king's children as well as the children of other noble families. Alcuin also taught the king. Einhard wrote of Charlemagne's "education":

> The King spent much time and labor . . . studying rhetoric, dialectics, and especially astronomy; he learned to reckon [calculate], and used to investigate the motion of the heavenly bodies most curiously, with an intelligent scrutiny. He also tried to write, and used to keep tablets and blanks in bed under his pillow, that at leisure hours he might accustom his hand to form the letters; however, as he did not begin his efforts in due season, but late in life, they met with ill success.[2]

THIS MOMENT IN HISTORY:

Charlemagne

How did Charlemagne's interest in education impact his generation and future generations?

____

____

____

____

____

____

____

____

THROUGH EYES OF FAITH:

The Value of Education

Some Christians are suspicious of higher education. What do Charlemagne's educational reforms suggest about how a Christian should view all levels of education?

____

____

____

____

____

____

____

____

Perhaps it was under Alcuin's influence that Charlemagne developed his deep concern for a better-educated clergy. He encouraged the church to establish schools to upgrade the literacy of the priests and monks. In a letter to church leaders, Charlemagne set forth what has been called the charter of education for the Middle Ages. In it, he said:

> Whence it happened that we began to fear lest perchance, as the skill in writing was less, so also the wisdom for understanding the Holy Scriptures might be much less than it rightly ought to be. And we all know well that, although errors of speech are dangerous, far more dangerous are errors of the understanding. Therefore, we exhort you not only not to neglect the study of letters but also with most humble mind, pleasing to God, to study earnestly in order that you may be able more easily and more correctly to penetrate the mysteries of the divine Scriptures.[3]

Charlemagne's educational reforms renewed interest in the Bible and the works of classical writers. For several centuries in western Europe there had been little interest in learning; few people could read or write. During that time many ancient manuscripts were lost or damaged; others were full of copyists' mistakes. One of the most important contributions of Charlemagne's reign was the rediscovery and preservation of these ancient works. In addition, God used the Carolingian scholars to preserve copies of the Bible.

Monasteries were the primary centers for studying, copying, and preserving ancient manuscripts; they were the "printing houses" and libraries of the Middle Ages. Monks undertook the painstaking process of making handwritten copies of earlier works. During this period, they developed a new and beautiful style of handwriting known as the **Carolingian minuscule**. This clean and simple writing style became the model for much of our "lowercase" writing today. Many manuscripts were illuminated with colorful illustrations.

Disintegration of Charlemagne's Empire

Although the effects of this renewed interest in learning lasted for centuries, Charlemagne's impressive empire deteriorated rapidly. Within a century after his death, the empire had collapsed, torn by civil war and pillaged by invaders.

Problems from Within

When Charlemagne died in 814, his empire passed to his only surviving son, Louis the Pious. During Louis's reign, a bitter rivalry broke out among his sons over which portion of the empire each would inherit. Even before Louis's death this rivalry led to civil war. The Bible tells us, "A brother offended is harder to be won than a strong city: and their contentions are like the bars of a castle" (Prov. 18:19).

After years of fighting, the brothers met at the city of Verdun to settle their differences. In the **Treaty of Verdun (843)**, they agreed to split the empire into three separate kingdoms: **Charles the Bald** received West Frankland; **Louis the German**, East Frankland; and the eldest brother, **Lothair**, retained the title of emperor and ruled the land between his brother's kingdoms. (See the map on p. 191.) Notice how closely the modern states of France, Germany, and Italy correspond to these divisions.

When Lothair died, Charles and Louis wasted little time in seizing portions of his kingdom. (Part of this territory is still know today as Lorraine, "Lothair's kingdom.") Political fragmentation characterized the last days of the empire as the Carolingian rulers persisted in their family strife. In addition, the successors to Charlemagne's grandsons were weak and incompetent rulers, as is demonstrated by the disrespectful surnames they were given; Louis the

Stammerer, Charles the Fat, Louis the Child, and Charles the Simple.

Problems from Without

During the ninth and tenth centuries, the Carolingian Empire offered little resistance to the foreign invaders that beset it on every side. From North Africa came Muslim raiders who devastated the Mediterranean coast of Europe. They captured Sardinia, Corsica, and Sicily and pillaged southern Italy. From the East came the **Magyars**, a group of Asiatic nomads who later became known as the Hungarians. They swept into the Danube region of southeastern Europe, where they ravaged the eastern borders of the empire.

The most feared invaders were the **Vikings**, or Norsemen. These Germanic tribes swooped down from the north out of the lands known today as Norway, Sweden, and Denmark. Fearless warriors, skilled seamen, and daring adventurers, Viking sailors braved the waters of the Atlantic to sail to Iceland, Greenland, and North America. Some sailed down the rivers of Russia, while others sailed along the coastal waters of Europe and into the Mediterranean region, plundering costal villages and towns. The Vikings struck terror into the hearts of the people of Europe; their swift raids left villages aflame, homes and crops destroyed, and churches and monasteries ransacked. Few in Europe felt safe from the attacks of the dreaded Norsemen. "From the fury of the Northmen, O Lord, deliver us" was a prayer offered in churches across western Europe.

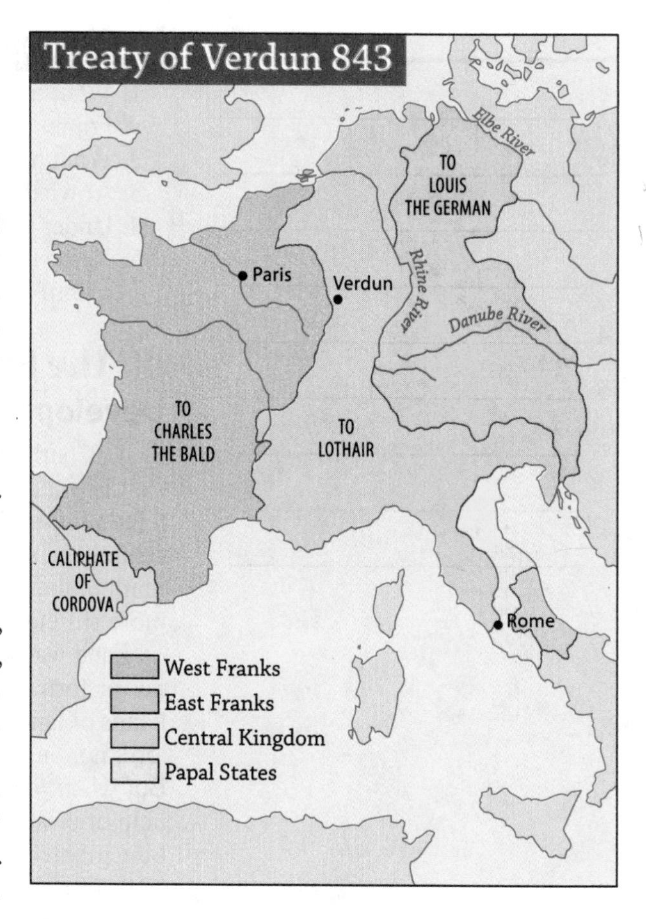

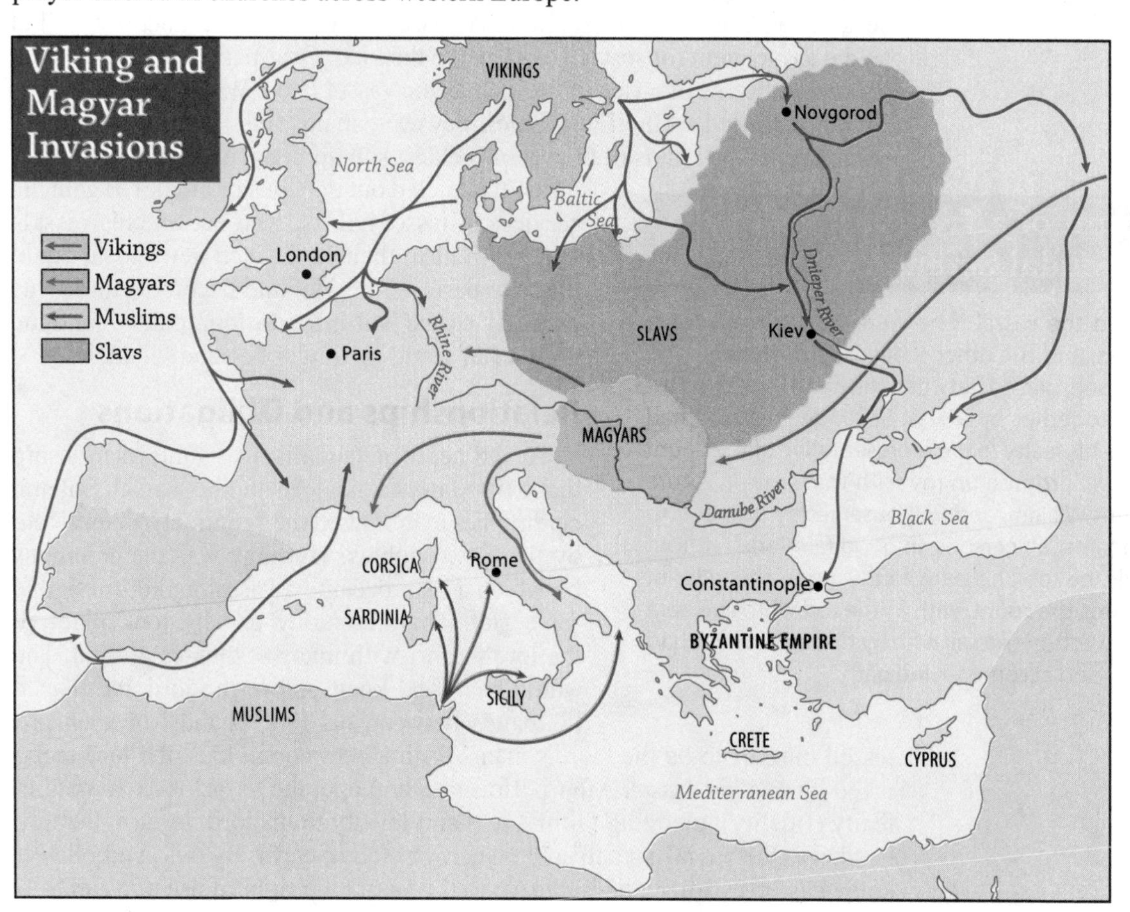

Section Quiz

1. __________
2. __________
3. __________

____
4. __________
5. __________

____

____

____

1. What man united the Frankish tribes and became known as "King of the Franks"?
2. What palace official became the real power behind the Frankish throne?
3. At what battle and in what year did Charles Martel defeat the Muslims?
4. Under whose rule did the Frankish empire reach its peak?
5. Name the treaty that split the Carolingian Empire into three parts, and identify the brothers and the portion of the kingdom which they received.

III. The Feudal System

Development

As Charlemagne's empire disintegrated, powerful nobles replaced the weak Carolingian kings. There arose a new political system in which local rulers offered the people protection in return for their services. This system, known as **feudalism**, was the form of government prevalent in western Europe from the ninth to the thirteenth centuries. It provided relative order and security until a more structured government emerged.

Land was the basis of wealth and power during the Feudal Age. Governing power formerly exercised by a central government gradually passed into the hands of landholding nobles, called **lords**. In theory, the king was the supreme lord, holding all the land in the kingdom by right of conquest or inheritance. But when foreign raiders threatened his territory, the king had to rely on the help of powerful nobles. In return for their services (usually military aid), the king granted them the use of landed estates. The land grants became known as **fiefs**, or in Latin, *feudum*, from which our word *feudal* comes.

A fief could be extremely large or very small. The recipient of such an estate became the king's **vassal** (servant). A vassal did not own the land, or fief, but held it as payment for service rendered to the king. Originally, the king granted his vassal the use of a fief for as long as the vassal lived. When the vassal died, the fief reverted to the king. Later, however, many fiefs became hereditary, remaining in the hands of the vassal's eldest son upon payment of a fee. Often a vassal parceled out portions of his fief to gain the services of lesser nobles, who became his vassals, and he, in turn, their lord. Each new vassal could likewise partition his fief and become a lord. This process, called **subinfeudation**, could continue until a fief could no longer be subdivided.

An Account of a Twelfth-Century Feudal Ceremony

The count asked the vassal if he were willing to become completely his man, and the other replied, "I am willing": and with his hands clasped, placed between the hands of the count, they were bound together by a kiss. Secondly, he who had done homage gave his fealty to the representative of the count in these words, "I will promise on my faith that I will in future be faithful to Count William, and will observe my homage to him completely against all persons, in good faith and without deceit." And thirdly, he took his oath to this upon the relics of the saints. Afterwards the count, with a little rod which he held in his hand, gave investitures to all who by this agreement had given their security and accompanying oath.

Relationships and Obligations

At the heart of feudalism was the relationship that existed between a lord and his vassal. Solemn ceremonies symbolized the "contract" entered into by these two nobles. **Homage** was the ceremony by which a man became a vassal and thus eligible for a fief. This ceremony usually took place in the lord's court with many witnesses present. The would-be vassal knelt before the lord and placed his hands between his lord's hands; he then professed himself to be the "lord's man." With a ceremonial kiss, the lord recognized him as his vassal. After performing homage, the vassal took an oath of fealty (fidelity), pledging faithfulness and loyalty to his lord. In turn, the lord handed to the vassal a small stick, lance, or clod of earth. By this symbolic act, known as **investiture**, the lord gave to the vassal the right of use of a fief.

In addition to the grant of a fief, the lord was obligated to guarantee his vassal protection and justice. The vassal's primary duty was to provide military service for his lord. He was expected to furnish a specified number of knights (for at least forty days a year) to assist the lord in his battles. Not all of the vassal's responsibilities were military, however. A vassal also agreed to supply financial payments, called **aids**, on special occasions such as when his lord's eldest son became a knight or when the lord's eldest daughter was married. Vassals attended the lord's court to give counsel and to assist in the administration of justice. In addition, the vassal was obligated to pay a ransom if his lord were captured in war. Although a vassal's duties were many and varied, he benefited from this feudal relationship. A fief gave a vassal authority and power; the greater the size of the fief, the greater the vassal's prestige. Often, through multiple alliances and exchanges of land, a knight became a vassal of more than one lord. This increased his dignity, but it also increased his obligations. It often led to conflicting loyalties, as when lords warred against one another. In the same way, problems arise when men try to serve two spiritual masters. It is indeed true, as Christ said, that "no man can serve two masters: for either he will hate the one, and love the other; or else he will hold to the one, and despise the other" (Matt. 6:24).

The Life of the Nobility

The Castle

The **castle** was the center of life for the nobility. It was not only the lord's home but also the local jail, the treasury, the armory, the court, and the seat of government. Modern books and films have romanticized daily life in the medieval castle. Yet, as impressive as feudal castles may have seemed from a distance, they were often damp, cold, musty, and dark. Tapestries and flowers

Bodiam Castle, England

were used to add warmth and cheer to the otherwise bleak surroundings. Feudal castles had few of the comforts and luxuries that we associate with the elegant, aristocratic palaces of a later day.

Castles were built primarily for defensive purposes. The word *castle* comes from the Latin word *castellum*, meaning "fort" or "fortress." At first castles were often just wooden blockhouses set on high mounds surrounded by a stockade and a ditch (moat). It was not until about the tenth century that castles assumed the features that most people think of today: massive stone walls, towering battlements, wide moats, and wooden drawbridges. It was the lord's responsibility to protect the inhabitants of the surrounding countryside. When invaders threatened the land, the local villagers fled into the safe confines of their lord's castle. High atop the castle's battlement, defenders could repel an attack with spears and arrows or by pouring molten metal or dropping large boulders on the heads of attackers.

Knighthood

Also important to the protection of life and property during the Middle Ages was the **knight**. In the early Middle Ages, anyone brave and strong enough could become one. Later, however, knighthood was restricted to the nobility.

The preparation for knighthood was long and hard. At age seven, a boy's initiation formally began. At that time his parents placed him in the care of a knight (often an uncle) for special training. For the next several years the youth, or **page**, developed both his mind and body. He studied academic subjects such as religion, science, and history; he also spent time learning to fence (fight with a sword), to ride a horse, and to hunt with falcons and dogs. In his midteens, the page became a **squire**, the personal servant of a knight. His training became more intense and his responsibilities greater. He cared for the knight's armor, weapons, and horse; he dressed his knight each morning and waited on him, his family, and guests as they ate.

The knight is symbolic of the feudal system and medieval society.

When he was about twenty-one, a squire became eligible for knighthood. Occasionally a man was knighted instantly on the battlefield in recognition of unusual bravery. More often, however, a squire received knighthood in a special religious ceremony. The squire spent the night before the ceremony praying before his armor, which lay on the altar of the church. The ceremony climaxed the next morning when the squire, kneeling before an elder knight or priest, was dubbed, or tapped on the shoulders with the flat side of a sword's blade. The ceremony often ended with a display of the young man's knightly skills.

The Code of Chivalry

The knight promised to live by a strict code of behavior, called the "code of chivalry." The word ***chivalry*** comes from the French word for *horseman* (i.e., a knight); it is closely related to the English word *cavalry*. A true knight was expected to be brave in battle, skillful with his weapons, honest and generous, and loyal to his lord. He never attacked an unarmed knight but gave him the opportunity to put on his armor before engaging him in battle. Likewise, it was improper for an entire company of knights to attack a single knight; they were to fight him one at a time.

The influence of the Roman church gradually pervaded the knightly code. According to the twelfth-century philosopher John of Salisbury, knights were to "defend the Church, assail infidelity, venerate the priesthood, protect the poor from injuries, pacify the province, pour out their blood for their brothers, and if need be lay down their lives."[4] The church not only tried to improve the conduct of the knights, but also attempted to place limitations on feudal warfare through decrees known as the **Peace of God** and the **Truce of God**. By the Peace of God the church forbade the pillage of her property and extended protection to all noncombatants in society. The Truce of God sought to limit fighting to specified weekdays by forbidding combat from Wednesday evening to Monday morning. Although often ineffective in enforcing these decrees, the church did help to improve the harsh and brutal conditions of the feudal period.

Tournaments and Jousts

Even in times of peace, the knight maintained his skills. He often went hunting and fishing, but his real love was fighting. When peaceful conditions kept him at home, he sometimes kept fit by staging a mock war, called a **tournament**. The typical tournament included two types of contests: the *joust* and the *melee*. Jousting was a competition between two knights on horseback who charged at each other, carrying lances with which each tried to unseat his opponent. The melee was a team competition. At a signal, the two sides rushed at each other on horseback and fought what amounted to a full-scale battle. Often they fought within a fenced area so that the battle would remain compact and thus more intense and exciting to watch. The weapons were usually blunted, but there were nonetheless many injuries and even some deaths. One historian states that the tournaments "satisfied the craving of both fighters and spectators for 'redblooded' excitement in a manner that reminds one of the Roman gladiatorial games, the Spanish bullfight, the rougher aspects of American football, and prize fighting."[5]

Section Quiz

1. What was land granted by kings to nobles in return for their service called?
2. What place was the center of life for the nobility?
3. What two stages of preparation did a young man go through to become a knight?
4. Name the strict code that governed knightly behavior.
5. What two types of activities were part of the typical tournaments among knights?

1. ______________________
2. ______________________
3. ______________________
   ____
4. ______________________
5. ______________________
   ____

IV. The Manor

Role

The **manor** was the home for the vast majority of people living in western Europe during the Middle Ages. It was the center of medieval society, a self-contained farming community controlled by a lord and farmed by peasants. The manorial system arose out of the economic and social conditions of the early medieval period; during that time trade decreased, the size and number of towns diminished, and money was rarely used as a medium of exchange. Most Europeans moved to large estates, where they relied on their own labor to produce their daily needs.

Because of the lack of trade, the manor had to be largely self-sufficient. Each manor usually had its own priest and skilled workers. Craftsmen made such items as furniture, shoes, tools, and woven cloth. The laborers on each manor produced their own food, built their own homes, and made their own clothing. They grew crops and raised cattle, sheep, and pigs; they constructed bridges and roads. About the only items the manor could not provide for itself were salt, iron, and tar, all of which had to be imported.

Manors varied from one locality to another. Factors such as climate and soil influenced the quality of life on the manor; the people on one manor might prosper, while those on another might barely eke out a living. Some manors were large estates composed of many villages and thousands of acres of land. Others were simply small villages with only a few hundred acres. Likewise there was a wide range in the population on the manors, from a dozen families to more than one hundred.

Description

The center of a typical manor was the village, usually located near a stream or at a crossroad. Here peasants lived in clusters of small cottages, which were one- or two-room huts with thatched roofs and walls of mud and straw. The peasants enjoyed few comforts or possessions; their homes had dirt floors, few if any windows (glass was a luxury), no chimneys, and meager furnishings. Next to each cottage was a small plot on which a peasant family could plant a vegetable garden and build a stable to house any livestock it might own. It was not uncommon for the livestock to be housed inside the cottage.

Two buildings dominated the manor: the lord's residence and the village church. Depending upon the size of the manor, the lord's dwelling might be a castle or a simple wooden building known as the manor house. In either case,

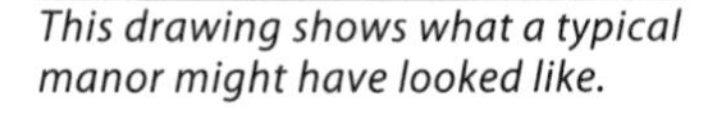

This drawing shows what a typical manor might have looked like.

it was situated on a high hill or some other defensible site. Usually the village was close by; when enemies attacked, the villagers sought refuge inside the fortified walls of the lord's house. Not far from the manor house stood the village church and the priest's home. The church steeple towered above the manor, directing the villagers' gaze heavenward. The church was not only the place of worship but also the place for village meetings, court sessions, and social gatherings.

Activities were not confined to the village. Villagers obtained building material and firewood from nearby forests and grazed their livestock in the pastures. They fished in streams and ponds and hunted for game in the manor's woodlands. The lord and villagers divided the cultivated fields on the manor. One-sixth to one-third of the arable land was set apart as the lord's **demesne** (dih MAYN)—the land reserved for the lord; the rest was alloted to the villagers. The village peasants worked together to plow the land, sow the seed, and harvest the crops; no one peasant had enough equipment or oxen to do the job alone. The open fields were divided into long, narrow strips. In each field, a villager held one or more of these strips. Often the lord's demesne was not a separate field but the most fertile strips in each open field.

During the early Middle Ages, most manors employed a **two-field system** of farming. Villagers planted crops on only half of the cultivated land, leaving the other half to lie fallow for a year to recover its fertility. The following year, they reversed the procedure.

Later a **three-field system** came into common use, especially in northern Europe. This system established a pattern of rotating planting among three fields. In the spring the peasants planted one field with barley, oats, or beans; in the fall they planted a second field with rye or wheat. In the meantime the third field was left fallow. This rotation increased the productivity of the land, because one crop put back into the soil the nutrients another took out.

People

The population on even the smallest manors reflected the medieval class structure: clergy, nobility, and peasantry. Throughout the Middle Ages the highest social status belonged to the clergy and the nobility. Every person on the manor, regardless of his class, had specific duties. The parish priest cared for the religious needs of the villagers, while the local lord provided protection and justice. Both the clergy and the nobility relied upon the support and provision of the peasants.

A small percentage of the people on the manor were **freemen**. These were the more privileged peasants who served as manorial officials or provided skilled labor, such as blacksmiths, millers, and carpenters. Some freemen owned their own land, while others rented land from the lord of the manor. Freemen did not have the same obligations as the average peasant. For example, freemen were often exempted from laboring in the lord's fields. Furthermore, they had the freedom to leave the manor. Although he had greater privileges, the freeman's living conditions differed little from those of the average peasant.

The majority of those living on a manor were the peasants known as the **serfs** (from the Latin *servus*, which means "slave"). The status of the serf was midway between the ancient slave and the medieval freeman. He had the use of a small portion of land and had opportunity to provide for himself and his family. Unlike the freeman, the serf was bound to the land on which he was born; he was not free to leave the manor without the lord's permission.

In return for the use of the lord's land and his protection, the serfs owed the lord various services and payments. These services took the form of labor; serfs were bound to work on the lord's demesne. They plowed his fields, sowed and harvested his crops, gathered his hay, and cared for his cattle. The lord might call upon them to build fences, clear woodland, or dig a moat for his castle. Usually the serfs devoted two or three days a week to working for their lord, an obligation known as **week work**.

Serfs also had to pay the lord—usually in produce—for the use of his land and its resources. Serfs gave the lord a portion of their crops, a share of the fish caught in the village stream, cheese in exchange for pasturing their cattle in the lord's fields, and a share of the firewood cut. In addition, the serfs were obligated to use the village mill and bakery owned by the lord. The lord took part of their grain and flour as a fee.

Daily Life

The only world most peasants ever knew was the manor on which they were born. It was their home—the place of their work, their worship, and their death—just as it had been for their ancestors before them. In fact, a peasant seldom traveled more than twenty miles from the place where he was born.

Each year there were two major holy days (holidays)—Easter and Christmas. Christmas brought a two-week celebration (alluded to in our carol "The Twelve Days of Christmas") and a great banquet at the lord's house. There were also other holidays, such as May Day (in the spring) and Harvest Day (much like our Thanksgiving).

Despite the holidays, life was hard for the peasant on the manor. He worked from sunrise to sunset. Yet despite all his labors, the average peasant barely managed to subsist. He suffered from both poverty and misery. What little money he could earn usually went either to the lord in rent and fees or to the church in tithes. Famines plagued the land and constant feudal wars ruined crops and killed livestock. Strenuous labor, filthy living conditions, poor diet, and lack of medical care combined to give the average peasant a very short lifespan.

Section Quiz

1. Where did the vast majority of people in Europe during the Middle Ages live?
2. What two buildings dominated the manor?
3. Name the term that described the peasant laborers on the manor.
4. Why did the peasants work for their lord and give him part of the crops they raised?

1. __________
2. __________
3. __________
4. __________

A Glance Behind

This chapter describes everyday life in the early Middle Ages. It was an age dominated by the church, feudalism, and the manor. With the exception of Charlemagne's brief empire, this age experienced little political unity. For the most part, Europe was under the strong authority of the Roman Catholic Church. But following the collapse of the Carolingian Empire, several feudal princes began to amass power and to slowly build strong feudal kingdoms in the midst of Europe's political disorder. These princes would one day rival the Roman church in influence and openly challenge the authority of the pope.

and a Glimpse Ahead

Notes

1. Einhard, *Life of Charlemagne*, trans. Samuel Epes Turner, Ann Arbor Paperbacks (Ann Arbor: The University of Michigan Press, 1969), pp. 50, 52.

2. Ibid., p. 54

3. Donald A. White, *Medieval History: A Sourcebook*, (Homewood, IL: The Dorsey Press, 1965), p. 239.

4. Sidney Painter, *Feudalism and Liberty* (Baltimore: Johns Hopkins Press, 1961), p. 93.

5. Loren C. MacKinney, *The Medieval World* (Reinhart and Co., 1938), p. 230.

Chapter Review

Can You Define?

catholic
pope
Roman sacramental system
mass
transubstantiation
clergy
laity
purgatory
mayor of the palace
feudalism
lords
fiefs
vassal
subinfeudation
homage
investiture
aids
castle
knight
page
squire
chivalry
tournament
manor
demesne
two-field system
three-field system
freemen
serfs
week work

Can You Identify?

Leo I
Petrine theory
seven sacraments
secular clergy
regular clergy
Benedictine Rule
Patrick
Boniface
Gregory I
Franks
Clovis
Merovingian House
"do-nothing kings"
Pepin II
Charles Martel
732
Pepin the Short
Carolingian House
Lombards
Donation of Pepin
Charlemagne
missi dominici
800
Alcuin
Carolingian minuscule
Treaty of Verdun (843)
Charles the Bald
Louis the German
Lothair
Magyars
Vikings
Peace of God
Truce of God

Can You Locate?

Rome
Tours
Lombardy
Aachen (Aix-la-Chapelle)
Verdun
Charlemagne's empire
Divisions after Treaty of Verdun

How Much Do You Remember?

1. What were the three institutions of medieval Europe? What social class represented each? What were their roles in society?
2. What did the word *church* mean to the majority of the people living during the Middle Ages?
3. What were the two divisions of the clergy? What were the duties of each?
4. Why was Charlemagne called "the Great"? How did he organize his realm? What were his contributions to the advancement of learning?
5. What three groups invaded Europe in the ninth and tenth centuries? What group caused the most damage? How?
6. What was the difference between a freeman and a serf?

What Do You Think?

1. Does the fact that the church was the dominant influence on medieval life make the Middle Ages an "age of faith"?
2. Why was it difficult for a person to know the gospel during the Middle Ages?
3. According to the Roman church, how is a person saved? Compare your answer to what the Bible teaches in Titus 3:5 and Ephesians 2:8–9.
4. Read Hebrews 10:10–14. How do these verses refute the Roman church's teaching concerning the mass?
5. Feudalism has been described as "chaos roughly organized." Is this description accurate?

9

"I am the Sun; the emperor, the moon."

Princes and Popes

The Holy Roman Emperor Henry IV humbling himself before Pope Gregory VII at Canossa in 1077. Engraving. Civica Raccolta Bertarelli, Milan, Italy

The collapse of the Carolingian Empire and the declining influence of the church made the ninth century in western Europe a period of widespread political chaos and moral corruption. Reforms beginning in the tenth century, however, strengthened the church and led to greater religious and temporal power for the papacy. Able German rulers revived the imperial tradition by establishing the Holy Roman Empire. In England and France, feudal kings gradually increased in influence over the noblemen. These changes brought about a struggle for power in Europe. Popes clashed with kings, and kings challenged nobles as each party sought to make its power supreme. Yet in the midst of the struggle, these rivals joined forces to rescue the Holy Land from the Muslims. Their efforts, called the Crusades, failed to accomplish their intended goal. They did, however, expose western Europe to the influences that would bring it out of the "Dark Ages."

According to English folklore, Robin Hood took a stand against medieval injustices. He is depicted here defying King John.

I. Reforms in the Church

By crowning Charlemagne emperor, Pope Leo III established an important precedent. Later popes claimed that this practice demonstrated their authority over civil rulers. In Charlemagne's day this supremacy existed only in theory. During the political disorder that followed the collapse of Charlemagne's empire, however, the papacy had opportunity to make real its claim of supreme political power. Nevertheless, the church was slow in asserting its leadership. Corrupt popes and worldly clergy caused the Roman church to lose much of its prestige and influence. The reforms of the eleventh through thirteenth centuries restored the church's prestige and brought the papacy to the height of its power.

Need for Reform

During the ninth century and the early part of the tenth, the Roman church sank deep in moral corruption. It amassed great wealth as churchmen neglected their religious duties for temporal gain. When the political conditions in Europe became worse, the church needed protection for its large landholdings. The greatest threat to the church's possessions was the Viking raiders. Churchmen secured protection from these and other enemies by entering into feudal relationships. They became vassals; their loyalties were divided between the church and feudal lords. Some kings and nobles were claiming that it was their right not only to appoint church officials but also to invest them with their religious authority—a practice known as **lay investiture**.

Before long it became commonplace for lay lords to appoint men with few spiritual qualifications to church offices in return for their political loyalty and financial favors. Unscrupulous men, enticed by the wealth and power of high church office, bought and sold church positions. The condition of the papacy was little better. Inept and immoral men filled the office, openly committing great wickedness and bringing disgrace upon the church. In addition, striving factions of nobles in Rome squabbled over the appointment of popes.

The scandalous conditions in the church prompted a reform movement. It began in **910** at a monastery in Cluny, France, and spread quickly throughout the Roman church. Members of this movement exposed and sought to remedy abuses within the church. They introduced measures to forbid **simony** (the buying and selling of religious or blessed articles or goods, which at the time extended even to the selling of church offices), to free the church from secular control resulting from lay investiture, and to restore the dignity and authority of the papacy.

One of the most influential of the reforming monastic orders was the **Cistercians** (sih STUR shunz). Monks of this order adopted lives of seclusion and strict discipline. They wore rough garments, abstained from meats, and worked hard in the fields. This order was made popular by its most zealous member, **Bernard of Clairvaux** (1091–1153). A man of deep piety and sincere devotion, Bernard demonstrated by his life the genuineness of his religious convictions. He was an outspoken critic of worldliness in the church and in society.

Rivalry Between Pope and Emperor

A primary goal of church reform was to rescue the papacy from the state of weakness and corruption into which it had fallen. In 1059, the **College of Cardinals** was created so that churchmen rather than Roman nobles or German kings could choose the popes. After almost two centuries of worthless popes, men of moral strength and able leadership restored the dignity and increased the power of the papal office. In fact, the papacy soon became the driving force of the reform movement.

Probably the greatest of the reforming popes was **Gregory VII** (1073–85). As a Benedictine monk, he had been a leading advocate of papal reform. He used his influence as pope to curb other abuses in the church and to strengthen his office. Gregory believed that the church was superior to the state; therefore, he wanted to free the church from secular control. This meant doing away with lay investiture.

In 1075 Gregory formally prohibited (on pain of excommunication) any layman from appointing a person to church office or investing a person with spiritual authority. The German emperor **Henry IV** refused to obey, insisting upon his right to appoint the bishops in his realm. He declared that Gregory was not pope but a "false monk." In retaliation, Gregory excommunicated him and freed Henry's subjects from their oaths of loyalty. The struggle between the two might have continued, but growing discontent among the German nobles prompted Henry to seek the pope's forgiveness. In the winter of **1077** at Canossa (a castle in northern Italy), the penitent Henry stood barefoot in the snow for three days, waiting for the pope to speak to him. Gregory had won, at least for the moment, a victory for the papacy.

The struggle over lay investiture did not end with Gregory and Henry. It continued until 1122, at which time the pope and the German emperor reached a compromise settlement. At the city of Worms, they signed an agreement—the **Concordat of Worms**—that recognized the right of the church to elect its own bishops and abbots and to invest them with spiritual authority. These elections, however, had to be held in the presence of the emperor or his representatives. In addition, the emperor retained the right to invest church officials with secular authority.

Church-State Relations

Whose power is greater—the church's or the state's? This question has been asked in nearly every age of history. The medieval world viewed both the church and the state as God's instruments, each possessing God-given authority and definite responsibilities in society. Even so, the powers asserted by one were often in direct conflict with those claimed by the other. Ever since the emperor Constantine had made Christianity an accepted religion of the Roman Empire, the roles of church and state had become less distinct.

The Bible tells us that God established both institutions. For this reason, the two should not be in conflict. Both are God's ministering agents for the good of society. The church is to be a bulwark of moral righteousness, striving to bring people to Christ through the preaching of the gospel; the state is to be a bulwark of justice and order, providing protection through its God-given authority. The Christian citizen has an obligation to both.

Sin has thwarted man's attempt to achieve an ideal church-state relationship. The church has often failed to provide moral leadership and has become entangled in temporal affairs. Likewise, the state has often overstepped its bounds of authority and has interfered with the church and the home. During the Middle Ages the tension between church and state led to an intense struggle for power. Satan encourages this conflict even today as he attempts to harm God's people and frustrate God's purpose.

New Religious Orders

In the thirteenth century, new religious orders arose, which continued the reforms begun by the Cluniac and Cistercian movements. Unlike earlier monastic orders whose members sought seclusion from society, the new Franciscan and Dominican orders emphasized service to one's fellow man. They labored to bring about reform by living and preaching among the people—especially those in the growing towns. Members of these orders were called **friars** ("brothers"). Renouncing worldly possessions, they pledged themselves to lives of poverty. Since the friars begged for their daily sustenance, these are sometimes referred to as **mendicant** ("begging") **orders**.

Francis of Assisi (uh SEE see; 1182–1226), the son of a rich merchant, was the founder of the Franciscan order. As a young man he exchanged his wealth for beggar's rags and devoted his life to preaching and ministering to the poor and sick. A contemporary of his, a Spanish nobleman named **Dominic** (1170–1221), founded the Dominican order. Dominic devoted his life to battling heresy. He believed that the best way for the church to combat heresy was to educate its members. Consequently the Dominican order earned a reputation in the field of learning; its members taught at Europe's finest universities and were among the church's greatest scholars. Combining their intellectual training with their zeal for fighting heresy, the Dominicans became the leaders of the Inquisition—a church court established to discover and try heretics.

These mendicant orders pledged their allegiance to the pope. They championed the cause of

Francis of Assisi and the Manger Scene

Of all the objects associated with Christmas, none is more familiar than the manger scene. Usually included in this portrayal of Christ's birth are figures of Mary, Joseph, shepherds, three wise men, an ox, and a donkey. The baby Jesus lies on a bed of hay in a wooden manger. From the Scriptures we know that there are several misconceptions in this traditional representation. For instance, the wise men did not come with the shepherds to the manger but arrived some time later (Matt. 2:11). Also, Scripture does not tell us how many wise men there were. Nor do we know what animals were present in the stable when Christ was born. Furthermore, Christ was probably laid in a stone manger, not a wooden one.

The man responsible for unintentionally popularizing these misconceptions was Francis of Assisi. To dramatize for the common people the events surrounding the birth of Christ, Francis tried to physically recreate the scene. He built the manger of wood, for wood was plentiful in his native land. (He had no way of knowing that mangers in Palestine were made of stone.) He had townspeople portray Mary, Joseph, the shepherds, and the wise men. Although the wise men were not actually present at the manger, Francis included them so that he might bring together the events related to the Christ child. Around the manger Francis placed an ox and ass, interpreting Isaiah 1:3 as referring to Christ's birth: "The ox knoweth his owner, and the ass his master's crib." At midnight on Christmas Eve 1223, Francis held an outdoor service using this manger scene. He hoped to show the people how Christ came in poverty and how He was born to a life of suffering and death. Because of his popularity and devout life, Francis's manger scene became the model which others copied.

The Basilica of San Francesco, where Francis of Assisi is buried

THROUGH EYES OF FAITH

The Problem of Worldliness

Although they tried to be godly and to avoid worldliness, in time many of the Franciscans and Dominicans lived very worldly lives. Why do you think this change occurred?

the papacy in its clashes with powerful bishops and princes. However, very shortly after their founding, many of these orders forsook poverty to gain wealth, abandoned others to serve themselves, and sacrificed spiritual power for temporal authority.

Zenith of the Papacy

The years of reform restored the church's prestige, tightened its hold over its members, and broadened its influence on medieval society. Nowhere was this power more evident than in the papacy. For centuries the popes had contended that their power exceeded that of kings; the truth of that claim was now certain. The battle over lay investiture and the formation of new religious orders had resulted in increased papal authority throughout Europe.

Innocent III

Papal power and prestige reached its zenith under Pope **Innocent III** (1198–1216). No pope before or after him exercised such extensive authority over both church and state. Innocent likened his authority to the sun and that of kings to the moon:

> The Creator of the universe set up two great luminaries [sources of light] in the firmament of heaven; the greater light to rule the day, the lesser light to rule the night. In the same way . . . he appointed two great dignities; the greater to bear rule over souls (these being, as it were, days), the lesser to bear rule over bodies (these being, as it were, nights). These dignities are the [papal] authority and the royal power. Furthermore, the moon derives her light from the sun, and is in truth inferior to the sun in both size and quality, in position as well as effect. In the same way the royal power derives its dignity from the [papal] authority.[1]

How was Innocent able to enforce this position when earlier popes had failed? A large measure of his success is due to the strength of the church, which he represented. By the thirteenth century the Roman church had matured into a large, wealthy, and powerful organization. By summoning the wide resources of the church, which were at his disposal, and by exploiting its strong influence on society, Innocent established his authority over all of Europe. He and his successors were especially zealous in humbling unsubmissive kings, even though the apostle Peter had commanded the believers to honor the king (1 Pet. 2:17). In addition, they worked to stamp out any individual or group that protested against papal authority.

Pope Innocent III holding the bull with which he raised revenue for the monastery
8th Century fresco. Sacro Speco (S. Scolastica), Subiaco, Italy

College of Cardinals

As the Roman church grew in size and power, the popes needed assistance in administering church affairs. Gathering together important church leaders from around the city of Rome, the popes gradually organized what is called the "College of Cardinals." The word *college* simply means "association" or "society." The term *cardinal* possibly comes from the Latin word *cardo*, which means "hinge." (Just as a hinge is vital to a door, so cardinals are vital to the operation of the church.)

Although the title "cardinal" goes back to the fifth century, it was not until the twelfth century that the College took the form it has today. The cardinals have two major functions: to advise and assist the popes in administering church affairs and, when a pope dies, to elect a new one (who is usually one of their own number). This procedure protected papal election from political influence.

Just as the pope is "king" of the Roman Catholic Church, the cardinals are the "princes." Each cardinal wears a bright red robe and red hat and has an exalted title, "Your Most Eminent Lord."

Papal Weapons

It was difficult for anyone to resist the ecclesiastical weapons that the popes directed against those who offended the church. Chief among the weapons in the church's arsenal were the following:

1. **Excommunication**—the punishment of an individual by depriving him of the sacraments and excluding him from the fellowship of the church. This was an especially powerful weapon in the hands of the pope, for churchmen believed that he controlled the gates to heaven and could through excommunication deprive an individual of any hope of eternal salvation.

2. **Interdict**—the suspension of public church services and of the administration of all sacraments (except baptism and extreme unction) in a given location. Popes often used this weapon against disobedient kings. By placing a king's realm under an interdict, the pope hoped that the suspension of spiritual blessings from the church would bring about a public outcry that would force the erring king to submit.

3. **Inquisition**—a special church court commissioned by the pope to stamp out heresy. Heresy, the holding of beliefs contrary to the teaching of the church, was the greatest of medieval crimes. Inquisitors were given special powers to seek out and judge those accused of heresy. They used torture to make the accused admit to heresy, whether he or she really was guily or not. Those who would not bend even under torture often faced death.

Character and Results of Reform

Sadly, many medieval reformers devoted more effort to rebuilding the church's prestige than to restoring its purity. Many were more interested in obtaining political power than in maintaining spiritual strength. The reforms provided no lasting solution to the church's difficulties, and often they compounded the very problems they were intended to correct. Though in many cases churchmen made outward changes, they failed to recognize the need for inward cleansing and forgiveness through Jesus Christ. They failed to see that genuine reform is possible only when hearts have been regenerated.

THROUGH EYES OF FAITH

Reforming the Church

If you were an influential person in medieval Europe, how would you attempt to reform the church? What if you were not an influential person?

___

___

___

___

___

___

___

___

___

___

___

___

The Inquisition

It is not without reason that one church historian has called the Inquisition "one of the most terrible engines of intolerance and tyranny which human ingenuity has ever devised." Started by Pope Gregory IX (1227–1241), the Inquisition was an organization of the Roman Catholic Church dedicated to uncovering and punishing heresy (teachings contrary to the Roman church). The Inquisitors, usually members of the Dominican order, were often well-educated and respected individuals. Nevertheless, they believed (as did the Roman church) that it was proper to force people to change their views by subjecting them to physical punishment.

The Inquisition operated in a methodical manner. A group of Inquisitors would come into a particular town, gather the people together, and then one of them would preach a sermon on the evils of heresy. The preacher urged those who held heretical views to confess them, promising that if they confessed voluntarily, the Inquisition would be lenient with them. After the sermon the Inquisitors took up lodging in the town and waited.

Over the next several days, people came to the Inquisition and confessed their heresies. While doing so they often mentioned the names of others who held similar views. After a set period of time the Inquisition no longer took voluntary confessions but began to call in those who had been accused of heresy by others. The accused person was not required to answer the Inquisition's summons, but if he did not do so he was presumed guilty and placed under arrest. The accused then had to stand trial before the panel of Inquisitors. He could not call any witnesses in his defense; he was not told who had accused him; and his trial was held in secret. The Inquisition did allow him to have a lawyer, but few attorneys ever agreed to help an accused heretic. The lawyers feared, and rightly so, that they too might be suspected of heresy. If during the trial the accused person steadfastly maintained his innocence, the Inquisitors used torture to force a confession. For example, they might pull his bones out of joint or burn parts of his body. Of course, when subjected to such suffering, the poor prisoner often readily confessed to anything.

Once the Inquisitors completed their last trial, they again gathered the whole town together. At this meeting one of the Inquisitors preached another sermon. Then he read the sentences handed down, beginning with the least severe and ending with the most severe. The punishments varied greatly. Some people had to do penance, some lost their property, and some were sentenced to prison. Those who refused to recant, however, were handed over to the secular authorities to be burned at the stake. After the executions, the Inquisitors moved on to the next town and began the process again.

Robert-Fleury, Joseph Nicolas (1797-1890). Galileo before the Holy Office of the Vatican. *Oil on canvas. Photo : Gérard Blot. Louvre, Paris, France*

By the end of the fifteenth century the Inquisition began to die out; however, Ferdinand and Isabella revived it in Spain. In addition, the success of the Protestant Reformation (see p. 292) prompted Pope Paul III (1534–49) to give the Inquisition a central organization called the Holy Office. Under this new organization, the Spanish Inquisition proved to be particularly barbaric as it tortured and killed suspected Protestants, Jews, and Muslims. By the early nineteenth century the Inquisition finally stopped its bloody activities, but the organization itself continued. Today it is called the Sacred Congregation for the Doctrine of the Faith.

Section Quiz

1. What was the practice called in which kings and nobles appointed church officials and invested them with their religious authority?
2. What pope and emperor had a showdown at Canossa in 1077? Which man won?
3. List the two new religious orders whose members begged for their daily sustenance. Identify the founder of each.
4. Under which pope did the papacy reach its zenith?
5. List and define the three major weapons used by the papacy during this period.

1. ____________________
2. ____________________
____
3. ____________________
____
____
____
4. ____________________
5. ____________________
____
____
____
____
____
____
____
____
____
____
____
____
____
____
____

II. A European Empire

Since the time of the Tower of Babel, many have dreamed of a universal empire that would unite all the peoples of the earth under one government. This concept took form in the tenth century with the founding of the Holy Roman Empire.

Founding of the German Kingdom

After the death of Charlemagne, his grandsons divided the Frankish empire (see p. 190). In East Frankland, the weak descendants of the ruler Louis the German offered little protection against the Magyars—savage horsemen who were terrorizing southeastern Europe. Local tribal leaders called **dukes** assumed the role of protectors. Each duke ruled like a king in his own territory, called a **duchy**. After the death of the last Carolingian king, the dukes elected one of their own to lead them against outside attackers.

The German nobles selected the Saxon duke **Henry the Fowler**, the first of the Saxon line of German kings. According to tradition, Henry was called "the Fowler" because the messengers who brought him the news of his election found him enjoying his favorite pastime—hunting game with hawks. As king, Henry I (919–36) forced the other dukes to acknowledge his royal status, but he permitted them to guide the internal affairs of their own territories. His chief concern was to strengthen his own duchy of Saxony so that he could build a strong base for his royal power. He repelled the raids of the Slavs and Magyars and expanded German territory eastward—a movement that would continue throughout German history.

Henry's son, **Otto I** (936–73), often called "the Great," became one of the strongest German kings. Unlike his father, he was not content with the mere title of king but sought to actually assert his royal authority over the other duchies. To aid him in his struggles with rival dukes, he relied on the support of high-ranking church officials, many of whom he had appointed to office. These powerful bishops and abbots served Otto as vassals, giving him their allegiance and supplying soldiers for his army. In addition to his conflict with the nobles, Otto won a great victory over the Magyars. After their defeat, the Magyars no longer menaced German territory. They settled in the lower Danube valley, where they are known today as the Hungarians.

Establishment of the Holy Roman Empire

Tenth-century Italy was divided into many warring factions. Fearing that a rival duke would seize northern Italy and threaten his monarchy, Otto crossed the Alps, took possession of Lombardy, and proclaimed himself king of Italy. Ten years later, in 962, he crossed the Alps again, this time marching his army into Rome. The pope, who had appealed to him for protection against the Roman nobles, crowned Otto emperor. Like Charlemagne, Otto had come

Germany's Cathedral of Magdeburg, where Otto the Great is buried

to the pope's rescue and in return had received the emperor's crown. Otto believed that his new role as protector made him superior to the pope, a claim disputed, of course, by the papacy.

The conquests and coronation of Otto revived the memory of the Carolingian and Roman empires. Later German kings considered themselves the successors of Charlemagne and the Roman caesars. Because of its alliance with the Roman church and its symbolic association with the empire of ancient Rome, the German empire became known as the **Holy Roman Empire**. But as the eighteenth-century French author and philosopher Voltaire observed, it was "neither holy, nor Roman, nor an empire." The empire was built on the union of Germany and Italy and on the alliance of the church and state, neither of which could provide a strong foundation.

Conflict Within the Empire

Conflict of Interest

Though the Holy Roman Empire founded by Otto I became the most powerful state in Europe, it experienced many internal conflicts. The first was a conflict of interest. The German rulers often intervened in Italian affairs. Otto's grandson, Otto III, built a palace in Rome and planned to make Rome the capital of the empire. Concerned for Italy's welfare, the German rulers neglected the affairs of their homeland. This lack of attention gave the German nobles an opportunity to increase their power. The divided interests of the Holy Roman emperors ultimately weakened their authority and hindered efforts to create a unified Italy and a unified Germany.

Holy Roman Empire about 1000

Conflict with Popes

Another conflict that plagued the empire was the struggle between the emperors and the popes. Beginning with Otto I, the emperors actively intervened in papal affairs. They even began choosing the popes. In addition, they continued the longstanding practice of appointing important church officials within their realm (a situation later to be resolved by the Concordat of Worms in 1122; see p. 202). As the Cluniac reforms spread throughout the Roman church, the popes began to challenge the emperor's authority, especially in the matter of lay investiture.

The most famous struggle over investiture was the one between the emperor Henry IV (1056–1106) and Pope Gregory VII. Although Gregory won a great victory over the emperor at Canossa in 1077 (see p. 202), the triumph was only temporary. Henry was humiliated but not defeated. Returning home, he crushed a rebellion of German nobles and then invaded Italy, seized Rome, and installed a new pope. Gregory VII, who fled, died a year later in exile. But the domination of the German emperors over the papacy did not continue. Soon other popes, such as Innocent III, were able to interfere in the political affairs of the empire and weaken the emperor's authority.

Conflict with Nobles

The third and perhaps most damaging conflict within the empire was the one between the German nobles and the Holy Roman emperors. For almost a century while the emperors had been preoccupied with Italian affairs, the German nobles had enjoyed great independence. The situation began to change, however, when a new royal line, the **Salian House** (1024–1125), succeeded the Saxon kings. The Salian kings (including Henry IV) were unsuccessful in their attempts to establish a strong, centralized monarchy that would weaken the power of the great nobles. After the death of Henry's son, who had died without an heir, civil war broke out among rival noble families who competed for the crown.

The civil wars further weakened the German monarchy and led to the development of feudalism throughout the empire. The large duchies in Italy and Germany broke up into many small states. Powerful nobles became feudal lords, forcing lesser nobles to become their vassals. During this period, several of the strongest nobles firmly established the practice of electing the German monarch. The power of the nobles was supreme in the land.

The Empire Under the Hohenstaufens

In 1152 the German princes hoped to bring an end to the civil wars by choosing as king a member of the **Hohenstaufen** (HO un SHTOU fun) family, **Frederick I** (1152–1190), also called Barbarossa ("Red Beard"). Frederick sought to restore the glory and stability of what he termed the "holy empire." Like previous German kings, Frederick meddled in Italian affairs. His expeditions brought strong papal opposition. Though most of Frederick's advances

Crown of the Holy Roman Empire (962?) made for the Emperor Otto I (912-973).

Gold, silver, precious stones. From Reichenau (?), Germany. Kunsthistorisches Museum, Vienna, Austria

into Italy ended in failure, he was successful in forming a marriage alliance between his son and the heiress of the kingdom of Sicily.

The last notable Hohenstaufen ruler was **Frederick II** (1215–1250), the grandson of Frederick I. Frederick was heir not only to the German throne but also to the throne of Sicily. The latter kingdom was established by the Normans in the eleventh century and included all of southern Italy. Frederick II grew up in Sicily, where he became acquainted with the Greek and Arab cultures. Later his court would become a leading center of culture. One of the most learned men of his day, he also distinguished himself as a patron of artists and scholars.

As a boy, Frederick was the ward of Pope Innocent III, the most powerful man in Europe. Innocent recognized the threat of having Hohenstaufen possessions encircling the Papal States. Therefore he secured the German throne for Frederick in return for his promise to give up the throne of Sicily. Shortly after Innocent's death, however, Frederick broke his promise. He devoted almost all his attention to Sicily and Italy, leaving the feudal princes of Germany relatively free from imperial interference. Frederick expanded his Italian holdings and might have united all of Italy under his control had it not been for the resistance of the papacy.

The death of Frederick II in 1250 was the beginning of the decline of the Holy Roman Empire. German kings still continued to call themselves Holy Roman emperors, but their contact with Italy was minimal. The attempts of the German emperors to unite Germany and Italy ended in failure. Their lack of success marked a long period of disunity for the two countries. Not until the late nineteenth century did Italy and Germany become unified national states.

Section Quiz

1. What German king founded the Holy Roman Empire? In what year did this take place?
2. What did the French philosopher Voltaire observe about the Holy Roman Empire?
3. What conflict of interest did many of the German emperors have?
4. From what family did the German princes choose a king in hopes of ending the period of civil war? List two emperors who belonged to this family.

1. ______________________
2. ______________________
____
____
3. ______________________
____
4. ______________________
____
____

III. Rise of Feudal Monarchies

England

The Anglo-Saxons Settle England

Roman authority over the Celts in Britain came to an end in the early fifth century. After nearly four hundred years of occupation, the Roman legions had to withdraw from the island in order to protect Roman territory on the Continent. Soon afterwards, Germanic tribes from northern Europe, such as the **Angles** and the **Saxons**, invaded Britain. They established their own independent kingdoms and transformed "Roman" Britain into England (or "Angle land," meaning the "land of the Angles").

In the ninth century, the Danes (Scandinavian Vikings) began to raid the land. The petty kingdoms of the Angles and Saxons had little success in resisting the Danes—that is, until the time of King **Alfred the Great** (871–99). Alfred, the ruler of the important Saxon kingdom of Wessex, defeated the Danes and pushed them back into northeastern England. He extended his rule over the southern part of England, laying the foundation for a unified English monarchy.

Alfred's success was not confined to the battlefield. He was an able ruler and a patron of learning. He built a navy to repel future Danish invasions—an undertaking that earned him the title "founder of the English navy." He strengthened the Anglo-Saxon practice of local government. His realm was divided into many local districts called **shires** (counties), governed by officials called *shire-reeves* (from which we get our word *sheriff*). He built churches, founded schools, and invited foreign scholars to his court. During his reign, scholars began to translate important literary works into the common language of the people. In addition, monks began to compile the ***Anglo-Saxon Chronicle***, which traces the history of England from Roman times to Alfred's day. The *Chronicle* was continued after Alfred; monks added current events and revised older passages.

Alfred was a man of strong character. He won the love and respect of his people as well as the admiration of later generations. Unlike many of the men who have been highly praised by historians, Alfred truly deserved the title "the Great." His life demonstrated that true greatness lies not in wealth or worldly fame, but in a man's character—not necessarily in what a man *does*, but in what he *is*.

Less than a century after Alfred's death, the Danes renewed their attacks. England fell to the Danish ruler **Canute**, who made England part of the Danish Empire, which also included Norway. Although Canute ruled England well, his successors were weak. The Anglo-Saxons eventually drove out the Danish rulers and placed **Edward the Confessor** on the throne.

THIS MOMENT IN HISTORY

Alfred the Great

How did Alfred contribute toward the development of local government? During Alfred's rule, what was the significance of important literary works being translated into the common language of the people?

Bronze statue of Alfred the Great erected in Winchester, England, to mark the millennium of his death

England in the Time of Alfred the Great

Britain's replica of the Bayeux Tapestry: The Battle of Hastings: Scene 2

William of Normandy Conquers England

Edward (1042–66) was a descendant of Alfred. He was called "the Confessor" because of his devotion to God. In January of 1066, he died without a direct heir. His cousin William, the French duke of Normandy, claimed the throne, asserting that Edward had promised it to him. The English nobles, however, refused to grant William the crown. Instead they elected **Harold**, the powerful earl of Wessex, king. William refused to be deprived of what he thought was rightfully his. Obtaining the blessing of the pope, he raised a large army, crossed the English Channel, and invaded England.

On October 14, 1066, the armies of William, duke of Normandy, and Harold, earl of Wessex, met in the famous **Battle of Hastings**. Much more was at stake than the English throne; the outcome of this battle altered the course of English history. Before the day ended, Harold had been killed and the Anglo-Saxons defeated. William, known as "the Conqueror," established a new line of English kings, the Norman dynasty.

William brought to England the centralized feudalism of Normandy and established himself as feudal lord over the entire country, which, in theory, was now his by right of conquest. He divided his holdings among his military followers, feudal vassals called **tenants-in-chief**. To maintain his power over all the feudal nobles, he required that all who became vassals through subinfeudation also swear allegiance to him as their lord. He also extended his authority over the English church; William—not the pope—appointed the bishops of his realm.

To determine the taxable resources that belonged to him as king, William commissioned a great survey. His royal officials traveled throughout the country gathering detailed information about property holders and their belongings. According to the *Anglo-Saxon Chronicle*, "there was not a single hide or rood [1/4 acre] of land, nor even was there an ox or a cow or a pig left that was not set down in his writings." The findings of the survey were collected in a record known as the ***Domesday Book***.

The Domesday Book

Why was William's census called the *Domesday Book*? Some historians have suggested that the name came from *Domus Dei*, the chapel in which the book was kept in Winchester Cathedral. It has also been suggested that because the book represented the official and final record of a person's holdings, it was compared by the common people to the coming Day of Judgment, or "doomsday," when God will open the Book of Life. Nevertheless, most scholars believe that the word *dome* comes from the Anglo-Saxon word *doom*, which means merely the judgment or decision of the king.

Reforms Strengthen Royal Authority

When William's sons William II and Henry I died without heir, the Norman line came to an end. After a period of dispute over rightful succession, the crown passed to the Plantagenet (or Angevin) family, founded by **Henry II** (1154–89), the great-grandson of William the Conqueror. A Frenchman, Henry possessed more wealth and territory outside of England than within. Through inheritance and marriage, he had gained landholdings in France that far surpassed those ruled directly by his feudal lord, the French king. This situation provoked jealous rivalry between the French and English thrones.

Henry strengthened royal authority in England by expanding the jurisdiction of the royal courts. Before this time, each lord had his own court for deciding cases concerning his vassals and serfs. Henry established circuit courts with justices who traveled throughout the land hearing cases. During Henry's time, the circuit courts usually heard only cases involving land disputes, but later other cases were handled also.

Before the circuit justices arrived in a shire, a jury composed of men of that district would make a list of **indictments** (accusations) of what crimes had been committed and who the suspected offenders were. (From this practice

Trial by Ordeal

One way the Anglo-Saxons attempted to determine the innocence or guilt of a person charged with a crime was trial by ordeal. There were four forms of trial by ordeal.

Trial by cold water. The charged person was taken to a pond, which was blessed by a priest. He was bound hand and foot and thrown into the water. If he floated, he was judged guilty, for the "holy water" had rejected him. If he sank, he was judged innocent, for the water had accepted him. He was then rescued—presumably in time to save his life; if not, his innocence supposedly merited entrance into heaven.

Trial by hot water. A person was forced to plunge his arm into boiling water. A priest would then wrap a bandage around his arm. After three days the bandage was removed. If the arm was blistered, the man was judged guilty; but if it had healed, he was judged innocent. Our saying "in hot water" probably comes from this ordeal.

Trial by hot iron. This ordeal was much like trial by hot water, except in this case a person had to carry a red-hot piece of iron in his hands for a prescribed distance.

Trial by morsel. A person was made to swallow a lump of dough. If he choked, he was judged guilty; if he did not, he was judged innocent.

The people of the Middle Ages falsely believed that God would immediately reveal guilt or innocence through these means. With the rise of the royal courts of Henry II, trial by ordeal gradually came to an end. By the time of King John's reign, it had all but disappeared from England. It then became the practice to determine the guilt or innocence of an accused person by the facts of the case rather than by an ordeal.

arose the modern-day grand jury, which decides whether there is sufficient evidence to hold an accused person for trial.) When the justice heard a case, he often relied on information supplied by a smaller jury of men acquainted with the facts of the case. Gradually, it became the accepted practice to have "twelve good and truthful men" serve on this jury, the forerunner of trial juries in America. Unlike their modern counterparts, however, these men gave evidence upon which the justice could render a verdict, instead of being the ones to hear the evidence and give the verdict.

As a result of Henry's judicial reforms, more cases were tried in the royal courts than in the feudal ones. The decisions of Henry's justices provided uniform laws for all of England and thus superseded the local feudal laws. This **common law** not only helped ensure justice but also helped to draw the English people together into a unified nation.

Henry hoped to strengthen his authority over the church by appointing his friend **Thomas à Becket** archbishop of Canterbury, the highest church office in England. Once in office, however, Becket became a bitter opponent of Henry's interference in church matters. The controversy reached a climax when Henry attempted to bring clerics who committed grave crimes to trial in royal, instead of church, courts. Becket resisted. Outraged by his opposition, Henry reportedly exclaimed, "What a pack of fools and cowards I have nourished in my house, that not one of them will avenge me of this turbulent priest!" Four knights, hearing the king's rash words, traveled to Canterbury and murdered the archbishop at his altar. Because of the popular uproar over Becket's death in 1170, the king abandoned his plans to control the clergy. Becket became a martyr and his tomb a popular shrine.

Magna Carta Limits Royal Power

After Henry's death his oldest son **Richard I** (1189–99) became king. Richard, known as "the Lion-Hearted," was an able warrior and an admired Crusader. Nevertheless, he contributed little to the English crown. He spent less than six months of his ten-year reign in England. His participation in the Kings' Crusade (see p. 221) and the defense of his French holdings from the king of France occupied most of his reign. While he was absent from England, his brother John and the king of France plotted to overthrow him. His reign provides the setting for the adventures of the legendary English hero Robin Hood.

The death of Richard elevated **John** (1199–1216) to the English throne. John was a more able ruler than Richard, but he lacked the strong personal qualities that had won his brother the trust and admiration of the people. John's weak will and cruel, unscrupulous ways brought him nothing but trouble. John's reign was marked by continual conflict with three formidable opponents: the French king, the pope, and the English nobles—all of whom got the better of him. The French king Philip II took advantage of John's weakness and extended his royal control over many of John's French possessions.

In the meantime, John clashed with Pope Innocent III over who would be the next archbishop of Canterbury. When the archbishop of Canterbury died in 1206 and John failed to appoint a new one, the monks at Canterbury decided that they would choose a new archbishop. (This choice was usually made with the approval of the king and the English bishops.) The monks sent the man of

Magna Carta

Certain provisions of the Magna Carta transcended the immediate occasion for which they were framed and became the bases of later political concepts.

No Taxation Without Representation. "No scutage [a feudal tax] or aid shall be imposed in our kingdom save by the common council of our kingdom." (Clause 12)

Trial by Jury and Due Process of Law. "No freeman shall be taken, or imprisoned, or dispossessed, or outlawed, or banished, or in any way injured, nor will we go upon him, nor send upon him, except by the legal judgment of his peers, or by the law of the land. To no one will we sell, to no one will we deny or delay, right or justice." (Clauses 39-40)

their choice to Rome to be confirmed by the pope. When John heard of this, he was outraged and had the bishops choose another man, who was also sent to Rome. When both men arrived in Rome, Innocent III refused to confirm either. Instead he selected a friend of his, an English cardinal named Stephen Langton, to be archbishop. When John refused to allow Langton into England (he had been out of the country for several years), trouble broke out.

The Magna Carta Memorial at Runnymede commemorates this great symbol of freedom under law

Innocent placed England under an interdict and excommunicated the king. Having no allies and threatened by a French invasion, John submitted to the pope, even to the point of becoming the pope's vassal and making England a fief of the papacy. Restored to the pope's graces, John was able to avert Philip's invasion of England. However, he was not able to put down a rebellion of the English barons (nobles).

The English barons were dissatisfied with John's reign. They resented his excessive taxes and his disregard for their feudal privileges. In 1215, the infuriated nobles revolted. At Runnymede, a meadow near London, they forced John to set his seal to the **Magna Carta** (Latin for "Great Charter"). Originally intended as a guarantee of feudal rights, the Magna Carta became one of the most important documents in English history. Later Englishmen looked to the Magna Carta as establishing the principle that the king's power is limited: the king is not above the law and can be removed for refusing to obey it.

Parliament Becomes an Important Institution

One of England's most gifted medieval kings was **Edward I** (1272–1307). He attempted to extend English rule over all of Britain—Wales, Scotland, and England. He conquered Wales and made his son Prince of Wales. (Since that time, it has been customary to confer the title "Prince of Wales" on the eldest male heir to the English throne.) Edward's attempts to subdue Scotland, however, met with fierce resistance.

Probably the most important and enduring contribution of Edward's reign was the development of **Parliament**. It had always been the custom of English kings to seek counsel from a group of advisers. The Anglo-Saxon kings had the **witan**, an assembly of the great men of the kingdom. William the Conqueror established the Great Council—also known as the ***curia regis*** ("king's council")—a feudal body composed of his chief vassals.

When Edward became king, he enlarged the membership of the Great Council to include representative knights from every shire and representative burgesses (citizens) from every town. The word *parliament* (from a French word meaning "to speak," or "to discuss") came to designate this expanded assembly. The meeting of Parliament during Edward's reign has been called the "Model Parliament," for it had the basic features of later Parliaments.

In the fourteenth century, members of Parliament met in two separate groups: the chief vassals in one, and the knights and burgesses in another. The members of the latter group were called the "Commons" because they represented the community. Their assembly became known as the House of Commons, and that of the chief feudal lords became known as the House of Lords.

Over the centuries, Parliament became more and more powerful. Edward had acknowledged that the king could not propose new taxes without the

THIS MOMENT IN HISTORY

Parliament

Why was the development of Parliament important for future democracies?

consent of Parliament. Therefore, he and his successors had to summon Parliament regularly to obtain needed revenue. The members of Parliament soon discovered that by withholding their approval of new taxes, they could force the king to hear their grievances. This **"power of the purse,"** as it came to be called, gradually transformed Parliament from an advisory body into a legislative body. Parliament served as a check on the king's power and in later centuries helped to convert English government into a limited monarchy.

France

The Capetians and Their Royal House

The kingdom of West Frankland, once the heart of the Carolingian Empire, broke up into many feudal realms soon after the death of Charlemagne. In 987 the great feudal lords chose the count of Paris, **Hugh Capet**, as their king, thus ending the weak rule of the Carolingian monarchs. Hugh founded a new royal line, the Capetian House, whose members built a strong monarchy in France.

Many factors helped the Capetian kings to steadily increase their power over the feudal lords. For instance, for over three hundred years every Capetian king had a son to succeed him. Therefore, no wars of succession threatened the stability of royal power. This power gradually increased as the size of the royal domain increased. Capetian rulers enlarged their possessions by conquest and through marriage alliances. They also developed an effective system of centralized government, which laid the foundation for the French national state. Furthermore, the Capetians found valuable allies in the church and townspeople. By tapping the wealth of the towns and the church, the Capetians won financial independence from the great feudal lords.

Philip II and Royal Expansion

Although the early Capetian monarchs bore the title of king, they actually ruled only a small area around Paris, known as the ***Île-de-France***. Like an island, it was surrounded by feudal lands ruled by the king's vassals. Many of these vassals were powerful lords possessing more land and authority than the French king. (Henry Plantagenet and William, duke of Normandy, are noted examples.)

The early Capetian kings were constantly struggling to maintain control of their feudal holdings. Not until the reign of the fifth Capetian king, Louis VI

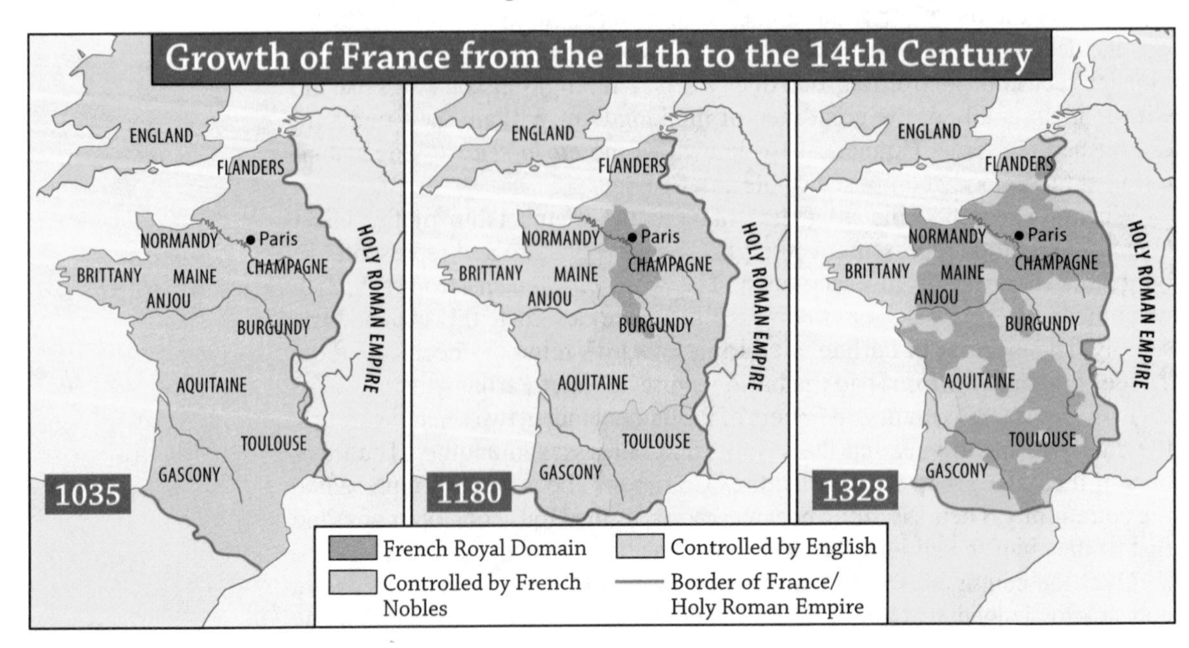

(1108–37), did the French king become master of his royal domain. For the first time the Capetians had a strong and solid base from which they would extend their royal power over the rest of the kingdom. It was **Philip II** "Augustus" (1180–1223), however, who became known as the real founder of France. By enlarging the territory under his rule and by increasing his power over his vassals, he began a period of Capetian greatness.

The chief obstacle to the expansion of royal power in France was the large amount of land held by the English kings. Although the Plantagenets were vassals of the French king, their landholdings in France far exceeded those ruled directly by the French king. Philip II attempted to deprive the English kings Henry II and Richard the Lion-Hearted of their continental holdings but met with little success. He found King John easier to deal with. A controversy broke out between John and one of his French vassals. When John refused to stand trial in Philip's court as the French monarch's vassal, Philip declared John's French lands forfeited. Because John had lost the support of his French vassals and had alienated the English nobles, he was defeated by Philip. John lost Normandy, Anjou, Maine, and Touraine to him. The French king had broken the power of King John in France and, in doing so, had tripled the size of his own royal domain.

Philip also increased the effectiveness of royal government. He replaced local feudal officials with new royal ones called ***baillis*** (bah YEE), or bailiffs, whom the king appointed and paid. Similar to Henry II's itinerant justices, these bailiffs collected royal taxes, enforced feudal rights, and administered justice, reinforcing the king's authority throughout his realm.

Philip's attempts to increase royal power in France met with one major setback. Shortly after taking a Danish princess as his wife, Philip had his marriage annulled by the French bishops. Pope Innocent III, who seized every opportunity to intervene in the internal affairs of the European states, refused to recognize the annulment. He excommunicated Philip and placed France under an interdict. Forced to back down, Philip took back his Danish wife; but in doing so, he had to put away another wife, whom he had married in the meantime.

Louis IX and Royal Dignity

Philip's grandson, King **Louis IX** (1226–1270), has been called the ideal medieval king. He combined sincere piety and just rule to build respect and loyalty for the French throne. His character is demonstrated in the instruction he gave to his son and heir:

> Fair son, the first thing I would teach thee is to set thine heart to love God. . . . If God send thee adversity, receive it in patience, and give thanks to our Saviour, and bethink thee that thou hast deserved it, and that He will make it turn to thine advantage. If he send thee prosperity, then thank Him humbly, so that thou become not worse from pride. . . . Maintain the good customs of thy realm, and abolish the bad. Be not covetous against thy people; and do not burden them with taxes and imposts save when thou art in great need. . . . See that thou hast in thy company men, whether religious or lay, who are right worthy, and loyal, and not full of covetousness, and confer with them oft: and fly and eschew the company of the wicked. Hearken willingly to the Word of God and keep it in thine heart . . . . Give often thanks to God for all the good things He has bestowed upon thee, so that thou be accounted worthy to receive more. In order to do justice and right to thy subjects, be upright and firm, turning neither to the right hand nor to the left, but always to what is just.

King Louis IX

Concerned about the welfare of his subjects, Louis IX made peace and justice the primary goals of his reign. He sought to protect the rights of all, regardless of their rank in society. Louis further expanded the jurisdiction of the royal courts over the feudal courts. He also established a permanent royal court at Paris, which served as the supreme court of the land. Fearful that his royal agents (the bailiffs) might infringe the feudal rights of his subjects, he appointed special men to search out abuses in the royal government. He was also the first French king to issue ordinances (i.e., legislation) without first consulting his chief vassals. His efforts at judicial reform earned him the title of "the French Justinian."

Louis IX led two crusades against the Muslims in North Africa. Although he was a zealous warrior, both of the campaigns failed. While on his second crusade, he contracted a disease and died. He is remembered in history as "Saint Louis."

Philip IV and Royal Strength

The climax of Capetian rule came during the reign of **Philip IV** (1285–1314). Known as "the Fair" (because of his handsome features), Philip IV further expanded royal power in France. He strengthened the organization and authority of the central government. As the royal government increased in size, the king needed greater revenue. Philip therefore taxed the French people as no French king before him had done.

The need for revenue led Philip to tax the French clergy also. Pope **Boniface VIII** stepped in and decreed that no king could impose a tax on clergy. Philip countered by refusing to allow gold and silver (especially the tithes of the French church) to be exported from France, thus decreasing the papal revenues. In another controversy, Philip defied Boniface's authority despite the threat of being excommunicated or having an interdict placed on his land (see p. 205). In doing so, he had the support of the French people. Their loyalty was gradually shifting away from the church and the papacy to the state and the French king.

To strengthen popular support for his policies, Philip summoned representatives from the church, nobility, and townspeople to meet at Paris. The meetings of these three estates (or classes) became known as the **Estates-General**. The king sought advice from this representative body, but he did not wait for its consent to enforce legislation or raise taxes. Thus the power of the French monarch grew without restraints such as those the English Parliament imposed on the English kings. This trend partly explains why the French government developed into an absolute monarchy, while the English government became a limited monarchy.

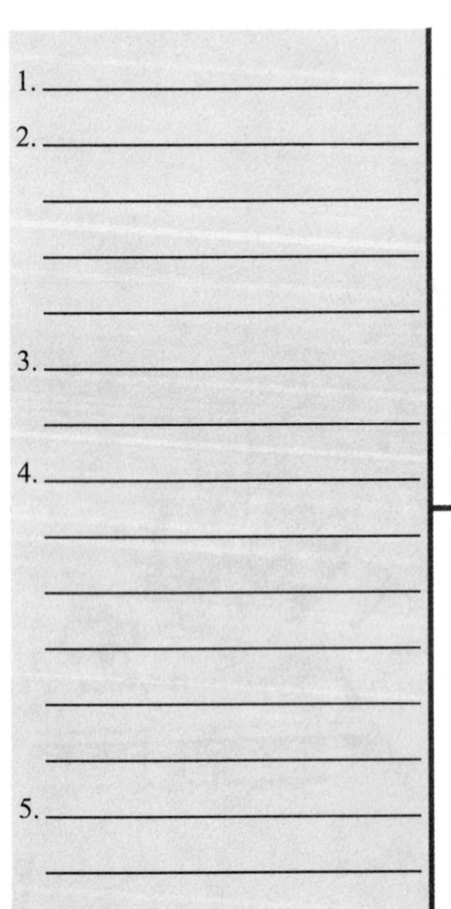

Section Quiz

1. What man defeated the Danes and laid the foundation for a unified English monarchy?
2. What two men struggled for the English throne in 1066? What was the name of the battle where this issue was settled? Who won?
3. On what document did English nobles force King John to affix his royal seal? In what year did this take place?
4. What ruling family came to power in France following the last of the Carolingian monarchs? List five kings in this section who belonged to this royal family.
5. List the English and the French advisory/representative assemblies that developed during this period and identify each with its respective country.

IV. Rescue of the Holy Land

For centuries tourists have flocked to see the land where Christianity began. Even in medieval times eager pilgrims from Europe journeyed to the Holy Land. They viewed Jerusalem as the center of the earth and revered the sites associated with the life of Christ as sacred and holy places. But these people journeyed to Jerusalem for much the same reasons that the Muslims went to Mecca: some wanted to demonstrate their piety; others hoped to earn forgiveness of sins. They believed that somehow they could draw nearer to God's presence by visiting the holy places.

For sure he must be sainted man
Whose blessed feet have trod the ground
Where the Redeemer's tomb is found.

Walter Scott, Marmion, *V.21*

Had these pilgrims walked "by faith, not by sight" (2 Cor. 5:7), they would have realized that we do not have to travel thousands of miles to draw near to God. God's Word tells us that we can "draw near with a true heart in full assurance of faith" (Heb. 10:22).

The Call

During the eleventh century, the Seljuk Turks advanced into the Near East. Moving into Palestine, they seized the holy places of Christendom and disrupted travel to the sacred sites. They invaded Asia Minor and threatened the security of Constantinople. Seeing his land in peril, the Byzantine emperor appealed to Christians in the West for help against the Turks. Pilgrims returning

A crusader castle near Sidon
Historic Views Of The Holy Land: The 1960s: Photographs of Charles Lee Feinberg, www.bible places.com, 2004.

from the Holy Land also called for the recovery of the holy places, recounting tales of terrible atrocities committed by the infidel Muslim Turks.

In 1095 Pope **Urban II** addressed a council of church leaders and French noblemen at Clermont, France. He called for a holy crusade to free the Holy Land from the Turks: "This royal city [Jerusalem] . . . situated at the center of the earth, is now held captive by the enemies of Christ. . . . She seeks, therefore, and desires to be liberated and ceases not to implore you to come to her aid." He called upon the feudal nobles to stop fighting one another and to join instead in fighting the Turks. He urged them to avenge the wrongs done by this "wicked race," to "enter upon the road to the Holy Sepulcher [the tomb where Christ was buried]," and to "wrest that land from the wicked race, and subject it to yourselves."

The response to Urban's moving appeal was overwhelming; those present enthusiastically answered, "It is the will of God!" Urban is reported to have replied: "Let these words be your war-cry when you unsheathe the sword. You are soldiers of the cross. Wear on your breasts or shoulders the blood-red sign of the cross. Wear it as a token that His help will never fail you, as the pledge of a vow never to be recalled." During the two centuries that followed, many Europeans were obsessed with the winning of the Holy Land. Wandering preachers spread the idea, causing thousands to answer the call. The people were convinced by the Roman church that their task was "God's work" and that they were fighting a "holy war." They went forth with the symbol of the cross sewn upon their garments. Those marked by a cross were called *Crusaders*, and their military campaigns became known as the **Crusades** (words derived from the Latin *crux*, meaning cross).

The Crusaders: Their Motives

What prompted the Crusaders to leave their homes and journey such long distances to fight the Turks? Some had a pious desire to serve Christ, to defend the church, and to rescue the Holy Sepulcher. At the same time there were those who desired adventure, seeking an escape from the humdrum life on the manor. Still others hoped to gain fame or fortune. Some knights joined a

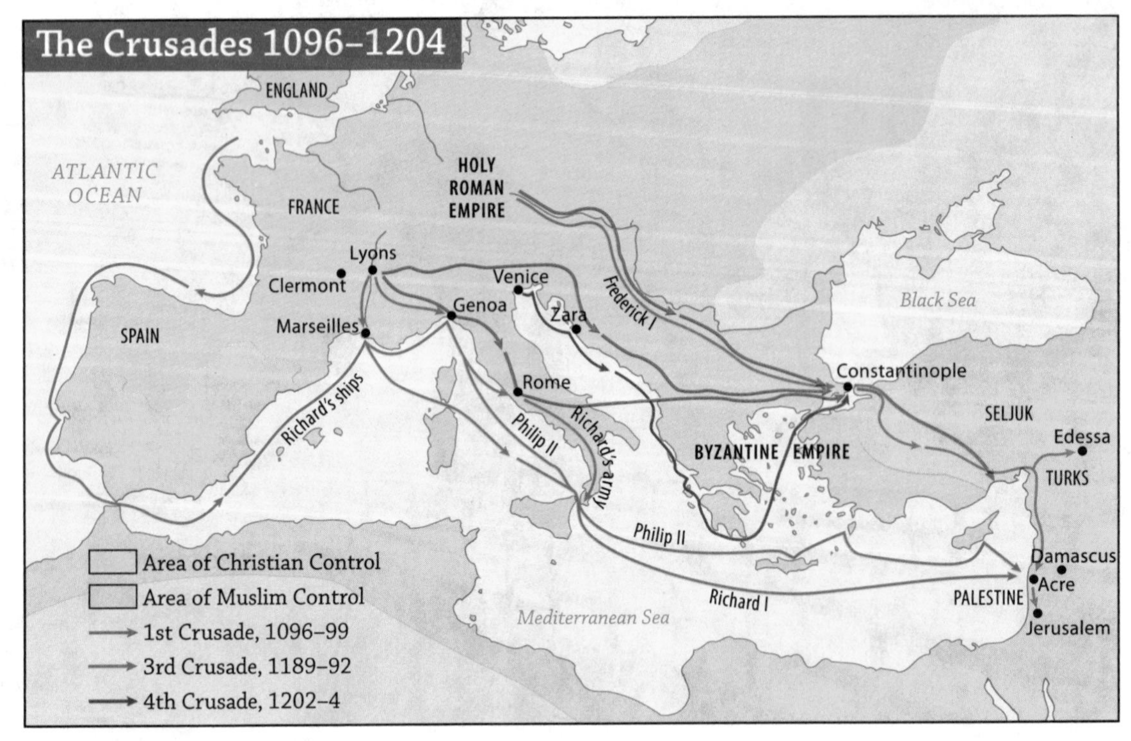

Crusade because they could enjoy their favorite pastime—fighting—and have in addition the blessing of the Roman church. Merchants incited by greed embarked on the Crusades looking for new opportunities for commercial gain.

The Roman church was a powerful force behind the Crusades. The promise of both earthly and heavenly rewards lured many into taking the Crusader's vow. Church leaders guaranteed the protection of the family and property of the Crusader while he was away. Criminals and debtors undertaking the "holy" cause received pardons. In fact, the popes proclaimed that participation in the Crusades was a substitute for penance. Hardened sinners were told they could earn forgiveness of sins by joining one of these campaigns. Furthermore, the Roman church assured the Crusaders that anyone who died while on a Crusade would be granted eternal life. Of course, this was a false assurance, given by church leaders who manipulated the credulous people. Notice the similarity of this false teaching of the Roman church to that of the Islamic religion (see p. 140). Both proclaimed their cause to be a holy war. Both promised paradise to their warriors who fell in battle.

The Campaigns

There were eight major Crusades between **1095** and **1291**. Some Crusaders traveled alone or in small bands; most, however, joined the large organized expeditions.

The First Crusade

Excitement mounted as the year of departure drew near for the first major expedition (1096–99) to the East. Masses of zealous peasants, eager to reach the Holy City, embarked on the long journey in advance of the main armies. These common people had few supplies and even less fighting experience. Those that survived the perilous journey found themselves no match for the Turks, who completely routed them.

The Crusaders' cause fared much better when the main body of knights reached Palestine. Despite the heat, a shortage of supplies, and dissension among their leaders, the Crusaders broke Muslim resistance and succeeded in capturing Jerusalem. In taking the city, they slaughtered its inhabitants. According to an exaggerated eyewitness account, the city was filled with corpses and blood. In the temple area alone, "men rode in blood up to their knees and bridle reins. Indeed," the account continues, "it was a just and splendid judgment of God that this place should be filled with the blood of unbelievers, since it had suffered so long from their blasphemies."[2]

Of all the Crusades, the first was the most successful. Besides winning the Holy City, the Crusaders established four small feudal kingdoms along the Mediterranean coastline. It was not long, however, before a new Muslim offensive threatened these "Crusader states." In response the Second Crusade was launched in 1147. Unlike the first, this second campaign ended in miserable failure, with the Western forces suffering defeat at the hands of the Turks.

The Kings' Crusade

In 1187 the Muslims recaptured Jerusalem under their new leader, **Saladin**. News of Saladin's victory stirred the Europeans to organize the Third Crusade, called the Kings' Crusade (1189–92). Three of the most powerful kings in Europe led the crusading armies: Frederick Barbarossa of Germany, Philip Augustus of France, and Richard the Lion-Hearted of England. This Crusade began as the largest of all, but troubles plagued the expedition from the start. Frederick accidentally drowned on the way to the Holy Land. Constant strife between Richard and Philip led Philip to return to France with his army shortly after his arrival in the Holy Land. Richard remained and defeated Saladin in many battles, but he did not succeed in taking Jerusalem. Richard and Saladin then agreed to a three-year truce that allowed Western pilgrims free access to the holy places in Jerusalem.

The "Diverted" Crusade

Unlike earlier Crusaders, who maintained the pretense of a religious undertaking, the participants of the Fourth Crusade (1201–4) abandoned the ideals of their predecessors and openly pursued political and economic ends. Venetian merchants agreed to transport the Crusaders to the East, but because of miscalculation, the Crusaders were unable to pay the transportation fees. To pay their way, they agreed to support a Venetian attack upon the city of Zara, a rival seaport in the Adriatic. The conquest of this city whetted the Crusaders' appetite for plunder and weakened their desire to reach the Holy Land. The Venetians realized this and diverted the Crusaders to Constantinople, Venice's chief rival. The wayward warriors never reached the Holy Land and never raised a sword against the Muslims. Instead, they attacked the Byzantines, who had originally requested their help against the Turks. In 1204 Constantinople fell to the Crusaders, who pillaged the city (see p. 131).

The Later Crusades

Crusaders continued to journey to the Holy Land throughout the thirteenth century, but they were no more successful than the earlier ones. The expeditions were poorly organized and lacked strong leadership. Meanwhile, attitudes in Europe were changing. With each failed Crusade, the religious zeal and fighting spirit so prevalent in Europe before the Crusades gradually subsided. Soon Europe became occupied with new expeditions. These were dominated by strong nations rather than the Roman church and motivated by commercial interests more than religious concerns. The Crusader was replaced by the explorer. The motto "take up the cross" was changed to "seek out and discover." And the recovery of the Holy Land gave way to finding new commercial routes to the Far East.

The Consequences

Although it is impossible to measure with exactness the effects of the Crusades upon western Europe, there is little doubt that they brought about several profound changes. The following are the most evident:

1. The Crusades weakened the feudal structure of Europe. Feudal nobles, seeking to raise money to go on Crusades, allowed the serfs to buy their freedom. Freed serfs left the manors with hopes of finding new opportunities in the growing towns. With the decline of the feudal structure came the emergence of strong nations ruled by kings. Under the pretext of financing the Crusades, several European kings gained the power to tax. Taxation provided badly needed revenues, which monarchs used to extend their powers.

2. The Crusades expanded the commercial activity of Europe. The Crusaders were amazed at the riches they found in the East. They came to know and desire such luxuries as sugar, spices, fruits, silks, cotton, and glass mirrors (which were obtained by Middle Eastern countries primarily through trade with the Orient). The heightened demand for these goods in Europe led enterprising individuals to import them. The increase in trade prompted the rise of a money

The Children's Crusade

In the summer of 1212 children by the thousands gathered in towns throughout France and many of the German states. Filled with religious zeal, they set out for the Holy Land convinced that God wanted to use them to free it from the Muslims. They took as their text Psalm 8:2: "Out of the mouth of babes and sucklings hast thou ordained strength because of thine enemies, that thou mightest still the enemy and the avenger." As they went forth they sang songs of praise to God. Later generations have associated the following song, traditionally known as "the Crusaders' Hymn," with the Children's Crusade.

Fairest Lord Jesus,
Ruler of all nature,
O Thou of God and man the Son!
Thee will I cherish,
Thee will I honor,
Thou my soul's glory, joy, and crown!

According to chronicles of the day, a young shepherd boy named Stephen from the town of Cloyes, France, had a vision. He claimed that Christ told him to lead a Crusade of children to the Holy Land. He journeyed to St. Denis just north of Paris, where he encouraged children to join him in a Crusade. Word spread quickly; by August, thousands of children had gathered. He told them that God had promised that the Mediterranean Sea would open for them so they could walk through on dry land just as the children of Israel had walked through the Red Sea. Following Stephen, they marched toward the sea.

When news of Stephen's vision reached Germany, another young boy, Nicholas, felt that he too was called to lead a Crusade. He attracted a large following in the city of Cologne. (Like St. Denis, Cologne was a pilgrim center. It had a shrine that supposedly housed the bones of the three wise men!) Of the thousands of children who left with Nicholas, only about a third reached the Mediterranean coast. When the sea did not open, they were sadly disillusioned; too weary to travel home, they remained in Italy.

Meanwhile, Stephen's group reached Marseilles, a Crusader port in southern France. They too discovered that the sea did not open for them. Many returned home, but about five thousand remained, still hoping for a miracle. It was then that two merchants offered the children free passage to the Holy Land. Thinking that this was God's miracle, they accepted. Of the seven ships that set sail, two were wrecked. The other five made their way to the North African coast, where the merchants sold the children into slavery. It was not until eighteen years later that the people of Europe found out what had happened. A priest who had accompanied the children, and who was himself enslaved, escaped and made his way back to Europe and told of the fate of the children.

Fort St. Jean in Marseilles, France; Marseilles was a Crusader port in southern France.

economy (as opposed to a barter system) and the need for banking services. It also incited Europeans to search for even greater profits by finding new routes to the wealth in the East.

3. The early Crusades strengthened the leadership of the papacy. The popes called for the Crusades, planned them, and collected taxes or tithes for their financing. They were thus able to extend their powers in both secular and sacred matters. As later Crusades failed, however, people became disillusioned and began to distrust the motives of the papacy. Respect for the crusading ideals and the papacy continued to diminish as popes called for Crusades to battle heretics in Europe and unruly German kings.

4. The Crusades opened new horizons to the people of medieval Europe. Contact with the East changed their narrow-minded attitudes and introduced them to other civilizations, such as the Byzantine and Muslim empires. In addition, the Crusades renewed interest in the knowledge of ancient Greece and Rome—knowledge that had been preserved by the civilizations in the East. And the Europeans' travel experiences and increased understanding of world geography gave impetus to the later period of exploration.

5. The Crusades offered important lessons for the Christian church. The Christian warriors believed they could accomplish God's work by using weapons of the flesh. Yet the Bible teaches that the Christian soldier is involved in a spiritual battle. His weapons should not be the weapons of this world. The Apostle Paul admonishes believers in 2 Corinthians 10:3–4: "For though we walk in the flesh, we do not war after the flesh: (For the weapons of our warfare are not carnal, but mighty through God to the pulling down of strong holds.)"

Section Quiz

1. What pope called for a holy crusade to free the Holy Land from the Turks? In what year did this occur?
2. How many major Crusades were there? Over what span of years did they occur?
3. What is the nickname of the Third Crusade? List the kings (with their countries) who went on this Crusade.
4. To where was the Fourth Crusade "diverted"? Who "diverted" the Crusade?

1. ______________________________

____

2. ______________________________

____

3. ______________________________

____

____

____

____

____

____

4. ______________________________

____

A Glance Behind

In many ways the Crusades were a dismal failure. The Holy Land was not permanently won, the Muslims were not driven out, and great crimes were committed against Eastern Europeans. Despite all this, the Crusades were not completely in vain. As always, God in His providence was at work, accomplishing His overall purpose in history. The results of the Crusades combined with other forces already at work brought about far-reaching positive changes in western Europe. In due course Europe entered into the modern age and anticipated a time of great spiritual revival—the Reformation—which you will read about in the next unit.

and a Glimpse Ahead

Notes

1. Henry Bettenson, ed., *Documents of the Christian Church* (New York: Oxford University Press, 1947), pp. 157–58.
2. Geoffroide Villehardouin and Jean, sire de Joinville, *Memoirs of the Crusades*, trans. Sir Frank Marzials (London: Dent, 1926), p. 321.

Chapter Review

Can You Define?

lay investiture
simony
friars
mendicant orders
excommunication
interdict
Inquisition
duke
duchy
Holy Roman Empire
shire
tenants-in-chief
indictment
common law
witan
curia regis
"power of the purse"
baillis
Estates-General
Crusades

Can You Identify?

910
Cistercians
Bernard of Clairvaux
College of Cardinals
Gregory VII
Henry IV
1077
Concordat of Worms
Francis of Assisi
Dominic
Innocent III
Henry the Fowler
Otto I
Salian House
Hohenstaufens
Frederick I
Frederick II
Angles
Saxons
Alfred the Great
Anglo-Saxon Chronicle
Canute
Edward the Confessor
Harold
Battle of Hastings (1066)
Domesday Book
Henry II
Thomas à Becket
Richard I
John
Magna Carta (1215)
Edward I
Parliament
Hugh Capet
Île-de-France
Philip II
Louis IX
Philip IV
Boniface VIII
Urban II
1095–1291
Saladin

Can You Locate?

Cluny
Canossa
Worms
Lombardy
England
Hastings
Normandy
Canterbury
Scotland
Anjou
Constantinople
Palestine
Jerusalem
Venice

How Much Do You Remember?

1. List three examples from this chapter of the conflicts between the papacy and European monarchs. Identify the names of the popes and rulers as well as the issue that prompted the controversy.
2. Identify the following records/document in English history: *Anglo-Saxon Chronicle, Domesday Book*, Magna Carta.
3. What did the reigns of Henry II of England and Philip II of France have in common?
4. List at least three motives that prompted Europeans to join the Crusades.
5. List five consequences of the Crusades.

What Do You Think?

1. The conflict between church and state was not just a medieval problem. In what ways is it evident today?
2. Compare the reigns of John of England and Louis IX of France in light of Proverbs 16:12.
3. Of the events discussed in this chapter, which one do you think had the greatest impact upon the church? What event had the greatest impact on each of the following: the Holy Roman Empire, England, France? Explain your answers.
4. What kinds of "holy wars" should Christians be prepared to fight? (See Eph. 6:10–18; 2 Cor. 10:3–5; 1 Tim. 1:18–19; 6:12.)

"Town air makes one free."

THE RESHAPING OF MEDIEVAL EUROPE

I. Revival of Trade
  - A. Trade Routes
  - B. Markets and Fairs
  - C. Money and Banking
  - D. The Medieval Church and Business Practices

II. Growth of Towns
  - A. Townsmen Gain Basic Freedoms
  - B. Merchants and Craftsmen Establish Guilds
  - C. A New Social Class Emerges
  - D. Town Life

III. Medieval Learning and Art
  - A. Universities
  - B. Philosophy and Theology
  - C. Medieval Science
  - D. Language and Literature
  - E. Art and Architecture

IV. Emergence of National States
  - A. War Between England and France
  - B. Reconquista in Spain and Portugal
  - C. Disunity in Italy and Germany

V. Decline of the Roman Church
  - A. Papal Humiliation
  - B. Papal Exile
  - C. Papal Schism

The growth of towns dramatically changed the social structures of medieval Europe.

In the last chapter, we discussed specifically the religious life of people in the Middle Ages. In this chapter, we will discuss the economic, social, and political developments of the Middle Ages, which reveal the beginnings of modern Western society. All of these aspects are intertwined. During the late medieval period (1200–1500), Europe experienced significant changes. Trade was pursued with renewed vigor, towns grew in size and importance, and a new social class emerged. Contact with other cultures sparked interest in learning and the arts, and national states began to appear. At the same time, the feudal and manorial systems weakened, and the church, once the dominant force in Europe, declined in strength and influence.

The Great Hall of Study at the University of Bologna

I. Revival of Trade

During the early Middle Ages, trade activity had diminished in Europe. Money was in short supply. Travel was often treacherous, as roads were poor, and robbers and pirates often threatened merchants on the trade routes. Towns, which were once the heart of economic activity, declined in size. The manors became the new economic centers of medieval Europe. Unlike towns and cities, manors did not depend upon trade but were virtually self-sufficient. The few items that could not be made or grown on a particular manor could be obtained by **barter**—exchanging goods for goods. For the most part, trade remained localized and relatively insignificant.

Trade Routes

The reopening of trade routes between western Europe and the East was a major factor in the revival of European commerce. During the early Middle Ages, Byzantine and Muslim merchants had dominated trade in the Mediterranean region. Later, however, enterprising Italian merchants, with their large fleets, began to seize trade rights in the Near East. Soon Italian cities such as Venice, Pisa, and Genoa gained a virtual monopoly on Mediterranean trade.

European commerce expanded as the Italian merchants became the middlemen in trade between Europe and the Orient. Once goods from the Far East reached the Mediterranean, Italian merchants transported them to Europe, where they were distributed to European markets. Traders who brought goods from the Orient reached the Mediterranean by three principal routes:

1. The southern route was almost entirely on water. Ships laden with goods from India and China sailed across the Arabian Sea and northward up the Red Sea. The goods were then hauled overland to the Nile River and transported to the Mediterranean.
2. The central route combined land and sea travel. Ships from the Far East carried goods to the Persian Gulf, where caravans transported the merchandise to Baghdad or Damascus. Other traders then brought them to port cities along the Mediterranean and Black seas.
3. The northern route, known as the "Silk Road," was an overland route across central Asia. It connected Beijing and Constantinople.

Italy controlled Mediterranean trade, but Flanders was the marketplace of northern Europe. The region of Flanders (which included parts of present-day Belgium, France, and Holland) lay at the crossroads of northern European trade routes. The Flemish, who were makers of fine cloth, had easy access to the markets of Europe.

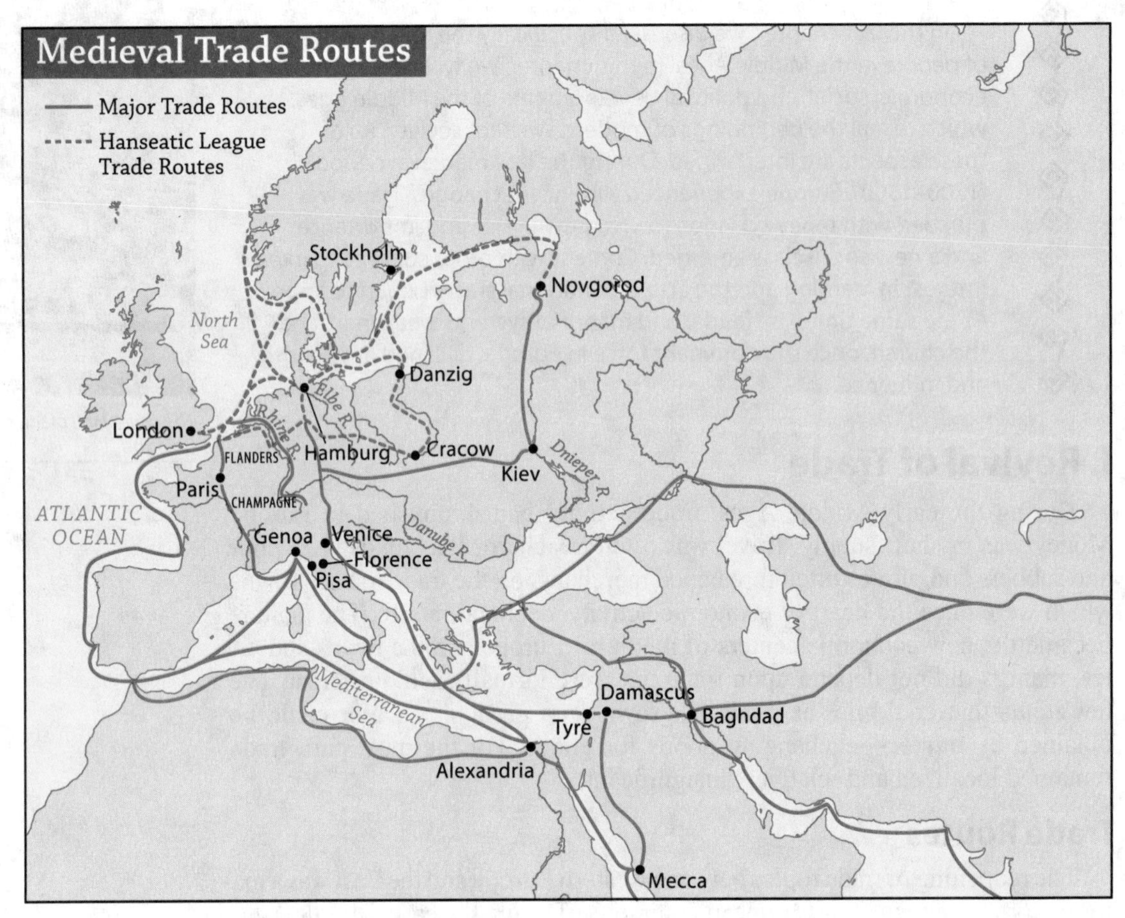

Markets and Fairs

As trade activity increased, so did the need for places where merchants could meet and exchange their goods. On the local level, markets became the primary centers for trade. Once a week traders met along important highways, in church courtyards, or in village squares. The goods sold there benefited both the people on the manor and those in the towns. The market offered incentive for the laboring serfs to produce more, for at the market they could sell their surplus produce. Many saved their money, desiring to buy goods or hoping one day to be able to buy their freedom from the manor. The market also offered craftsmen and merchants an opportunity to peddle their wares. Thus these places of trade met the demands of the local population. Townspeople obtained surplus food from the manors, and the people of the manor acquired articles made and sold by local craftsmen and merchants.

On a larger scale than the markets were the trade fairs, which attracted merchants from all over Europe as well as many foreign countries. These fairs were sometimes great regional or international events. They were held annually and could last from several days to several weeks. Because they were held in nearly every part of Europe, fairs were often scheduled in sequence so that merchants could attend one after the other.

Fairs provided a meeting place for East-West trade. Italian middlemen and foreign merchants from Constantinople, Damascus, and Alexandria brought spices, silks, precious gems, cotton, linen, rugs, and dyes from the East. Peddlers and town merchants bought these "luxury" items and distributed them locally. In return, foreign merchants purchased local products such as wool, grain, timber, and fish.

The most famous and important of the medieval fairs were held in Champagne, a region in northeastern France. This province became an important trade center for merchants traveling between Flanders and Italy. At almost any time during the year, fairs were being held in the towns of this region, each one lasting about six weeks.

Fairs such as the ones at Champagne were more than just places to exchange goods; they were festive occasions.

> The neighboring lords and their families came to see and to buy and to enjoy the diversions of the fair. The monks from the abbey and the secular clergy mingled with the throng. No doubt many an artisan and many a runaway serf from the neighboring manors was drawn hither by the strange sights and sounds and the gay-colored crowd. Mountebanks, jugglers, and musicians of every description vied in their efforts to attract the crowd; men with trained monkeys, dogs, or dancing bears, wrestlers, wandering minstrels singing ancient lays, fakers without number were there to entertain and astonish the populace. There were gathered as in modern fairs the thief, the pick-pocket, the cutpurse, the thug, the prostitute, beggars. Often the sergeants were hard pressed to maintain order in this heterogeneous mob.[1]

Jan Gossaert, Portrait of a Merchant, *c. 1530.*
Ailsa Mellon Bruce Fund, Image © 2005 Board of Trustees, National Gallery of Art, Washington

Money and Banking

The barter system in use during the early Middle Ages could not meet the expanding demands of the trade fairs. Therefore, money gained wider use as a means of exchange. This development helped trade and provided a standard of value for the purchase and sale of goods. Feudal lords and commercial towns began minting their own coins. Their values varied greatly, depending upon the amount and purity of the metal contained in them. Certain coins of high quality became widely accepted as mediums of exchange. One, for example, was the **florin**, a gold coin minted by the city of Florence.

Because most merchants did not know the value of coins minted outside their own region, **moneychangers** grew in importance at the markets and trade fairs throughout Europe. These men were experienced in judging the approximate value of coins, discovering counterfeit currency, and determining one currency's value in relation to another. Merchants could be assured of the value of a foreign currency that they accepted for their goods. If the merchants wanted that currency exchanged into their own, moneychangers were also ready to perform that service—for a fee, of course.

They did more, however, than just evaluate and exchange money for merchants. They provided many other services that we commonly associate with modern banks. Since they dealt constantly with money, moneychangers went to great lengths to protect their own funds. Realizing this, other merchants began entrusting their surplus cash to the moneychangers for safekeeping. The moneychangers then became moneylenders. Kings, nobles, and even popes borrowed from them to finance their activities. For example, a king might borrow money to finance a crusade to the Holy Land. He risked great danger, however, by carrying large sums on his journey. It was much safer and more convenient to obtain a letter of credit in Europe. (Letters of credit were much like our modern checks.) Once he reached the Holy Land, he could present the letter of credit to another moneychanger and receive cash in return. It is not surprising to learn that our word *bank* comes from the Italian ***banca***, which means "bench," referring to the table of a moneychanger.

The Medieval Church and Business Practices

There was little economic freedom in Europe during much of the medieval period. Most people had little opportunity or incentive to improve their way of life. Feudal lords held virtual monopolies over the economic life on the manors. In addition, the teaching of the Roman church discouraged economic activity.

In a day when religion dominated society, it was quite natural for the church to shape the economic ideas of Europe. The church viewed with suspicion those individuals involved in trade. Did not the Bible teach "Lay not up for yourselves treasures upon earth, . . . for where your treasure is, there will your heart be also" (Matt. 6:19, 21)? Poverty was upheld as a virtue. Since seeking the riches of this world often leads one to greed and the hoarding of wealth, the Roman church sought to place restraints upon business.

Every man had a particular place in society and was expected to work for the common good of society, not just for himself. It was considered selfish and rebellious for one to try to improve his own status in life or to involve himself in trade solely for profit.

Metsys, Quentin. The Moneylender and His Wife, *1514.*

Inv.: INV 1444. Photo Daniel Arnaudet. Louvre, Paris, France

Profit resulting from the sale of goods or services was deemed acceptable only if the seller did not take advantage of the buyer. The church advocated a **"just price"** for goods sold—a price that included the cost of materials, a fair return for labor expended, and a reasonable profit. According to the church it was wrong to sell an item for more than it was worth or to buy it for less than its actual value. If any man received a profit greater than his needs, he was expected to give it to charity.

Furthermore, the medieval church prohibited **usury**—the practice of charging interest for the use of lent money. Usury was considered a sin. The church assumed that anyone who borrowed money was in great need. Therefore, for someone to profit from a loan made to a brother in need was definitely wrong. Such a loan should be an act of charity, not a money-making venture. The revival of trade altered this doctrine. Merchants borrowed money not because of poverty but for business investment. Soon it became acceptable to charge interest on loans made for investment purposes. Profit made on such loans was considered a fitting reward for the risk taken since loss was an equal possibility.

In spite of the church's teaching, the revival of trade and changes in business methods brought new opportunities and incentives to much of Europe's population. Sound economic principles made Europe prosperous: the dignity of labor, the legitimacy of profit, freedom of exchange, and individual responsibility—not group responsibility—for economic matters. More and more people were gaining financial independence.

Section Quiz

1. Who served as middlemen in trade between Europe and the Orient?
2. What were the primary centers of trade on the local level in Europe? What were the centers of trade for large-scale international trade?
3. Where did we get our word for *bank*?
4. What is the term for charging interest for the use of lent money? What institution condemned this practice during the Middle Ages?

1. ____________________
2. ____________________
____
3. ____________________
____
4. ____________________
____

II. Growth of Towns

Towns, like trade, did not entirely disappear in the West during the Middle Ages. Even so, Europe could boast few cities that could compare in size and population to the many bustling cities of the Roman Empire. Renewed trade, however, stimulated the growth of towns. Towns provided needed markets and were important centers of exchange.

By the eleventh century, active forces at work in Europe began to give shape to the forerunners of the modern city. Better farming methods led to increased agricultural production. Townspeople who wished to devote their full energy to a specific trade or craft could depend upon others to produce surplus food. An increased food supply boosted Europe's population. As Europe's population grew, so did its towns. Some towns revived within the decayed walls of old Roman cities, while others sprang up at locations important to trade: crossroads, bridges, fords, river mouths, and harbors. Still others were built near castles, churches, and monasteries.

Bellinzona, Switzerland; located between Northern Italy and the Alps region, this area was a Roman military fortress. In the twelfth century a city began growing around the fortress, and today it is the capital city of the Swiss canton Ticino.

Townsmen Gain Basic Freedoms

Merchants and craftsmen, who lived in the growing urban centers, did not fit into the medieval class structure. They were not lords, vassals, or serfs. And their labor contributed little to the agricultural output of the local manor. Nevertheless, nearly every town was subject to some feudal lord.

Townsmen having common interests soon banded together to gain freedom from feudal interference and to secure local self-government. They achieved this independence in a variety of ways. Some towns bought privileges from feudal lords who were willing to grant certain liberties in exchange for large sums of money. Other lords bestowed these privileges freely, for a thriving town meant greater revenues from sales taxes and tolls (a fee paid for some privileges, such as traveling on a road or crossing a bridge). Nevertheless, there were some lords who did not want to relinquish control at any cost. In such cases towns often revolted and fought for their freedom.

The privileges granted a town by a feudal lord were usually written down in a legal document called a **charter**. This document outlined the rights and freedoms of the townspeople. The more favorable the charter, the greater the number of people attracted to settle in the town. While liberties varied from town to town, most townsmen shared certain basic freedoms:

1. **Free Status.** The most important privilege enjoyed by a townsman was that of being a freeman. No matter what his previous status, a man who lived in a town for a year and a day was considered free. A serf, for example, who ran away from his manor and managed to escape capture by living in a town for one year, broke all ties with his manor. An old German proverb said, "Town air makes one free."

2. **Exemption from Manorial Obligations.** Town charters usually exempted townsmen from laboring for the lord of the manor. The townsmen as a group, not as individuals, owed service to the lord. This service was usually rendered in the form of a cash payment.

3. **Town Justice.** Townsmen also won the privilege of administering their own justice. Instead of being tried in a feudal court and judged by feudal customs, a townsman was tried in the court of his town and was judged by town people and town customs.

4. **Commercial Privileges.** The chief commercial freedom granted to townsmen was the right to buy and sell freely in the town market. The merchants were free from feudal interference and were protected from competition by outside merchants.

Merchants and Craftsmen Establish Guilds

Merchants and craftsmen in growing towns banded together to protect their common commercial interests. They formed organizations called **guilds**, whose primary function was to regulate the business activity of a given town. By acting together, town merchants gained greater security, discouraged outside competition, and increased profits. Guilds also provided aid to members in need. They established schools and cared for the poor, widows, and orphans. Powerful guilds helped towns obtain favorable charters and played an important role in town governments.

There were two types of guilds: merchant and craft. The earliest type was the merchant guild. It guarded the trade interests of merchants by giving them a monopoly of a town's trade. The guild restricted outsiders from doing business in town except upon payment of a heavy fee. The guild also fixed prices at which goods could be bought and sold at the town market.

Guild halls in Ghent, Belgium

At first each town had only one guild. But as a town's trade grew and became more specialized, each merchant guild divided into many craft guilds. There were guilds for the town's bakers, tanners, shoemakers, butchers, wheelwrights, and other craftsmen. Each craft guild regulated the hours its members worked, the wages earned, and the number of employees hired. Members of a particular craft guaranteed the quality of their products. They punished members who used shoddy materials, dealt dishonestly, or sold goods cheaper than the established price.

Within each craft guild, there were three classes of members—apprentices, journeymen, and masters. A young boy began his training as an **apprentice**. He entered the home of a master craftsman and was expected to work hard in return for his food, lodging, and training. It was the master's responsibility to teach the young apprentice not only the skills of the trade, but also proper conduct. At the end of his apprenticeship—a period varying from two to seven years—the young man became a **journeyman**, or "day-laborer." He could then seek employment and earn wages as a skilled worker. Usually a journeyman remained at the home of his master and worked at his master's shop.

Every journeyman looked forward to the day when he could become a master himself. This required years of experience, as well as funds to open a shop. To become a **master**, a journeyman had to undergo an oral examination, present an example of his workmanship (called a "master piece"), and take an oath to conduct himself according to the regulations of the guild. Once approved

THIS MOMENT IN HISTORY

Hanseatic League

In what ways could the Hanseatic League have interfered with relationships between countries? How could the League have helped relationships between countries?

___

___

___

___

___

___

by the other masters of the guild, the new master could open his own shop and take on his own apprentices and journeymen.

Sometimes towns formed associations to promote and protect their mutual commercial interests. The most famous of these was the **Hanseatic League**, composed of more than seventy German cities in northwestern Europe. The *Hanse* (German for "guild") sought to organize and control trade in Sweden, Russia, Flanders, and England. Although the *Hanse* primarily sought commercial privileges, it also became a powerful political force. It negotiated treaties, maintained its own navy, and even waged war against other countries.

A New Social Class Emerges

In early feudal society, a great social and economic gulf had separated the nobility and the peasants. With the growth of towns during the eleventh and twelfth centuries, however, a new social class arose, commonly referred to as the **middle class**. It was composed of merchants, bankers, craftsmen, and skilled laborers. These were the "men of the town" known as *burgesses* in England, *bourgeois* in France, and *burgers* in Germany. (The word *burg* means "a walled town.") The members of this new class had freedom and money. They were energetic, independent, mobile, and growing in number and power. Their

The Black Death

Death swept across Europe in the fourteenth century. A form of plague known as the Black Death (because of the dark blotches it left on its victims' skin) slew at least one-fourth of the population of Europe. Some historians maintain that half of the people of Europe died. So great was the suffering and social upheaval that many people believed that the end of the world was at hand.

The plague spread to Europe from Asia, carried by the rats and fleas in merchant ships. During the Middle Ages, however, people did not know the cause of the disease. This uncertainty made the plague even more fearsome. The Black Death seemed uncaused and unstoppable. Members of every social and economic class fell to its onslaught. Men sought above all to save themselves. One witness of the plague wrote, "One citizen avoided another, hardly any neighbor troubled about others, relatives never or hardly ever visited each other. Moreover, such terror was struck into the hearts of men and women by this calamity, that brother abandoned brother, and the uncle his nephew, and the sister her brother, and very often the wife her husband. What is even worse and nearly incredible is that fathers and mothers refused to see and tend their children, as if they had not been theirs."[2]

The widespread destruction brought out the best and worst in mankind. Some devout men viewed the plague as the judgment of God and turned to Him. They devoted themselves to the treatment of the ill and the easing of suffering wherever possible. Others, however, gave free reign to their lusts. Their philosophy became "Eat, drink, and be merry; for tomorrow we die." Instead of being humbled by the terror, they became bolder in their sin.

Filling a mass grave at night during the Plague of London, c. 1665. Approximately 100,000 died in London.

world was the town market, and their livelihood was trade. The middle class contributed to the decline of feudalism and helped shape modern society.

Most noblemen considered the middle class a threat to their position in society. Social ranking, formerly determined by birth or landholding, had gradually shifted toward those who possessed the greatest amounts of money and goods. A nobleman's wealth was in his land; a merchant's wealth was his money or goods. While the nobleman usually spent the money he derived from his land, the merchant invested his money, often at great risk, to gain more wealth. Soon many merchants, bankers, and master craftsmen possessed goods, clothes, and dwellings to rival those of the feudal lords.

By challenging the nobility's social position, the middle class also weakened the nobility's political authority. By the twelfth century, most towns had gained some degree of self-government. Although townsmen were able to regulate trade within their own town, they realized that the sectionalism produced by feudalism and the tolls and sales taxes levied by feudal lords hindered widespread trade. As a result, the middle class desired the stable and uniform government a national king could offer rather than the localism of feudal lords. Kings who had previously relied on nobles to supply revenue and soldiers now could draw upon the rich resources of the towns and the middle class, usually in the form of taxes.

THROUGH EYES OF FAITH

Public Health

Many of the health hazards of the Middle Ages resulted from poor sanitation and the lack of education about human health. Does a Christian have biblical reasons for being concerned about proper sanitation and public health in general? If so, what are they?

____

____

____

____

____

____

____

Town Life

Medieval towns were small. By the thirteenth century, only a few, such as Paris, Rome, Venice, and Florence, had populations over fifty thousand. The typical town averaged only about five thousand people. Most towns were enclosed by thick walls for protection. As the population of the town grew, conditions became overcrowded. Old walls had to be torn down and new ones built to create more room. Because land space within walled towns was limited, houses were crowded together along narrow streets. It was not uncommon for houses to be four or five stories high. The upper stories of houses often extended out over the streets.

The streets below were dark, crooked, and filthy. The townspeople tossed their garbage into open gutters lining the roads. According to medieval writers, the stench from some towns could be smelled miles away. Poor sanitation caused disease, and epidemics spread rapidly, carried throughout the town by the pigs, rats, and dogs that roamed the streets.

Although town life was not easy or comfortable, it was often exciting. During the day the streets hummed with the noise of merchants and peddlers selling their wares, of craftsmen plying their trade, and of children playing in the streets. The center of activity was the town square. Here visiting merchants displayed dazzling items from foreign lands. Within the square's large open space, the town's militia drilled, boys played soccer, and actors performed. Lining the square were the town hall, various guild halls, and the towering cathedral.

Narrow street in Bergamo, Italy

Section Quiz

1. ______
2. ______
3. ______
4. ______
5. ______

1. What factors contributed to the growth of towns in medieval Europe?
2. List four basic freedoms shared by most townspeople.
3. What was the primary function of a guild?
4. What were the three classes of members of craft guilds?
5. What new social class arose with the rise of towns in the eleventh and twelfth centuries? What were the chief occupations of the people of this class?

III. Medieval Learning and Art

The Middle Ages is often considered an age of ignorance and superstition—a "dark" age of learning. While there was little formal education of the masses throughout much of this period, education never completely died out. Learning continued, primarily under the influence of the Roman church. The monks constituted the vast majority of the educated. The primary centers of education were the monasteries and cathedrals. The church, however, was often more interested in maintaining existing knowledge than in pursuing new ideas.

A basic part of medieval education was the liberal arts curriculum, which was divided into two groups of studies: the **trivium**, consisting of grammar (Latin), rhetoric (effective speaking), and logic; and the **quadrivium**, consisting of arithmetic, geometry, astronomy, and music. A medieval bishop-historian described his education:

> [I was taught] by means of grammar to read, by dialectic [logic] to apprehend the arguments in disputes, by rhetoric to recognize the different meters, by geometry to comprehend the measurement of the earth and of lines, by [astronomy] to contemplate the paths of the heavenly bodies, by arithmetic to understand the parts of numbers, by harmony to fit the modulated voice to the sweet accent of the verse.[3]

During the twelfth century, a revival of learning swept across Europe. It was brought about by several factors:

1. Political and economic conditions in Europe were improving, producing a climate more favorable for intellectual and cultural pursuits.
2. Europe's contact with the Byzantine and Arab civilizations exposed Europe to new ideas. These cultures transmitted to Europe not only their own knowledge but also the preserved learning of ancient Greece and Rome. New avenues of study opened as Justinian's code of laws, the works of Aristotle, and Greek and Arab medical writings became available in Europe.
3. As towns grew and the functions of government expanded, there was an increasing need for education. A theological training was no longer sufficient to meet all the needs of law and business. Greater numbers of people—including some from the rising middle class—were seeking entrance into the ranks of the educated.

Universities

Probably the most important development during this period was the rise of the university. These new centers of learning gradually replaced most of the old monastery and cathedral schools of the Roman church. In the late Middle Ages students were little concerned about the town or school in which they studied. They were more interested in who their teacher was. Students traveled

University Life

University life has changed significantly over the years. Early universities had no campuses, buildings, laboratories, or athletic facilities. Classes met wherever the teacher could find a place to lecture. All lectures were conducted in Latin. Students sat on the floor, on straw, or on small benches. They took notes on wax tablets or parchment, if they could afford it. Few students had textbooks—books were too scarce and too expensive. Sometimes students pooled their resources to buy a textbook, which they shared.

Medieval Universities

While the academic setting has changed dramatically over the centuries, some things about university life never change. For example, many students will still write home only when they are in need of money.

This letter from a medieval student to his parents could well have been written by his modern counterpart: "This is to inform you that I am studying at Oxford with the greatest diligence, but the matter of money stands greatly in the way of my promotion, as it is now two months since I spent the last of what you sent me. The city is expensive and makes many demands; I have to rent lodgings, buy necessaries, and provide for many other things which I cannot now specify. Wherefore I respectfully beg your paternity by the promptings of divine pity that you may assist me, so that I may be able to complete what I have well begun."[4]

In another letter, a father writes to his son who is away at school. The contents of the letter would not seem out of place in modern society: "It is written, 'he also that is slothful in his work is brother to him that is a great waster.' I have recently discovered that you live dissolutely and slothfully, preferring license to restraint and play to work and strumming a guitar while the others are at their studies, whence it happens that you have read but one volume of law while your more industrious companions have read several. Wherefore I have decided to exhort you herewith to repent utterly of your dissolute and careless ways, that you may no longer be called a waster and that your shame may be turned to good repute."[5]

all over Europe to find the best instructor in their subject area. A master teacher attracted many students, who paid him a fee to teach them. As the number of teachers and students grew in a given locality, the scholars—like craftsmen—formed educational guilds for privileges and protection. At first any association of people, such as a guild, was called a ***universitas***. But gradually the term came to designate those united for the common purpose of education.

Two of the earliest universities were at Bologna in northern Italy and at Paris. Students organized the university at Bologna and formed a guild to ensure adequate instruction from their teachers and to protect against being overcharged for food and rent by the townspeople. The university at Paris grew out of an old cathedral school. Unlike Bologna, it was supervised by a guild of masters or professors, not students. Each school offered training in specialized areas of study. Bologna became a leading center for the study of law; Paris, for liberal arts and theology. These schools served as models for other universities.

Rules for Teachers Set Down by Students at Bologna

A professor might not be absent without leave, even a single day, and if he desired to leave town, he had to make a deposit to ensure his return. If he failed to secure an audience of five for a regular lecture, he was fined as if absent—a poor lecture indeed which could not secure five hearers! He must begin with the bell and quit within one minute after the next bell. He was not allowed to skip a character in his commentary, or postpone a difficulty to the end of the hour, and he was obliged to cover ground systematically, so much in each specific term of the year.[6]

Philosophy and Theology

The schools and universities of twelfth-century Europe provided a home for the new intellectual movement known as **Scholasticism**. It was characterized by a renewed interest in theology and philosophy. In their search for understanding, the "Schoolmen" (from which we get the term *scholasticism*) relied on two sources of knowledge: faith and reason. They tried to harmonize the teachings of the church (faith) and the writings of Greek philosophers (reason). Although the Schoolmen or "Scholastics" acknowledged the necessity of faith, they attempted to use logic and philosophy to explain and defend the church's teaching. They did not seek to discover new knowledge but sought to support that which already existed. By applying the test of reason to the teaching of the church, they hoped to show the reasonableness of the Christian faith.

Three of the most noted Scholastic thinkers were Anselm, Peter Abelard (AB uh LARD), and Thomas Aquinas (uh KWY nus). The earliest of these was **Anselm** (1033–1109), the archbishop of Canterbury whose view of reason and faith may be summed up by his following statement:

> I do not try, Lord, to attain Your lofty heights, because my understanding is in no way equal to it. But I do desire to understand Your truth a little, that truth that my heart believes and loves. For I do not seek to understand so that I may believe; but I believe so that I may understand. For I believe this also, that "unless I believe, I shall not understand."[7]

THROUGH EYES OF FAITH

Faith and Reason

From what you have read here about these three scholastics, which most closely followed biblical truth?

____

____

____

____

____

____

Anselm realized that faith is essential to proper understanding. Nevertheless, he did not reject reason. He is best remembered for his use of logical arguments to support two major doctrines of the Christian faith: the existence of God and the satisfaction concept of the atonement (the belief that Christ's death on the cross satisfied God's holiness and justice and redeemed fallen man).

Unlike Anselm, **Peter Abelard** (1079–1141) advocated the frequent asking of questions as the "first key to wisdom." Abelard, a popular teacher of philosophy and theology at Paris, governed his studies by the following principle: "By doubting we arrive at inquiry (asking critical questions), and through inquiry we perceive the truth." In his most famous work, *Sic et non* ("Yes and No"), Abelard listed 158 questions concerning important articles of faith. With each question he presented pro and con statements of earlier church scholars. He thereby demonstrated that contradictory views existed. Abelard did not attempt to answer the questions that he raised; he did hope that the questions would prompt his students to search for truth through critical reasoning. Nevertheless, many church leaders viewed his emphasis upon reason as dangerous to the teachings of the church.

Scholasticism reached its height under **Thomas Aquinas** (1225?–74), called "the prince of the Schoolmen." Aquinas believed that certain truths could be understood by man's reason and that others could be perceived by faith alone. Since both man's reason and man's faith are gifts from God, Aquinas saw no real contradiction between them. In his *Summa Theologica* he attempted to demonstrate in a systematic fashion that the teachings of the church were in harmony with the logic and philosophy of Aristotle.

By reconciling the teachings of the church and the writings of Aristotle, the Scholastics hoped to settle the controversy between faith and reason. (The problem, however, was not with faith and reason, but was in the Scholastics' sources for their faith and reason.) Although they did consult the Bible, they gave an unwarranted priority to Aristotle's teachings. This attempt to apply human reasoning to spiritual truth often led them into error. Many of them placed Aristotle's system above faith, making spiritual truth dependent upon a human system. Furthermore, their overemphasis on reason took them beyond profitable learning and left them with empty speculations. For example, they asked such foolish questions as "Are angels brighter in the morning or in the evening?" "At what hour of the day did Adam sin?" and "Will a man at the resurrection recover all his fingernail clippings?" Neglecting the Bible as the source of faith and the guide for reason, they gave "heed to fables and endless genealogies, which minister questions, rather than godly edifying which is in faith" (1 Tim. 1:4).

In their attempts to explain their faith, the Scholastics revealed many contradictions in the church's teaching. These were not contradictions in Scripture but in the fallible decrees of popes and councils and in the opinions of early church scholars. In later centuries people would take their eyes off the church and look elsewhere for a more reliable source of truth. God used the Scholastics to prepare for the coming of the Reformation—a period in which men once again recognized the Bible as the only infallible source of truth.

Medieval Science

In medieval times people devoted little attention to science. Medieval thinkers focused upon the world to come and placed little emphasis upon the present physical world. In their opinion, faith and reason were the only sure guides to knowledge. Science was merely a secondary source of knowledge, which at best could only confirm truths that theology and philosophy had already established.

Magic and superstition clouded medieval science. Astrologers sought to interpret the future from the position of the stars, while alchemists attempted to transform nonvaluable metals into gold. What little scientific knowledge that did exist had been handed down from ancient sources. Churchmen compiled this information into handbooks of knowledge called encyclopedias. Because these compilers did not question the accuracy of their sources or conduct any experiments themselves, they often passed down gross misconceptions and falsehoods.

The body of scientific knowledge increased during the twelfth and thirteenth centuries as Greek and Muslim works began to circulate in Europe. For the most part European "scientists" were content to accept the findings of the past without verification. Nevertheless, there were some who began to critically reexamine inherited scientific ideas. One of the best known of these new scientific thinkers was the Englishman **Roger Bacon** (1214?–94). He was keenly aware of the obstacles facing scientific advancement: "There are four principal stumbling blocks to comprehending truth, which hinder well-nigh every scholar: the example of frail and unworthy authority, long-established custom, the sense of the ignorant crowd, and the hiding of one's own ignorance under the show of wisdom."[8]

Although not the first to conceive of the idea, he advocated observation and experimentation as tests for scientific conclusions. Thanks to Bacon and others, science was beginning to free itself from the shackles of mysticism, superstition, and unreliable authority. Nevertheless, it was not until a later day that scholars grasped the full importance of this scientific method.

Roger Bacon and the Future

In a fascinating letter, the thirteenth-century English scientist and philosopher Roger Bacon forecast what he believed would become of the technological achievements of the future. Some of his predictions demonstrate astonishing foresight.

He predicted, for example, improvements in ships which would "do away with the necessity of rowers, so that great vessels, both in rivers and on the sea, shall be borne about with only a single man to guide them and with greater speed than if they were full of men." The modern reader can easily imagine trains or cars when Bacon describes "carriages [which] can be constructed to move without animals to draw them, and with incredible velocity."

Long before the twentieth century, men dreamed of building flying machines. Bacon was one of these dreamers. His idea, however, was unlike modern airplanes: "Machines for flying can be made in which a man sits and turns an ingenious device by which skillfully contrived wings are made to strike the air in the manner of a flying bird." Bacon's predictions demonstrate that scientific inquiry is not just experimentation and observation. Scientists need healthy imaginations too.

Language and Literature

The language of the learned during the Middle Ages was Latin. It was firmly established in the universities and governments throughout Europe and was the official language of the Roman Catholic Church. It was not the spoken language of the common people, however. The common tongue varied from region to region; French, German, Italian, Spanish, and English were among

Chaucer's Pilgrims

Chaucer's *Canterbury Tales,* written in the late fourteenth century, gives a wonderful picture of medieval England. The following two selections are from his descriptions of the twenty-nine pilgrims. Because of the changes in the language over the last six hundred years, the English of Chaucer's day is rather difficult for the modern reader to understand.

A KNYGHT ther was, and that a worthy man,
That fro the tyme that he first bigan
To riden out, he love chivalrie,
Trouthe and honour, fredom and curteisie.

A MARCHANT was ther with a forked berd,
In mottelee, and hye on horse he sat;
Upon his heed a Flaundryssh bever hat,
His bootes clasped faire and fetisly.

Chaucer from a fifteenth-century manuscript of Canterbury Tales

Statue of Dante Alighieri in Florence, Italy

those spoken. By the twelfth century, writers began to use the common spoken language, or **vernacular**, in literature.

Among the earliest forms of vernacular literature were the heroic epics—long narrative poems that celebrated the adventures of legendary heroes. Many of these epics have become national treasures: the English *Beowulf*, the French *Song of Roland*, the German *Song of Nibelungs*, and the Spanish poem about El Cid.

Wandering minstrels called **troubadours** popularized the vernacular in lyric poetry. They traveled from castle to castle singing their songs of love and adventure to noblemen and their ladies. They also popularized stories about knights, chivalry, and love. Probably the best-known of these medieval romances are the tales of King Arthur and the Knights of the Round Table.

The two greatest writers of the late medieval period were Dante and Chaucer. **Dante Alighieri** (DAHN-tay ah-lee-GYAY-ree) (1265–1321) was an Italian poet. His *Divine Comedy* ranks as one of the most brilliant works in all literature. In this long poem Dante takes an imaginary journey through hell, purgatory, and paradise. His work reflects the religious beliefs, social order, and political turbulence of the late Middle Ages.

Geoffrey Chaucer (CHAW sur) (1340?–1400) was a prominent English poet. His masterpiece, *The Canterbury Tales*, presents a collection of stories told by pilgrims on their way to visit the tomb of Thomas à Becket at Canterbury (see p. 214). Chaucer used his skill as a storyteller and his insight into human behavior to depict English life and customs. By their masterful use of the vernacular in literature, both Dante and Chaucer aided the development of their native languages.

Art and Architecture

The art of the Middle Ages was primarily religious. Since laymen were illiterate, the church used the visual arts to teach Bible stories. Artists depicted Bible characters and popular "saints" of the church with certain characteristics. These symbols helped the observer identify the painted or sculptured figures.

For example, John the Baptist is always shown wearing an animal skin and carrying a staff with a cross on top. The skin illustrates the fact that "John was clothed with camel's hair" (Mark 1:6). The cross symbolizes his message: "Behold the Lamb of God, which taketh away the sin of the world" (John 1:29).

The most prominent form of medieval art was religious architecture. The people of Europe poured much of their wealth and energy into building impressive cathedrals. An eleventh-century French monk described the architectural revival that began about the year 1000:

> There occurred, throughout the world, especially in Italy and Gaul, a rebuilding of church basilicas. Notwithstanding the greater number were already well established and not in the least in need, nevertheless each Christian people strove against the others to erect nobler ones. It was as if the whole earth, having cast off the old . . . were clothing itself everywhere in the white robe of the church.[9]

Symbolism in Medieval Art

In this painting entitled *The Coronation of the Virgin,* the Italian artist Antonio da Imola portrays the Roman Catholic teaching of the crowning of the Virgin Mary as the queen of heaven. A number of Bible characters and medieval "saints" are gathered around Christ and Mary watching this event. Like many other works of art from the Middle Ages, this painting reflects a mixture of biblical truth and Roman Catholic legend or extrabiblical teaching.

Most medieval paintings contain a great deal of symbolism. In *The Coronation,* da Imola paints several "saints" with telltale attributes—characteristics that would enable the medieval viewer to easily identify the painted figure. For example, Augustine of Hippo is shown dressed in black, holding a bishop's crosier (a staff similar to a shepherd's crook), and wearing a miter (a tall, pointed hat worn by bishops). The artist portrays Francis of Assisi bearing stigmata (wounds in the hands and feet similar to Christ's). Francis supposedly received these marks as a reward because of his great holiness. The martyr Catherine of Alexandria is seen holding a spiked wheel—the instrument of torture associated with her death. Lucy of Syracuse holds her eyes in a dish. According to legend, she cut them out because their beauty was a stumbling block to a young man who ardently admired her.

The painting also contains a number of Bible characters. For example, Peter is the older man with a short gray beard. Although da Imola did not do so, many artists portrayed Peter with keys (Matt. 16:18–19), a book (for his epistles), a cross (John 21:18–19), or a fish (Matt. 4:18–19). Da Imola portrays Paul with a brown beard and bald head. He holds a sword, which symbolizes his martyrdom. Mary Magdalene is shown with long hair and ointment in her hand. The medieval world believed that it was she who anointed Jesus's feet and wiped them with her hair (Luke 7:36–38). Lastly, the artist paints the archangel Gabriel with wings, holding a lily in his hand. The lily, found throughout this painting, is a symbol of purity.

Antonio Checchi, called Guidaccio da Imola. The Coronation of the Virgin
From the collection of the Museum & Gallery at Bob Jones University

Cathedral of Notre Dame in Paris, an example of Gothic architecture

From 1050 to about 1150 the prevalent architectural style in Europe was **Romanesque** (ROH muh NESK) ("Roman-like"). Romanesque builders modified the rectangular Roman basilica (which earlier church architects had copied) and constructed churches in the shape of a Latin cross. Thick walls supported the tremendous weight of stone vaults and ceilings. Other features included rounded arches, heavy columns, and small doors and windows. The interiors of these churches were dark and gloomy.

Beginning about the thirteenth century, architects devised a way to support stone vaults and ceilings by the use of "flying" or external buttresses. These supports made it pos-

Medieval Hymns

Although most of the hymns we sing today are of recent origin, there are several medieval hymns that have remained famous to this day. Two of these, probably written by companions of Francis of Assisi, illustrate the religious ideas of the Middle Ages. The first, known as the *Stabat Mater*, is a hymn devoted to the Virgin Mary. Based upon John 19:25, the hymn begins as follows:

At the Cross, her station keeping,
Stood the mournful mother weeping,
Where he hung, the dying Lord.

The second hymn, the *Dies irae* (based upon Zeph. 1:15), portrays the fearful day of judgment when both sinners and saints will tremble before the wrath of God. The first few lines of Sir Walter Scott's well-known translation set the tone for this piece:

That day of wrath, that dreadful day,
When heaven and earth shall pass away,
What power shall be the sinner's stay?
How shall he meet that dreadful day?

Although the above hymns are rarely if ever sung in Protestant churches, there are other medieval hymns that are often sung. In 1225 Francis of Assisi wrote his "Canticle of the Sun, and Hymn of Creation"—a poem praising God for the glories of His creation. This poem, which has seven stanzas in its English paraphrase, begins with these words:

All creatures of our God and King,
Lift up your voice and with us sing
Alleluia, alleluia!
Thou burning sun with golden beam,
Thou silver moon with softer gleam;
O praise him, O praise him,
Alleluia, alleluia, alleluia!

Another much-loved hymn came from the pen of Bernard of Clairvaux, who wrote a seven-part poem that speaks of Christ's suffering on the cross. The final part speaks of the head of Christ:

O sacred Head, now wounded,
With grief and shame weighed down,
Now scornfully surrounded
With thorns, Thine only crown;
O sacred Head, what glory,
What bliss till now was Thine!
Yet, though despised and gory,
I joy to call Thee mine.

Finally, there is what many regard to be the finest of all medieval hymns—"Jesus, the Very Thought of Thee." Although tradition has ascribed this poem to Bernard, the authorship is uncertain. It is a hymn that every Christian should be able to sing from the heart:

Jesus, the very thought of Thee
With sweetness fills the breast.
But sweeter far Thy face to see,
And in Thy presence rest.

Jesus, our only joy be Thou,
As Thou our prize wilt be;
In Thee be all our glory now,
And through eternity.

sible for cathedrals to have higher ceilings, thinner walls, and larger windows and doors. This new style was called **Gothic**. In contrast to the dark and heavy elements of the Romanesque, Gothic architecture was light and delicate. The spacious and lofty Gothic cathedrals created an atmosphere of dignity and serenity. Their high towers and pointed arches soared toward heaven, inviting people to turn their thoughts toward God. Another feature of Gothic architecture was stained-glass windows. They added beauty, light, and color to the interior of churches. They also served as a type of "visual Bible." By arranging the glass pieces, artists illustrated biblical stories in vivid colors.

Section Quiz

1. List three factors that aided a revival of learning during the twelfth century.
2. What were two of the earliest universities begun in Europe? How did they differ?
3. What is the name of the new intellectual movement characterized by a renewed interest in theology and philosophy? What did the philosophers and theologians of this movement try to harmonize?
4. What clouded the work of medieval science?
5. Who were the two greatest writers of the late Middle Ages? Identify each man's native country and the title of his most important work.

1. ______________________

____

____

2. ______________________

____

____

____

3. ______________________

____

4. ______________________

____

5. ______________________

____

____

____

____

____

IV. Emergence of National States

Nation-states emerged in the late Middle Ages as people in certain regions became more fully aware of their common traditions, language, and religion. This awareness was the foundation of national feeling. Accompanying the growth of nation-states was the rise of national monarchies. The monarchy served as the symbol of national pride. The independent king ruling a group of people having common interests formed the basis of the early nation-state. Royal power steadily increased in the fourteenth and fifteenth centuries while feudalism gradually declined. As differences among the various people in Europe became more distinct and as national feeling mounted, boundaries between nation-states began to solidify. By 1500 the major states of Europe were established. The medieval age was passing; the modern age was at hand.

War Between England and France

During the fourteenth and fifteenth centuries, England and France were embroiled in a long struggle known as the **Hundred Years' War**. Intermittent battles and broken truces spanned the years from 1337 to 1453. What began as a conflict between feudal lords ended as a rivalry between two emerging nation-states. The war contributed to the decline of feudalism in England and France and stimulated the growth of national feeling in each country.

Causes

For centuries English and French monarchs had confronted one another on the matter of English holdings in France. Although Philip II had drastically reduced the size of the English possessions, the king of England still held on to the duchy of Aquitaine. More fuel was added to this flame of discord when the French monarch attempted to take possession of the rich commercial territory of Flanders. This act threatened England's profitable wool trade. War finally erupted after the last Capetian king died without a male heir. The English king, **Edward III**, whose mother was the sister of the three previous French kings, claimed to be the rightful heir to the French throne. But the French nobles were unwilling to give the crown to the long-time rival of the French monarchs. Instead, they chose Philip VI of the house of Valois (vah LWAH) as king.

Conflict

English forces crossed the Channel and won several major victories over the French—at Crécy (kray SEE) in 1346, at Poitiers (pwah TYAY) in 1356, and at Agincourt (AJ in KORT) in 1415. Their success was due in large part to new battle tactics and weapons. The English relied on archers armed with **longbows**. Arrows shot by these powerful weapons could penetrate a suit of armor. With the longbow English archers had greater range and accuracy than their French counterparts, who used the conventional crossbow. Through the strategic deployment of bowmen and knights in battle, the outnumbered English completely routed the French.

The Battle of Crécy

During the first half of the Hundred Years' War, the outnumbered English forces won a series of impressive victories over the French. Superior English weaponry and discipline made the difference. No battle demonstrates this more clearly than that of Crécy.

In 1346 King Edward III of England invaded France. After landing in Normandy, the English marched along the coast en route to Paris. Edward knew it would be difficult to capture Paris; so he turned his forces northward to join his allies in Flanders. The French pursued them, and the two armies met on August 26 near the village of Crécy, some one hundred miles south of Paris.

The English took up their position on a sloping ridge. Their knights dismounted and prepared to fight alongside the infantry. Armed with deadly longbows, the archers placed themselves slightly forward in wedges. In the center of the English line was a series of irrigation terraces that provided additional protection. The English also lined up a new weapon—the cannon. King Edward directed the battle from his headquarters in a nearby windmill. His troops readied themselves for the enemy attack.

The French forces, however, were in chaos. Three times as large as the English invasion forces, the French army was poorly organized. The French king, Philip VI, was indecisive. Some of his advisers urged an immediate attack. Others advised waiting. According to one account of the battle, Philip ordered the attack but then changed his mind. Unfortunately, by the time he had reconsidered, the army had started moving and could not be easily stopped. Also many of the French knights, hungry for a battle with the English, disregarded the king's order to withdraw.

A skilled longbow archer could send an arrow a distance of 270 yards.

The large but confused French army moved forward to confront the enemy. The first line of the French forces, mercenary crossbowmen from Genoa, surged up the hill. Before they ever reached the English, a shower of arrows, as one writer put it, "fell like snow" upon them. Trying to escape the "feathered death" of the arrows, the Genoese fell back. Enraged, the French knights behind them slashed at the Genoese with their weapons and rode their horses directly over them toward the English. Some of the angry Genoese began firing their crossbows at the French.

The English longbows continued to pour down death upon the French. The longbow shot with greater accuracy and distance than any other kind of bow and could even pierce armor. Volley after volley from the English archers whistled through the air into the ranks of the French.

The brave French charged on into the slaughter. Waves of knights swept up the slope, only to die in the face of the staunch English defense. At one point the French pressed in on the area commanded by the Prince of Wales, heir to the English throne. The prince sent a message to his father asking for reinforcements. From his windmill, King Edward answered, "Let the boy earn his spurs!" The prince's forces fought on without reinforcements and drove the French back.

The battle continued on into the night. Finally, the weary French army fell back and melted away. King Philip fled the battlefield. The sun came up the next morning on corpses of thousands of French soldiers. The English lost at most only a few hundred. England had scored a decisive victory in her campaign against the French throne.

The English nonetheless had little to show from their victories over the French. Decades of constant skirmishes had left them drained of resources. Political unrest at home decreased their zeal for fighting a foreign war. For the French, the war was one of humiliation and destruction. They not only suffered one defeat after another but also saw their countryside pillaged by the English knights.

Even though the English won most of the battles, the French eventually won the war. What turned the tide for the French was a surge of nationalism inspired by a simple peasant girl named **Joan of Arc**. Believing that heavenly voices had directed her to drive the English out of France, she roused the weak French king to action, rallied the dispirited French troops, and accompanied the French army into battle. She was captured by the enemy and burned at the stake in 1431, but her example stirred the nation. The French succeeded in bringing the war to an end.

Consequences

The English defeat was actually a blessing in disguise. No longer did the English kings concentrate their efforts on holding their French possessions. Instead they began to build a strong nation-state at home. The war also furthered the cause of nation-making in France. The rivalry over the English presence in France had stirred French nationalism. This bolstered the cause of the French kings as they continued to increase their royal powers.

In England—After a century of fighting on French soil, the English troops returned home only to become involved in civil war. Two rival families, the houses of York and Lancaster, fought for the English throne. The series of conflicts between these noble families is known as the **Wars of the Roses**. (The emblem of the House of York was a white rose; the emblem of the House of Lancaster, a red rose.) The struggle ended after thirty years when Henry Tudor defeated Richard III at the battle of Bosworth Field. Henry was crowned King **Henry VII** (1485–1509). He founded the powerful Tudor dynasty. During the sixteenth century, the Tudors firmly established the power of the English monarchy and built the English nation into a major European power—a position she held for over four hundred years.

King Henry VII by Unknown artist
Date: 1505, National Portrait Gallery, London

Henry has a red rose in his hand for the house of Lancaster.

In France—Weary of the death and destruction, the Estates-General had during the war allowed the French king to levy a royal land tax called a ***taille*** (TAH yuh) with which he could maintain a strong army and thereby defeat the English. The eventual success over the English greatly increased the power of the French king. Unlike the English king, who had to depend upon Parliament for funds, the French king could raise money without consent of the Estates-General. There was no check upon his growing power.

Reconquista in Spain and Portugal

Nation-states did not develop as quickly in the Iberian Peninsula (see map on p. 246) as they had in England and France. The peninsula had long been primarily a Muslim land (see p. 141). In the eleventh century a few small non-Muslim states in the north began a concerted effort to drive out the **Moors** (Spanish Muslims). By the late thirteenth century, warriors of the ***Reconquista*** ("reconquest") had successfully reclaimed all of the peninsula except for the kingdom of Granada.

As the Moors were being driven out, the small northern states expanded into the reclaimed land. Three principal kingdoms emerged: Portugal, Castile, and Aragon. Like most other European states, these kingdoms experienced struggles between a developing monarchy and feudal nobles. There arose in each kingdom the equivalent to an Estates-General or Parliament—the **Cortes**, a council composed of nobles, clergy, and representatives of the cities. The expulsion of the Moors, together with the support from the growing towns and the decline of feudalism, increased the power of each king above that of his feudal nobles and Cortes.

Iberian Peninsula 910

Spain 1400

The nation of Spain was created when **Ferdinand**, heir to the throne of Aragon, married **Isabella**, heiress to the throne of Castile. (The kingdom of Portugal remained independent.) Ferdinand and Isabella firmly established their royal power in the new nation. They began the Spanish Inquisition, a systematic persecution of Muslims and Jews. Inquisitors later directed their attacks against Christians who opposed the Roman Catholic Church. Ferdinand and Isabella completed the *Reconquista* by driving the Moors out of Granada in **1492**. In that same year Christopher Columbus, who was under their Spanish sponsorship, landed in the New World.

Disunity in Italy and Germany

In contrast to the rising tide of nationalism and strong monarchies in England, France, Spain, and Portugal, Germany and Italy remained divided into many small regional states. "Germany" and "Italy" were geographic expressions, not unified nations.

The collapse of the Hohenstaufen house in the thirteenth century brought an end to German interference in Italy. Italy was left divided among the kingdom of Naples, the Papal States, and powerful northern cities such as Florence, Venice, Genoa, and Milan. There was little opportunity for national unity while each region struggled to prevent the others from becoming too powerful. Despite its political turmoil and disunity, Italy prospered commercially and later gave birth to the period of cultural achievement known as the Renaissance (see Chapter 11).

Imperial authority declined in Germany with the fall of the Hohenstaufens. Small territorial states emerged. The office of emperor remained, but the real power of government passed into the hands of the great nobles. By the middle of the fourteenth century, a written constitution known as the **Golden Bull** established the **Diet** of the Holy Roman Empire. The Diet was the German equivalent to the English Parliament and the French Estates-General. The most important members of the Diet were the seven electors (three archbishops and four noble princes) who selected the German emperors. The electors generally chose weak men as emperors in order to protect the power of the German nobility. In addition, they passed the imperial crown from one family to another so that no single family would acquire too much power. While other lands were striving toward national unity, the German electors specifically sought to avoid it.

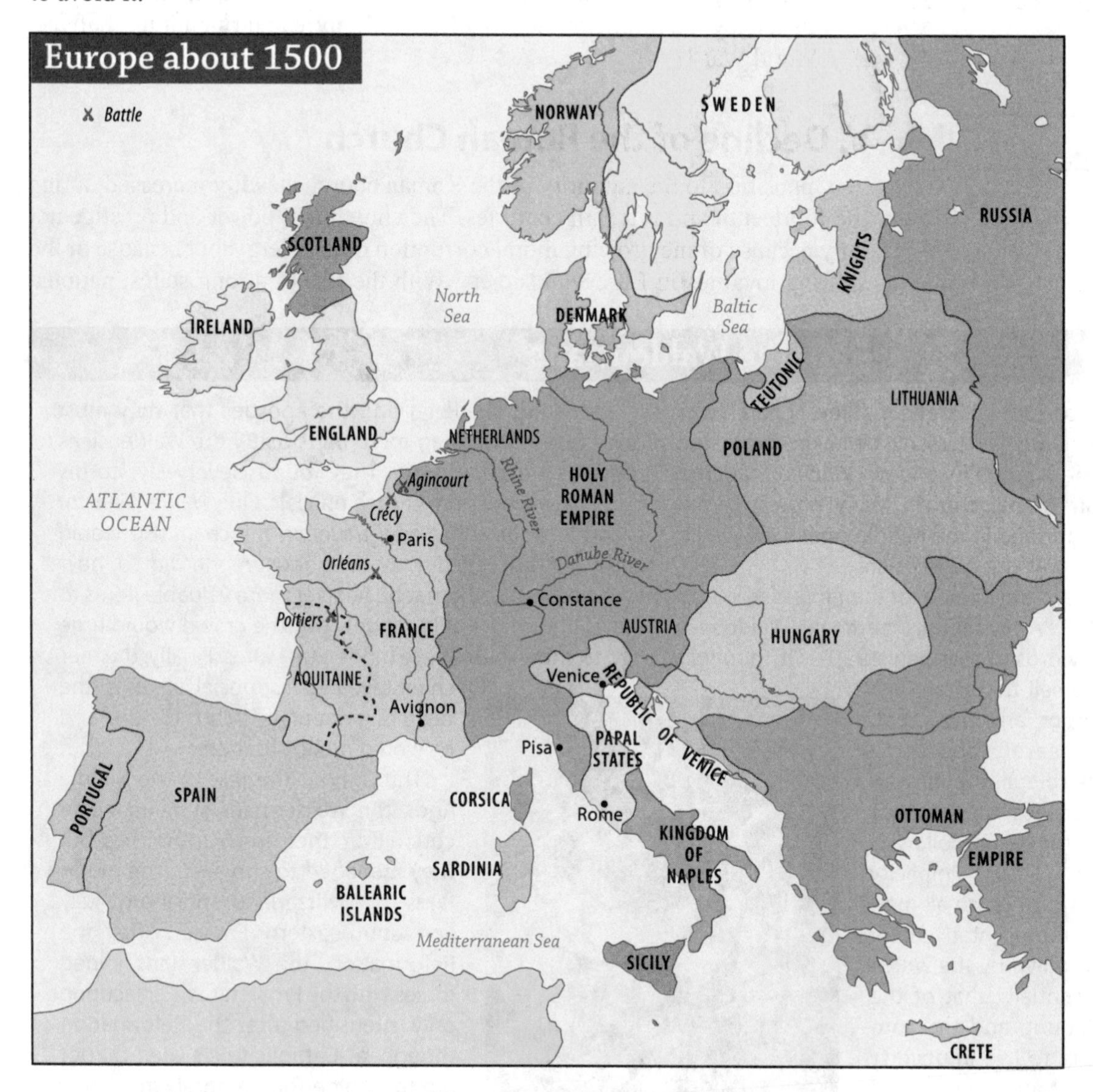

Despite the efforts of the German nobles, the **Hapsburg** family built a strong base of power among the southern German states. These states became known collectively as Austria. (Members of the Hapsburg family ruled from the city of Vienna until after World War I.) After 1438 only members of this family were elected to the German throne. Emperor **Maximilian I** (1493–1519) greatly enlarged the Hapsburg possessions through marriage. His first marriage brought the rich region of the Low Countries (modern Belgium and Holland) under his rule. His second marriage brought him Milan. He also formed a marriage alliance between his son and the daughter of Ferdinand and Isabella of Spain. In this way Spain, the Low Countries, the Holy Roman Empire, and territory in the New World (the Spanish possessions) came under Hapsburg rule.

Section Quiz

1. ______________________

____

2. ______________________

____

3. ______________________

____

4. ______________________

____

5. ______________________

1. What two nations fought during the Hundred Years' War? What were the dates for this war?
2. Which side won most of the battles of this war? What side won the war?
3. What people did the Spanish and Portuguese seek to drive out of the Iberian Peninsula? What was this effort called?
4. What was the German constitution called? What assembly did it establish?
5. Following the collapse of the Hohenstaufen house, what family came to occupy the throne of the Holy Roman Empire and ruled it until after World War I?

V. Decline of the Roman Church

Opposition to the authority of the Roman church steadily increased during the fourteenth and fifteenth centuries. The church lost power and prestige not only because of the growing moral corruption of the clergy, but because of the shifting loyalties in European society. With the rise of strong states, national

The Waldensians

The increasing corruption of the medieval church was not unnoticed by Christians. Many believers protested strongly against the immorality and worldliness that characterized the institutional church. Many protest movements arose and vanished in the Middle Ages. One which outlasted all others was the Waldensians.

The Waldenensians are named for their founder, Waldo of Lyons (died 1217). A prosperous merchant, Waldo was moved by Jesus's words in Matthew 19:21—"If thou wilt be perfect, go and sell that thou hast, and give to the poor, and thou shalt have treasure in heaven: and come and follow me." He sold all that he had and gave the proceeds to the poor. Then Waldo, and others who followed him, began living a life of simplicity and poverty, seeking to go to all men. As he told a papal representative later, "We have decided to live by the words of the Gospel, essentially that of the Sermon on the Mount, and the commandments, that is, to live in poverty without concern for tomorrow."

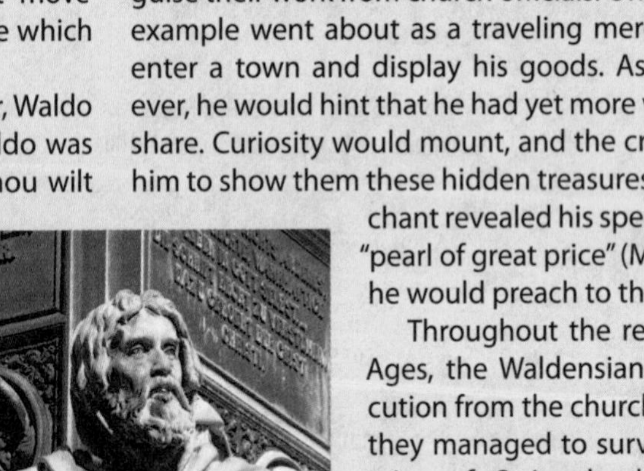

Waldo of Lyons

In the beginning the Waldensians did not differ from other reform movements such as that of Francis of Assisi. The Waldensians, however, remained laymen instead of becoming priests. They went about preaching and began to translate parts of the Bible into the common language. Their preaching and translating drew the opposition of the church hierarchy, who considered them ignorant laymen, and the pope condemned the movement.

Declaring like Peter and the apostles that they must "obey God rather than men" (Acts 5:29), the Waldensians continued their ministry. They found clever ways to disguise their work from church officials. One Waldensian, for example went about as a traveling merchant. He would enter a town and display his goods. As he did so, however, he would hint that he had yet more valuable items to share. Curiosity would mount, and the crowd would urge him to show them these hidden treasures. Finally, the merchant revealed his special "wares"—the "pearl of great price" (Matt. 13:46)—and he would preach to them.

Throughout the rest of the Middle Ages, the Waldensians suffered persecution from the church authorities, but they managed to survive in the mountains of Switzerland, northern Italy, and southeastern France. After the Reformation, the Waldensians joined forces with the Protestants. Persecution only intensified after the Reformation, though, as Catholic rulers tried to root out the Waldensians entirely from their domains. Some Waldensians fled. One group, for instance, settled in North Carolina in 1893 and built a thriving bakery business. Only in the nineteenth and twentieth centuries were the Waldensians finally able to gain the right to worship freely. As protestors against corruption of the medieval church even before the Reformation, the Waldensians won the praise of English poet John Milton as "them who kept [God's] truth to pure of old / When all our Fathers worship't sticks and Stones."

loyalties began to overshadow church loyalty. Many kings no longer tolerated papal interference in their lands. Furthermore, the expansion of knowledge challenged the traditions of the church, and a critical spirit of inquiry gradually replaced the passive acceptance of the church's teachings. In addition, the steady growth of wealth in European society turned people's attention from spiritual concerns to earthly gain. In fact, members of the clergy who should have been examples of spirituality were often the ones most desirous of temporal wealth and power.

The growing weakness of the church was most evident in the declining power of the papacy. From its zenith under Pope Innocent III, the papacy had fallen into disgrace. It lost not only its hold on the kings of Europe but also its position of leadership in the church.

Papal Humiliation

The decline of the papacy began under Pope **Boniface VIII** (1294–1303). He sought to control Europe in the highhanded manner of Innocent III. But times had changed; the arrogant demands of Boniface met with resistance.

He suffered a series of humiliating defeats at the hands of the French king Philip IV. Trouble began when Philip decided to levy a tax on the French clergy. The pope denounced this, but his words went unheeded. The conflict intensified when Philip arrested a criminal bishop and brought him before a royal court to stand trial. Boniface ordered Philip to release the bishop. When Philip refused, Boniface issued the famous papal **bull** (an official papal document) ***Unam Sanctam*** (1302). In this strong statement of papal supremacy, Boniface asserted that "it is altogether necessary to salvation for every human being to be subject to the Roman pontiff."

Philip, supported by the French people, defied the pope. He accused Boniface of heresy and sought to bring him to trial. Philip's agents, accompanied by a band of soldiers, traveled to the papal residence and took the pope captive. But the people of the town aided Boniface, and he was soon freed. The aged pope, however, did not recover from the shock and humiliation of the ordeal. He died a month later.

The papal palace at Avignon

Papal Exile

National feeling and royal power triumphed over the demands of the papacy. A short time after the death of Boniface, a Frenchman was elected to the papal office. He, however, never set foot in Rome but moved the papal capital from Rome to Avignon (AH vee NYAWN), a city in modern France. From **1309 to 1377** the popes—all Frenchmen—resided at Avignon. This period is known as the "**Babylonian Captivity** of the Church," or the Avignon Exile. Although the popes were not actually held captive, they did fall under the influence of the French kings.

During the Avignon years, the papacy declined even further. The rising tide of nationalism caused the English, Germans, and Italians to resent a "French-controlled" papacy. In addition, critics of the church denounced the wealth and corruption that marked the Avignon court. Some of the popes raised new church taxes and sold church offices to maintain their lives of luxury. The Avignon popes were

THROUGH EYES OF FAITH

Great Schism

In what ways might the Great Schism have helped as well as hindered those who would trust in Christ as their Savior?

for the most part able administrators of the church bureaucracy, but they had little concern for spiritual matters. Once again calls for reform echoed across Europe.

Papal Schism

The papacy returned to Rome in 1377, but the pope died soon after taking up residence in the city. The French-dominated College of Cardinals, threatened by a Roman mob, elected an Italian as pope. Several months later, the cardinals declared the election invalid and elected a new pope, who moved back to Avignon. The Roman church now had two popes—one in Rome and one in Avignon. Both men claimed to be the rightful pope, and each excommunicated the other. For forty years this **Great Schism** divided the allegiance of the nations of Europe.

In 1409 church leaders met at Pisa to resolve the schism within the church. The council deposed both popes and appointed a new one. But the other two refused to relinquish their office and the church now had three popes. The matter was finally settled at the **Council of Constance** (1414–18). This large gathering of church leaders succeeded in deposing the other claimants to the papal office and secured the election of Martin V as the sole pope. The council healed the schism and restored the papacy to Rome. But because it was unwilling to initiate any meaningful reforms, it failed to stop the growing criticism of the church's doctrine and practice. As a result, the "Babylonian Captivity" and the Great Schism added more fuel to the smoldering discontent that would soon flame into the Protestant Reformation.

Section Quiz

1. Who issued the papal bull *Unam Sanctam*? What did it assert?
2. To what city was the papacy "exiled"? What is this period called?
3. What church council finally settled the Great Schism?

A Glance Behind

From 1200 to 1500 medieval Europe underwent many changes that helped lay the foundations of modern Western society. Trade revived, towns grew, and national states came into existence. Though the Renaissance and the Reformation mark the end of the historical period known as the Middle Ages, certain medieval institutions and practices continued to exist for several centuries. For example, Latin remained the language of the educated, and the nobility retained their prominent place in society.

Some medieval institutions, such as the jury system, the Roman Catholic Church, and the university have continued to the present. An understanding of the Middle Ages, therefore, helps in the understanding of our own culture.

and a Glimpse Ahead

Notes

1. James W. Thompson, *An Economic and Social History of the Middle Ages* (New York: The Century Co., c. 1928), p. 602.
2. Boccaccio, *Decameron*, trans. Richard Aldington (New York: Garden City Pub. Co., Inc., 1930), p. 4.
3. Gregory of Tours, *History of the Franks*, trans. Ernest Brehant (New York: Octagon Books, 1973), p. 248.
4. C. H. Haskins, *Studies in Medieval Culture* (Oxford: Oxford Univ. Press, 1929), p. 10.
5. Ibid., p. 15.
6. James W. Thompson and Edgar Nathan Johnson, *An Introduction to Medieval Europe* (New York: Norton, 1937), p. 730.
7. Anselm, *Proslogion*, trans. M. J. Charlesworth, 1.
8. Thompson and Johnson, p. 716.
9. E. G. Holt, ed. *Literary Sources of Art History* (Princeton Univ. Press, 1947), p. 3.

Chapter Review

Can You Define?

barter
banca
"just price"
usury
charter
guilds
apprentice
journeyman
master
middle class
trivium
quadrivium
universitas
Scholasticism
vernacular
troubadours
Romanesque
Gothic
nation-state
taille
Reconquista
Cortes
Golden Bull
Diet
bull
"Babylonian Captivity"
Great Schism

Can You Identify?

florin
moneychangers
Hanseatic League
Anselm
Peter Abelard
Thomas Aquinas
Roger Bacon
Dante Alighieri
Geoffrey Chaucer
Hundred Years' War
Edward III
longbow
Joan of Arc
Wars of the Roses
Henry VII
Moors
Ferdinand
Isabella
1492
Hapsburgs
Maximilian I
Boniface VIII
Philip IV
Unam Sanctam
1309–77
Council of Constance

Can You Locate?

medieval trade routes
Flanders
Champagne
Paris
Bologna
Crécy
Poitiers
Agincourt
Iberian Peninsula
Granada
Portugal
Castile
Aragon
Austria
Netherlands
Avignon
Pisa
Constance

How Much Do You Remember?

1. Name three factors that encouraged the revival of trade in medieval Europe.
2. In what ways did the church influence business practice?
3. Identify the important contributions and written works of the Scholastic thinkers Anselm, Peter Abelard, and Thomas Aquinas.
4. List characteristics distinguishing Romanesque and Gothic architecture.
5. What were the causes of the Hundred Years' War? What effect did this war have on England? on France?
6. Give the key events and people in the following outline of the decline of the medieval church from 1302 to 1418.
   I. Papal humiliation
   II. Papal exile
   III. Papal schism

What Do You Think?

1. Compare modern labor unions with medieval guilds.
2. Was medieval science truly "scientific"? Explain your answer.
3. Why was the period of the exile of the papacy in Avignon called the "Babylonian Captivity of the Church"?

The Awakening World

"The Awakening World" may seem a strange title for Unit IV. Had the world been asleep before? The word *awakening* here signifies a new expansion of man—geographically, mentally, and, most important, spiritually. The Renaissance recaptured the artistic excellence of the ancients and taught men again to use their God-given talent and reason. The explorers revealed the immensity of the world and brought exciting, unknown lands to the attention of Europe. In the midst of these achievements of mind and body, God sent an "expansion" of the soul, the spiritual revival known as the Reformation. Greater than all the beautiful works of the Renaissance artists, more dramatic than all the discoveries of the explorers, more influential than all the kings and wars of the era was a simple sentence penned by the apostle Paul and proclaimed by a former German monk named Martin Luther: "The just shall live by faith."

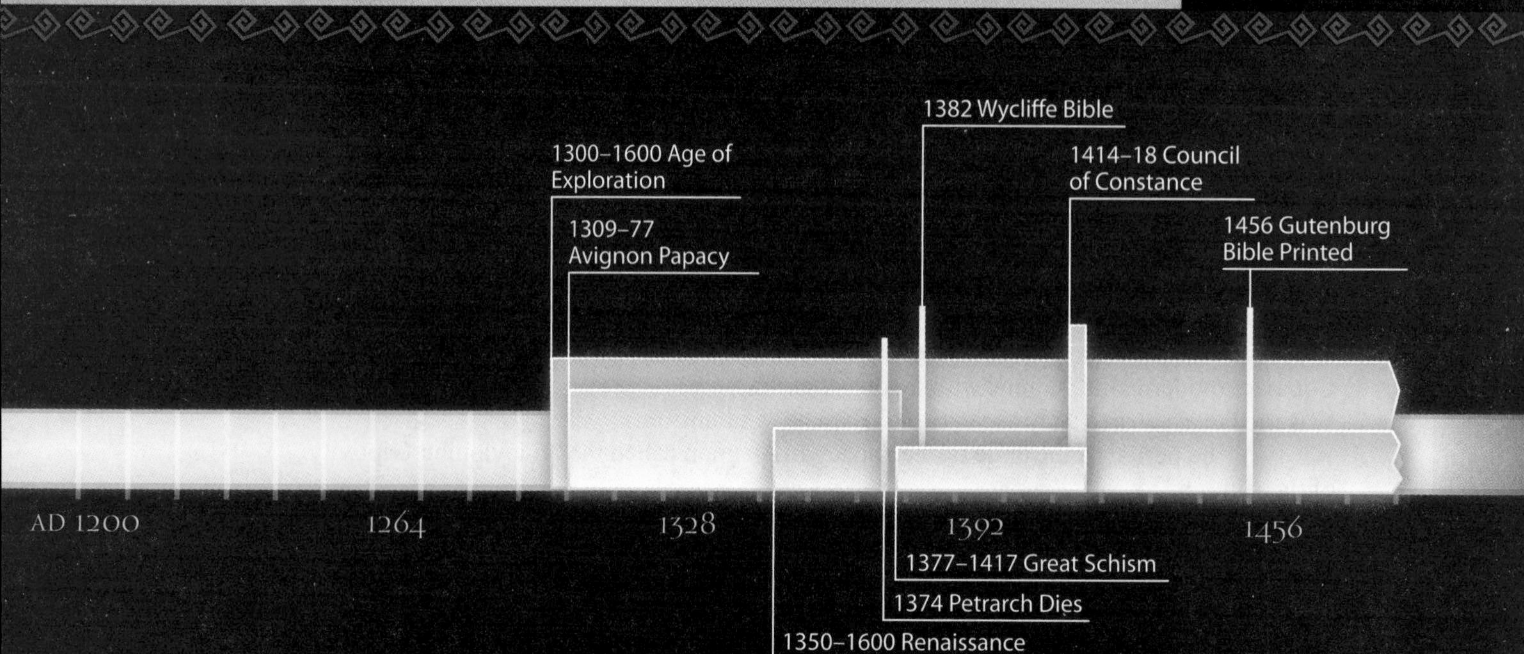

1492 Columbus Sails to America
1493 Line of Demarcation
October 31, 1517 Ninety-five Theses
1521 Diet of Worms
1530 Augsburg Confession
1534 Henry VIII Becomes Head of the English Church
1536 *Institutes of the Christian Religion*
1545–63 Council of Trent
1588 Spanish Armada
1598 Edict of Nantes
1607 Jamestown Founded
1608 Quebec Founded
1611 King James Version

11

"What is man, that thou art mindful of him?"

THE RENAISSANCE

Florence, Italy—birthplace of the Renaissance

A new age was dawning in Europe in the fourteenth century. The Western world was on the threshold of a widespread revival in learning and of a brilliant flowering of the arts. This period of change in Europe from the fourteenth century through the sixteenth century is known as the **Renaissance** (REN uh sahns), a French word meaning "rebirth." The spirit of this age is evident in the confident outburst of a young German: "What a century! What genius! It is sheer joy to be alive. . . . Learning flourishes, men are spiritually quickened. O Barbarism, take a rope and prepare for extinction!"[1] This chapter focuses on the intellectual and artistic developments that constituted this transformation in Western civilization.

Florence

I. Characteristics of the Renaissance

Contrast with the Middle Ages

The Renaissance man considered the time in which he lived a sharp break with the ignorance and superstition of the Middle Ages. To him the medieval period was but a backward, unimportant interval between the achievements of classical culture and the glory of his own "modern" age. He failed to realize that the Renaissance was the culmination of gradual changes that had begun during the Middle Ages.

The Renaissance attitude toward life differed sharply from the medieval outlook. The Renaissance man's hearty zest for living was a far cry from the sober, otherworldly concerns of earlier generations, who were consumed with the welfare of their souls and with the work of the church. People during the Middle Ages fixed their thoughts on the future joys of heaven. The dusty past and the troubled present were of little interest or importance. The Renaissance man, on the other hand, gloried in the past and lived with enthusiasm in the present. The future could take care of itself, or so he thought.

Focus on Man

The Renaissance emphasized human individuality, ability, and dignity. In medieval times the group—not the individual—had been all-important (for example, the church, a guild, or a particular social class). During the Renaissance, however, the reverse was true. People of this age praised the wonders of human achievement. They conceived of the ideal man as one with diverse interests and talents.

This renewed focus on man's capacities has been called **humanism**. Unlike modern secular humanism, Renaissance humanism did not abandon belief in God. But like every movement that puts undue emphasis upon human ability, it led to the false assumption that man is basically good. "There is nothing to be seen more wonderful than man," wrote an Italian humanist. Shakespeare's immortal character Hamlet declares, "What a piece of work is a man, how noble in reason, how infinite in faculties, in form and moving, how express and admirable in action, how like an angel in apprehension."

Created in God's image and given dominion over creation, man does possess a unique position in God's universe. But God's image in man was badly marred by the

Humanism

Humanism is an overemphasis on human worth and ability, leading man to glorify himself instead of God. There have been many historical expressions of humanism. The Greek humanists, for example, emphasized the uniqueness of man above the animals; they taught that man's reason was the standard of truth. Like the Greeks, most of the Renaissance humanists praised human accomplishment and talent. Although most of them were church members and acknowledged the existence of God, many Renaissance humanists were primarily interested in classical learning.

While its historical forms may vary, humanism inevitably leads people away from God and spiritual concerns. It promotes the false idea that man is good and that he is superior to God. Secular humanism of the twenty-first century altogether rejects belief in God and worships man as God. The pride of humanism, however, will not go unpunished.

The lofty looks of man shall be humbled, and the haughtiness of men shall be bowed down, and the Lord alone shall be exalted in that day. For the day of the Lord of hosts shall be upon every one that is proud and lofty, and upon every one that is lifted up; and he shall be brought low.

Isaiah 2:11–12

Fall in the Garden of Eden. Because of Adam's disobedience, man is basically sinful. He is in need of a Savior.

The godly man acknowledges that God is the source of all wisdom and the giver of all talents and abilities (James 1:17). The psalmist David said to God, "I will praise thee; for I am fearfully and wonderfully made" (Ps. 139:14). He humbly recognized man's true character and the source of understanding.

> *When I consider thy heavens, the work of thy fingers, the moon and the stars, which thou hast ordained; what is man, that thou art mindful of him? and the son of man, that thou visitest him? For thou hast made him a little lower than the angels, and hast crowned him with glory and honour. Thou madest him to have dominion over the works of thy hands: thou hast put all things under his feet. . . . O Lord our Lord, how excellent is thy name in all the earth!*
>
> *Psalm 8:3–6, 9*

Because many people in Renaissance society misunderstood man's true nature, much of their culture was devoid of eternal values, biblical ethics, and godly living.

Revival of Learning

The expansion of trade and the growth of town and national governments during the later Middle Ages increased the need for well-educated laymen with professional skills. Merchants, bankers, lawyers, clerks, and diplomats—to name only a few—needed a well-rounded education to meet the demands of an increasingly complex society. Renewed business activity also indirectly sparked interest in classical literature. Lawyers needing to draw up business contracts and other legal documents turned to Roman law to see how the ancients had handled such matters. In the process of their research they discovered the writings of Cicero and other Latin authors. Interest in classical literature prompted men to collect and study this literature.

Tower of Palazzo Vecchio, Florence, Italy

Soon a new course of study—the **humanities**—became popular in the West. The humanities, also known as the liberal arts, included the study of history, science, and grammar, as well as classical literature and philosophy. Those who studied the liberal arts were known as **humanists**. Unlike the Scholastics of the Middle Ages, most Renaissance humanists did not study to prepare for service in the church. Instead they prepared themselves for life in the secular world.

The goal of Renaissance education was to develop well-rounded individuals. Humanists, who considered ignorance the source of evil, looked to education as the remedy for sin. They criticized medieval man for being ignorant and narrow-minded, and they praised men of their own day for their zest for life, wide interests, and quest for knowledge. They scorned the medieval practice of passively accepting ideas without questioning their accuracy. Renaissance man was more critical. He examined established ideas to discern whether they were trustworthy.

Renaissance humanists greatly admired the classical age of ancient Greece and Rome. They praised the amazing versatility that the ancients had possessed.

Cicero received special honor, for he was not only a renowned scholar, lawyer, and statesman but also an eloquent orator and master of literary expression. By following the example of the ancients, the humanists believed they could reshape their own age according to classical values. They stimulated a "rebirth" of interest in the literature, art, and philosophy of the classical age.

This fascination with classical culture led to an intense search for ancient manuscripts. Men went to great lengths and spent vast fortunes to obtain classical works. They found many Latin manuscripts in the libraries of monasteries where they had lain neglected and forgotten for centuries. Although Greek works were rare in the West, many had been preserved in the East by the Byzantine and Muslim civilizations. As the humanists recovered these precious works, they examined them to determine their accuracy and authenticity. Essential to such an investigation, of course, was a thorough knowledge of the classical languages. This need gave rise to the renewed study of Greek and classical Latin during the Renaissance period.

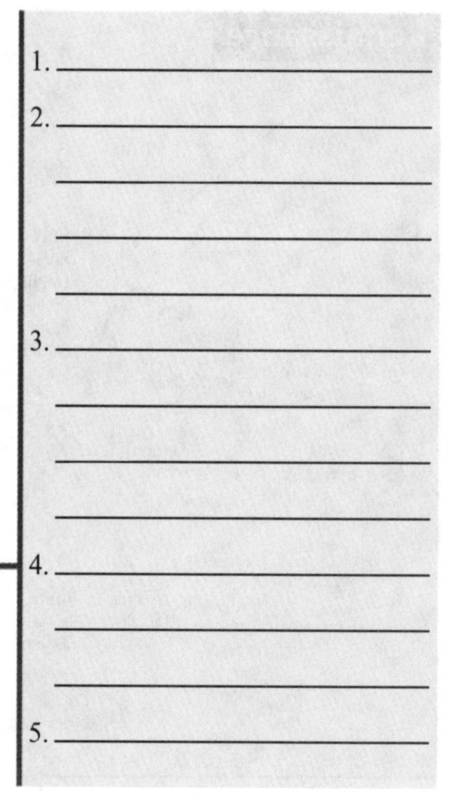

Section Quiz

1. What is the name of the period during the fourteenth through the sixteenth centuries in European history in which learning and the arts revived and flowered?
2. Define *humanism.*
3. What new course of study became popular in Europe during the Renaissance? What subject disciplines were included in this course of study?
4. What was the goal of Renaissance education?
5. What period of history did the Renaissance humanists admire?

II. Course of the Renaissance

The Renaissance began in Italy. This land had been the center of the ancient Roman Empire; even in the fourteenth century, the Italians thought of themselves as Romans. In their long history Italians had also come into close contact with the Byzantine and Islamic civilizations. Several cities in northern Italy had maintained trade and cultural ties with the East during the Middle Ages. When commerce began to revive throughout Europe during the eleventh and twelfth centuries, the Italian cities rose to prominence. Their control of the Mediterranean trade routes to the East brought them great riches. To display their newly acquired wealth, these cities commissioned talented artists to design buildings, decorate churches, and carve statues for public squares. Affluent bankers and merchants became sponsors or **patrons** of these artists. No longer were artists dependent solely on the church for support.

Perhaps the most famous of the Renaissance patrons, apart from the church itself, were the members of the **Medici** (MED uh CHEE) **family**. The Medici were prominent Italians who had become extremely wealthy through commerce and banking. Their riches gained them political control of the city of Florence. They also used their vast financial resources to promote learning and the arts. They sponsored searches for manuscripts, established a public library (one of the first in Europe), and commissioned great works of painting, sculpture, and architecture. The most notable and most generous patron of the Medici family was **Lorenzo de Medici** (1469–1492), called *Il Magnifico* ("The Magnificent").

Florentine 15th Century or Florentine 16th Century, probably after a model by A. Verrocchio and O. Benintendi, Lorenzo de' Medici, *1478/1521.*

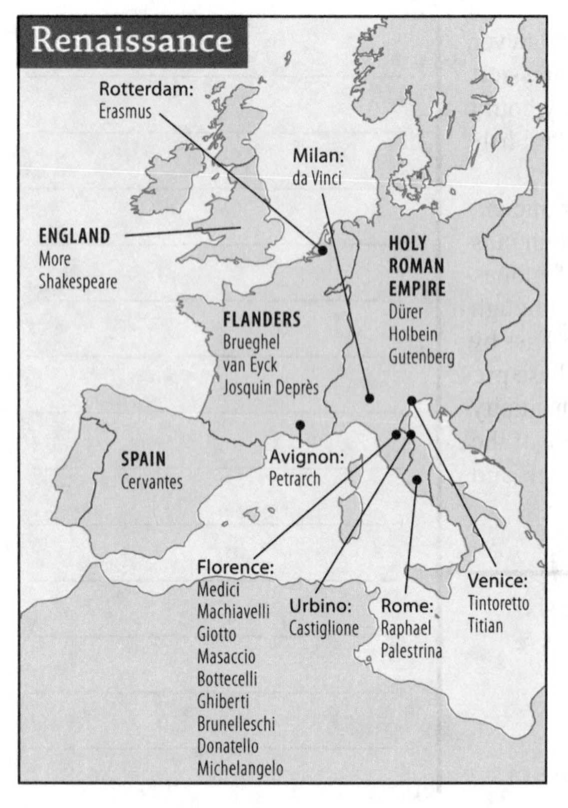

Matteo Nigetti (1560-1649). Chapel of the Princes (or Cappella dei Principi), Basilica di San Lorenzo, Florence, Italy

During his rule the city of Florence became the most influential city of the Renaissance movement.

Until about 1500 the Renaissance was primarily an Italian movement. As the sixteenth century began, however, enthusiasm for art and learning spread throughout Europe. It was carried abroad by students who had studied in Italy and by merchants who traded with Italian cities. The Renaissance took hold in England, France, Germany, and the Netherlands. At first the people of these lands copied the Italians, but before long they developed their own ideas and styles.

Thought and Literature

Italian Humanist Writers

The city of Florence, home of the powerful Medici, was the birthplace of the Renaissance. This bustling city was the center of Italian commerce. Members of the wealthy class, who sponsored art and learning, made Florence the center of culture in Italy. Most of the writers, painters, sculptors, and architects of the early Renaissance lived in this city.

At the beginning of the fourteenth century, Florentine writers gave expression to the growing secular attitudes. They looked to the literature of ancient Greece and Rome for inspiration. Their study of the classics stirred a rebirth of learning in Europe.

Petrarch—The pioneer of Renaissance humanism and one of the most important figures in Italian literature was **Francesco Petrarch** (1304–1374), the son of a Florentine merchant. As a youth he followed his father's wishes and entered law school. But his real love was the classical writings of Greece and Rome. His father did not approve of his spending more time reading these ancient works than studying law. One day he found his son's copies of the classics and threw them into the fire. But then, moved by Petrarch's grief, he managed to snatch two works from the flames.

After his father's death, Petrarch gave up his study of law and devoted his life to the classics. He searched monastic and church libraries to find ancient manuscripts, which he collected and studied. He composed his own Latin poems, modeling them after classical poetry. These he considered his best works. Later generations, however, remember him best for his vernacular writings. In sonnets (fourteen-line poems) and letters to his friends, he expressed human interest and emotions. Petrarch wrote about nature, his pride in his homeland, and his love for Laura (the woman he idealized). His love poetry had an immense influence on later writers. Of Laura he wrote the following:

> He for celestial charms may look in vain
> Who has not seen my fair one's radiant eyes,
> And felt their glances pleasingly beguile.
> How can Love heal his wounds, then wound again,
> He only knows who knows how sweet her sighs,
> How sweet her [conversation], and how sweet her smile.

In letters addressed to his heroes of the past—Cicero, Virgil, and Livy—Petrarch places his own day on an equal plane with the days of ancient Rome. Because Petrarch led the way in reviving interest and study in classical literature, he is known as the Father of Humanism.

Castiglione—Another Italian, **Baldassare Castiglione** (CAHS tee LYOH nay; 1478–1529), wrote one of the most famous books on etiquette (social behavior) published during the Renaissance. The topic of good manners was popular at that time. As more people acquired wealth and moved into a higher social class, they were eager to behave in an acceptable manner. In his book *The Courtier*, Castiglione describes the ideal Renaissance gentleman. He presents the courtier or gentleman as a man of character, well-educated, courageous, and courteous. Such a man should demonstrate the nobility of his character whether on the battlefield or in the fashionable places of society. *The Courtier* became an immediate bestseller and was translated into many different languages. It set the standard for courtly behavior all over Europe.

Raphael, Portrait of Baldassare Castiglione
Louvre, Paris, France

Rules for Proper Conduct

Besides *The Courtier*, other books of etiquette circulated in Europe during the Renaissance. *The Book of Manners*, written by Giovanni della Casa (1503–1556), is typical of such publications. The following excerpts typify the author's advice.

> A man should never boast of his birth, his honors or his wealth, and still less of his brains.
>
> It is not a polite habit . . . to carry your toothpick either in your mouth, like a bird making its nest, or behind your ear.
>
> You should also take care, as far as you can, not to spit at mealtimes, but if you must spit, then do so in a decent manner.
>
> Refrain as far as possible from making noises which grate upon the ear, such as grinding or sucking your teeth.
>
> Anyone whose legs are too thin, or exceptionally fat, or perhaps crooked, should not wear vivid or parti-colored hose, in order not to attract attention to his defects.
>
> A man must . . . not be content to do things well, but must also aim to do them gracefully.[2]

Machiavelli—One of the most influential Renaissance writers was the Florentine public official and political thinker **Niccolo Machiavelli** (MAH kyah VEL ee; 1469–1527). From 1489 to 1512 he worked as a diplomat for the Florentine Republic. During these years he was able to observe firsthand the political developments in Europe.

He was deeply disturbed by the unrest and division in his native land. Italy at this time was divided into a number of competing, warring states. Many of these relied on mercenary soldiers led by men called ***condottière*** (KAHN duh TYEHR ee) to fight their battles. Even the papacy was involved in these petty conflicts. The popes acted like secular rulers as they sought to expand the boundaries of the Papal States. The kings of France and Spain added to the turmoil by fighting several wars over these troubled regions.

Machiavelli wrote several important and influential works on government. The most important and controversial of these is an essay called *The Prince*. In this work Machiavelli reflects upon the political conditions of his day. He tells his readers that the successful ruler must do what is expedient and not be governed by principles of right and wrong. Such a man uses force when necessary, for "it is much safer to be feared than loved." Although Machiavelli probably wrote *The Prince* as merely an objective description of Italian politics, later

THROUGH EYES OF FAITH

Machiavelli's *The Prince*

Consider Machiavelli's statement "It is much safer to be feared than loved." How should a Christian governor view the use of fear and love? Are both being loved and feared to be desired or is neither?

____

____

____

____

____

____

____

____

____

THIS MOMENT IN HISTORY

Machiavelli's *Discourses on the First Ten Books of Livy*

Explain the ways this work may have contributed to the design of the United States government.

____
____
____
____
____
____
____
____
____

rulers took his "advice" and embraced this wicked system as the ideal political philosophy.

Perhaps a better source of Machiavelli's own political views is his *Discourses on the First Ten Books of Livy*. In this work he examines the politics of ancient Rome and derives lessons for rulers of his day. Favoring a republican form of government, he writes that "when there is combined under the same constitution a prince, a nobility, and the power of the people, then these three powers will watch and keep each other reciprocally in check."

Whatever Machiavelli's motives were, his works, particularly *The Prince*, promoted the concept of the secular state—one freed from moral restraints and religious principles. In succeeding centuries the idea that "might makes right" became popular with many of Europe's rulers. They justified the use of any method necessary (including deceit and brute force) to maintain their political power. The ideal of morally responsible governments and rulers seemed to fade from view as Europe entered what is called the "Age of Absolutism" (see Chapter 14).

Northern Humanist Writers

Despite the strong Italian influence over the Renaissance in northern Europe, the emphasis of northern humanists differed from that of their Italian counterparts. The northern humanists generally had a greater interest in religious matters than the Italian humanists. Their religious concern led to a greater emphasis upon church reform in the north. Accordingly, northern humanists gave more attention to Christian rather than classical sources. They placed the study of the Hebrew Old Testament and the Greek New Testament above the writings of Cicero, Virgil, and other ancients.

Erasmus—Perhaps the most honored and influential scholar of the Renaissance was **Erasmus** of Rotterdam (1466?–1536). As a young man he entered a monastery, but he spent little time there. Instead he traveled throughout Europe obtaining an education in Latin and Greek. He distinguished himself as the foremost scholar of Europe and was widely acclaimed as the prince of humanists.

Erasmus did much to prepare the way for the Protestant Reformation even though he himself refused to break with the Roman Catholic Church.

In his most famous work, *The Praise of Folly*, he uses satire to point out the evils and follies of Renaissance society.

He became a leading advocate of church reform and was an outspoken critic of monasticism, the ignorance and worldliness of the clergy, and the church's

In The Praise of Folly, *the character Folly describes how the people of this world have followed her teachings. These illustrations by Hans Holbein give examples of those whom Erasmus thought exhibited folly.*

A theologian full of excommunications and useless speculations

A pilgrim to Rome with no real purpose in his trip

A self-important logician who always believes he is right

empty ritualism. His interest and skill in biblical studies led him to publish his first edition of the Greek New Testament in 1516. In the preface Erasmus tells his readers his position on translating Scripture:

> I strongly dissent from those who are unwilling to have the Scriptures translated into the vernacular and read by the ignorant, as if Christ taught so complicated a doctrine that it can hardly be understood even by a handful of theologians. . . . It is perhaps reasonable to conceal the mysteries of kings, but Christ seeks to divulge his mysteries as much as possible. I should like to have even the most humble women read the [Gospels] and the Epistles of St. Paul. . . . Would that the plowboy recited something from them at his plowshare, that the weaver sang from them at his shuttle, and that the traveler whiled away the tedium of his journey with their tales.[3]

Dürer, Albrecht (1471-1528). Erasmus of Rotterdam, *1526, engraving (B107).*

The great reformer Martin Luther used Erasmus's Greek New Testament in making his German translation of the New Testament. Many others, including the translators of the King James Version, have used Erasmus's text as the basis for translating the New Testament into the common languages of the people.

More—A close friend of Erasmus was the English humanist Sir **Thomas More** (1478–1535). More was a man of deep piety who spent regular hours in prayer. He exercised his responsibility as a father to "train up a child in the way he should go" (Prov. 22:6). He held daily devotions in his home, requiring even the household servants to attend. Before each meal he had one of his children read a portion of Scripture.

More devoted much of his life to the service of his country. His interest in social and political matters prompted him to write a book setting forth his

Gutenberg

A resourceful German named **Johannes Gutenberg** helped to significantly change the course of history. He is generally recognized as the man to put movable-type printing into use in Europe. The Chinese had developed movable-type printing in the eleventh century, but there is no evidence that their accomplishments were known in Europe. Gutenberg's greatest achievement was his edition of the Bible, which was printed in 1456.

The advent of movable-type printing is a landmark in the history of the Western world. The cost of books dropped dramatically because they no longer needed to be copied by hand and because they could be produced in large quantities. In addition, printing eliminated many of the errors which characterized older handwritten books. It paved the way for the rapid spread of ideas and stimulated the growth of education. In the past students had to memorize everything they heard in the classroom because the teacher was usually the only one who had a book. With printing, students could afford to purchase their own books. It is no coincidence that between 1450 and 1517 a total of twenty-five new universities and colleges were established in Spain, France, Germany, and England.

In the seventeenth century Sir Francis Bacon, an English philosopher and author, wrote that there were three inventions that "changed the appearance and state of the whole world." They were the compass, gunpowder, and movable-type printing. These inventions may not seem significant to us, but they shaped Europe almost to the same extent that television and computers are shaping the present age.

views on the ideal government. This work, entitled *Utopia* (meaning "nowhere"), is the story of an imaginary state built upon Christian principles and Plato's philosophy. More was dismayed by the greed of the nobility and the plight of the poor in English society. He believed that if men would govern themselves by a sense of community and brotherly love, they could achieve political, social, and economic equality. According to More, the three deadliest sins of the English community were sloth (laziness), greed, and pride. In Utopia, all men would be compelled to work. Thus everyone would have economic security, and all sloth and greed would be eliminated. All pride was to be centered in the state.

More was not the first nor the last person to conceive of an ideal state. Throughout history men have set forth a variety of views. Nevertheless, to have a perfect state, society would have to be composed of perfect men and women. Since "all have sinned, and come short of the glory of God" (Rom. 3:23), it is impossible for man to achieve this goal.

More entered the service of Henry VIII (the king of England) because, as he said, "If better men did not go into politics, worse ones would." Although he served Henry well, he was beheaded for treason when he refused to take an oath recognizing Henry as head of the church in England. At the scaffold he said, "I die the king's loyal servant, but God's first." Despite the corruption in the Renaissance papacy, More still believed in the pope's supremacy in the church.

Cervantes—The foremost Spanish writer of the late Renaissance is **Miguel de Cervantes** (sur VAN tez; 1547–1616). His novel *Don Quixote* (DAHN kee-HO-tay) is one of the most enduring works in all of literature. It is a satire on chivalry and on the chivalric literature that was popular in Cervantes's day. The main character, Don Quixote, imagining himself to be a knight, puts on a suit of armor, mounts an old horse, and gallops around the Spanish countryside seeking to right the world's wrongs. In doing so he makes a fool of himself.

MR. WILLIAM
SHAKESPEARES
COMEDIES,
HISTORIES, &
TRAGEDIES.
Published according to the True Originall Copies.

LONDON
Printed by Isaac Iaggard, and Ed. Blount. 1623.

Title page of a collection of Shakespeare's works, dated 1623.

William Shakespeare, Used by permission of the Folger Shakespeare Library

Accompanying Don Quixote on his many adventures is his faithful squire Sancho Panza, whom Cervantes presents as the more practical, down-to-earth person. Through this work Cervantes pokes fun at outmoded medieval ideas. At the same time he presents a vivid picture of life in sixteenth-century Spain.

Shakespeare—Renaissance literature reached its peak in the works of **William Shakespeare** (1564–1616), who is generally considered the greatest playwright of all time and the finest poet in the English language. Shakespeare, the son of a prosperous trader, was born and reared in Stratford-upon-Avon, a small town northwest of London. As a young man he went to London, where he became a successful actor and playwright. His fame spread during his early career after he published two long narrative poems. Shakespeare gained financial success as a leader and a stockholder in a prominent London theatrical group called the Lord Chamberlain's Men, later known as the King's Men. He purchased stock in two playhouses, the most famous of which was the Globe Theatre, where most of his plays were performed.

Shakespeare's lifework includes 154 sonnets and at least thirty-seven plays. His dramatic works are classified as histories, comedies, and tragedies. The tragedies, including *Hamlet*, *Othello*, *King Lear*, and *Macbeth*, are generally recognized as his greatest works. Fourteen of his plays are set in Italy. This delighted English audiences, for in true Renaissance spirit they looked to Italy as the birthplace of learning. Several of Shakespeare's plays reflect the surge of national pride in England. In his history play *Richard II*, he penned these words:

> This royal throne of kings, this sceptred isle,
> This earth of majesty, this seat of Mars,
> This other Eden, demi-paradise,
> This fortress built by Nature for herself
> Against the infection and the hand of war,
> This happy breed of men, this little world,
> This precious stone set in the silver sea,
> Which serves it in the office of a wall,
> Or as a moat defensive to a house,
> Against the envy of less happier lands;
> This blessed plot, this earth, this realm, this England.

Shakespeare has left an indelible print upon Western culture. His works have had an enormous impact upon later authors. Few libraries in the world could contain all of the books that have been written about his life and work. Shakespeare's poems and plays have been the object of careful study by every generation since his death. His literary genius enriched the English language and influenced its development. Many of the phrases and expression that he coined are part of everyday speech in modern society. His plays, which have been translated into many languages, have worldwide appeal. A master of character portrayal, Shakespeare probed the depths and complexity of human existence as few writers ever have.

Section Quiz

1. Apart from the church, what family was the most famous patron of Renaissance learning and art? Who was the most noted patron of this family?
2. Who is called the Father of Humanism because he led the way in reviving interest and study in classical literature?
3. What contribution did Johannes Gutenberg make to European history?
4. What work of Erasmus did later reformers and Bible translators use?
5. What Englishman is generally considered the greatest playwright of all time?

1. ____________________
   ____
2. ____________________
3. ____________________
   ____
4. ____________________
5. ____________________

The Visual Arts

The visual arts clearly express the spirit and attitudes of the Renaissance. As in any age, there were both men who sought to honor the Lord with their work and those who did not. Many artists during this period used their God-given talents to bring glory to their Creator. Others, however, used their abilities to make a name for themselves, arrogantly trying to outdo one another. These were quick to boast of their ability. They measured themselves by the praise of men and had little concern for God's standard:

> *For we dare not make ourselves of the number, or compare ourselves with some that commend themselves: but they measuring themselves by themselves, and comparing themselves among themselves, are not wise. But we will not boast of things without our measure, but according to the measure of the rule which God hath distributed to us . . . not boasting of things without our measure, that is, of other men's labours. . . . But he that glorieth, let him glory in the Lord. For not he that commendeth himself is approved, but whom the Lord commendeth.*
>
> *2 Corinthians 10:12–13, 15, 17–18*

Renaissance artists drew their inspiration from the classical world. They broke with the artistic traditions of the Middle Ages in the following ways:

Crucifix, *Francesco di Vannuccio*
From the Bob Jones University Collection

1. Renaissance art emphasized the present physical world. Medieval art had emphasized the spiritual realm and the life to come.
2. Secular patrons often supported the Renaissance artists. During the Middle Ages the church of Rome had almost exclusively patronized the artists.
3. Most Renaissance artists were extremely proud of their work and wanted their names known and their works praised. Medieval artists, on the other hand, had worked primarily for the glory of God and the church and usually did not gain any personal recognition.
4. Renaissance artists gave a realistic, three-dimensional aspect to their works. Medieval art was flat and two-dimensional.
5. Most Renaissance portrait painters frequently painted kings, merchants, and other important secular individuals. Medieval painters usually portrayed church leaders, biblical characters, or saints of the church.
6. Painting and sculpture were the most popular media during the Renaissance. The glory of medieval art was its architecture.

Early Italian Painters

***Giotto*— Giotto di Bondone** (JAWT-toh dee bone-DOH-nay; 1266?–1337) is the most famous painter of the early Italian Renaissance. He is often called the Father of Renaissance Painting. He opened a new era of art in the Western world. Before his time, figures in paintings were stiff and flat; medieval artists painted expressionless people and set them against a plain gold background. This practice created an impression of calm serenity—a heavenly atmosphere. Giotto, however, sought to make painting more natural. His figures were more realistic and exhibited human feelings. He also tried to create a three-dimensional look in his paintings by making greater use of backgrounds.

Giotto is most famous for his **frescoes** (paintings on wet plaster) on the walls of the town church at Padua. Although he tried to make his painting as realistic as possible, he never fully mastered the technique of **perspective**—portraying a three-dimensional appearance on a flat surface.

Masaccio—Florentine artists of the fifteenth century achieved greater realism in their paintings by creating works that gave a sense of life, action, depth, and feeling. Early in the century **Masaccio** (mah ZAHT chee oh; 1401–28) added new techniques to painting. By means of shading (contrasting light and dark), he created a three-dimensional effect in his painting. This technique enabled him to portray human figures with a realism that had been missing in the works of previous painters.

Botticelli—In the late fifteenth century, **Sandro Botticelli** (BOT ih CHEL ee; 1444?–1510) added another dimension to Renaissance art: movement. He depicted forms with bold line and gave clarity and a sense of activity to his characters. With their flowing hair and wispy garments, his painted figures seemed

Savonarola: Preacher of Righteousness

A generation before the Reformation, a Dominican friar named **Girolamo Savonarola** (SAV uh nuh ROLL uh; 1452–1498) sought to bring moral reform to the city of Florence and to the Roman church. He opposed the corrupt rule of the Medici family and severely criticized Pope Alexander VI, a man notorious for his bribery, fornication, robbery, blasphemy, and murder. Savonarola warned the Florentines of a coming day of judgment and called upon them to repent of their wicked ways. At the height of his popularity, crowds of ten to twelve thousand people flocked to hear his sermons. He soon became the leading religious figure in the city.

As a result of his preaching, the secular culture that dominated the city began to change. For example, people built great bonfires into which they threw playing cards, gambling dice, immoral books and pictures, and objects of luxury. Not everyone, however, enthusiastically accepted the reforms that Savonarola had begun. Alexander VI, perhaps the most wicked of all the popes, sought to silence him. He prohibited him from preaching, but Savonarola continued to boldly denounce the sins of Rome. Alexander then tried to buy his silence by offering to make him a cardinal, but Savonarola refused. He finally excommunicated him, but Savonarola ignored his action.

The people of Florence, intimidated by the pope's action and weary of Savonarola's strict preaching, abandoned the friar. He was arrested, tortured, tried, and condemned to die by hanging. The crowds that had once gathered to hear him preach gathered to watch him die. Savonarola was hanged, his body was burned, and his ashes were cast into the Arno River. (His ashes were scattered so that nobody could preserve them as relics.)

In the eyes of his contemporaries, Savonarola was a failure. The city had cast aside his reforms and had consented to his execution. God, however, does not measure success or failure on the basis of popular approval. He rewards those of His servants who are faithful—even unto death.

Sandro Botticelli, The Adoration of the Magi, *early 1480's.*

Andrew W. Mellon Collection, Image © 2005 Board of Trustees, National Gallery of Art, Washington

to move and sway. Botticelli's early paintings reflected the humanistic spirit prevalent in the Medici court. He painted pagan themes of classical mythology. But when the Medici family was expelled from Florence, Botticelli fell under the influence of the preaching of the monk Savonarola. He became a convert, and his painting took on a more religious and moral outlook.

High Renaissance Painters

The artistic achievement of the Italian Renaissance culminated in the early sixteenth century. During this period, known as the High Renaissance, the center of culture shifted from Florence to Rome. The papacy became the major patron of Italian artists. High Renaissance artists mastered the painting techniques that the Italian artists of the fifteenth century had pioneered. The most famous High Renaissance painters are Leonardo da Vinci, Raphael, and Michelangelo.

***Leonardo da Vinci*—Leonardo da Vinci** (duh VIN-chee; 1452–1519) is probably the best example of the so-called Renaissance man. He displayed interest in a wide range of fields. He was an accomplished sculptor, architect,

Leonardo da Vinci and His Notebooks

Though remembered primarily for his great artistic abilities, Leonardo da Vinci was extremely interested in science and technology. He studied nature and conceived of numerous inventions, recording all his thoughts and observations in notebooks. Today we have about 5,700 pages of his notes, all of which are written in "mirror script." Since Leonardo was left-handed he found it easier to write from right to left. His notes may be read properly—that is, from left to right—only when viewed in a mirror.

Leonardo originally began his notebooks to help him in his painting. He studied plant life and the human body in order to make his paintings more realistic. Some of his plant drawings are so accurate that they could be used in a modern botany textbook. He often used cross-sections and cutaway views to better understand the objects of his study.

While much of Leonardo's work was designed to improve his artistic abilities, he was also interested in knowledge for its own sake. An intelligent and imaginative man, he invented many things. With the help of modern technology—as well as some alterations—many of them have proved workable. He devised, among other things, a chain drive (used on bicycles), ball bearings, a jack, an odometer, a device for measuring humidity, and a life belt for those who were shipwrecked. His work foreshadowed prefabricated houses, submarines, and automobiles. In the area of military science, Leonardo invented a tank which was powered from the inside by hand cranks, and a triple-tier machine gun. While one set of guns was being fired, another was cooling, and the third was being reloaded.

Of all Leonardo's inventions, those that proved to be the least workable were his flying machines. Although flying fascinated Leonardo almost more than any other subject, he never fully grasped its principles. He did, however, diagram two objects that are used today in modified form. One of them is a helical screw (from the Greek word *helix*— "spiral"). This object is the forerunner of the propeller as well as the helicopter. The second object is Leonardo's version of the parachute.

An artist's rendering of some of Leonardo's sketches

painter, musician, and poet. He also studied anatomy, botany, geology, astronomy, engineering, and mathematics.

As a young man Leonardo received training in painting and sculpture at Florence. Distinguishing himself as a painter, he was admitted into the Florentine painters' guild. But he believed that the restrictions of the guild stifled his creative talents. He was eager to explore new ideas; the city of Florence, he thought, was much too dependent on the classical age. Therefore in 1482 he sought a position in Milan under the sponsorship of the duke of Milan. In a letter he wrote to his prospective patron, Leonardo proudly listed his qualifications:

> And in short, according to the variety of cases, I can contrive various and endless means of offence and defense [that is, weaponry].... In time of peace I believe I can give perfect satisfaction and to the equal of any other in architecture and the composition of buildings, public and private; and in guiding water from one place to another.... I can carry out sculpture in marble, bronze, or clay, and also I can do in painting whatever may be done, as well as any other, be he whom he may.[4]

While in Milan, Leonardo painted his famous mural *The Last Supper* on a wall in a monastery. The painting illustrates his mastery of perspective and exemplifies the Renaissance love for balance. He vividly depicts the intense feelings of the disciples when Christ announced that one of them would betray Him. Although in a deteriorated state, this mural remains one of the most famous religious paintings of all time. Perhaps Leonardo's most famous work is his painting the *Mona Lisa*.

Raphael (1483-1520). Madonna del Granduca, 1505.

Galleria Palatina, Palazzo Pitti, Florence, Italy

Raphael—Raffaello Sanzio (1483–1520), better known as **Raphael** (RAF ay el), completed an enormous number of paintings and frescoes in his short lifetime. His interest in painting undoubtedly began at home, for his father was a painter. As a young man Raphael studied the works of the masters in order to perfect his own technique. He soon became one of the most beloved painters of his time.

Raphael is famous for his paintings of sweet-faced Madonnas in which he idealized motherhood. He sought to express the peace and quiet joy of life rather than its anguish and strain. He is also known for the magnificent frescoes that he painted to decorate the papal residence in Rome. *The School of Athens* is an excellent example of his work; it displays balance, harmony, and perspective. In this painting he creates a spacious setting in which are gathered the great philosophers and scientists of the classical world.

Michelangelo—**Michelangelo Buonarroti** (MY-kul-AN-juh-lo BWAWN-uh-RAW-tee; 1475–1564) is one of the most famous artists in all of history. His contemporaries praised his artistic masterpieces. As a young boy he exhibited unusual skill in sculpting. It is said that he learned how to handle a chisel and hammer before he could read and write. When he told his father that he wanted to study painting and sculpture, his father was furious. His father believed manual labor was beneath the dignity of the family. But when Michelangelo displayed little interest or ability in school, his father apprenticed him to a leading Florentine artist. While an apprentice, the talented youth caught the

Michelangelo Buonarroti (1475-1564). Creation of the Stars and of the Planets. *Detail of the Sistine ceiling.*
Sistine Chapel, Vatican Palace, Vatican State

eye of Lorenzo de Medici, who took Michelangelo into his household as his adopted son.

In 1508 Pope Julius II asked Michelangelo to paint the ceiling of the **Sistine Chapel** in the Vatican (the papal residence in Rome). Protesting that he was a sculptor and not a painter, Michelangelo began the mammoth project reluctantly. After four years of working on scaffolds nearly seventy feet above the floor, he finished painting the 5,800-square-foot ceiling. The original plan had called for only twelve figures; however, when Michelangelo finished the project, he had painted over three hundred figures, most of which were ten to eighteen feet tall. This magnificent fresco depicts the story of Creation, the Fall, the Flood, and the Redemption of man as prophesied by the Old Testament prophets. Nearly a quarter of a century later he painted the front wall of the chapel with his conception of the last judgment. This painting is filled with violent, frenzied action portraying a dynamic Christ calling the saved to heaven and condemning the lost to hell.

Venetian Painters

During the late Renaissance the city of Venice became a leading center of culture. It is located on a cluster of islands at the northern end of the Adriatic Sea. Numerous canals dissect the city and serve as streets along which gondolas, or flat-bottomed boats, transport people around the city. Its merchant fleet was once the strongest sea power in the Mediterranean region. Its merchants controlled the important trade routes to the East. The economic prosperity it enjoyed encouraged cultural activity. Wealthy merchants built grand palaces and commissioned artists to adorn the city with magnificent works of art. The beautiful, wealthy, and proud city of Venice became known as the Queen of the Adriatic.

Venice, however, was wicked and materialistic. The citizens eagerly pursued luxury, pleasure, and prestige. Each year the city staged elaborate pageants; beneath all the glitter and pomp was a city sunk deep in moral decay.

Even the art of Venice mirrored its materialism, attesting to the Venetian love for money, precious gems, rich clothing, decoration, and festive occasions. Artists painted wealthy merchants, proud city officials, and beautiful women. These paintings, filled with radiant color and light, reflect the city's secular and sensuous spirit.

Titian—Tiziano Vecelli (1477–1576), known as **Titian** (TISH un), was the leading figure of the Venetian school of painting. He ranks with Michelangelo as one of the foremost painters of the Renaissance. A prolific painter known for his rich use of color, Titian is especially remembered for his portraits. His work contains a freshness, warmth, and vitality missing in the serene Renaissance portraits of southern Italy. He captured on canvas the personality of his subject, not just the physical appearance. His fame spread throughout Europe. He painted pictures for the Holy Roman Emperor and the kings of Spain and France, becoming one of the few Renaissance painters to grow wealthy through his work.

Titian (Tiziano Vecellio) (c. 1488–1576). The Pilgrims at Emmaus. *1535.*
Oil on canvas. Louvre, Paris, France.

Tintoretto—**Tintoretto** (1518–1594) was the last of the great sixteenth-century Venetian painters. He was born Jacopo Robusti but is known by his nickname Tintoretto (Italian for "little dyer") because his father was a dyer by profession. In his painting he sought to combine the bright colors of Titian and the masterful drawing of Michelangelo. His work exhibits a dramatic excitement full of tension and action.

Northern European Artists

Dürer—The German painter **Albrecht Dürer** (DOOR ur; 1471–1528) is sometimes called the "Leonardo of the North." Like Leonardo, he was accomplished in many different fields: writing, designing, engraving, and painting. He had a high regard for Italian art and was the first northern artist to travel to Italy for the express purpose of studying art. His painting illustrates his love for both classical and religious themes. He also had a keen interest in nature, an interest reflected by his amazingly accurate watercolors of floral scenes. Although Dürer is a celebrated painter, he is best remembered for his woodcarvings and engravings, which were used to illustrate printed books. He is the first artist to sign even his most insignificant drawings. His "signature" consisted of a capital A straddling a capital *D*.

Albrecht Dürer, Knight, Death and Devil, *1513.*
Gift of W. G. Russell Allen, Image © 2005 Board of Trustees, National Gallery of Art, Washington

Holbein—Another celebrated German painter is **Hans Holbein** (HOHL bine) the Younger (1479?–1543). He is considered the finest portrait painter of the Northern Renaissance. He traveled throughout Europe, working in many countries—especially England. Holbein became the official court painter of Henry VIII, the king of England. He not only painted portraits of Henry, his wives, and his son but also designed Henry's clothes, jewelry, and tableware. This German master also painted the portraits of leading figures of the Northern Renaissance, such as Erasmus and Sir Thomas More.

Jan van Eyck, The Arnolfini Portrait
© The National Gallery, London

Van Eyck's masterful painting of an Italian financier and his wife displays the enormous advance in realism that the artist achieved through his use of oil paints. In addition, the subject matter—which is not overtly religious—illustrates the secular interests that grew during the Renaissance. Note the realistic details, such as the mirror in the background showing the backs of the artist's subjects.

Van Eyck—One of the founders and an outstanding representative of the Flemish school of painters was **Jan van Eyck** (van IKE; 1370?–1440?). In his early career he illustrated manuscripts; this art form required careful attention to minute details. Van Eyck's concern for detail carried over to his large paintings. He was one of the first to use oil paints, a medium that allowed him to achieve greater realism in his painting.

Brueghel—During the fifteenth century, Flemish painters created a distinctive style of art known for its realism, landscapes, and scenes of contemporary life. In the sixteenth century **Pieter Brueghel** (BROY gul; 1525?–69) helped develop and perfect this style. He is best remembered for his **genre painting**, a type of painting that depicts scenes of everyday life. These works show the peasants in their daily activities: farming in the fields, hunting in the woods, and dancing in the village square. When he painted biblical events, he depicted them as though they took place in Flanders.

Architects and Sculptors

Both architects and sculptors were influenced by the spirit of humanism. They greatly admired the art of the classical world. Renaissance architecture and sculpture, like painting, also reflected the new secular concerns of the Renaissance Age. In the medieval period the primary function of architecture had been to glorify God through the building of magnificent cathedrals. During the Renaissance, however, architects also designed and built spacious palaces and comfortable villas for powerful princes and wealthy merchants. Similarly, sculpture that had been used during the Middle Ages to decorate churches now graced town squares and homes of the wealthy.

Ghiberti—About the year 1401 the leading men of Florence held a contest to select an artist to design a set of bronze doors for one of the entrances to the baptistery of Florence. Among the many artists who entered the competition were **Lorenzo Ghiberti** (gee BEHR tee; 1378–1455) and **Filippo Brunelleschi** (BROO nuh LES kee; 1377?–1446). According to the contest rules, each participant had to present a sculptured relief depicting the story of the sacrifice of Isaac. Ghiberti's work was judged the best. He gloated over his victory:

> To me was conceded the palm of victory by all the experts and by all those who had competed with me. To me the honor was conceded universally and with no exception. To all it seemed that I had at that time surpassed the others without exception, as was recognized by a great council and an investigation of learned men . . . highly skilled from the painter and sculptors of gold, silver, and marble. There were thirty-four judges from the city and the other surrounding countries. The testimonial of the victory was given in my favor by all . . . . It was granted to me and determined that I should make the bronze door for this church.[5]

Ghiberti, however, would have done well to heed God's admonition in 1 Samuel 2:3—"Talk no more so exceeding proudly; let not arrogancy come out of your mouth: for the Lord is a God of knowledge, and by him actions are weighed."

For the next two decades Ghiberti worked on the doors. The finished doors contained twenty-eight panels depicting New Testament stories. The city later commissioned him to do a second set of doors. This time he chose to depict stories from the Old Testament. According to Michelangelo, Ghiberti designed the ten panels on these doors "so fine that they might fittingly stand at the Gates of Paradise." Ghiberti himself said, "Of all my work it is the most remarkable I have done and it was finished with skill, correct proportion, and understanding."

The Florence Cathedral, showing Brunelleschi's dome (left) and Giotto's bell tower (right)

Brunelleschi—Disgusted with losing the competition to design the doors of the baptistery in Florence, Brunelleschi turned from sculpture to architecture. He traveled to Rome where he studied Roman monuments. He later returned to Florence and defeated Ghiberti in a competition to design and construct a dome for the cathedral of Florence. Not since the days of ancient Rome had such a magnificent and lofty dome been constructed in the West. His dome was the crowning glory of the Florence cathedral. Most of the domes designed during the Renaissance conformed to his model.

Donatello—**Donatello** (1386?–1466) was the leading sculptor of the early Renaissance. He was born in Florence and as a young boy served as an assistant to Ghiberti. He later accompanied Brunelleschi to Rome, where both studied classical statues. Although strongly influenced by these classical works, he gave to his sculpture a new realism and expression. He mastered the art of sculpting freestanding statues. One of his most revolutionary works was his statue of David, whom he depicted as a young Florentine shepherd boy. Donatello also cast the first full-scale equestrian statue (man on horseback) since Roman times. His realistic, freestanding statues later inspired the most outstanding sculptor of the Renaissance—Michelangelo.

Michelangelo's Pietà

Michelangelo—Michelangelo was a man of many talents. He was a noted painter (see pp. 267–68), sculptor, architect, engineer, and poet. While in his early twenties he completed one of his most famous masterpieces, the *Pietà* (pyay TAH; an Italian term meaning "pity" or "compassion"). It depicts the virgin Mary mourning over the crucified Christ. When the work was unveiled, one viewer exclaimed, "This cannot be the work of some unknown artist. It must be the work of our master in Milan." Hearing this, Michelangelo returned later that night and carved into the ribbon across Mary's chest, "Michelangelo Buonarroti, Florentine, made this."

In sculpting the *Pietà*, Michelangelo went beyond usual artistic methods of portraying subjects realistically because he wanted to express what he considered to be the ideal. The sculpture contains a number of contradictions.

For example, Michelangelo portrays Christ after the Crucifixion without any disfigurement; in fact, the figure of Christ is a model of physical perfection. Though dead, He looks full of life. Perhaps Michelangelo had in mind the teaching of Scripture in Revelation 1:18—"I am he that liveth, and was dead; and, behold, I am alive for evermore." Another interesting feature is that Mary is presented as a young girl—one too young to be the mother of Christ. Michelangelo created this distortion of historical fact in order to emphasize the purity of Mary. Furthermore, though the figure of Christ is life-sized, Mary is larger than life. It is estimated that if she were to stand, she would be eight to nine feet tall. When questioned about these discrepancies, Michelangelo said, "The hands execute but the eye judges." To the admiring eye these distortions are not readily apparent.

Another famous work by Michelangelo is his marble statue of David. Like many of the Renaissance artists, Michelangelo glorified the human body. His David, standing eighteen feet high, is the embodiment of Michelangelo's vision of a perfect specimen of young manhood.

Music

The most prominent type of musical composition during the early Middle Ages was known as **plainsong**, or Gregorian chant. Sung to Latin words, these simple single-lined melodies became the official music of the Roman Catholic Church and were a vital part of medieval church services. For the most part, medieval music was mystical and spiritual in nature; its purpose was to appeal not to the senses and emotions of its listeners but to their spirits. Medieval music attempted to remove the listener from the cares of the world.

Lute

Renaissance music was more secular. Like the visual arts, it did not remain under the exclusive patronage of the church. With the advent of the printing press, copies of music became more available. Both the number of musicians and the popular interest in music increased. Music moved into the palaces of the nobles and the homes of the middle class. Even ordinary people could purchase printed song books. "How-to-do-it" books instructed would-be musicians in how to play a musical instrument. By far the most popular instrument of the day was the lute. This instrument, which resembles a pear-shaped guitar, was most widely used to accompany singers. More music was composed and performed during the Renaissance than in any previous period in history.

Josquin Deprès

One of the leading figures in music during the early Renaissance was the Flemish composer **Josquin Deprès** (ZHOHZ-kan duh-PREH; 1450?–1521). His life and music mark the transition between medieval and modern times. His contemporaries hailed him as one of the foremost composers of the day. Martin Luther said of him, "He is the master of notes; they do as he bids; as for the other composers, they have to do as the notes will."

With a simple and charming style, Josquin composed both sacred and secular works. He is best remembered for his masses (music sung during the mass service), hymns, and more than one hundred **motets**—unaccompanied Latin songs that combined different melodies and words with a plainsong melody. Less serious were his **chansons**, lighthearted songs that set secular lyric poems to music.

In the latter part of his life, Josquin served as the court composer for his good friend King Louis XII of France. On one occasion when Louis forgot to fulfill a promise that he made to Josquin, the composer devised an unusual way to remind the king. At the next church service the choir sang a newly composed motet about those who break their promises.

Palestrina

The most famous composer of church music during the Renaissance was the Italian composer Giovanni Pierluigi (1526?–1594). He is better known as **Palestrina**, taking his name from the town of his birth. As a boy he sang in his town's church choir; later he served as the organist and choirmaster of the Palestrina Cathedral.

During his lifetime, Palestrina composed more than nine hundred musical pieces. He also revised many of the old Gregorian chants. By the sixteenth century, church music had become so complicated that it became difficult to understand what the choir was singing. Commissioned by the papacy, Palestrina simplified much of the church's official music. He was the master of **polyphonic** music (consisting of many melodies), which he composed for choirs to sing without accompaniment. In his own day he was hailed as the Prince of Music.

Section Quiz

1. During the High Renaissance, what city became the culture center of Italy?
2. List the three most famous painters of the High Renaissance period; for each, give the title of one of his masterpieces.
3. What beautiful, wealthy city, called the Queen of the Adriatic, became the center of culture during the late Renaissance? Identify two leading painters from this city.
4. Identify a Northern Renaissance artist for each of the following: portrait painting, genre painting, woodcarvings and engravings, detailed realism through oil painting.
5. Who was the most famous composer of church music during the Renaissance? What type of music did he master?

1. ______________________
2. ______________________

____

____

____

____

____

3. ______________________

____

____

4. ______________________

____

____

____

____

____

____

____

5. ______________________

____

III. Consequences of the Renaissance

The Renaissance and the Reformation that followed it are in many respects exact opposites. The Renaissance was a secular age; men placed confidence in human ability and gloried in human achievement. Artists and scholars, who looked to classical Greece and Rome for inspiration and authority, helped stir a great revival in learning and the arts. The Reformation was a religious age; men placed confidence in God and gloried in God's salvation. Men of God, who looked to the Scriptures as the sole authority, helped stir a great spiritual revival.

Despite these differences, it would be wrong to assume that there was no connection between the Renaissance and the Reformation. Every period of history is preparatory to the age that follows. In God's providence, the age of the Renaissance prepared western Europe for the coming age of the Reformation (which we will discuss in the next chapter).

Positive

The Renaissance shaped the tools that were useful to the Reformation movement. In this sense the Renaissance made the Reformation possible. *First*, the Renaissance provoked a spirit of inquiry. Men no longer meekly accepted the authority of the Roman church. Instead they critically evaluated its teaching for themselves. This critical spirit encouraged men to turn their attention back to the simplicity of first-century Christianity.

Second, it revived interest in the literature and languages of antiquity. In their search for classical sources, Renaissance humanists recovered many

Christian sources—manuscripts of the Old and New Testaments. The discovery of these manuscripts led to a renewed interest in the biblical languages (Greek and Hebrew) and in the study of the Bible itself.

Third, it developed movable-type printing. The new publishing industry made possible the inexpensive production of written material. The printed page would be instrumental in spreading the ideas of the reformers throughout Europe.

Fourth, it made education more widely available to the common person. More people were now able to read what was being printed.

Fifth, it stressed the importance of the individual, thus restoring the proper emphasis on individual responsibility—the obligation each person has to God and to his fellow man.

Negative

The Renaissance's secular emphasis helped weaken moral restraints and thereby made the need for reform more readily apparent. The church, which should have been the example of moral righteousness, was steeped in worldliness and wickedness. Renaissance clergy and popes reveled openly in luxury and immorality. It has been said that "the moral corruption of Rome and Italy in the latter half of the fifteenth century and the early part of the sixteenth is the best justification of the Protestant Reformation." Similarly, the humanists, who sought to imitate the best of the classical world, often embraced its evils.

The revival of classical literature and art carried in it the danger of a revival of heathenism in religion and morality. The worship of classical forms led to the worship of classical ideas. Some humanists and artists combined culture with Christian faith and devoted their genius to the cause of truth and virtue, but the majority silently or openly worshiped the pagan gods of Greece and Rome rather than the God of the Bible. The dazzling glory of classical antiquity obscured the humble beauty of Christianity.[6]

A Glance Behind

Throughout history people have sought to reach a proper balance between life on earth and life in the world to come. The medieval world "tipped the scale" toward the world to come. People of that age often were careless about the past, believing that it had little bearing on their present lives. Likewise, they merely existed in the present, resigning themselves to all its evils. Their eyes were fixed on the future, anticipating the glories that awaited.

The Renaissance world reacted against the otherworldly interest of the Middle Ages. But in doing so, people of the Renaissance placed too much emphasis on the things of this world. They gloried in the past, finding there the inspiration and example for the present. At the same time, their enthusiasm for life led them to exalt the present, but often to the neglect of the future.

It was the Reformation that sought to restore the proper balance between this life and the life to come. The reformers found their guide for life in the Word of God, which puts past, present, and future in proper perspective:

> *For the grace of God that bringeth salvation hath appeared to all men, teaching us that, denying ungodliness and worldly lusts, we should live soberly, righteously, and godly, in this present world; looking for that blessed hope, and the glorious appearing of the great God and our Saviour Jesus Christ.*
>
> *Titus 2:11–13*

and a Glimpse Ahead

Notes

1. Lewis W. Spitz, *The Renaissance and Reformation Movements* (Chicago: Rand McNally, 1971), p. 5.
2. Selections from *The Renaissance: Maker of Modern Man* (National Geographic Society, 1970), p. 93, and John R. Hale, et al., *Renaissance* (New York: Time-Life Books, 1965), p. 57.
3. *The Renaissance: Maker of Modern Man*, p. 300.
4. E. G. Holt, *Literary Sources of Art History* (Princeton: Princeton UP, 1947), p. 170.
5. Ibid., pp. 87–88.
6. Spitz, p. 17.

Chapter Review

Can You Define?

Renaissance
humanism
humanities
humanists
patrons
frescoes
perspective
genre painting
plainsong
motets
chansons
polyphonic

Can You Identify?

Medici family
Lorenzo de Medici
Francesco Petrarch
Baldassare Castiglione
Niccolo Machiavelli
condottière
Erasmus
Thomas More
Johannes Gutenberg
Miguel de Cervantes
William Shakespeare
Giotto di Bondone
Masaccio
Sandro Botticelli
Girolamo Savonarola
Leonardo da Vinci
Raphael
Michelangelo Buonarroti
Sistine Chapel
Titian
Tintoretto
Albrecht Dürer
Hans Holbein
Jan van Eyck
Pieter Brueghel
Lorenzo Ghiberti
Filippo Brunelleschi
Donatello
Josquin Deprès
Palestrina

Can You Locate?

Florence
Rotterdam
Rome
Milan
Venice
Flanders

How Much Do You Remember?

1. How did the Renaissance man's attitude toward life differ from the medieval man's?
2. List three reasons why Italy was the home of the early Renaissance.
3. Identify the title of one important work authored by each of the following: Petrarch, Castiglione, Machiavelli, Erasmus, More, Cervantes, and Shakespeare.
4. In what ways did the northern European humanists differ from the humanists of Italy?
5. List four ways Renaissance art differed from medieval art.

What Do You Think?

1. Many of the Renaissance artists boasted of their talent and ability. What should be the Christian's attitude toward his talents and abilities? What does the Bible say about this in 2 Corinthians 10:12–18?
2. The Renaissance men believed it was important to have a broad education in the humanities. Today many educators emphasize the importance of specialized study. What are the strengths of each position?
3. "The printing press was the most important invention of the Renaissance period." Do you agree or disagree with this statement? Why?

12

"Scripture alone, faith alone, grace alone"

THE REFORMATION

William Farel, John Calvin, Theodore Beza, and John Knox: Wall of the Reformers Monument, Geneva, Switzerland

On November 10, 1483, in the mining town of Eisleben located in the heart of Germany, a son was born to Hans and Margaretta Luther. Before this boy had reached the age of ten, European explorers had sailed to the southern tip of Africa and had landed in the New World. The age of exploration and discovery had begun. Meanwhile, the Renaissance was flourishing in Italy and was beginning to spread to northern Europe. Throughout Europe a spirit of nationalism was stirring. Men busied themselves in much religious activity; even so, there was little true godliness.

This was the age in which the young Martin Luther grew up. This son of German peasants became one of the leading figures of the sixteenth century. Through God's leading he initiated the Protestant Reformation and was an outspoken leader during its early years. This religious movement began during the early sixteenth century as a protest against the corruption in the Roman Catholic Church. Luther and other Protestant reformers exposed the false doctrines of Catholicism, such as the equal authority of tradition and Scripture, papal infallibility, and indulgences (the sale of grace to obtain heaven), that had clouded God's Word for centuries. The reformers reasserted biblical truth and the authority of the Word of God. Through their efforts and the moving of God in the hearts of men, Europe experienced a great spiritual awakening. The hold of the Roman Catholic Church on the populace was broken, and many Protestant churches came into existence.

Martin Luther nails his Ninety-Five Theses on the door of the castle church in Wittenberg, Germany

I. Forerunners

The spiritual revival that swept across Europe during the sixteenth century was the culmination of centuries of activity. For many generations men had attempted to curb the abuses in the church. Most reforming efforts, however, were directed only against its most visible evils. Only a few men recognized the need for doctrinal purity and deeper moral reform. Attempting to stir inward reform, they attacked the church's corrupt teaching as well as its corrupt practices. These brave men held to the Bible as the sole authority for the Christian faith. Asserting that Christ was the only head of the church, they rejected the authority of the pope. God used these stalwarts of the Faith to prepare the way for the later reformers of the Reformation Era.

John Wycliffe

One of the strongest voices of protest against the wickedness in the Roman church came from the Englishman **John Wycliffe** (WIK lif; 1320?–84). Wycliffe was a fearless preacher, a distinguished scholar, and a patriotic leader. Long associated with the University of Oxford, he earned fame as a teacher, lecturer, and theologian. Nevertheless, it is for his work as a religious reformer that he is best remembered. Because many of his convictions and teachings were later embraced by the sixteenth-century reformers, he has been called the Morning Star of the Reformation.

From his study of the Bible, Wycliffe became convinced that the church as it had come to be dominated by Roman Catholicism had strayed from its original purity both in doctrine and practice. Through sermons, lectures, and writings, he opposed the temporal power and wealth of the Roman church. He sought to purge the church of its corrupt clergy. Wycliffe denounced monastic orders, criticized the practice of confessing sins to a priest, and denied the doctrine of transubstantiation (the belief that during the Holy Eucharist the bread and wine are transformed into the actual body and blood of Christ).

John Wycliffe

English people, in spite of persecutions for heresy, persisted in gathering secretly to read Wycliffe's English Bible.

Detail of The Reading of Wycliffe's English Bible *by George Clausen*

Palace of Westminister Collection

He, as well as other Englishmen of his day, resented the claims of the papacy upon the church in England. But Wycliffe went a step further than his countrymen in proclaiming the papacy to be an institution "full of poison." He preached Christ as the only head of the church. The pope, he said, "is not the head, life or root except perchance of evildoers in the church." He called the pope "the antichrist" and "the leader of the army of the devil."

Wycliffe upheld the Bible as the supreme authority for all believers, clergy as well as laity. He believed that every Christian should study the Bible and that God's Word is the only source of spiritual truth and the only accurate presentation of the way of salvation. Wycliffe contended that a knowledge of Scripture would expose the error in the practice and teaching of the Roman Catholic Church and would start true reform. For this reason, he initiated the translation of the Bible from Latin into English so that more people could discover the truths found in Scripture. This first complete English translation of the Bible—known as the Wycliffe Bible—was finished in 1382. Wycliffe also trained men, mostly laymen, to preach the gospel. By groups of twos, these servants of the Lord, barefoot and clad in coarse garments, went out with staffs in hand (a symbol of their pastoral office) to live and preach among the people.

Wycliffe's reforming efforts met with stiff opposition. Church leaders sought to suppress his teaching, which they condemned as heretical. In 1384 Wycliffe died from a stroke, but his death did not end the persecution. For more than a century after his death, the church attempted to completely eradicate his teaching and followers in England. Many of his followers, known as **Lollards**, were imprisoned, tortured, and burned at the stake.

John Huss

The flame of truth could not be extinguished. Wycliffe's views soon spread to the Continent (mainland Europe), where they influenced the Bohemian reformer **John Huss** (1369?–1415). From the city of Prague, Huss challenged the Bohemian people to oppose the worldliness in the church. Huss, who taught and defended many of Wycliffe's beliefs, was accused by church leaders of spreading heresy. Though excommunicated, he remained steadfast in his beliefs and continued to be a popular preacher.

In 1414 church leaders met in the city of Constance to settle the pressing disputes over the papal schism (see p. 250) and church reform. Sigismund, the Holy Roman Emperor, wishing to settle the question of heresy in Bohemia, summoned Huss to the **Council of Constance**, giving him a promise of imperial protection. Huss traveled to Constance expecting to have opportunity to defend his teaching from the Word of God. But soon after his arrival, church leaders had him imprisoned and placed on trial for teaching heresy. Not shown from God's Word that he was in error, Huss refused to renounce his beliefs. In spite of the emperor's promise of protection, the council condemned him to die at the stake.

The day of execution came, and Huss was led to the stake. Moments before the fire was kindled, he was asked to **recant** (renounce his beliefs) and thereby save his life. He responded, "I shall die with joy today in the faith of the gospel which I have preached." Although the flames ended his earthly life, his influence remained strong, and the work for reform continued. His Bohemian brethren, stirred by his death, vigorously adhered to his teaching despite increased persecution by the Roman church.

The same council that condemned Huss to death also reexamined the writings of Wycliffe. The Roman church formally condemned Wycliffe as a heretic on 260 different counts and ordered his writings to be burned. His enemies at the council also ordered his body to be dug up and burned—an act that supposedly signified his condemnation to hell. More than a decade passed, however, before this order was carried out. In 1428, forty-four years after his death, Wycliffe's bones were dug up and burned. His ashes were thrown into a nearby stream.

The Roman church seemingly triumphed over Wycliffe and Huss. Both men had called attention to the deplorable condition of the church; neither, however, had been able to initiate any widespread or lasting reform. In the providence of God, the time was not yet ripe. The task of breaking the grip of the Roman church was left for a later generation. Nevertheless, these "reformers before the Reformation" faithfully stood for truth and boldly opposed the errors of Roman Catholicism. In doing so, they prepared the way for the Protestant Reformation.

This rock marks the place where Huss was burned at the stake.

Chaucer and Wycliffe

In *The Canterbury Tales* Geoffrey Chaucer, a contemporary of John Wycliffe, ridicules the clergy of his day. His description of a monk and a friar displays the popular contempt for the selfish desires and worldly interests of many members of the clergy. In contrast to these examples of religious hypocrisy, Chaucer presents the tale of a town parson who is materially poor but rich in true godliness.

A good man was there of religion,
And a poor PARSON OF A TOWN,
But rich he was of holy thought and work.
He was also a learned man, a clerk,
That Christ's gospel truly would preach;
His parisshens devoutly would he teach.

This noble ensample to his sheep he gave,
That first he wrought, and afterward he taught.
Out of the gospel he the words caught,
And this figure he added eke thereto,
That if gold rust, what shall iron do?
For if a priest be foul, on whom we trust,
No wonder is a lewed [ordinary] man to rust.

To drawen folk to heaven by fairness,
By good ensample, this was his business.
But it were any person obstinate,
What so he were, of high or low estate,
Him would he snybben sharply for the nonys.
A better priest I trowe that nowhere none is.
He waited after no pomp and reverence,
He maked him a spiced conscience,
But Christ's lore and his apostles twelve
He taught, but first he followed it himself.

Section Quiz

1. What Englishman's protest against the Roman church prior to the Reformation period earned him the title Morning Star of the Reformation?
2. What did this "pre-reformer" uphold as the supreme authority for all believers? What great work did he do in order to expose the corruption of the Roman church to the English people?
3. What English author presented contrasting views of the clergy of his day—the hypocrisy of a wealthy, worldly monk with the godliness of a poor town parson? What was the title of his work?
4. What city is associated with the life and ministry of John Huss?
5. What council condemned Huss to be burned at the stake? What other man did this council condemn as a heretic?

1. ____________________
2. ____________________
____
____
3. ____________________
____
4. ____________________
5. ____________________
____

Cranach, Lucas the Elder (1472–1553).
Portrait of Martin Luther.
Germanisches Nationalmuseum, Nuremberg, Germany

II. Beginning

The name **Martin Luther** is inseparably linked to the Reformation period. His courageous stand against the Roman Catholic Church sparked the religious upheaval known as the Protestant Reformation.

Luther's Early Life

Strict discipline characterized Martin Luther's early training both at home and at school. At the age of eighteen he entered the University of Erfurt, where he became acquainted with both Scholastic and classical studies. It was also at the university that he saw a complete Bible for the first time.

After graduation Luther planned to obey the wishes of his father and prepare for a legal career. But these plans, as well as the course of his life, changed suddenly during the summer of 1505. While returning to Erfurt after a visit with his parents, Luther was caught outside in a violent thunderstorm. When a lightning bolt struck nearby, Luther, thinking himself near death, cried out in terror, "Saint Anne, help me! I will become a monk." To the shock of his parents and friends, Luther remained true to his vow. Soon after returning to Erfurt, he entered an Augustinian monastery.

Luther spent his days in the monastery zealously performing good works, which he hoped would earn him his salvation. In 1507 he was ordained a priest. A few years later he was made professor of Bible at the newly formed university at Wittenberg and became a pastor of the town church. Though a respected monk, pastor, and teacher, he was filled with doubt and despair over his own salvation. How could he, a sinner, stand before a just and holy God? His good works offered no relief from his burden of guilt and sin. Through his study of Scripture, however, Luther soon discovered that no amount of good works could justify a sinner before God; justification was by faith alone. Luther later described his spiritual awakening:

> Night and day I pondered until I saw the connection between the justice of God and the statement that "the just shall live by faith" [Rom. 1:17]. Then I grasped that the justice of God is that righteousness by which through grace and sheer mercy God justifies us through faith. Thereupon I felt myself to be reborn and to have gone through open doors into paradise. The whole of Scripture took on a new meaning, and whereas before the "justice of God" had filled me with hate, now it became to me inexpressibly sweet in greater love. This passage of Paul became to me a gate to heaven.[1]

This doctrine transformed Luther's life, and to the day of his death, it was the heart of his preaching. ***Sola fide*** (justification by faith alone) became the rallying cry of the Reformation movement.

Controversy

In 1514 Pope **Leo X** (1513–21) launched a campaign to complete the rebuilding of St. Peter's Basilica in Rome. Because of the lavish spending of the Renaissance popes, the papal treasury was drained of funds. In order to raise the needed money, Leo sent out agents to sell certificates of **indulgences**, which, according to Catholicism, granted pardon from the punishment of sins. In 1517 one of these agents, a Dominican friar named **Johann Tetzel**, began selling indulgences near Luther's parish at Wittenberg. People flocked to see Tetzel, believing they could purchase forgiveness for sins. He told them that by buying an indulgence a person could free a relative from suffering in purgatory. He is said to have preached, "As soon as a coin in the coffer rings, right then a soul from purgatory springs." Martin Luther had concluded that salvation was God's free gift and detested the exploitation of his people in the name of religion. From his pulpit he railed against the abuses accompanying the sale of indulgences.

Raphael (1483–1520). Pope Leo X Medici (1475–1521) with cardinals Giulio de Medici (later Pope Clement VII, 1478–1534), and Luigi de Rossi, 1517.

Oil on wood. Inv. Galleria Palatina 40. Uffizi, Florence, Italy

Leo X's issuance of indulgences was nothing new for the Roman church. For centuries, popes had granted certificates of pardon. It was the position of the Roman church that although Christ died to save men from hell, they still had to do penance or suffer in purgatory as punishment for their individual sins. The popes maintained that they had the power to suspend these punishments for specific individuals. This practice rested in the theory that the saints did more good works than necessary to get themselves into heaven. Their "excess works," along with the merits of Christ's perfect life, were to be collected in a type of bank, the **treasury of saints**. (The theory of gaining heaven by merit and thus having excess or extra to place in a bank used for salvation is Roman Catholic tradition and not rooted in biblical teaching.) The pope served as "treasurer" and could dispense these extra good works. At first, popes granted indulgences only to those people who performed some special work, such as giving money to charity or fighting on a crusade. However, by the time of the Renaissance, popes were selling indulgences to raise money for their own projects. This is one of the extra-biblical practices which drove Luther to produce his Ninety-five Theses, questions for Rome to answer.

Though Tetzel's methods were scandalous, his cash boxes overflowed with money for Leo's building program. Nevertheless, there were a few sincere church members who questioned the practice of selling indulgences. They wondered why the pope, if he were truly the keeper of the treasury of saints, did not give these merits out freely to all, or why, if he could pardon one soul from purgatory, he did not pardon everyone. Luther raised these same questions. He had been dismayed to find that members of his congregation who had purchased indulgences were unwilling to change their wicked ways. Concern for the spiritual well-being of his parishioners prompted Luther's protests. His opposition to the sale of indulgences shook all of Christendom.

Luther's Break with Rome

The Ninety-five Theses

On **October 31, 1517**, Martin Luther, dressed in his professor's gown, stood outside the castle church in Wittenberg, Germany. On the church's wooden door, which served as a kind of public bulletin board for the university and town, he posted a lengthy document. It contained a list of ninety-five theses, or statements, concerning the sale of indulgences, which Luther proposed as topics for a scholarly debate. Little did he realize he would stir up a great controversy. Almost overnight the **Ninety-five Theses** became a symbol of defiance against the corruption and hypocrisy of Rome. By questioning indulgences, Luther inadvertently—but providentially—challenged the whole system of Roman Catholicism.

Wittenberg Castle church where Luther nailed his Ninety-five Theses

The hammer blows that nailed Luther's protest to the church door rang throughout Germany. Within weeks, printed copies of his Ninety-five Theses circulated widely in Germany and received a sympathetic welcome among the people. Many of them were disgusted with Tetzel's evil ways; others looked for an occasion to stop the flow of German money into the papal coffers at Rome. Indulgence sales dropped off sharply, a fact that angered Tetzel and upset church officials. They denounced Luther as a heretic and urged the people to take action against him. At first Pope Leo X refused to get involved in what he considered a minor quarrel among monks. But when funds stopped coming in for St. Peter's Basilica, he was prompted to action.

The Leipzig Debate

Opponents of Luther, thinking him to be nothing more than an ignorant and misguided monk, sought to engage him in debates in order to show him the error of his ways. But Luther, armed by years of diligent study of the Scriptures and guided by the Spirit of God, was more than their match. The climax of this confrontation occurred in the debate at Leipzig (LIPE sig) during the summer of 1519. Here Luther met the formidable scholar **Johann Eck**, a champion of Catholicism. The three-week debate centered on the question of authority in the church. Luther asserted that the pope had human rather than divine authority and that he could err just as any other man. The great reformer insisted that Scripture was the only reliable authority. Eck charged that Luther was holding views similar to those of John Huss, whom the Council of Constance had condemned as a heretic a century earlier. In response Luther maintained that not all of Huss's teachings were heretical—a position that led him to the conclusion that even church councils might err.

The Leipzig debate only widened the breach between Luther and Rome. Luther had entered the debate believing himself to be a good Roman Catholic; in his mind all he had done was to call attention to a few corrupt practices that other sincere Catholics had found equally offensive. But because he renounced the authority of popes and councils, he was driven to the Scriptures for guidance. He soon became even more firmly convinced that the Bible alone is the sole authority for the Christian faith.

In the months that followed, Luther wrote a series of pamphlets intended to rouse the German people to action. He wanted them to take a stand against the corrupt Roman system. Because the papacy failed to take the initiative, he called upon civil rulers to reform the church. He attacked the sacramental system of the church, stating that it distorted the true meaning of salvation. He maintained that every believer was a priest and that each had the freedom to approach God personally through faith (Eph. 2:18; 1 Pet. 2:9).

The Road to Worms

The pope was unable to take serious action against Luther. One reason for this was that Luther was the subject of one of the most respected and powerful territorial princes in all of Germany, Frederick the Wise, Elector of Saxony. Frederick opposed the idea of having any of his subjects stand trial outside of Germany—especially if that trial were to take place in Italy.

In June of 1520, the pope finally heeded the counsel of his advisers. He issued a papal bull that condemned Luther for advancing heretical doctrines and gave him sixty days to recant. If he did not do so, he would be excommuni-

Luther's Trip to Rome

In the fall of 1510, while still a monk, Luther traveled to Rome on business for the Augustinian order. He had eagerly anticipated the trip; in Rome there would be many opportunities to visit sacred shrines and venerate relics of the saints. Luther considered Rome a holy city—a place where he could draw closer to God.

What he found, however, deeply disturbed him. Renaissance Rome was a city given over to wickedness. Even church leaders indulged in sins of every kind. Prostitution and other forms of sexual immorality flourished. Greed and ambition controlled the actions of both clergy and laity. During his visit Luther encountered stories of how Pope Alexander VI (1492–1503) had used treachery and murder to accomplish his purposes.

St. Peter's Basilica in Rome

As a reformer, Luther used his experiences in Rome and other cities to illustrate the corruption of the Roman Catholic Church. On one occasion in 1537 Luther told a group of friends, "I wouldn't have missed being in Rome for a great deal of money. I wouldn't have believed it if I hadn't seen it for myself. For so great and shameless is the godlessness and wickedness there that neither God nor man, neither sin nor disgrace are taken seriously. All godly persons who've been there testify of this, and this is the witness of all the ungodly who have returned from Italy worse than they had been before."[2]

cated. At a public gathering near the city gate of Wittenberg, Luther responded to the pope's ultimatum; he ceremoniously tossed the papal bull into a bonfire. By this act he sealed his separation from Rome. As expected, a few weeks later he was formally excommunicated from the Roman church.

The newly crowned German emperor, **Charles V**, sensing Luther's strong public support, refused to condemn him without a hearing. In the spring of 1521 he summoned Luther to the city of Worms [VOHRMS] to appear before the German Diet. The emperor gave Luther the promise of imperial protection to and from Worms, but Luther's friends reminded him of what had happened to John Huss in a similar situation. Despite their warnings, Luther proceeded to Worms to defend the truth before the imperial Diet.

On the afternoon of April 17, 1521, Luther stood before the emperor, princes, and bishops of the Holy Roman Empire at the **Diet of Worms**. He was given no chance to defend his teaching. Instead he was simply asked whether a number of books lying on a table in front of him were his writings and whether he would recant the heresy contained in them. To the first question Luther answered yes; to the second, he asked for time to consider his answer. On the next day the questions were again put to him, and he was asked to give a clear and simple reply. With firmness of conviction, he gave his memorable declaration:

> Unless I am convinced by the testimony of the Scriptures or by clear reason (for I do not trust either in the pope or in councils alone, since it is well known that they have often erred and contradicted themselves), I am bound by the Scriptures I have quoted and my conscience is captive to the Word of God. I cannot and I will not retract anything, since it is neither safe nor right to go against conscience. I cannot do otherwise; here I stand, may God help me. Amen.

THROUGH EYES OF FAITH

Standing for Truth

As Luther faced intense controversy he no doubt faced the temptation to compromise what he viewed as scriptural truth. How should you view confrontation with error when you are convinced from Scripture that what you are defending is true?

____

____

____

____

____

____

After the Diet of Worms, Luther stayed a few months at Wartburg Castle, taking the name Junker Jörg (Knight George).

Dürer, Albrecht (1471–1528). Philipp Melanchthon. 1526
Engraving. Graphische Sammlung, Kunstmuseum, Düsseldorf, Germany

Luther left the city. The emperor soon afterwards issued an edict declaring Luther an outlaw of the empire. He banned Luther's writings, forbade anyone to give him aid, and demanded that he be seized and turned over to the authorities. If captured, Luther was to suffer the fate of a condemned heretic—death. God, however, was not through with this man. Luther lived for twenty-five years under the imperial edict and died a natural death in 1546. During these years the truth of God's Word, which he so boldly defended, took root in the hearts and lives of men and women all over Europe.

Progress in Germany

Continuation of Luther's Work

Despite the Edict of Worms, the doctrines of the Reformation continued to spread rapidly. They were proclaimed from pulpits, heralded from street corners, and circulated in printed pamphlets. Perhaps the greatest help to the reforming cause in Germany was Luther's translation of the New Testament (and later the whole Bible) into German. This work, based upon Erasmus's Greek New Testament, created widespread enthusiasm for the Bible among all classes of German people. The power and beauty of its expression helped to create a standard German language for all Germany.

Luther's work did not stop with his translation of the Bible. In order to make the principles of the Reformation so clear that even a child could understand them, he wrote his *Shorter Catechism.* In question-and-answer form, this catechism gives instruction in the fundamental doctrines of Scripture. Luther also used music as a means of teaching the gospel. He urged the people to sing doctrinal hymns at home, work, and church. His own hymn, "A Mighty Fortress Is Our God," called the "victory hymn of the Reformation," is one of the best-known and most-loved hymns of the Christian church.

As the followers of Luther's teaching increased in number, it soon became necessary to frame an official statement of Lutheran beliefs. In 1530 **Philipp Melanchthon**, Luther's close friend and coworker, drew up the **Augsburg Confession**, which clearly sets forth the chief doctrines for which Luther and his followers contended. This document became the doctrinal standard for the Lutheran Church and has remained that church's most highly respected statement of faith.

Preoccupation of Charles V

One reason for the rapid spread of Lutheran doctrine was Charles V's preoccupation with the political affairs of Europe. Charles, the crowned ruler of the Holy Roman Empire, was also the ruler by inheritance of the Hapsburg possessions of Spain, Sicily, Naples, the Netherlands, and Austria, plus territory in the New World. His vast holdings gave him great power, but many problems as well. He was constantly defending the borders of his far-flung possessions, putting down revolts, and repelling invasions.

Between the years 1522 and 1546, Charles fought several wars with his chief rival, **Francis I**, the king of France. The French king was particularly concerned that his country was encircled by Charles's possessions. Meanwhile, Charles was faced with another threat. The Ottoman Turks, led by **Suleiman** (1520–66), invaded the eastern portion of his empire. By the early 1540s Charles had halted the Turkish advance and had signed a truce with the French king. He could now turn his attention to the religious situation in the German states. But over twenty years had elapsed since the Diet of Worms. Lutheranism was firmly established.

In 1546, the year of Luther's death, Charles began his attack on the German Protestants. For nearly nine years his imperial and pro-Catholic forces waged war against the anti-imperial and Protestant forces of German princes. In 1555 a compromise settlement was finally reached in the **Peace of Augsburg**. It allowed each prince the right to choose whether his territory would be Lutheran or Roman Catholic. The people within a given territory had to either accept the choice of their prince or move elsewhere. The peace only postponed the religious and political problems in Germany; in 1618 war would break out once again.

Titian (Tiziano Vecellio) (c. 1488–1576). Charles V.
Alte Pinakothek, Munich, Germany

Section Quiz

1. What pope launched a fundraising drive to rebuild St. Peter's Basilica? What did his agents sell in order to raise the needed money?
2. What did Luther post on the door of the castle church in Wittenburg? Give the day, month, and year in which this event took place.
3. At the Leipzig debate, Eck charged that Luther was holding views similar to what earlier reformer? What conclusion did Luther reach as a result of this debate?
4 To what city was Luther summoned to appear before the princes, bishops, and emperor of the Holy Roman Empire? Who was the emperor who presided over the assembly?
5. What settlement ended the civil war that broke out among the Catholic and Protestant princes of Germany? What compromise was reached by this settlement?

1. ____________________

____

2. ____________________

____

3. ____________________

____

____

4. ____________________

____

5. ____________________

____

____

____

____

____

III. Spread

The Protestant Reformation was not confined to the land of Germany. Nor was Luther its only leader. God raised up reformers in many lands who protested the abuses of Roman Catholicism and sought to restore biblical Christianity. Though the reformers often differed on matters of biblical interpretation, they were in agreement with the key doctrines of the Reformation movement: "Scripture alone, faith alone, grace alone!"

Switzerland

Switzerland was one of the first places outside Germany to feel the influence of the Protestant Reformation. The Swiss Confederation began in 1291

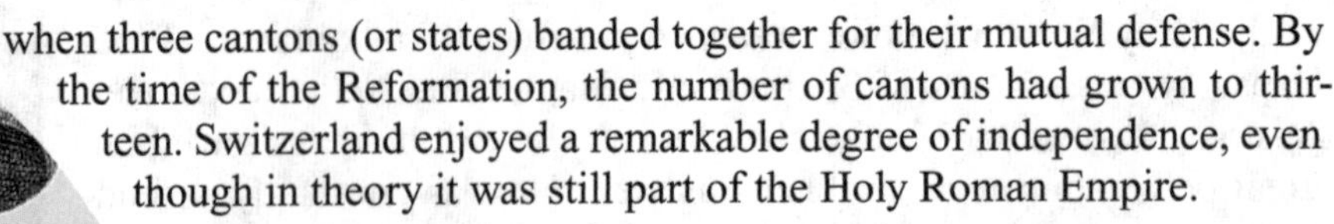

when three cantons (or states) banded together for their mutual defense. By the time of the Reformation, the number of cantons had grown to thirteen. Switzerland enjoyed a remarkable degree of independence, even though in theory it was still part of the Holy Roman Empire.

Zwingli in Zurich

An early leader of the Swiss Reformation was **Ulrich Zwingli** (ZWING lee). He was born in 1484 in a small village in the northern German-speaking region of Switzerland. He studied at several leading universities, where he developed a keen interest in the classics. His training acquainted him with Erasmus, under whose influence he began to study the Bible. As a young man, Zwingli was ordained a Roman Catholic priest. Early in his ministry, however, he realized that there was corruption in the Roman church. He soon became an outspoken critic of its abusive practices. In 1519 Zwingli became the priest of the largest church in Zurich, one of the leading towns in the Swiss Confederation.

Ulrich Zwingli

While in Zurich, Zwingli was exposed to Luther's writings for the first time. Through Luther, he came to understand that salvation comes only by the grace of God through faith. With the support of the Zurich city council, Zwingli began to make significant changes in his church. These changes aroused Roman Catholic opposition, but Zwingli ably defended his position at several public debates. For one such occasion, he drew up his *Sixty-seven Conclusions*. These articles, similar in style to Luther's Ninety-five Theses, set forth Zwingli's belief in the Bible as the sole rule of faith. He rejected Roman Catholic teaching concerning the mass, celibacy of priests, purgatory, and the primacy of the pope. He declared that Christ is the only way to salvation—that He alone is the eternal high priest, the only mediator between God and man.

Although Zwingli had received a great amount of enlightenment through reading Luther's writings, he disagreed with Luther's view of the Lord's Supper. In an effort to create a united Protestant front and to settle their doctrinal differences, Zwingli and Luther met at Marburg, Germany, in October of 1529. Both men were in general agreement on the doctrines of the Trinity, the person of Jesus Christ, the work of the Holy Spirit, justification by faith, original sin, and baptism. However, at this meeting Zwingli maintained that the Lord's Supper is only a symbolic remembrance of Christ's death. Luther, on the other

The Term *Protestant*

The term *Protestant* dates back to the early days of the Reformation. In April of 1529 representatives of the German states gathered in the city of Speyer to discuss the religious situation in Germany. At that meeting the Roman Catholic majority attempted to halt the progress of the Reformation, hoping to eventually suppress it altogether. They passed an edict which, among other things, required the Lutheran princes to guarantee the religious liberty of Roman Catholics living under their rule. At the same time, however, Roman Catholic princes could deny religious liberty to Lutherans living in their territories. The Lutheran princes opposed the entire edict, stating that they would "protest and testify publicly before God" that they would agree with "nothing contrary to His Word." It is from their courageous protest that the word *Protestant* comes. Today the term refers to anyone who holds to the biblical teachings of the Reformation in opposition to Roman Catholicism.

hand, believed that in the Lord's Supper, Christ is literally present *in, with,* and *under* the elements of bread and wine. (Non-Lutherans call this view *consubstantiation.*) Neither reformer would change his mind, and so after three days of discussion the conference ended without resolving the issue.

Zwingli did not live long after this meeting. Civil war broke out in Switzerland between the cantons that embraced Protestantism and those that remained Roman Catholic. In 1531 Zurich went to war against some neighboring Catholic districts. Zwingli accompanied the troops as a chaplain and was killed at the Battle of Kappel as he sought to aid a wounded soldier. Others carried on Zwingli's reforms in Zurich. Some of his followers joined the ranks of the Lutherans, while others merged with the followers of another famous reformer, John Calvin.

The Anabaptists

Although Zwingli and his followers dominated the religious and political life of Zurich, there were those who were not satisfied with his reforms. Some of them met together in 1525 and organized their own congregation, calling themselves the Swiss Brethren. Among other things, these men opposed the practice of infant baptism. All those who joined their ranks and who had been baptized as infants were rebaptized. For this reason their enemies called them **Anabaptists** (from a Greek word which means "baptize again"). The Swiss Brethren did not call themselves "rebaptizers" because they did not believe infant baptism to be valid in the first place. When the city council tried to force the Zurich Anabaptists to conform to the religious practices of the city, the men refused to change their beliefs. Persecution followed. Some of them were imprisoned, others fled the city, and several were martyred.

Other groups that opposed infant baptism sprang up in Europe. These various religious bodies were grouped under the common title "Anabaptist," even though on other issues they were often in sharp disagreement. Some Anabaptists had revolutionary ideas and twisted Scripture to support their false doctrines. Others wanted nothing more than to be left in peace to worship God freely and to study His Word. Because of the wrongdoing of a few, however, all Anabaptists had a bad reputation. The apostle Paul reminds us in the New Testament that if we are not careful to guard our actions, we can bring reproach upon the "name of God" (1 Tim. 6:1) and upon the "word of God" (Titus 2:5).

In spite of their wide differences, most Anabaptist groups held certain beliefs in common. For instance, most believed that only true believers should be members in the local church. In most areas of Europe at this time all the inhabitants of a particular community were considered church members regardless of their spiritual condition. Second, most Anabaptists believed in the separation of church and state—that is, they rejected state interference in their affairs. In addition, many of them believed it was wrong for Christians to hold political office. Third, many Anabaptists believed that a Christian should not take up arms against anyone, even in time of war. This belief is called **pacifism**.

Unfortunately, many of the early Anabaptists also questioned the doctrine of justification by faith alone. They feared that this teaching might encourage people to think that justification apart from good works allowed them to sin as much as they wanted and still have forgiveness from God. These Anabaptists did not understand, as most of the other reformers did, that the Bible teaches that justification—although by faith without works (Gal. 3:11; Eph. 2:8–9)—always results in good works in the life of the justified believer (Eph. 2:10).

Most of the Anabaptist groups died out. However, the Mennonites, founded by Menno Simons, and the Amish, founded in the seventeenth century by Jacob Amman, have continued to the present day.

Calvin at Geneva

The most famous and influential Protestant reformer after Martin Luther was **John Calvin**. He was born in 1509 in northwestern France. As a young man, he studied both law and theology at the universities of Orléans, Bourges, and Paris. Since the Reformation was in full swing during Calvin's student days, Luther's ideas were undoubtedly being discussed at the French universities. From his later writings, it is evident that Calvin diligently searched the Scriptures during these years to determine the validity of Reformation doctrine. Sometime around 1533 Calvin was converted and became a Protestant.

His* Institutes**—About a year after Calvin's conversion, the king of France intensified his persecution of French Protestants. Calvin fled his native land and sought refuge in the Swiss city of Basel, where he finished one of the most significant and influential books on theology ever written. ***The Institutes of the Christian Religion, published in 1536 when Calvin was just twenty-six, sets forth Christian doctrine in a systematic outline.

At the heart of Calvin's system of theology is his strong belief in the sovereignty of God. Calvin believed that God "predestines" all things according to His own will. As the sovereign Creator of the universe, God foreordains or predestines who will be saved (the elect). Everything God does is for His glory, although finite man does not understand God's ways.

His Years at Geneva—In 1536, while returning from a visit to France, Calvin stopped for the night at the beautiful city of Geneva in the French-speaking part of Switzerland. He intended to spend only one night there, but God had other plans. The Protestants of Geneva asked Calvin to stay and become their pastor and teacher. Though he was hesitant at first, he finally agreed, taking up the work of the Reformation that others had already begun in the city.

Calvin applied his teaching concerning God's sovereignty to everyday life in Geneva. He sought to build a Christian community based upon the Word of God. Taking the Bible, especially the Old Testament, as his law book, Calvin made sure that the city statutes conformed to scriptural teaching. He stressed the independence of church and state, but he believed that both were subject

Cathedral of St. Peter in Geneva where Calvin preached

to the rule of God. He asserted that the duty of the state was to promote piety, punish evildoers, and assist the church by providing an atmosphere that would encourage godliness in the lives of church members. The Geneva city council adopted his teaching and issued orders forbidding dancing, drunkenness, and gambling and requiring everyone to attend church services. Opposition mounted to Calvin's strict discipline, however, and in 1538 the city council banished him. Later, problems in Geneva prompted the city to beg Calvin to return and become their spiritual leader once again. In 1541 Calvin returned; he remained there until his death in 1564.

Under Calvin's leadership, the city of Geneva became a leading center of the Protestant Reformation. Calvin's influence, however, reached far beyond Geneva. During his lifetime, many Protestants who had fled Catholic persecution in other countries came to Geneva for protection. Others came to study Calvin's theology. As they returned to their native lands, they passed Calvin's ideas on to others. Many Protestant churches adopted Calvin's system of theology, calling themselves the Reformed churches. This name is still widely used today.

John Calvin

England

Cries for reform had echoed in England since the days of John Wycliffe. His persecuted followers, the Lollards, opposed papal tyranny and preached the authority of the Word of God. During the sixteenth century, efforts for reform intensified in England as Luther's writings were widely circulated and read. The English Reformation, which did not have a dominant leader like Luther or Calvin, was influenced by two important factors.

The first factor was *the publication of English translations of the Bible.* One cannot overemphasize the importance that the Word of God had in bringing about spiritual revival in Europe. The Bible itself instructs us that "faith cometh by hearing, and hearing by the word of God" (Rom. 10:17). During the late fifteenth and early sixteenth centuries, the Bible was translated and printed in the native languages of almost every European country. In England a number of versions of the Bible were published and distributed. These were translated from the ancient tongues into the common language of the English people. A readable, understandable Bible helped increase knowledge of God's Word and helped show the English people (as it did people in other lands) the extra-biblical teaching of the Roman Catholic Church.

The second factor was *the involvement of the English rulers*. The English Reformation began as a political movement under the direction of the English crown. During the sixteenth century, members of the **Tudor family** occupied the throne. There were five Tudor rulers in all: Henry VII, the founder of this royal line; his son Henry VIII; and Henry VIII's three children—Edward VI, Mary I, and Elizabeth I. Under the Tudors, England broke with the papacy—the authority of the pope over the church in England was no longer recognized. For the most part, the English people supported the crown. They were filled with national pride and resented the claims of a foreign pope on their land. At first the majority of Englishmen remained in the Roman Catholic Church. But a growing number became increasingly dissatisfied with Rome and embraced Protestantism. Political motives gradually gave way to spiritual concerns as the truth of God's Word found acceptance in the hearts of a growing number of English people.

Holbein, Hans the Younger (1497–1543). Portrait of Henry VIII, King of England. 1540
Galleria Nazionale d'Arte Antica, Rome, Italy

The Break with Rome Under Henry VIII

King **Henry VIII** (1509–47) was on the throne of England when the Protestant Reformation began in Germany. He branded Martin Luther a heretic and wrote a book attacking Luther's teaching. The pope promptly proclaimed Henry "Defender of the Faith." Nevertheless, Henry later broke with Rome also, though not for the same reasons that motivated Luther. Henry wanted to divorce his wife Catherine of Aragon, the daughter of Ferdinand and Isabella of Spain. Catherine had been married to Henry's older brother, who had died soon after the wedding. Contrary to church doctrine, the pope permitted Henry to marry Catherine. Because she had borne him no sons to continue the Tudor line, Henry said that he had sinned and that God was punishing him (see Lev. 20:21).

The pope, not wishing to offend Catherine's nephew, the powerful emperor Charles V, refused to grant Henry the divorce. Therefore, Henry decided to take matters into his own hands. He appointed a new archbishop of Canterbury, **Thomas Cranmer**, who declared Henry's marriage to Catherine invalid and legalized his new marriage to Anne Boleyn. In 1534, Henry had Parliament pass the Act of Supremacy, which made the king the "supreme head" of the church in England. This act completed the break between England and the papacy. It also placed the English church under the direct control of the state. Even so, during Henry's day, the English church remained true to Roman teaching and practice.

Protestant Gains Under Edward VI

When Henry VIII died in 1547, his son **Edward VI** succeeded him to the throne. Edward, a frail boy, was only nine years old when he became king. He was strongly influenced by his advisers, who were sympathetic to the Protestant Reformation. As a result, sweeping changes were made in the English church. Parliamentary acts legalized the marriage of clergymen, abolished many Catholic ceremonies, and required church services to be in English rather than in Latin. In addition, the clergy were required to use the *Book of Common Prayer* in their churches. This prayer book was drawn up by Thomas Cranmer, who had become a leading voice of Protestantism in England. It contains Bible readings and prayers for special occasions and also prescribes orders of worship for various church services.

The statement of faith known as the *Forty-two Articles* reveals the extent of Protestant gains during Edward's reign. Formulated by Cranmer and issued by Edward, it became the official creed of the English church. The document sets forth the major Protestant doctrines of justifi-

Coblitz, Louis (1814-1863). After Holbein: King Edward VI of England (1537-1553).
Oil on canvas. Inv.: MV 3194. Photo Arnaudet. Chateaux de Versailles et de Trianon, Versailles, France

cation by faith alone and the sole authority of the Bible. It renounces transubstantiation and recognizes only two sacraments—baptism and the Lord's Supper.

Catholic Reaction Under Mary I

The sickly Edward died of tuberculosis at the age of sixteen (1553). His half sister Mary succeeded him to the throne. **Mary I**, the daughter of Henry VIII by Catherine of Aragon, was a devout Roman Catholic. She sought to restore Roman Catholicism to England by compelling Parliament to repeal the religious laws passed during Edward's reign. She removed several thousand clergymen from office who had Protestant sympathies or who had married.

Mor, Anthonis (1519–1576). Queen Mary of England (Mary Tudor, 1516–1558), second wife of Philip II of Spain.
Museo del Prado, Madrid, Spain

As political and religious opposition mounted against Mary's pro-Catholic policies, she revived laws against heresy and began to persecute the Protestants. Hundreds of Englishmen fled to Germany and Switzerland. Many who remained in England were imprisoned; some became martyrs at the stake. The most famous victims of Mary's persecution were two bishops, Hugh Latimer and Nicholas Ridley. They were condemned to be burned at the stake. As the fire was lit, Latimer said to Ridley, "We shall this day light such a candle, by God's grace, in England, as I trust shall never be put out." Mary next turned her fury to Thomas Cranmer, the man who had declared her mother's marriage invalid. Charged with heresy and facing death, Cranmer weakened. He signed statements renouncing his Protestant beliefs and acknowledging the authority of the pope over the church in England. Nevertheless, he was sentenced to die at the stake. On the day of his execution he publicly condemned his previous weakness and boldly reaffirmed his Protestant convictions. As the flames came up about him, he thrust the hand that had signed the recantations into the fire so that "this unworthy hand" was consumed first.

Persecution continued until Mary's death in 1558. During her five-year reign, nearly three hundred leaders were martyred. But instead of wiping out Protestantism in England, her actions only increased anti-Catholic sentiment and earned her the name Bloody Mary.

Break with Rome Confirmed Under Elizabeth

When Mary I died, her half-sister **Elizabeth I** (1558–1603) became queen. Her forty-five-year reign marks one of the greatest periods in English history. Elizabeth never married, but she was so devoted to her country that it has been said she was married to the throne of England. A strong and determined woman, she ruled England effectively during a crucial period of its history. During her long reign she was a symbol of stability and strength. The English affectionately called her Good Queen Bess.

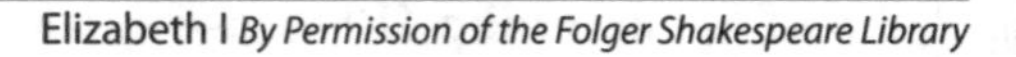

Elizabeth I *By Permission of the Folger Shakespeare Library*

History of the English Bible

To Tytus.

Salute Prisca and *Aquila/and the housholde of Onesyphorus. *Erastus abode at Corinthum. But *Trophymus lefte I sycke at Myletum. Make spede to come before wynter. Eubolus/ and Pudens/and Lynus/and Claudia/and all the brethren salute the. The Lorde Iesus Christe be with thy sprete. Grace be with you/Amen.

¶The seconde Epistle vnto Timothe/wrytten from Rome/when Paul was presented the seconde tyme before the Emperoure Nero.

The Epistle of the Apostle saynct Paul to Tytus.

¶Paul exhorteth Titus to ordeyne Bysshoppes in every cytye/declareth what maner of men they ought to be and chargeth Titus to rebuke soch as withstande the Gospell.

The fyrst Chapter.

Paul the seruaunt of God/ and an Apostle of Iesu Christ/to preache the fayth of Gods electe/ and the knowledge of the trueth/ which leadeth vnto godlynesse vpon the hope of eternall lyfe/ which God *that can not lye/ hath promysed before ye tymes of the worlde:but at thys tyme hath opened hys worde thorow preachynge/ which is commytted vnto me accordynge to the commaundement of God oure Saueour. *Vnto Tytus my naturall sonne after the commun fayth. Grace/mercy/and peace from God the father/ and from the Lorde Iesu Christ oure Saueoure.

First page of Titus from a Tyndale New Testament

The history of the English Bible begins with John Wycliffe, who believed that everyone should have the opportunity to read God's Word. In 1382 he and his followers produced the first complete English translation of the Scripture—a translation made from the Latin Vulgate. (Wycliffe did not know Hebrew or Greek.) Although the common people were eager to know what the Bible had to say, the clergy strongly opposed Wycliffe's work. The archbishop of Canterbury described Wycliffe as "the very herald and child of anti-Christ, who crowned his wickedness by translating the Scripture into the mother tongue." Nevertheless, the religious and political authorities could not destroy God's Word. Wycliffe's translation survived, and some of its wording even found its way into the Authorized (King James) Version. For example, the phrase "strait is the gate, and narrow is the way" (Matt. 7:14) and the words "beam" and "mote" (Matt. 7:3) come from Wycliffe's translation.

William Tyndale (1492–1536), an able Hebrew and Greek scholar, produced the first English Bible translated directly from the ancient biblical languages. Forced to flee his native England, Tyndale went to Germany, where his New Testament was published in 1525. The authorities in England, however, made every effort to seize or purchase these New Testaments as they were smuggled into the country. On one occasion, a London merchant who was Tyndale's friend sold numerous copies at a high price to the bishop of London. Although the bishop had the copies destroyed, Tyndale used the money he received from the

THROUGH EYES OF FAITH

English Reformation

How did God use the bad situation of Henry VIII's divorce to carry the Reformation more fully into England? What does this tell you about God's control of history?

____

____

____

____

____

____

The Church of England—Though reared a Protestant, Elizabeth favored a moderate solution to England's religious problems. She restored Protestantism to England; yet she did not totally alienate the English Roman Catholics. Like her father, she had Parliament pass an Act of Supremacy (1559) which rejected papal authority. This act affirmed the queen's position over the Church of England; however, it changed her title from "Supreme *Head*" to "Supreme *Governor*," the latter being less offensive to the Roman Catholics. Under Elizabeth, Cranmer's *Forty-two Articles* were revised to become the *Thirty-nine Articles*—another Protestant statement of faith.

The attempt by Elizabeth to settle England's religious problems through compromise is known as the **Elizabethan Settlement**. It laid the foundation for the Church of England, also known as the **Anglican Church**. This institution became the established state church of England and has as its creed the *Thirty-nine Articles*. While the Anglican Church embraced Protestant doctrines, it did not alter its church government, nor did it abolish certain established rituals that were not expressly forbidden in Scripture. The Anglican Church retained such things as clerical vestments (robes) and candles on the communion table.

War with Spain—England's shift toward Protestantism did not go unopposed by Roman Catholics outside of England. England's most formidable Catholic opponent was King Philip of Spain. **Philip II** (1556–98) was the son of the

sale to finance a better printing of the New Testament! He also managed to publish part of the Old Testament, but before he could translate and publish all of it, he was captured in Belgium. Condemned as a heretic, he was strangled and then burned at the stake.

Tyndale died, but his work was not in vain. Others used what he had done to produce new translations. A year before Tyndale died, Miles Coverdale (1488–1569) published a translation of the entire Bible. Since he did not know Greek or Hebrew, he relied heavily upon Luther's German translation, the Latin Vulgate, and Tyndale's work. Two years later one of Tyndale's friends, John Rogers, produced the so-called Matthew's Bible. (He published it under the pseudonym of Thomas Matthew.) This was not really a new translation, because Rogers simply combined parts of Coverdale's work with sections of the Old Testament that Tyndale had translated but never published. In 1539 Coverdale himself revised Matthew's Bible. When it was published it measured 16 1/2 by 11 inches and received the name Great Bible because of its size. This was the first version of the English Bible specifically authorized to be read publicly in the churches. For almost thirty years it was the only version that could be used legally in England.

Bible translation work did not cease, however. During the reign of Mary I, some of the most important Protestant leaders fled to Geneva to escape death. While there, these men produced a Bible in 1560 that contained, in their words, "most profitable annotations upon all the hard places." Known as the Geneva Bible, this was the first English version to have numbered verses. This version also used italics to indicate words that were not actually found in the Greek and Hebrew manuscripts. Within a short time, the Geneva Bible became very popular, especially among the Puritans.

In an effort to weaken the popularity of this unauthorized version, the Church of England commissioned a new translation. It came out in 1568 and became known as the Bishop's Bible. In spite of its official status, it never gained wide acceptance. The culmination of all this early translation work occurred at the beginning of the seventeenth century. King James I authorized a group of about fifty scholars to produce a new revision of the Bible. Following the king's orders, these men used the Bishop's Bible as their guide and consulted other English translations and certain Hebrew, Greek, and Latin manuscripts—especially the Greek New Testament that had been edited by Erasmus.

To make their work more efficient and to guard against errors, the translators divided themselves into six committees. Each committee was assigned a particular task. For example, one group translated Genesis through 2 Kings. Once a particular committee completed a portion of its work, it would send the portion to the others for evaluation and revision.

In 1611 the scholars delivered their work to the king's printer for publication. The King James Version was a masterpiece, but at first many people resented it. For example, the Pilgrims dogmatically rejected it. They had grown to love the familiar phraseology of the older English versions and did not want to change. But with the passage of time, this beautiful translation won the hearts of the English-speaking world.

Hapsburg emperor Charles V. When Charles abdicated in 1556, Philip became the ruler of the Hapsburg territories in Spain, the Netherlands, and the New World. One of the strongest defenders of the Roman Catholic Church, he worked hard to stamp out Protestantism. He stopped the spread of the Reformation in his realm by turning the Spanish Inquisition against the Protestants. As leader of the strongest Catholic country in the world, Philip sought to bring England back into the fold of the Roman Catholic Church.

Shortly before becoming king, Philip had married Mary I, the Roman Catholic queen of England. A child born of that union would no doubt have been reared a Roman Catholic and would have been by right the next ruler of England and Spain. But in God's providence Mary died childless, and her Protestant sister Elizabeth became queen. Philip sought to marry Elizabeth. But while he was wooing her, Elizabeth was secretly working against Spain. She encouraged her sea captains (men such as Francis Drake) to plunder Spanish ships returning with treasure from the New World. She also aided the Dutch in their revolt against the Spanish ruler.

Because Elizabeth opposed Philip's political and religious involvement in various parts of Europe, he began plotting her overthrow. He conspired to have Elizabeth killed and have her cousin Mary Stuart—the former queen of Scotland—crowned queen of England. The plot was discovered, however, and Elizabeth had Mary put in prison and later executed.

THIS MOMENT IN HISTORY

Elizabeth I

Why would the English people refer to Elizabeth as Good Queen Bess? In what ways was her reign positive for England?

____

____

____

____

____

____

Vroom, Hendrik Cornelisz. Sea battle between the Spanish Armada and English naval forces, c. 1600.
Oil on canvas. Landesmuseum Ferdinandeum, Innsbruck, Austria

Exasperated and angry, Philip decided to invade England. He amassed a great fleet of 130 ships which was to sail to the Netherlands, pick up a large Spanish army, and transport the invasion force to England. In 1588 this fleet, called by some the Invincible Armada, set sail from Spain with the pope's blessing. Philip is said to have spent hours on his knees praying for the success of his plans. But God did not hear his pleas. The large, unwieldy Spanish galleons were no match for the smaller, more maneuverable English ships, under the command of the daring Sir **Francis Drake**. The battered Spanish fleet turned north only to be overtaken by fierce storms that wrecked many Spanish vessels along the coast of Scotland and Ireland. The Invincible Armada limped back to Spain with only about half of the number of ships that it had set out.

The defeat of the **Spanish Armada** had a significant impact upon world history. First, it preserved England from both Spanish and Roman Catholic domination. Second, it accelerated the decline of Spain, which during the period of exploration had been one of the richest and strongest European countries. The battle weakened Spanish sea power and as a result weakened Spain's position in the New World. Finally, it established England as a sea power at the very time English colonial expansion was under way. The way was opened for English Protestants, instead of Spanish Catholics, to settle in America.

English Protestants acknowledged God's help in their victory. They had no doubt that the "Protestant wind" that had wrecked the Spanish fleet came from God, for "the Lord hath his way in the whirlwind and in the storm, and the clouds are the dust of his feet" (Nah. 1:3). They could agree with 2 Chronicles 16:9—a verse that applies to both individuals and nations: "The eyes of the Lord run to and fro throughout the whole earth, to shew himself strong in behalf of them whose heart is perfect toward him."

The Puritans—Though Protestantism had triumphed in England, not all Protestants were in agreement with the Church of England. Many believed that the Anglican Church retained too many of the "trappings of popery."

They wished to "purify" the church of those practices that reminded them of Roman Catholicism. Thus originated their nickname—the **Puritans**. Other Englishmen saw no hope of bringing about change in the English church. Those who removed themselves from the church were therefore known as **Separatists**. Englishmen with Catholic leanings were not satisfied with the Church of England either. They hoped to bring the Church of England back in line with Roman Catholicism.

Neither the Protestants nor the Catholics were satisfied with Elizabeth's solution to England's religious problems. As a result, England experienced much political and religious agitation during the seventeenth century.

Scotland

The leader of the Protestant Reformation in Scotland was **John Knox** (1505–72). In 1547 he was taken prisoner by the French; he served for nineteen months as a galley slave on a French ship. When released he went to England, where he became a noted preacher during the reign of Edward VI. When Mary I came to the throne, he fled to Geneva, where he was greatly influenced by John Calvin.

He returned to Scotland in 1559. Through fiery preaching, he attacked the evils of Roman Catholicism. It was said of him, "Others lop off branches, but this man strikes at the root." Under his leadership Scotland threw off Catholicism and became a Protestant nation. The Scottish parliament rejected papal authority, abolished the mass, and adopted

John Knox's house, Edinburgh, Scotland

Nursery Rhymes

According to many traditional accounts, some of the most familiar Mother Goose rhymes were written during the Reformation Era. Childhood verses such as "Jack and Jill," "Little Boy Blue," and "Little Jack Horner" were probably penned during this period. Since it was not safe at this time to be openly critical of government or church officials, rhymes were a convenient way of poking fun at those in authority. For example, "Little Miss Muffet" satirizes the relationship between John Knox and Mary Stuart.

Little Miss Muffet
Sat on a tuffet,
Eating her curds and whey;
There came a big spider,
And sat down beside her,
And frightened Miss Muffet away.

Miss Muffet is Mary Stuart, who at the age of eighteen sat down as queen upon the throne of Scotland. At first Mary enjoyed herself, but before long the reformer John Knox "sat down beside her." Knox publicly condemned her scandalous behavior and her Roman Catholic beliefs. In addition, he had several discussions with her. Political problems finally forced Mary to flee Scotland and take refuge in England with her cousin, Queen Elizabeth. In the popular mind, however, it was John Knox who had frightened the young queen away.

Another familiar nursery rhyme is "Three Blind Mice":

Three blind mice, see how they run!
They all ran after the farmer's wife,
Who cut off their tails with a carving knife,
Did you ever see such a sight in your life,
As three blind mice?

In this rhyme "the farmer's wife" is Mary I, the Roman Catholic queen of Tudor England. The "three blind mice" are the churchmen Cranmer, Ridley, and Latimer, who tried to prevent Mary from reinstating Roman Catholicism in England. In response to their efforts, Mary "cut off their tails"—she had the men arrested and executed.

for the Scottish church a Calvinistic statement of faith drawn up by Knox. They established the Presbyterian Church in Scotland.

The Reformation in Scotland flourished even though Scotland had a Catholic queen, **Mary Stuart** (1542–87). Mary was less than a week old when her father, King James V, died and she was proclaimed queen of Scotland. She grew up in France, however, the homeland of her mother, while her mother acted as her regent in Scotland. In 1561 the young queen returned to Scotland only to find that her Catholic and French upbringing alienated the nationalistic Scottish Protestants.

Her downfall came when she was implicated in plotting her husband's death. To make matters worse, she married her husband's suspected murderer. Forced to abdicate, she fled to England, leaving behind her infant son James VI, the next king of Scotland. When Elizabeth I died in 1601, James VI was invited to assume the English throne; he was crowned King James I of England.

The Netherlands

The Netherlands (which included at that time the modern-day countries of the Netherlands and Belgium) was one of the many territories ruled by Charles V. When Charles abdicated, this territory came under the control of his son, Philip II. Because Philip was both Spanish and Catholic, many of his subjects disliked him. Not long after he became king, Protestant unrest in the Netherlands prompted Philip to send troops to put down the trouble. His troops severely persecuted the Protestants there, causing them to break out in armed revolt in 1568. The Protestants fought bravely under their leader, William of Orange, also called **William the Silent**, and for a time even many of the Roman Catholics living in the southern part of the Netherlands turned against Spanish rule.

The war dragged on for years, but the Netherlands, aided by the English, managed to hold off the Spanish troops. In 1581 the Protestant areas of the Netherlands declared their independence from Spain. The Roman Catholic area (modern Belgium) remained under Spanish control. William was murdered a few years later, but the Dutch Protestants, nevertheless, won a truce with Spain in the early seventeenth century.

France

The writings of Luther flowed into France, arousing widespread interest in the Reformation. The works of John Calvin also had a strong influence there. By the middle of the sixteenth century, there were more than two thousand Protestant congregations in France, and perhaps as many as half of the nobles had become Protestants. Despite these gains, France remained a thoroughly Catholic country. The government, fearful of the growing political and religious power of Protestantism, fiercely persecuted the **Huguenots** (French Protestants).

One of the most shocking incidents occurred in 1572. Catherine de Medici, the mother of the French king and the real power behind the throne, instigated a massacre of the Huguenots in Paris. Very early on the morning of August 27 (St. Bartholomew's Day), bands of Roman Catholics began roving the city, breaking into homes and murdering their unsuspecting and helpless occupants. These grisly deeds occurred throughout France.

By the time the massacre had ended, an estimated twenty thousand Huguenots had been murdered. Although many people condemned the **St. Bartholomew's Day Massacre**, Philip II of Spain praised it, stating that it was "of such value and prudence and of such service, glory, and honor to God and universal benefit to all Christendom that to hear of it was for me the best

François Dubois, Le Massacre de la Saint-Barthélemy.
vers 1572–1584, Huile sur bois, 94 x 154 cm. Musée cantonal des Beaux-Arts de Lausanne

and most cheerful news which at present could come to me." Even the pope ordered a special celebration in Rome.

The massacre, needless to say, increased the tension between the French Roman Catholics and the Protestants, whose differences had already led to civil war. Civil war broke out once again, this time over the question of who would rule France. The Valois family, which had ruled France since the fourteenth century, was dying out. Two other families were seeking the throne. One of these, the Guise family, was Roman Catholic and traced its line back to Charlemagne. Another family, the **Bourbon** family, was Huguenot and traced its ancestry back to Louis IX.

Henry of Navarre, the head of the Bourbon family and the leader of the Huguenots, emerged victorious in the struggle for the throne. He declared himself to be Henry IV (1589–1610), the king of France. However, there was one serious problem. The majority of Frenchmen were Roman Catholic and did not want a Protestant king. To please the people and secure the throne he had so eagerly sought, Henry IV became a Roman Catholic. He supposedly remarked, "Paris is well worth a mass." Although Henry IV deserted his Huguenot followers, he did grant them a certain amount of religious toleration in the famous **Edict of Nantes** (1598). But, as we shall see in Chapter 14, this period of toleration did not last.

Section Quiz

1. What city and country are associated with the ministry of the reformer Ulrich Zwingli?
2. List three beliefs that many of the early Anabaptist groups held in common.
3. What influential work on theology did John Calvin write? What city associated with his ministry became a leading center of the Protestant Reformation?
4. Following England's break with the Roman Catholic Church, what became the state church of England?
5. Who was the fiery Scottish preacher who advanced the cause of the Reformation in Scotland? What Protestant church became the state church in Scotland?

1. ______________________

2. ______________________
____
____
____
____
____
____
____

3. ______________________
____
____

4. ______________________

5. ______________________
____

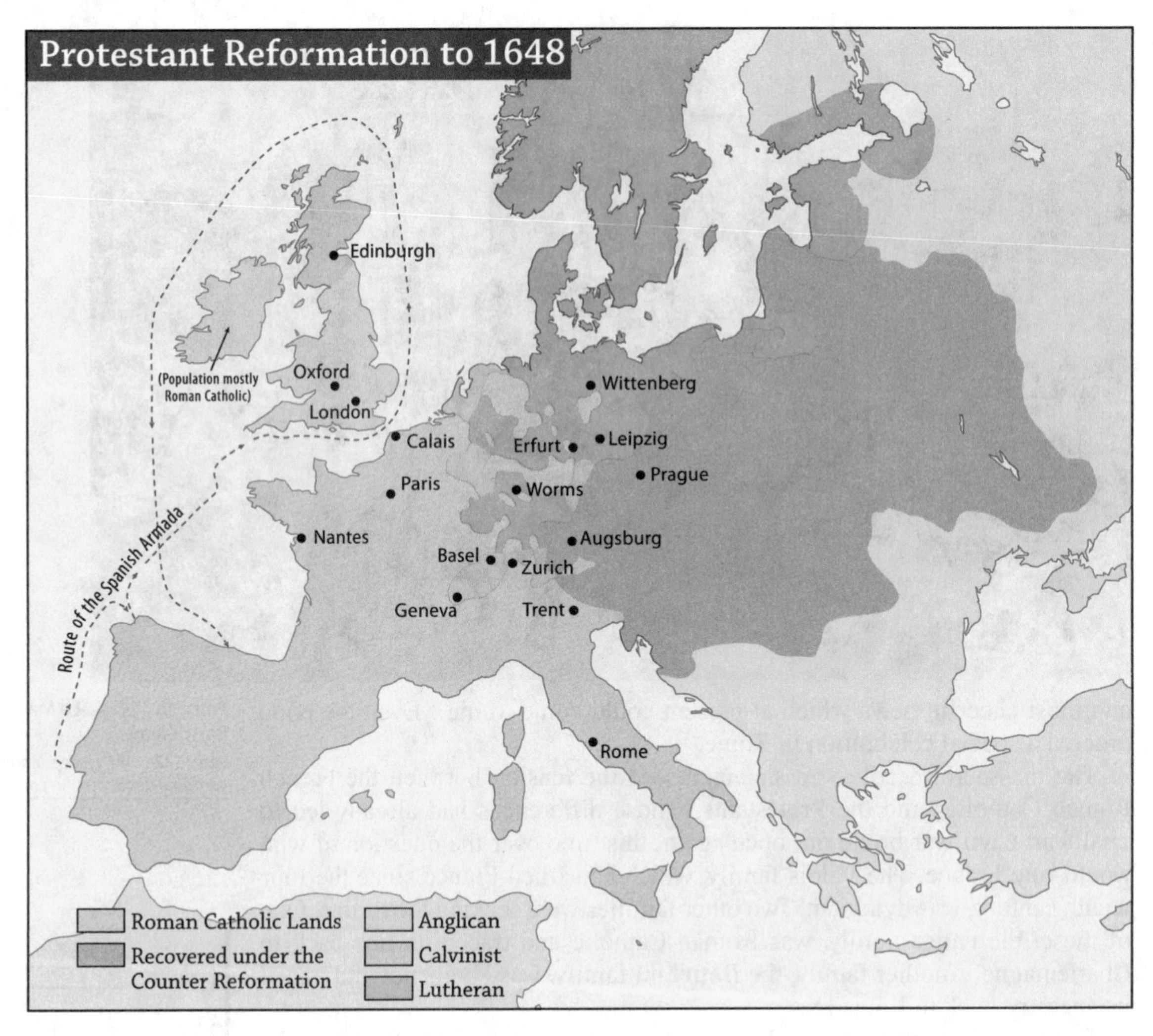

IV. The Counter Reformation

In the early stages of the Reformation it seemed that the Roman Catholic Church was fading because of the efforts of the reformers. Northern Europe as well as many areas of eastern Europe had rejected the Roman church. A strong Protestant movement was under way in France. There were even small Protestant groups in such Catholic strongholds as Spain and Italy. In an effort to prevent further losses to the Protestants, the Roman Catholic Church promoted reforms of its own. In the late Middle Ages, as criticism against corruption in the church mounted, Catholics attempted to correct the problem. However, it was not until the sixteenth century, when large numbers left the Roman church, that its leaders became seriously concerned about the need for reform.

The Catholic Reformation is often called the **Counter Reformation**. (The word *counter* means "to oppose.") The Protestant leaders had directed their efforts primarily against false doctrine. Most Catholic reformers, on the other hand, attempted to clean up the church by correcting some of the outward moral problems. They failed to see that the root of their problems was doctrinal error.

Jesuits

The Society of Jesus, or the **Jesuits**, was instrumental in promoting the Counter Reformation. This new religious order was founded by the Spanish soldier **Ignatius Loyola** (loy OH luh; 1491?–1556). While recovering from a battle injury, Loyola underwent a religious experience in which he determined to devote his life to the Roman church. In 1540 the Jesuit order officially came into existence. Unlike those in other religious orders, the Jesuits took a special vow of absolute obedience to the pope.

From its beginnings the purpose of the Jesuit order was to suppress heresy and to promote Roman Catholic education. The Jesuits realized the importance of careful training. Those who wanted to become members of the organization had to go through two years of probation. During that time the prospective member studied the *Spiritual Exercises* written by Loyola and learned to be completely submissive to those in authority. "We ought always to be ready to believe that what seems to us white is black if the hierarchical Church so defines it," Loyola once said. If the two-year probation period ended successfully, an individual became a member of the Jesuit society. He usually continued his studies, sometimes spending a total of fifteen years in preparation for his work.

The Jesuits used every means available to promote their own order and to turn people back to the Roman church. They believed it was perfectly proper to do wrong in order to accomplish something good. For example, some Jesuits taught that it was acceptable to murder someone—even a ruler—if that death furthered Catholic purposes. They infiltrated schools and government circles, attacking Protestantism and spreading the Counter Reformation wherever they went. They were also zealous missionaries. Of the many Jesuit missionaries, the best known is Francis Xavier (1506–52), who traveled to India, China, and Japan.

Montanes, Juan Martinez (1568–1649).
St. Ignatius.
Statue. University Chapel, Seville, Spain

Inquisition

To stop the spread of Protestantism, Pope Paul III (1534–49) reorganized the **Inquisition**. It brought terror and death to Protestants in strong Roman Catholic areas such as Spain. The Inquisition operated on the assumption that anyone accused of heresy was guilty until proved innocent. After being arrested (which usually occurred at night), the accused would stand before an inquisitor. Without knowing what charges had been brought against him or who had brought them, the accused person would be asked to confess his wrong. If mild methods of persuasion failed to produce a confession, the Inquisition used barbaric torture. Those who still refused to cooperate with the Inquisition were burned at the stake. The family of the accused often suffered as well through arrest or loss of property.

Index

When Gutenberg introduced movable-type printing in Europe, the price of books and pamphlets dropped sharply. Previously only the rich could afford books, but by the sixteenth century many people could purchase printed material. Printed copies of the Bible and books written by the reformers circulated throughout Europe. Realizing the impact that the printed page was having on the spread of the Reformation, the Roman church tried to regulate what its members read. In 1559 the Roman Catholic Church established the ***Index of Prohibited Books***, which condemned, among other things, forty-eight allegedly heretical editions or versions of the Bible. Only those books that received an ecclesiastical license had official church approval. Even today, books officially sanctioned by the Roman church contain inside the front cover the Latin words *imprimatur* ("let it be printed") and *nihil obstat* ("nothing hinders").

Council of Trent

Twenty-five years after the beginning of the Protestant Reformation, Pope Paul III called a church council to discuss doctrinal questions and to propose needed reform. Charles V, the Holy Roman Emperor, had demanded such a council because the religious division in Germany was increasing. He wanted to end the division and to restore unity to his land. Fearful of what a general church council might do, Pope Paul III structured it in such a way that the pope's representatives, as well as the other Italian delegates, controlled the proceedings. The outcome was predetermined. In 1545 the council held its first meeting in Trent, a city of northern Italy. Church leaders did not meet on a continuous basis but gathered for an extended period of time on three separate occasions. In 1563 the Council of Trent held its last session.

The **Council of Trent** is significant for two major reasons. The council explicitly condemned many of the biblical principles upon which Protestantism is based. Most importantly it rejected the doctrines of justification by faith alone and the sole authority of the Scripture. This sealed the break between Protestant and Roman Catholic churches. Also the council set forth a complete doctrinal position of the Roman church. It made its position binding upon all Roman Catholics. The Roman Catholic Church did not tolerate any deviation from the decrees of the council.

Section Quiz

1. ______________________
2. ______________________
   ____
3. ______________________
4. ______________________
5. ______________________
   ____

1. What was the name for the Catholic Reformation that sought to stop the spread of the Protestant movement?
2. What new religious order was formed to suppress heresy and promote Roman Catholic education? Who was the founder of this order?
3. What church court of the Roman Catholic Church focused its attention on finding out and punishing those accused of holding Protestant beliefs?
4. What did the Roman Catholic Church issue to regulate what its members could read?
5. At what council did the Roman Catholic Church set forth its doctrinal position? Who was the pope that called this council?

A Glance Behind

The Reformation broke the hold of the Roman Catholic Church on religious life in western Europe. This religious upheaval, however, produced changes in all areas of European society. It reasserted the dignity of everyday labor and encouraged the spread of lay education and the founding of schools. The Reformation's emphasis on individual responsibility furthered democratic and representative forms of government as opposed to absolute monarchies. The inquisitive spirit it helped foster led to the birth of modern science. Thus many of the freedoms and privileges that we enjoy today come directly or indirectly from the Protestant Reformation.

and a Glimpse Ahead

Notes

1. Roland H. Bainton, *Here I Stand: A Life of Martin Luther* (New York: Mentor Books, 1950), pp. 49–50.
2. Martin Luther, *Table Talk*, ed. and trans. Theodore G. Tappert, *Luther's Work*, vol. 54 (Philadelphia: Fortress Press, 1967), p. 237.

Chapter Review

Can You Define?

recant
sola fide
indulgences
treasury of saints
pacifism
Elizabethan Settlement
Counter Reformation

Can You Identify?

John Wycliffe
Lollards
John Huss
Council of Constance
Martin Luther
Leo X
Johann Tetzel
October 31, 1517
Ninety-five Theses
Johann Eck
Charles V
Diet of Worms
Philipp Melanchthon
Augsburg Confession
Francis I
Suleiman
Peace of Augsburg (1555)
Ulrich Zwingli
Anabaptists
John Calvin
The Institutes of the Christian Religion
Tudor family
Henry VIII
Thomas Cranmer
Edward VI
Mary I
Elizabeth I
Anglican Church
Philip II
Francis Drake
Spanish Armada (1588)
Puritans
Separatists
John Knox
Mary Stuart
William the Silent
Huguenots
St. Bartholomew's Day Massacre
Bourbon
Henry of Navarre
Edict of Nantes (1598)
Jesuits
Ignatius Loyola
Inquisition
Index of Prohibited Books
Council of Trent

Can You Locate?

Oxford
Prague
Erfurt
Wittenberg
Leipzig
Worms
Augsburg
Zurich
Basel
Geneva
Trent

How Much Do You Remember?

1. List three beliefs that Wycliffe and Huss held to that caused the Roman Catholic Church to condemn them as heretics.
2. In contrast to the position of the Roman Catholic Church, what did Luther teach concerning salvation, the priesthood, the Bible, and the authority of the pope and church councils?
3. For each of the following reformers, identify the country in which he ministered and any important works he authored: Wycliffe, Huss, Luther, Zwingli, Calvin, Knox.
4. Identify the response of each of the following monarchs of England toward the Protestant Reformation: Henry VIII, Edward VI, Mary I, Elizabeth I.
5. List four ways the Roman Catholic Church sought to further the Counter Reformation in opposition to the Protestant Reformation.

What Do You Think?

1. We know that history is under God's control. Can you list some evidences of how God "made the world ready" for the Protestant Reformation?
2. How do you account, humanly speaking, for the fact that Huss died a martyr's death, while Luther lived a full life and died a natural death?
3. What part did the Word of God have in bringing about the Reformation?
4. Analyze the response of European rulers to the Protestant Reformation. List various motives that you think they had in supporting or opposing the Reformation.

13

"For Gold, Glory, and God"

EXPLORATION AND DISCOVERY

The Half Moon

They that go down to the sea in ships, that do business in great waters; these see the works of the Lord, and his wonders in the deep.
Psalm 107:23–24

The two hundred years from 1450 to 1650 marked the great age of European exploration and discovery. Men crossed uncharted waters, braved violent storms, and suffered starvation and disease as they sailed to distant parts of the globe. What prompted these explorers to face untold perils? Most desired wealth; some sought adventure and fame; others sought to spread the gospel to heathen lands. But whether motivated by greed, pride, or compassion, these explorers helped open up the continents of North and South America, the coast of Africa, and part of Asia to European trade and colonization.

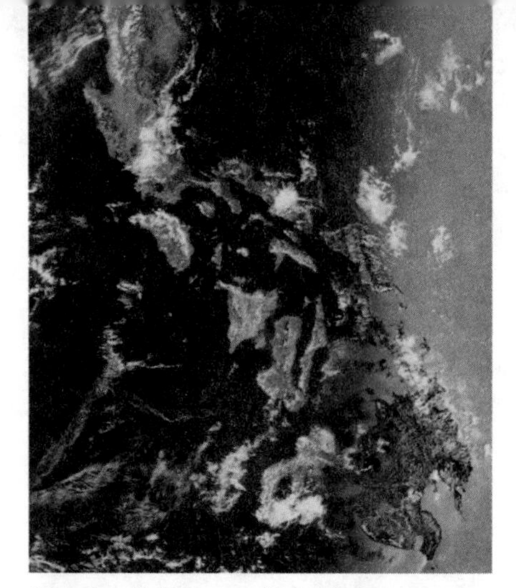

Magellan died on a small island in the Philippines in his attempt to circumnavigate the earth. Only eighteen of his more than two hundred men completed the voyage.

I. Preparation for Discovery

Several developments in Europe gave rise to this Age of Exploration. The Crusades awakened interest in lands beyond Europe's borders. Travelers such as **Marco Polo** stirred the popular imagination with tales of strange customs and unbelievable riches in the Far East. The Renaissance provided western Europe with the means, namely navigational equipment and finances, to reach the Orient. In the endeavor to reach the East, Europeans discovered the New World.

Motives for Exploration

Search for New Trade Routes

Spurred by the Crusades and the stories of Marco Polo and others, Europeans reopened trade routes with the East. They imported numerous luxury items from China, India, and the Spice Islands (located north of Australia). Merchants traded for diamonds, rubies, and other gems as well as for silk and for expensive porcelain (china). Spices, such as cloves and cinnamon, were in great demand. Europeans used them to flavor and preserve food and as ingredients in drugs and perfumes.

All these items came across Asia to Europe by way of the Middle East. But there were many problems for traders along this long route. Much of the terrain was rugged and difficult to cross. In addition, local rulers charged trading caravans for the privilege of passing through their territory; taxes and tolls drove up the prices of the products. Furthermore, the Italians held a monopoly on Oriental trade. Merchants from Genoa controlled the northern routes that came overland from Asia, and those from Venice controlled the southern routes that ran along the coast of India, up the Persian Gulf, and across the desert to Palestine. (See map on p. 228.) Not only were Italians draining gold from the rest of Europe, but they were also keeping traders from other European countries from getting a share of the profits.

Marco Polo and the Awakening of Curiosity

Marco Polo was only seventeen when he set off on a journey that would revolutionize the world. He was accompanying his father, Nicoló, and his uncle Matteo, both Venetian traders, on their second voyage to the little-known kingdom of Cathay (China). The year was 1271.

For four years the three men traveled eastward, finally reaching the city of Cambaluc (Beijing), the capital of Cathay. Young Marco Polo quickly became a favorite of the ruler, Kublai Khan. He learned the languages of the court and by the age of twenty-three became the Khan's adviser. The Polos lived in Cathay for seventeen years, traveling and seeing sights that few Europeans ever dreamed of. In 1292 they began the long journey home. When they arrived in Venice, their old friends did not recognize them; most at first refused to believe their stories, but the travelers convinced them by producing a wealth of gems that they had received in Cathay.

Three years after his return to Italy, Marco was captured while fighting in a local war and jailed in Genoa. To pass the time, he recounted his adventures to a fellow prisoner, who recorded them in what was soon to become a very popular book: *The Book of Sir Marco Polo Concerning the Kingdoms and Marvels of the East.* The work was far more accurate than the few other books about Cathay that were available in Europe at that time. Its readers were astonished by the tales of a strange black rock (coal) that the Mongols burned. They thrilled to the description of fantastic riches in gold, spices, and many other luxuries. They wondered about the islands of "Cipango" (Japan) that Polo described. More importantly, they learned of the great sea (the Pacific) that lay beyond Asia.

Nearly two centuries after Polo, a man from Genoa read this book and wondered if the ocean to the west—the Atlantic—might be the same one that Polo saw. This man's name was Christopher Columbus.

In the 1400s these problems became more acute when the Ottoman Turks became a major power in the Middle East. This warlike people attacked caravans and destroyed trading posts. The Europeans, who still craved Eastern luxuries, needed to find a new route to the Orient. Some wondered if it might be possible to get to the East entirely by sea, avoiding the Turks, the Italian traders, and all the tolls and taxes. The quest began in earnest in the late fifteenth century. Adventurers sailed south and east around Africa; others sailed west across the Atlantic; and some even tried to find a Northwest Passage through Arctic ice.

Quest for Gold

For many years there had been stories circulating in Europe that there was gold—lots of gold—somewhere in Africa. Europeans, however, knew very little about this huge continent. The northern coast, naturally, was well known to travelers. But few if any Europeans had traveled south into the heart of the continent. Occasionally African traders arrived in Mediterranean ports, bringing gold from the interior, but no European knew exactly where this gold came from. Not surprisingly, many wanted to find it. Explorers were willing to take great risks to obtain wealth, but they often suffered great losses instead. They should have heeded Proverbs 15:16, which says, "Better is little with the fear of the Lord than great treasure and trouble therewith."

Desire for Adventure and Glory

While some explorers craved great riches, others sought the thrill of adventure and the praise of men. Undoubtedly the Renaissance, which encouraged a spirit of curiosity and emphasized individual achievement, played a part in these desires. Men risked their lives, sailing through unknown waters and traveling to distant lands. Through their daring adventures, they hoped to achieve worldly fame. While several explorers did become famous for their exploits, many more died in the quest for glory. The Bible teaches that glory or fame is not something one should go looking for. The writer of Proverbs reminds us that "for men to search their own glory is not glory" (25:27). How much better it is for people to seek the praise of God rather than the praise of others.

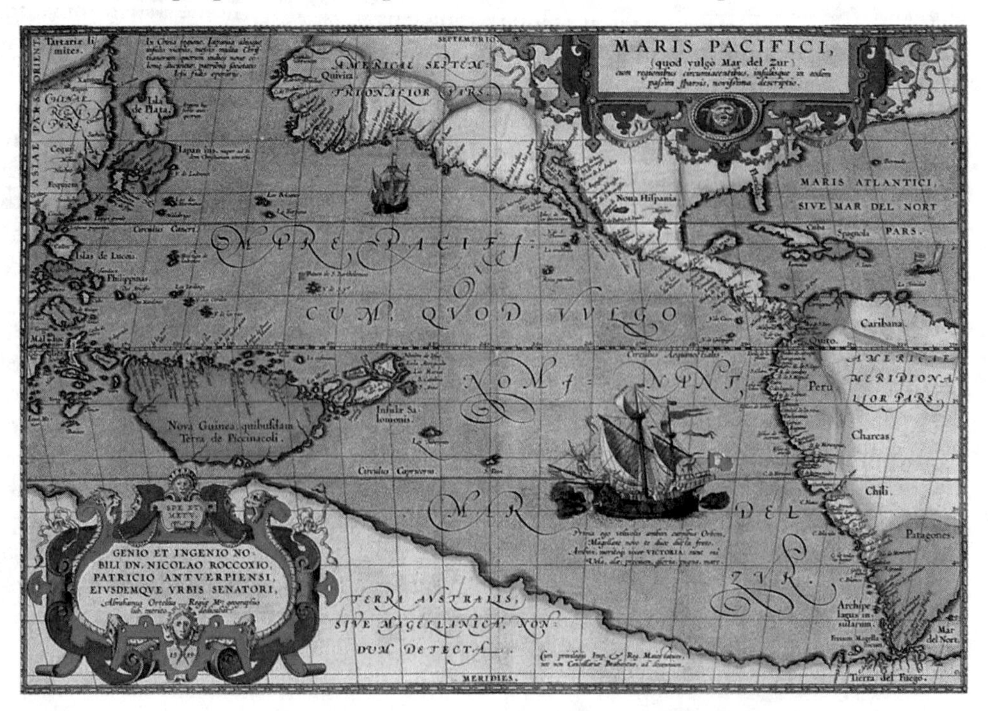

This 1589 map represents one of the earliest known depictions of what is now America's western coast.

Religious Concerns

Though overlooked or neglected by some historians, religious concern also motivated many explorers. The crusading spirit was alive in Europe, for the Muslim threat was still very real. Even as late as the fifteenth century, the Moors still controlled the southern portion of the Iberian Peninsula. After the fall of Constantinople to the Ottoman Turks in 1453, Europeans feared a full-scale Muslim invasion of eastern Europe. European rulers searched for ways to stop further Muslim victories.

There were rumors of a king in Africa named **Prester John**, supposedly a wealthy and powerful Christian who wanted to help the Europeans fight the Muslims. During the fifteenth century, explorers sailed along the west coast of Africa searching for Prester John's kingdom. They hoped to enlist his help; by attacking from both the north and south, their combined forces could defeat the Muslims. Prester John was not to be found.

Not all of Europe's religious zeal was directed against the Muslims. Some explorers went out seeking to spread the gospel to heathen people, who needed to hear of salvation in Jesus Christ alone. Most of the early explorers were Roman Catholics. Although they won converts to the Roman Catholic Church, they failed to lead people to Christ.

Competition Among European Nations

Exploration was also sparked by the commercial rivalry among the nations of Europe. As Italian merchants brought precious gems, spices, and silks from the East, Europeans were filled with great excitement, but also with great envy. Non-Italian merchants wanted to profit from the Oriental trade, and kings wanted to increase their countries' wealth and power. As the explorers traveled to unknown regions, they claimed their discoveries for the country they sailed for. The European countries were eager to start trade with the people of newly discovered lands. Nations established trade settlements and encouraged colonization in order to protect their commercial interests.

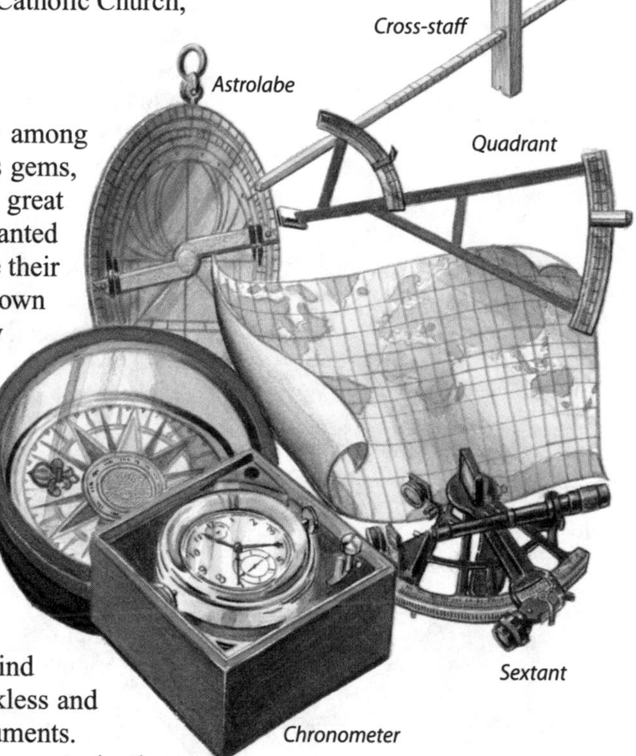

Navigational instruments

Tools for Exploration

Navigational Aids

Three things were of great importance to explorers: accurate maps to guide them to their destination, a compass to tell them in what direction they were actually going, and some kind of "locator" instrument to tell them their position. On a trackless and featureless ocean, they needed accurate and trustworthy instruments.

Maps—Maps of the known world became much more accurate in the fifteenth century. Italian mapmakers drew up sailing charts based upon the reports of traders and fishermen. These maps were fairly reliable guides for sailing in the Mediterranean Sea or along the European coast, but they were of little help to the explorers. These men sailed in uncharted waters. As they returned from their voyages, they updated their maps to include their discoveries. With the invention of printing, these maps were widely distributed, opening the door for further exploration.

Instruments—The **compass** greatly aided sailors in navigation and mapmaking. Invented by the Chinese, the early compass was a magnetized needle floating in a bowl of water on a piece of reed or cork. In the late 1300s, Europeans mounted the compass on a stiff card marked with the cardinal points (north, south, east, and west). This small improvement made a great difference to sailors, who could now use the instrument easily on a moving ship. The compass became an invaluable tool; it helped sailors determine direction and follow a definite course.

Sailors also relied on more complicated instruments to determine their position on an unmarked ocean. The three most common instruments—the astrolabe, the quadrant, and the cross-staff—measured the angle between a star (usually the North Star) and the horizon. From this information the sailor could determine his **latitude**, or distance from the equator. With any one of these instruments, the captain of a ship, even though out of sight of land, could compute his position with some degree of accuracy. They did have two major drawbacks, however. They were useless in cloudy weather, and they were not very accurate when used on the rolling deck of a ship.

Seagoing Vessels

It was not until about 1400 that ships were built to sail long distances over wide and sometimes stormy seas. Early ships in the Mediterranean Sea had made great use of oars. An oared ship would need such a large crew to travel the ocean that it could not possibly carry enough supplies to feed all the men. Oceangoing vessels, therefore, needed to use sails. But of the two types of sails in use, neither would be right for a long ocean voyage. The Arabs used triangular sails, which made their boats easily maneuverable, even when the wind changed directions. This kind of sail, however, could power only a small craft. Such vessels would not be large enough to carry the needed supplies and then return with enough spices to make a trip profitable. On the other hand, the northern sailors, such as the Vikings, used square sails, which could power a larger ship and required a smaller crew. But these ships were not very maneuverable.

The solution came in the middle of the fifteenth century with the building of the versatile **caravel**. This light, fast vessel was popular with the early explorers. It had several masts on which were mounted large square sails to provide power and smaller triangular sails to provide maneuverability. The caravel's high sides and its broad and deep construction made it suitable for ocean travel.

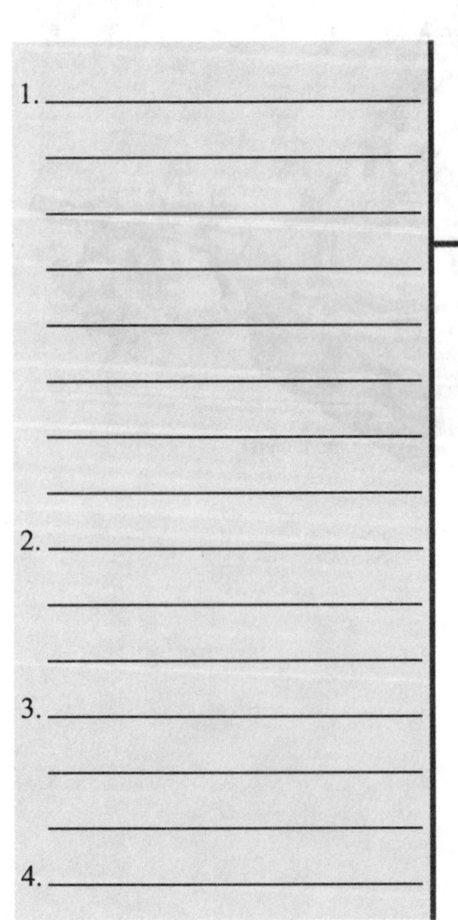

Section Quiz

1. List five motives that prompted European explorers to "seek out and discover."
2. What man's account of his travels awakened European curiosity in the Orient? In what Asian land did he spend seventeen years? In whose court did he serve as an adviser?
3. What three things were of great importance to the early explorers?
4. What light, fast vessel was popular with the early explorers of the late fifteenth century?

II. Process of Discovery

The early explorers were pioneers. They set sail across vast, unexplored oceans with uncertain prospects of ever returning home. While some never returned, others brought back the exciting news of their discoveries. They told of new routes to the Orient, of great riches to be gained, of new lands to be explored, and of heathen people that needed to be evangelized. Europe eagerly responded to the challenge. The explorers were followed by merchants, soldiers, settlers, and missionaries. Through trade along the African coast and in Asia, and through colonization in the New World, Europe rapidly extended its influence around the world.

Portugal and Spain

Portugal and Spain were the leading nations of the Age of Exploration. Several factors accounted for their early success. Shipping had long been a principal industry in these lands; Portugal and Spain were bounded by the waters of the Atlantic Ocean and the Mediterranean Sea. Because the Italians had gained a monopoly on trade in the Mediterranean, sailors from the Iberian Peninsula turned southward to the coast of Africa and westward across the Atlantic in search of new trade routes to the East. Furthermore, the experienced Portuguese and Spanish sailors were greatly aided by the navigational and mapmaking skills they had learned from the Moors. A strong motivating force behind their drive for discovery was the crusading spirit, which was still very much alive in the peninsula. (The last Muslim stronghold in the Iberian Peninsula was not conquered until 1492.) The Portuguese and Spanish sailors set sail to spread Roman Catholicism and to battle the Muslims.

Portugal Rounds Africa

***Prince Henry the Navigator*—Prince Henry** (1394–1460), called "The Navigator," was largely responsible for Portugal's early success in exploration. Although he never went on an expedition, he has been called "the greatest figure in the history of exploration." As a youth, he was fascinated with the great land of Africa to the south. How big was it? Where was the source of the gold that came out of its interior? Where was Prester John's kingdom? These questions led Prince Henry to start a school of navigation on the coast of Portugal. It was not a *school* in our sense of the word; it was more like a *storehouse* of knowledge about navigation. He attracted to his palace geographers, astronomers, mapmakers, and sea captains. Under his sponsorship, these men improved navigational instruments, drew up more accurate maps, and developed the caravel. Henry sent sailors out to explore the coast of Africa and to bring back all the information they could find. On each voyage, Henry's sailors went farther south along Africa's coast. They had not yet reached the equator when he died in 1460, but his accomplishments laid the foundation for the achievements of two other men who would finish the job that he had begun.

Bartolomeu Dias—In 1487, nearly thirty years after Prince Henry's death, the king of Portugal sent **Bartolomeu Dias** down the coast of Africa to find a sea route to India. As he neared the southern tip of the continent, a fierce storm blew his ships out of sight of land for thirteen days. When he finally sighted land again, he noticed that the sun rose on the ship's right instead of its left; he was therefore heading north. He rightly concluded that he had rounded the tip of Africa during the storm and that indeed there might be an all-water route to the Orient. When his men refused to go any farther, he turned around and headed back to Portugal. As he rounded the tip of Africa again, he sighted

THIS MOMENT IN HISTORY

Prince Henry

List the ways Prince Henry's interest in navigation helped promote exploration.

____

____

____

____

____

____

____

____

The Cape of Good Hope

a huge rocky cape, which he named "The Cape of Storms." The king later changed its name to "The Cape of Good Hope" because he hoped that Dias had finally found a direct water route to India.

Vasco da Gama—Ten years after Dias's discovery, the king of Portugal selected **Vasco da Gama** to lead an expedition around the Cape of Good Hope to India. In 1497, with a fleet of four ships, da Gama set sail from Lisbon, Portugal. He did not follow the African coast all the way to the Cape of Good Hope as Dias had done. Instead, he made a great westward sweep to gain more favorable winds and currents. At one point he was actually closer to South America than to Africa. He stayed out of sight of land for fourteen weeks before reaching the tip of Africa. (In following centuries, wind-driven vessels followed this route pioneered by da Gama.)

Nearly a year after leaving Portugal, da Gama arrived in India. He was the first European to reach the great subcontinent by sailing around Africa. He told those who met him, "We have come to seek Christians and spices." But he found Muslim merchants living there who controlled trade in the region and opposed his efforts to trade with the Indians. Despite many obstacles, he was able to trade for spices—enough to pay for the voyage sixty times over!

The Portuguese swiftly took advantage of da Gama's discovery of the ocean route to India. They soon not only controlled this water route but also broke the Muslim trade monopoly in the Indian Ocean. The Muslim fleet was no match for the heavy artillery on the Portuguese ships. It was not long before ships laden with spices were a familiar sight in Portuguese ports.

Spain Sails Westward

Christopher Columbus—When Dias returned from his voyage around the Cape of Good Hope, an Italian named **Christopher Columbus** heard his report: India could be reached by sailing around the tip of Africa. But Columbus, who had studied the writings of the ancient geographer Ptolemy and the traveler Marco Polo, believed that he could reach Japan and China by sailing west—that Japan was perhaps as close as three hundred miles from Portugal. For many years he tried without success to persuade the king of Portugal to finance his voyage westward. But the king's advisers declared the undertaking to be impossible. In Spain Columbus was finally able to secure support for his voyage from King Ferdinand and Queen Isabella. In August of **1492** he set sail from Spain with three ships: the *Niña*, the *Pinta*, and the *Santa Maria*.

Columbus was a devoted Catholic who wrote that he believed he was commissioned by God to spread the gospel in distant lands. He was confident that his voyage would be a success. His men, however, did not share his optimism. After weeks of being out of sight of land, they demanded that the ships turn back. Columbus was able to persuade them to continue for two or three more days. Two days later, on the morning of October 12, he sighted land and named it San Salvador ("Holy Savior"). He thought that he was near the East Indies; actually he was in the Bahamas. He sailed south to

Landing of Columbus *by John Vanderlyn, located in the Rotunda of the U.S. Capitol*

The Naming of America

When Columbus landed on an island in the Caribbean in 1492, he mistakenly assumed that he had succeeded in reaching Asia. Upon his return, most Europeans believed his reports, but when later expeditions failed to bring back any riches, doubts began to arise. An Italian merchant named Amerigo Vespucci sailed west to settle the uncertainty. What he found was not a water route to the Orient but a new continent. He was the first European to reach and explore one of two landmasses that now bear his name—South America.

Hearing of Amerigo Vespucci's discovery, a German mapmaker named Martin Waldseemöller began to sell maps of the new continent. Proposing that the land be named after its discoverer, he referred to it as "America." The name was accepted, and soon people applied it to the large landmass to the north of the Spanish possessions as well. They called it "North America."

Cuba, which he thought was Marco Polo's Cathay, and to Hispaniola, which he identified as Cipango (Japan).

In three later voyages he explored further in the Caribbean and landed on the South American continent in what is now Venezuela. He never found the great riches he was looking for, and as long as he lived, he believed that he had reached Asia. Although he was mistaken as to where his voyages had taken him, his discovery was nonetheless of great importance. He opened up a "New World" that attracted European exploration and colonization for centuries following. Sadly, he also opened up an Indian slave trade.

Columbus was not the first to discover the New World, however. The Vikings had made the voyage from Europe in the tenth and eleventh centuries. A few historians even think that the ancient Phoenicians landed in South America before the time of Christ. But in God's plan, the lands of the New World remained virtually unknown to Europe until the sixteenth century—a time when Europe was also rediscovering the truth of God's Word. During the seventeenth century the New World, especially North America, became a haven for Christians who fled from political and religious persecution in Europe.

Line of Demarcation—As a result of Columbus's discoveries, Spain began to compete with Portugal for trade rights and new territory. To avoid disputes with Portugal, Spain asked Pope Alexander VI to divide the world between them. In 1493 he issued a bull, which drew a **Line of Demarcation** running north and south down the middle of the Atlantic Ocean. (See map on p. 310.) Portugal, he said, could claim lands to the east of the line, while Spain could claim those to the west. After negotiations between Spain and Portugal, it was agreed the following year to move the line farther to the west.

This agreement between Spain and Portugal had several important results.

1. It encouraged Portugal to colonize in Africa and the East Indies, which were east of the line.

2. It gave Spain the right to nearly all of the New World with one exception—the line cut across Brazil, giving that land to the Portuguese, who later explored and settled there. That is why even today the language of Brazil is Portuguese, while the rest of South America speaks Spanish.

3. It cut Spain off from going east around Africa to get to India and China. To remain competitive, Spain had to find a westward route. It was not long before she found a sailor who would do it.

THROUGH EYES OF FAITH

Christianization in the New World

Why do you think that God timed the Age of Exploration and the Reformation simultaneously? What results are benefiting us today because of this "coincidence"?

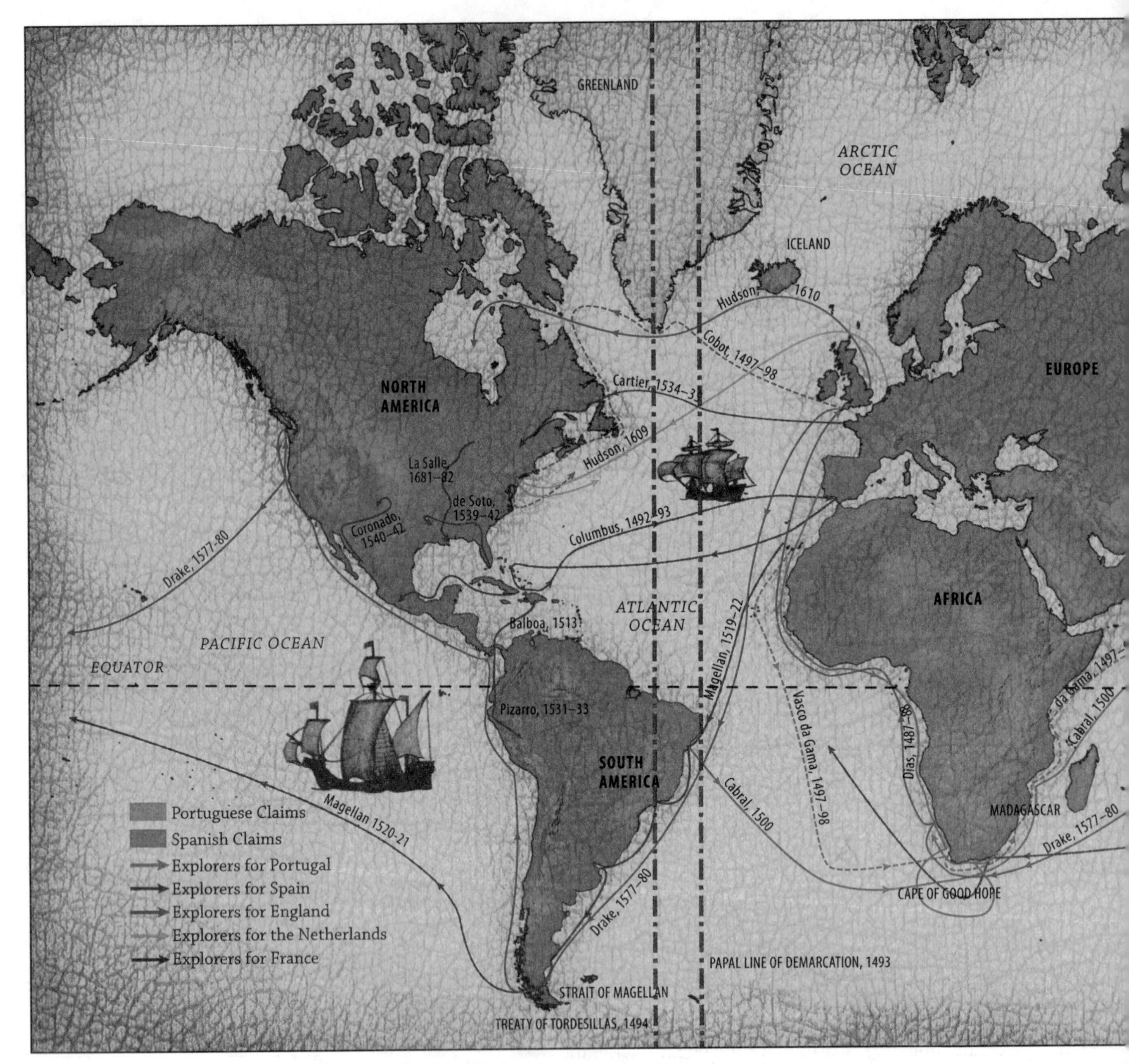

Ferdinand Magellan—In September of 1519 **Ferdinand Magellan** set out with a fleet of five ships to do what Columbus had failed to accomplish. By this time he knew that Columbus had found not the Orient, but an intervening landmass. He thought that he could sail around its southern end and then get to the Spice Islands through Spanish territory. He sailed from Spain to the coast of South America, where he spent the winter. There he saw natives who were so large that he named them Patagonians ("Big Feet"). He then sailed around the southern tip of South America through what we now call the Strait of Magellan. There one of his five ships deserted, and he lost a second in a severe storm. When he finally reached the ocean to the west, he appreciated its calmness so much that he named it *Pacific* ("peaceful").

As the three ships sailed westward across the Pacific, they ran out of supplies, and many of the sailors starved to death. Finally they reached the

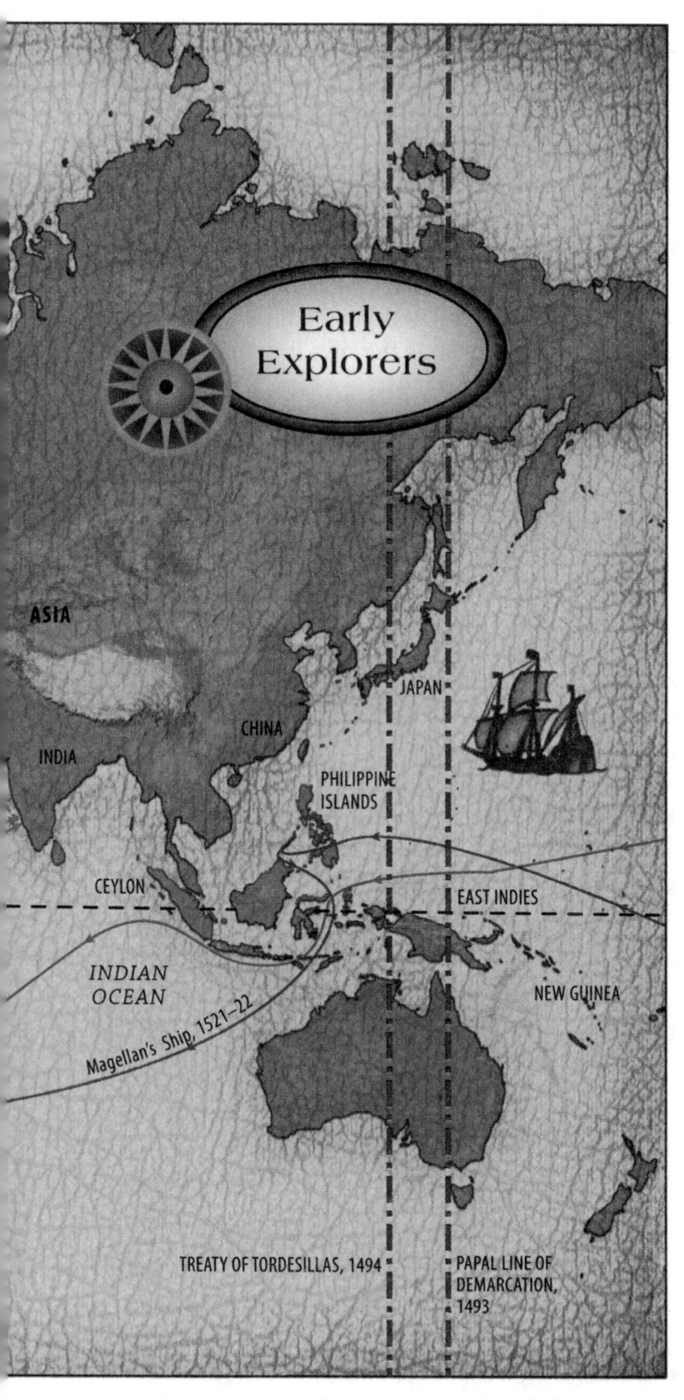

Ferdinand Magellan

Philippines, but there Magellan was killed by natives when he tried to help a local ruler in a tribal conflict. Magellan's crew continued the voyage without him, reaching the Spice Islands, where they took on a large cargo of spices. With only one ship remaining, they sailed around Africa and back to Spain. The ship returned with only eighteen of the more than two hundred men who had started the journey. This three-year-long, tragic voyage, the first **circumnavigation** of the earth, has been called "the greatest single human achievement on the sea." Furthermore, it demonstrated that one great body of water covered the earth's surface and confirmed the fact that the world was round—something the Bible had already affirmed: "It is he that sitteth upon the circle of the earth" (Isa. 40:22). Magellan's voyage also made it clear to Europeans that the discoveries of Columbus were not as near to Asia as Columbus had hoped.

1. ____________________

____

2. ____________________

____

3. ____________________

4. ____________________

____

5. ____________________

____

Section Quiz

1. What two European nations led the way during the Age of Exploration?
2. What member of the Portuguese ruling family greatly aided the Age of Exploration? What nickname did he earn?
3. Da Gama's discovery led to the Portuguese establishment of an all-water route to what land?
4. For whom are North and South America named? What German mapmaker popularized the name for these continents?
5. Who settled the trade disputes between Spain and Portugal by dividing the world between the two countries? What was the dividing line called?

Europe and the New World

Amerindian Civilizations

When Columbus landed in the Bahamas, he thought he had reached the East Indies. He thus called the natives whom he found there "Indians." These peoples had lived in North and South America for several thousand years before the Europeans arrived. They had probably crossed the Bering Strait between Asia and Alaska and then moved rapidly southward.

Of the Indian groups in North America, some were farmers and lived in villages; others, because they were hunters, followed the herds. Many worshiped nature: the sun, the moon, the wind, and the mountains. Most tribes believed in a "Great Spirit" as well as a number of lesser spirits, which they believed watched over them. For many years they had no knowledge of the one true God. The North American Indians did not normally form large nations but lived in small groups or tribes. All the tribes in a particular region, however, were very similar. There are five main regions in which these Indians lived: the Northeast, the Southeast, the Plains, the Southwest, and the West Coast.

Mesa Verde in southwest Colorado; ruins of the ancient dwellings of the Ancestral Puebloans

1. The Northeastern Indians, unlike other tribes, formed a five-tribe confederation led by the Iroquois (IHR uh kwoy). They are known for their use of wampum, or shell money, and for their birch-bark canoes.

2. The Southeastern Indians were most famous as "mound builders"; they built burial and ceremonial mounds, many of which still exist.

3. Farther west, the Plains Indians roamed the grasslands, hunted buffalo, lived in tepees, and fought often with other tribes. They did not use horses, however, until the Spaniards brought them to the New World.

4. The Indians of the Southwest are often called "cliff dwellers." They built villages, called pueblos, out of adobe, or sun-dried brick. Many of these villages were built into the sides of cliffs in order to provide protection from would-be attackers. The cliff dwellers were the most peaceable of the North American Indians.

5. The last major group of Indians, those of the West Coast, are remembered for their totem poles, which they carved out of tree trunks to depict their local gods.

The Indians of Central and South America were more highly civilized than those in North America. They built large cities, traded with their neighbors, and created art and literature of extremely high quality. Nevertheless, they remained very pagan and superstitious peoples. Three cultures in particular—the Mayas, Aztecs, and Incas—are of special importance.

Catlin, George (1796-1872). Bull Dance, Mandan O-kee-pa ceremony, 1832. Oil on canvas.
Smithsonian American Art Museum, Washington, DC, USA

Maya—The **Mayan** civilization, which flourished from the fourth century through the tenth century, was noted for its artistic and intellectual achievements. Like that of the ancient Greeks, the Mayan civilization was not a unified nation but consisted of many city-states located in the Yucatán (YOO kuh TAN) Peninsula in southeastern Mexico. They built great pyramids, temples, altars, paved highways, and other structures. The Mayas developed hieroglyphics and studied astronomy with as much dedication as the ancient Egyptians. They computed the length of a year almost exactly (to 365 1/4 days), built astronomical observatories, and developed a system of mathematics that even included the concept of zero as a placeholder. The Mayas worshipped many false gods, the most common of which was a feathered serpent. During the ninth and tenth centuries, the Mayan civilization declined; her centers of culture were abandoned. The Indians themselves lived in the area until the coming of the Spaniards. When the Spanish arrived, they found only traces of the Mayan civilization.

Aztec—The **Aztecs** established their civilization after the Mayan civilization had declined. Around the year 1345 they founded the city of

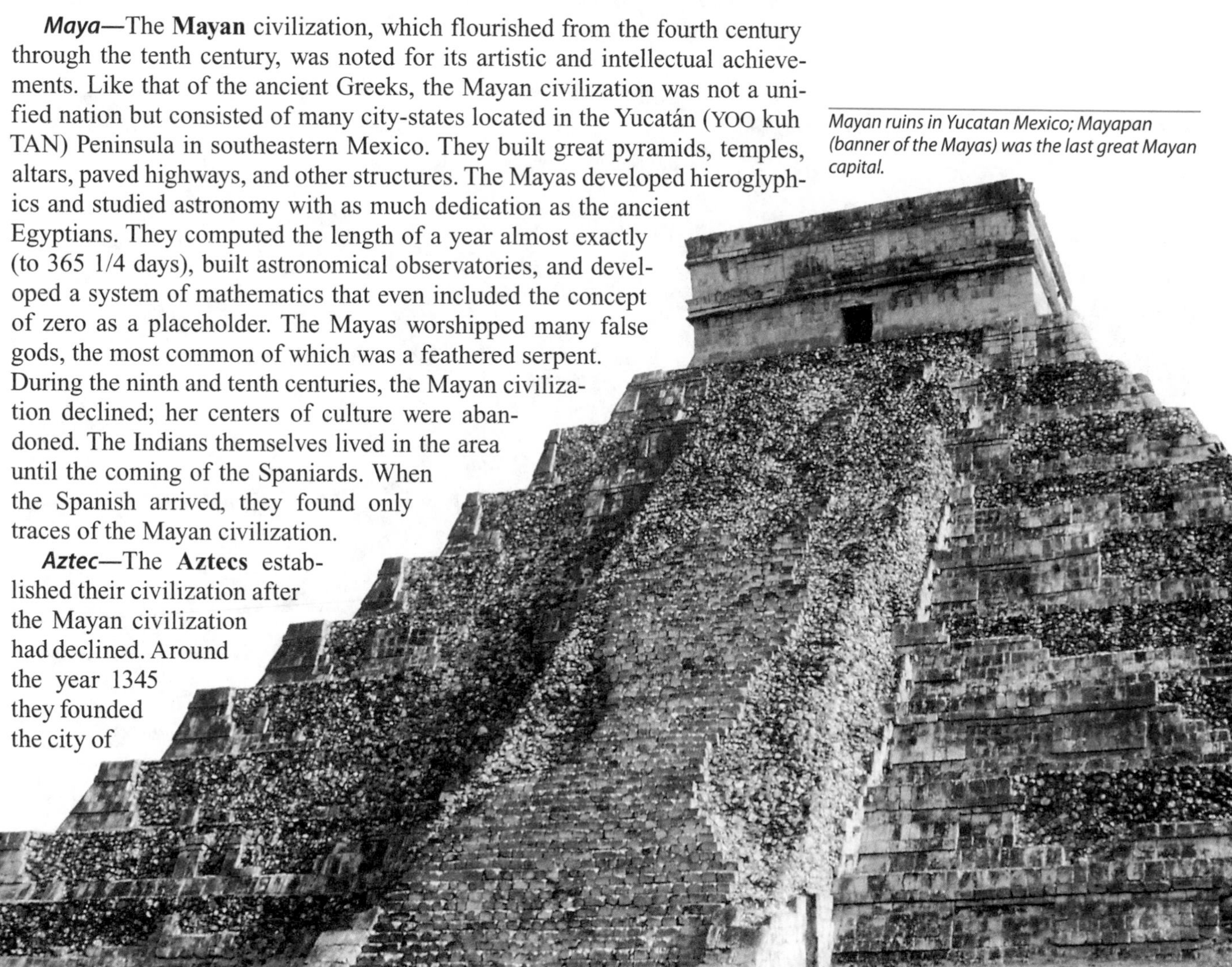

Mayan ruins in Yucatan Mexico; Mayapan (banner of the Mayas) was the last great Mayan capital.

Tenochtitlán (tay NOACH tee TLAHN) on an island in the middle of a lake in central Mexico. This walled city, connected to the mainland by several four-mile-long bridges, had a huge pyramid temple as well as about twenty other beautiful temples. Describing the network of canals throughout the city, one of the first Europeans to see the city called Tenochtitlán "the Venice of the New World."

The Aztecs were fighters. Every able-bodied Aztec man had to serve in the army. With a vicious and well-trained force, they conquered more than five million people and collected tribute from them all. They were better fighters than governors, however, and never developed a real empire. The army often took prisoners of war to sacrifice to their gods. Sometimes the priests even ate the flesh of their human sacrifices.

Inca—The **Inca** empire, which was at its height from about 1380 to 1570, flourished along the western coast of South America where Peru is today. Inca families lived in tightly organized communes in which several families shared possessions. Most Incas were farmers, raising maize (corn), potatoes, and cotton. All of the communes were closely controlled by the ruler—"the Inca"—whom the people worshiped as a god.

Unlike the Mayas and the Aztecs, the Incas ruled a genuine empire. They not only conquered neighboring peoples but also took over their lands and ruled them absolutely. Among the peoples they conquered, they abolished human sacrifices and cannibalism. They planned their cities carefully and connected them with well-constructed roads. Of the road between Cuzco, the Inca capital, and Quito, one Spanish conqueror said, "The roads constructed by the Romans in Spain . . . are not to be compared to it." The roads even crossed deep

The ruined city of Machu Picchu (meaning "old peak") in the Andes Mountains of modern Peru is one of the best preserved treasures of Inca culture. Located nearly eight thousand feet above sea level, Machu Picchu was apparently unknown to the Spanish and was discovered by an American explorer in 1911.

canyons on a type of suspension bridge, which was strong enough to hold up under heavy use. Using these roads the Incas set up a courier system that could deliver messages over one hundred fifty miles per day.

Spanish Exploration

The early Spanish explorers who came to the New World found that the Indian tribes could be easily conquered. Spain, which claimed rights to this land, sent **conquistadors** ("conquerors") to search for riches, to convert the Indians to Catholicism, and to establish Spanish authority. By using their firearms and horses, which the terrified Indians had never seen, small bands of Spanish soldiers were able to subdue entire Indian tribes and empires.

But the conquistadors were often cruel to the Indians they had come to "convert." Many of these men used the same ruthless methods to gain both riches and "converts." They saw no conflict in their quest for both, even though God's Word instructs us that "no man can serve two masters: for either he will hate the one, and love the other; or else he will hold to the one, and despise the other. Ye cannot serve God and mammon [riches]" (Matt. 6:24). Often their desire for wealth and fame overshadowed their religious zeal, making their evangelistic efforts a mockery of the gospel.

Balboa—The first notable conquistador was **Vasco Núñez de Balboa**. He came to the New World in search of adventure but soon found himself working on a farm on the island of Hispaniola. Dissatisfied and heavily in debt, he stowed away aboard a ship bound for the mainland, where a new colony was to be established. He joined the colony as a soldier, but by plotting against those in charge, he was able to win control of it. Under his leadership the colony moved to a site on the coast of Panama.

Balboa knew that complaints had been lodged against him before the king of Spain. The only way to gain royal favor, he concluded, would be to find gold or make some striking discovery. He heard rumors of a great ocean to the west and of a people wealthy with gold. In 1513, with a force of some two hundred men, he began cutting his way westward across what is today Panama, making his way through the heavy jungle of the isthmus (a narrow strip of land connecting two larger landmasses). After three weeks he and his men neared the western coast. Balboa, wanting to be the first European to see the new ocean, ordered his men to wait while he walked to the crest of a small mountain. There he saw a great body of water, which he named the "South Sea"; Magellan renamed it "Pacific" seven years later.

Balboa sent word of his discovery back to Spain, hoping to receive a royal commendation. But in the meantime he was arrested on trumped-up charges made by a jealous rival and was beheaded.

Cortés—In 1519 **Hernando Cortés**, called "the greatest of the conquistadors," landed on the shore of Mexico. After sinking his ships so that none of his soldiers would desert, he moved his army inland toward the Aztec capital. When the Aztec king, **Montezuma**, heard of their approach, he thought that Cortés might be the returning god Quetzalcoatl (ket SAHL koh AH t'l), or at least his representative. (Their chief god, Quetzalcoatl, was supposed to return to them someday from across the sea.) Instead of fighting Cortés, Montezuma welcomed him with gifts of gold and jewels, which only intensified the Spaniard's greed. Cortés himself had said, "We Spaniards suffer from a disease that only gold can cure."

After a time of uneasy peace, war broke out. The Spanish guns took their toll as the Spaniards massacred hundreds of Aztecs. Montezuma was stoned to death by his own people as a traitor. In 1521, after a four-month siege, Cortés finally defeated the Aztecs and destroyed the city. On its ruins he began to

Cortez and Montezuma at Mexican Temple *by Constantino Brumidi is located in the Rotunda of the U.S. Capitol*

build what is now Mexico City. This city later became one of the capitals of New Spain; one of the several **viceroys**, or "assistant kings," which the Spanish king appointed to oversee affairs in the New World, lived here.

Cortés and his men were not satisfied with their successes. Some soldiers headed north, still lusting for gold. Others fought over their newly acquired treasures. Cortés finally returned to Spain in 1539 and died eight years later, a discouraged and frustrated man. He had found great riches, but he was not satisfied. The writer of Ecclesiastes reminds us, "He that loveth silver shall not be satisfied with silver; nor he that loveth abundance with increase: this is also vanity" (5:10). Cortés spent his life acquiring treasure on earth, but he had laid up no treasure in heaven (Matt. 6:19–21).

Pizarro—**Francisco Pizarro** (pih ZAHR oh) was probably the cruelest of all the conquistadors. He came to the New World for one reason: to find gold. He accompanied Balboa in his march across the Isthmus of Panama. After Balboa's execution, he decided to find the people to the south—the Incas—who were rumored to be very wealthy. In 1531 he and his men set out for Peru by ship. After landing on the coast, they marched through jungles for six months, plundering villages as they went. Raiding the Inca empire, they captured **Atahualpa** (AH tah WAHL pah), the Inca ruler, and held him for ransom. Atahualpa promised to fill a room with gold and silver to buy his release. After receiving a ransom of over thirteen thousand pounds of gold and nearly twice as much silver (enough to make all his men rich), Pizarro broke his promise and executed the Inca. With only a handful of men, he had conquered the great Inca empire.

Two years later Pizarro founded the city of Lima, which is today the capital of Peru. Soon afterwards other Spaniards, as greedy as Pizarro and jealous of his gold, attacked and

The Requirement

Before the conquistadors made war on the Indians, they were required to read to the Indians a document issued by the king of Spain. The statement, known as the ***requerimento***, informed the Indians that the eternal God gave the pope in Rome the authority over all men. (Pope Boniface VIII, in the 1302 *Unam Sanctam* said, "... we declare, we proclaim, we define that it is absolutely necessary for salvation that every human creature be subject to the Roman Pontiff.") The pope in turn had given Spain authority over the New World. It invited the Indians to embrace the Roman Catholic religion and to become loyal subjects under Spanish rule. If they refused, the document warned that "with the help of God, we [the Spanish] shall powerfully enter into your country and shall make war against you in all ways and manners that we can, and shall subject you to the yoke and obedience of the Church and of Their Highnesses. We shall take you and your wives and your children, and shall make slaves of them, and as such shall sell and dispose of them as Their Highnesses may command. And we shall take your goods, and shall do you all the mischief and damage that we can, as to vassals who do not obey and refuse to receive their Lord and resist and contradict him." The *requerimento* gave legal justification to those Spaniards who massacred unsubmissive Indians. It mattered little to them that none of the Indians were able to understand the document because it was read in Spanish. Nor did it seem to bother the conquistadors to sometimes read the document when no Indians were present to hear it.

killed him in his home. Pizarro had found more gold in the New World than anyone else, but greed—his own greed and that of others—prevented anyone from enjoying it. Like Pizarro, most other conquistadors died violently, fighting to keep the gold which they thought would help them to enjoy life.

Las Casas—Not all Spaniards who came to the New World were after gold. In 1502 **Bartolomé de Las Casas** (1474–1566), a Roman Catholic friar, arrived in the Americas as a missionary to the Indians. Deeply distressed over the cruelty of his countrymen, he wrote several works decrying the abuse of the Indians in the New World. He described, for example, the death of one Indian chief who was being burned at the stake. A priest told him to become a Christian so he could go to heaven. The man refused, saying that he did not want to go to any place where there were Christians. Unfortunately, the Indians, like many people today, were turned away from the gospel by the lives of people who claimed to be Christians but were not.

This painting of Las Casas by Constantino Brumidi is hanging in the Senate wing of the Capitol.

Las Casas devoted his life to improving the plight of the Indians in the New World. In 1542 he helped pass the "New Laws," which protected the Indians from being made slaves. Previously, the Spanish had forced the natives to work on plantations where they were overworked and mistreated. These new laws forbade this practice. Las Casas also opposed the common Roman Catholic practice of giving people the choice of converting to Christianity (Catholicism) and being allowed to live as slaves or refusing the church and being killed. No man, he said, could be converted by force; real conversion comes only to those who are persuaded gently. Though he was correct that people must never be forced to believe, he saw conversion only as "joining the church" and relying on good works. Real conversion is the result of God's Spirit's working in men's hearts and their repenting from sin and turning to Jesus Christ, Who alone can give salvation.

The Legend of El Dorado

Many of the early explorers came to the New World with only one thing in mind: gold. The story that excited them more than any other was the legend of El Dorado. According to American Indian folklore, El Dorado ("the gilded one") was the name of both a wealthy ruler and his fabulous city. This land supposedly possessed untold amounts of gold dust—so much, in fact, that each morning the ruler sprinkled his body with gold dust and each evening washed it off in a lake. It was said that his people threw golden statues and jewelry into the lake as offerings to their gods and that gold was so plentiful that gold dust clung to the roots of plants when they were pulled up out of the ground.

Explorers hunted all over northern South America in search of this magnificent ruler and his country. Many men lost their lives in this land of rugged mountains and fierce Indian tribes. No one ever found El Dorado, of course, for it did not exist except in legend. Years later American poet Edgar Allan Poe wrote a somber poem about the search for El Dorado. In his poem an explorer, wearied by long years of vain searching, "met a pilgrim shadow" and asked "Where can it be—/ This land of Eldorado?" The shadow grimly answered:

"Over the mountains
Of the moon,
Down the valley of the shadow,
Ride, boldly ride,"
The shade replied—
"If you seek for Eldorado!"

Those who searched for El Dorado were like those in Proverbs 13:7: "There is that maketh himself rich, yet hath nothing."

Further Spanish Explorations—Spanish exploration was not confined entirely to Latin America. Rumors of "a land of gold" to the north enticed other explorers to the regions of what is now the United States. In 1539 **Hernando de Soto**, who served with Pizarro in Peru, landed near Tampa Bay, Florida, in search of "golden" cities. In his exploration of the southeastern United States, he discovered the great Mississippi River. Though he did not find gold, his expedition led the way for further exploration of the North American continent.

Another explorer of the lands to the north was **Francisco Vásquez de Coronado** (KOR uh NAH doh). He set out from Mexico in 1540 to find the "Seven Cities of Cibola," which were reportedly rich in gold. He led his expedition into what is now New Mexico and Arizona and then on through what is now Kansas and Texas. Some of his men went westward and discovered the Grand Canyon.

Neither de Soto nor Coronado realized the value of the lands they explored. Since there was no gold, they said it was a waste of time to explore further. Because of these two expeditions, the Spaniards decided to concentrate their efforts on the land they already held, leaving most of North America open for other European nations to explore.

French, Dutch, and English Exploration

When the pope gave Spain and Portugal rights to all newly discovered lands in 1493, the other nations of Europe objected. King Francis I of France commented sarcastically, "I should like to see Adam's will, wherein he divided the earth between Spain and Portugal." After Magellan's voyage, most Europeans realized that the land to the west was indeed not Asia, but a new world; and the French, Dutch, and English sought to claim some of it for themselves.

French Explorers—The first great French explorer in the New World was **Jacques Cartier** (kar TYAY), who made three voyages to what is now eastern Canada. In 1534 he sailed to Newfoundland and Labrador, which was so desolate that he remarked, "I am rather inclined to believe that this is the land God gave to Cain."

A replica of Henry Hudson's ship, Half Moon

On his second voyage (1535) he sailed up the Saint Lawrence River to an Iroquois Indian village. The view from a nearby mountain was so impressive that Cartier named the site Montreal (French for "Mount Royal"). Today one of the largest cities in Canada stands there. Like many explorers of his day, Cartier was certain that there existed a water route—the so-called Northwest Passage—which would take him to the Pacific Ocean and from there to the Orient but he was unsuccessful in finding one.

Some seventy years after Cartier, **Samuel de Champlain** (sham PLANE), called the "Father of New France," explored and colonized the area around the Saint Lawrence River. In 1608 he founded the city of Quebec. He worked closely with the local Indians, who led him to two of the Great Lakes (Ontario and Huron) and to what we now call Lake Champlain. Like Cartier, he was looking for a route west to China.

Another noted French explorer was Jesuit missionary **Jacques Marquette** (mar KET). In 1673 he and a friend, **Louis Joliet** (JOH lee ET), explored the Mississippi River. They paddled canoes downstream to a point in southern Arkansas before turning back. In 1682 Sieur de La Salle (luh SAL) traveled to the mouth of the Mississippi River and claimed the entire Mississippi Valley for France. He called it "Louisiana" in honor of King Louis XIV of France.

Dutch Explorers—The most famous explorer for the Netherlands was the Englishman **Henry Hudson**, whom the Dutch hired to find a shorter route to the East. He explored the northeastern coast of America in his ship the *Half Moon*. In 1609 he entered the Hudson River, thinking it might be the Northwest

Life at Sea

Life at sea was full of hardships during the Age of Exploration. In return for their hard labor, sailors were paid very little and were fed the worst sorts of food imaginable. Since many ships remained at sea for long periods of time, the sailors often had to live for months on a dreary diet of biscuits (hardtack), salt beef, salt fish, and beer. The salted meat was tough, usually stank, and often had maggots in it. The biscuits were usually of poor quality. Some sailors jokingly refused to eat those biscuits that were not infested with maggots, stating that they did not want to eat something that even the maggots had refused. All ships carried barrels of water, but within a short time the water became stagnant and undrinkable. It became discolored, gave off a terrible odor, and was full of tiny organisms. Unfortunately, the only thing on board that did not spoil was the liquor.

One disease that plagued sailors and caused the deaths of many was a vitamin-C deficiency called scurvy. It caused the gums to become swollen and bloody (loosening the teeth in the process) and caused the limbs to become swollen and discolored. Although no one knew about vitamin C at the time, various sea captains stumbled upon a cure for scurvy, finding that fresh fruit and vegetables stopped it. Since fresh produce could not be carried on long sea voyages, the British navy made it compulsory in 1798 for their ships to carry lime juice. Because of this practice, British sailors acquired the nickname "limeys."

Green lime

Passage. He continued upriver to where Albany, New York, now stands. His exploration gave the Dutch a claim to the region. In 1621 the Dutch founded the city of New Amsterdam, which is today New York City.

English Explorers—The English began exploring the New World soon after Columbus's first voyage. They hired an Italian sailor named **John Cabot** to lead the first English expedition to North America. After a six-week voyage across the Atlantic, Cabot dropped anchor off the coast of Canada. The first European after the Vikings to set foot on the North American mainland, he returned to England and was rewarded by King Henry VII. In 1498 Cabot made a second voyage to the New World, this time accompanied by his son Sebastian. They explored the northern coast of North America. Though they did not find gold or spices, they found rich fisheries off the Newfoundland coast. The two expeditions to the New World were the basis for England's claim on America. The Cabots paved the way for the founding of English colonies on the North American continent a century later.

Like the Spanish, the English also looked for gold. But they went about obtaining it much differently. For the most part, the English did not engage in the extreme cruelty to the natives that was typical of the Spaniards. The English brought their families and sought to develop the land, not exploit it. Their first permanent settlement was **Jamestown**, founded in **1607** near the mouth of Chesapeake Bay. Under the leadership of Captain **John Smith** they built a village and began to explore the land. In 1608 much of the village burned down, and the few settlers had almost given up when a new governor, Lord de la Warr, arrived. The influx of new settlers and fresh supplies gave new life to the struggling colony.

This English settlement, the first of many in the New World, was the beginning of what would later become the United States of America. Most of the freedoms that Americans have enjoyed—freedom of religion, freedom of

Statue of John Smith

THROUGH EYES OF FAITH

Eastern-Western Relations

How do you think that these initial encounters with Westerners affected Easterners' view of the West? What about their view of Christianity? Do you think this view helped or hindered the cause of Christ when missionaries arrived in the East decades later?

speech, and many others—came from the influence of Protestant settlers who came to North America during the seventeenth century.

Europe and the Orient

The West Reaches the East

Europe's exploration efforts were not limited to the New World; in fact, her main interests were on the other side of the world in the Orient. Spain was largely excluded from this area by treaty with Portugal (although she did colonize the Philippines). Portugal, the Netherlands, and England, however, traded and colonized extensively in the East.

The Portuguese—Soon after da Gama returned from his historic voyage, the Portuguese, under the leadership of **Pedro Cabral**, established a trading post in India. From this small beginning they were able to establish numerous trading posts throughout the Indian Ocean. Their fully armed ships gave them an insurmountable advantage over Muslim and native traders in the region.

In 1506 **Affonso de Albuquerque** (AL buh KUR kee) was named the viceroy of Portuguese holdings in the East. He discouraged cruelty to the natives and led his men in setting up trading posts and plantations along the trade routes to support and protect Portuguese traders. Under his leadership the Portuguese began to build a vast commercial empire. They captured and controlled the entrances to the Persian Gulf and the Red Sea. Shortly after Albuquerque's death they pushed farther eastward. By 1520 they had taken Ceylon (present-day Sri Lanka) and the town of Banten on the island of Java. The latter controlled one of the two water entrances to the Far East. Since the Portuguese already controlled the other entrance at the straits of Malacca, they were in an excellent position to dominate all of the sea trade between Europe and Asia. In 1542 they began trading with Japan; in 1557 they founded the colony of Macao on the Chinese mainland.

The Portuguese "eastern empire," however, had some fatal weaknesses. It was spread out too widely for the little country of Portugal to administer and defend effectively. Furthermore, since many sailors died at sea, Portugal's manpower was drained to a critical point. (About one voyage in seven ended in disaster.) Finally, the cruelty of the traders—despite Albuquerque's reforms—caused the Asians to hate them. With the lack of cooperation essential for successful trading, Portuguese commercial interests were hampered. When other European nations began to compete for the business in the East, the Asians granted it to them.

The Dutch—The Dutch were not a wealthy people in the sixteenth century, but they were experienced sailors. When prices soared under the Portuguese monopoly, the Dutch decided to go directly to the source for their Asian goods. In 1596 they settled on Java and Sumatra and expelled the Portuguese from the key city of Banten. They later captured the main Spice Islands and founded the city of Batavia, which became a key port and trading post in the East Indies. They soon became the only nation with which Japan would trade. They also began trading with Formosa (modern Taiwan) and seized the island of Ceylon. By the middle of the seventeenth century, Dutch control extended from Persia to Japan.

In order to provide fresh water, vegetables, and meat for ships making the long voyage around Africa to the Indies, the Dutch in 1652 established a settlement at the Cape of Good Hope at what is now Cape Town, South Africa. The mild climate of the cape attracted many settlers; before long it became a sizable colony.

The English—When England defeated the Spanish Armada in 1588, she realized that she had enough sea power to carry on a busy trade with the East.

In 1591, almost a century after da Gama, English merchant-seamen made a trading voyage to India. Although they started late, the English far surpassed the Portuguese in long-range influence in the Orient. They followed the Dutch into the East Indies, trading alongside them for several years. Soon, however, they turned their main attention to India. England seized control of the Persian Gulf and opened trade on both the east and west coasts of India. This was the beginning of England's influence in India—an influence that she continued to expand well into the nineteenth century.

The East Responds to the West

China and Japan resented Western intervention in their affairs. The same satisfied attitude that had kept them from exploring other lands also kept them from welcoming traders to their own land. They had been secure in their traditions, and they did not take kindly to European sailors who attempted to claim their properties for unknown kings and their souls for Roman popes. The Portuguese, who were the first to come to the East, were especially tactless and cruel, and by 1550 there had already been several bloody battles between Chinese and Portuguese soldiers. The people of China resisted the European way of life as well as Christianity. They wanted to be left alone. The Chinese did allow, however, the Portuguese to colonize the port city of Macao, but for this privilege the Portuguese had to pay $30,000 per year in tribute. Except for isolated instances, there was no direct trade between China and the European countries for many years.

Initially, Japan was more friendly to the Europeans than China was. The Japanese welcomed **Francis Xavier**, the famous Jesuit missionary. Later, however, the government, influenced by Buddhism, expelled the foreign missionaries who had followed Xavier to Japan. Those who stayed were severely persecuted. More trouble broke out in 1639 when the Japanese emperor learned that Portuguese trading ships were smuggling in Catholic missionaries disguised as merchants. Furious, he commanded that any Portuguese who came to Japan be killed on sight. Some traders who did not think the emperor was serious learned otherwise and paid with their lives. The Japanese did allow a few Dutch ships to trade in their ports, but for the most part Japan, like China, was a "closed" country to European travelers.

Section Quiz

1. List the five major groups of Indian tribes in North America.
2. What were the three major native Indian cultures of Central and South America?
3. After crossing the Isthmus of Panama, Balboa saw what body of water? What did he call it? Who gave it its present name?
4. List the country for which each of the following explorers sailed and claimed territory in the New World: Jacques Cartier, Samuel de Champlain, Henry Hudson, and John Cabot.
5. List the Oriental possessions gained by each of the following countries during the Age of Exploration: Portugal, the Netherlands, and England.

1. ______________________________
____
____
____
____

2. ______________________________
____
____

3. ______________________________
____
____

4. ______________________________
____
____
____

5. ______________________________
____
____
____

III. Parallel to Discovery: The Commercial Revolution

During the fifteenth and sixteenth centuries, Europe underwent many political, social, religious, and aesthetic changes. There were also many economic changes. The ownership of land no longer was considered the basis of wealth. Money became the medium of exchange in trade. As new sources of gold and spices were discovered in distant lands and used as a medium of exchange, wealth was redefined. Soon after the earliest explorers had returned home, commercial ventures were organized to establish trade ties with newly discovered peoples across the seas. Before long, great wealth was coming into Europe from around the world. Europe's business thinking and practice changed. These changes are known as the **Commercial Revolution**.

Mercantilism: Nations Acquiring Wealth

The dominant economic system of the Age of Exploration is known as **mercantilism**. Mercantilists believed that the newly found wealth should benefit the mother country. As a result, European nations kept tight control over their country's economy. A nation's strength and greatness was believed to rest upon its wealth, that is, the amount of gold and silver it possessed. For this reason, the goal of mercantilistic nations was to obtain as much precious metal as possible. To achieve this goal, nations sought to acquire colonies, to become self-sufficient, and to maintain a favorable balance of trade.

Under mercantilism, colonies existed for the good of the mother country. They supplied the mother country with raw materials and provided markets where goods from the mother country could be sold. The colonies were not allowed to produce anything that the mother country produced, for that would be competition. Nor were the colonies allowed to trade with anyone but the mother country. Mexico, for example, had to buy everything it needed from Spain, and whatever it produced had to be sold to Spain. Likewise, it was not allowed to trade directly with other Spanish colonies; for Mexican products to reach Peru, for example, they had to be shipped across the ocean to Spain and then back again to Peru. Thus the mother countries became wealthier and wealthier, and the colonies usually suffered.

By establishing colonies, European nations hoped to become self-sufficient. They did not want to purchase goods from other European countries, for that would drain their own supply of gold and silver.

Instead they desired to export more than they imported, and thus bring more gold and silver into their national treasury. This was considered to be a "favorable balance of trade." But mercantilism had its weaknesses. Under this system the government regulated a nation's economic activity, creating national monopolies that deterred competition. More often than not, the interests of the government

Spanish gold doubloons and pieces of eight salvaged from a 1715 wreck; the pieces of eight are cut from an eight-ounce piece of molten silver and stamped with the shield of Philip V of Spain and the cross.

superseded the interests and welfare of the people—especially those in the colonies.

Mercantilists did not view trade as a "two-way street" benefiting both buyer and seller. They thought of it only in terms of the seller, who obtained gold and silver for his product. This one-sided foreign trade, in which goods went out of a country and gold and silver came in, was often a detriment to a country's agriculture and industry. Under this system the goods and crops a nation produced were deemed important only if they could be traded abroad for gold and silver.

Once gold and silver were obtained by a mercantilistic country, the wealth was seldom used to benefit the people. These precious metals were hoarded. But as Solomon (who possessed great amounts of gold and silver) says in Ecclesiastes 5:13: "There is a sore evil which I have seen under the sun, namely, riches kept for the owners thereof to their hurt." God does not want us to hoard the resources and riches which He has provided for our use. He wants us to invest and use what we have for His glory and not for our own selfish gain.

Capitalism: Individuals Advancing Wealth

The opportunity for acquiring great wealth was open not only to national states but also to private individuals. During this period another economic system—**capitalism**—developed side by side with mercantilism. Unlike mercantilism, the goal of capitalism was not simply to acquire wealth, but to advance wealth. Enterprising individuals used what money they had to make more money. They invested their wealth, often at great risk, in hopes of making a profit.

Many of the early capitalists were bankers. They made money by buying and selling bills of exchange, by safeguarding money for others, and by exchanging money. They often invested their own resources in business ventures such as financing trade voyages. But sea travel at this time was perilous: it was not uncommon for the stormy seas to send ships to the bottom of the ocean or for pirates to seize a ship's cargo. Such disasters could bring financial ruin to an individual. For this reason, men organized **companies** in which they pooled their resources; they shared the gains as well as the losses.

From this practice arose the **joint-stock company**. People invested money in such companies; in return they were issued stock certificates showing the amount of money they invested. The invested money became part of the company's **capital**, or supply of money. The company then used this capital to finance a business venture. If a profit was made, it was given to the stockholders, or contributors (also called investors), in the form of **dividends**. They shared in both the profits and the losses.

There were many joint-stock companies during the Age of Exploration. Three are especially important. The English East India Company, founded in 1600 with only a small amount of capital, began trading mostly in India. It was astonishingly successful. Profits for the years 1609–13, for example, averaged almost 300 percent each year (that is, investors received back every year dividends three times their original investment). The Dutch East India Company, founded in 1602, traded in the East Indies (such as Java and Sumatra). It too made great profits, paying dividends of 18 percent each year for many years. The French Company of New France traded in Canada, mainly for furs. All these companies did more than just trade, however. They set up bases, or settlements, to make their work more permanent.

Another method of getting people to help finance an enterprise was to post in a public place a **prospectus**—details of a proposed business venture. People

The East Indiaman "Warley" *(BHC3707) 1801, by Robert Salmon*
© National Maritime Museum, London

wrote their names below the prospectus, stating that they would help share the cost of the enterprise. If it was a success, they would share in the profits; if it was a failure, they agreed to sustain the loss. It is from this practice that we get the word **underwriter**, which today we use to describe an insurance company. One of the earliest insurance companies was Lloyds of London. It was founded in 1688 by a group of men who underwrote voyages to the New World.

Section Quiz

1. What are the changes in Europe's business thinking and practice during the fifteenth and sixteenth centuries called?
2. What was the dominant economic policy of most European nations during the Age of Exploration?
3. What was the purpose of colonies under this economic policy?
4. Using wealth to make more wealth describes what economic policy?

1. ______________________________

____

2. ______________________________
3. ______________________________

____

4. ______________________________

A Glance Behind

It was not accidental that the Age of Exploration occurred at the same time as the Reformation. While explorers were discovering new lands across the seas, theologians were rediscovering the truth of God's Word. In God's timing, these discoveries occurred simultaneously. Instead of bearing the message of Catholicism, many Europeans disseminated the message of the reformers to distant parts of the globe. Furthermore, the discovery of the New World—in particular, North America—provided a safe haven for those who were persecuted for the name of Christ on the European continent.

and a Glimpse Ahead

Chapter Review

Can You Define?

compass
latitude
caravel
Line of Demarcation
circumnavigation
conquistadors
viceroy
Commercial Revolution
mercantilism
capitalism
company
joint-stock company
capital
dividends
prospectus
underwriter

Can You Identify?

Marco Polo
Prester John
Prince Henry
Bartolomeu Dias
Vasco da Gama
Christopher Columbus (1492)
Ferdinand Magellan
Mayas
Aztecs
Incas
Vasco Núñez de Balboa
Hernando Cortés
Montezuma
Francisco Pizarro
Atahualpa
Bartolomé de Las Casas
Hernando de Soto
Francisco Vásquez de Coronado
Jacques Cartier
Samuel de Champlain
Jacques Marquette
Louis Joliet
Henry Hudson
John Cabot
Jamestown (1607)
John Smith
Pedro Cabral
Affonso de Albuquerque
Francis Xavier

Can You Locate?

Spice Islands
Cathay (China)
Cape of Good Hope
Lisbon
Indian Ocean
Bahamas
Hispaniola
Cuba
Brazil
Strait of Magellan
Pacific Ocean
Bering Strait
Yucatán Peninsula
Mexico
Tenochtitlán
Peru
Isthmus of Panama
Lima
Mississippi River
Montreal
Saint Lawrence River
Quebec
New Amsterdam
Jamestown
Ceylon
Java
Formosa

How Much Do You Remember?

1. What new navigational instruments aided the explorers in their travels?
2. List four reasons why Portugal and Spain led other European nations in the Age of Exploration.
3. List the important contribution that each of the following explorers made to the Age of Exploration: Bartolomeu Dias, Vasco da Gama, Christopher Columbus, and Ferdinand Magellan.
4. How did the Indians of Central and South America differ from those of North America?
5. What was the Chinese and Japanese attitude toward the European traders?

What Do You Think?

1. In what ways do you think the Renaissance influenced the Age of Discovery?
2. How does 1 Timothy 6:9–10 relate to the motives of many of the explorers? How does Proverbs 16:16 relate to their goals?
3. What discovery of the Age of Exploration do you think had the greatest impact on history?
4. What effect did the defeat of the Spanish Armada in 1588 have on the history of North America?
5. Mercantilism and capitalism are both economic policies—how do they differ?

GLOSSARY

A

Abbasid Caliphate that marked the peak of the **Muslim** empire; during this caliphate the political unity of the Muslim world collapsed (Ch. 6)

Abrahamic Covenant God's covenant to Abraham in which He promised Abraham descendants, a land for his descendants, and a Messiah that would come through his seed (Ch. 2)

aids Financial payments by a **vassal** to a **lord** on special occasions (Ch. 8)

Allah The god of **Islam** (Ch. 6)

Anabaptists Group that rejected infant baptism and rebaptized each other (Ch. 12)

anarchy The breakdown of government and order (Ch. 3)

ancestor worship Worship of a family's ancestors (Ch. 7)

Anglican Church Church of England; the established state church of England which has as its creed the *Thirty-nine Articles* (Ch. 12)

Anglo-Saxon Chronicle Document that traces the history of England from Roman times to Alfred's day (Ch. 9)

Anglo-Saxons Germanic tribes from northern Europe that invaded Britain after the Romans left (Ch. 9)

anthropomorphic Having human forms or attributes (Ch. 3)

apprentice First class in a craft **guild**; lived in the home of a **master** and learned trade skills and proper conduct (Ch. 10)

aqueducts Structures built to supply water to cities (Ch. 5)

archon Chief magistrate of the Athenian council of nobles (Ch. 3)

artifacts Objects made by humans (Ch. 1)

Aryans A fair-skinned people who came from central Asia sometime after 1500 BC and subdued the non-Aryan people of northwest India; established **Sanskrit** (Ch. 7)

astrology The practice of trying to interpret human events and destiny by the position of the planets and stars (Ch. 2)

astronomy The study of celestial bodies (Ch. 2)

Athena Goddess of wisdom; patron of the city of Athens (Ch. 3)

Augsburg Confession A confession written by Philipp Melanchthon that set forth the chief doctrines that Luther and his followers contended (Ch. 12)

augustus Co-emperor of half the Roman Empire under Diocletian's plan (Ch. 5)

autocratic Ruling with unlimited authority (Ch. 7)

Avesta The sacred writings of Zoroastrianism (Ch. 2)

Aztec Central American civilization that flourished after the Mayan civilization; conquered by the Spanish (Ch. 13)

B

Baal Pagan god of the Canaanites (Ch. 2)

Babel City in Shinar (southeastern Mesopotamia) that had a great tower; place where languages were formed (Ch. 1)

Babylonian Captivity (1) Seventy-year exile of Israel in Babylon (Ch. 2); (2) The period from 1309 to 1377 when the papal court dwelt in Avignon, France (Ch. 10)

baillis French royal officials whom the king appointed and paid (Ch. 9)

banca "Bench"; the table of the moneychangers (Ch. 10)

barbarians A Roman term for all those outside the empire who did not share in the Greek or Roman cultures (Ch. 5)

barter Exchanging goods for goods (Ch. 10)

Battle of Hastings Battle in England between the Normans and the Anglo-Saxons; William the Conqueror established the Norman dynasty (Ch. 9)

Battle of Manzikert Battle in Asia Minor between the **Seljuk Turks** and the Byzantines; established Turkish control of Asia Minor (Ch. 6)

Battle of Tours Defeat of the **Muslims** by the Franks; stopped the Muslim advance into Europe (Ch. 6)

Bedouins Arab nomads who traveled through the harsh desert wilderness in independent bands searching for pastureland and water for their livestock (Ch. 6)

Benedictine Rule A standard of discipline and order that strictly regulated the life of monks; the most popular system of rules in medieval Europe; designed by Benedict of Nursia (Ch. 8)

Bourbon French royal family; descended from Louis IX (Ch. 12)

Brahman The great Hindu god who supposedly permeates everything in the universe (Ch. 7)

Buddhism Eastern religion founded by Siddhartha Gautama (Buddha); a religion built upon works and moral behavior (Ch. 7)

bull An official papal document (Ch. 10)

Bushido An unwritten military code that governed the conduct of the **samurai** (Ch. 7)

Byzantine Empire The Eastern Roman Empire after the Western Roman Empire fell (Ch. 6)

C

caesar The assistant of an **augustus** (Ch. 5)

caliphs Successors of Muhammad who directed the affairs of **Islam** and exercised spiritual, political, and military authority (Ch. 6)

calligraphy The art of beautiful writing (Ch. 6)

capital Supply of money (Ch. 13)

capitalism Economic system designed to advance wealth (Ch. 13)

caravel A ship with large square sails to provide power and smaller triangular sails to provide maneuverability (Ch. 13)

Carolingian House The Frankish royal house named after Charlemagne (Ch. 8)

Carolingian Miniscule Clean and simple writing style developed during Charlemagne's reign; became the model for much of our "lowercase" writing today (Ch. 8)

caste system A system of rigid social groups in India (Ch. 7)

castle The center of life for the nobility; the **lord**'s home, the local jail, the treasury, the armory, the court, and the seat of government (Ch. 8)

catholic "Universal"; "encompassing all"; the term of early Christians for the universal church (Ch. 8)

chansons Lighthearted songs that set secular lyric poems to music (Ch. 11)

charter A legal document that outlined the privileges granted to a town by a feudal **lord** (Ch. 10)

Chinese characters Sixty-five thousand characters that represent complete ideas, objects, and sounds (Ch. 7)

chivalry A **knight**'s strict code of behavior (Ch. 8)

Christian worldview Composed of three central truths: (1) God made the world and everything in it; (2) this world has fallen into a sad and broken condition because of human sin; and (3) God is working to redeem this world to Himself; see **worldview** (Ch. 1)

circumnavigation Sailing around the world (Ch. 13)

Cistercians Monastic order whose monks adopted lives of seclusion and strict discipline; made popular by Bernard of Clairvaux (Ch. 9)

civilization Human existence lived in cities or under their influence (Ch. 1)

clan (1) A number of families from a common ancestor (Ch. 4); (2) A group of families claiming descent from a common ancestor; the basic social, political, and religious unit in Japan (Ch. 7)

clergy Those who took "Holy Orders" in special service to the church (Ch. 8)

College of Cardinals The Roman Catholic assembly of cardinals that chooses a new **pope** (Ch. 9)

Commercial Revolution The economic changes in European business practice and thinking during the fifteenth and sixteenth centuries (Ch. 13)

common law Uniform laws in England determined by justices (Ch. 9)

company An organization of inventors who pooled their resources, sharing gains as well as losses (Ch. 13)

compass A magnetized navigation device that greatly aided sailors during the age of exploration (Ch. 13)

Concordat of Worms Recognized the right of the church to elect its own bishops and abbots and to invest them with spiritual authority; the elections had to be held in the presence of the emperor or his representatives (Ch. 9)

condottière Leaders of mercenaries that fought in Italy during the late fifteenth and sixteenth centuries (Ch. 11)

Confucianism Eastern religion founded by Confucius that was based on relationships (Ch. 7)

conquistadors "Conquerors" sent from Spain to the New World to search for riches, to evangelize the Indians, and to establish Spanish authority (Ch. 13)

consul Annually elected leaders of the Roman Republic who held the **imperium** (Ch. 4)

Cortes Spanish council composed of nobles, **clergy**, and representatives of the cities (Ch. 10)

Council of Constance Fifteenth-century Roman Catholic Church council that ended the **Great Schism** and burned John Huss (Ch. 10, 12)

Council of Nicaea Church council in 325 that affirmed the doctrines of Christ's deity and the Trinity (Ch. 5)

Council of Trent The **Counter-Reformation** council that condemned justification by faith alone and the sole authority of Scripture, set forth a complete doctrinal position of the Roman Church, and sealed the break between Protestant and Roman Catholic churches (Ch. 12)

Counter-Reformation Another term for the Catholic Reformation that opposed the Protestant Reformation (Ch. 12)

Creation Mandate First command from God revealing that man's reason for being is to subdue the earth and exercise dominion over it; found in Genesis 1:28 (Ch. 1)

crucifixion Death on a cross (Ch. 5)

Crusades Military expeditions from the West to free the East from the **Muslims** (Ch. 6, 9)

culture The physical and mental environment developed through human thought and labor (Ch. 1)

cuneiform The earliest known form of writing (Ch. 2)

curia regis The Great Council; an English feudal body composed of chief **vassals**; "king's council"(Ch. 9)

D

Delian League Defensive alliance of Greek city-states led by Athens against the Persians (Ch. 3)

demesne The land reserved for the **lord** (Ch. 8)

democracy Rule by the people (Ch. 3)

Diaspora The scattering of the Jewish people (Ch. 2)

Diet The German equivalent of the English Parliament and the French **Estates-General** (Ch. 10)

Diet of Worms The **Diet** in 1521 at which Martin Luther reaffirmed the views expressed in the books that he had written (Ch. 12)

dividends Profit given to the stockholders of a **joint-stock company** (Ch. 13)

divine providence Biblical teaching that God has planned all of human history (Ch. 1)

divine sovereignty God's complete and permanent authority over this world (Ch. 1)

"do-nothing kings" Seventh-century **Merovingian** kings who reigned but did not rule; the power went to the **mayor of the palace** (Ch. 8)

Domesday Book A survey of property taken in England when William the Conqueror conquered England (Ch. 9)

Donation of Pepin The lands of the **Lombards** that were given to the **pope** by Pepin the Short; became the Papal States (Ch. 8)

Dorians Invaders that conquered the **Mycenaean civilization** around 1200 BC (Ch. 3)

duchy A **duke**'s territory (Ch. 9)

duke Local Germanic tribal leader (Ch. 9)

dynastic rule The rule of one family (Ch. 7)

E

Eastern Orthodox Church Made up of various national churches that refused to recognize the Church of Rome's claim of control (Ch. 6)

Edict of Milan Edict of Constantine that made Christianity legal in 313 (Ch. 5)

Edict of Nantes Edict of Henry IV that gave the **Huguenots** a certain amount of religious toleration (Ch. 12)

Elizabethan Settlement The attempt by Elizabeth to settle England's religious problems through compromise (Ch. 12)

empire The rule of one people over another (Ch. 2)

Epic of Gilgamesh Epic Babylonian poem that describes the adventures of Gilgamesh and includes an account of a universal flood (Ch. 2)

Epicureanism Philosophy that teaches that true happiness comes only as man frees his mind from fear and his body from pain (Ch. 5)

Estates-General French representative body composed of **clergy**, nobility, and townspeople (Ch. 9)

Etruscans One of Italy's earliest civilizations; lived in northern Italy and contributed to the development of Roman culture (Ch. 4)

evaluation of historical sources Examination of a given record for its internal consistency and believability (Ch. 1)

excommunicate To punish an individual by depriving him of the sacraments and excluding him from the fellowship of the church (Ch. 9)

F

fasces A small bundle of rods which enclosed an axe; symbol of the **imperium** (Ch. 4)

Fertile Crescent Crescent-shaped fertile region encompassing Mesopotamia and the land of Canaan (Ch. 2)

feudalism A political system in which local rulers offered the people protection in return for their services (Ch. 8)

fief Land grants given in return for services (Ch. 8)

Five Pillars of Islam Certain religious duties that **Islam** requires every **Muslim** to perform in order to reach heaven; (1) reciting the simple confession "There is no God but **Allah**, and Muhammad is his prophet"; (2) reciting prayers five times daily while facing toward Mecca; (3) giving alms (money) to the poor; (4) fasting from sunrise to sunset during the sacred month of Ramadan; (5) making a pilgrimage to Mecca (Ch. 6)

florin A gold coin minted by the city of Florence (Ch. 10)

Four Noble Truths The center of Buddha's teachings; (1) Suffering is part of all existence; (2) Suffering has a cause—selfish desires; (3) Suffering can be overcome by destroying selfish desires; (4) If man follows the Eightfold Path, he will destroy selfish desires and end all suffering (Ch. 7)

Franks The most powerful Germanic people in the early Middle Ages; kingdom ruled by the **Merovingian House** and the **Carolingian House** (Ch. 8)

freemen Privileged peasants who served as manorial officials or provided skilled labor, such as blacksmiths, millers, and carpenters (Ch. 8)

frescoes Paintings on wet plaster (Ch. 11)

friars Members of the **mendicant orders** (Ch. 9)

Fujiwara A **clan** that took over Japan by marrying their daughters to the sons of the imperial family (Ch. 7)

G

genre painting A type of painting that depicts scenes of everyday life (Ch. 11)

geocentric theory Theory that the earth is the center of the universe (Ch. 5)

gladiator Warrior who fought in the Roman Colosseum (Ch. 5)

Golden Bull Established the **Diet** of the Holy Roman Empire (Ch. 10)

Golden Horde Mongol state based in Russia; founded by Batu Khan; the strongest Mongol state in western Asia (Ch. 7)

gospel The teaching that Jesus Christ died in the place of sinful humans so that they might be forgiven of their sins and be able to claim as their own the righteousness of Jesus Christ (Ch. 5)

Gothic Light and delicate fourteenth-century architecture with flying buttresses, higher ceilings, thinner walls, larger windows and doors, and stained glass windows (Ch. 10)

Great Schism The period from the late fourteenth to early fifteenth century during which the Roman Catholic Church had two to three men claiming to be the **pope** (Ch. 10)

"Greek fire" An explosive mixture of naphtha oil, sulfur, and saltpeter (Ch. 6)

guilds Organizations whose primary function was to regulate the business activity of a given town (Ch. 10)

Gupta Empire Fourth-century Indian empire under which India had perhaps its greatest era of prosperity and achievement (Ch. 7)

H

Hagia Sophia Cathedral in Constantinople built by Justinian; finest example of Byzantine architecture (Ch. 6)

Hanseatic League An association composed of more than seventy German cities in northwestern Europe; sought to organize and control trade in Sweden, Russia, Flanders, and England (Ch. 10)

Hapsburgs German noble family that built a strong base of power (Austria) among the southern German states; ruled the **Holy Roman Empire** after 1438 (Ch. 10)

Hegira The flight of Muhammad from Mecca to Medina; year 1 of the **Muslim** calendar (Ch. 6)

Hellenic Greek culture (Ch. 3)

Hellenistic Similar to Greek culture (Ch. 3)

Helots Original Spartans who were enslaved by the **Dorians** (Ch. 3)

hierarchical Structure with levels of authority (Ch. 5)

hieroglyphics A form of picture writing (Ch. 2)

Hinduism Indian religion that has no formal statement of doctrine but is based on the **Vedas** and **Upanishads**; serves as the unifying influence in India's diverse society (Ch. 7)

historical interpretation Interpreting events by integrating the perceived meaning and significance of the events (Ch. 1)

historical synthesis Gathering the useful information and weaving the facts together into a narrative of the past (Ch. 1)

history The study of the record of the past acts of God and man on earth from its creation to the present, based on the best surviving evidence (Ch. 1)

Hohenstaufens German royal family that rose to prominence in the twelfth century (Ch. 9)

Holy Roman Empire The name of the German empire because of its alliance with the Roman Catholic Church and its symbolic association with the empire of ancient Rome (Ch. 9)

homage The ceremony by which a man became a **vassal** and thus eligible for a **fief** (Ch. 8)

Huguenots French Protestants (Ch. 12)

human depravity The doctrine that every aspect of every human's being (body, mind, will, and emotions) has been marred by the Fall and is opposed to God's will (Ch. 1)

humanism A renewed focus on man's capacities (Ch. 11)

humanists Those who studied the liberal arts (Ch. 11)

humanities (1) Formal study of human thought and culture (Ch. 3); (2) The liberal arts; the study of history, science, and grammar, as well as classical literature and philosophy (Ch. 11)

Hundred Years' War War between England and France during the fourteenth and fifteenth centuries; won by the French (Ch. 10)

Huns Nomadic tribe led by Attila, whose advance west forced Germanic tribes to seek refuge in Roman territory (Ch. 5)

I

icon Painted images of Christ and the saints (Ch. 6)

Ile-de-France The small area around Paris owned by the Capetians (Ch. 9)

Iliad An epic poem of the Greek Dark Ages written by Homer (Ch. 3)

image of God A complex of qualities possessed by all humans that reflects part of God's own personality (Ch. 1)

imperator An ancient title given to the commander of a victorious army; head of the Roman Empire (Ch. 4)

imperium The king's authority in Rome (Ch. 4)

Inca South American **empire** from the fourteenth to the sixteenth centuries (Ch. 13)

Index of Prohibited Books A list of books that the Roman Catholic Church has condemned (Ch. 12)

indictment Accusation (Ch. 9)

indulgences Certificates that supposedly granted pardon from the punishment of sins (Ch. 12)

Inquisition A special church court commissioned by the **pope** to stamp out heresy (Ch. 9, 12)

The Institutes of the Christian Religion Theological book written by John Calvin; one of the most significant and influential books on theology ever written (Ch. 12)

interdict The suspension of public church services and of the administration of all sacraments (except baptism and extreme unction) in a given location (Ch. 9)

investiture Symbolic act by which the **lord** gave to the **vassal** the right to use a **fief** (Ch. 8)

Islam A religion based on the teaching of Muhammad (Ch. 6)

J

Jamestown First English permanent settlement in the New World; located in Virginia (Ch. 13)

Jesuits Roman Catholic religious order founded by Ignatius Loyola that suppressed heresy and promoted Roman Catholic education (Ch. 12)

jihad Islamic "holy war" (Ch. 6)

joint family Extended family that includes the children, grandchildren, wives, and close blood relatives of a common ancestor (Ch. 7)

joint-stock company A company in which people invested money and in return were issued stock certificates showing the amount of money they hadinvested (Ch. 13)

journeyman Second class of a craft **guild**; "day laborer"; could seek employment and earn wages as a skilled worker (Ch. 10)

"just price" A price that included the cost of materials, a fair return for the labor expended, and a reasonable profit (Ch. 10)

Justinian Code A systematic arrangement of laws that clarified Roman legal principles (Ch. 6)

K

Kaaba A sacred shrine at Mecca that housed hundreds of pagan idols; Muhammad destroyed the idols of the Kaaba and turned it into the center of Islamic worship (Ch. 6)

knight Medieval warriors who protected life and property and lived by the "code of **chivalry**" (Ch. 8)

Koran The sacred book of the **Muslims** (Ch. 6)

L

laity Those who did not take "Holy Orders" (Ch. 8)

latitude Distance from the equator (Ch. 13)

Law of the Twelve Tables Foundation of Roman civil law; the first written law code in Rome; hung in the **Roman Forum** (Ch. 4)

lay investiture Claim of kings and nobles not only to appoint church officials but also to invest them with their religious authority (Ch. 9)

League of the Seven Hills League of seven villages on the banks of the Tiber River; the beginning of the city of Rome (Ch. 4)

Line of Demarcation Line of separation in the Atlantic Ocean that decided the areas that could be colonized by Spain and Portugal (Ch. 13)

Lollards Followers of John Wycliffe (Ch. 12)

Lombards Germanic people who through conquest moved into northern Italy (Ch. 8)

longbow English bow that could shoot arrows able to penetrate suits of armor (Ch. 10)

lord Landholding noble in **feudalism** (Ch. 8)

M

Magna Carta A guarantee of feudal rights; one of the most important documents in English history because it showed that the king was under the law (Ch. 9)

Magyars A group of Asiatic nomads who later became known as the Hungarians (Ch. 8)

manor The center of medieval society, a self-contained farming community controlled by a **lord** and farmed by peasants (Ch. 8)

Mare Nostrum The Roman term for the Mediterranean Sea; "our sea" (Ch. 4)

mass The Roman Catholic service in which the Holy Eucharist is offered (Ch. 8)

master Third class of a craft **guild**; could open his own shop and take on **apprentices** and **journeymen** (Ch. 10)

Maya Central American civilization from the fourth through the tenth centuries; noted for its artistic and intellectual achievements (Ch. 13)

mayor of the palace Principal palace official under the **Merovingian House** (Ch. 8)

Medici family Prominent Italians who had become extremely wealthy through commerce and banking; controlled the city of Florence (Ch. 11)

mendicant orders Monastic orders that labored to bring about reform by living and preaching among the people; they begged for their daily sustenance (Ch. 9)

mercantilism Economic system that held that the wealth of colonies should benefit the mother country (Ch. 13)

Merovingian House First royal line of the **Franks** (Ch. 8)

middle class Social class primarily composed of merchants, bankers, craftsmen, and skilled laborers (Ch. 10)

Middle Kingdom Chinese term reflecting the belief that China was the center of the earth (Ch. 7)

minaret A tower that is a part of or adjacent to a **mosque** (Ch. 6)

Minoan civilization An early civilization in the Aegean region based on the island of Crete; established trade with the **Fertile Crescent** and Egypt (Ch. 3)

missi dominici Messengers sent in pairs by Charlemagne throughout his **empire** to ensure the enforcement of his policies on the local level (Ch. 8)

monarchy Rule by one (Ch. 3)

monasticism The lifestyle of withdrawing from all worldly cares and possessions and practicing strict discipline and religious exercises (Ch. 5)

moneychangers Men experienced in judging the approximate value of coins, discovering counterfeit currency, and determining one currency's value in relation to another (Ch. 10)

monotheism Belief in only one God (Ch. 2)

Moors Spanish **Muslims** (Ch. 10)

mosaic Inlaid pieces of glass or stone in wet cement or plaster (Ch. 6)

mosque Place of **Muslim** worship (Ch. 6)

motets Unaccompanied Latin songs that combined different melodies and words with a plainsong melody (Ch. 11)

movable type Separate printing blocks for each character (Ch. 7)

muezzin One who calls faithful **Muslims** to prayer five times a day from a **minaret** (Ch. 6)

Mughul Turkish-Mongol dynasty in India around the sixteenth century; founded by Babur (Ch. 7)

Muslim Follower of **Islam**; "submitter to **Allah**" (Ch. 6)

Mycenaean civilization Early Greek civilization on the mainland of Greece; borrowed heavily from the **Minoan civilization** (Ch. 3)

N

nation Very large group of people (usually including many cities) who have in common the same land area and the same language (Ch. 1)

nation-state An independent group of people having common interests and ruled by a king (Ch. 10)

"New Rome" Constantine's name for Constantinople (Ch. 6)

Nika Revolt A popular uprising crushed by Justinian early in his reign; the turning point of Justinian's reign (Ch. 6)

Ninety-five Theses A list of statements concerning the sale of indulgences that Martin Luther proposed as topics for a scholarly debate (Ch. 12)

O

Odyssey An epic poem of the Greek Dark Ages written by Homer (Ch. 3)

oligarchy Rule by a few (Ch. 3)

Olympiad Four-year period between Olympic games; became a Greek means of dating historical events (Ch. 3)

organization A system of rules, regulations, and accountability that governs all who take part in the functions of a city (Ch. 1)

Ottoman Turks The **Muslim** invaders who sacked Constantinople and killed the last Byzantine emperor (Ch. 6)

P

pacifism Refusal to take up arms against anyone, even in time of war (Ch. 12)

page A boy placed under the care of a knight for the purpose of becoming a **knight** (Ch. 8)

Parliament The English representative body consisting of two houses, the House of Commons and the House of Lords; had the **"power of the purse"** (Ch. 9)

pater The father in the Roman family; exercised sole authority in the family (Ch. 4)

Parthenon Most spectacular temple in Athens; dedicated to **Athena** (Ch. 3)

patriarch Bishop of one of the five important cities of the empire—Jerusalem, Antioch, Alexandria, Rome, or Constantinople (Ch. 5)

patrician The aristocratic class in Rome made up of wealthy landowners and noble families (Ch. 4)

patrons Sponsors of artists (Ch. 11)

Pax Romana "Roman Peace"; 31 BC to 180 (Ch. 5)

Pax Sinica "Chinese Peace" established by the Han Dynasty (Ch. 7)

Peace of Augsburg Allowed each German prince the right to choose whether his territory would be Lutheran or Roman Catholic (Ch. 12)

Peace of God Decree by which the church forbade the pillage of her property and extended protection to all noncombatants in society (Ch. 8)

Peloponnesian League A league of Greek city-states led by Sparta with the intention of thwarting the goals of Athenian democracy (Ch. 3)

Peloponnesian War Greek civil war between Athens and her allies and Sparta and her allies (Ch. 3)

perspective Artistic technique of portraying a three-dimensional appearance on a flat surface (Ch. 11)

Petrine theory Roman Catholic theory that Christ made Peter the first **pope** and gave him supreme authority over the church on earth; Peter subsequently transferred this office and its authority to those who succeeded him as bishop of Rome (Ch. 8)

pharaoh Ruler of Egypt (Ch. 2)

philosophers Men who sought the answers to the basic questions of life through human reasoning ability (Ch. 3)

plainsong Gregorian chant; simple, single-lined melody (Ch. 11)

plebeian The common class in Rome made up of farmers, traders, and craftsmen (Ch. 4)

plebiscite A resolution of the Council of Plebeians (Ch. 4)

polis City-state; basic political unit of Greece (Ch. 3)

polygamy Marriage of a husband to more than one wife (Ch. 7)

polyphonic Consisting of many melodies (Ch. 11)

polytheism Belief in many gods (Ch. 2)

pontifex maximus "Greatest pontiff"; title of the Roman emperors (Ch. 5)

pope The bishop of Rome; first used of the bishop of Rome in 452 and generally accepted as his title by the end of the sixth century; the head of the visible church in the West (Ch. 8)

"power of the purse" A representative body's power to approve all new taxes; a means of forcing the king to hear grievances (Ch. 9)

primary sources Records produced during the time period being studied, usually by those involved in the events being studied (Ch. 1)

princeps "First citizen" (Ch. 5)

prospectus Details of a proposed business venture (Ch. 13)

publican Tax collector for the Roman Republic in the provinces (Ch. 4)

Punic Wars Three wars between Carthage and Rome (Ch. 4)

purgatory a place of temporary punishment where souls bound for heaven must go after death to atone for their "minor" unconfessed sins or for sins for which they have not done sufficient penance (Ch. 8)

Puritans Those who wanted to purify the **Anglican Church** of those practices that reminded them of Roman Catholicism (Ch. 12)

Q

quadrivium Liberal arts curriculum consisting of arithmetic, geometry, astronomy, and music (Ch. 10)

R

recant Renounce one's beliefs (Ch. 12)

Reconquista The reconquest of the Iberian Peninsula, which was held by the **Muslims** (Ch. 10)

regular clergy Clergy who lived according to a monastic rule (Ch. 8)

Renaissance The revival of learning in Europe from the fourteenth century through the sixteenth century (Ch. 11)

republic Form of government in which voting citizens exercise power through elected officials under law (Ch. 4)

requerimento Statement that the **conquistadors** read to the Indians explaining that the **pope** had given Spain authority over the New World

Roman Forum The center of Roman government (Ch. 4)

Roman sacramental system A system of religious acts which Roman Catholics believe automatically grant grace (spiritual benefit) by their very performance; see **seven sacraments** (Ch. 8)

Romanesque The prevalent architectural style in Europe from 1050 to 1150 (Ch. 10)

Rus The Slavic designation of the Norsemen; "rowers" or "seafarers" (Ch. 6)

S

St. Bartholomew's Day Massacre Massacre of **Huguenots** throughout France on August 27, 1572 (Ch. 12)

sacraments Baptism, confirmation, penance, the Holy Eucharist, matrimony, holy orders, and extreme unction; see **Roman sacramental system** (Ch. 8)

Salian House German royal house that tried to bring the German nobles under royal control (Ch. 9)

samurai Japanese warrior (Ch. 7)

Sanskrit Early Indian language established by the **Aryans** (Ch. 7)

satrapies Provinces in the Persian Empire (Ch. 2)

Scholasticism A twelfth-century intellectual movement that was characterized by a renewed interest in theology and philosophy (Ch. 10)

secondary sources Records that explain or interpret **primary sources** (Ch. 1)

secular clergy Conducted religious services, administered the sacraments to the laity, and supervised the business and property of the church (Ch. 8)

seed of the serpent Humans yet to be born who would prove to have the same deceptive, God-defying nature that Satan evidenced that day in the garden (Ch. 1)

seed of the woman Future humans who would prove to be loyal to their Creator (Ch. 1)

Seljuk Turks Nomadic tribes from central Asia that adopted Arab culture and the Islamic religion (Ch. 6)

Senate The most important and most powerful body of the Roman Republic (Ch. 4)

Separatists Those who removed themselves from the **Anglican Church** (Ch. 12)

Septuagint Greek translation of the Hebrew Old Testament (Ch. 5)

serfs Majority of those living on a **manor**; their status was midway between the ancient slave and the medieval freeman (Ch. 8)

sheriff One who governed a **shire** (Ch. 9)

Shintoism A Japanese form of nature worship that attributed deity to anything in nature that was awe-inspiring or extraordinary; stressed the supremacy of the sun goddess and the divine descent of the emperor; a religion of feeling (Ch. 7)

shires Districts in England set up by Alfred the Great (Ch. 9)

shogun "Great general"; military ruler of Japan; held the real power over the Japanese government from 1192 to 1868 (Ch. 7)

simony The buying and selling of religious or blessed articles as well as church offices (Ch. 9)

Sistine Chapel A chapel in the Vatican; Michelangelo painted the ceiling (Ch. 11)

Slavs A group that settled in Eastern Europe after the Germanic tribes migrated west; the largest people group in Russia (Ch. 6)

Sola fide Justification by faith alone; Reformation doctrine that a person is not justified before God by works or faith and works but by faith alone (Ch. 12)

Spanish Armada A great fleet of 130 ships that was to sail to the Netherlands, pick up a large Spanish army, and transport the invasion force to England; defeated by the English and storms in 1588 (Ch. 12)

specialization An individual's commitment to concentrate on a given endeavor necessary for human existence (Ch. 1)

squire The personal servant of a **knight** (Ch. 8)

steppes Vast grassy plains extending from western China to eastern Europe (Ch. 7)

Stoicism Philosophy that taught that the highest good is the pursuit of courage, dignity, duty, simplicity of life, and service to fellow men (Ch. 5)

sub-Saharan Africa The part of Africa south of the Sahara (Ch. 7)

subinfeudation Parceling out portions of a **fief** to gain the services of lesser nobles (Ch. 8)

Swahili The native African language of the east African city-states; contained elements of Arabic, Persian, and Indian (Ch. 7)

syllogism A three-step logical process of thinking (Ch. 3)

synagogues Centers of worship for the "scattered" Jews (Ch. 5)

Table of Nations Genesis 10; lists the descendants of Shem, Ham, and Japheth according to the nations that arose from their families (Ch. 1)

Taika Reform Mid-seventh-century restructuring of Japanese government to weaken the strength of the local **clan** chieftains; known as the "Great Change"(Ch. 7)

taille French royal land tax (Ch. 10)

Taoism Founded by Lao-tzu; encouraged people to live in harmony with nature ; became the basis of mystical, magical, and superstitious elements in Chinese society (Ch. 7)

Tartars Fierce Mongolian warriors from central Asia that attacked Russia in the thirteenth century (Ch. 6)

tenants-in-chief Military followers who were feudal **vassals** (Ch. 9)

theocracy Government directly by God (Ch. 2)

three-field system A pattern of rotating planting among three fields leaving one fallow each year (Ch. 8)

topography The physical features of the land (Ch. 7)

tournament A mock war; included two types of contests, the joust and the melee (Ch. 8)

tradition The handing down of information by word of mouth from generation to generation (Ch. 1)

transubstantiation Roman Catholic belief that during the Holy Eucharist the priest transforms the bread and wine into the actual body and blood of Christ (Ch. 8)

treasury of saints Roman Catholic doctrine of the storehouse of the "excess works" of the saints and the works of Christ; used in the dispensing of **indulgences** (Ch. 12)

Treaty of Verdun Treaty between Charles the Bald, Louis the German, and Lothair to divide Louis the Pious's kingdom (Ch. 8)

Tribal Assembly Another name for the **plebeian** assembly in Rome (Ch. 4)

tribe A number of **clans** united by common beliefs and living in a particular region (Ch. 4)

tribunes Ten men, elected by the Council of Plebeians, who protected the rights and interests of the common people (Ch. 4)

triumvirate Rule of three men (Ch. 4)

trivium Liberal arts curriculum consisting of grammar, rhetoric, and logic (Ch. 10)

troubadours Wandering minstrels who popularized the vernacular in lyric poetry (Ch. 10)

Truce of God Decree which limited fighting to specified weekdays by forbidding combat from Wednesday evening to Monday morning (Ch. 8)

Tudor family The ruling family of England during the sixteenth century (Ch. 12)

two-field system Planting crops on only half of the cultivated land, leaving the other half to lie fallow for a year to recover its fertility (Ch. 8)

tyranny Government headed by a tyrant who gained complete control of it—usually by force (Ch. 3)

U

Umayyad Caliphate that was a hereditary dynasty centered in Damascus (Ch. 6)

Unam Sanctam Papal **bull** by Boniface VIII; stated that obedience to the pontiff was necessary for salvation (Ch. 10)

underwriter One who wrote his name below the **prospectus**, pledging to help share the cost of the enterprise (Ch. 13)

universitas Those united for the common purpose of education (Ch. 10)

Upanishads Philosophical essays elaborating on the teaching of the **Vedas** (Ch. 7)

usury The practice of charging interest for the use of lent money (Ch. 10)

Vandals A Germanic tribe that established a kingdom in North Africa; sacked Rome after the **Visigoths** (Ch. 5)

Varangians Swedish Norsemen who plundered Slavic villages during the eighth and ninth centuries (Ch. 6)

vassal Recipient of a **fief**; owed allegiance to a **lord** (Ch. 8)

Vedas Collection of religious literature that contains the early traditions and religious beliefs of the people of India (Ch. 7)

vernacular Common spoken language (Ch. 10)

viceroy An "assistant king" appointed by the Spanish king to oversee affairs in the New World (Ch. 13)

veto A way for tribunes to stop unjust acts of **patrician** officials (Ch. 4)

Vikings Germanic tribes from Scandinavia that were explorers and warriors; the most feared invaders of their day (Ch. 8)

Visigoths A Germanic tribe that settled in the Eastern Roman Empire; defeated the Romans at the battle of Adrianople and later sacked Rome (Ch. 5)

Wars of the Roses Series of conflicts between the houses of York and Lancaster over the English throne (Ch. 10)

week work Obligation of **serfs**; devoting two or three days a week to work for the **lord** (Ch. 8)

wheel of life Cycle of rebirths in reincarnation (Ch. 7)

witan Anglo-Saxon assembly of the great men of the kingdom (Ch. 9)

world soul Another name for the **Brahman** (Ch. 7)

worldview A perspective from which we may examine and interpret the universe and everything in it (Ch. 1)

written records More accurate records of the past such as private letters, inventory lists, inscriptions, diaries, and journals (Ch. 1)

Yamato clan Japanese **clan** that forged a unified state; claimed divine lineage for the emperor (Ch. 7)

Zeus "King of gods and man"; ruler of Mount Olympus (Ch. 3)

ziggurats Pyramidlike structures that had terraces at different levels along their exterior (Ch. 2)

INDEX

T

PHOTOGRAPH CREDITS

The following agencies and individuals have furnished materials to meet the photographic needs of this textbook. We wish to express our gratitude to them for their important contribution.

Alamy
American Antiquarian Society
Amoret Tanner/fotoLibra
APVA Preservation Virginia
AP/Wide World Photos
Architect of the Capitol
The Art Institute of Chicago
Art Resource, NY
John Bean
Bibliothèque nationale de France
Bildarchiv Preussischer Kulturbesitz
Bob Jones University Collection
Edvard Braekke (ebrakke)/TrekEarth.com
The Bridgeman Art Library
Bridgeman-Giraudon
British Library
The British Museum
George Bush Presidential Library
Calvin College
Jimmy Carter Library
Chemical Heritage Foundation Image Archives
Chicago Historical Society
William J. Clinton Library
George R. Collins
Colonial Williamsburg Foundation
Corbis
CNP – Ministère de la Culture
Dr. Stewart Custer
Department of Defense
Naomi Duguid/Asia Access
Dundee Central Library, Mary Slessor Collection
Eastman Chemicals Division
Ursula Edelmann - ARTOTHEK/Frankfurt, Städelsches Kunstinstitut
Egyptian Tourist Authority
Dwight D. Eisenhower Library
European Commission
Dr. Charles Lee Feinberg
Gene Fisher
Fisher Scientific Company
Folger Shakespeare Library
Fondation du Château de Chillon
French Embassy Press and Information Division
German Information Center
Getty Images/Hulton Archive
Desmond Groves, London
Paul Halsall
Carol Highsmith
HMSO and Queen's Printer for Scotland
HolyLandPhotos.org
Webb Hudspeth
The Huntington Library, San Marino, California
Institute of Human Origins
Imperial War Museum, London
IMSS - Florence
istockphoto.com
Italian Tourist Agency
Lyndon B. Johnson Library
JupiterImages
Dr. Tim Keesee
Kunsthistorisches Museum, Vienna
Lars Göhler/India-Picture.com
Alan Laughlin, City of Edinburgh Council
Library of Congress
Map Resources
The Metropolitan Museum of Art
Missouri Historical Society
Morristown National Historical Park
Andrés Morya – Hinojosa
Musée cantonal des Beaux-Arts, Lausanne
Musée du Louvre, Paris, France
Museum & Gallery at Bob Jones University
NASA
National Archives
National Archives of Canada
National Gallery of Art, Washington D.C.
National Gallery, London
National Library of Medicine
National Maritime Museum, London
National Park Service
National Portrait Gallery, London
National Trust
Naval Historical Center
New Netherland Museum
Henri Nissen
North Wind Picture Archives
NTPL/Andrew Butler
Office de Tourisme de Nîmes France
Gerald Oskoboiny
Overseas Missionary Fellowship
The Oxyrhynchus Papyri Project, Oxford/Egypt Exploration Society
Palace of Westminister Collection
PhotoDisc/Getty Images
Photos For Me
Punch, Ltd. www.punch.co.uk
Wade Ramsey
Reading Borough Council
Ronald Reagan Library
Réunion des Musées Nationaux
Ed Richards
Franklin Delano Roosevelt Library
Russian Gospel Ministries
Russian National Library
Saudi Aramco World
Smithsonian American Art Museum, Washington, DC
Stephen Eric Wood/DHD Multimedia Gallery
Stock Montage
Swabia Tourism Bureau
Sword of the Lord
Robert Thom, courtesy of Pfizer, Inc.
Time Life Pictures
Todd Bolen/BiblePlaces.com
The Tudor Group/Johnnie Rutter
Harry S Truman Library
University of Bologna
UN Photo Library
Unusual Films
USAID
U.S. Air Force
U.S. Army
U.S. Department of State
United States Holocaust Memorial Museum
U.S. Navy
Western Pennsylvania Conservancy/Harold Corsini
The White House
Wikimedia
William L. Krewson/BiblePlaces.com
Winston Churchill Memorial and Library
Wittenberg Culture
John Wolsieffer
Yale Divinity School Library

Cover, Book A
Photos For Me/CORBIS

Cover, Book B
Department of Defense

Front Matter, Book A
www.istockphoto.com/David Shawley iii; www.istockphoto.com/Eileen Morris v (top); www.istockphoto.com/Gustavo Fadel v (bottom); www.istockphoto.com/Robert Creigh vi (top); Wittenberg Culture, www.wittenberg.de vi (bottom); PhotoDisc/Getty Images viii (top right); www.istockphoto.com/Riccardo Bissacco ix (background bottom right)

Front Matter, Book B
www.istockphoto.com/David Shawley iii; Library of Congress v, vi (top); www.istockphoto.com/Daniel Reiche vi (bottom)

Unit I Opener
SEF/Art Resource, NY xiv–xv

Chapter 1
NASA Glenn Research Center (NASA-GRC) 2; © 2006 JupiterImages/Photos.com. All rights reserved. 3 (top right), 18; Public Domain 3 (top left), 6 (top); Todd Bolen/BiblePlaces.com 3 (center top); © 2006 JupiterImages 3 (center bottom), 9; Library of Congress 3 (bottom); PhotoDisc/Getty Images 6 (bottom), 8, 13, 16, 24 (bottom); The Oxyrhynchus Papyri Project, Oxford/Egypt Exploration Society 7; From the Bob Jones University Collection 10, 20; © National Portrait Gallery, London 11; AP/Wide World Photos 15 (top); Institute of Human Origins 15 (center); CNP – Ministère de la Culture 15 (bottom); © 2006 JupiterImages/Ablestock.com. All rights reserved. 19; Dr. Stewart Custer 21; Photo from the book "Noah's Ark Uncovered," Scandinavia 2005/Courtesy of Henri Nissen 23; Kunsthistorisches Museum, Vienna 24 (top); Unusual Films/Wade Ramsey 24 (center)

Chapter 2
Todd Bolen/BiblePlaces.com 28, 33; www.istockphoto.com/Eileen Morris 29; Unusual Films/Wade Ramsey 30, 47, 51; © North Wind Picture Archives. All Rights Reserved. 32; Gene Fisher 34; www.istockphoto.com/Julia Chernikova 35; Photograph © 1982 The Metropolitan Museum of Art 36; Egyptian Tourist Authority 37; © Copyright The Trustees of The British Museum. 38; www.istockphoto.com/Hayley Easton 39; © 2006 Map Resources. All Rights Reserved. 40 (top); Stephen Eric Wood/DHD Multimedia Gallery © Damon Hart-Davis 40 (bottom); © 2006 JupiterImages/Photos.com. All rights reserved. 41; George Baramki Azar/*Saudi Aramco World*/PADIA 42; From the Bob Jones University Collection 44

Chapter 3
PhotoDisc/Getty Images 54, 55 (top), 58 (bottom), 61, 75; © 2006 Map Resources. All Rights Reserved. 55 (bottom); www.HolyLandPhotos.org 56 (top), 73 (center left); Nimatallah/Art Resource, NY 58 (top); www.istockphoto.com/Leeman 60; www.istockphoto.com/David Shawley 67; Photograph © 1992 The Metropolitan Museum of Art 69; Unusual Films/Wade Ramsey 72, 73 (top left); Musée du Louvre, Paris, France 73 (top right); www.istockphoto.com/Andreas Guskos 73 (bottom left); www.istockphoto.com/George Cairns 73 (bottom center); www.istockphoto.com/Marje Cannon 73 (bottom right)

Chapter 4
Unusual Films/Wade Ramsey 76; © 2006 Map Resources. All Rights Reserved. 77; Todd Bolen/BiblePlaces.com 78; William L. Krewson/BiblePlaces.com 79 (top); www.istockphoto.com/Riccardo Bissacco 80 (background), 95; © 2006 JupiterImages/Ablestock.com. All rights reserved. 82; PhotoDisc/Getty Images 85, 93 (background); www.istockphoto.com/Iwona Adamus 87; Photograph © 1986 The Metropolitan Museum of Art 89; Scala/Art Resource, NY 92

Chapter 5
From the Bob Jones University Collection 96, 111; Bildarchiv Preussischer Kulturbesitz/Art Resource, NY 98; Todd Bolen/BiblePlaces.com 101, 105 (bottom), 113; William L. Krewson/BiblePlaces.com 103 (top), 116; Gerald Oskoboiny 103 (center, bottom); © 2006 JupiterImages/Ablestock.com. All rights reserved. 104; Unusual Films/Wade Ramsey 105 (top); © 2006 JupiterImages/Photos.com. All rights reserved. 106 (top); George R. Collins 106 (bottom); Photo Office de Tourisme de Nîmes France 107 (top); www.istockphoto.com/Zastavkin 107 (bottom); Published by permission, *Historic Views Of The Holy Land: The 1960s: Photographs of Charles Lee Feinberg,* www.bibleplaces.com, 2004. 109; www.HolyLandPhotos.org 112; Photograph © 1986 the Metropolitan Museum of Art 117; Unusual Films 118, 119; Museum & Gallery at Bob Jones University 121

Unit II Opener
www.istockphoto.com/Terry J Alcorn 124–125

Chapter 6
www.istockphoto.com/Murat Baysan 126; PhotoDisc/Getty Images 127 (top), 128, 143; www.istockphoto.com/Yusuf Demirelli 127 (bottom); www.istockphoto.com/Eliana Dulinsky 130; Paul Halsall, Internet History Sourcebooks Project 132; From the Bob Jones University Collection 133 (top both); www.istockphoto.com/Gustavo Fadel 133 (bottom); © 2006 Map Resources. All Rights Reserved. 134; www.istockphoto.com/Denis Ryssev 135; Photo taken by Ali Mansuri/Wikipedia 137; Dick Doughty/Saudi Aramco World/PADIA 139

Chapter 7

PhotoDisc/Getty Images 146, 147 (top), 156, 163; © 2006 Map Resources. All Rights Reserved. 147 (bottom), 160, 162 (top), 167, 170; © 2006 JupiterImages/ Photos.com. All rights reserved. 149, 150, 162 (bottom); © Lars Göhler/India-Picture.com 152; © 2006 JupiterImages/Ablestock. com. All rights reserved. 153; Corbis 158; Naomi Duguid/Asia Access 164; Nik Wheeler/Saudi Aramco World/PADIA 166; www.istockphoto.com/Vadim Rumyantsev 171; Edvard Braekke (ebrakke)/TrekEarth. com 172; Photograph © 1983 The Metropolitan Museum of Art 173

Unit III Opener

© CW Images/Alamy 176–177

Chapter 8

www.istockphoto.com/Robert Creigh 178; From the Bob Jones University Collection 180; www. istockphoto.com/Natalia Bratslavsky 181; www.istock-photo.com/Peter Hibberd 182; www.istockphoto.com/Dale Robins 184; www.istockphoto. com/Cristian Lupu 185; Réunion des Musées Nationaux/Art Resource, NY 187; Erich Lessing/ Art Resource, NY 188; Joern Sackermann/Alamy 189; www.is-tockphoto.com/Craig Stanton 193; www.istockphoto.com/Andrew Dernie 194

Chapter 9

SEF/Art Resource, NY 200; Library of Congress 201; © 2006 JupiterImages/Photos.com. All rights reserved. 203; Scala/Art Resource, NY 204; Réunion des Musées Nationaux/Art Resource, NY 206; Bildarchiv Monheim GmbH/Alamy 208 (top); © 2006 Map Resources. All Rights Reserved. 208 (bottom), 216; Erich Lessing/Art Resource, NY 209; Peter Brogden/Alamy 211; Copyright Reading Borough Council (Reading Museum Service). All rights reserved. 212–13; © NTPL/Andrew Butler 215; Missouri Historical Society 217; Published by permission, *Historic Views Of The Holy Land: The 1960s: Photographs of Charles Lee Feinberg,* www.bibleplaces. com; www.istockphoto.com/free-photoagency 223

Chapter 10

www.istockphoto.com/Emanuele Gnani 226; University of Bologna 227; © 2006 Map Resources. All Rights Reserved. 228, 237, 247; National Gallery of Art, Washington D.C. 229; Réunion des Musées Nationaux/Art Resource, NY 230; Andrés Morya – Hinojosa 231; © 2006 JupiterImages/Ablestock.com. All rights reserved. 233; HIP/Art Resource, NY 234; www.istock-photo.com/marco bernes 235; The Huntington Library, San Marino, California 240 (top); www.istock-photo.com/Sean Patrick Henry 240 (bottom); From the collection of the Museum & Gallery at Bob Jones University 241; PhotoDisc/ Getty Images 242, 249; The Tudor Group/Johnnie Rutter/www. tudorgroup.co.uk 244; © National Portrait Gallery, London 245; Webb Hudspeth 248

Unit IV Opener

© 2006 JupiterImages/Brand X Pictures/Steve Allen 252–253

Chapter 11

© 2006 JupiterImages/Photos. com. All rights reserved. 254; www.istockphoto.com/Jocelyn Lin 255, www.istockphoto. com/Ogen Perry 256; National Gallery of Art, Washington D.C. 257, 265, 269 (bottom); Scala/Art Resource, NY 258, 268; Erich Lessing/Art Resource, NY 259, 269 (top); From *In Praise of Folly*/Public Domain 260 (bot-tom all); Foto Marburg/Art Resource, NY 261 (top); German Information Center 261 (bot-tom); By Permission of the Folger Shakespeare Library 262; From the Bob Jones University Collection 264; Alinari/Art Resource, NY 267; © National Gallery, London 270; Italian Tourist Agency 271 (top); Todd Bolen/BiblePlaces.com 271 (bot-tom); PhotoDisc/Getty Images 272

Chapter 12

www.istockphoto.com/Glen Rodgers 276; German Information Center 277 (top); Webb Hudspeth 277 (bottom), 279; Palace of Westminister Collection 278; Scala/Art Resource, NY 280, 285, 290 (top); Erich Lessing/Art Resource, NY 281, 284 (top), 291 (top), 294; Wittenberg Culture, www.wittenberg.de 282; www. istockphoto.com/Marc C. Johnson 283; Foto Marburg/Art Resource, NY 284 (bottom), 299; J. H. Merle d'Aubigne, *History of the Reformation of the Sixteenth Century*, American Tract Society, public domain 286; Corbis 288; Library of Congress 289; Réunion des Musées Nationaux/Art Resource, NY 290 (bottom); Folger Shakespeare Library 291 (bottom); Unusual Films 292; Alan Laughlin, City of Edinburgh Council 295 (top); © 2006 JupiterImages 295 (bottom); J.-C. Ducret, Musée can-tonal des Beaux-Arts, Lausanne 297

Chapter 13

Photo courtesy of New Netherland Museum/www.newnetherland.org 302, 318; NASA 303; Courtesy of Morristown National Historical Park 304; www.istockphoto. com/Michael Bischof 307; Architect of the Capitol 308, 316, 317; © 2006 Map Resources. All Rights Reserved. 310–11; Library of Congress 311; www.istock-photo.com/Ashok Rodrigues 312; Smithsonian American Art Museum, Washington, DC/Art Resource, NY 313 (top); © 2006 JupiterImages/Ablestock.com. All rights reserved. 313 (bot-tom); John Wolsieffer 314; www. istockphoto.com/David Freund 319 (top); Courtesy of the APVA Preservation Virginia 319 (bot-tom); Gene Fisher 322–23 (all); © National Maritime Museum, London 324

Unit V Opener

Réunion des Musées Nationaux/ Art Resource, NY 354–55

Chapter 14

Library of Congress 356; www. istockphoto.com/René Mansi 357; From the Bob Jones University Collection 358 (top), 373; © National Gallery, London 358 (bottom); Bridgeman-Giraudon/ Art Resource, NY 359, 366; www. istockphoto.com/michel mory 361; www.istockphoto.com/Ryan KC Wong 362; Erich Lessing/Art Resource, NY 364 (top), 367, 368; Swabia Tourism Bureau 364 (bot-tom); Musée du Louvre, Paris, France 369; © 2006 JupiterImages 370 (top), 371 (bottom); © National Portrait Gallery, London 370 (bottom); National Trust/ Art Resource, NY 371 (top); Public Domain/from Wikipedia 372; Bildarchiv Preussischer Kulturbesitz/Art Resource, NY 375; National Archives of Canada/C-139911 376

Chapter 15

Photographic Department, IMSS-Florence 380, 382 (top); Library of Congress 381; 390, 393 (center), 394, 396 (top), 403; Erich Lessing/Art Resource, NY 382, (bottom) 384 (top left); NASA 383 (top); Nimatallah/ Art Resource, NY 383 (bot-tom); Snark/Art Resource, NY 384 (top right), 387; Painting by Robert Thom, Courtesy of Pfizer, Inc. 385 (top), 386; Fisher Scientific Company 385 (bottom left); Courtesy of the Chemical Heritage Foundation Image Archives 385 (bottom right); © British Library/HIP/Art Resource, NY 389; © National Portrait Gallery, London 395; Courtesy, American Antiquarian Society 396 (bottom); National Gallery of Art, Washington D.C. 397, 398 (bottom), 399 (bottom); www.istockphoto. com/Tiago Fernandes 398 (top); From the Bob Jones University Collection 399 (top); PhotoDisc/ Getty Images 400; © 2006 JupiterImages 401; Public Domain 402; © National Maritime Museum, London 404

Chapter 16

Library of Congress 406, 424 (both), 430; Unusual Films 407; PhotoDisc/Getty Images 408, 412; George R. Collins 409, 410 (both); Photograph © 1992 The Metropolitan Museum of Art 411; © 2006 JupiterImages 415, 421; Réunion des Musées Nationaux/Art Resource, NY 417, 427; French Embassy Press and Information Division 418; Erich Lessing/Art Resource, NY 420; Bridgeman-Giraudon/Art Resource, NY 422; National Gallery of Art, Washington D.C. 425; © National Maritime Museum, London 426; © 2006 Map Resources. All Rights Reserved. 428

Unit VI Opener

© 2006 JupiterImages/Ablestock. com. All rights reserved. 432–33

Chapter 17

© 2006 JupiterImages/Ablestock. com. All rights reserved. 434; PhotoDisc/Getty Images 435 (top); Bridgeman-Giraudon/Art Resource, NY 435 (bottom), 442; © 2006 JupiterImages 436, 453 (top, center), 454 (top, center), 457 (right), 458; © 2006 Map Resources. All Rights Reserved. 437, 439, 447(bottom), 449 (top); Bibliothèque nationale de France 441 (all); Library of Congress 443, 444, 446, 451 (bottom), 454 (bottom), 456, 457 (left); Amoret Tanner/fotoLibra 447; Evert A. Duyckinck, *Portrait Gallery of Eminent Men and Women of Europe and America* (New York: Johnson, Wilson and Company, 1873) 448 (top, center), 450; Scala/Art Resource, NY 448 (bottom); National Archives 449 (bottom); Dr. Tim Keesee 451 (top); © Ursula Edelmann - ARTOTHEK/Frankfurt, Städelsches Kunstinstitut 453 (bottom); Fondation du Château de Chillon 455; Photography © The Art Institute of Chicago 459 (top); National Gallery of Art, Washington D.C. 459 (bottom), 460

Chapter 18

www.istockphoto.com/Chris Schmidt 462; Library of Congress 463 (top), 465 (bottom), 466, 468 (Clermont, Wright brothers, plane, Henry Ford, Model Ts), 471 (both), 473, 474, 475 (top), 476, 478, 480 (bottom), 481, 483 (bot-tom); © 2006 Map Resources. All Rights Reserved. 463 (bottom); © North Wind Picture Archives - All rights reserved. 465 (top), 468 (Fulton); © 2006 JupiterImages 468 (Stephenson), 483 (top); Eastman Chemicals Division 470; Evert A. Duyckinck, *Portrait Gallery of Eminent Men and Women of Europe and America* (New York: Johnson, Wilson and Company, 1873) 475 (bottom), 485 (top); *Sword of the Lord* 480 (top); National Library of Medicine 482; National Gallery of Art, Washington D.C. 485 (bottom), 486 (bottom), 487; Photograph © 1999 The Metro-Metropolitan Museum of Art 486 (top)

Chapter 19

The Royal Cake or The Western Empires sharing China between them. L-R: Queen Victoria (1837–1901), Kaiser Wilhelm II (1859–1941) by French School, (19th century), © Private Collection/ Archives Charmet/The Bridgeman Art Library, Nationality/copyright status: French/out of copyright 490; www.istockphoto.com/ Emrah Türüdü 491; © 2006 Map Resources. All Rights Reserved. 492, 506, 511, 513; National Archives 494 (both); John Bean 496 (top, center); PhotoDisc/Getty/ Photographer: Glen Allison 496 (bottom); Library of Congress

497 (top), 508 (background), 509 (top); *The Battle of Araure*, 1828 by Salas, Tito (b. 1887) © Private Collection/Index/The Bridgeman Art Library, Nationality/copyright status: Venezuelan/in copyright until 2060 497 (bottom); *The Battle of Maipu on the 5th April*, 1818, printed by Raffet (lithograph) by Spanish School (19th Century) © Private Collection/Index/The Bridgeman Art Library, Nationality/copyright status: Spanish/out of copyright 498; William Carey after Robert Home NPG D2182, © National Portrait Gallery, London 502; Permission British Library WD 2460 503 (top); © North Wind Picture Archives 503 (bottom); Overseas Missionary Fellowship 504; Special Collections, Yale Divinity School Library 505 (top); Chicago Historical Society P&S 1932.21 505 (bottom left); © National Portrait Gallery, Smithsonian Institution/Art Resource, NY 505 (bottom right); Two slave collars, c.1790 (iron) by English School, (18th century), Private Collection/© Michael Graham-Stewart/The Bridgeman Art Library, Nationality/copyright status: English/out of copyright 508 (foreground) ; Dundee Central Library, Mary Slessor Collection 509 (bottom); © 2006 Stock Montage 510; U.S. Navy photo by Photographer's Mate Airman Christopher J. Newsome 512

Unit VII Opener

NASA Headquarters - GReatest Images of NASA (NASA-HQ-GRIN) 516–17

Chapter 20

National Archives 518, 519 (top), 524 (both), 525, 527 (bottom left), 528, 532 (top), 533, 534, 538; Library of Congress 519 (bottom), 521, 527 (top), 529, 532 (bottom right), 535; www.istockphoto.com/Lisa Kyle Young 520; Reproduced with the permission of Punch, Ltd. www.punch.co.uk 522; © 2006 Map Resources. All Rights Reserved. 523, 525 (both), 530, 537; The Trustees of the Imperial War Museum, London 526; Getty Images/Hulton Archive 527 (bottom right); AP/Wide World Photos 532 (bottom left); Ed Richards 539 (both)

Chapter 21

Time Life Pictures/Getty Images 544; National Archives 545, 548, 553 (bottom), 558, 560 (all), 561 (top right, bottom); Getty Images/Hulton Archive 546, 551 (top); Library of Congress 547 (all), 550, 551 (bottom), 553 (top), 554 (bottom), 555, 557, 561 (top left), 565 (center, bottom); © 2006 JupiterImages 552; © 2006 Map Resources. All Rights Reserved. 554 (top); Russian Gospel Ministries 556; Courtesy of Calvin College 559, 562 (bottom all); United States Holocaust Memorial Museum 562 (top); AP/Wide World Photos 563; National Gallery of Art, Washington D.C. 564; Western Pennsylvania Conservancy/Harold Corsini 565 (top)

Chapter 22

Naval Historical Center 568, 589 (bottom); NARA/National Park Service 569 (top); AP/Wide World Photos 569 (bottom), 570 (bottom); NARA/Harry S Truman Library 570 (top); National Archives 571, 572, 575, 578 (bottom), 585 (both), 586 (top), 587, 588, 589 (top), 590 (both), 591 (top), 594 (top), 595 (top right, bottom right), 596 (top); © 2006 Map Resources. All Rights Reserved. 573 (both maps), 577, 591 (bottom), 593; Getty Images/Hulton Archive 573 (bottom), 576, 578 (top), 579 (bottom), 582; Franklin Delano Roosevelt Library 574; Library of Congress 579 (top), 581 (bottom both), 592, 594 (bottom); BJU Press Files 580, 581 (top), 584 (bottom); United States Holocaust Memorial Museum 583; Ed Richards 584 (top); The Trustees of the Imperial War Museum, London 586 (bottom); U.S. Air Force 595 (left); Carol Highsmith 596 (bottom); UN Photo Library 597

Chapter 23

German Information Center 600, 607, 616 (top), 621 (top right), 630; National Archives 601, 604 (bottom), 610 (center), 611 (Nixon, Brezhnev), 612 (both), 616 (bottom); Winston Churchill Memorial and Library in the United States at Westminster College, Fulton Missouri 602, 622; © 2006 Map Resources. All Rights Reserved. 603, 609, 623, 624; Library of Congress 604 (top), 610 (bottom), 611 (Kennedy, Ford, Stalin, Khrushchev), 614 (top), 625 (top), 627; AP/Wide World Photos 605 (left), 610 (top), 615 (top), 616 (center), 617, 620 (top), 625 (center, bottom), 629 (both); Getty Images/Hulton Archive 605 (right); U.S. Department of State 608; National Park Service 611 (Truman); Dwight D. Eisenhower Library 611 (Eisenhower); Lyndon B. Johnson Library 611 (Johnson, Kosygin); The White House 611 (Carter); Ronald Reagan Library 611 (Reagan, Gorbachev), 619, 620 (bottom), 628 (top); George Bush Presidential Library 611 (Bush), 628 (bottom); Public Domain/from Wikipedia 611 (Andropov, Chernenko); U.S. Navy 614 (bottom); NASA 615 (center), U.S. Air Force photo 615 (bottom); Dr. Tim Keesee 621 (top left); William J. Clinton Library 621 (bottom); Corbis 626; Naval Historical Center 631; David Johnson/The White House 632

Chapter 24

AP/Wide World Photos 634, 635 (bottom both), 640, 641 (bottom), 642 (bottom), 645 (top), 646, 650, 651, 652, 654 (top), 656 (both), 657 (top), 658 (bottom both), 661 (all); Department of Defense 635 (top), 649 (bottom), 660 (center, bottom), 662 (center left), 663 (bottom both); European Commission 636; www.istockphoto.com/Gaspar Avila 637 (top left); www.istockphoto.com/Daniel Reiche 637 (top right); © 2006 Map Resources. All Rights Reserved. 637 (bottom), 645 (bottom), 649 (top), 655 (left), 662 (bottom), 663 (top); Desmond Groves, London 638; George Bush Presidential Library 639; The White House 641 (top), 642 (top), 660 (top), 662 (top left); Public Domain/from Wikipedia 654 (bottom); Jimmy Carter Library, National Archives 657 (bottom); Paul Morse/The White House 658 (top); PhotoDisc/Getty Images 659; U.S. Army photo by Staff Sgt. Kyle Davis 662 (top right)

Epilogue

2006 JupiterImages/Ablestock.com. All rights reserved. 666; Colonial Williamsburg Foundation 667 (top); PhotoDisc/Getty Images 667 (bottom)

Chapter 1 Activity pages

© Copyright The Trustees of The British Museum SA1 (top); © The British Museum/HIP/Art Resource, NY SA1 (bottom); Bildarchiv Preussischer Kulturbesitz/Art Resource, NY SA2 (top); Photograph (detail) by Bruce and Kenneth Zuckerman, West Semitic Research, with the collaboration of the Ancient Biblical Manuscript Center. Courtesy Russian National Library (Saltykov, Shchedrin) SA2 (bottom)

Chapter 2 Activity pages

PhotoDisc/Getty Images SA10 (background)

Chapter 3 Activity pages

www.istockphoto.com/Marje Cannon SA20 (background)

Chapter 4 Activity pages

PhotoDisc/Getty Images SA28 (background); © 2006 Map Resources. All Rights Reserved. SA34

Chapter 5 Activity pages

PhotoDisc/Getty Images SA38

Chapter 6 Activity pages

www.istockphoto.com/Murat Baysan SA46

Chapter 7 Activity pages

www.istockphoto.com/Henry Lucenius SA56; © 2006 Map Resources. All Rights Reserved. SA60, SA62

Chapter 8 Activity pages

www.istockphoto.com/Craig Stanton SA63

Chapter 9 Activity pages

Peter Brogden/Alamy SA68; © 2006 Map Resources. All Rights Reserved. SA78

Chapter 10 Activity pages

PhotoDisc/Getty Images SA82

Chapter 11 Activity pages

PhotoDisc/Getty Images SA86

Chapter 12 Activity pages

www.istockphoto.com/Glen Rodgers SA96; © 2006 Map Resources. All Rights Reserved. SA104

Chapter 13 Activity pages

John Wolsieffer SA106

Chapter 14 Activity pages

www.istockphoto.com/Ryan KC Wong SA114

Chapter 16 Activity pages

PhotoDisc/Getty Images SA132; © 2006 Map Resources. All Rights Reserved. SA138

Chapter 17 Activity pages

© 2006 JupiterImages/Ablestock.com. All rights reserved. SA142

Chapter 19 Activity pages

National Archives SA164; © 2006 Map Resources. All Rights Reserved. SA165

Chapter 20 Activity pages

National Archives SA176, SA183, SA184, SA185 (Bismarck, Ferdinand), SA186 (Pershing); Library of Congress SA185 (Wilhelm II); © 2006 JupiterImages SA185 (Wilson); Public Domain SA185 (Foch); AP/Wide World Photos SA186 (York)

Chapter 21 Activity pages

National Archives SA188, SA197 (Hitler); © 2006 Map Resources. All Rights Reserved. SA196; Library of Congress SA197 (Stalin, Hindenburg, Roosevelt); © 2006 JupiterImages SA197 (Mussolini)

Chapter 22 Activity pages

Naval Historical Center SA200; © 2006 Map Resources. All Rights Reserved. SA202, SA204, SA206; National Archives SA213 (Chamberlain, Eisenhower), SA214 (MacArthur); Franklin Delano Roosevelt Library SA213 (Churchill); NARA/Harry S Truman Library SA213 (Chiang Kai-shek); Library of Congress SA213 (Charles de Gaulle); SA214 (Truman)

Chapter 23 Activity pages

U.S. Navy SA216; © 2006 Map Resources. All Rights Reserved. SA218, SA220; Public Domain/from Wikipedia SA227 (Mao Zedong); Library of Congress SA227 (Kennedy, Kruschev), SA228 (Ho Chi Minh, Thatcher); National Archives SA227 (Nixon), SA228 (Brezhnev); Ronald Reagan Library SA227 (Reagan), SA228 (Gorbachev); AP/Wide World Photos/NARA SA228 (Castro)

Chapter 24 Activity pages

Department of Defense SA232, SA246 (Hussein); © 2006 Map Resources. All Rights Reserved. SA234, SA236; William J. Clinton Library SA245 (Yeltsin); Public Domain/from Wikipedia SA245 (Putin); © Crown copyright material is reproduced with the permission of the Controller of HMSO and Queen's Printer for Scotland. SA245 (Blair); USAID SA246 (Karzai); Eric Draper/The White House SA246 (Bush)

WORLD HISTORY

STUDENT ACTIVITIES

Third Edition

Name ______________________________

WORLD HISTORY 1 ACTIVITY 1

Making Proper Use of Historical Sources

Page 7 of the student text explains that the historian produces a historical account through evaluation of historical sources, synthesis of those sources into a historical narrative, and an interpretation of that narrative for his readers. This student activity helps you understand this process by having you produce a historical account of one of the most famous events from ancient history: the fall of Babylon to Cyrus in 539 BC. Historians know about this event through many different sources. This activity will focus on four of the most important sources. Read each source and then answer the questions at the end.

The Nabonidus Chronicle

The Nabonidus Chronicle is a cuneiform tablet now located in the British Museum, London. It is an official Babylonian account of the reign of Nabonidus, the last ruler of the Babylonian empire. Though damaged, it is possible to piece together the Babylonian account of the fall of Babylon. Throughout this source, *Akkad* is another word for Babylonia, and *Gobryas* is probably the man called "Darius the Median" in the Book of Daniel.

> In the month of Tishri [September/October], when Cyrus fought at Opis on the Tigris river against the troops of Akkad, the people of Akkad he destroyed. . . . On the fourteenth day [of Tishri] Sippar was captured without fighting. Nabonidus fled. On the sixteenth day Ugbaru [called elsewhere Gobryas], the governor of Gutium, and the troops of Cyrus without fighting entered Babylon. Afterwards when Nabonidus returned he was taken captive in Babylon. . . . In the month of Marchesvan [October/November], the third day, Cyrus entered Babylon. . . . Peace was established in the city. . . . Gobryas, his governor, placed governors in charge of Babylon. (Translation and commentary from Raymond Philip Dougherty, *Nabonidus and Belshazzar: A Study of the Closing Events of the Neo-Babylonian Empire* [New Haven: Yale University Press, 1929], 169–72.)

The Cyrus Cylinder

The Cyrus Cylinder is a clay cylinder also located in the British Museum. As an official record of the deeds of Cyrus, the first Persian emperor, it records the fall of Babylon from the perspective of the conquerors. This account attributes Cyrus's victory to Cyrus's claim that he was more committed to Marduk, the god of the Babylonians.

> [Marduk] sought a righteous prince according to his heart's desire who would grasp his hands. Cyrus, the king of Anshan, whose name he uttered, [Marduk] proclaimed for lordship over everything. . . . Marduk, the great lord, the protector of his people, looked joyfully upon his pious deeds and his righteous heart. [Marduk] decreed [Cyrus's] march upon his city, Babylon. . . . Without encounter and battle [Marduk] caused [Cyrus] to enter into the midst of Babylon, his city. Nabonidus, the king who did not [honor] [Marduk,] [Marduk] delivered into [Cyrus's] hands. . . . [The people of Babylon]

Cyrus Cylinder, Babylonian, from Babylon, southern Iraq, c. 539–530 BC. This clay cylinder represents a declaration of good kingship. It is inscribed in Babylonian cuneiform with an account by Cyrus, king of Persia of his conquest of Babylon in 539 BC and capture of Nabonidus, the last Babylonian king.

rejoiced in his sovereignty (and) their countenances shone. . . .
I am Cyrus, king of the world. . . . When I had entered into the midst of Babylon in peace, I took the seat of lordship in the palace of princes amidst jubilation and rejoicing. . . . My numerous troops advanced peacefully into the midst of Babylon. . . . The inner part of Babylon and all its cities I cared for in peace. . . . (As to) their dwellings, I repaired their dilapidation; I removed their ruins. (Translation and commentary from Raymond Philip Dougherty, *Nabonidus and Belshazzar: A Study of the Closing Events of the Neo-Babylonian Empire* [New Haven: Yale University Press, 1929], 176–78)

The History of Herodotus

Herodotus (484–425 BC) is known as the Father of History. He was a Greek historian who lived about a century after the fall of Babylon. His famous history recounts, among other things, descriptions of his travels, the Peloponnesian Wars, and the fall of Babylon to Cyrus.

Herodotus (ca. 484–430/20 BC). Greek historian. Roman portrait bust.

> A battle was fought at a short distance from the city, in which the Babylonians were defeated by the Persian king, whereupon they withdrew within their defences. Here they [the Babylonians] shut themselves up, and made light of [Cyrus's] siege, having laid in a store of provisions for many years in preparation against this attack. . . . [Cyrus] placed a portion of his army at the point where the river enters the city, and another body at the back of the place where it issues forth, with orders to march into the town by the bed of the stream, as soon as the water became shallow enough. . . . [H]e turned the Euphrates by a canal into the basin, which was then a marsh, on which the river sank to such an extent that the natural bed of the stream became fordable. Hereupon the Persians who had been left for the purpose at Babylon by the river-side, entered the stream, which had now sunk so as to reach about midway up a man's thigh, and thus got into the town. Had the Babylonians been apprised of what Cyrus was about, or had they noticed their danger, they would never have allowed the Persians to enter the city, but would have destroyed them utterly. . . . Such, then, were the circumstances of the first taking of Babylon. (*The History of Herodotus*, book 1, chapters 190–91)

The Book of Daniel

The biblical account of Babylon's fall to the Persians can be found in Daniel 5. Daniel's account focuses on an aspect of this event that the other accounts ignore. It gives special attention to a drunken feast held in Babylon by Belshazzar (the son of Nabonidus and the ruler of Babylon during his father's long absences). It also mentions Darius the Median, known in the Nabonidus Chronicle as "Gobryas."

> Belshazzar the king made a great feast to a thousand of his lords, and drank wine before the thousand. Belshazzar . . . commanded to bring the golden and silver vessels which his father Nebuchadnezzar had taken out of the temple which was in Jerusalem. . . . They drank wine, and praised the gods of gold, and of silver, of brass, of iron, or wood, and of stone. In the

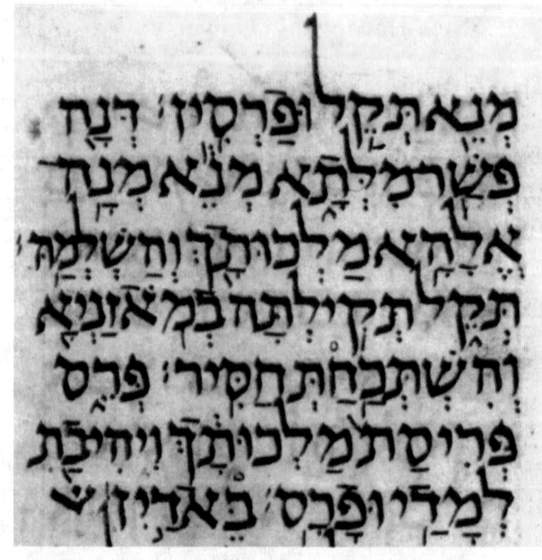
מנא תקל ופרסין׃ דנה
פשר מלתא מנא מנה
אלהא מלכותך והשלמה
תקל תקילתה במאזניא
והשתכחת חסיר׃ פרס
פריסת מלכותך ויהיבת
למדי ופרס׃ באדין

A portion of Daniel's account of the fall of Babylon from the Leningrad Codex, one of the most important Old Testament manuscripts. These words record Daniel's interpretation of the handwriting on the wall. (Daniel 5:25-28)
Bruce and Kenneth Zuckerman, West Semitic Research.

same hour came forth fingers of a man's hand, and wrote over against the candlestick upon the plaister of the wall of the king's palace: and the king saw the part of the hand that wrote. . . . Then came in all the king's wise men: but they could not read the writing, nor make known to the king the interpretation thereof. . . .Then was Daniel brought in before the king. . . . Then Daniel answered and said before the king, . . . This is the interpretation of the thing: MENE; God hath numbered thy kingdom, and finished it. TEKEL; Thou art weighed in the balances, and art found wanting. PERES; Thy kingdom is divided, and given to the Medes and Persians. Then commanded Belshazzar, and they clothed Daniel with scarlet, and put a chain of gold about his neck, and made a proclamation concerning him, that he should be the third ruler in the kingdom. In that night was Belshazzar the king of the Chaldeans slain. And Darius the Median took the kingdom, being about threescore and two years old.

Evaluation of Historical Sources

1. Of these sources, which one is most reliable? Why?

____

____

2. Of these sources, which one is probably the least reliable? Why?

____

____

Historical Synthesis

Using the reliable sources, weave the events they record into a narrative of thirteen points. After stating the event, be sure to indicate in parentheses your source. To help get you started, the first two events have been filled in.

1. Cyrus's troops defeated a Babylonian force at Opis on the Tigris River in the month of Tishri. (Nabonidus Chronicle)
2. A few days later, on the fourteenth day of Tishri, Cyrus took the city of Sippar without a fight. (Nabonidus Chronicle)
3. ______________________________
4. ______________________________

   ____
5. ______________________________
6. ______________________________
7. ______________________________

   ____

   ____
8. ______________________________

   ____

   ____

9. ______________________________

10. ______________________________

11. ______________________________

12. ______________________________

13. ______________________________

Historical Interpretation

1. What does the Cyrus Cylinder identify as the reason for the fall of Babylon?

2. What does Herodotus's account seem to identify as the reason for the fall of Babylon?

3. According to the Book of Daniel, why did Babylon fall?

4. If you were writing a history of ancient civilizations, what would you identify as the cause of Babylon's fall? How would you derive present significance from the fall of Babylon?

Name ______________________

WORLD HISTORY 1 ACTIVITY 2

Sin and Civilization

The student text defines *civilization* as "human culture characterized by cities." It then defines a *city* as "a complex cultural institution in which humans share core values and a desire to improve the quality of their existence through specialization and organization" (p. 16). This student activity is designed to show what makes a civilization sinful. The questions that follow will ask you to consider the different parts of the definition of *city* and what the Bible states about what makes a city sinful.

Specialization and Organization

Cities arise as humans develop specialization of tasks and an organization structure to protect the network of specialization. Is the Bible critical of specialization and organization?

1. Exodus 18:17–22 ______________________

2. Romans 12:3–8 ______________________

Desiring to Improve One's Quality of Life

People agree to accept the sacrifices and challenges of specialization and organization, in part, to improve their quality of life. This improvement is usually of three kinds: (1) an increase in pleasure, (2) an increase in wealth or possessions, and (3) an increase in knowledge, skill, or understanding. Does the Bible teach that it is wrong to pursue these three improvements?

1. Genesis 3:6 ______________________

2. Genesis 2:9 ______________________

3. 1 Timothy 4:1–5 ______________________

4. Mark 10:29–30 ______________________

5. Proverbs 25:2 ______________________________

6. 1 Corinthians 1:30–31 ______________________________

Core Values

In a civilization people are able to join together to improve their quality of life because they share certain core values. A civilization's core values are its citizens' beliefs about what is most important in life. Although disagreement over core values is present in every civilization, all civilizations do still have a dominant worldview—one that can be accurately represented in a list of the values that tend to characterize the people of that civilization. What does the Bible teach about the core values of the following civilizations?

1. Babel: Genesis 11:4, 8 ______________________________

2. Israel: Deuteronomy 6:4–6, 10–14 ______________________________

3. Sodom: Ezekiel 16:49–50 ______________________________

4. New Jerusalem: Revelation 21:9–11; 21:22–22:5 ______________________________

Conclusion

1. If a civilization is pervasively wicked, what has made it wicked?

2. If a civilization can justly be called righteous, what makes it righteous?

3. How may a Christian glorify God through his involvement in a sinful civilization?

Name ______________________

WORLD HISTORY 1 ACTIVITY 3

Foundations for the Study of History

Fill in the following blanks.

The Christian worldview presented in the Bible is composed of three central truths:

(1) ______________________

(2) ______________________

(3) ______________________

Match the appropriate term with its definition.

A. culture	C. specialization	E. city
B. divine providence	D. human depravity	

_____ 1. Every aspect of every human's being (body, mind, will, and emotions) has been stained by the Fall.

_____ 2. The division of labor that is part of the culture of every city.

_____ 3. A complex cultural institution in which humans share core values and a desire to improve the quality of their existence.

_____ 4. There is no event that is out of God's control or that does not help to accomplish His purpose for this world.

_____ 5. The physical and mental environment developed through human thought and labor.

Fill in each blank with the appropriate term.

6. A ____________ is a large group of people (usually including many cities) who have in common the same land area, the same customs, and the same language.

7. A ______________ is a perspective from which we may examine and interpret the universe and everything in it.

8. __________________ refers to a system of rules, regulations, and accountability that governs all who take part in the functions of the city.

9. The __________________ is a complex of qualities possessed by all humans that reflects part of God's own personality.

Write a description of the following terms.

10. Historical synthesis ______________________

____

11. Table of Nations ______________________

____

12. Creation Mandate ______________________

____

____

Name ____________________

WORLD HISTORY 2 ACTIVITY 1

Questions and Timeline

Identify the person, civilization, place, event, and/or date for each of the following questions. Identify in parentheses the civilization each person represents. Then record the appropriate information on the timeline on the next page.

Section I:

1. United the land of Mesopotamia and is remembered for his code of laws (year reign began) ____________________
2. Established the first known empire (year reign began) ____________________

Section II:

3. Age when Egypt became a great world power (year age began) ____________________
4. Age in Egypt when Khufu built the great pyramid at Giza (year age began) ____________________
5. Age when Egyptian pharaohs directed their attention to projects that would benefit the country as a whole (year age began) ____________________

Section III:

6. The Israelites led out of Egypt by Moses ____________________
7. Jews carried into Babylon ____________________
8. Began to settle Asia Minor with their army commanders as kings (year began) ____________________
9. Came from Ur and began Israel's history (birth year) ____________________
10. King whose army destroyed Jerusalem and carried the Jews into exile for seventy years (year reign began) ____________________
11. Israel's southern kingdom capital that the Chaldeans destroyed ____________________

Section IV:

12. Led the Assyrian army to destroy Samaria and took captive the ten northern Hebrew tribes (year destroyed) ____________________
13. Used by God to free His people from their captivity in Babylon ____________________
14. City destroyed by the Chaldeans and the Medes ____________________
15. Was killed by the Medes and Persians after using the golden vessels from God's temple in Jerusalem ____________________

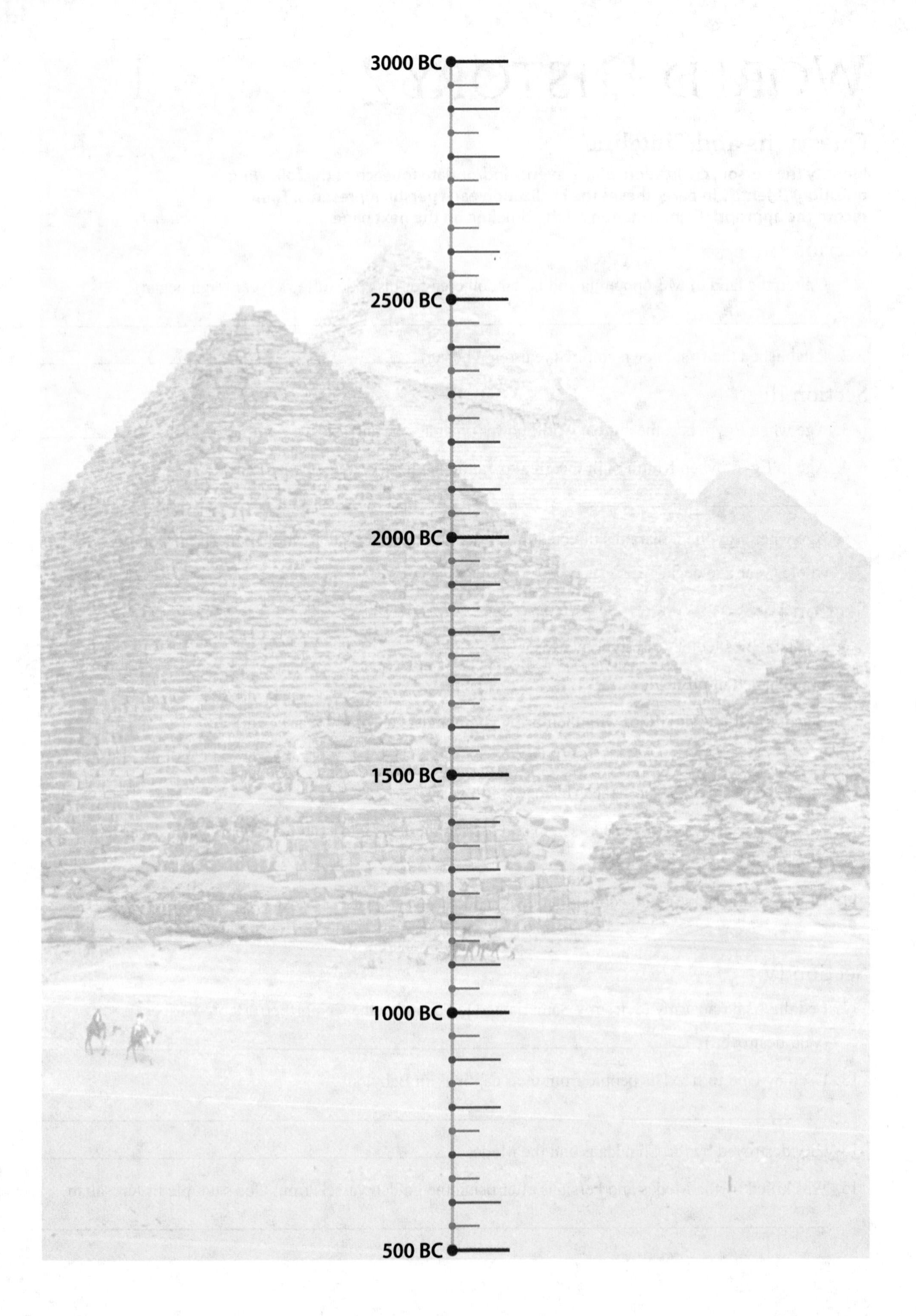
3000 BC
2500 BC
2000 BC
1500 BC
1000 BC
500 BC

Name ____________________

WORLD HISTORY 2 ACTIVITY 2

Spread of Civilization

Complete the chart. For each civilization write its capital, its main leaders, and its main accomplishments. The accomplishments are listed below the chart.

Civilization	Century (BC)	Capital(s)	Leader(s)	Accomplishments
Akkadian				
Amorite				
Egyptian				
Hittite	15th	Hattushash		
Phoenician				
Aramean				
Hebrew	11th			
Assyrian	8th			
Chaldean	7th			
Persian	6th			

astrology
Avesta
code of Hammurabi
cuneiform
destruction of Jerusalem
destruction of Samaria
Epic of Gilgamesh
first known alphabet
first known empire
"go-between" language
hieroglyphics
iron weapons
monotheism
papyrus
postal system
rebuilding of Jerusalem
satrapies
solar calendar
units of sixty
ziggurats
Zoroastrianism

Name ______________________

WORLD HISTORY 2 ACTIVITY 3

Word Origins

One smart way to remember words is to learn their origins and the meaning of their root words. Use your textbook and a dictionary to find the country where these words originated and the meaning of their roots. Then answer the questions that follow.

1. astrology ______________________
2. astronomy ______________________
3. Avesta ______________________
4. Baal ______________________
5. cuneiform ______________________
6. delta ______________________
7. Diaspora ______________________
8. empire ______________________
9. hieroglyphics ______________________
10. monotheism ______________________
11. pharaoh ______________________
12. polytheism ______________________
13. satrap ______________________
14. theocracy ______________________
15. ziggurat ______________________
16. List all of the ancient languages that provided source words for the list above.

    ____
17. Which ancient language provided the most source words in the list above?

    ____
18. Which word above was derived from a letter in an ancient alphabet?

    ____
19. Which two words above were derived from Hebrew words in the Old Testament?

    ____
20. Which root word appears three times in the words above?

    ____
21. Which root word appears twice in the words above?

    ____

Name ____________________

WORLD HISTORY 2 ACTIVITY 4

Map Study: Ancient Near East

I. Label each of the following regions, cities, and special features on the Ancient Near East map.

Regions	Cities (identify with •)	Special Features
Assyria	Babylon	Arabian Desert
Canaan	Damascus	Euphrates River
Egypt	Jerusalem	Jordan River
Hittites (Anatolia)	Memphis	Mediterranean Sea
Lydia	Nineveh	Nile River
Media	Sardis	Persian Gulf
Persia	Susa	Red Sea
Phoenicia	Thebes	Sinai Peninsula
Sumer	Tyre	Tigris River
Syria		

II. Shade the Fertile Crescent with a colored pencil.

III. Identify the following.

1. first Egyptian capital ____________________
2. Egyptian capital in Moses' day ____________________
3. capital of Amorites and Chaldeans ____________________
4. first major iron producers ____________________
5. first kingdom with a solar calendar ____________________
6. first used coins ____________________
7. traders of purple ____________________
8. leading city of Phoenicia ____________________
9. Aramean capital ____________________
10. Hebrew capital ____________________

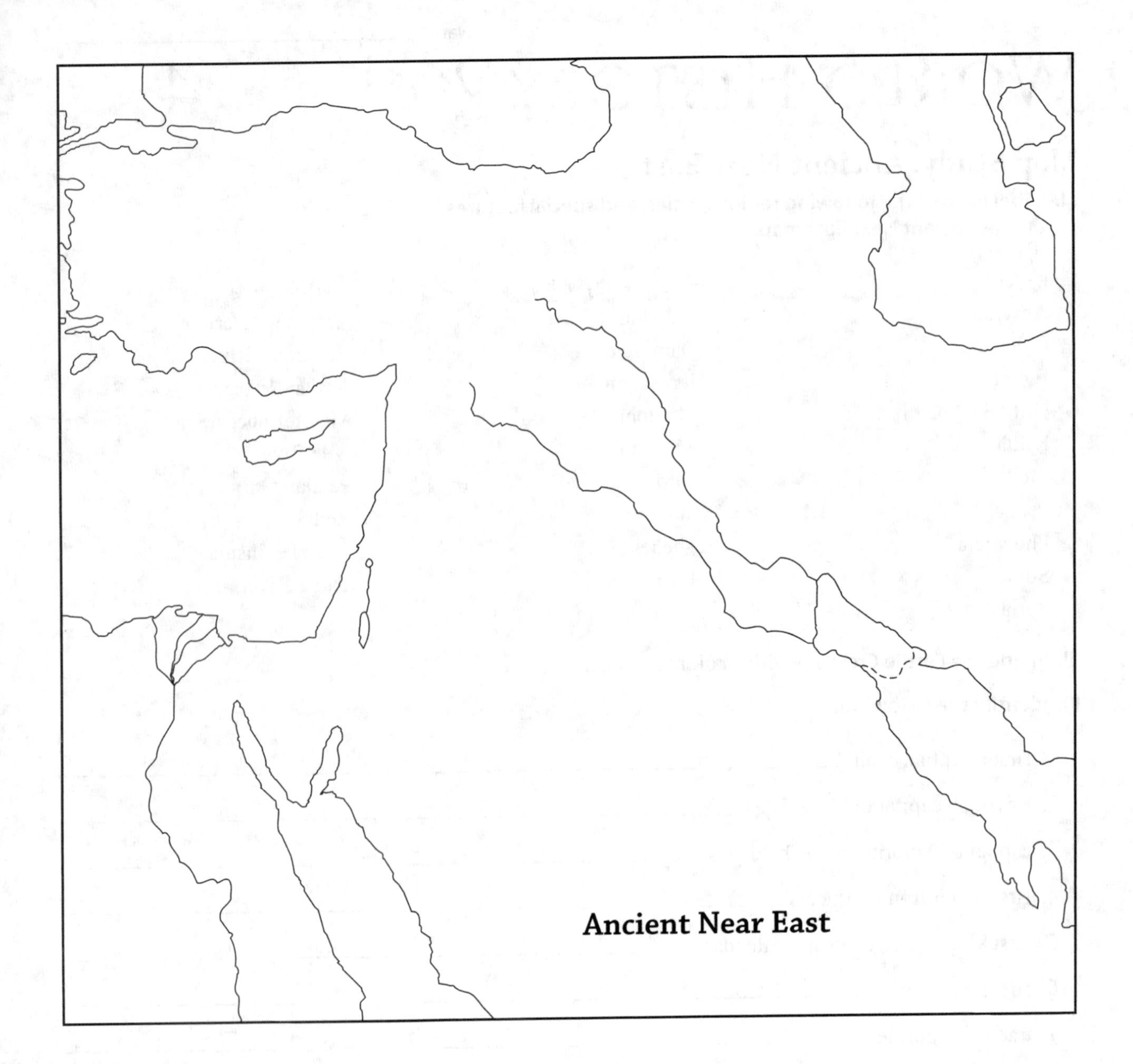
Ancient Near East

Name ____________________

WORLD HISTORY 2 ACTIVITY 5

Israel's Walk Through the Nations— A Firsthand View of the Ancient World

The nation of Israel had dealings with every major civilization in the ancient Near East. The Bible's references to Hittites, Amorites, and other peoples often just sound like names. Now that you have studied the ancient world, you should be able to see these people through the eyes of an Israelite. Your Bible gives you a firsthand look at these ancient nations.

Use your textbook and the Bible to answer the questions below. (You may want to refer to the Unit 1 timeline in your textbook to see the parallel chronology of events in Israel and the rest of the world.)

Patriarchal Period (2166–1876 BC)

1. If indeed Abraham lived among the Sumerians in the city of Ur, his forefathers would have been alive during the reign of Sargon himself. However, in Abraham's day the Akkadian civilization had fallen into decay, threatened by Amorite invaders. Based on your textbook, give some details about the daily life of the Sumerians.

   a. writing ____________________

   b. religion ____________________

   c. temple towers ____________________

2. When Abraham arrived in Canaan, he found that many Amorites had invaded the region. Abraham's son, **Isaac**, was alive when the **Amorites**—led by King **Hammurabi**—captured Ur and the rest of Mesopotamia. Isaac's cousin Laban was living in Mesopotamia when all this took place. The Amorites did not fight against the Hebrews until after Moses led them to the Promised Land.

   a. What law code ruled the land when Jacob fled from Esau to live with his uncle Laban in Mesopotamia? ____________________

   b. Why did God tell Abraham that his people would have to wait four hundred years in Egypt before they came back to take the land of the Amorites (Gen. 15:12–16)?

   ____

   c. Where in Canaan were Amorites living when Joshua fought against them (Num. 13:29)?

   ____

   d. What physical characteristics did the Amorites have (Amos 2:9–10)?

   ____

Egyptian and Wilderness Period (1876–1406 BC)

3. Abraham temporarily sojourned in Egypt during its **Middle Kingdom**. Pharaoh even sought to marry Abraham's wife, Sarah. Years later, Abraham's grandson, Jacob, took all the Israelites down into Egypt to live with his son, **Joseph**, who had become a leader among the **Egyptians**. Joseph's sons, Ephraim and

Manasseh, were possibly still alive when Hyksos warriors invaded Egypt and ended the Middle Kingdom.

a. In what type of language did Joseph write? ______

b. What river enabled Egypt to prosper in the midst of famine (see Gen. 41:1–4; Deut. 11:10–11)?

______

c. In what city was the pharaoh living when Joseph first appeared before his throne?

______

d. What type of family did Joseph's wife come from (Gen. 41:45)?

______

e. What Hebrew occupation was offensive to the Egyptians (Gen. 46:31–34)? ______

f. What did the Egyptians do with Joseph's body (Gen. 50:26)? ______

4. The **Egyptians** who overthrew the Hyksos and founded the **New Kingdom** were "warrior-kings." They built a large empire. When **Moses** was born, the greatest conqueror in Egyptian history—**Thutmose III**—was probably pharaoh. To ensure that the Israelites did not revolt while he was away fighting wars, Thutmose forced the Israelites into slave labor, constructing government buildings. Thutmose's heir, probably **Amenhotep II**, opposed Moses' efforts to free his people.

a. Name a female pharaoh who ruled over the Israelites. ______

b. What new implements of war did the Egyptians adopt from the Hyksos (Exod. 14:5–9, 23–28)?

______

c. What two Egyptian cities did the Hebrews build out of bricks (Exod. 1:9–11)?

______

d. Based on your textbook, what do you think Moses learned in the royal school (Acts 7:22)?

______

______

Conquest and Judges Period (1406–1050 BC)

5. Abraham knew some **Hittites** who had moved into Canaan—he purchased his burial place from a generous Hittite. Many years later Moses' successor, **Joshua**, arrived in Palestine—"the land of the Hittites"—hoping to crush the small Hittite city-states there. Joshua did not utterly defeat them. The Hebrews later broke God's law and intermarried with the Hittites. During the age of the judges, Hittites from Asia Minor (north of Israel) fought against the Egyptians (in the south). Their preoccupation with each other left the petty kings in Canaan free to oppress the Hebrews.

a. Why do you think Rebekah disliked Esau's two wives (see Gen. 26:34–35, 36:2)?

______

b. Why did Joshua's twelve spies fear the Hittites of Palestine (see Num. 13:26–33)?

______

c. Why was God angered by Israel's intermarriage with the Hittites (see Judg. 3:5–6, Ezra 9:1–3)?

d. What rumor caused the Arameans (Syrians) to withdraw from their siege of Samaria (2 Kings 7:6-7)?

United and Divided Kingdom (1050–586 BC)

6. Because of Assyria's rising threat, the **Arameans** (Syrians) and Israel's other neighbors were unable to concentrate their strength against the newly established kingdom of Israel. Eventually, the **Assyrians** began to be a menace to Israel too. Although the Bible never mentions it, King **Ahab** (Ahaabu) of Israel forged an alliance with his enemies, the Arameans, to stop the advance of Assyrian king Shalmaneser III at the battle of Qarqar (853 BC). When King **Jehu** (Jaua) usurped Ahab's throne, however, the alliance fell apart, and Assyria was able to force the weakened Jehu to pay tribute. (On an obelisk that Shalmaneser had carved for himself, Jehu is pictured bowing before the Assyrian king.)

   A century later the great Assyrian King Tiglathpileser III conquered Damascus and forced Israel and Judah to pay him tribute. Soon afterward King **Sargon II** destroyed Samaria. Later Sennacherib tried to take Jerusalem but failed. The prophet **Isaiah** lived during the reigns of all of these Assyrian kings. He prophesied the destruction of Samaria and encouraged **Hezekiah** to trust that God would preserve Judah.

   a. Jonah was a prophet during the reign of Jeroboam, who ascended the throne about thirty-five years after Jehu's death. Why did Jonah, a citizen of Israel, dislike Assyria?

   b. How did Jehu's treatment of his enemies compare to Assyria's treatment of her enemies (2 Kings 10:1–8)?

   c. In Sennacherib's own monument recounting his victories, he boasted that he made King Hezekiah "a prisoner in Jerusalem, his royal residence, like a bird in a cage." He also boasted, "Hezekiah himself, whom the terror-inspiring splendor of my lordship had overwhelmed and whose irregular and elite troops which he had brought into Jerusalem, his royal residence, in order to strengthen it, had deserted him, did send me, later, to Nineveh, my lordly city, together with 30 talents of gold, 800 talents of silver, precious stones, antimony, large cuts of red stone, couches inlaid with ivory, chairs inlaid with ivory, elephant-hides, ebony-wood, boxwood, and all kinds of valuable treasures, his own daughters, concubines, male and female physicians. In order to deliver the tribute and to do obeisance as a slave he sent his personal messenger" (James B. Pritchard, ed., *Ancient Near Eastern Texts*, p. 288). What do you think this declaration shows about Sennacherib's pride? Why was it an empty boast?

Exile Period (586–538 BC)

7. When Nineveh was destroyed in 612 BC, no one was sure what would happen to the Assyrian empire. At the great battle of Carchemish in 605 BC, when Prince **Nebuchadnezzar** led the **Chaldeans** to victory against the Egyptian pharaoh Necho, Nebuchadnezzar made it clear who now controlled the old empire. When his father died that year, Nebuchadnezzar was crowned king. However, King **Jehoiakim** of Judah failed to appreciate this sudden reversal in world power. The prophecies of **Jeremiah** fell on deaf ears. Jehoiakim rebelled that same year but was defeated. Among the captives taken was the boy **Daniel**. Jehoiachin rebelled again in 597 BC—after only three months on the throne. He was defeated and taken captive to Babylon, along with **Ezekiel** and others. In 586 BC Nebuchadnezzar destroyed Jerusalem altogether.

   a. Why was Jeremiah condemned for treason (Jer. 21:8–10; 32:1–5; 34:1–4; 38:1–6)?

   ____

   b. List some of the sights that the Jews of the Diaspora—such as Ezekiel and Daniel—would have seen in Babylon. ____

   ____

   c. What are some of the things Daniel would have learned in the royal school?

   ____

   d. What Chaldean ruler's own testimony is in the Bible (Dan. 4:34–37)? ______________

Period of Persian Rule (538–332 BC)

8. The night that Belshazzar blasphemed God during his drunken feast, the **Persian** army of **Cyrus the Great** (538–529 BC) captured his great capital, Babylon. To win the allegiance of the former peoples of the Chaldean empire, Cyrus was wise and merciful, allowing exiles to return to their lands. For example, he allowed the Jews to return to Jerusalem to rebuild the temple.

   Cyrus placed an officer named Darius the Mede over the former Babylonian empire. (He was not related to a later Persian king, Darius the Great, 521–486 BC). This Darius raised **Daniel** to a top position in Babylon. A later Persian ruler, Xerxes (or Ahasuerus, 486–464 BC), married a Jewish exile named **Esther**. His successor, Artaxerxes (464–425 BC), allowed **Ezra** to take the treasures of the temple back to Jerusalem. Thirteen years later Artaxerxes allowed **Nehemiah** to return to Jerusalem, along with many exiles, to rebuild the walls of the city.

   a. How many provinces, each ruled by a prince, were under Darius the Mede (Dan. 6:1–3)?______________

   b. What Jew became the leading minister in Artaxerxes' empire (Esther 10:1–3)? ______________

   c. What Persian king's decree is included in the Bible (Ezra 7:11–26)? What form of writing did he use? ____

   d. What famous road would Nehemiah have used during the first leg of his journey from Susa to Jerusalem (Ezra 8:31–32)? What would the Jews have seen while traveling on the road?

   ____

   e. Ezra gave the king's message to one of the Persian governors (Ezra 8:36). From your reading of the textbook, what title did the governors have? ______________

Name ______________________

WORLD HISTORY 3 ACTIVITY 1

Questions and Timeline

Identify the person, place, event, civilization, and/or date for each of the following questions. Then record the appropriate information on the timeline on the next page. If the answer spans a number of years, draw a bracket and label.

Section I:

1. Invaded Mycenaeans ______________________
2. Epic poems about the Greek Dark Ages ______________________
3. Earliest center of civilization in Aegean region (year flourished)

____

Section II:

4. Led Athens in taking a step toward democracy (year assumed office of archon)

____

5. The Greek political system that developed (year development began)

____

Section III:

6. The devastating war that pitted Greek against Greek (year began)

____

7. Athens most influential leader (year leadership began) ______________________
8. Led a Persian force that landed twenty-five miles north of Athens (year landed)

____

9. Where the Greeks defeated the Persian fleet (year defeated) ______________________

Section IV:

10. Became king and with his conquering armies amassed a huge empire (year reign began)

____

Section V:

11. The Father of Medicine (birth year) ______________________
12. Tutored Alexander the Great (birth year) ______________________
13. The Father of Philosophy (birth year) ______________________
14. Established a school of philosophy and science called the Academy (birth year)

____

15. Philosopher who lived in Athens during her golden age and whose motto was "Know thyself" (birth year) ______________________

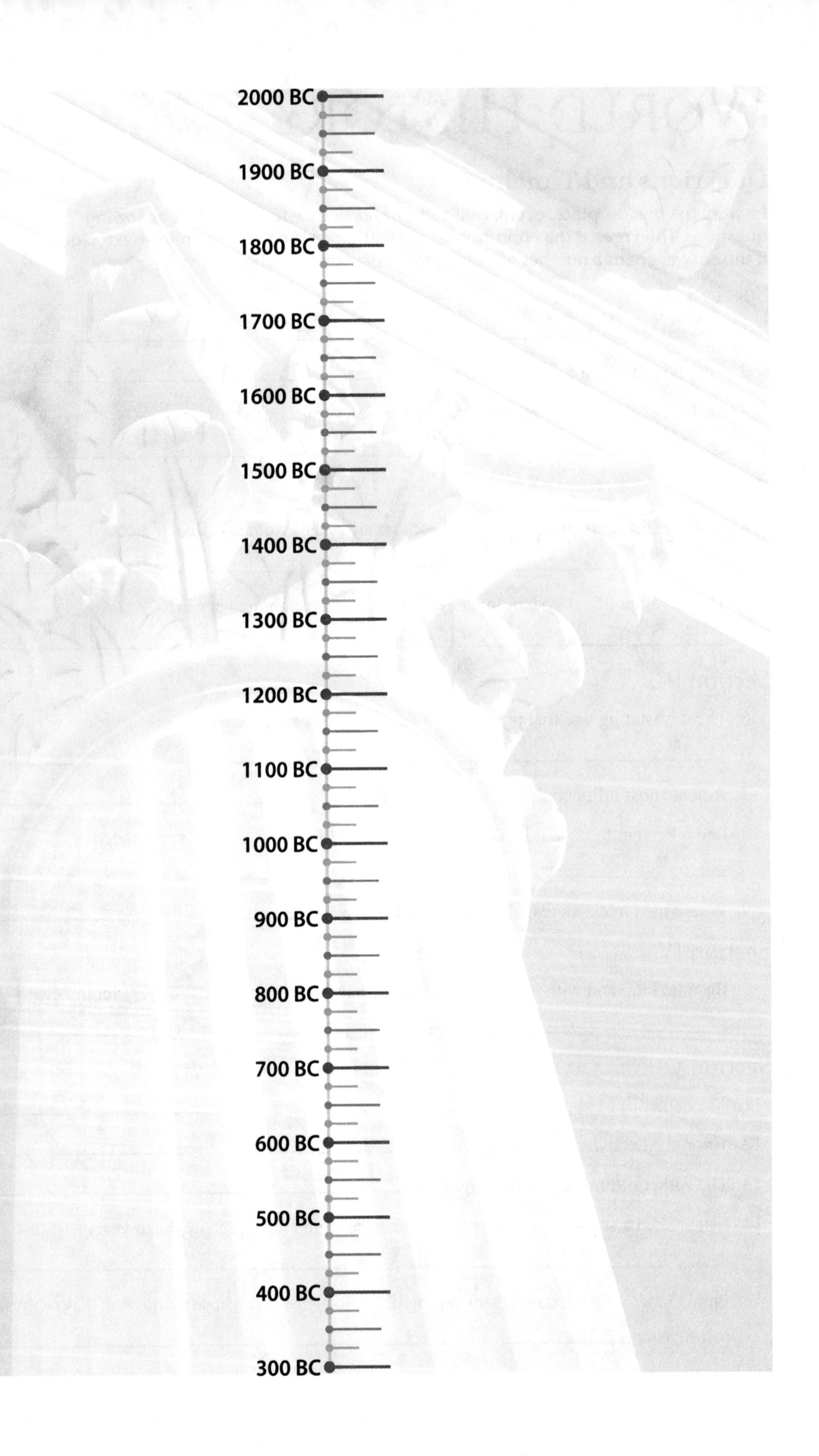
2000 BC
1900 BC
1800 BC
1700 BC
1600 BC
1500 BC
1400 BC
1300 BC
1200 BC
1100 BC
1000 BC
900 BC
800 BC
700 BC
600 BC
500 BC
400 BC
300 BC

Name ____________________

WORLD HISTORY 3 ACTIVITY 2

Odyssey Excerpts

Read the excerpts from Homer's *Odyssey,* translated by Samuel Butler, that tells of Ulysses' (Odysseus) travels home after the fall of Troy. Answer the questions.

Excerpt I—Book I:

Opening paragraph

TELL ME, O MUSE, of that ingenious hero who traveled far and wide after he had sacked the famous town of Troy. Many cities did he visit, and many were the nations with whose manners and customs he was acquainted; moreover he suffered much by sea while trying to save his own life and bring his men safely home; but do what he might he could not save his men, for they perished through their own sheer folly in eating the cattle of the Sun-god Hyperion; so the god prevented them from ever reaching home. Tell me, too, about all these things, O daughter of Jove, from whatsoever source you may know them.

1. How is Ulysses described?

____

2. Why was Ulysses unable to save his men?

____

Excerpt II—Book II:

Antinous (one of Penelope's suitors) speaking to Telemachus (Ulysses/Odysseus' son) about Penelope

. . . And then there was that other trick she played us. She set up a great tambour frame in her room, and began to work on an enormous piece of fine needlework. "Sweet hearts," said she, "Ulysses is indeed dead, still do not press me to marry again immediately, wait—for I would not have skill in needlework perish unrecorded—till I have completed a pall for the hero Laertes, to be in readiness against the time when death shall take him. He is very rich, and the women of the place will talk if he is laid out without a pall."

This was what she said, and we assented; whereon we could see her working on her great web all day long, but at night she would unpick the stitches again by torchlight. She fooled us in this way for three years and we never found her out, but as time wore on and she was now in her fourth year, one of her maids who knew what she was doing told us, and we caught her in the act of undoing her work, so she had to finish it whether she would or no. . . .

3. What was the trick that Penelope played on her suitors?

____

____

4. How did the suitors discover Penelope's trick?

____

5. How much time had passed before Penelope's trick was revealed?

____

Excerpt III—Book XXI:

Penelope tells the suitors what they must do to win and marry her.

MINERVA now put it in Penelope's mind to make the suitors try their skill with the bow and with the iron axes, in contest among themselves, as a means of bringing about their destruction. . . . [A]nd Penelope stepped upon the raised platform, where the chests stood in which the fair linen and clothes were laid by along with fragrant herbs: reaching thence, she took down the bow with its bow case from the peg on which it hung. . . . she went to the cloister where the suitors were, carrying the bow and the quiver, with the many deadly arrows that were inside it. . . When she reached the suitors, she stood by one of the bearing-posts supporting the roof of the cloister, holding a veil before her face, and with a maid on either side of her. Then she said: "Listen to me you suitors, who persist in abusing the hospitality of this house because its owner has been long absent, and without other pretext than that you want to marry me; this, then, being the prize that you are contending for, I will bring out the mighty bow of Ulysses, and whomsoever of you shall string it most easily and send his arrow through each one of twelve axes, him will I follow . . . ."

6. What did Penelope tell the suitors they must do to win her?

____

7. Who gave Penelope the idea?

____

Excerpt IV—Book XXI:

After all the suitors have tried in vain to string Ulysses' bow, Ulysses in a beggar's disguise strings the bow and shoots the arrow through the ax handles.

Ulysses, when he had taken it up and examined it all over, strung it as easily as a skilled bard strings a new peg of his lyre and makes the twisted gut fast at both ends. Then he took it in his right hand to prove the string, and it sang sweetly under his touch like the twittering of a swallow. The suitors were dismayed, and turned colour as they heard it; at that moment, moreover, Jove thundered loudly as a sign, and the heart of Ulysses rejoiced as he heard the omen that the son of scheming Saturn had sent him.

He took an arrow that was lying upon the table—for those which the Achaeans [Penelope's suitors] were so shortly about to taste were all inside the quiver—he laid it on the centre-piece of the bow, and drew the notch of the arrow and the string toward him, still seated on his seat. When he had taken aim he let fly, and his arrow pierced every one of the handle-holes of the axes from the first onwards till it had gone right through them, and into the outer courtyard.

8. What occurred when Ulysses strung his bow?

____

____

9. Who would soon taste of all the arrows in Ulysses's quiver?

____

Name ______________________

WORLD HISTORY 3 ACTIVITY 3

Types of Government

Complete the chart. Note how a "republic" combines the best of these elements in the next chapter.

	Definition	Examples from Ancient Greece	Advantages	Disadvantages
Monarchy				
Oligarchy				
Tyranny				
Democracy			Athens attained cultural heights unparalleled in the ancient world. Each adult male citizen shared in the responsibility of ruling his city.	Too much liberty and freedom without restraint leads to anarchy (the breakdown of government and order).

Name ____________________

WORLD HISTORY 3 ACTIVITY 4

Facts to Remember

Answer the questions.

1. Which city-state headed the Peloponnesian League? ____________________
2. Where was the Minoan civilization located? ____________________
3. Whose thirty-year leadership led Athens to unparalleled cultural heights in the ancient world?
____
4. Who were the Helots?
____
5. Which epic poems did Homer write? ____________________
6. Which Persian king crushed a Greek revolt and sought to punish Athens for her part in the rebellion?
____
7. Under whose leadership did Athens take a step toward democracy?
____
8. Which Greek civilization was begun by invaders from the north?
____
9. What was an archon?
____
10. What is the difference between a monarchy and an oligarchy?
____
11. Define *anthropomorphic.*
____
12. In which city-state alliance did Athens become the leader?
____
13. Which war pitted Greek against Greek? ____________________
14. Under whose leadership did Athens establish a "rule of the people"?
____
15. Why did Xerxes invade Greece?
____
16. Why did the Greek city-states disunite after Sparta's victory in the Peloponnesian War?
____
____
____

Name ____________________

WORLD HISTORY 3 ACTIVITY 5

Map Study: Ancient Greece

I. Using the maps in this chapter, label each of the following regions, cities, and special feature on the Ancient Greece map.

Regions	Cities (Identify with •)	Special Features
Attica	Athens	Aegean Sea
Crete	Corinth	Black Sea
Ionia	Knossos	Hellespont
Macedonia	Sardis	Marathon
Peloponnesus	Sparta	Salamis
Rhodes	Troy	Thermopylae
		Mediterranean Sea

II. Identify the following.

1. capital of the Minoan civilization ____________________
2. strait between Europe and Asia ____________________
3. narrow pass that protected Attica from overland invasion ____________________
4. bay where the first Persian army landed in Greece and was crushed ____________________
5. bay where the Persian invasion fleet was destroyed in 480 BC ____________________
6. Trojan horse ____________________
7. "school of Greece" ____________________
8. city ruled by a military oligarchy ____________________
9. city with first democracy in history ____________________
10. city of Pericles ____________________
11. home of Alexander the Great ____________________
12. earliest center of civilization in Aegean Sea area ____________________

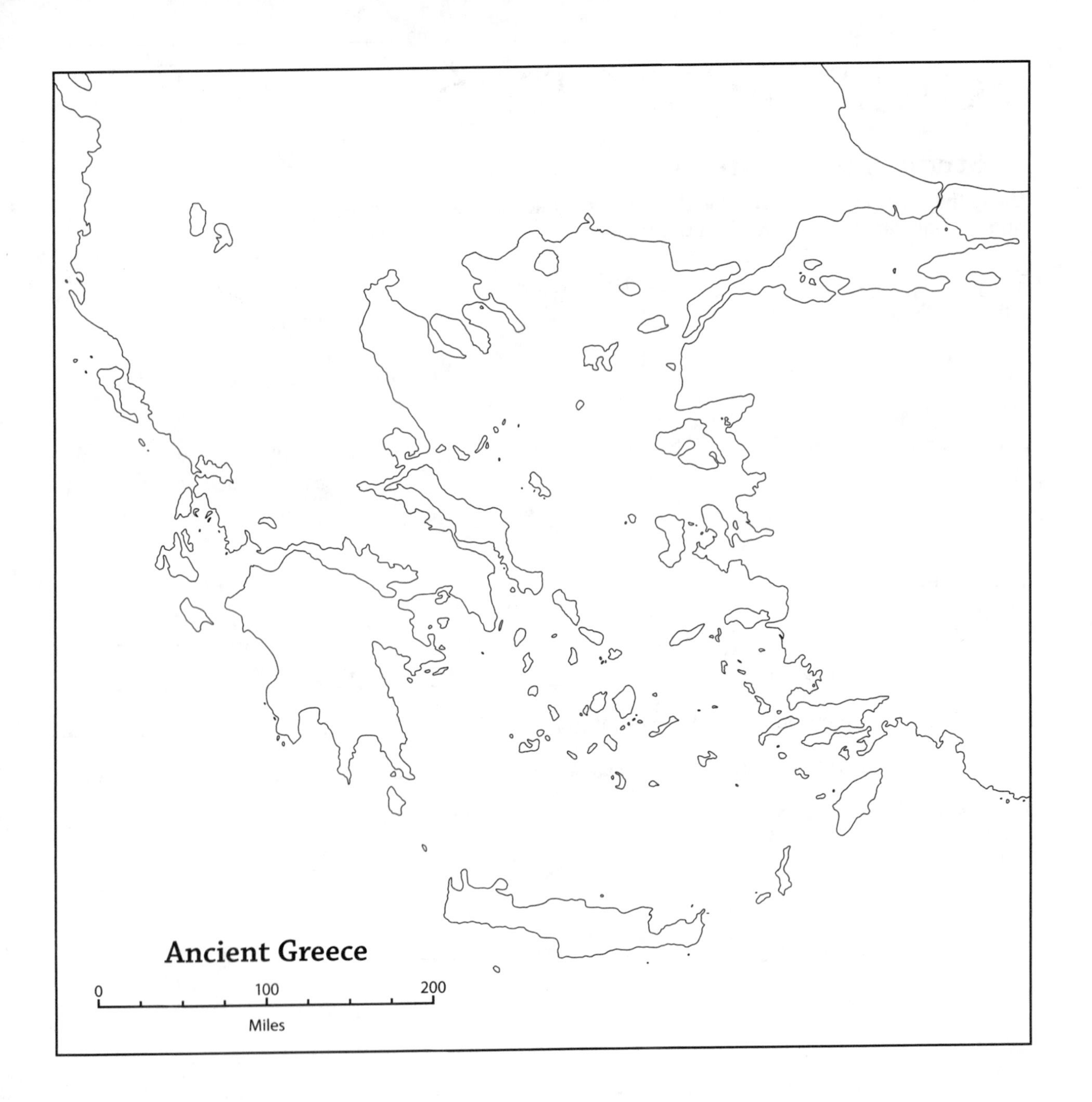
Ancient Greece
0
100
200
Miles

Name ______________________________

WORLD HISTORY 4 ACTIVITY 1

Questions and Timeline

Identify the person, place, event, civilization, and/or date for each of the following questions. Then record the appropriate information on the timeline on the next page.

Section I:

1. City founded by Romulus and Remus (year founded)

   ____

2. Established one of Italy's earliest civilizations (bracket time period)

   ____

Section II:

3. The foundation of Roman law that was hung in the Roman Forum (year law hung)

   ____

4. Established in place of the monarchy (year established)

   ____

5. Plebeian assembly that gained power to pass laws binding upon all people of Rome (year gained power)

   ____

Section III:

6. Battle where the Romans suffered one of their worst defeats (year)

   ____

7. He led attacks on Rome at the beginning of the Second Punic War (year war began)

   ____

8. Began over the control of Sicily (year war began)

   ____

9. He aroused Roman action against Carthage, beginning the Third Punic War (year war began)

   ____

10. The battle during the Second Punic War where the Carthaginian army was defeated by the Romans (year)

    ____

Section IV:

11. He was murdered in the Senate on the Ides of March (year murdered)

    ____

12. Battle that Antony and Cleopatra lost (year)

    ____

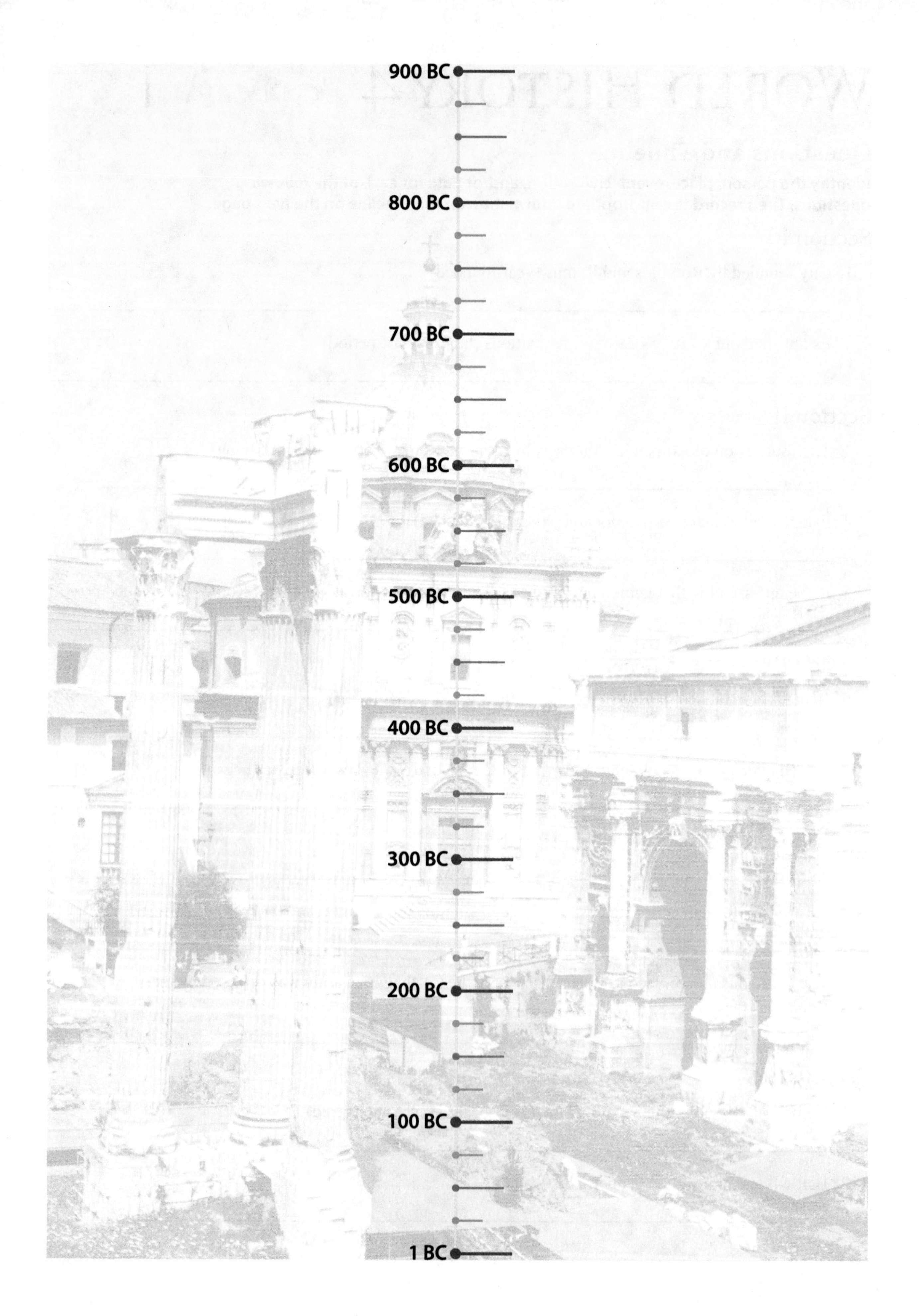
900 BC
800 BC
700 BC
600 BC
500 BC
400 BC
300 BC
200 BC
100 BC
1 BC

Name ______________________

WORLD HISTORY 4 ACTIVITY 2

Roman vs. American Republic

Complete the chart comparing the Roman Republic and the modern American Republic. You may need to use an encyclopedia or a U.S. history textbook.

		Roman Republic	United States Republic
Written Law	Date the Monarch Was Overthrown		
	Name and Date of the Written Law of the Land		
	Purpose of the Written Law		
Separation of Powers	Main Body That Passed Laws and Controlled Finances		
	Term of Office for Senators		
	Secondary Body That Passed Laws		
	Term of Office for Tribunes/ Representatives		
	Name of the Executive Who Carried Out Laws		
	Term of Office for the Executive		
	Commander of the Army		
	Supreme Judge		

Checks and Balances		Roman Republic	United States Republic
	Checks on the Executive's Power		
	Checks on the Senate's Power		
	Checks on the Representative Assembly's Power		

Name ______________________

WORLD HISTORY 4 ACTIVITY 3

Lessons from History

The fortunes (and misfortunes) of the Roman Republic provided lessons for the Western civilizations that came later, including America. Match each term or event with the lesson that it *best* illustrates.

A. power of the Roman *pater*
B. limit of consuls to one-year terms and co-rule
C. revolt of the Latins against Rome
D. Law of Twelve Tables
E. decrease of the Tribal Assembly's power during the Punic Wars
F. Cato's speeches
G. Rome's conquest of the East
H. loyalty of Rome's subjects during the Second Punic War
I. publicans
J. murder of the Gracchi brothers
K. Marius's military reforms and civil war
L. breakdown of the triumvirate

_____ 1. High taxes breed corruption.

_____ 2. Reliance on violence to solve problems simply encourages more violence.

_____ 3. Foreign conquest creates more problems than it solves.

_____ 4. Rivalry between nations continues until one is completely destroyed.

_____ 5. The backbone of a strong civilization is strong families.

_____ 6. In time of war, people are willing to give up their political freedoms so that experienced leaders can see them through the crisis.

_____ 7. After overthrowing their monarchs, republics fear too much power in one man's hands.

_____ 8. Republics need written laws so that the people can appeal to them against corrupt judges.

_____ 9. Alliances between many equal states usually break down because one state grows more powerful.

_____ 10. When leaders share power, one leader always gains the preeminence.

_____ 11. Fair and generous treatment of conquered enemies reaps long-term benefits.

_____ 12. A "professional" army is dangerous in a republic.

Thought Questions

What terms or events from this chapter illustrate the following lessons?

13. Civilizations create many legends to glorify their founders.

____

14. Winning battles can be so costly that a nation loses the war.

____

15. Competition over trade often leads to war.

____

16. Nations can win a war even after a whole army is annihilated.

____

17. In every republic the government is split into rival parties or factions.

____

18. National strength is the result of unity among diverse groups. _______________

19. Man recognizes the tendency of governments to strive to increase their power unjustly and must therefore place limits on government to balance that power.

____

20. Excess ambition can prevent even good leaders from sharing power for the good of their nation.

____

Name ____________________

WORLD HISTORY 4 ACTIVITY 4

Map Study: The Roman Republic

I. Using the maps in this chapter, label each of the following regions, cities, battle sites, and special features on the map.

Regions	Cities (identify with •) and Battle Sites (identify with *)	Special Features
Corsica	Actium	Adriatic Sea
Gaul	Cannae	Alps
Macedonia	Carthage	Apennines
North Africa	Rome	Mediterranean Sea
Sardinia	Syracuse	Tiber River
Sicily	Zama	Tyrrhenian Sea
Spain		

II. Identify the following.

1. Mare Nostrum ____________________
2. major Greek colony on Sicily ____________________
3. island where the Punic Wars began ____________________
4. low mountains dividing the Italian Peninsula ____________________
5. high mountains protecting Italy from northern invasion ____________________
6. Hannibal's greatest victory ____________________
7. Scipio's victory over the Carthaginians ____________________
8. region conquered by Pompey ____________________
9. region conquered by Julius Caesar ____________________
10. decisive battle that brought an end to the 478-year-old Roman Republic ____________________

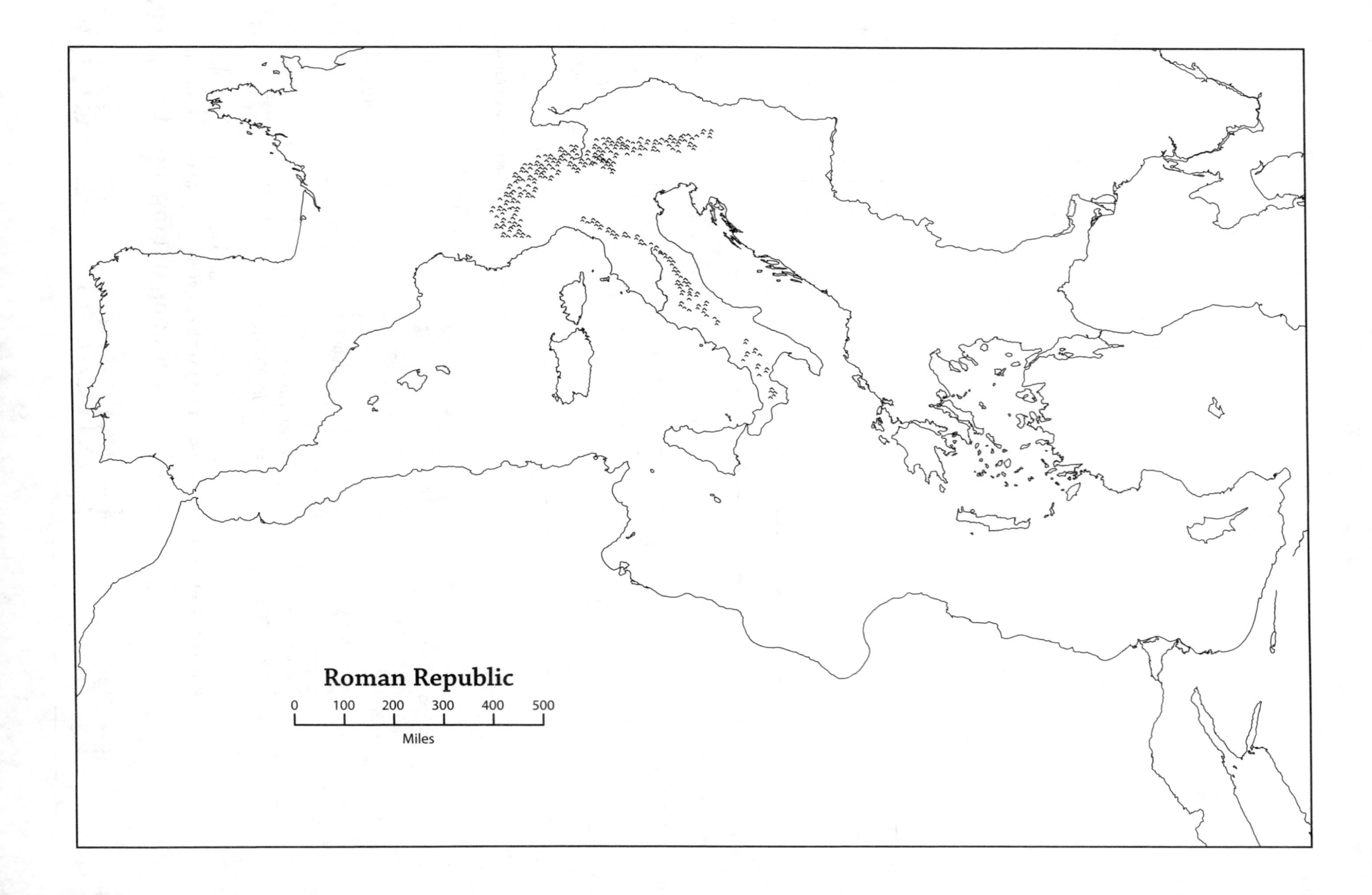
Roman Republic
0
100
200
300
400
500
Miles

Name ______________________

WORLD HISTORY 4 ACTIVITY 5

Rise and Fall of the Roman Republic

For each event, write its cause, significant people, and its effects on the government of Rome. (The causes and effects are listed on the next page.) Then answer the questions.

Causes	Events	People	Effects on Roman Government
good farmland ford on a trade route	League of the Seven Hills (8th century BC)	Romulus Remus	1. strong family (*pater*) 2. patricians and plebeians 3. imperium of the king
	establishment of the republic (509 BC)		
	first Council of Plebeians (5th century)		
	Law of Twelve Tables (450 BC)		
	Tribal Assembly (287 BC)		
	defeat of the Greeks in southern Italy (256 BC)		
	First Punic War (264–214 BC)		
	Second Punic War (218–201 BC)		
	wars against Macedonia (200–167 BC)		
	Third Punic War (149–146 BC)		
	land reforms (133–122 BC)		
	first civil war (88–82 BC)		
	second civil war (49–45 BC)		
	third civil war (44–31 BC)		

Causes	Effects on Roman Government
• assassination of Caesar on the Ides of March • nobility's hatred of Etruscan kings • plebeian demand for equal political power • plebeian demand for legal equality • poverty of small farmers following foreign wars • Roman competition with Carthage over Sicily • Roman competition with Carthage over Spain • Roman revenge against Carthage's allies • Roman expansion into southern Italy • plebeian warriors' demand for representation • Roman jealousy of Carthage's recovery • rivalry between Tribal Assembly and the Senate • rivalry within the triumvirate	• beginning of the Senate • beginning of Roman sea power • Caesar's reforms and public works • creation of provinces ruled by governors • demand of tribute from provinces • end of the republic • establishment of a dictator for life • first consuls • first "professional" army • foundation of Roman civil law • plebeian laws binding all people • plebiscites • policy of mercy toward conquered subjects • reign of an imperator • Roman mastery of the western Mediterranean • Roman mastery of the eastern Mediterranean • Senators' first use of murder to preserve power • Senate's triumph over the Tribal Assembly • tribunes' veto power • utter destruction of Rome's rival

Review Questions

Answer these questions based on the textbook and the chart on the previous page.

1. Which three significant people are not Romans? ______________________________

2. Who was the Gracchus brothers' grandfather? Julius Caesar's uncle? ______________________________

3. Which famous Romans were murdered? ______________________________

4. Which famous people committed suicide? ______________________________

5. How many years passed between the establishment and end of the republic? ______________________________

6. What event came between the famous Second Punic War and the infamous Third Punic War?

   ____

7. When did Rome begin fighting wars for evil motives (revenge and tribute)?

   ____

8. Which event resulted in Rome's mastery of the entire Mediterranean? ______________________________

9. Which event do you think marks the turning point in the republic, when it began to decline? (Hint: This event was followed by poverty for farmers, failed reform, violence, and civil war.)

   ____

10. The Senate held heated debates throughout the foreign wars. One side argued for isolationism (avoidance of foreign entanglements). The other argued for expansionism, fulfilling Rome's destiny of greatness. Which view do you think would have been best for the republic? Why?

    ____

    ____

    ____

Name ______________________

WORLD HISTORY 5 ACTIVITY 1

Questions and Timeline

Identify the person, place, event, and/or date for each of the following.
Then record the appropriate information on the timeline on the next page.

Section I:

1. His reign began the *Pax Romana* (year reign began) ______________________

Section II:

2. Was destroyed by the eruption of Mount Vesuvius ______________________
3. Was considered the greatest orator of his day (birth year) ______________________
4. Promoted the theory that the earth was the center of the universe (birth year) ______________________
5. His death ended the *Pax Romana* (death year) ______________________
6. The most famous Greek writer in the Roman Empire (birth year) ______________________
7. Historian who lived during the Augustan Age and wrote a history of Rome (birth year) ______________________
8. Was called the "poet of the Augustan Age" (birth year) ______________________
9. Called the "Homer of Rome" (birth year) ______________________
10. Tutored Nero and was one of the leading Stoics of the Roman Empire (birth year) ______________________
11. Considered to be the greatest exponent of Epicureanism (birth year) ______________________

Section III:

12. Roman emperor at the time of Christ's death (year reign began) ______________________
13. Emperor who began the first official Roman persecution of Christianity (year reign began)
    ____
14. Destroyed by Roman commander Titus (year destroyed) ______________________
15. Emperor who made Christianity the exclusive religion of the empire (year reign began)
    ____
16. Event making Christianity legal ______________________
17. Affirmed Christ's deity and the doctrine of the Trinity ______________________
18. Emperor under whom Christianity was made legal (year reign began) ______________________
19. Emperor during the most violent widespread Roman persecution of Christians (year reign began)
    ____

Section IV:

20. Visigoths defeated the Roman army and killed the emperor ______________________
21. A non-Roman was placed on the Roman throne ______________________
22. Leader of the Huns called the "scourge of god" (year reign began) ______________________

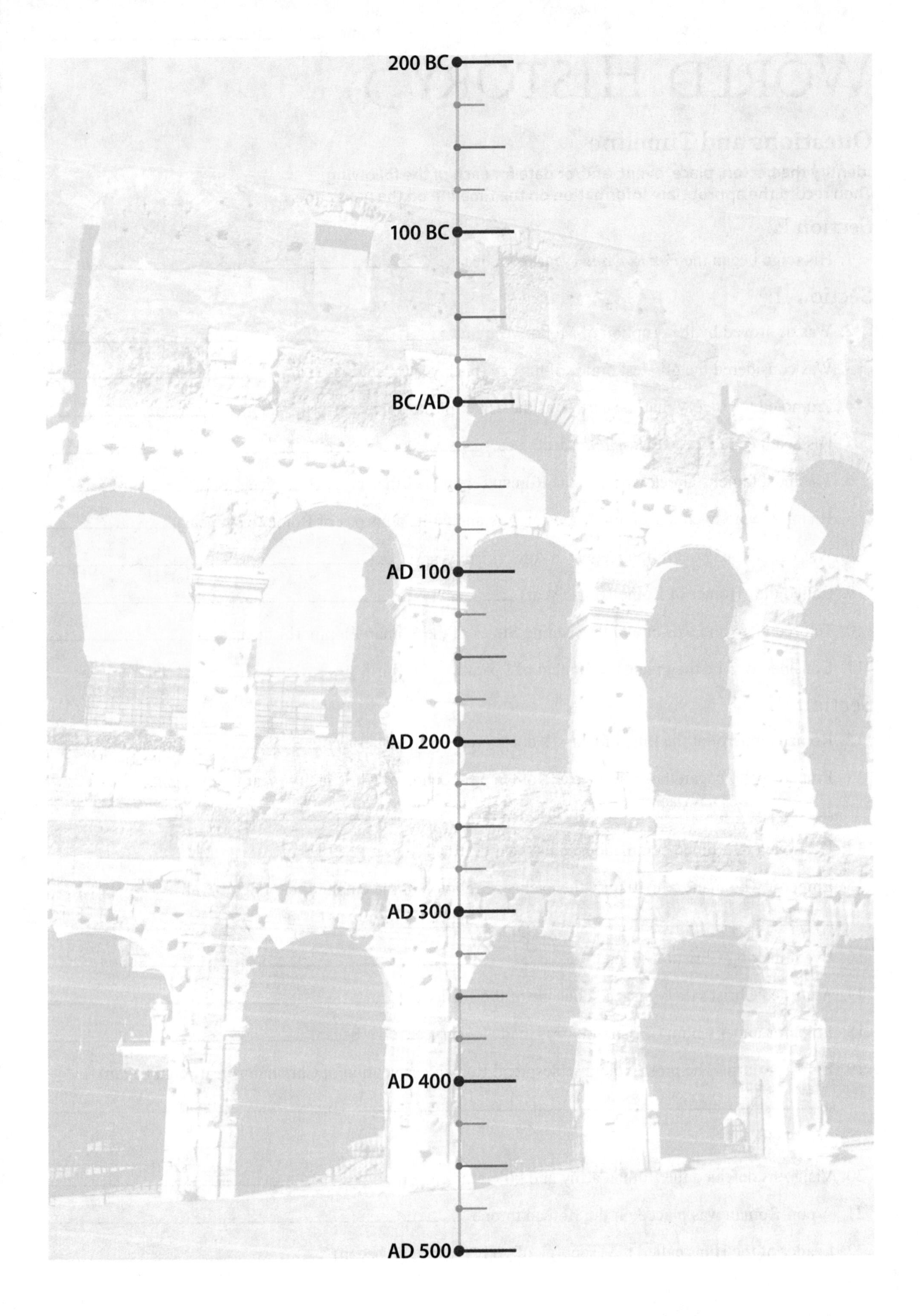
200 BC
100 BC
BC/AD
AD 100
AD 200
AD 300
AD 400
AD 500

Name ______________________

WORLD HISTORY 5 ACTIVITY 2

The Bedrock of Western Civilization

Give the contributions of each ancient civilization to the West. (Do not forget the Greek contributions during the *Pax Romana*.) List all relevant terms, people, and writings.

	Greek Civilization	Roman Civilization
Politics		
Warfare		
Law		
Philosophy		
Science		
Medicine		
Mathematics		
Poetry		
History		
Architecture		

Name ______________________________

WORLD HISTORY 5 ACTIVITY 3

Josephus Discusses Masada

Read the excerpt from *The Works of Josephus* and answer the questions.

. . . Upon this top of the hill, Jonathan the high priest first of all built a fortress, and called it Masada: after which the rebuilding of this place employed the care of king Herod, . . . for the report goes how Herod thus prepared this fortress on his own account, as a refuge against two kinds of danger; the one for fear of the multitude of the Jews, lest they should depose him, and restore their former kings to the government; the other danger was greater and more terrible, which arose from Cleopatra queen of Egypt, who did not conceal her intentions, but spoke often to Antony, and desired him to cut off Herod, and entreated him to bestow the kingdom of Judea upon her. And certainly it is a great wonder that Antony did never comply with her commands in this point, as he was so miserably enslaved to his passion for her; nor should any one have been surprised if she had been gratified in such her request. So the fear of these dangers made Herod rebuild Masada, and thereby leave it for the finishing-stroke of the Romans in this Jewish war.

1. How is Masada described and where is it located?

____

2. Who first built Masada and named it?

____

3. Why did Herod rebuild the fortress?

____

4. What fear did Herod have concerning the Jews?

____

____

5. Whom did Herod fear aside from the Jews and why?

____

____

6. Why did Herod think Cleopatra could be granted her request?

____

7. For whom was Masada the finishing-stroke?

____

Name ______________________

WORLD HISTORY 5 ACTIVITY 4

Map Study: The Roman Empire

I. Using the maps in this chapter, label each of the following regions, cities, rivers, and seas on the Roman Republic map.

Regions	Cities (Identify with •)	Rivers and Seas
Britain	Milan	Tyrrhenian Sea
Spain	Rome	Mediterranean Sea
Gaul	Corinth	Adriatic Sea
North Africa	Athens	Aegean Sea
Sicily	Philippi	Rhine River
Italy	Constantinople	Danube River
Germania	Nicaea	Black Sea
Greece	Ephesus	Caspian Sea
Macedonia	Antioch	Tigris River
Asia Minor	Jerusalem	Euphrates River
Cyprus	Alexandria	Nile River
Syria		Red Sea
Judea		
Egypt		

II. Identify the following.

1. region of Jesus' birth ______________________
2. first use of the term "Christians" (Acts 11:19–26) ______________________
3. central city of the early church, "Jewish cradle" of Christianity ______________________
4. edict that made Christianity legal in AD 313 ______________________
5. council that settled the Trinitarian controversy in AD 325 ______________________
6. patriarchate regarded as the "first among equals" ______________________
7. "New Rome" built by Constantine at Byzantium ______________________
8. first patriarchate to be overrun by barbarians ______________________

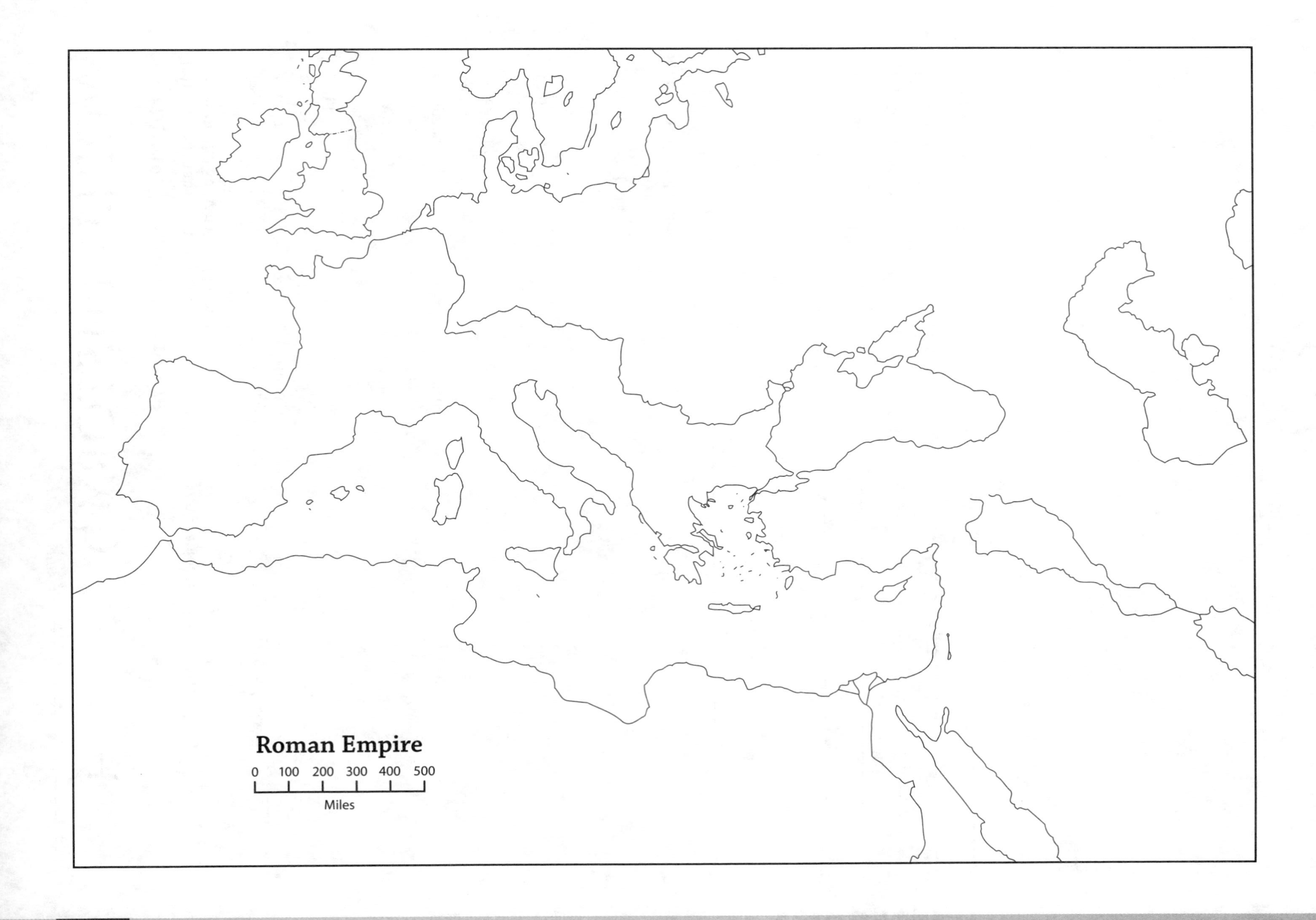
Roman Empire
0 100 200 300 400 500
Miles

Name ____________________

WORLD HISTORY 5 ACTIVITY 5

Beginning of Church History

Place the descriptions at the bottom of the chart into the appropriate period. Those that involve Christians belong under "church history." The rest belong under "secular history."

Secular History	Period	Church History
	Augustus (31 BC –AD 14)	
	Tiberius (14–37)	martyrdom of Stephen (33?)
	Nero (54–68)	
	the Flavians, including Titus (69–96)	last book of the New Testament death of the apostle John (96?)
	Marcus Aurelius (161–80)	execution of Justin Martyr (165?)
rapid succession of twenty-six emperors	civil wars (235–84)	
	Diocletian (284–305)	
	Constantine (306–37)	
death of the previous emperor at the Battle of Adrianople (378)	Theodosius (379–95)	
	attacks on Rome (410–76)	

Alaric
Arius
Attila the Hun
Horace
Livy
Ovid
Virgil
governorship of Pilate
Seneca's Stoicism
Augustine's *City of God*
birth of Christ
Crucifixion of Christ
conversion of Augustine
beginning of *Pax Romana*
end of *Pax Romana*
reign of the philosopher-king
death of the Apostle Paul
beginning of Jewish uprising
Colosseum
Constantinople
augustus and caesar
Edict of Milan
Council of Nicaea
destruction of Jerusalem
eruption of Mount Vesuvius
fall of Rome
sack of Rome
first official Roman persecution of Christians
first empire-wide persecution of Christians
worst persecution of Christians
Christianity becomes Rome's official religion
first division of the empire
final division of the empire

Review Questions

Answer these questions based on the textbook and your timeline.

1. What term describes the period from 31 BC to AD 180? ______
2. Which of Octavian's titles identified him as the chief priest? ______
3. What title signifying honor and majesty did the Senate give Octavian? ______
4. Under which emperor did Latin literature flourish? ______
5. Which Roman historian wrote 142 books on Roman history? ______
6. Who wrote the *Aeneid* to glorify ancient Rome? ______
7. Which Roman poet described the dangers of a life of luxury? ______
8. Which Roman poet living after the death of Octavian longed for a return to the republic? ______
9. Who was emperor when Christ was born? ______
10. What Roman procurator had Jesus crucified? ______
11. Who was the first Christian martyr? ______
12. From which historian do we learn about the destruction of Jerusalem in AD 70? ______
13. How many years did the *Pax Romana* last? ______
14. What was going on in church history about the time that the city of Pompeii was buried by Vesuvius? ______
15. Approximately how many centuries passed between Rome's first official persecution of Christians and the first empire-wide persecution? ______
16. What Stoic philosopher tutored the first emperor to persecute Christians? ______
17. What philosopher-king was the emperor when Justin Martyr was executed? ______
18. What significant event in church history took place during the troubled years between 235 and 284? ______
19. Compare the events preceding and following the Edict of Milan. How did this edict begin a new epoch in church history? ______
20. What part did the emperor play in the Council of Nicaea? ______
21. Eusebius of Caesarea (260–339) wrote the first history of Christianity, called *Ecclesiastical History.* What famous people and events was he able to observe firsthand? ______
22. What famous heretic is included in your timeline? ______
23. What two barbarians are included in your timeline? ______
24. What event sparked the writing of the *City of God*? ______
25. How many years did the Roman Empire last in the west? ______

Name ______________________

WORLD HISTORY 6 ACTIVITY 1

Questions and Timeline

Identify the person, place, event, and/or date for each of the following.
Then record the appropriate information on the timeline on the next page.

Section I:

1. broke out in Constantinople and threatened to topple Emperor Justinian (year) ______________________
2. called "New Rome" and dedicated by Constantine (year) ______________________
3. where Seljuk Turks annihilated the Byzantine army (year) ______________________
4. instituted the first great period of Byzantine history and culture (year reign began)

   ____
5. collapse of the western part of this empire (year) ______________________
6. led the Byzantine Empire's military reach to its height (year reign began)

   ____
7. ended when the Ottoman Turks sacked Constantinople and killed the emperor (year)

   ____

Section II:

8. ruler who led Kiev to reach the zenith of its power (year reign began)

   ____
9. the ruler and year that Russia adopted Byzantine Christianity ______________________
10. gained control of Novgorod and began Russian history (year reign began)

    ____

Section III:

11. the "flight" of Muhammad to Medina (year) ______________________
12. first caliph after Muhammad's death (year became caliph) ______________________
13. claimed to be the last and greatest prophet of Allah (birth year)

    ____
14. Muslim forces stopped by Franks (year) ______________________

300
400
500
600
700
800
900
1000
1100
1200
1300
1400
1500

Name ______________________

WORLD HISTORY 6 ACTIVITY 2

Defend Your Faith: The Koran vs. the Bible

In order to defend your faith against Islam, you need to learn some basics about the heart of the Islamic faith—the Koran. Muslims revere the Koran as God's final revelation to mankind. Below are the main passages that cover such important topics as the nature of God, sin, and salvation.

Three great questions divide Christians and Muslims: Is Allah the same as Jehovah? Is Muhammad a greater prophet than Jesus Christ? Is man saved by good works or by grace? As you answer the questions below, you will see that the Koran contradicts every important doctrine of Scripture.

As you read the selections below, remember that Allah, not Muhammad, is the speaker.

Sura 2. The Chapter of the Heifer

Call to Believe (2:21–23)

> If you are in doubt about what we have revealed to our servant, then bring a sura [chapter] like it, and call your witnesses other than Allah, if you tell the truth. But if you do not do it—and you shall surely not do it—then fear the fire whose fuel is men and stones, prepared for misbelievers.
>
> But bear the glad tidings to those who believe and work righteousness, that for them are gardens beneath which rivers flow. Whenever they are provided with fruit there from they will say, "This is what we were provided with before," and they shall be provided with the like; and there are pure wives for them therein, and they shall dwell therein forever.

Importance of Fighting (2:186–215)

> Fight in Allah's way with those who fight with you, but do not transgress. Truly, Allah does not love those who transgress.
>
> Kill them wherever you find them, and drive them out from whence they drive you out; for sedition is worse than slaughter; but do not fight them by the Sacred Mosque until they fight you there. Then kill them, for such is the recompense of those that misbelieve.
>
> But if they desist, then, truly, Allah is forgiving and merciful.
>
> But fight them that there be no sedition and that the religion may be Allah's; but, if they desist, then let there be no hostility save against the unjust.
>
> The sacred month for the sacred month; for all sacred things demand retaliation; and whoever transgresses against you, transgress against him like as he transgressed against you; but fear Allah, and know that Allah is with those who fear. . . .
>
> They will not cease from fighting you until they turn you from your religion if they can; but whoever of you is turned from his religion and dies while still a misbeliever; these are those whose works are vain in this world and the next; they are the fellows of the Fire, and they shall dwell therein forever.
>
> Truly, those who believe, and those who flee, and those who wage war in Allah's way; these may hope for Allah's mercy, for Allah is forgiving and merciful.

1. How does the Koran's description of heaven contradict the Bible (Matt. 22:29–30)?

____

2. What phrase in the Koran contradicts the Bible's view of works (Eph. 2:4–9)?

____

3. How does the Koran's view of fighting differ from Jesus's view (Matt. 5:38–39, 26:52)?

____

Sura 3. The Chapter of Imran's Family

Story of Jesus's Birth (3:40–53)

[Recall] when the angel said, "O Mary! truly, Allah gives you the glad tidings of a Word from Him; his name shall be the Messiah Jesus the son of Mary, regarded in this world and the next and of those whose place is near to Allah. And he shall speak to people in his cradle, and when grown up, and shall be among the righteous."

She said, "Lord! how can I have a son, when man has not yet touched me?"

He said, "Thus Allah creates what He pleases. When He decrees a matter He only says 'Be' and it is; and He will teach him the Book, and wisdom, and the Law, and the Gospel, and he shall be a prophet to the people of Israel [saying] "I have come to you with a sign from Allah, namely, that I will create for you out of clay the form of a bird, and I will blow thereon and it shall become a bird by Allah's permission; and I will heal the blind from birth, and lepers; and I will bring the dead to life by Allah's permission; and I will tell you what you eat and what you store up in your houses. Truly, in that is a sign for you if you are believers. And I will confirm what is before you of the Law, and will surely make lawful for you some of that which was prohibited from you. I have come to you with a sign from your Lord. So fear Allah and follow me, for Allah is my Lord, and your Lord, so worship Him—this is the right path.'". . .

[Recall] when Allah said, "O Jesus! I will make you die and take you up again to me and will clear you of those who misbelieve, and will make those who follow you above those who misbelieve, at the day of judgment, then to me is your return. I will decide between you concerning that wherein you disagree. And as for those who misbelieve, I will punish them with grievous punishment in this world and the next, and they shall have none to help them." But as for those who believe and do what is right, He will pay them their reward, for Allah does not love the unjust.

That is what we recite to you of the signs and of the wise reminder. Truly the likeness of Jesus with Allah is as the likeness of Adam. He created him from earth, then He said to him "Be," and he was—the truth from thy Lord, so do not be of those who are in doubt.

Abraham Not a Jew or a Christian (3:58–61, 78–84)

O people of the Book, why do you dispute about Abraham, when the Law and the Gospel were not revealed until after him? What! do you not understand? Here you are, disputing about what you have some knowledge of; why then do you dispute about what you have no knowledge of? Allah knows and you do not know.

Abraham was not a Jew, nor yet a Christian, but he was a 'Hanif, a Moslem, and not of the idolaters. Truly, the people most worthy of Abraham are those who follow him and his prophets, and those who believe; Allah is the patron of the believers. . . .

Say, "We believe in Allah, and what has been revealed to you, and what was revealed to Abraham, and Ishmael, and Isaac, and Jacob, and the tribes, and what was given to Moses, and Jesus, and the prophets from their Lord—we will make no distinction between any of them—and we are unto Him resigned. Whoever craves other than Islam for a religion, it shall surely not be accepted from him, and he shall, in the next world, be of those who lose." . . .

Truly, those who misbelieve after believing, and then increase in misbelief, their repentance shall not be accepted; these are those who err.

Encouragement to Persevere (3:138–41)

Muhammad is but an apostle; apostles have passed away before his time; what if he die or is killed, will you retreat upon your heels? He who retreats upon his heels does no harm to Allah at all; but Allah will recompense the thankful. It is not for any soul to die, save by Allah's permission written down for an appointed time; but he who wishes for the reward of this world we will give him of it, and he who wishes for the reward of the future we will give him of it, and we will recompense the grateful.

How many prophets have myriads fought against! yet they did not give way at what befell them in Allah's way. Nor were they weak, nor did they demean themselves—Allah loves the patient. And their word was only to say, "Lord, forgive us our sins and our extravagance in our affairs; and make firm our footing, and help us against the misbelieving people!"

4. What parts of this story of Jesus are not in the Bible?

 ____

 ____

 ____

5. Why does the Koran say to minimize the uniqueness of Jesus, whose birth, death, and Resurrection were so amazing?

 ____

6. How does the Bible refute the Koran's claims about Abraham (John 8:39–58)?

 ____

 ____

7. What limitations did Muhammad face that Jesus Christ did not (John 10:17–18; Heb. 4:15)?

 ____

 ____

Sura 5. The Chapter of the Table

Allah's Three Revelations: The Law, Gospel, and Koran (5:48–53)

Truly, we have revealed the Law in which is guidance and light. The prophets who were resigned did judge thereby those who were Jews. . . . He who will not judge by what Allah has revealed, these are the unjust.

And we followed up the footsteps of these [prophets] with Jesus the son of Mary, confirming that which was before him and the Law, and we brought him the Gospel, wherein is guidance and light, verifying what was before it of the Law, and a guidance and an admonition unto those who fear. Then let the people of the Gospel judge by that which is revealed therein. For whoever will not judge by what Allah has revealed, these are the evildoers.

We have revealed to you [Arabs] the Book [Koran] in truth verifying what was before it, and preserving it. Judge then between them by what Allah has revealed, and do not follow their lusts, turning away from what is given to you of the truth.

For each one of you have we made a law and a pathway; and had Allah pleased He would have made you one nation, but He will surely try you concerning that which He has brought you. Therefore be emulous in good deeds; your return is to Allah altogether, and He will let you know concerning that about which you dispute.

Christians' Mistaken View of Jesus (5:76–81)

They misbelieve who say, "Truly, Allah is the Messiah the son of Mary"; but the Messiah said, "O children of Israel! worship Allah, my Lord and your Lord." Truly, he who associates anything with Allah, Allah hath forbidden him Paradise, and his resort is the Fire, and the unjust shall have none to help them.

They misbelieve who say, "Truly, Allah is the third of three." For there is no Allah but one, and if they do not desist from what they say, there shall touch those who misbelieve amongst them grievous woe.

Will they not turn again towards Allah and ask pardon of Him? for Allah is forgiving and merciful.

The Messiah the son of Mary is only a prophet: prophets before him have passed away; and his mother was a faithful woman; they both used to eat food. See how we explain to them the signs, yet see how they turn aside!

Say, "Will you serve, other than Allah, what can neither hurt you nor profit you?" but Allah, He both hears and knows.

Say, "O people of the Book! do not exceed the truth in your religion, and do not follow the lusts of a people who have erred before, and who lead many astray, and who go away from the level path."

8. How do the Koran's claims about Allah's revelation contradict the Bible's teachings about God's revelation (John 5:45–47; 12:47–48; Heb. 1:1–2)?

____

____

9. In Sura 4:169–70, the Koran says Allah could not have a son because it would diminish his glory. What "proof" in 5:76–81 verifies that Jesus was only a prophet (i.e., only human)? How do these two suras contradict the Bible's view of Christ's humanity (Heb. 2:9–18)?

____

____

____

____

Sura 19. The Chapter of Mary (19:16–37)

And mention Mary in the Book, when she retired from her family into an eastern place, and she took a veil [to screen herself] from them, and we sent to her our spirit [Gabriel], and he took for her the semblance of a well-made man.

She said, "Truly, I take refuge from you in the Merciful One, if you are pious."

He said, "I am only a messenger of your Lord to bestow on you a pure boy."

She said, "How can I have a boy when no man has touched me, and when I am no harlot?"

He said, "Thus says your Lord, It is easy for me! and we will make him a sign to man, and a mercy from us; for it is a decided matter."

So she conceived him, and she retired with him into a remote place. And the labor pains came upon her at the trunk of a palm tree, and she said, "O that I had died before this, and been forgotten out of mind!"

And he [Jesus] called to her from beneath her: "Grieve not, for your Lord has placed a stream beneath your feet, and shake the trunk of the palm tree towards you. It will drop on you fresh dates fit to gather; so eat, and drink, and cheer your eye; and if you see any mortal, say, 'Truly, I have vowed a fast to the Merciful One, and I will not speak with a human being today.' "

Then she brought it [the baby] to her people, carrying it. They said, "O Mary! you have done an improper thing! O sister of Aaron! your father was not a bad man, nor was your mother a harlot!"

So she pointed to him, and they said, "How are we to speak with one who is in the cradle a child?"

He said, "Truly, I am a servant of Allah. He has brought me the Book, and He has made me a prophet, and He has made me blessed wherever I am; and He has required of me prayer and almsgiving so long as I live, and piety towards my mother, and has not made me a miserable tyrant; and peace is upon me the day I was born, and the day I die, and the day I shall be raised up alive."

That is Jesus, the son of Mary—the word of truth about which you dispute!

Allah could not take to himself any son! celebrated be His praise! when He decrees a matter He only says to it, "Be," and it is; and, truly, Allah is my Lord and your Lord, so worship Him; this is the right way.

10. The Koran relies on some apocryphal stories that are not in the Bible. Can you find one of them?

____

11. Like the Jews, Muslims stumble over the doctrine of the Virgin Birth of Christ. How does the Koran's account of Christ's birth differ from the biblical story (Luke 1:26–38)?

____

____

12. Jesus' death and Resurrection do not have the same significance in the Bible and the Koran. How do they differ (Luke 1:67–79; 2:25–35)?

____

____

____

____

Sura 23. The Chapter of Believers (23:103–113)

And when the trumpet shall be blown, there shall be no [claims of family] relation between them on that day, nor shall they question each other!

And he whose [weighing] scales are heavy—they are the prosperous. But he whose scales are light—these are they who lose themselves, in hell to dwell forever! The fire shall scorch their faces, and they shall curl their lips therein! "Were not my signs recited to you? and you said that they were lies!" They say, "Our Lord our misery overcame us, and we were a people who did err! Our Lord! take us out there from, and if we return, then shall we be unjust."

He will say, "Go you away into it and do not speak to me!"

Truly, there was a part of my servants who said, "Our Lord! we have believed, so pardon us, and have mercy upon us, for you are the best of the merciful ones."

And you took them for a jest until you forgot my reminder and did laugh thereat. Truly, I have recompensed them this day for their patience; truly, they are happy now.

13. What is the greatest difference between this description of God's judgment and the Bible descriptions (Matt. 7:21–23, 24:31, 25:31–46; Rom. 14:8–12; 2 Cor. 5:9–10; Rev. 20:11–15)?

____

____

____

14. The idea of a sacrifice for sins does not appear in the Koran. Sura 7:41 says Paradise is "an inheritance for that which you have done." Later, Sura 11:116 says, "Truly, good works remove evil works." How do these statements contradict 1 Peter 1:3–5?

____

Extra Research

The other major passages in the Koran that mention Christ are Sura 2:81; 4:152–57, 169–70; 5:109–120. Look them up and describe any conflicts you find with the Bible.

Name ______________________

WORLD HISTORY 6 ACTIVITY 3

Map Study: The Byzantine and Islamic Empires and Early Russia

I. Using the maps in this chapter, label each of the following regions, cities and battles, and special features on the Byzantine and Islamic Empires and Early Russia map.

Region	Cities (identify with •) and Battle Sites (identify with *)	Special Features
Arabia	Alexandria	Arabian Sea
Asia Minor	Baghdad	Baltic Sea
Egypt	Constantinople	Black Sea
Franks	Cordova	Bosporus
Greece	Damascus	Caspian Sea
Italy	Jerusalem	Danube River
North Africa	Kiev	Dnieper River
Persia	Mecca	Euphrates River
Russia	Medina	Mediterranean Sea
Spain	Moscow	Nile River
Sweden	Novgorod	Persian Gulf
	Rome	Red Sea
	Toledo	Sahara Desert
	Tours	Tigris River
	Venice	

II. Identify the following

1. capital of the Byzantine Empire ______________________
2. site of Nika Revolt ______________________
3. region conquered by the Seljuk Turks after the Battle of Manzikert ______________________
4. Constantinople's chief commercial rival ______________________
5. Constantinople's chief patriarchal rival ______________________
6. region where Cyril and Methodius did missionary work ______________________
7. original home of Varangians ______________________
8. Rurik's capital ______________________
9. Vladimir I's capital ______________________
10. Yaroslav's "Mother of Russian Cities" ______________________
11. region settled by Ishmael's descendents ______________________
12. "holy city" of Islamic pilgrims ______________________
13. first Muslim city converted during the Hegira ______________________

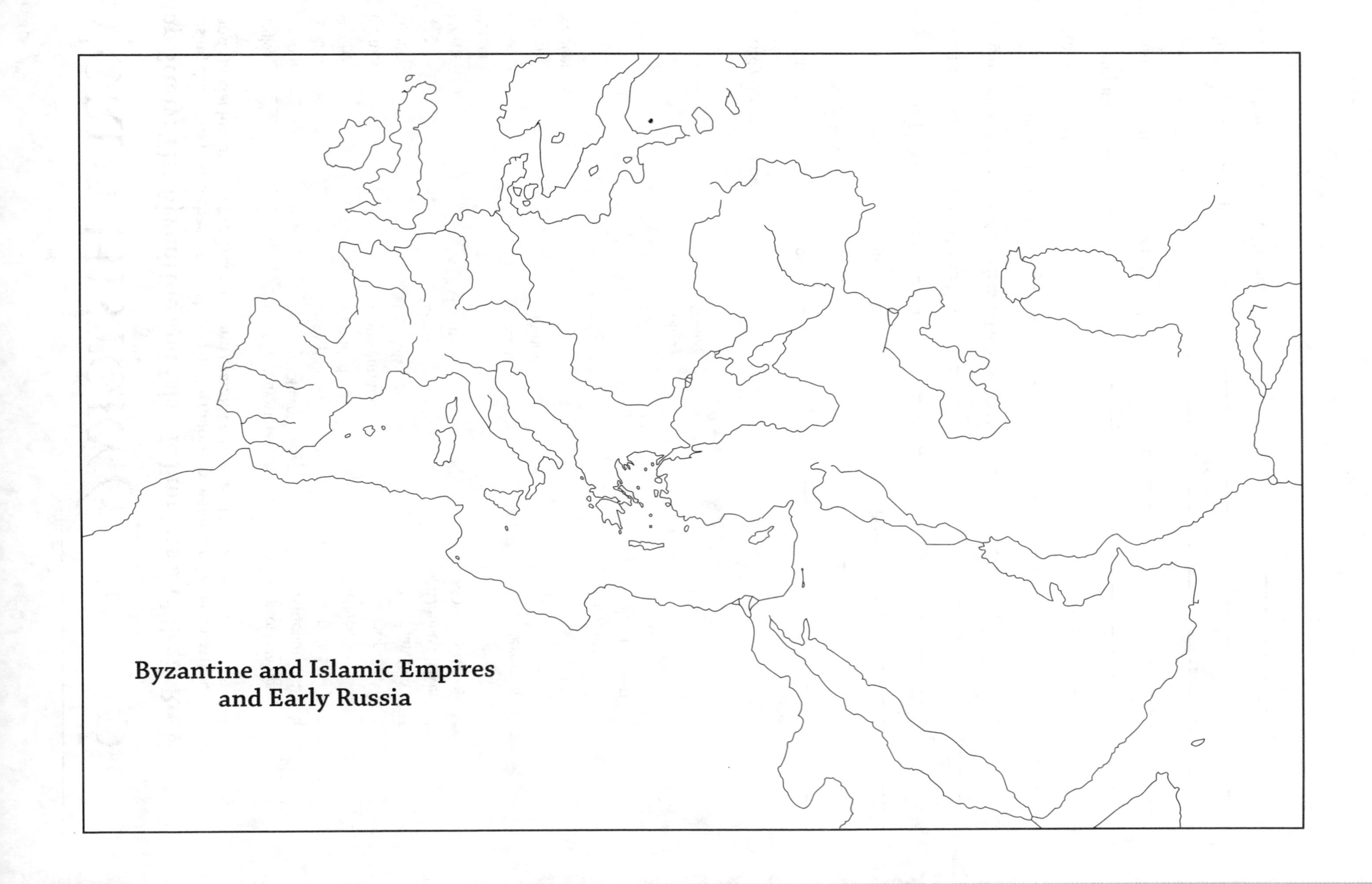
Byzantine and Islamic Empires
and Early Russia

Name ____________________

WORLD HISTORY 7 ACTIVITY 1

Questions and Timeline

Identify the person, place, dynasty, and/or date for each of the following questions. Beside each answer, identify in parentheses the country, civilization, or kingdom each represents. Then record the appropriate information on the timeline on the next page.

Section I:

1. Religion founded by Siddhartha Gautama (approximate year) ____________________
2. Earliest civilization (two cities) on Indus River (year) ____________________
3. Threatened India with his armies (year) ____________________

Section II:

4. The most honored teacher in Chinese history (year of birth) ____________________
5. Dynasty establishing the *Pax Sinica* (year established) ____________________
6. Earliest known Chinese dynasty (year established) ____________________
7. Dynasty known for the consolidation of existing structures into the Great Wall (year established)

   ____
8. Dynasty in which Chinese culture flourished (year established)

   ____
9. Dynasty in which Li Po, Chinese poet, lived (year dynasty established)

   ____
10. Legendary founder of Taoism (year of birth) ____________________

Section III:

11. Powerful individuals who held the real power over the Japanese government (year power began)

    ____

Section IV:

12. Given the title of "universal ruler" (year title given) ____________________
13. Moscow ruler who refused to pay tribute to the Mongols (year reign began)

    ____
14. Established the Mughal dynasty (year established) ____________________
15. Dynasty established by Kublai Khan in China (year established)

    ____

Section V:

16. Mali's most famous ruler (year rule began) ____________________

2400 BC
2200 BC
2000 BC
1800 BC
1600 BC
1400 BC
1200 BC
1000 BC
800 BC
600 BC
400 BC
200 BC
BC/AD
200
400
600
800
1000
1200
1400
1600

Name ______________________

WORLD HISTORY 7 ACTIVITY 2

Far Eastern Religions

Place in the blank the letter of the religion that matches each description below. Some have more than one answer.

A. Buddhism B. Confucianism C. Hinduism D. Shintoism E. Taoism

_____ 1. native to China

_____ 2. native to India

_____ 3. native to Japan

_____ 4. no primary human founder

_____ 5. founded by Siddhartha Gautama

_____ 6. founded by K'ung Fu-tzu

_____ 7. founded by Lao-tzu

_____ 8. *Vedas* and *Upanishads*

_____ 9. Nirvana

_____ 10. ignores the worship of gods

_____ 11. worship of many gods

_____ 12. worship of ancestors

_____ 13. worship of the emperor

_____ 14. belief that human life is a cycle of rebirths

_____ 15. belief that suffering is caused by selfish desires

_____ 16. emphasis on outward religious rituals

_____ 17. promoted an active way of life, meeting the needs of society

_____ 18. promoted a passive way of life, finding personal enlightenment

_____ 19. goal of reuniting with the world soul

_____ 20. belief that peace is achieved through human works

_____ 21. religion adopted by Asoka, the most famous Mauryan ruler of India

_____ 22. religion adopted by Prince Shotoku, one of the most famous rulers of Japan

Thought Questions

Look up these verses and discuss how they refute a major teaching of Far Eastern religion.

1. wheel of life (Heb. 9:27)

____

2. world soul (Ps. 113:4–6; 1Tim. 6:16; Col. 1:16–17)

____

3. Eightfold Path/tao (Eph. 2:8–9)

____

4. Confucian ethics (Matt. 22:37–40)

____

Name ____________________

WORLD HISTORY 7 ACTIVITY 3

Contrasts in Asia

Use terms and phrases to complete the chart. Include every geographic feature and bold-faced term that you can. (Write small!)

	India	China	Japan
geographic borders			
geographic features			
family life and social groups			
most influential class of people	Brahmans (priests)		
discoveries and inventions			
main religions			
degree of political unity among tribes/ clans			
capitals	Mohenjo-Daro, Harappa Pataliputra	various early capitals	
main empires and dynasties (with dates, if given)			
main rulers			
contacts with Muslims and the West			
contact with the Mongols			Kublai Khan's failed naval invasions (1274, 1281)

Name ____________________

WORLD HISTORY 7 ACTIVITY 4

Map Study: Civilizations of Asia

I. Using the maps in this chapter, label each of the following regions, cities, and special features on the Asia map.

Regions	Cities (identify with •)	Special Features
Korea	Baghdad	Arabian Sea
China	Constantinople	Bay of Bengal
India	Delhi	Ganges River
Japan	Harappa	Gobi Desert
Mongolia	Mohenjo-Daro	Great Wall
Russia	Moscow	Himalayas
	Nara	Huang He (Yellow River)
	Beijing	Indian Ocean
	Samarkand	Indus River
		Khyber Pass
		Pacific Ocean
		Sea of Japan
		Volga River
		Yangtze River
		Yellow Sea

II. Identify the following.

1. two leading cities of India's earliest civilization ____________________
2. fertile river valley where India's earliest civilization flourished ____________________
3. fertile river valley where China's early Shang dynasty flourished ____________________
4. Aryan invasion route through the mountains into India ____________________
5. country where K'ung Fu-tzu lived ____________________
6. country where Buddha lived ____________________
7. country ruled by the legendary emperor Jimmu Tenno ____________________
8. country ruled by Asoka ____________________
9. country ruled by Akbar ____________________
10. Middle Kingdom ____________________
11. geographic barrier in northern China ____________________
12. geographic barrier in western China ____________________
13. country where Taoism arose ____________________
14. country where Shintoism arose ____________________
15. first country to produce silk and porcelain ____________________
16. "Third Rome" after the fall of Constantinople ____________________

17. first permanent Japanese capital ______

18. region where Mongols first lived ______

19. Kublai Khan's capital ______

20. Babur's capital ______

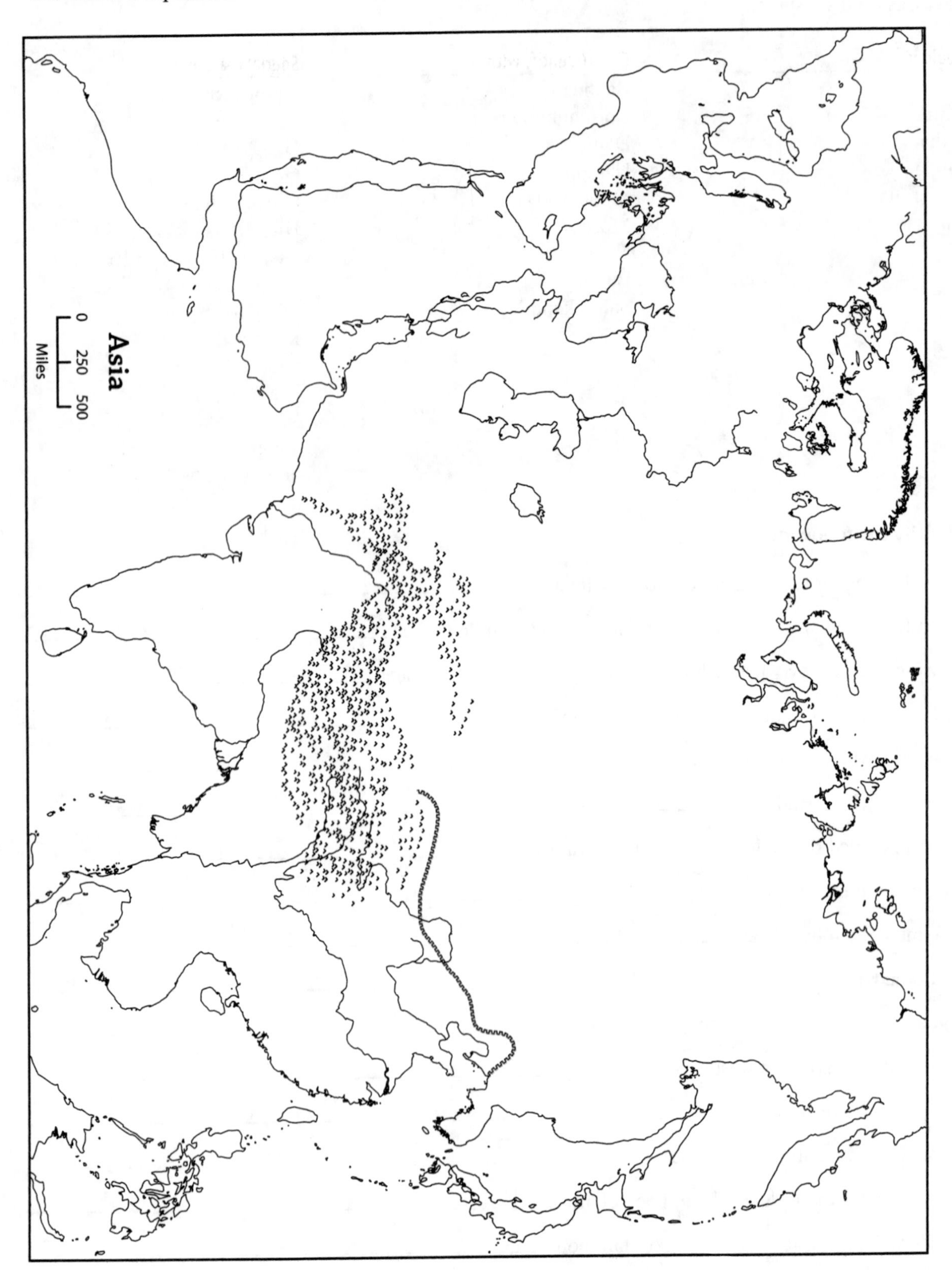

Name ____________________

WORLD HISTORY 7 ACTIVITY 5

Map Study: Early Africa

I. Using the map in Section V of the chapter and additional resources, label each of the following regions, cities, and special features on the Africa map.

Regions	Cities (identify with •)	Special Features
Egypt	Cairo	Indian Ocean
Benin	Mecca	Red Sea
Kush	Meroë	Mediterranean Sea
Aksum	Aksum	Atlantic Ocean
Madagascar	Mogadishu	Zambezi River
Zanzibar	Kilwa	Congo River
	Sofala	Lake Chad
	Zimbabwe	Niger River
	Timbuktu	Nile River
		Atlas Mountains
		Sahara Desert
		Kalahari Desert
		Orange River

II. Identify the following.

1. prosperous city-state that received goods from interior tribes and kingdoms and sold them to Arab sea traders ____________________
2. the kingdom of Kanem-Bornu thrived on these shores ____________________
3. Mansa Musa's capital city ____________________
4. fell to Aksum kingdom ____________________
5. an important kingdom of the forest kingdom that came into contact with the Europeans at the end of the Middle Ages ____________________
6. provided a base for the kingdoms of Ghana, Mali, and Songhai as its waters drew travelers crossing the Sahara ____________________
7. mountains in the northwest section of Africa ____________________
8. desert in Africa's southern portion ____________________
9. large island in the Indian Ocean off Africa's east coast ____________________
10. early African kingdom that embraced Christianity ____________________
11. city that Mansa Musa visited on his trip to Mecca, astonishing people with his wealth ____________________
12. desert in the northern part of Africa ____________________

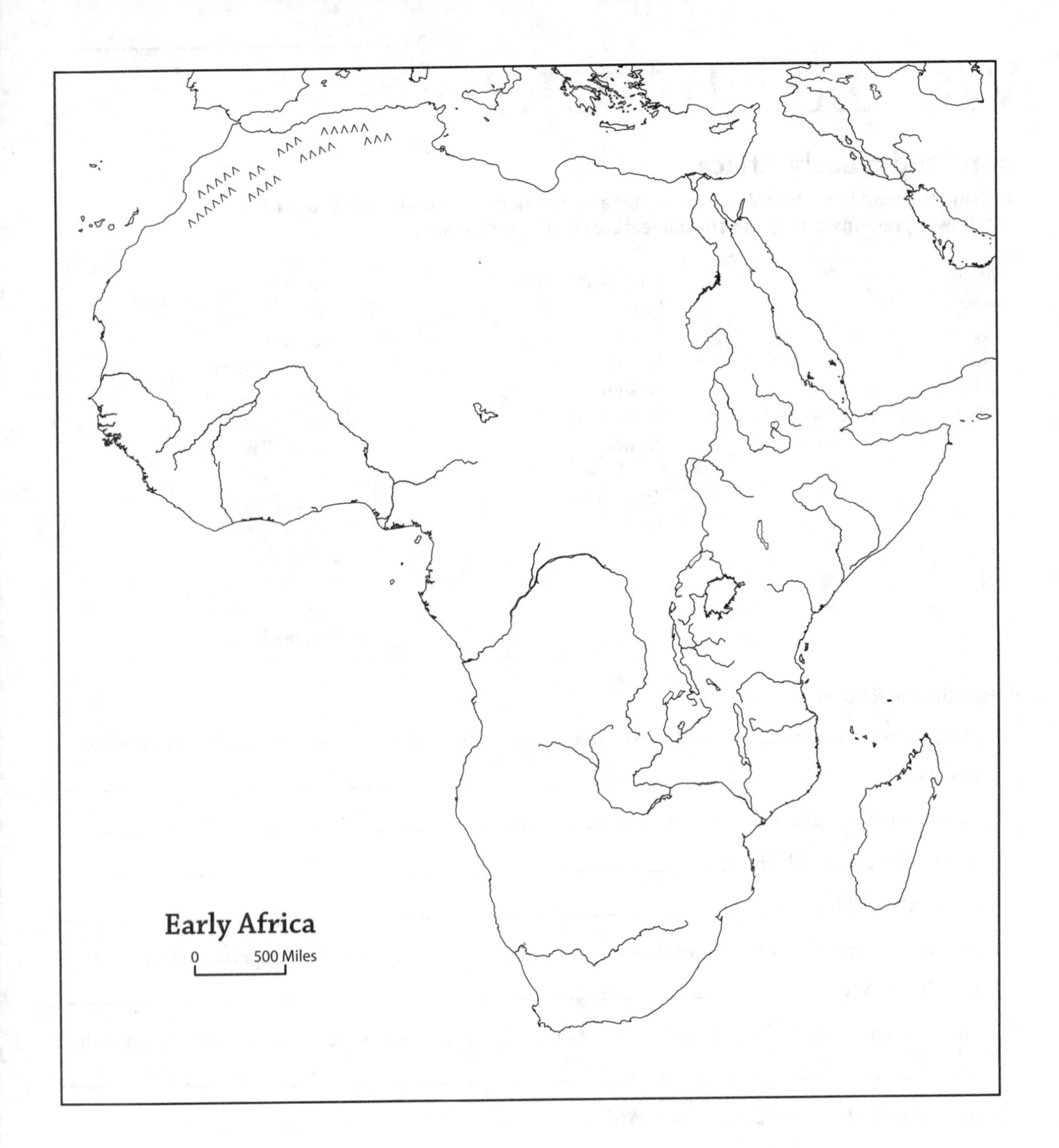
Early Africa
0 500 Miles

Name ______________________________

WORLD HISTORY 8 ACTIVITY 1

Questions and Timeline

Identify the person, place, event, and/or date for each of the following questions. Then record the appropriate information on the timeline.

Section I:

1. threatened Rome; persuaded by Leo I to spare the city (year city threatened) ______________
2. took the gospel to Ireland (birth year) ______________
3. recognized as the first true pope (year became pope) ______________
4. known as the "Apostle of the Germans" (birth year) ______________

Section II:

5. battle where the Muslims were defeated in France (year) ______________
6. became head of the Frankish tribe in northern Gaul (year became tribal head) ______________
7. ruling house established when Pepin the Short became king (year reign began)

   ____
8. king under whose rule the Frankish kingdom reached its peak (year reign began)

   ____
9. document that settled the dispute between Charlemagne's sons and divided the empire (year)

   ____

Name ____________________

WORLD HISTORY 8 ACTIVITY 2

Roman Catholic Religion vs. the Bible

Match each teaching of the Roman Catholic Church with the passage of Scripture that it most clearly contradicts.

A. Jeremiah 44:24–27
B. Matthew 15:1–9
C. Mark 6:3
D. Luke 2:22, 24 (Leviticus 12:8)
E. John 16:7–14
F. Romans 1:7
G. Romans 14:5
H. 1 Timothy 2:5
I. Hebrews 12:22–23
J. 1 Peter 5:2–3

_____ 1. The universal church is synonymous with the Roman Catholic Church.

_____ 2. Christ made Peter the first pope and gave him supreme authority over the church on earth (Petrine theory).

_____ 3. The pope is the vicar, or substitute, of Christ on earth.

_____ 4. Saints are Christians who perform miracles or die a martyr's death.

_____ 5. Dead saints intercede before God's throne on the behalf of living Christians.

_____ 6. Mary should be adored as the queen of heaven.

_____ 7. Mary never sinned.

_____ 8. Mary remained a virgin throughout her life.

_____ 9. The Roman church, not the individual, is the final authority in interpreting the Scriptures.

_____ 10. Tradition is equal in authority to the Scriptures.

A. Matthew 15:9
B. Luke 22:19
C. Romans 5:17
D. 1 Corinthians 1:17
E. 2 Corinthians 5:8
F. Ephesians 2:8–9
G. Ephesians 6:10–18
H. Hebrews 10:10–14
I. 1 John 1:7–2:2
J. Revelation 1:4–6

_____ 11. The Roman sacramental system is necessary for salvation.

_____ 12. Baptism washes away original sin.

_____ 13. Through penance a church member earns forgiveness for sin.

_____ 14. During the holy eucharist, the priest sacrifices Christ anew.

_____ 15. During the mass, the priest transforms the bread and wine into the actual body and blood of Christ.

_____ 16. Through holy orders certain men are set apart as priests.

_____ 17. Only through the sacraments can God be properly worshiped.

_____ 18. Those who properly view and honor relics will receive extra grace.

_____ 19. The clergy are the only warriors of the church.

_____ 20. Dead souls must go to purgatory before they can enter heaven.

Name ______________________

WORLD HISTORY 9 ACTIVITY 1

Questions and Timeline

Identify the person, place, event, and/or date for each of the following questions. Then record the appropriate information on the timeline on the next page.

Section I:

1. the founder of the Franciscan order (year born) ______________________
2. created so that churchmen, not nobles or kings, could choose the popes (year created) ______________________
3. agreement recognizing the right of the church to elect its own bishops and abbots and invest them with spiritual authority (year) ______________________
4. the greatest of the reforming popes (year became pope) ______________________
5. pope under whom the papacy reached its zenith (year became pope) ______________________

Section II:

6. ruler whose death marked the decline of the Holy Roman Empire (year of death) ______________________
7. first of the Saxon line of German kings (year reign began) ______________________

Section III:

8. event establishing the Norman dynasty in England (year) ______________________
9. developed the English "Model" Parliament (year reign began) ______________________
10. ruled the Saxon kingdom of Wessex and strengthened the practice of local government (year reign began) ______________________
11. a bitter opponent of Henry II's interference in church matters (year murdered) ______________________
12. document that King John was forced to sign at Runnymede (year) ______________________
13. has been called the ideal medieval king (year reign began) ______________________
14. developed the French Estates-General (year reign began) ______________________
15. became known as the real founder of France (year reign began) ______________________
16. founded the Capetian royal line where members built a strong feudal monarchy in France (year reign began) ______________________

Section IV:

17. called for a holy crusade to free the Holy Land from the Turks (year crusade called) ______________________
18. recaptured Jerusalem, stirring the Europeans to organize the Third Crusade (year Jerusalem recaptured) ______________________

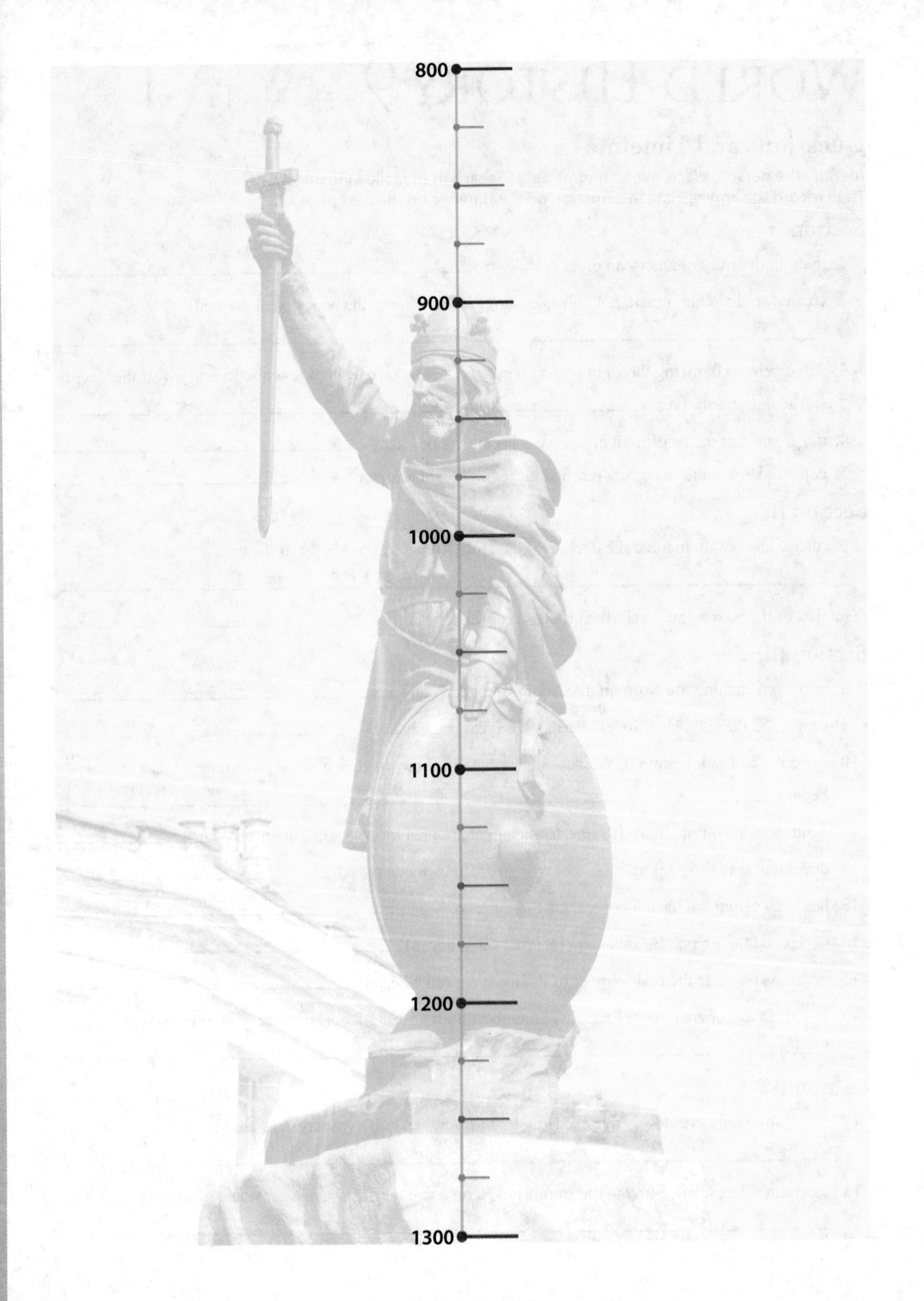
800
900
1000
1100
1200
1300

Name ____________________

WORLD HISTORY 9 ACTIVITY 2

Solving the Problems of Government

Throughout history, countries have faced the same basic problems of effective government. For each problem, summarize the solutions implemented by various governments of the past. Each summary should include the terms given in parentheses. (Use the index to find information from earlier chapters.)

1. **Taxation:** How did the government collect taxes?

   Roman Empire (publicans, census):

   ____

   ____

   ____

   ____

   Carolingian Empire:

   ____

   ____

   ____

   ____

   England (*Domesday Book*, Magna Carta):

   ____

   ____

   ____

   ____

   France (*baillis*, Estates-General):

   ____

   ____

   ____

   ____

2. **Bureaucracy:** How did the government implement laws efficiently?

   Roman Empire (provincial governors, coemperors, and caesars):

   ____

   ____

   ____

   ____

Carolingian Empire (*missi dominici*):

England (shires, tenants-in-chief):

France (*baillis*):

3. **Justice:** How did the government uphold laws and judge criminals?

Roman Empire (Law of Twelve Tables, individual rights):

Carolingian Empire:

England (royal courts, jury, indictments, common law):

France:

4. **Limited Government:** How could citizens influence government decisions?

Roman Empire (Senate, Tribal Assembly, veto):

Carolingian Empire:

England (Magna Carta, Parliament, "power of the purse"):

France (Estates-General):

5. **Religion and Morals:** How did the government control and promote religion and morals?

Roman Empire (emperor worship, *pontifex maximus*):

Carolingian Empire (Aix-la-Chapelle):

England (lay investiture, Thomas à Becket):

____

____

____

____

France (Boniface VIII, tithes):

____

____

____

____

Extra Credit: On a separate sheet of paper, discuss how the following governments solved the problems above: ancient Egypt, Israel's monarchy, Persian Empire, Athenian Empire, Byzantine Empire, Islamic empires, ancient India, ancient China, and the Holy Roman Empire.

Name ____________________

WORLD HISTORY 9 ACTIVITY 3

The Shifting Power of the Feudal Monarchs

Write the name of each king beside the date his reign began. Then write the corresponding act(s) or event(s) for each, using the list at the bottom of each page.

Rise of Limited Monarchy in England		
Date	**English King**	**Significant Acts/Events**
878		a. ____ b. ____ c. ____
1030		united all of England
1042		____
1066		____
1066		a. ____ b. ____ c. ____ d. ____
1154		a. ____ b. ____
1215		____
1272		a. ____ b. ____ c. ____
	Result:	Parliament's "power of the purse" provided a powerful check on royal power, contributing to the rise of limited government.

Rise of Absolute Monarchy in France		
Date	**French King**	**Significant Acts/Events**
987		a. ______ b. ______
1108		______
1180		a. ______ b. ______
1226		a. ______ b. ______ c. ______
1285		______
Result:		The French king controlled taxation without restraints, contributing to the rise of absolute government.

united southern England
conquered Wales
became master of Île-de-France
tripled royal domain
elected king by French lords
elected king by nobles (witan)
started the long Capetian line of kings
forced all vassals to swear allegiance to him
forced to sign Magna Carta
died without a direct heir
compiled the *Anglo-Saxon Chronicle*
Domesday Book
introduced shires and shire-reeves
created tenants-in-chief
established the *curia regis*
created a common law
installed royal *baillis*
established circuit courts under royal control
established a permanent royal court in Paris
called the first ("model") parliament
summoned Estates-General for "advice"
issued ordinances without consulting vassals
gave dignity to royal office
acknowledged that Parliament must approve new taxes

Name ______________________

WORLD HISTORY 9 ACTIVITY 4

Modified True/False

If the statement is true, write *true* in the blank. If it is false, change the underlined words to make the statement true.

______________________ 1. The practice of lay investiture allowed men with few spiritual qualifications to take church offices.

______________________ 2. The buying and selling of church offices is called excommunication.

______________________ 3. Bernard of Clairvaux was the most famous Cistercian reformer.

______________________ 4. The word *mendicant* means "brother."

______________________ 5. Urban II was known as the reform pope.

______________________ 6. The Franciscan order became closely associated with the Inquisition.

______________________ 7. When a pope dies, the College of Cardinals elects a new pope.

______________________ 8. In 910 King Henry IV of Germany stood in the snow at Canossa to beg the pope's forgiveness.

______________________ 9. The papacy reached its zenith under Innocent III.

______________________ 10. Simony was used by the pope to suspend public church services and the administration of all sacraments in a given region.

______________________ 11. Frederick Barbarossa established the Holy Roman Empire.

______________________ 12. The Holy Roman Empire consisted of Italy and France.

______________________ 13. Emperor Henry IV belonged to the Salian family, which tried unsuccessfully to strengthen the monarchy in Germany.

______________________ 14. Richard II was the "founder of the English navy."

______________________ 15. William of Normandy divided England among his vassals, called sheriffs.

______________________ 16. An English county is known as a *baillis*.

______________________ 17. The Norman duke William defeated the last Anglo-Saxon king in 1066 at the Battle of Hastings.

______________________ 18. In English law, a jury would make a list of accusations, or interdicts, listing all crimes and suspected criminals.

______________________ 19. Thomas à Becket opposed the efforts of King John to control the English clergy.

______________________ 20. The Magna Carta established the principle that the king's power is limited.

______________________ 21. The Anglo-Saxon assembly of the country's leaders was called the witan.

______________________ 22. *Curia regis* means "power of the purse."

_____________ 23. Hugh Capet was able to triple the size of the French kingdom by breaking the power of King John of England.

_____________ 24. Louis VI is called "Saint Louis."

_____________ 25. In 1204 Constantinople fell to the Seljuk Turks.

Name ____________________

WORLD HISTORY 9 ACTIVITY 5

Map Study: Europe in the Middle Ages

I. Using the maps in this chapter, label each of the following regions, cities, battle sites, and special features on the Europe in the Middle Ages map on the following page.

Regions	Cities (identify with •) and Battle Sites (identify with *)	Special Features
England	London	North Sea
France	Canterbury	English Channel
Normandy	Hastings	Rhine River
Spain	Paris	Danube River
Holy Roman Empire	Marseilles	Black Sea
Byzantine Empire	Genoa	Mediterranean Sea
Seljuk Turks	Venice	Atlantic Ocean
Palestine	Rome	
	Constantinople	
	Jerusalem	

II. Identify the following

1. where Thomas à Becket was killed ____________________
2. the Holy Land ____________________
3. French duchy of William the Conqueror ____________________
4. where the College of Cardinals met ____________________
5. battle that marked the end of the Anglo-Saxon reign in England ____________________
6. separates France from England ____________________
7. the Holy City ____________________
8. "Christian" city pillaged in 1204 by Crusaders who were supposed to fight the Muslims ____________________
9. "land of the Angles" ____________________
10. Constantinople's rival city ____________________

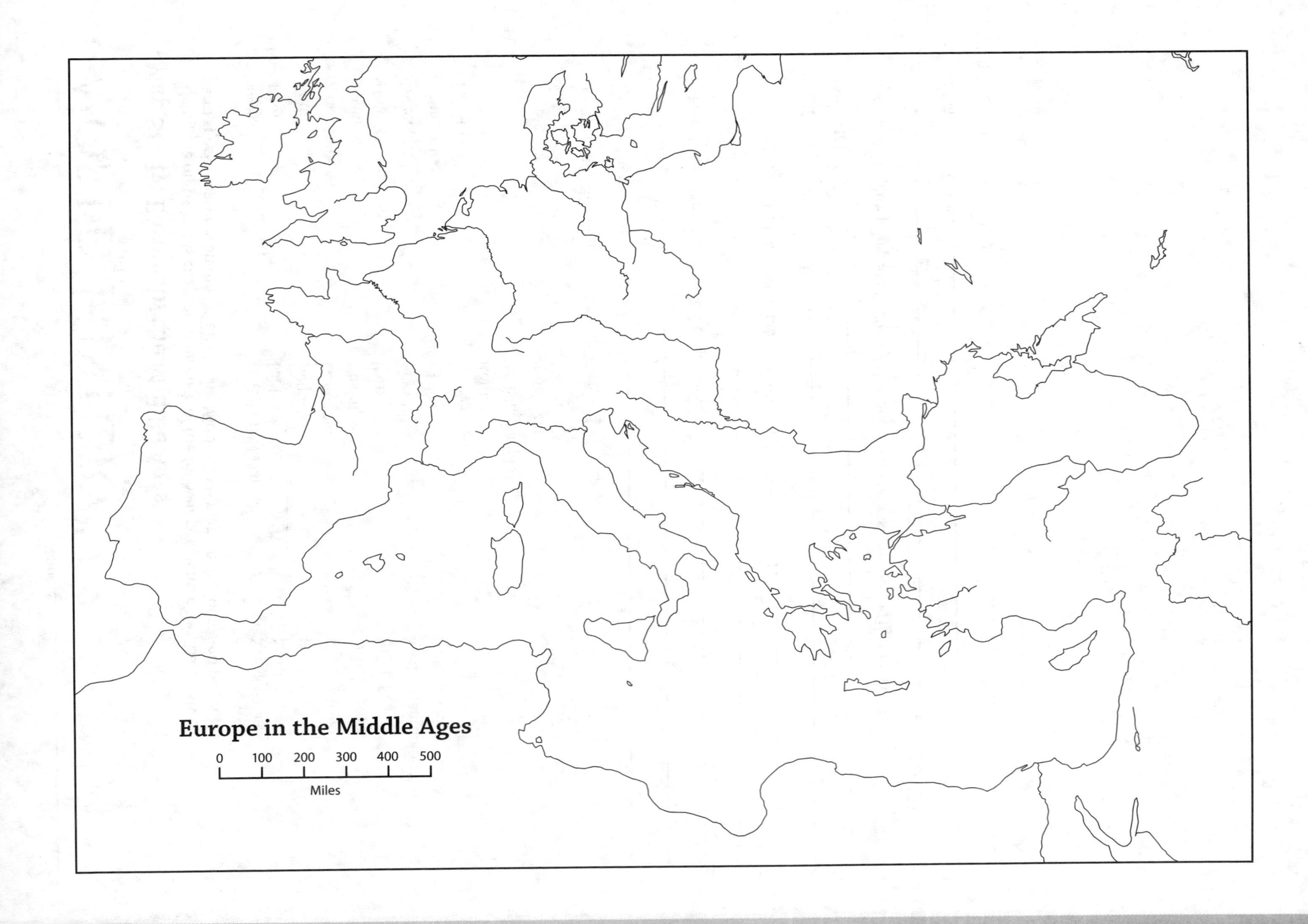
Europe in the Middle Ages
0
100
200
300
400
500
Miles

Name ____________________

WORLD HISTORY 10 ACTIVITY 1

Business and Labor Relations in the Bible

Today's workers and employers face the same kinds of problems that the workers and employers of the medieval era faced. Look up each Scripture passage and identify its teaching by writing its letter in the correct blank.

Workers

A. Proverbs 14:23
B. Proverbs 30:8–9
C. Ecclesiastes 9:10
D. Matthew 20:8–15
E. Luke 3:14
F. Philippians 4:11
G. Colossians 3:22
H. 2 Thessalonians 3:10
I. Titus 2:9

_____ 1. All labor is valuable.

_____ 2. Whatever work you do, do it with all your might.

_____ 3. Work to please God, not your employer.

_____ 4. Seek only enough money to keep you from stealing or becoming greedy.

_____ 5. Be content with your wages.

_____ 6. Learn to be content in whatever condition you live.

_____ 7. Accept whatever pay scale your employer chooses.

_____ 8. If a man will not work, he should not eat.

_____ 9. Do not talk back to your employer.

Employers

A. Deuteronomy 24:15
B. Job 31:13–14
C. Proverbs 22:16
D. Proverbs 27:18
E. Philippians 2:4
F. Colossians 4:1

_____ 10. Be concerned about the things that others need, not just your own needs.

_____ 11. Do not exploit workers to increase your riches.

_____ 12. Pay workers their wages promptly.

_____ 13. Pay your workers what is just and fair.

_____ 14. Listen to the concerns of your workers.

_____ 15. Praise workers who faithfully serve you.

Banks

Describe how the following verses might have affected medieval banking, from the point of view of both the Roman Catholic establishment as well as the emerging merchant class.

1. Proverbs 23:4 and 1 Timothy 6:10 ____________________

2. Exodus 22:25 and Luke 6:35 ____________________

3. Proverbs 11:1 ____________________

Name ______________________

WORLD HISTORY 10 ACTIVITY 2

Questions and Timeline

Identify the person, event, and/or date for each of the following.
Then record the appropriate information on the timeline on the next page.

Section III

1. Called "the Prince of the Schoolmen" (birth year) ______________________
2. Wrote *Divine Comedy* (birth year) ______________________
3. Advocated the frequent asking of questions as the "first key to wisdom" (birth year) ______________________
4. English scientific thinker who said that there were four principal stumbling blocks to comprehending truth (birth year) ______________________
5. Wrote *Canterbury Tales* (birth year) ______________________
6. Used logical arguments to support the existence of God and the satisfaction concept of the atonement (birth year) ______________________

Section IV

7. The long struggle between England and France (year it began) ______________________
8. Founded the English Tudor dynasty (year reign began) ______________________
9. Drove the Moors out of Granada (year) ______________________
10. Expanded the Hapsburg possessions to include Spanish territory in the New World (year reign began) ______________________
11. Inspired French nationalism toward the end of the Hundred Years' War (year of death) ______________________

Section V

12. Began the period when all French popes resided at Avignon (year began) ______________________
13. Famous papal bull issued by Boniface VIII (year issued) ______________________
14. A forty-year period when two men claiming to be the rightful pope divided the allegiance of the nations of Europe (year began) ______________________
15. Restored the papacy to Rome and healed the schism (year began) ______________________

1000
1100
1200
1300
1400
1500

Name ______________________

World History 10 Activity 3

Map Study: Europe About 1500

I. Using the map on page 247, label each of the following regions, cities, and special features. Using colored pencils, color each region a different color.

Regions
- Portugal
- Spain
- Ottoman Empire
- Aquitaine
- France
- Scotland
- England
- Ireland
- Norway
- Sweden
- Russia
- Denmark
- Lithuania
- Poland
- Teutonic Knights
- Holy Roman Empire
- Netherlands
- Austria
- Hungary
- Republic of Venice
- Papal States
- Kingdom of Naples
- Crete
- Sicily
- Corsica
- Sardinia
- Balearic Islands

Cities (identify with •)
- Paris
- Constance
- Avignon
- Rome
- Venice
- Pisa

Special Features
- North Sea
- Baltic Sea
- Atlantic Ocean
- Mediterranean Sea

II. Identify the following.

1. nation for which Joan of Arc inspired nationalism during the Hundred Years' War ______________________
2. place where the "Babylonian Captivity" occurred ______________________
3. nation created when Ferdinand and Isabella married ______________________
4. region where Chaucer lived ______________________
5. city where Abelard was a popular teacher of philosophy and theology ______________________
6. region where the Wars of the Roses were fought ______________________
7. French duchy held by the English king ______________________
8. region that remained independent during Ferdinand and Isabella's reign ______________________
9. city where a council healed the Great Schism and restored the papacy to Rome ______________________
10. region in which the Golden Bull established a Diet ______________________

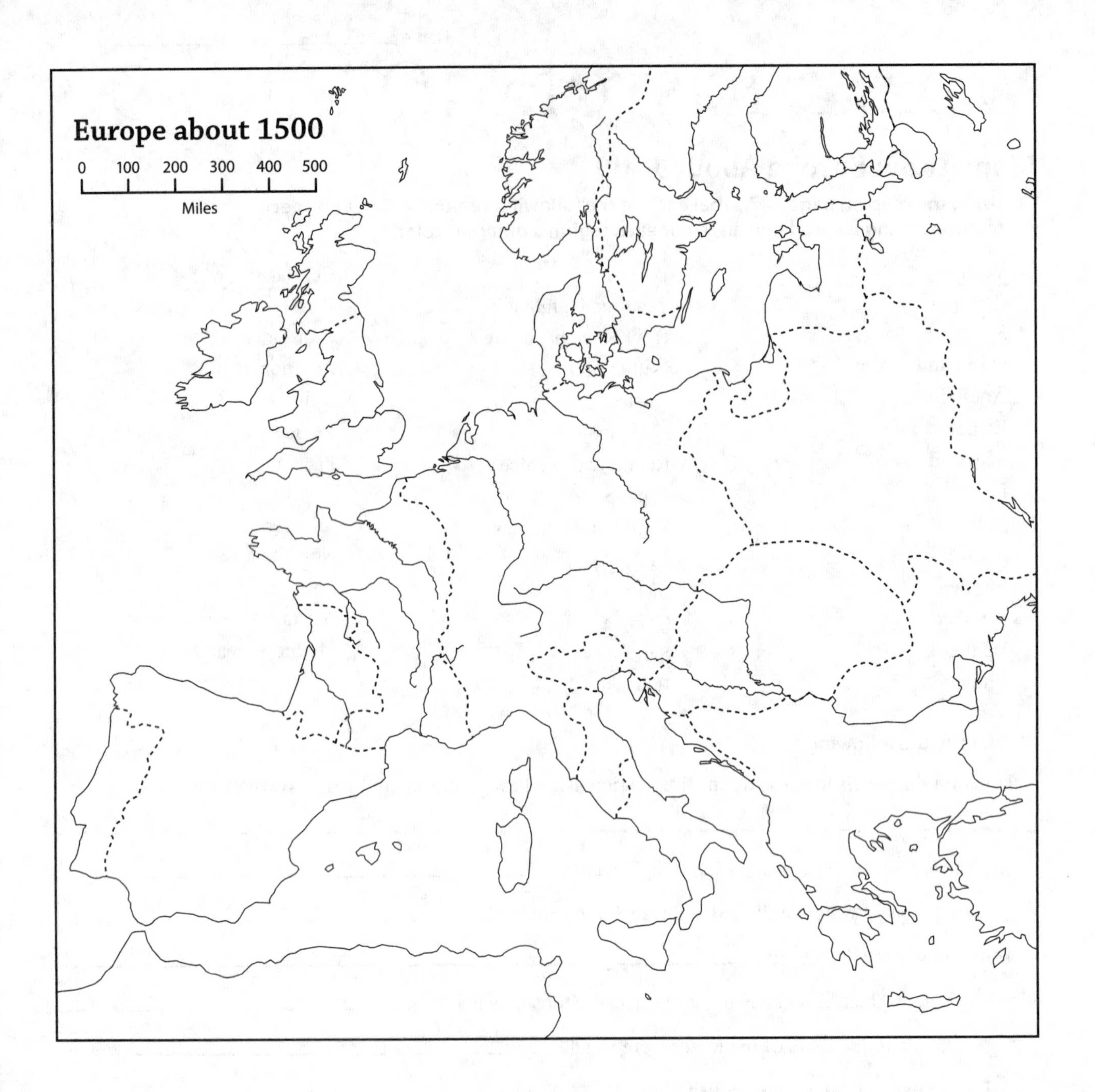
Europe about 1500
0
100
200
300
400
500
Miles

Name ____________________

WORLD HISTORY 11 ACTIVITY 1

Questions and Timeline

Identify the person and/or date for each of the following questions. In parentheses, beside each answer, identify the individual's city, country, or region. Then record the appropriate information on the timeline on the next page.

Section II

1. Wrote *The Prince* (birth year) ____________________
2. Wrote *The Praise of Folly* (birth year) ____________________
3. Considered the greatest playwright of all time (birth year) ____________________
4. Often called the Father of Renaissance Painting (birth year) ____________________
5. Best example of the so-called Renaissance man (birth year) ____________________
6. Sometimes called the "Leonardo of the North" (birth year) ____________________
7. Was hailed as the Prince of Music in his day (birth year) ____________________
8. During his rule, his city became the most influential city of the Renaissance movement (year rule began) ____________________
9. His greatest achievement was his edition of the Bible (year printed)
   ____
10. Wrote *Don Quixote* (birth year) ____________________
11. Idealized motherhood in his paintings of sweet-faced Madonnas (birth year)
    ____
12. Sculpted the *Pietà* (birth year) ____________________
13. Martin Luther said of him, "He is the master of notes." (birth year)
    ____
14. Wrote *Utopia* (birth year) ____________________
15. Known as the Father of Humanism (birth year) ____________________
16. Prolific painter known for his use of color and especially remembered for his portraits (birth year)
    ____

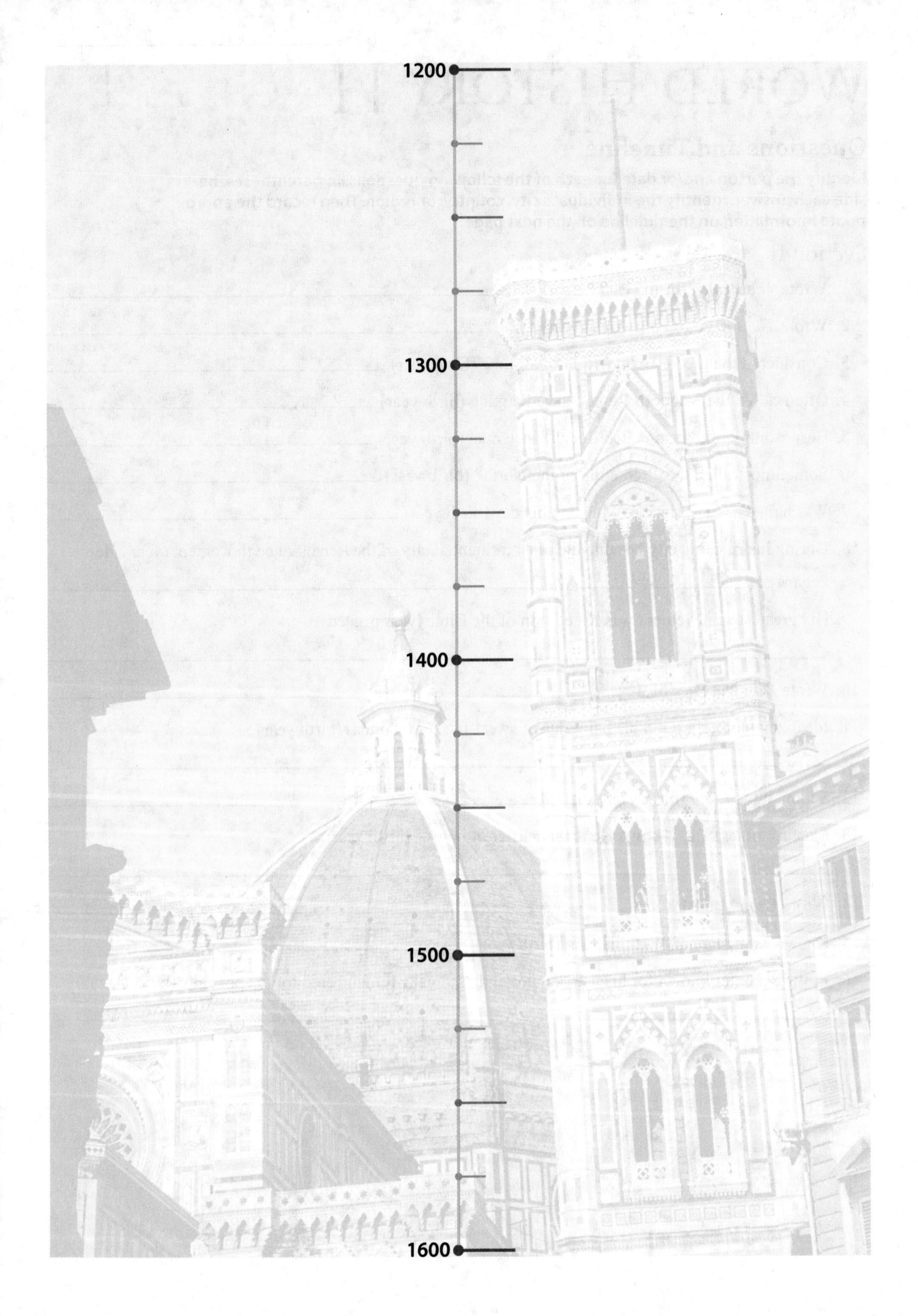
1200
1300
1400
1500
1600

Name ______________________

WORLD HISTORY 11 ACTIVITY 2

Machiavelli's *The Prince*

Machiavelli is the "grandfather of modern political science." Until he wrote *The Prince*, most governments had based their authority and decisions on a moral foundation rooted in religion. Perhaps the greatest single shift in the modern world has been the changed role of God in government. Read the main chapters in *The Prince* and answer the questions.

Chapter XIV: *That Which Concerns a Prince on the Subject of the Art of War*

A prince ought to have no other aim or thought, nor select anything else for his study, than war and its rules and discipline. For this is the sole art that belongs to him who rules. It is of such force that it not only upholds those who are born princes, but it often enables men to rise from a private station to that rank. On the contrary, when princes have thought more of ease than of arms they have lost their states. The first cause of your losing it is to neglect this art; and what enables you to acquire a state is to be master of the art. . . . A prince who does not understand the art of war, over and above the other misfortunes already mentioned [in earlier chapters], cannot be respected by his soldiers, nor can he rely on them. He ought never, therefore, to have out of his thoughts this subject of war, and in peace he should addict himself more to its exercise than in war. This he can do in two ways, the one by action, the other by study.

As regards action, he ought above all things to keep his men well organized and drilled, to follow incessantly the chase, by which he accustoms his body to hardships, and learns something of the nature of localities, and gets to find out how the mountains rise, how the valleys open out, how the plains lie, and to understand the nature of rivers and marshes, and in all this to take the greatest care. Which knowledge is useful in two ways. Firstly, he learns to know his country, and is better able to undertake its defence. Afterwards, by means of the knowledge and observation of that locality, he understands with ease any other locality which it may be necessary for him to study hereafter; because the hills, valleys, and plains, and rivers and marshes that are, for instance, in Tuscany, have a certain resemblance to those of other countries, so that with a knowledge of the aspect of one country one can easily arrive at a knowledge of others. The prince that lacks this skill lacks the essential which it is desirable that a captain should possess. For it teaches him to surprise his enemy, to select quarters, to lead armies, to array the battle, to besiege towns to advantage. . . .

But to exercise the intellect the prince should read histories, and study there the actions of illustrious men, to see how they have borne themselves in war, to examine the causes of their victories and defeats, so as to avoid the latter and imitate the former; and above all do as an illustrious man did, who took as an example one who had been praised and famous before him, and whose achievements and deeds he always kept in his mind, as it is said Alexander the Great imitated Achilles, Caesar Alexander, Scipio Cyrus. And whoever reads the life of Cyrus, written by Xenophon, will recognize afterwards in the life of Scipio how that imitation was his glory, and how in chastity, affability, humanity, and liberality Scipio conformed to those things which have been written of Cyrus by Xenophon. A wise prince ought to observe some such rules, and never in peaceful times stand idle, but increase his resources with industry in such a way that they may be available to him in adversity, so that if fortune changes it may find him prepared to resist her blows.

1. How does the first sentence of the chapter contradict God's purpose of government, stated in Romans 13:3–4?

______

______

______

2. According to Machiavelli, in what two ways should princes study war during peacetime?

______

Chapter XV: *Concerning Things for Which Men, and Especially Princes, Are Praised or Blamed*

It remains now to see what ought to be the rules of conduct for a prince towards subject and friends. And as I know that many have written on this point, I expect I shall be considered presumptuous in mentioning it again, especially as in discussing it I shall depart from the methods of other people. But, it being my intention to write a thing which shall be useful to him who apprehends it, it appears to me more appropriate to follow up the real truth of a matter than the imagination of it. For many have pictured republics and principalities which in fact have never been known or seen, because how one lives is so far distant from how one ought to live, that he who neglects what is done for what ought to be done, sooner causes his ruin than his preservation. For a man who wishes to act entirely up to his professions of virtue soon meets with what destroys him among so much that is evil.

Hence it is necessary for a prince wishing to hold his own to know how to do wrong, and to make use of it or not according to necessity. Therefore, putting on one side imaginary things concerning a prince, and discussing those which are real, I say that all men when they are spoken of, and chiefly princes for being more highly placed, are remarkable for some of those qualities which bring them either blame or praise. Thus it is that one is reputed liberal, another miserly; one is reputed generous, one rapacious; one cruel, one compassionate; one faithless, another faithful; one effeminate and cowardly, another bold and brave; one affable, another haughty; one lascivious, another chaste; one sincere, another cunning; one hard, another easy; one grave, another frivolous; one religious, another unbelieving, and the like. And I know that every one will confess that it would be most praiseworthy in a prince to exhibit all the above qualities that are considered good. But because they can neither be entirely possessed nor observed, for human conditions do not permit it, it is necessary for him to be sufficiently prudent that he may know how to avoid the reproach of those vices which would lose him his state; and also to keep himself, if it be possible, from those which would not lose him it; but this not being possible, he may with less hesitation abandon himself to them. And again, he need not make himself uneasy at incurring a reproach for those vices without which the state can only be saved with difficulty. For if everything is considered carefully, it will be found that something which looks like virtue, if followed, would be his ruin; while something else, which looks like vice, yet followed brings him security and prosperity. . . .

3. Find every occurrence of the words *real*, *imagine*, and *imagination* in this excerpt. On what basis does Machiavelli derive his "rules of conduct for a prince"? Why is this wrong?

______

______

4. How does the first sentence of paragraph 2 contradict King Solomon's advice to princes (Prov. 16:12)?

____

____

5. According to Machiavelli, why is it unimportant for "prudent" princes to worry about virtue and vice (i.e., character)?

____

____

____

Chapter XVII: *Concerning Cruelty and Clemency, and Whether It Is Better to Be Loved Than Feared*

Coming now to the other qualities mentioned above, I say that every prince ought to desire to be considered clement and not cruel. Nevertheless he ought to take care not to misuse this clemency. Cesare Borgia was considered cruel; notwithstanding, his cruelty reconciled the Romagna, unified it, and restored it to peace and loyalty. . . . Therefore a prince, so long as he keeps his subjects united and loyal, ought not to mind the reproach of cruelty; because with a few examples he will be more merciful than those who, through too much mercy, allow disorders to arise, from which follow murders or robberies. For these tend to injure the whole people, while those executions which originate with a prince offend the individual only.

Of all princes, it is impossible for the new prince to avoid the imputation of cruelty, owing to new states being full of dangers. Hence Virgil, through the mouth of Dido, excuses the inhumanity of her reign owing to its being new, saying:

Res dura, et regni novitas me talia cogunt
Moliri, et late fines custode tueri.

["... against my will, my fate, a throne unsettled, and an infant state. Bid me defend my realms with all my powers, and guard my shores with these severities."]

Nevertheless he ought to be slow to believe and to act, nor should he himself show fear, but proceed in a temperate manner with prudence and humanity, so that too much confidence may not make him incautious and too much distrust render him intolerable.

Upon this a question arises: Would it be better to be loved than feared or feared than loved? It may be answered that one should wish to be both. But, because it is difficult to unite them in one person, it is much safer to be feared than loved, when, of the two, either must be dispensed with. Because this is to be asserted of men in general, that they are ungrateful, fickle, false, cowardly, covetous, and as long as you succeed they are yours entirely; they will offer you their blood, property, life and children, as is said above, when the need is far distant; but when it approaches they turn against you. That prince who, relying entirely on their promises, has neglected other precautions, is ruined. Friendships that are obtained by payments, and not by greatness or nobility of mind, may indeed be earned, but they are not secured, and in time of need cannot be relied upon. Men have less scruple in offending one who is beloved than one who is feared. For love is preserved by the link of obligation which, owing to the baseness of men, is broken at every opportunity for their advantage; but fear preserves you by a dread of punishment which never fails.

Nevertheless a prince ought to inspire fear in such a way that, if he does not win love, he avoids hatred; because he can endure very well being feared while he is not hated, which will always be as long as he abstains from the property of his citizens and subjects and from their women. But when it is necessary for him to proceed against the life of someone, he must do it on proper justification and for manifest cause, but above all things he must keep his hands off the property of others, because men more quickly forget the death of their father than the loss of their patrimony. Besides, pretexts for taking away the property are never wanting. For he who has once begun to live by robbery will always find pretexts for seizing what belongs to others; but reasons for taking life, on the contrary, are more difficult to find and sooner lapse. But when a prince is with his army, and has under control a multitude of soldiers, then it is quite necessary for him to disregard the reputation of cruelty, for without it he would never hold his army united or disposed to its duties.

Among the wonderful deeds of Hannibal this one is enumerated: that having led an enormous army, composed of many various races of men, to fight in foreign lands, no dissensions arose either among them or against the prince, whether in his bad or in his good fortune. This arose from nothing else than his inhuman cruelty, which, with his boundless valour, made him revered and terrible in the sight of his soldiers, but without that cruelty, his other virtues were not sufficient to produce this effect. Shortsighted writers admire his deeds from one point of view and from another condemn the principal cause of them. That it is true his other virtues would not have been sufficient for him may be proved by the case of Scipio, that most excellent man, not of his own times but within the memory of man, against whom, nevertheless, his army rebelled in Spain; this arose from nothing but his too great forbearance, which gave his soldiers more license than is consistent with military discipline. . . .

Returning to the question of being feared or loved, I come to the conclusion that, men loving according to their own will and fearing according to that of the prince, a wise prince should establish himself on that which is in his own control and not in that of others. He must endeavour only to avoid hatred, as is noted.

6. Why does Machiavelli believe princes should choose cruelty over clemency? Do you think this view is based on his study of King Solomon (Prov. 20:28)?

____

____

____

7. Why does Machiavelli believe princes should try to be feared rather than loved?

____

Chapter XVIII: *Concerning the Way in Which Princes Should Keep Faith*

Everyone admits how praiseworthy it is in a prince to keep faith, and to live with integrity and not with craft. Nevertheless our experience has been that those princes who have done great things have held good faith of little account, and have known how to circumvent the intellect of men by craft, and in the end have overcome those who have relied on their word. You must know there are two ways of contesting, the one by the law, the other by force. The first method is proper to men, the second to beasts. But because the first is frequently not sufficient, it is necessary to have recourse to the second. Therefore it is necessary for a prince to understand how to avail himself of the beast and the man. This has been figuratively taught to princes by ancient writers, who describe how

Achilles and many other princes of old were given to the Centaur Chiron to nurse, who brought them up in his discipline; which means solely that, as they had for a teacher one who was half beast and half man, so it is necessary for a prince to know how to make use of both natures, and that one without the other is not durable. A prince, therefore, being compelled knowingly to adopt the beast, ought to choose the fox and the lion; because the lion cannot defend himself against snares and the fox cannot defend himself against wolves. Therefore, it is necessary to be a fox to discover the snares and a lion to terrify the wolves. Those who rely simply on the lion do not understand what they are about. Therefore a wise lord cannot, nor ought he to, keep faith when such observance may be turned against him, and when the reasons that caused him to pledge it exist no longer. If men were entirely good, this precept would not hold, but because they are bad, and will not keep faith with you, you too are not bound to observe it with them. Nor will there ever be wanting to a prince legitimate reasons to excuse this nonobservance. Of this endless modern examples could be given, showing how many treaties and engagements have been made void and of no effect through the faithlessness of princes; and he who has known best how to employ the fox has succeeded best.

But it is necessary to know well how to disguise this characteristic, and to be a great pretender and dissembler. Men are so simple, and so subject to present necessities, that he who seeks to deceive will always find someone who will allow himself to be deceived. . . .

It is unnecessary for a prince to have all the good qualities I have enumerated, but it is very necessary to appear to have them. And I shall dare to say this also, that to have them and always to observe them is injurious, and that to appear to have them is useful; to appear merciful, faithful, humane, religious, upright, and to be so, but with a mind so framed that should you require not to be so, you may be able and know how to change to the opposite.

You have to understand this, that a prince, especially a new one, cannot observe all those things for which men are esteemed, being often forced, in order to maintain the state, to act contrary to faith, friendship, humanity, and religion. Therefore it is necessary for him to have a mind ready to turn itself accordingly as the winds and variations of fortune force it, yet, as I have said above, not to diverge from the good if he can avoid doing so, but, if compelled, then to know how to set about it.

For that reason, let a prince have the credit of conquering and holding his state, the means will always be considered honest, and he will be praised by everybody because the vulgar are always taken by what a thing seems to be and by what comes of it; and in the world there are only the vulgar, for the few find a place there only when the many have no ground to rest on.

8. What animal trait was praised by Machiavelli but despised by Jesus (Luke 13:32)?

____

9. List the reasons that Machiavelli gives to justify the prince's deception. Be prepared to refute each reason.

____

____

____

____

Name ______________________

WORLD HISTORY 11 ACTIVITY 3

Art Appreciation

Examine the paintings on the pages listed below. Based on your reading about each painter, answer these questions.

Botticelli's *The Adoration of the Magi* [National Gallery of Art, p. 265]

1. Give three examples of movement that Botticelli captured on the canvas.

____

____

2. How does this painting incorporate perspective?

____

____

3. Was this painting from Botticelli's early or late career?

____

____

Dürer's *Knight, Death and Devil* [National Gallery of Art, p. 269]

4. How does the natural background in this engraving reflect Dürer's German roots?

____

5. What honored humanist did Dürer engrave on page 261?

____

6. How does this engraving imitate Titian's skill in bringing out the personality traits of the subject?

____

____

7. What features does the signature on page 261 have in common with the signature for *Knight, Death and Devil* (p. 269)?

____

Van Eyck's *The Marriage* [National Gallery, London, p. 270]

8. List three examples of van Eyck's careful attention to minute details.

____

____

____

Name ____________

WORLD HISTORY 11 ACTIVITY 4

Middle Ages vs. the Renaissance

Summarize the contrasts between the Middle Ages and the Renaissance. (Review Chapter 10 for this activity.)

		Middle Ages	Renaissance
World View	Importance of the Past		
	Importance of the Present		
	Importance of the Future		
	Importance of the Individual		
Human Nature	Basic Nature of Man		
	The Ideal Man		
	Honored People of the Past		
	Code of Conduct		
	Source of Evil		
	Remedy for Sin		
Education	Main Topics of Education		
	Goal of Education		
	Language(s) of Learning		
	Attitude Toward Traditional Ideas		
Government	Business Practice		
	Principles of Government		
	Favorite Form of Government		

		Middle Ages	Renaissance
Literature	Most Popular Forms of Literature		
	Main Topics of Literature		
Art	Main Patrons of the Arts		
	Most Popular Media of Art		
	Elements of Italian Art		
	Most Popular Subjects of Northern European Art		
	Popular Architectural Styles		
Music	Most Popular Types of Composition		
	Melodies		
	Purpose of Music		

Name ____________________

WORLD HISTORY 12 ACTIVITY 1

Questions and Timeline

Identify the person, event, and date for each of the following questions. Then record the appropriate information, with the city, country, or region in parentheses, on the timeline on the next page.

Section I

1. Bohemian reformer (birth year) ____________________
2. Called the Morning Star of the Reformation (birth year) ____________________

Section II

3. Event where Luther was given no chance to defend his teaching (year) ____________________
4. Pope who sent out agents to sell certificates of indulgences (year became pope)

   ____
5. Drawn up by Melanchthon to set forth Luther's chief doctrines (year)

   ____
6. Made "justification by faith alone" the heart of his preaching (birth year)

   ____
7. Became the symbol of defiance against the corruption and hypocrisy of Rome (year)

   ____
8. Settlement that allowed each German prince the right to choose whether his territory would be Lutheran or Roman Catholic (year) ____________________
9. Led the Ottoman Turks who invaded the eastern portion of Charles V's empire (year reign began)

   ____

Section III

10. Made the sovereignty of God the heart of his theology (birth year) ____________________
11. Was nine years old when he became king and achieved Protestant gains in his country during his reign (year reign began) ____________________
12. Was called Good Queen Bess (year reign began) ____________________
13. The Act of Supremacy made him head of the church (year reign began) ____________________
14. Revived pro-Catholic policies and was called "Bloody Mary" by some (year reign began)

    ____
15. Was said of him, "Others lop off branches, but this man strikes at the root" (birth year)

    ____
16. Fleet sent by Philip II to invade England but was defeated (year)

    ____

17. Huguenot massacre instigated by Catherine de Medici (year)

____

18. Document that granted a certain amount of religious toleration to the Huguenots (year)

____

Section IV

19. First of three meetings leading to the break between Protestant and Roman Catholic churches (year)

____

20. Established by Roman Catholic Church to regulate what its members read (year)

____

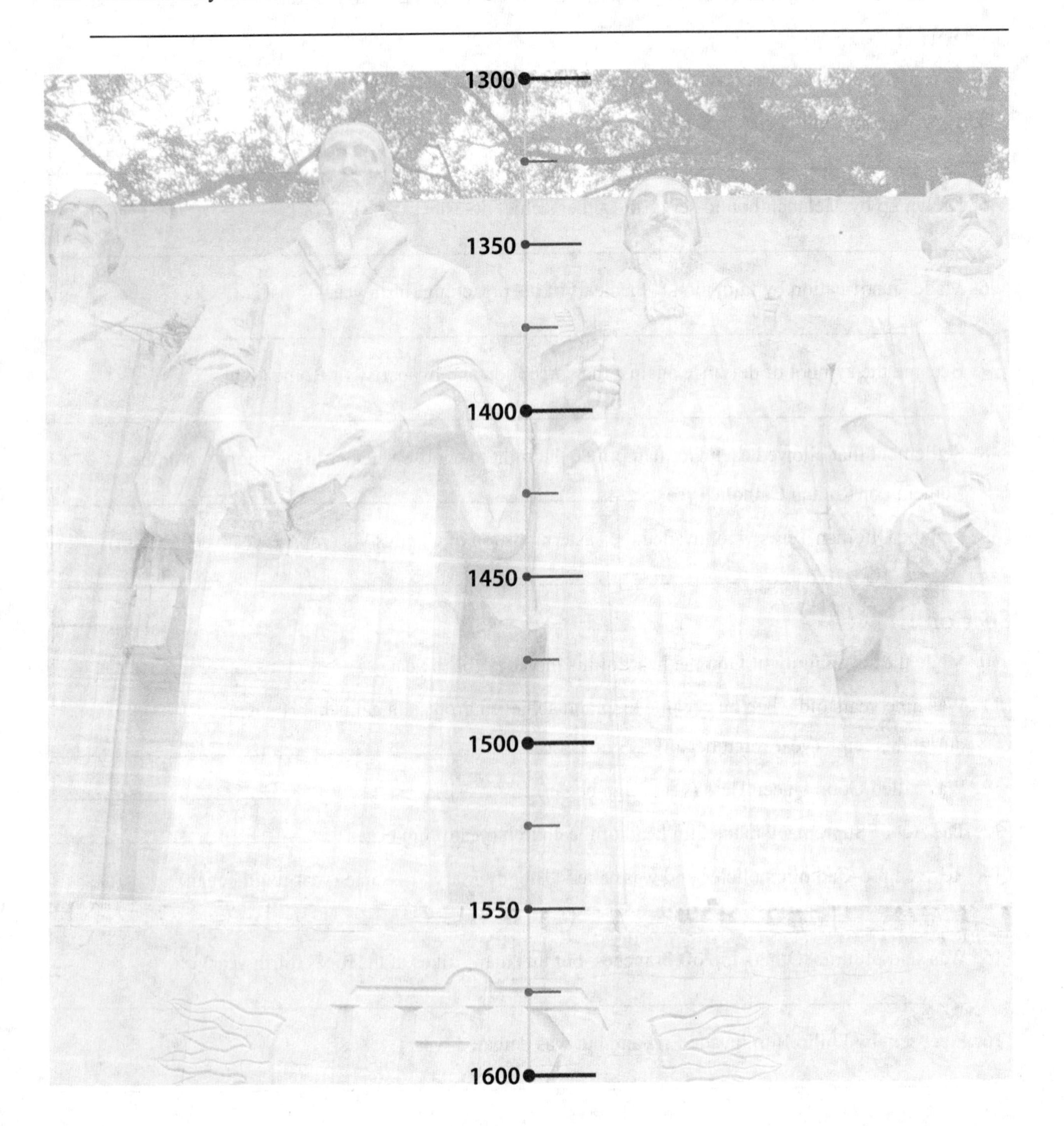

Name ____________________

WORLD HISTORY 12 ACTIVITY 2

Rise of Religious Liberty and the Modern Secular State

I. Studying the Reformation helps us understand the transition to the modern secular (nonreligious) state. Before this time, kings controlled the religion of their people. The idea of religious liberty did not take hold in Europe until after a series of bloody religious wars had broken the power of Roman Catholicism. Complete the chart showing the relationship between political changes and the Reformation. The events are listed at the end of the chart (p. SA100). (Events are listed in the order they appear in the book. A few events are from past chapters.)

Period	Political Developments		Reformation and Counter Reformation	
Forerunners of the Reformation (1300s–1400s)	1291	Holy Roman emperors fail to unite Germany. Switzerland breaks from Holy Roman Empire.		
	1302		1309	
	1337		1377	
			1382	
	1414		1415	
	1453		1456	
	1492	Columbus discovers America.		

Period	Political Developments		Reformation and Counter Reformation	
Beginning of the Reformation (1500–1530)			1514	
			1516	
			1517	
			1519	
			1521	
	1522		1525	
			1529	
			1530	
Spread of the Reformation (1530–55)	1533	The pope refuses to let Henry VIII of England divorce Catherine of Spain	1534	
			1536	
			1540	Loyola's Jesuit order becomes official.
			1542	Pope Paul III reorganizes the Inquisition.
	1546		1545	
	1553			
	1555			

Period	Political Developments		Reformation and Counter Reformation	
Challenges to the Reformation (1556–1600)	1556		1556	Thomas Cramner is burned at the stake.
	1558		1559	
	1561		1565	
	1568		1572	
	1588			
	1589		1598	
Final Stages of the Reformation (1600–1700)	1618	Protestants revolt in Bohemia against the Holy Roman emperor, sparking the Thirty Years' War.	1619	The Thirty Years' War spreads to Germany, becoming the bloodiest religious war in European history.
			1620	English Separatists found Plymouth Colony in America.
			1630	English Puritans found Massachusetts Bay Colony in America.
	1635	France joins the Protestants in the Thirty Years' War to prevent Hapsburg victory.		
	1642	Catholic king Charles I sparks civil war in England.	1649	Oliver Cromwell wins the English civil war and creates a Puritan republic.

Period	Political Developments		Reformation and Counter Reformation	
	1648	Peace of Westphalia ends the Thirty Years' War, guaranteeing (1) the independence of Protestant Netherlands and Switzerland and (2) the freedom of German princes to choose their religion.		
	1660	Parliament restores a Roman Catholic as king of England.		
	1668	The Glorious Revolution requires a Protestant to sit on the English throne.	1689	The Act of Toleration grants religious toleration in England.

Political Developments:

Turks destroy Constantinople.

Philip IV of France defies Pope Boniface VIII.

Hundred Years' War begins between France and England.

Spain completes the *Reconquista*.

Holy Roman emperor calls Council of Constance.

Hapsburg Charles V is preoccupied by wars with the French king Francis I and the Turk Suleiman.

Charles V sparks civil war in Germany.

German princes sign Peace of Augsburg.

Bloody Mary becomes queen of England.

Protestant Elizabeth I becomes queen of England.

Philip II becomes ruler of Hapsburg lands.

The Spanish Armada fails to defeat England.

Mary Stuart returns from Catholic France to Scotland.

Dutch Protestants, led by William of Orange, revolt against Spain.

The Protestant Henry of Navarre wins civil war in France.

Reformation and Counter Reformation:

The Babylonian Captivity of the Papacy begins.

The Great Schism begins.

The German Gutenberg uses movable type to print the first Bible.

Erasmus publishes the Greek New Testament.

The English Wycliffe Bible is completed.

Holy Roman emperor executes John Huss of Bohemia.

Leo X approves indulgences for St. Peter's Basilica.

German Luther posts Ninety-five Theses.

Luther debates Eck at Leipzig.

Charles V condemns Luther at Worms.

Melanchthon writes *Augsburg Confession.*

Zwingli and Luther fail to agree at Marburg.

First Anabaptists organize in Switzerland.

Calvin publishes *Institutes* in Switzerland.

England breaks with the papacy by passing the Act of Supremacy.

England approves the Elizabethan Settlement.

John Knox brings Calvinism to Scotland.

French Catholics commit the St. Bartholomew's Day Massacre.

The Edict of Nantes grants religious toleration in France.

The Council of Trent first meets.

Rome establishes the *Index*.

The Council of Trent completes official Catholic doctrine.

II. Answer the following questions based on the textbook and the chart on the previous pages. Be sure to examine the events under "Final Stages of the Reformation." (You will study these events in more detail in Chapter 14.)

1. What two major events, which you studied in previous chapters, occured while Wycliffe translated the Bible?

   a) political development ______________________________

   b) religious development ______________________________

2. What political development distracted the Holy Roman emperor Charles V soon after he condemned Luther at Worms? ______________________________

3. What two important developments from the Renaissance preceded Luther's posting of the Ninety-five Theses? How do you think these developments aided the Reformation?

   a) Gutenberg ______________________________

   b) Erasmus ______________________________

4. During the "beginning of the Reformation" (1500–1530), what two reforming groups arose in Switzerland, separate from the Lutherans? ______________________________

5. Which two important religious teachers/leaders/organizers won many followers during the critical "spread of the Reformation" period (see chart)? ______________________________

6. For what political reason did the king of England break from the papacy—an unintentional boost to the cause of Protestantism? ______________________________

7. Protestantism faced its greatest political danger between 1546 and 1589. What dangers threatened Protestantism in each country, and how were the threats miraculously resolved?

   a) Germany ______________________________

   b) England ______________________________

   c) Scotland ______________________________

d) Netherlands ____________________

____

____

e) France ____________________

____

____

8. What document marks the beginning of religious toleration in these countries?

   a) Germany ____________________

   b) France ____________________

   c) England ____________________

9. What occurred in all of the above countries before religious toleration was granted?

   ____

10. What two events during the 1600s guaranteed the place of Protestantism in Europe?

   ____

11. What two events during the 1600s guaranteed the spread of Protestantism to America?

   ____

Name ____________________

WORLD HISTORY 12 ACTIVITY 3

Map Study: The Protestant Reformation

I. Using the map in this chapter and additional sources, label the following regions and cities on the Protestant Reformation map. Using colored pencils, color each religious region a different color.

Regions	Cities (identify with •)
England	Augsburg
France	Basel
Scotland	Calais
Spain	Edinburgh
	Geneva
	Leipzig
	London
	Nantes
	Oxford
	Paris
	Prague
	Rome
	Trent
	Wittenberg
	Worms
	Zurich

II. Identify the following.

1. country of the Lollards ____________________
2. region where John Huss ministered ____________________
3. university where Luther taught ____________________
4. city where Luther was condemned ____________________
5. peace treaty (1555) ending Germany's religious war ____________________
6. city where Huss challenged people to oppose worldliness in the church ____________________
7. three-week debate between Johann Eck and Luther ____________________
8. country led by Henry VIII ____________________
9. original homeland of the Huguenots ____________________
10. city where the St. Bartholomew's Day Massacre began ____________________
11. edict granting religious toleration to Protestants in France ____________________
12. council that set Roman Catholic doctrine ____________________

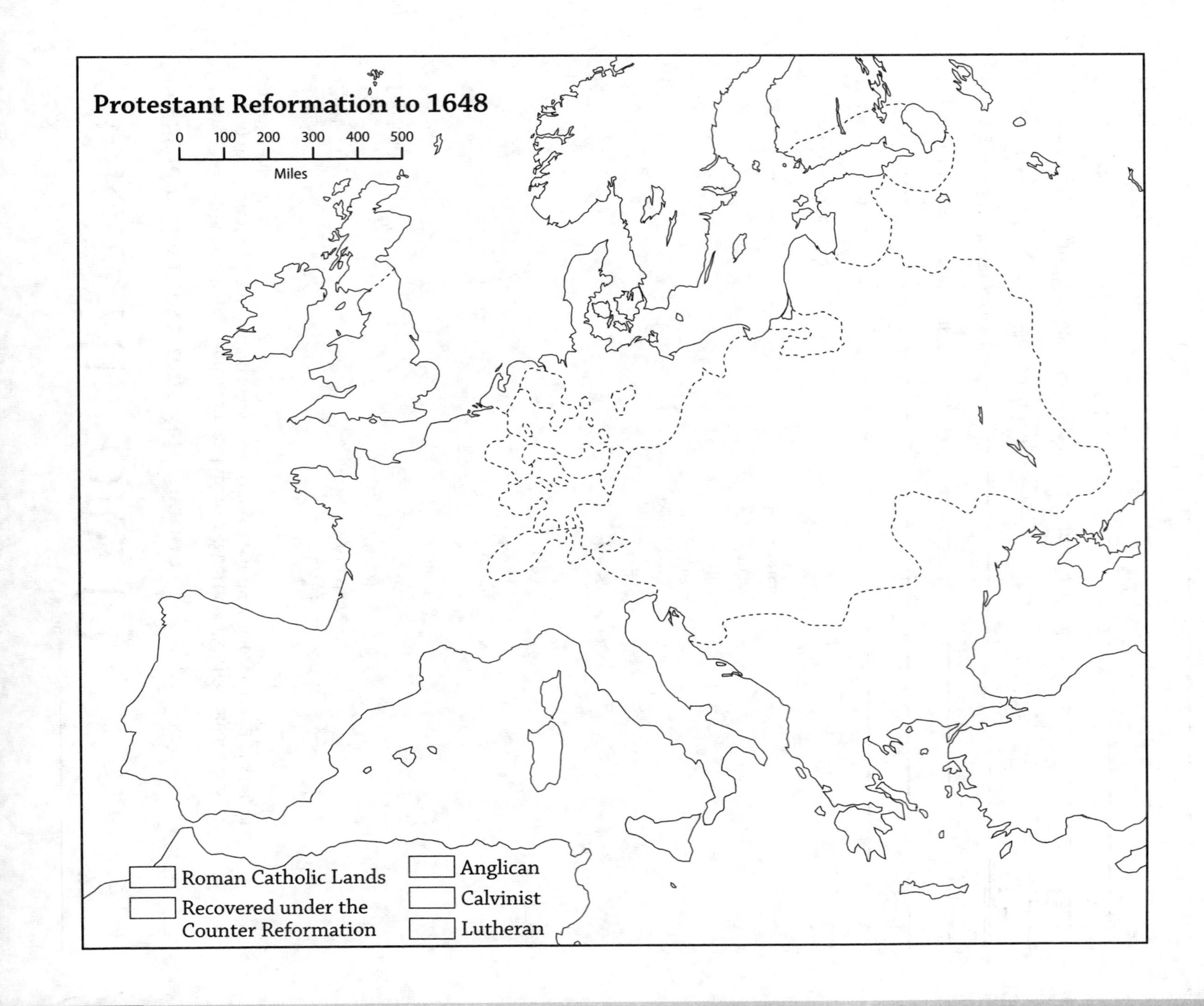
Protestant Reformation to 1648
0
100
200
300
400
500
Miles
Roman Catholic Lands
Recovered under the Counter Reformation
Anglican
Calvinist
Lutheran

Name ____________________

WORLD HISTORY 13 ACTIVITY 1

Questions and Timeline

For each of the following questions, identify the person, event, and/or date, placing the city, country, or region in parentheses. Then record the appropriate information on the timeline on the next page.

Section I

1. Explorer whose tales of strange customs and riches in the Far East stirred the popular imagination (year he went to Cathay) ____________________
2. Event which caused Europeans to fear a full-scale Muslim invasion (year occurred) ____________________

Section II

3. Sent by his king down Africa's coast to find a sea route to India (year sent) ____________________
4. Explorer supported by King Ferdinand and Queen Isabella who sailed west to reach Japan and China (year sailed) ____________________
5. Called "The Navigator" and largely responsible for his country's early exploration success (year of birth) ____________________
6. Established by Pope Alexander VI to divide the world between two countries (year established) ____________________
7. Selected by his king to lead an expedition around the Cape of Good Hope to India (year sailed) ____________________
8. Named the Pacific Ocean and commanded one of his ships that later completed the first circumnavigation of the world (year sailed) ____________________
9. Explorer, called "the greatest of the conquistadors," who landed on Mexico's shores (year landed) ____________________
10. Roman Catholic friar who wrote several works expressing concern over Indian abuses in America (year arrived in America) ____________________
11. First notable conquistador who cut across today's Panama and was the first European to see the Pacific Ocean (year began to cross Panama) ____________________
12. Landed near today's Tampa Bay, Florida, and eventually discovered the Mississippi River (year landed in Florida) ____________________
13. Considered to be the cruelest conquistador; raided the Inca empire (year set out for Peru) ____________________
14. Set out from Mexico to find the "Seven Cities of Cibola" (year set out) ____________________

15. First great explorer from his country who sailed to Newfoundland and Labrador (year sailed)

____

16. First permanent English settlement in the New World (year founded) ______________

17. Explorer who gave the Dutch a claim to the Hudson River region (year entered the Hudson River)

____

18. Two men who explored the Mississippi River (year exploration began)

____

19. City founded by Champlain when he explored the Saint Lawrence River area (year founded)

____

20. Was named viceroy of his country's holdings in the East; discouraged cruelty to the natives (year named viceroy) ______________

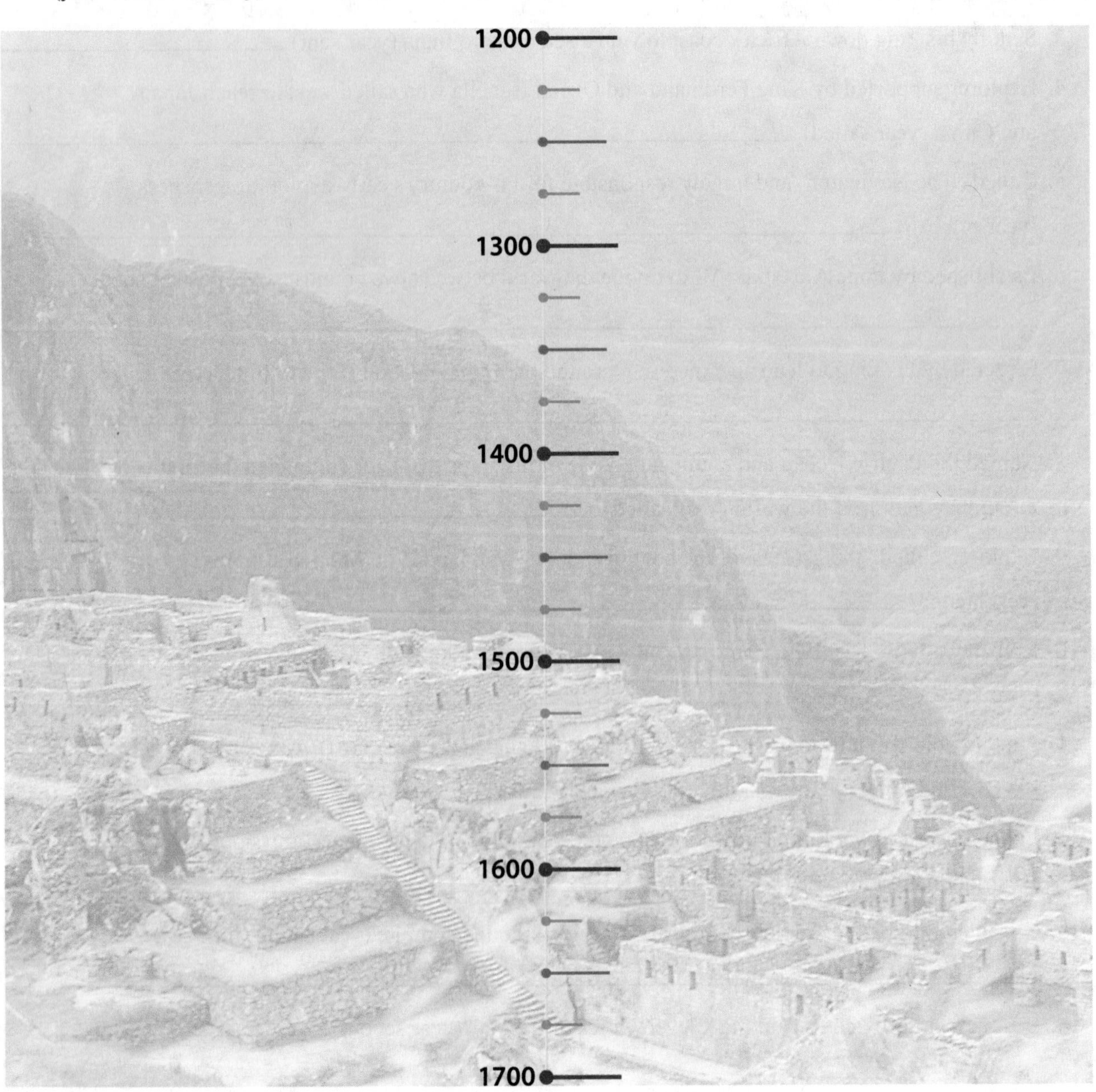

Name ______________________________

WORLD HISTORY 13 ACTIVITY 2

Map Study: Early Explorers

I. Using the map in this chapter and additional sources, first draw the routes of these explorers using a different color for each: Balboa, Cabot, Cartier, Columbus, Cortes, da Gama, Dias, Hudson, and Magellan. Next label each of the following regions and special features on the Early Explorers map.

Regions

Aztec
Cathay (China)
Cipango (Japan)
Cuba
England
France
Holland (Netherlands)
Inca
India
Maya
Philippines
Portugal
Spain

Special Features

Atlantic Ocean
Arctic Ocean
Cape of Good Hope
Indian Ocean
Isthmus of Panama
Mississippi River
Pacific Ocean
St. Lawrence River
Strait of Magellan

II. Identify the following.

1. ocean that Columbus crossed ______________________________
2. Dias's "Cape of Storms" ______________________________
3. Asian country that da Gama opened to Europe by a new sea route ______________________________
4. first European country to set up colonies along the African coast ______________________________
5. dangerous waters where Magellan lost two ships ______________________________
6. peaceful ocean named by Magellan ______________________________
7. islands where Magellan was killed ______________________________
8. Indian civilization that disappeared before Europeans arrived ______________________________
9. civilization conquered by Cortés ______________________________
10. civilization conquered by Pizarro ______________________________
11. region explored by Balboa ______________________________
12. river explored by Marquette and Joliet ______________________________
13. land ruled by Montezuma ______________________________
14. land ruled by Atahualpa ______________________________
15. region centered in Tenochtitlán ______________________________
16. river where Champlain founded Quebec ______________________________
17. two Far East countries that closed their ports to European trade

    ____

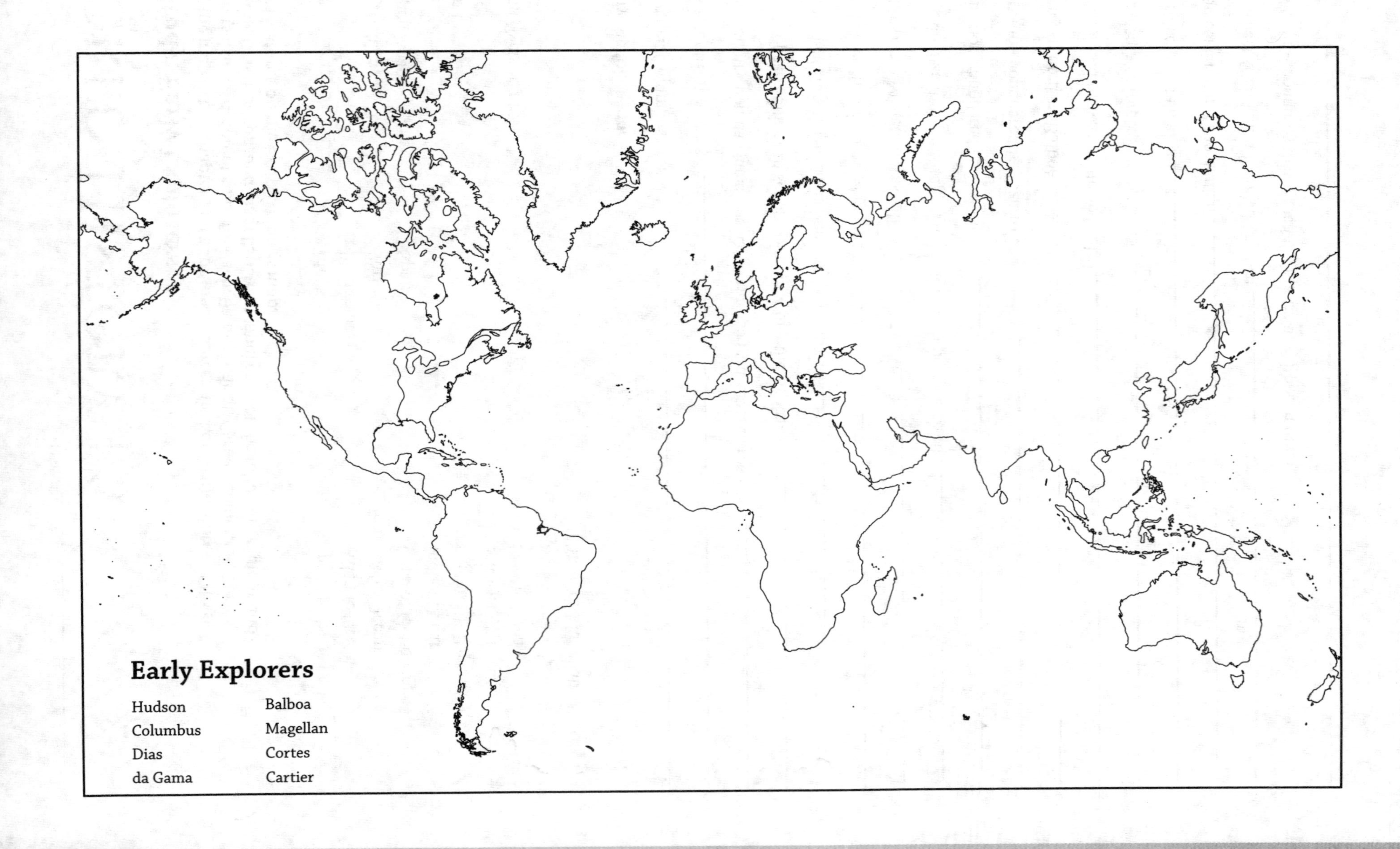
Early Explorers
Hudson
Columbus
Dias
da Gama
Balboa
Magellan
Cortes
Cartier

Name ______________________

WORLD HISTORY 13 ACTIVITY 3

Unsolved Mysteries: The Voyages of John Cabot

The details of John Cabot's voyages to America remain largely a mystery. We do not have any of his log books or handwritten accounts. The only reliable sources for the first trip are three short letters written by two men who apparently had met Cabot. All we know for sure about the second voyage is that (1) the king commissioned him and (2) his ships ran into trouble before they reached America. Accounts do not agree: Were the ships lost? Did Cabot reach America and die? Did Cabot return to England?

These three short letters disagree even about the first trip. Yet Cabot's achievement formed the basis for England's claim to North America. Read the following letters. Compare and contrast the accounts of Lorenzo and Raimondo by answering the questions at the end of the readings.

Letter from Lorenzo Pasqualigo to His Brothers

London, 23rd August, 1497

Our Venetian, who went with a small ship from Bristol to find new islands, has come back, and says he has discovered, 700 leagues off, the mainland of the country of the Gran Cam, and that he coasted along it for 300 leagues, and landed, but did not see any person. But he has brought here to the king certain snares spread to take game, and a needle for making nets, and he found some notched trees, from which he judged that there were inhabitants. Being in doubt, he came back to the ship. He has been away three months on the voyage, which is certain, and, in returning, he saw two islands to the right, but he did not wish to land, lest he should lose time for he was in want of provisions. This king has been much pleased. He says that the tides are slack, and do not make currents as they do here. The king has promised for another time, ten armed ships as he desires, and has given him all the prisoners, except such as are confined for high treason, to go with him, as he has requested; and has granted him money to amuse himself till then. Meanwhile, he is with his Venetian wife and his sons at Bristol. His name is Zuam Calbot, and he is called the Great Admiral, great honor being paid to him, and he goes dressed in silk. The English are ready to go with him, and so are many of our rascals. The discoverer of these things has planted a large cross in the ground with a banner of England, and one of St. Mark, as he is a Venetian; so that our flag has been hoisted very far away.

First and Second Despatches of Raimondo di Soncino to the Duke of Milan

24th August, 1497

Some month afterwards His Majesty sent a Venetian, who is a distinguished sailor, and who was much skilled in the discovery of new islands, and he has returned safe, and has discovered two very large and fertile islands, having, it would seem, discovered the seven cities 400 leagues from England to the westward. These successes led His Majesty at once to entertain the intention of sending him with fifteen or twenty vessels.

18th December, 1497

My most illustrious and most excellent Lord,

Perhaps amidst so many occupations of your Excellency it will not be unwelcome to learn how this Majesty has acquired a part of Asia without drawing his sword. In this kingdom there is a certain Venetian named Zoanne Caboto, of gentle disposition, very expert in navigation, who, seeing that the most serene Kings of Portugal and Spain had occupied unknown islands, meditated the achievement of a similar acquisition for the said Majesty. Having obtained royal privileges securing to himself the use of the dominions he might discover, the sovereignty being reserved to the Crown, he entrusted his fortune to a small vessel with a crew of 18 persons, and set out from Bristo, a port in the western part of this kingdom. Having passed Ibernia, which is still further to the west, and then shaped a northerly course, he began to navigate to the eastern part, leaving (during several days) the North Star on the right hand. Having wandered thus for a long time, at length he hit upon land, where he hoisted the royal standard, and took possession for his Highness, and, having obtained various proofs of his discovery, he returned. The said Messer Zoanne, being a foreigner and poor, would not have been believed if the crew, who are nearly all English, and belonging to Bristo, had not testified that what he said was the truth. This Messer Zoanne has the description of the world on a chart, and also on a solid sphere which he has constructed, and on which he shows where he has been; and, proceeding towards the east, he has passed as far as the country of the Tanais. And they say that there the land is excellent and [the climate?] temperate, suggesting that brasil and silk grow there. They affirm that the sea is full of fish, which are not only taken with a net, but also with a basket, a stone being fastened to it in order to keep it in the water; and this I have heard stated by the said Messer Zoanne.

The said Englishmen, his companions, say that they took so many fish that this kingdom will no longer have need of Iceland, from which country there is an immense trade in the fish they call stock-fish. But Messer Zoanne has set his mind on higher things, for he thinks that, when that place has been occupied, he will keep on still further towards the east, where he will be opposite to an island called Cipango, situated in the equinoctial region, where he believes that all the spices of the world, as well as the jewels, are found. He further says that he was once at Mecca, whither the spices are brought by caravans from distant countries. Having inquired from whence they were brought and where they grow, they answered that they did not know, but that such merchandize was brought from distant countries by other caravans to their home. They further say that they are also conveyed from other remote regions. So he adduced this argument, that if the eastern people tell those in the south that these things come from a far distance from them, presupposing the rotundity of the earth, it must be that the last turn would be by the north towards the west. It is said that in this way the route would not cost more than it costs now, and I also believe it. What is more, this Majesty, who is wise and not prodigal, reposes such trust in him because of what he has already achieved, that he gives him a good maintenance, as Messer Zoanne has himself told me. It is said that before long his Majesty will arm some ships for him, and will give him all the malefactors to go to that country and form a colony, so that they hope to establish a greater depot of spices in London than there is in Alexandria. The principal people in the enterprise belong to Bristo. They are great seamen, and, now that they know where to go, they say that the voyage thither will not occupy more than 15 days after leaving Ibernia. I have also spoken with a Burgundian, who was a companion of Messer Zoanne, who affirms all this, and who wishes to return because the Admiral (for so Messer Zoanne is entitled) has given him an island, and has given another to his barber of Castione, who is a Genoese, and both look upon themselves as Counts. Nor do they look upon my Lord the Admiral as less than a Prince. I also believe that some poor Italian friars are going on this voyage, who have all had bishoprics promised to them. If I had made friends with the Admiral when he was about to sail, I should have got an archbishopric at least. But I have thought that the benefits reserved for me by your Excellency will be more secure. I would venture to pray that, in the event of a vacancy taking place in my absence, I may be put in possession, and that I may not be superseded by those who, being present, can be more diligent than I, who am reduced in this country to eating at each meal ten or twelve kinds of victuals, and to being three hours at table every day, two for love of your Excellency, to whom I humbly recommend myself. London, 18 Dec. 1497.

Your Excellency's most humble servant,
Raimundus

1. How is Cabot's name spelled?

   Lorenzo: ______________________________

   Raimondo: ______________________________

2. In what town did the expedition begin?

   Lorenzo: ______________________________

   Raimondo: ______________________________

3. How many leagues is it to the New World?

   Lorenzo: ______________________________

   Raimondo: ______________________________

4. What is the name of the land that Cabot explored?

   Lorenzo: ______________________________

   Raimondo: ______________________________

5. What potential wealth was discovered in the New World?

   Lorenzo: ______________________________

   Raimondo: ______________________________

6. What contacts did Cabot have with the natives?

   Lorenzo: ______________________________

   Raimondo: ______________________________

7. What type of land claims did Cabot make in the New World?

   Lorenzo: ______________________________

   Raimondo: ______________________________

8. What were the king's plans for a second voyage (number of ships and men, goals)?

   Lorenzo: ______________________________

   Raimondo: ______________________________

   ____

Name ______________________

WORLD HISTORY 13 ACTIVITY 4

The Explorers

For each explorer give the hiring country, his nationality (if different), the areas he explored, and his accomplishments. Refer to previous chapters if necessary.

	Explorer	Dates of Exploration	Employing Country	Nationality (if different)	Accomplishments
Early Discovery	Marco Polo	1271–95			
	Bartolomeu Dias	1487–88			
	Christopher Columbus	1492–1504			
	John Cabot	1497–98			
	Vasco da Gama	1497–1503			
	Amerigo Vespucci	1499–1500 1501–2	Spain Portugal		
	Pedro Alvares Cabral	1500–1501	Portugal		Brazil; da Gama's route
Spanish Exploration	Juan Ponce de León	1513	Spain		Florida
	Vasco Núñez de Balboa	1513–14			
	Ferdinand Magellan	1519–21		Portuguese	
	Hernando Cortés	1519–36			
	Giovanni da Verrazano	1524	France	Italian	North American coastline
	Francisco Pizarro	1531–35			
	Jacques Cartier	1534–42			
	Hernando de Soto	1539–42			
	Francisco Vasquez de Coronado	1540–42			
English and French Exploration	Sir John Hawkins	1562–67	England		West Indies
	Sir Francis Drake	1567–95			
	Sir Martin Frobisher	1576–78	England		Labrador, Baffin Island
	Sir Humphrey Gilbert	1578–83	England		Newfoundland
	John Davys	1585–1605	England		Baffin Bay, South Seas
	Samuel de Champlain	1603–15			
	Henry Hudson	1609, 1610–11			
	William Baffin	1612–16	England		Baffin Bay
	Jacques Marquette and Louis Joliet	1673			
	Sieur de La Salle	1682			
	Vitus Bering	1725, 1728	Russia	Danish	Siberia, Bering Strait
	James Cook	1768–78	England		Pacific Ocean